The Cariff's

May 1995

The Cariff's

May 1995

Best Holiday
Foods & Crafts

McCall's
Best Holiday Foods & Crafts

By the
Food Editors of McCall's

Edited by
Elaine Prescott Wonsavage

NEWFIELD PUBLICATIONS, INC.

Design
Ted Bertz
Graphic Design Inc.
Art Direction
Kimberly Kubik

Senior Writer/Copy Editor
Meg Beutel

Recipe Editor
Ruth Pomeroy

Editorial Coordinator
Dorcas Comstock

Production Assistant
Diane Syc

Published by
Newfield Publications, Inc.
4343 Equity Drive
Columbus, OH 43216

Printed in the
United States of America

ISBN 0-8374-1764-3

CONTENTS

INTRODUCTION
7

ONE

A CELEBRATION OF THANKSGIVING
8

Flight of Fancy 10
Turkey With a Citrus Twist 14
Sensational Stuffings 18
The Noble Bird and
　All the Trimmings 22
　Wonderful Ways With Turkey ... 24
　Fabulous Fixin's 26
　Finales for the Feast 28
　Second-Day Spectaculars 30
Great Holiday Dinners 42
　An American Indian
　　Thanksgiving 42
　A New England
　　Thanksgiving 44
　A Creole Thanksgiving 46

Thanksgiving With a Light
　Touch 52
　Trim 'n' Tasty Trimmings 53
　Lighter-Than-Air Desserts 54
Feasts for a Few 58
Make-It-Yourself Thanksgiving
　Centerpieces 64
　Thanksgiving Flower Basket .. 64
　Pumpkin-In-Bloom 66
　Autumn Glory Arrangement 68

TWO

'TIS THE SEASON FOR PARTIES
70

Savory Ways To Say 'Welcome' .. 72
O Tidings of Comfort and Joy 76
Parties To Put You on the Map .. 80
　Tex-Mex Fiesta 80
　Cajun Dinner 82
　Nantucket Supper 84
　Pacific Northwest Dinner 86
Kids' Stuff 94
Terrific Tarts & Tortes 98
Sweet Finishes They Won't
　Forget 104
30-Minute Menus for the Holiday
　Season 108
　Rush-Hour Supper 109
　A Trim-The-Tree Favorite 110
　Before-The-Pageant Dinner ... 111
　Gift-Wrappers' Buffet 112
　Carolers' Delight 113
　Decorate-The-House Special .. 114
　A Before-The-Theater Treat .. 115
　Shoppers' Night Special 116
　Christmas Eve Supper 117

THREE

DECK THE HALLS...
118

America's Most Enchanting
　Decorations 120
　Northeast 121
　Midwest 122
　South 124
　Southwest 126
Collect Your Own Christmas
　Magic 128
Wreaths That Say 'Welcome' ... 132
　Wreaths That Say Welcome
　　in Every Room 134
　Wonderful Wreaths To
　　Make at Home 136
Home-For-The-Holiday
　Arrangements 140
O Tannenbaum, O Tannenbaum,
　Thou Tree Most Fair
　and Lovely! 146
Handmade Treasures for
　Your Tree 150

FOUR

HOLIDAY GIFTS WITH A HOME-MADE TOUCH
156

FOODS TO GIVE

Fabulous Fruitcakes 158
Homemade for the Holidays 162
Preserved Presents 162
Snacks and Nibbles 163
Festive Spreads 163
Sweet Treats 164
Party Panache 166
The Sweetest Gift 167
Bountiful Baskets To Make
  and Take 180

CRAFTS TO GIVE

Sweet and Spicy Holiday
  Baskets 182
Once Upon a Time 184
These Are a Few of Our Favorite
  Things 188
All Done Up in Ribbon 198
The Season's Fanciest
  Footwork 202
It's a Wrap 210
Surprise Packages 214
Wrapped With Imagination...
  and Almost No Money 216
Gift Wraps That Go
  Everywhere 218

FIVE

VISIONS OF GINGERBREAD
222

Classic Cookie Houses 224
Bake Your Own
  Victorian Village 244

SIX

FESTIVE FOODS FOR JOYOUS CELEBRATIONS
252

Luscious Feasts for the Festival
  of Lights 254
A Favorite Pot Roast Dinner .. 254
A Classic Hanukkah Meal 256
A World of Sweet Seasonal
  Breads 262
A Holiday Feast To
  Remember 268
Classic Christmas Feasts 272
Little Women 272
*Amahl and the Night
  Visitors* 274
The Wind in the Willows 276
As the British Feast
  at Christmas 282
Christmas Dinner With a
  Southern Accent 288
Winter Wonderland 292
Your Favorite Yuletide Treats .. 300
'Toys' With a Timeless Flavor .. 310
Simple Make-And-Bake
  Cookies 314
A Sweet Enchanted Forest 320
Heavenly Holiday Desserts 326

SEVEN

WELCOME THE NEW YEAR
332

Freeze-Ahead Party
  Hors d'Oeuvres 334
Ring in the New Year...
  The Low-Calorie Way 338
An Elegant New Year's Eve 342
A Bountiful Winter Buffet 344
Party Givers Guide
  to Beverages 348
*A Champagne Toast to the
  New Year* 349
Nonalcoholic Beverages 350
Coffee 352
Teatime 354
Hot Wine Drinks 356
Sweet Endings for the
  New Year 358
A Year Full of Special
  Delights 362

INDEX
373

Recipes 373
Crafts 383

INTRODUCTION

The holiday season "officially" begins with Thanksgiving and ends on New Year's Day. But the preparation and anticipation usually extend far beyond these exciting weeks. Many of us are on the lookout all year long for spectacular recipes, unique gifts and delightful decorations to help make the coming season even more joyous and memorable than the last.

You need look no further than the pages of this book for the very best assemblage of festive foods and imaginative crafts that embrace the wonderful spirit of the holidays. For Thanksgiving, you'll find a cornucopia of delectable recipes for the bird (and not just turkey), the trimmings and desserts...plus beautiful floral centerpieces that are surprisingly simple to make. 'Tis the season for parties, and our company-pleasing hors d'oeuvres, buffets and sweets are ideal for any style of entertaining. You'll be amazed at the variety of fabulous, hand-crafted wreaths, arrangements and ornaments to deck the halls and every other part of the house. Our collection of homemade gifts offers something for everyone on your list: fabulous cakes and cookies, adorable toys and stitchery and dozens of clever wrapping ideas. An elaborate Victorian mansion and cozy log cabin are among our many enchanting gingerbread houses to bake and build. For Hanukkah, we've selected traditional menus to commemorate the Festival of Lights. For Christmas, we set before you classic, elegant feasts and a heavenly assortment of sweet breads, cakes, cookies, pies and tortes. Our New Year's celebration includes easy, timesaving buffet menus; spirited and nonalcoholic beverages; plus a calendar of monthly delights to keep that special holiday feeling alive throughout the year.

Think of this book as your complete guide to the very best that the season has to offer. Need we say more? Well, just two words: Happy Holidays!

ONE

A CELEBRATION OF THANKSGIVING

The true meaning of Thanksgiving can be described by just two words—*thankfulness* and *togetherness*.

Two other words—*abundance* and *variety*—can describe the many foods and ways in which we all celebrate this uniquely American holiday. For some, turkey is a must; for others, it's goose. In some homes, family tradition means Great-Grandma's sausage stuffing and hearty mincemeat pie; in others, the menu changes from year to year. Some gatherings number 20 people; others, just two or four. What you'll find in this section is an abundance of recipes and menus, from a spectacular hors d'oeuvre "turkey" to traditional and nontraditional ideas on stuffings and trimmings to light desserts—each guaranteed to enhance a variety of entertaining styles. We've also included tips on buying, cooking and carving a turkey as well as scrumptious recipes for the day after. And for that special homemade touch, we show you how to make three fabulous floral arrangements.

Have a very happy Thanksgiving!

Let's talk turkey—not your usual bird, but one that doubles as a magnificent hors d'oeuvre. Use a hearty bread and rolls as the body, neck and head. Then construct colorful plumage from skewered shrimp, vegetables, cheese, olives, salami and other favorite finger foods. Make a "comb" by standing Belgian endive and red-pepper strips in cream cheese. The "nest" is fried vermicelli! This do-ahead masterpiece is worth the extra effort: It makes 40 appetizer servings and is guaranteed to get oohs and aahs from gobbling guests. Instructions begin on page 12.

JOHN UHER

FLIGHT OF FANCY

continued from page 10

FANTASY BIRD HOLIDAY APPETIZER
(pictured)

3 cups water
1 cup dry white wine
1 small onion, coarsely chopped
1 clove garlic, minced
1 teaspoon salt
8 black peppercorns
2 lb medium-small-size raw shrimp (about 40 per lb)
1 large head (1¾ lb) cauliflower
1 large bunch (1¾ lb) broccoli
1 large carrot
2 medium green peppers (4 to 5 inches high)
1 small red pepper
24 medium radishes
12 green onions

DRESSING
⅔ cup olive oil
⅓ cup tarragon-flavored vinegar
1 teaspoon sugar
1 teaspoon salt
¼ teaspoon ground white pepper
1 small clove garlic, pressed

DILL-YOGURT DIP
1 container (8 oz) plain yogurt
½ cup mayonnaise
2 tablespoons grated onion
2 tablespoons snipped fresh dill or 1 teaspoon dried dillweed
½ teaspoon salt

BIRD'S NESTS
1 pkg (1 lb) vermicelli or thin spaghetti (see Note)
Salad oil for frying (about 1 quart)

1 pkg (8-inch-long) bamboo skewers (you will need about 42)
1 pkg (12-inch-long) bamboo skewers (you will need about 66)
1 can (15 oz) baby corn, drained
1 (7-inch-long) cucumber
1 pkg (1 lb) part-skim mozzarella cheese, cut into ¾-inch cubes
1 pkg (6- or 8-oz) cocktail frankfurters (about 16)
1 pkg (8 oz) mild Cheddar cheese, cut into ¾-inch cubes
1 can (6 oz) pitted large ripe olives, drained
2½-to-3-lb oval or round loaf, firm whole-grain bread (10 inches long, 8 inches wide, 4½ inches high)
2 oval French rolls (about 5 inches long) or cut ends of French baguette
Decorative wooden picks or toothpicks (you will need about 60)
1 rectangular hard roll (about 4 inches long), or cut a middle section of baguette
1 pkg (8 oz) sliced hard salami
1 pkg (6 oz) sliced turkey breast
2 large Belgian endives
10 large pimiento-stuffed olives
1 pkg (3 oz) cream cheese

DAY AHEAD

1. Prepare steps 1 to 18: In large saucepan, combine water, white wine, chopped onion, minced garlic, 1 teaspoon salt and the peppercorns. Bring to boiling; simmer 5 minutes; add shrimp; cover; remove from heat; let stand 15 minutes. Drain shrimp, discarding cooking liquid and other particles. Shell and devein shrimp, leaving tail segment on, if desired. Wrap shrimp in foil; refrigerate until ready to assemble skewers.

2. With sharp knife, cut cauliflower and broccoli flowerets off stems in 2-inch lengths. (Cut large flowerets in half lengthwise. Refrigerate stems for another use, such as soup stock.)

3. Pare carrot. With long sharp knife, cut ¼-inch-deep, V-shape wedges along length of carrot, at ¼-inch intervals. Slice carrot crosswise into ¼-inch slices.

4. Cut green peppers in quarters lengthwise; remove and discard stems, ribs and seeds. Cut each pepper quarter in half crosswise. With scissors, make four 1½-inch-deep cuts in each pepper piece, starting from the crosswise cut and cutting toward but not through rounded end.

5. Cut red pepper in half lengthwise; remove and discard stem, ribs and seeds. With scissors, cut a solid V-shape piece of red pepper lengthwise from each pepper half, about 3 inches wide at the top and tapering to a point at bottom of pepper. From pepper trimmings, cut a triangular piece (1 inch long, ½ inch wide) for the bird's beak. Also from trimmings, cut 16 (1¼-by-¼-inch) strips of pepper for bird's comb. Wrap and refrigerate small pieces overnight.

6. In 5- or 6-quart kettle, bring 2 quarts water to boiling. Add cauliflowerets; cook 1½ minutes. With slotted spoon, remove cauliflower to colander; rinse immediately with cold water to stop cooking; drain well. In same boiling water, repeat procedure with broccoli, cooking 1½ minutes. Cook green-pepper pieces 30 seconds; cook the two large red-pepper triangles 1 minute (do not cook small

red-pepper pieces); cook carrot slices 4 minutes. Wrap and refrigerate all vegetables.

7. Trim and discard ends from radishes. With small, sharp paring knife, cut 5 or 6 shallow "petals" around side of each radish to make a "rose." Place radish roses in bowl of cold water; refrigerate.

8. Trim and discard root ends from green onions. Trim green tops off, leaving a 3-inch piece of onion. With sharp knife, make 1-inch-deep lengthwise cuts, ⅛ inch apart, at both cut ends of each onion; place onions in bowl of cold water; refrigerate overnight so ends curl to form brushes.

9. Make Dressing: In 1½-cup jar with tight-fitting lid, combine all dressing ingredients; cover; shake to blend; refrigerate overnight.

10. Make Dill-Yogurt Dip: In small bowl, combine all dip ingredients; cover; refrigerate overnight.

11. Make Bird's Nests: In 8-quart saucepot, bring 3 quarts water to boiling. Add vermicelli, a little at a time, stirring constantly; return to boiling; boil 5 minutes. Drain in colander; do not rinse. Vermicelli will be sticky and hold together. When cool enough to handle, on tray or cookie sheet, form vermicelli into 15 loose piles or nests, about 3 to 4 inches in diameter. Meanwhile, in deep 12-inch skillet or wok, heat about 1 inch oil (be sure oil is no more than one-third the depth of pan) to 375F on deep-frying thermometer. With large slotted utensil, lower four or five nests, one at a time, into hot oil. (Oil will bubble up in the beginning and subside.) Cook until nests are light golden-brown—3 to 4 minutes on each side; use two slotted utensils to turn them. Remove nests from skillet; drain well on paper towels. Repeat with remaining nests. Salt lightly, if desired. Store nests on tray at room temperature, loosely covered, until next day.

12. To assemble skewers, have two or three large trays or jelly-roll pans on hand. Thread 12 ears of baby corn, through the large ends, onto 12 (8-inch) skewers; place on tray. Set aside remaining corn. (When threading ingredients, to prevent foods from breaking, turn skewers as you insert into food.)

13. Drain onion brushes. Thread onion brushes crosswise onto 12 (8-inch) skewers; push 2 inches down from tip of skewer. Thread green-pepper sections

through uncut ends to make "tulips." Place skewers on tray. Set aside remaining pepper pieces.

14. Thread 2 or 3 shrimp, with tails aligned in same direction, onto each of 24 (12-inch) skewers; place on tray. Set aside remaining shrimp.

15. With fork, score skin of cucumber lengthwise. Cut cucumber crosswise into ¼-inch slices. Thread a cucumber slice vertically onto each of 18 (12-inch) skewers; push on skewer about 2 inches down; thread a broccoli floweret onto tip of each skewer. Place on tray. Set aside remaining broccoli and cucumber.

16. Drain radishes. Thread a mozzarella cube, 4 inches down, onto each of 24 (12-inch) skewers. Thread a radish rose; then insert points of skewers about 1 inch into a caulifloweret. Place on tray. Set aside leftover cauliflowerets and cheese, if any.

17. Thread a frankfurter vertically onto each of 16 (8-inch) skewers; push 4 to 5 inches down. Next, thread a Cheddar-cheese cube, a ripe olive and, at the tip, a carrot slice vertically; place on tray. Set aside leftover olives, carrot slices and cheese, if any.

18. Cover trays of skewered ingredients with plastic wrap; refrigerate. Arrange all leftover ingredients on serving plates; cover, and refrigerate.

NEXT DAY

19. About 4 hours before serving: Remove trays of skewers from refrigerator. Shake dressing well; brush only the shrimp and vegetables on skewers on both sides with dressing. Brush other plates of ingredients, except cheese, with leftover dressing. Cover, and return to refrigerator.

20. Place loaf of bread on large serving tray. (It is best to work with a high, oval loaf to achieve the most realistic bird shape. If one end of loaf is higher than the other, use the higher end to form the tail with the skewers. If bread is round, trim with serrated knife to make an oval shape.)

21. With knife, cut one French roll in half crosswise. With tapered ends of roll facing toward center of oval loaf, secure both halves of roll with wooden picks under tail end of loaf, to elevate it. (This will help later on to balance the weight of the skewers in the tail.)

22. To make head of bird, with sharp knife, trim 1 to 1½ inches off one end of remaining French roll, making it rounded, to form back of bird's head. To form neck, trim both ends of rectangular roll to a 45-degree angle, making sure that both angles are parallel. At end of oval loaf, opposite tail, place neck at right angle to loaf, and secure with two 8-inch skewers inserted through center of roll, leaving an inch of skewer showing; attach head to neck with same skewers.

23. To make it easier to insert skewers in oval loaf, with serrated knife, starting in center of oval loaf, score a line ¹⁄₁₆ inch deep across entire width of loaf. Working toward tail end, repeat scoring, 1 inch apart, making five scored lines in all. In space below last scored line, with metal skewer, punch about 16 holes an inch apart through crust, to facilitate inserting last set of skewers.

24. To make bird's tail, remove skewers from refrigerator. Insert corn skewers into first scored line in center of body of bird, spacing them evenly about 1 inch apart. Place longest corn ears in center of scored line and shortest ones at ends. Place the onion-pepper "tulips" in second scored line. Place shrimp skewers behind onion-pepper skewers. Place cucumber-broccoli skewers in the next line behind shrimp. Insert radish-cauliflower skewers in last line. Finally, insert frankfurter skewers into pre-formed holes at end of loaf. (If tail end of bread becomes top-heavy and tips downward, place fried vermicelli nests underneath tail end for balance.)

25. To cover top front of bird: Form salami slices into cone shapes. Fold turkey slices in half. With wooden picks, secure salami cones and folded turkey, in overlapping rows, across top and breast of bird.

26. Separate Belgian endives into leaves. With picks, secure large leaves, beginning from back to front, across lower sides of body to front in two or three overlapping rows. Set aside small leaves for the comb.

27. Arrange the two large triangular red-pepper pieces, one overlapping the other, to cover lower front of breast.

28. Cut stuffed olives in half lengthwise. With picks, attach olives, end to end, around base of neck.

29. Unwrap cream cheese; cut lengthwise into four strips. Starting at top center of bird's head, press one cheese strip onto roll, running cheese to back of head. Place two more cheese strips at base of first cheese strip, crosswise, in T shape. Reserve ½ teaspoon cream cheese from remaining strip; set aside. (Wrap and refrigerate remaining strip of cream cheese for another use.)

30. To make bird's comb, select 15 or 16 reserved small endive leaves. Insert leaves straight up along cream-cheese strips, beginning with the smallest leaves at front of comb and building to large leaves at back of head. Intersperse red-pepper strips between endive leaves. For bird's beak, secure small triangular red-pepper piece at tapered end of head with a pick.

31. To form bird's eyes, divide reserved ½ teaspoon of cream cheese in half. Flatten each half into a ⅓-inch diamond shape; place a piece on each side of head; cut two small triangles from a ripe olive; place a piece in center of each eye.

TO SERVE

32. Arrange some of the vermicelli nests around base of bird. Place remaining nests in a basket to serve alongside. Serve skewers and plates of ingredients with Dill-Yogurt Dip. (When all food and skewers have been removed from bird, the leftover bread and rolls may be wrapped and frozen for use in making stuffing or bread crumbs.) *Makes about 40 appetizer servings. Dip makes 1½ cups.*

Note: Two cans (5-ounce size) chow-mein noodles or two cans (7-ounce size) fried potato sticks may be used around base of bird, instead of the fried-vermicelli birds nests. ■

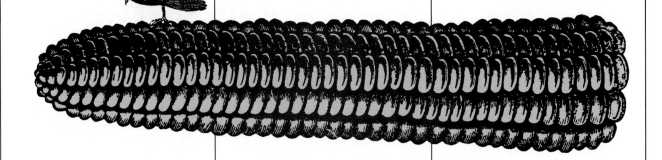

TURKEY WITH A CITRUS TWIST

This splendid Turkey à l'Orange is a delicious variation on the usual holiday bird. It's filled with a crunchy Pecan Stuffing, glazed with sweet orange sauce, adorned with a Candied Orange-Ring Chain and surrounded by cranberry-filled orange shells. Recipes and a complete Thanksgiving-dinner menu, plus turkey buying and roasting tips, begin on page 16.

continued from page 14

THANKSGIVING DINNER
(Planned for 12)
MUSHROOM CONSOMME
ROAST TURKEY A L'ORANGE*
PECAN STUFFING*
ORANGE-GIBLET SAUCE*
FRESH-CRANBERRY SAUCE IN
ORANGE SHELLS*
CANDIED ORANGE-RING CHAIN*
BUTTERED FRESH GREEN BEANS
SALAD OF TOSSED GREENS
WITH AVOCADO
HOT BUTTERED ROLLS
PUMPKIN CHEESECAKE*
HOT MINCEMEAT PIE*
HARD SAUCE*
FRESH-FRUIT BOWL
NUTS IN SHELL
BEAUJOLAIS OR CHILLED WHITE WINE
COFFEE
*Recipes given for starred dishes.

ROAST TURKEY A L'ORANGE
(pictured)

14- to 16-lb ready-to-cook turkey
Pecan Stuffing, recipe follows
½ cup (1 stick) butter or margarine, melted
Salt
Pepper
1 cup Beaujolais
2½ cups water
1 celery stalk, cut up
1 medium onion, peeled and quartered
1 medium carrot, pared and cut up
4 black peppercorns
1 bay leaf
½ cup orange marmalade
Orange-Giblet Sauce, recipe follows

1. Remove giblets and neck from turkey; wash and set aside for broth. Wash turkey thoroughly inside and out. Pat dry with paper towels. Remove and discard any excess fat.

2. Prepare Pecan Stuffing. Preheat oven to 325F.

3. Spoon some of stuffing into neck cavity of turkey. Bring skin of neck over back; fasten with poultry pin.

4. Spoon remaining stuffing into body cavity; do not pack. Insert four or five poultry pins at regular intervals. Lace cavity closed with twine, bootlace fashion; tie.

5. Bend wing tips under body, or fasten to body with poultry pins. Tie ends of legs together. Insert thermometer in inside of thigh at thickest part.

6. Place turkey in shallow roasting pan. Brush with some of butter; sprinkle with salt and pepper. Add wine.

7. Roast, uncovered and brushing occasionally with remaining butter and pan drippings, about 4½ hours, or until meat thermometer registers 185F. Leg joint should move freely. When turkey begins to turn golden, cover with a loose tent of foil, to prevent overbrowning.

8. Meanwhile, place giblets (reserve liver) and neck in a 2-quart saucepan. Add water, then celery, onion, carrot, ½ teaspoon salt, the peppercorns and bay leaf.

9. Bring to boiling; reduce heat; simmer, covered, 2½ hours, or until giblets are tender. Discard neck. Remove giblets from broth; chop coarsely. Strain cooking broth, pressing vegetables through sieve with broth. Measure broth; there should be 1½ cups. Set aside.

10. Remove foil. Spread turkey with marmalade; roast 10 minutes longer. Place turkey on heated serving platter. Remove twine and poultry pins. Let stand 20 to 30 minutes before carving. Meanwhile, make Orange-Giblet Sauce.

11. To serve: Garnish with Fresh-Cranberry Sauce in Orange Shells, recipe follows. Pass Orange-Giblet Sauce.

12. If desired, decorate turkey with Candied Orange-Ring Chain, recipe follows. *Makes 16 servings.*

PECAN STUFFING

12 cups fresh white-bread cubes
1 cup coarsely chopped pecans
½ cup chopped parsley
1 tablespoon poultry seasoning
2 teaspoons salt
½ teaspoon pepper
½ cup (1 stick) butter or margarine
3 cups chopped celery
1 cup chopped onion

1. In large bowl, combine bread cubes, pecans, parsley, poultry seasoning, salt, pepper; toss to mix well.

2. In hot butter in medium skillet, sauté celery and onion until golden — 7 to 10 minutes.

3. Add to bread mixture; toss lightly until well mixed.

4. Use to fill prepared turkey. *Makes 12 cups*, enough to stuff a 16-pound turkey.

ORANGE-GIBLET SAUCE

Fat from drippings
Liver from turkey
3 tablespoons brandy
3 tablespoons coarsely grated orange peel
¾ teaspoon chopped garlic
¼ cup all-purpose flour
1 tablespoon catsup
Dash pepper
1½ cups broth from giblets
½ cup red wine
¼ cup orange juice
1 cup orange sections

1. Strain drippings into a 4-cup measure. Skim fat from surface; reserve.

2. In 2 tablespoons reserved fat in large skillet, brown liver; remove from heat. Heat brandy slightly; ignite; pour over liver. Remove liver; chop. In same skillet, in 1 tablespoon fat, sauté orange peel and garlic 3 minutes.

3. Pour 1 cup drippings back into roasting pan. Add flour. Cook, over medium heat, stirring, until flour is browned. Add catsup, pepper, giblet broth, wine, orange juice, liver, orange-peel mixture and chopped giblets.

4. Bring to boiling, stirring to dissolve browned bits in pan. Reduce heat; simmer 10 minutes. Add orange sections; heat 1 minute. *Makes 4 cups.*

FRESH-CRANBERRY SAUCE IN ORANGE SHELLS

4 cups fresh cranberries
1½ cups sugar
1½ cups water
4 medium oranges (optional)

1. Wash cranberries; remove any stems (if frozen, don't thaw).

2. In large saucepan, combine sugar with water; bring to boiling, stirring until sugar is dissolved. Cook, uncovered and stirring occasionally, 10 minutes.

3. Add cranberries; return to boiling. Reduce heat; simmer, uncovered, 8 to 10 minutes. Remove from heat.

4. Turn into a bowl; refrigerate, to chill well before serving.

5. If desired, make orange shells: With sharp knife, cut oranges in half crosswise, making a zigzag pattern. Scoop out pulp (to use another time). Fill shells with cranberry sauce. *Makes 4 cups.*

CANDIED ORANGE-RING CHAIN

5 large navel oranges
1½ cups sugar
½ cup light corn syrup
2 cups water
1 drop red food color (optional)

1. With 2¼-inch round cookie cutter, cut four rounds of orange peel from each orange (pressing cutter and turning into orange). With 1½-inch round cookie cutter, cut out centers of large rounds to make rings.

2. In heavy, 4-quart Dutch oven, combine sugar, corn syrup, water and red food color, if desired. Bring to boiling, stirring constantly until sugar is dissolved. Boil, uncovered, 10 minutes.

3. Add orange rings; reduce heat; simmer 50 to 60 minutes, or until rings are glazed. Remove from heat.

4. Turn into a shallow dish, so rings are covered with syrup. Cover; let stand at room temperature several hours.

5. To assemble chain: Make a cut in half of the rings, and interweave with remaining rings, alternating cut and uncut rings. Secure cut rings with small piece of toothpick.

PUMPKIN CHEESECAKE

GRAHAM-CRACKER CRUST
1½ cups graham-cracker crumbs
2 tablespoons granulated sugar
½ cup (1 stick) butter or margarine, melted

CHEESE FILLING
4 pkg (8-oz size) cream cheese, at room temperature
1¼ cups granulated sugar
4 eggs
2 teaspoons vanilla extract
1 teaspoon grated lemon peel
1½ cups mashed pumpkin
¼ cup heavy cream
1½ teaspoons ground cinnamon
1½ teaspoons ground ginger
¼ teaspoon ground nutmeg

1 cup heavy cream, chilled
2 tablespoons confectioners' sugar
Chocolate curls

1. Preheat oven to 350F. Make Graham-Cracker Crust: In medium bowl, combine crumbs, 2 tablespoons granulated sugar and the butter; mix well with fork.

2. Grease bottom and side of a 10-inch springform pan.

3. With back of spoon, press crumb mixture to the bottom and halfway up the side of the prepared pan. Bake 8 minutes, or just until golden-brown. Remove to wire rack to cool.

4. Make Cheese Filling: In large bowl of electric mixer, at high speed, beat the cheese until light and fluffy.

5. Beat in granulated sugar and eggs, one at a time, beating well after each addition. Add vanilla, lemon peel, pumpkin, ¼ cup cream, the cinnamon, ginger and nutmeg; mix until well blended and smooth. Pour mixture into springform pan.

6. Bake 60 minutes. Turn off heat. Let cheesecake stand in oven 1 hour. Remove to wire rack to cool completely. Refrigerate 3 hours or overnight.

7. Before serving: With spatula, carefully loosen crust from side of pan. Remove side of springform pan.

8. In medium bowl, combine heavy cream and confectioners' sugar. With electric mixer, beat until stiff.

9. Turn cream into pastry bag with number-5 star tip. Pipe a ruching around edge; then make rosettes, 1½ inches

apart. Arrange chocolate curls between rosettes. Cut cheesecake into wedges. *Makes 10 to 12 servings.*

HOT MINCEMEAT PIE

1 jar (1 lb, 12 oz) prepared mincemeat
2 cups chopped, pared tart apple
1 cup coarsely chopped walnuts
2 tablespoons light-brown sugar
¼ cup sherry
1 pkg (11 oz) piecrust mix
1 egg yolk
1 tablespoon water
Hard Sauce, recipe follows

1. In large bowl, combine mincemeat, apple, walnuts, brown sugar and sherry; mix well.

2. Prepare piecrust mix as package label directs. Form into a ball.

3. On lightly floured surface, roll out half of pastry to form a 12-inch circle. Fit into a 9-inch pie plate. Preheat oven to 425F.

4. Turn mincemeat filling into pie shell; trim pastry to the edge of the pie plate.

5. Roll out remaining pastry to form a 12-inch circle. Make several slits near center for steam vents; adjust pastry over filling. Trim pastry evenly, leaving a ½-inch overhang all around. If desired, roll the trimmings ⅛ inch thick, and cut out several leaf shapes, for decoration.

6. Fold edge of top crust under bottom crust; press together to seal. Crimp edge decoratively. Lightly brush top, but not edge, with egg yolk beaten with water. Arrange leaves on top. Brush with egg-yolk mixture.

7. Bake 30 to 35 minutes, or until crust is golden-brown.

8. Meanwhile, make Hard Sauce.

9. Partially cool pie on wire rack. Serve warm with Hard Sauce. *Makes 12 servings.*

HARD SAUCE

⅔ cup (1⅓ sticks) butter or margarine, softened
2 teaspoons vanilla extract, or 1 or 2 tablespoons sherry
2 cups unsifted confectioners' sugar

1. In small bowl of electric mixer, at high speed, cream butter until light.

2. Add vanilla or sherry and confectioners' sugar; beat until smooth and fluffy. *Makes about 1½ cups.*

TURKEY TIPS

Don't "wing it."....Follow our guidelines for a picture-perfect turkey dinner.

BUYING—Most of the turkeys today are sold frozen in vacuum-packed plastic bags. Before you buy, check the bag for any punctures or tears: *Don't* buy the turkey if the bag is punctured or torn. For turkeys under 12 pounds, allow about 1 pound per person; turkeys over 12 pounds should yield about ¾ pound per serving. When selecting the size of a turkey, keep in mind that it must fit into your oven along with any other dishes that need baking! Check to see if directions for thawing and roasting come with the turkey. If they do, follow them carefully. If they don't, follow our directions below.

THAWING—The best and safest thawing method is to partially open the plastic bag and place the bird on a large tray or roasting pan in the refrigerator—allow about 24 hours for every 5 pounds. If you don't have that much time, you can safely thaw the bird in its original plastic wrapping by immersing it in cold water, changing the water every hour. This method takes about 8 hours to thaw a 12-pound turkey. If you have a microwave oven, check the manufacturer's guidebook for defrosting directions. Room-temperature thawing is *not* recommended because parts of the turkey could become warm enough for spoilage to begin. Once thawed, remove the plastic and the giblets, then cover the turkey with wax paper or plastic wrap and keep refrigerated until ready to stuff and cook.

STUFFING—A small 6- to 8-pound turkey holds very little, so it's better to bake the stuffing separately during the last 45 minutes of roasting time. When stuffing a larger bird, allow about ½ cup stuffing per pound, filling the neck and body cavity loosely, as the stuffing will expand during cooking. It is very important to stuff the turkey just before it goes into the oven. *Do not* stuff the bird the night before or even several hours before roasting—bacteria can grow in the warm, moist stuffing and may cause food poisoning. Spoon extra stuffing into a casserole and refrigerate. Bake 40 to 45 minutes before serving. To speed preparation, you can mix the dry ingredients for the stuffing the night before. Do not freeze stuffing in a cooked or uncooked turkey.

continued on page 21

SEN·SATIONAL STUFFINGS

What would a traditional Thanksgiving turkey be without the stuffing? Just a hollow bird! To fill your holiday turkey with succulent flavors, we've developed an array of untraditional but sensational stuffings, using very traditional Thanksgiving ingredients.

Cranberries aren't just for sauce —try them as the main ingredient in a Cranberry-Orange Stuffing made with chopped Brazil nuts and raisin bread. If you usually serve oysters raw on the half shell, think of them instead in a rich stuffing made the Maryland way with onions, celery and thyme. Cornbread joins with breakfast-sausage meat, savory sage and thyme for an old-fashioned New England flavor. And mashed yams give a Southern accent to a stuffing that gets its crunch from chopped pecans and toasted bread cubes.

These are all made-from-scratch stuffings. But if you prefer to start with your favorite packaged mix, just add sautéed fresh mushrooms, a touch of onion and parsley and some extra herbs and spices. Who's to know? For recipes, see page 20.

GEORGE RATKAI

continued from page 18

CRANBERRY-ORANGE STUFFING

½ cup (1 stick) butter or margarine
½ cup chopped onion
½ cup chopped celery
1 pkg (6 oz) chopped Brazil nuts (1 cup)
2 cups fresh cranberries, washed
½ cup sugar
½ cup orange juice
1 tablespoon grated orange peel
2 loaves (1-lb size) raisin bread
1½ teaspoons salt
½ teaspoon poultry seasoning
½ teaspoon dried savory leaves
⅛ teaspoon pepper

1. Preheat oven to 350F.
2. In hot butter in medium skillet, sauté onion, celery and Brazil nuts about 5 minutes.
3. Add cranberries, sugar and orange juice and peel; cook over medium heat, stirring constantly, until cranberries start to pop. Remove from heat; let stand 20 minutes.
4. Cut bread slices into ½-inch cubes, to measure 10 cups. Spread the bread cubes on a cookie sheet. Place in oven 5 minutes, or until lightly toasted.
5. Turn cubes into large bowl. Add salt, poultry seasoning, savory and pepper; toss to mix.
6. Add cranberry mixture; toss lightly until well mixed.
7. Use to fill prepared turkey. *Makes 12 cups,* enough to stuff a 16-pound turkey.

JOANNE'S MARYLAND OYSTER STUFFING

½ cup (1 stick) butter or margarine
1 cup chopped onion
1 cup chopped celery
¼ teaspoon dried thyme leaves
¼ teaspoon salt
Dash pepper
1½ lb firm-type sliced white bread, cut into cubes
2 pints small oysters
1 egg

1. In hot butter in Dutch oven, sauté onion and celery, stirring until golden—about 5 minutes. Remove from heat.
2. Stir in thyme, salt and pepper. Add bread cubes; toss lightly to mix well.
3. Drain oysters, reserving liquid. Add oysters to bread mixture; toss lightly to combine.
4. In small bowl, combine ½ cup oyster liquid and the egg; beat with fork to blend well. Add to bread mixture; toss lightly to combine. *Makes 10 cups,* enough stuffing for a 12-to-14-pound turkey.
Note: Or you may turn stuffing into a lightly buttered 2-quart casserole. Bake at 350F, ¾ hour, or until oysters curl.

SAUSAGE-CORNBREAD STUFFING

1 pkg (10 or 12 oz) cornbread mix
1 lb sausage meat
4 cups chopped celery
3 cups chopped onion
1 cup chopped green pepper
¼ cup chopped parsley
1½ teaspoons rubbed savory
1½ teaspoons dried sage leaves
1½ teaspoons dried thyme leaves
1½ teaspoons salt
½ teaspoon pepper
1 can (13¾ oz) chicken broth, undiluted
3 eggs, slightly beaten

1. Prepare cornbread mix as package label directs. Cool.
2. In large skillet, sauté sausage meat, stirring, until lightly browned. Add celery, onion, green pepper and parsley; sauté 8 to 10 minutes.
3. Crumble cooled cornbread into large bowl. Add sausage meat, vegetables, savory, sage, thyme, salt and pepper. Gradually add chicken broth and eggs, tossing lightly with fork. *Makes about 10 cups,* enough for a 12-pound turkey.

SWEET-POTATO-PECAN STUFFING

4 cups mashed, cooked sweet potatoes or yams
2 cups (4 sticks) butter or margarine, melted
3 cups finely chopped onion
2 cups finely chopped celery
2 cups coarsely chopped pecans
1½ teaspoons salt
1½ teaspoons dried thyme leaves
1½ teaspoons dried marjoram leaves
½ teaspoon dried sage
¼ teaspoon pepper
8 cups toasted bread cubes

1. In large bowl or kettle, beat sweet potatoes with portable electric mixer until smooth; beat in 1 cup butter.
2. In remaining hot butter in large skillet, sauté onion and celery, stirring, until onion is golden—about 5 minutes. Add to potato, along with pecans, salt, thyme, marjoram, sage and pepper; mix well. Add bread cubes; stir until well combined. Cool before using. *Makes 10 cups,* enough for a 12-pound turkey.

FRESH-MUSHROOM STUFFING

1 cup (2 sticks) butter or margarine
1 cup finely chopped onion
1½ lb fresh mushrooms, washed and coarsely chopped
1 pkg (8 oz) herb-stuffing mix
½ cup chopped parsley
2 teaspoons dried marjoram leaves
1 teaspoon poultry seasoning

½ teaspoon salt
½ teaspoon ground nutmeg
⅛ teaspoon pepper

1. In hot butter in large skillet, sauté onion and mushrooms, stirring, about 5 minutes; remove from heat.
2. In large bowl or kettle, combine stuffing mix, parsley, marjoram, poultry seasoning, salt, nutmeg and pepper; toss to mix well. Add sautéed onion and mushrooms and the drippings in skillet. With two forks, toss lightly. *Makes about 8 cups,* enough for a 10-pound turkey.

CHESTNUT STUFFING

1 cup (2 sticks) butter or margarine
1 cup chopped onion
4 cups coarsely chopped celery
¼ cup chopped parsley
6 cups dry white-bread cubes
4 cans (about 4 lb) water-packed chestnuts (see Note), well drained and broken into pieces
2 teaspoons salt
¼ teaspoon pepper
⅛ teaspoon ground nutmeg
¼ cup light cream or half-and-half
¼ cup white wine

1. In hot butter in large skillet, sauté onion, celery and parsley, stirring, about 5 minutes.
2. In large kettle, combine bread cubes, chestnuts, salt, pepper and nutmeg; toss to mix well.
3. Combine cream and wine; mix well. Add to bread mixture, along with vegetables and drippings in skillet. Toss lightly, using two large forks. *Makes 13 cups,* enough to fill a 16-pound turkey.
Note: Or use fresh chestnuts: To roast, make a slit in each shell with a sharp knife. Bake at 500F for 15 minutes. Remove shells and skins.

MASHED-POTATO STUFFING

10 medium potatoes (3 lb)
Boiling water
1 tablespoon salt
½ cup (1 stick) butter or margarine
1 cup chopped onion
½ cup chopped celery
4 cups toasted bread crumbs (see Note)
2 teaspoons salt
1 teaspoon rubbed sage
1 teaspoon dried thyme leaves
3 eggs, beaten

1. Pare potatoes; quarter. In 2 inches boiling water in large saucepan, cook potatoes with 1 tablespoon salt, covered, until tender—20 minutes. Drain well; return to saucepan.

2. Beat with portable electric mixer (or mash with potato masher) until smooth. Heat slowly over low heat, stirring, to dry out—about 5 minutes.

3. In hot butter in medium skillet, sauté onion and celery 5 minutes, or until tender.

4. Add mashed potato to onion-celery mixture, along with bread crumbs, salt, sage and thyme. Beat with wooden spoon to mix well. Beat in eggs. Use potato mixture to stuff turkey. *Makes 10 cups,* enough for a 12-pound turkey.

Note: Toast white bread; grate on fine grater.

MAKE-AHEAD RAISIN STUFFING

½ cup (1 stick) butter or margarine
⅓ cup finely chopped onion
1 lb ground chuck
1 pkg (15 oz) seeded dark raisins
¼ cup chopped parsley
1 tablespoon Worcestershire sauce
¼ teaspoon salt
¼ teaspoon pepper
2 quarts coarsely grated fresh white-bread crumbs (see Note 1)
1 can (10¾ oz) condensed chicken broth, undiluted
1 egg

1. In hot butter in 5-quart kettle, sauté onion until tender. Add chuck; cook, stirring until meat is no longer red.

2. Add raisins, parsley, Worcestershire, salt, pepper; cook over low heat, covered, 10 minutes. Remove from heat.

3. Stir in bread crumbs, chicken broth and egg until well blended.

4. To freeze: Turn stuffing into foil-lined 2-quart casserole; fold foil over stuffing. Freeze solid. Remove from casserole; overwrap with foil, plastic wrap, or moisture-vaporproof freezer paper. Seal; label; freeze.

5. To serve: Reheat on top of range if oven space is used for roasting turkey. Unwrap frozen stuffing; replace in casserole; cover tightly with lid or foil. Place on rack in large kettle. Add 1 inch boiling water to kettle; steam, covered, 2 hours. Water in kettle should boil gently; add more water as needed. (Stuffing may also be reheated in oven at 325F. Completely unwrap frozen stuffing. Place in a 2-quart casserole; bake, covered, 2 hours, or until heated through.) *Makes 12 servings,* enough for a 12-pound turkey.

Note 1: Or use 2 packages (8-oz size) herb-seasoned stuffing, and increase the chicken broth to 2 cans.

Note 2: If desired, do not freeze stuffing. Use at once to stuff turkey; do not store prepared stuffing in refrigerator. ∎

TURKEY WITH A CITRUS TWIST

continued from page 17

ROASTING—Before roasting, tie the turkey legs to the body and close body cavity with metal skewers or by sewing with heavy thread. Twist the wing tips under the back. Place the bird, breast up, on a rack in a shallow roasting pan. Brush with cooking oil or margarine. To control browning and help keep the breast meat moist, make a tent of aluminum foil that barely touches the bird. Baste occasionally with drippings. Remove the foil during the last 30 minutes of roasting for final browning.

TIMETABLE FOR ROASTING UNSTUFFED TURKEY
(Foil-Tent Method)

Weight of unstuffed, ready-to-cook turkey (pounds)	Cooking time for foil-tent method, at 325F (hours)
6 to 8	2¼ to 3¼
8 to 12	3 to 4
12 to 16	3½ to 4½
16 to 20	4 to 5
20 to 24	4½ to 5½

Turkey is done when meat thermometer in thigh registers 180 to 185F, or breast temperature registers 170 to 175F and leg joint moves freely.

TIMETABLE FOR ROASTING STUFFED TURKEY

Weight of unstuffed, ready-to-cook turkey (pounds)	Cooking time in uncovered pan, at 325F (hours)
6 to 8	3 to 3½
8 to 12	3½ to 4½
12 to 16	4½ to 5½
16 to 20	5½ to 6½
20 to 24	6½ to 7

Turkey is done when meat thermometer in thigh registers 180 to 185F, or breast temperature registers 170 to 175F and leg joint moves freely.

CARVING—For perfect timing, the turkey should be ready about 30 minutes before serving. Let it stand on a heated serving platter to absorb the juices and make carving easier. Remove stuffing before carving. To carve, first remove leg by cutting to the joint between the thigh and body of turkey. Press leg outward, bend back and cut through. Place leg on a plate and cut thigh from drumstick at joint. Slice dark meat from thigh, leaving drumstick whole, if desired. Next, with knife held parallel to the table, make a long cut to the bone at the base of the breast just above the wing joint. Cut off the wing. Slice the white meat in thin, even slices, each ending at the base cut. Arrange on a platter with the dark meat.

STORING—Scoop out all the extra stuffing, place in a covered container or in moistureproof wrapping, and refrigerate. Remove the meat that's left on the bones. Store whatever you plan to use in the next few days in the refrigerator. Then, to freeze the rest, separate the large slices from the smaller pieces and freeze in individual packets the types and amounts of meat you'll need for recipes you plan to use. To package for freezing, wrap meat securely in heavy-duty foil, making several double folds over each opening. Seal with freezer tape, and mark the contents with a freezer pencil. Don't forget to date the packages. For cooked turkey to retain its good quality, you'll need to use it within 6 months. Leftover gravy can be frozen, or stored in the refrigerator for up to two days. And don't throw out the carcass: It makes delicious turkey broth to use for soup now or to freeze for use later. Be sure to reheat broth or gravy to the boiling point before serving. ∎

THE NOBLE BIRD AND ALL THE TRIMMINGS

Thanksgiving is a day for counting our blessings as we gather for a sumptuous turkey feast. House to house across America the reason for celebrating is the same, but the foods of this celebration are often uniquely different. There are so many ways to prepare the bird, such a wealth of succulent go-alongs and feast-crowning desserts, that no two holiday dinners need be, or should be, alike. Here we bring you an ample sampling of the delicious possibilities. Opposite is the time-honored roast turkey, adorned with a string of cranberries, surrounded by sautéed sausages and served with a smooth Giblet Gravy. But turn the page and you'll find entirely different ways to present the bird, ranging from a robust Alsatian recipe to an exotic fruit-decked fowl. Accompanying our Golden Roast Turkey, opposite, is a creamy Winter-Squash Soup and a flaky lattice-topped Cranberry-Apple Pie. Included, too, are other exciting accompaniments—appetizers and relishes; potatoes and vegetables; pies, cakes and other sweets. We've also collected some second-day spectaculars that make the leftovers as appealing in taste as in their appearance. Recipes begin on page 32.

Braised Turkey Roll, above, is a one-dish meal ideal for a small family gathering. We've seasoned ours with onion, garlic and spices; bathed it in wine; and added turnips and carrots to all cook in the same liquid.

Roast Turkey in White Wine, above, is basted in a delicately spiced wine sauce and served tropical-style with glazed pears and kumquats, sautéed bananas and small clusters of green grapes.

Turkey With Orange Sauce, above, borrows a French-accented fruit-and-wine basting, more commonly used with duckling. Serve turkey garnished with watercress and fluted mushroom caps on orange slices.

Roast Turkey, Alsatian Style, left, with an apple-onion stuffing, is roasted on a juicy bed of sauerkraut, then served with tasty bratwurst, sautéed apple rings and French fries.

FABULOUS FIXIN'S

Baked Stuffed Onions, above, are big Spanish onions hollowed into cups, drizzled with butter, then filled with a mixture of mushrooms, bacon and herbs.

Cauliflower With Shrimp Sauce, above, is a gourmet dish with a simple secret: a can of cream-of-shrimp soup mixed with light cream and tomato juice.

Broccoli With Lemon Sauce, below, rings a serving dish with forest-green flowerets, then heaps the center with a lemon-accented froth of sauce.

Creamed Spinach and Potatoes Au Gratin, opposite, has rosettes of mashed potatoes around a lightly seasoned spinach cream, all sprinkled with cheese and baked till golden.

Cream-Cheese-Frosted Pumpkin Cake, above, is a light and springy tempter slathered with snowy swirls of creamy frosting and crowned with crunchy pecan halves.

Clove Cake With Caramel Frosting, above, is a moist, hearty spiced treat enveloped in sweet caramel and beautifully studded with chopped walnuts.

Pumpkin Meringue Pie, above, tops everyone's favorite Thanksgiving dessert with rosettes of easy-bake meringue...one rosette for each heavenly slice!

Mincemeat-Apple Pie, above, is today's answer to the old-fashioned two-pie choice. A lattice-topped work of art, combining two fillings, it is equally delicious with rum sauce or whipped cream.

Toasted-Coconut-Ice-Cream Mold, opposite, is a showy freeze-ahead marvel with toasted coconut both inside and out. Serve with Dark Chocolate Sauce.

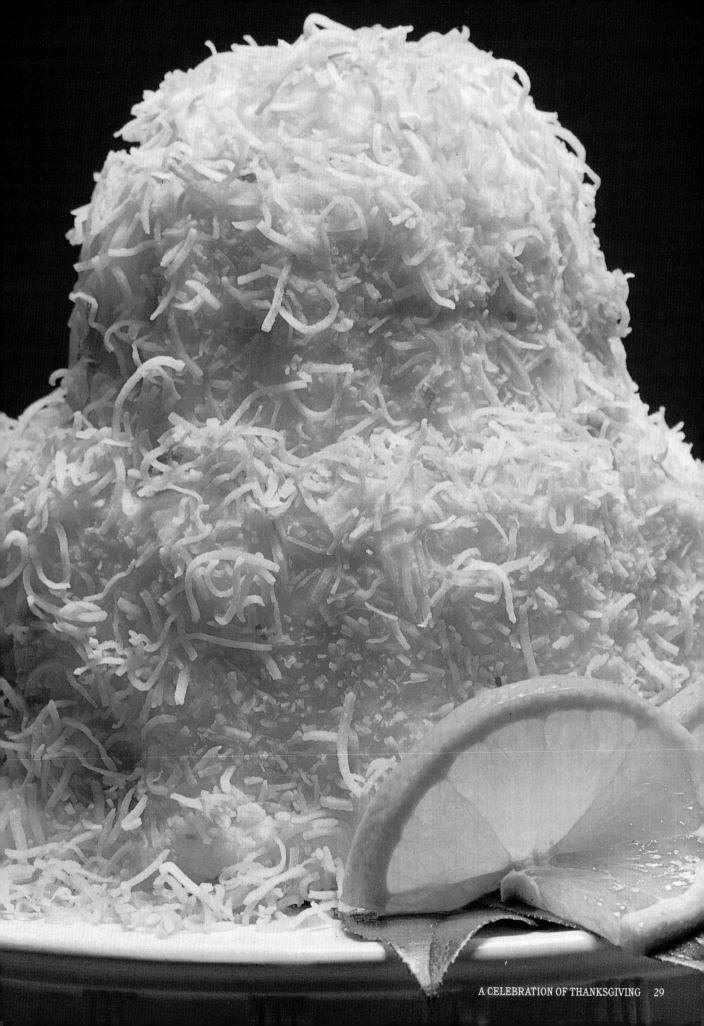

Sweet-And-Pungent Turkey, above, in typical oriental style, is a delightful contrast of tastes and textures. The green-onion flower garnish is easy to make—we tell you how on page 41.

Deluxe Turkey Pie, above, is a colorful medley of vegetables, sausage and cut-up cooked turkey that bakes "under cover" in a delicately seasoned sauce. It's a first-rate appetite-pleaser.

Turkey-And-Vegetable Pie, left, mixes peas or corn, cooked turkey and potatoes into a marvelous flaky-pastry-topped meal-in-one. You'll get requests for seconds for this tasty dish!

continued from page 22

MENU FOR THANKSGIVING DINNER

WINTER-SQUASH SOUP*

OR

LOBSTER BISQUE WITH SHERRY

GOLDEN ROAST TURKEY*

THANKSGIVING DRESSING*

GIBLET GRAVY*

CRANBERRY-ORANGE-APPLE RELISH*

SPICED CRANBERRIES*

CREAMED SPINACH AND
POTATOES AU GRATIN*

BROCCOLI WITH LEMON SAUCE*

AVOCADO-AND-FRESH-FRUIT
SALAD BOWL

HOT ROLLS   BUTTER

CRANBERRY-APPLE PIE*

TOASTED-COCONUT-ICE-CREAM MOLD*

CIDER   RED OR WHITE WINE

COFFEE

*Recipes given for starred dishes.

WINTER-SQUASH SOUP
(pictured)

1 butternut squash, about 3 lb (see Note 1)
2 cans (10¾-oz size) condensed chicken
    broth, undiluted
¼ teaspoon salt
Dash white pepper
1 cup heavy cream
¼ teaspoon ground nutmeg

1. Preheat oven to 400F. Bake whole squash about 1 hour, or until tender when pierced with a fork.

2. Let squash cool slightly. Cut in half lengthwise; discard seeds. With a spoon, scoop squash pulp from the skin.

3. In electric blender, combine half of squash pulp and 1 can broth; blend at low speed until well combined, then at high speed until smooth. Turn into a bowl. Repeat with remaining squash and broth. Stir in salt and pepper.

4. Refrigerate soup, covered, overnight.

5. At serving time, heat squash mixture just to boiling. Gradually stir in ½ cup cream; cook slowly until heated through. Taste and correct seasoning, if necessary.

6. Meanwhile, beat remaining cream just until stiff.

7. Serve soup very hot. Garnish each serving with a spoonful of whipped cream; sprinkle with nutmeg. *Makes 6 servings.*

Note 1: Or use 3 packages (12-ounce size) frozen squash, partially thawed.

Note 2: This recipe may easily be doubled to serve 12.

GOLDEN ROAST TURKEY
(pictured)

14- to 16-lb ready-to-cook turkey
Choice of Thanksgiving Dressings, recipes
    follow
1 cup (2 sticks) butter or margarine,
    melted
Salt
Pepper
Giblet Gravy, recipe follows

1. Remove giblets and neck from turkey; wash, and set aside. Wash turkey thoroughly inside and out. Pat dry with paper towels. Remove and discard any excess fat.

2. Prepare your choice of Thanksgiving Dressing. Preheat oven to 325F.

3. Spoon some of dressing into neck cavity of turkey. Bring skin of neck over back; fasten with poultry pin.

4. Spoon remaining dressing into body cavity; do not pack. Insert 4 or 5 poultry pins at regular intervals. Lace cavity closed, with twine, bootlace fashion; tie.

5. Bend wing tips under body, or fasten to body with poultry pins. Tie ends of legs together. Insert meat thermometer in inside of thigh at thickest part.

6. Place turkey on rack in shallow roasting pan. Brush with some of butter; sprinkle with salt and pepper.

7. Roast, uncovered and brushing occasionally with remaining butter and pan drippings, about 4½ hours, or until meat thermometer registers 185F. Leg joint should move freely. When turkey begins to turn golden, cover with a square of butter-soaked cheesecloth or a loose tent of foil, to prevent too much browning.

8. While turkey roasts, cook giblets and neck as directed in Giblet Gravy.

9. Place turkey on heated serving platter. Remove cheesecloth or foil, twine and poultry pins. Let stand 20 to 30 minutes before carving. Meanwhile, make gravy. *Makes 14 to 16 servings.*

THANKSGIVING DRESSINGS

OLD-FASHIONED DRESSING

12 cups fresh white-bread cubes
½ cup chopped parsley
1 tablespoon poultry seasoning
2 teaspoons salt
½ teaspoon pepper
½ cup (1 stick) butter or margarine
3 cups chopped celery
1 cup chopped onion

1. In large bowl, combine bread cubes, parsley, poultry seasoning, salt and pepper; toss to mix well.

2. In hot butter in medium skillet, sauté celery and onion until golden—7 to 10 minutes.

3. Add to bread mixture; toss lightly until well mixed.

4. Use to fill prepared turkey. *Makes 12 cups,* enough to stuff a 16-pound turkey.

CORNBREAD-OYSTER DRESSING

1 cup water
1½ cups (3 sticks) butter or margarine
2 pkg (8-oz size) cornbread-stuffing mix
1½ pints fresh oysters, or 3 cans (7-oz
    size) frozen oysters, thawed
½ cup chopped onion
½ cup chopped green pepper
½ cup chopped celery
1 teaspoon salt
½ teaspoon dried rosemary leaves
¼ teaspoon pepper

1. In 6-quart Dutch oven or kettle, heat 1 cup water and 1 cup of the butter until butter is melted. Remove from heat.

2. Add stuffing mix; toss to mix well.

3. Drain oysters; cut in half.

4. In remaining butter in medium skillet, sauté oysters, onion, green pepper and celery until onion is golden—5 to 7 minutes. Stir in salt, rosemary and pepper.

5. Add to stuffing mixture; toss lightly until well mixed.

6. Use to fill prepared turkey. *Makes 12 cups,* enough to stuff a 16-pound turkey.

GIBLET GRAVY
(pictured)

Turkey giblets and neck, washed
3 cups water
1 stalk celery, cut up
1 medium onion, peeled and quartered
1 medium carrot, pared and cut up
1 teaspoon salt
4 black peppercorns
1 bay leaf
1 can (10¾ oz) condensed chicken broth
⅓ cup all-purpose flour

1. Refrigerate liver until ready to use.

2. Place rest of giblets and neck in a 2-quart saucepan. Add water, the celery, onion, carrot, salt, peppercorns and bay leaf.

3. Bring to boiling; reduce heat; simmer, covered, 2½ hours, or until giblets are tender. Add liver; simmer 15 minutes longer. Discard neck. Remove giblets from broth, and chop coarsely. Set aside.

4. Strain cooking broth, pressing vegetables through sieve with broth. Measure broth; add enough undiluted canned broth to make 2½ cups. Set aside.

5. When turkey has been removed from roasting pan, pour drippings into a 1-cup measure. Skim fat from surface,

and discard. Return ⅓ cup drippings to roasting pan.

6. Stir in flour until smooth. Stir, over very low heat, to brown flour slightly. Remove from heat. Gradually stir in broth.

7. Bring to boiling, stirring; reduce heat; simmer, stirring, 5 minutes, or until gravy is thickened and smooth. Add the chopped giblets; simmer 5 minutes. *Makes about 3 cups.*

CRANBERRY STRING

Thread washed cranberries on a string, using a large darning needle and heavy-duty thread.

SAUTEED LINK SAUSAGES

Place 1 pound pork-sausage links in a heavy skillet with water 1 inch deep. Cook over medium heat until water is evaporated. Then sauté gently 15 to 20 minutes, turning until sausages are nicely browned all over and cooked through.

WONDERFUL WAYS WITH TURKEY

TURKEY WITH ORANGE SAUCE
(pictured)

8½-lb ready-to-cook turkey
1 large unpeeled orange
1 large onion
Salt
Pepper
¼ cup (½ stick) butter or margarine, melted
1 can (10¾ oz) condensed chicken broth

ORANGE SAUCE
3 tablespoons sugar
Water
2 navel oranges
2 tablespoons cornstarch
1 chicken-bouillon cube
½ teaspoon salt
¾ cup ruby port

Orange slices
Sautéed fluted mushroom caps
Watercress sprigs

1. Preheat oven to 325F. Remove giblets and neck from turkey; wash and set aside. Wash turkey thoroughly inside and out. Pat dry with paper towels. Remove and discard any excess fat.

2. Cut unpeeled orange into wedges. Peel onion, and cut into wedges.

3. Sprinkle neck and body cavities of turkey with salt and pepper. Place some of orange and onion wedges in neck cav-ity. Bring skin of neck over back, and fasten with poultry pin.

4. Stuff body cavity with remaining orange and onion wedges, the heart and cut-up gizzard. Omit liver. Close body cavity with poultry pins; lace with twine. Tie ends of legs together; bend wing tips under body.

5. Place turkey, breast side up, on rack in shallow roasting pan. Place neck in pan, also. Brush turkey with some of melted butter; sprinkle with salt and pepper. Insert meat thermometer in inside of thigh at thickest part.

6. Roast, uncovered and brushing occasionally with remaining melted butter, combined with ½ cup undiluted chicken broth, about 3 hours, or until meat thermometer registers 185F. Leg joint should move freely. (Reserve rest of broth.)

7. Place turkey on heated platter. Remove twine and poultry pins. Let stand in warm place 20 minutes before carving.

8. While turkey is roasting, start making Orange Sauce: In medium saucepan, heat sugar just until melted and light golden-brown. Carefully stir in ¼ cup water. Continue cooking over low heat until well blended and sugar is dissolved. Set aside.

9. Cut peel from 1 navel orange into 2-inch-long julienne strips. Place in small saucepan; add water to cover; boil 3 minutes; drain. Peel other orange. Section oranges over bowl, to reserve juice.

10. Add reserved undiluted chicken broth to drippings in roasting pan; bring to boiling, stirring to dissolve browned bits. Strain into a 2-cup measure; discard neck. Skim off and discard fat. Return dripping mixture to pan. Mix cornstarch with orange juice; add to pan along with bouillon cube and salt. Bring to boiling, stirring mixture constantly until mixture thickens; reduce heat; simmer 5 minutes.

11. Add port, sugar syrup, orange peel and the orange sections, and stir until the sauce is heated through.

12. To serve: Pour some of sauce over turkey; pass rest in sauceboat. Garnish platter with orange slices, mushroom caps and watercress. *Makes 8 servings.*

ROAST TURKEY IN WHITE WINE
(pictured)

10- to 12-lb ready-to-cook turkey
1½ teaspoons salt
½ teaspoon pepper
1 teaspoon dried thyme leaves
1 teaspoon dried rosemary leaves
½ cup (1 stick) butter or margarine, melted
1 cup chopped celery
1 medium onion, sliced
4 whole cloves
1 cup white wine

SAUCE
Water
3 tablespoons all-purpose flour
½ cup white wine
2 chicken-bouillon cubes
Dash pepper

Glazed-Fruit Garnish, recipe follows

1. Remove giblets and neck from turkey; wash, and set aside. Wash turkey thoroughly inside and out. Pat dry with paper towels. Remove and discard any excess fat.

2. Preheat oven to 400F.

3. Mix salt, ½ teaspoon pepper, the thyme and rosemary; sprinkle half the mixture inside turkey. Place heart and cut-up gizzard inside turkey; omit liver. Bring skin of neck over back; fasten with poultry pin. Bend wing tips under body, or fasten to body with poultry pins. Tie ends of legs together.

4. Place turkey, breast side up, in shallow roasting pan without rack. Brush half the butter over turkey. Sprinkle with remaining salt-and-pepper mixture. Insert meat thermometer in inside of thigh at thickest part.

5. Roast, uncovered and brushing with remaining butter, 40 minutes, or until lightly browned. Remove from oven. Reduce temperature to 350F.

6. Add celery, onion, cloves and turkey neck to roasting pan. Pour 1 cup wine over turkey. Cover pan tightly with foil.

7. Roast, basting every 30 minutes with pan juices, 2 hours. Remove foil; roast ½ hour longer, or until meat thermometer registers 185F. Leg joint should move freely.

8. Remove turkey from roasting pan to heated serving platter; remove twine and poultry pins. Turkey should stand in warm place 20 minutes before carving.

9. Make Sauce: Bring drippings in pan to boiling, stirring to dissolve browned bits. Boil, uncovered, 5 minutes. Discard neck. Strain into a 4-cup measure. Skim off all fat, and discard. Add water to liquid to measure 2½ cups; pour back into roasting pan. In small bowl, mix flour and ½ cup wine until smooth. Stir into pan; add bouillon cubes and pepper; simmer, stirring occasionally, 5 minutes. Strain; pour into sauceboat. There will be 2½ cups sauce.

10. To serve: Decorate platter with Glazed-Fruit Garnish. Pass Sauce. *Makes 10 to 12 servings.*

continued on page 34

continued from page 33

GLAZED-FRUIT GARNISH

¼ cup (½ stick) butter or margarine
½ cup light-brown sugar, firmly packed
2 tablespoons light corn syrup
2 cans (1-lb, 1-oz size) pear halves, drained
12 preserved kumquats
3 medium bananas
2 tablespoons lemon juice
1 lb green grapes, washed and divided into clusters

1. In large skillet, combine butter, sugar and corn syrup; cook over medium heat, stirring, until sugar is dissolved and mixture boils.
2. Place pear halves and kumquats in single layer in skillet; cook, uncovered, 5 minutes. Turn pear halves; cook 3 minutes, or just until glazed. Remove pears and kumquats; keep warm.
3. Peel bananas; cut in half lengthwise, then in half again. Sprinkle with lemon juice. In same pan, sauté banana halves, turning once, 3 to 5 minutes.
4. Arrange glazed fruit and grapes around turkey, as pictured.

TURKEY PAPRIKASH

9- to 10-lb ready-to-cook turkey
Paprika
Salt
Pepper
3 cloves garlic, slivered
¼ cup (½ stick) butter or margarine
1 onion, peeled and quartered
4 chicken-bouillon cubes
2 cups water
½ cup all-purpose flour
1 teaspoon Worcestershire sauce
1 pint dairy sour cream, at room temperature
Noodles and Mushrooms, recipe follows

1. Remove giblets and neck from turkey; wash, and set aside. Wash turkey thoroughly inside and out. Pat dry with paper towels. Remove and discard any excess fat.
2. Preheat oven to 400F.
3. Sprinkle 1 teaspoon paprika, 1 teaspoon salt and ½ teaspoon pepper inside body cavity. Place garlic in cavity. Bring skin of neck over back; fasten with poultry pin. Bend wing tips under body; tie ends of legs together.
4. Place turkey, breast side up, on rack in shallow roasting pan.
5. Melt butter in small saucepan. Stir in 1 teaspoon paprika, ½ teaspoon salt and ¼ teaspoon pepper. Brush some of mixture over turkey, coating completely. Insert meat thermometer in inside of thigh at thickest part.

6. Roast, uncovered, 20 minutes. Baste with remaining butter mixture; roast 20 minutes longer.
7. Meanwhile, in medium saucepan, combine giblets, neck, onion, bouillon cubes, 3 tablespoons paprika, ¼ teaspoon pepper and the 2 cups water. Bring to boiling; cover; reduce heat, and simmer 30 minutes. Remove liver and neck; discard.
8. Remove turkey from oven. Pour giblet mixture into pan. Cover turkey lengthwise and crosswise with strips of heavy-duty foil, to form a loose tent over turkey. Crimp foil to edge of pan, to seal completely.
9. Reduce oven temperature to 325F.
10. Return turkey to oven; roast 3 hours, or until meat thermometer registers 185F. Leg joint should move freely.
11. Remove turkey from roasting pan to heated serving platter. Remove twine and poultry pin. Turkey should stand in warm place 20 minutes before carving.
12. Make Paprika Sauce: Remove giblets from roasting pan; set aside. Strain liquid into medium bowl. Skim off fat, reserving ⅓ cup fat and discarding rest. Reserve liquid.
13. In roasting pan, blend reserved fat with flour until smooth. Add 2 teaspoons paprika, 1¼ teaspoons salt and the Worcestershire. Gradually stir in 2 cups reserved liquid.
14. Bring to boiling, dissolving browned bits in pan and stirring constantly until sauce thickens. Reduce heat; simmer 2 minutes. Remove from heat. Gradually stir in sour cream; heat over low heat, but do not boil. Add finely chopped giblets, if you wish. Keep warm.
15. To serve: Spoon Noodles and Mushrooms around turkey on platter. Ladle some sauce over turkey, if desired; pass remaining sauce. *Makes 8 to 10 servings.*

NOODLES AND MUSHROOMS

1 lb wide noodles
½ lb fresh mushrooms
½ cup (1 stick) butter or margarine

1. In large saucepan, cook noodles as package label directs.
2. While noodles cook, slice mushrooms and sauté in hot butter until lightly browned—3 to 5 minutes.
3. Drain noodles. Place in large bowl. Pour mushrooms and butter over them, and toss lightly. *Makes 8 to 10 servings.*

ROAST TURKEY, ALSATIAN STYLE
(pictured)

¼ cup (½ stick) butter or margarine
2 cups chopped onion
1 large apple, unpared and chopped
1 can (1 lb, 11 oz) sauerkraut
1 medium potato, pared and grated
1 tablespoon caraway seed
½ teaspoon salt
¾ teaspoon pepper
6- to 7-lb ready-to-cook turkey
1 large apple
1 large onion
5 slices bacon
¼ cup (½ stick) butter or margarine, melted

Sautéed Apple Rings, recipe follows
Bratwurst, recipe follows
French-Fried Potatoes, recipe follows

1. Preheat oven to 325F.
2. Melt ¼ cup butter in large skillet. Add chopped onion and chopped apple; sauté 10 minutes. Add sauerkraut, grated potato, caraway seed, salt and ½ teaspoon pepper.
3. Bring to boiling; reduce heat; simmer, uncovered, 5 minutes.
4. Meanwhile, remove giblets and neck from turkey; wash, and set aside. Wash turkey thoroughly inside and out. Pat dry with paper towels. Remove and discard any excess fat.
5. Core apple; cut into wedges. Peel onion, and cut into wedges.
6. Place some of apple and onion wedges in neck cavity. Bring skin of neck over back, and fasten with poultry pin.
7. Stuff body cavity with remaining apple and onion wedges, heart and cut-up gizzard. Omit liver and neck. Close body cavity with poultry pins, lace with twine. Tie ends of legs together; bend wing tips under body.
8. Turn sauerkraut mixture into shallow roasting pan. Place turkey, breast side up, on sauerkraut. Sprinkle ¼ teaspoon pepper over turkey. Place bacon slices evenly over turkey. Insert meat thermometer in inside of thigh at thickest part.
9. Roast turkey, uncovered, 1½ hours. Remove bacon from turkey; add to sauerkraut. Brush turkey with some of melted butter.
10. Roast, uncovered and brushing occasionally with remaining melted butter, 1 hour and 15 minutes longer, or until meat thermometer registers 185F. Leg joint should move freely.
11. Remove turkey from roasting pan to heated serving platter; remove twine and poultry pins. Turkey should stand in warm place 20 minutes before carving. Keep sauerkraut warm in oven in roast-

ing pan. Meanwhile, prepare Sautéed Apple Rings, Bratwurst and French-Fried Potatoes, if desired.

12. To serve: Remove bacon from sauerkraut, and discard. Gently stir sauerkraut. Remove with slotted spoon, and place around turkey. Arrange Sautéed Apple Rings, Bratwurst and French-Fried Potatoes as pictured. Garnish with parsley, if desired. *Makes 6 servings.*

SAUTEED APPLE RINGS

Core 3 large apples; cut each crosswise into 4 rings. In 3 tablespoons hot butter or margarine, sauté rings, turning once, just until tender—4 to 5 minutes. Keep warm.

BRATWURST

In 1 tablespoon butter, sauté 1 pound bratwurst, turning frequently, until well browned—20 to 25 minutes. Keep warm.

FRENCH-FRIED POTATOES

Fill large skillet or deep-fat fryer one-third full with salad oil; slowly heat to 375F on deep-frying thermometer. Meanwhile, pare 3 large baking potatoes (about 2 pounds); cut lengthwise into quarters. Fry potatoes, a single layer at a time, in hot oil about 10 minutes, or until golden-brown and tender. Drain on paper towels. Keep warm.

BRAISED TURKEY ROLL
(pictured)

4-lb ready-to-cook turkey roll
3 tablespoons butter or margarine
1½ cups thinly sliced onion
2 cloves garlic, crushed
1 can (10¾ oz) condensed chicken broth
1⅓ cups dry white wine
1 sprig parsley
1 sprig fresh tarragon or ½ teaspoon dried tarragon leaves
1 bay leaf
½ teaspoon salt
¼ teaspoon dried thyme leaves
4 black peppercorns
4 white turnips (1¼ lb)
6 large carrots (1 lb)
⅓ cup all-purpose flour

1. Remove turkey roll from plastic bag. Pat dry with paper towels.
2. Heat butter in a 6-quart Dutch oven.

Brown turkey roll well on all sides, turning with tongs or 2 wooden spoons.

3. Move roll to one side of Dutch oven. Add onion and garlic; sauté until golden.

4. Add undiluted chicken broth, 1 cup wine, the parsley, tarragon, bay leaf, salt, thyme and peppercorns. Insert meat thermometer into center of turkey roll. Simmer, covered, 1 hour.

5. Pare and quarter turnips. Peel carrots; halve crosswise. Add turnip and carrot to Dutch oven; simmer, covered, 45 to 60 minutes longer, or until meat thermometer registers 185F.

6. Remove turkey roll and vegetables to heated serving platter. Remove string from roll. Keep warm.

7. Make gravy: Strain stock into a 4-cup measure; skim off fat, and discard. Measure liquid. You should have about 3 cups. Return liquid to Dutch oven.

8. In small bowl, mix flour with remaining wine, to make a smooth paste. Stir into liquid; bring to boiling, stirring until thickened. Reduce heat; simmer 2 minutes.

9. Pour some of gravy over turkey roll. Pass the rest. Garnish roll with fresh tarragon sprigs and parsley, if desired. *Makes 6 servings.*

FABULOUS FIXIN'S

CREAMED SPINACH AND POTATOES AU GRATIN
(pictured)

MASHED POTATOES
8 medium potatoes (about 2½ lb)
1 tablespoon salt
½ cup milk
¼ cup (½ stick) butter or margarine
⅛ teaspoon white pepper
Dash ground red pepper
2 egg yolks

CREAMED SPINACH
2 pkg (10-oz size) chopped spinach
2 tablespoons butter or margarine
¼ cup chopped onion
3 tablespoons all-purpose flour
1½ cups light cream
¾ teaspoon salt
⅛ teaspoon white pepper
⅛ teaspoon ground nutmeg

1 tablespoon grated Parmesan cheese

1. Make Mashed Potatoes: Pare potatoes; cut in quarters. Cook in 1 inch boiling water with 1 tablespoon salt, covered, until tender—20 minutes. Drain well; return to saucepan.

2. Beat with portable electric mixer (or mash with potato masher) until smooth. Heat slowly, stirring, over low heat, to dry out—about 5 minutes.

3. In saucepan, heat milk and ¼ cup

butter until butter melts—don't let milk boil.

4. Gradually beat hot milk mixture into potato until potato is smooth, light and fluffy; beat in ⅛ teaspoon white pepper, the red pepper and egg yolks.

5. Make Creamed Spinach: Cook spinach as label directs. Drain very well on paper towels. In hot butter in medium saucepan, over medium heat, sauté onion 5 minutes.

6. Remove from heat. Stir in flour. Gradually stir in cream. Bring to boiling, stirring. Add drained spinach, salt, pepper and nutmeg; cook 3 minutes.

7. Grease a shallow 9-inch round baking dish. With a pastry bag and a number-5 tip, make 9 or 10 large rosettes around edge with the mashed potatoes. Fill center with the creamed spinach. Sprinkle all over with Parmesan cheese.

8. To serve: Preheat oven to 425F. Bake 15 minutes, or until hot and golden. *Makes 8 servings.*

BAKED STUFFED ONIONS
(pictured)

6 sweet Spanish onions (about 4 lb)
4 chicken-bouillon cubes
1 can (3 oz) chopped mushrooms, drained
4 slices bacon
1 cup soft bread crumbs
2 tablespoons chopped parsley
1 teaspoon dried marjoram leaves
1 teaspoon salt
⅛ teaspoon pepper
3 tablespoons butter or margarine
½ teaspoon paprika

1. Peel onions; cut a thin slice from top of each. Place onions in large saucepan or small kettle; add bouillon cubes and 2 quarts water. Bring to boiling; reduce heat, and simmer until almost tender—30 to 35 minutes. Drain, and let cool.

2. Preheat oven to 400F.

3. With small knife or teaspoon, remove centers of onions, leaving outside layers about ½ inch thick. Invert to drain.

4. Chop centers fine; measure 1 cup. Chop mushrooms fine.

5. Sauté bacon until crisp; crumble. Reserve bacon fat.

6. In medium bowl, combine crumbled bacon, chopped onion, mushrooms, bread crumbs, parsley, marjoram, salt and pepper; toss with a fork, to mix well. Mix in 2 tablespoons reserved bacon fat.

7. Melt butter in shallow baking dish; add paprika. Place onions in dish, brushing all over with butter mixture. Fill onions with stuffing; bake 20 minutes. *Makes 6 servings.*

continued on page 36

continued from page 35

CAULIFLOWER WITH SHRIMP SAUCE
(pictured)

2 heads cauliflower (2 lb each)
2 tablespoons lemon juice
2 teaspoons salt
1 can (10¾ oz) condensed cream-of-shrimp soup
½ cup light cream or half-and-half
½ cup tomato juice

1. Trim leaves and stems from cauliflower; wash thoroughly. Make two ½-inch-deep gashes across stems. Brush tops with lemon juice.
2. Place cauliflower, stem ends down, on rack in shallow roasting pan. Add enough water to just cover stems. Add salt to water.
3. Bring to boiling; steam gently, covered, 40 to 45 minutes, or until stems of cauliflower are tender. (Use sheet of foil if pan has no cover.)
4. Meanwhile, turn soup into medium saucepan.
5. Stir in cream and tomato juice; bring to boiling, stirring frequently. Keep warm.
6. Drain cauliflower very well; place in heated serving dish. Spoon sauce over top. *Makes 8 to 10 servings.*

BROCCOLI WITH LEMON SAUCE
(pictured)

2½ to 3 lb broccoli
Salt
2 eggs, separated
2 tablespoons heavy cream
2 tablespoons lemon juice
4 tablespoons (½ stick) butter or magarine

Lemon slices (optional)

1. Trim broccoli; wash thoroughly. Split each stalk lengthwise into halves or quarters, depending on size.
2. Place broccoli in large saucepan. Add boiling water to almost cover; add 1 teaspoon salt. Cook, covered, 10 minutes, or until tender. Drain. Keep warm.
3. Meanwhile, in top of double boiler, beat egg yolks with cream and ¼ teaspoon salt until thickened and light colored. Gradually beat in lemon juice.
4. Place over hot, not boiling, water; cook, beating constantly with wire whisk, until mixture thickens slightly. Remove double boiler from heat, but leave top over hot water.
5. Add butter, ½ tablespoon at a time, beating after each addition until butter is melted. Remove top from hot water.
6. In small bowl, beat egg whites until soft peaks form when beaters are slowly raised. Fold into yolk mixture.
7. Arrange broccoli on heated serving platter. Top with sauce, and, if desired, garnish with lemon slices. *Makes 6 to 8 servings.*

CANDIED SWEET POTATOES AND APPLES

1 cup light-brown sugar, firmly packed
¾ cup light corn syrup
½ cup (1 stick) butter or margarine
¼ teaspoon salt
6 pared, cooked, large sweet potatoes, halved lengthwise (4 lb); or 2 cans (1-lb, 12-oz size) vacuum-packed sweet potatoes
2 medium red apples
1 tablespoon lemon juice

1. In large, heavy skillet, combine sugar with corn syrup, butter and salt.
2. Bring to boiling over low heat, stirring until butter melts and sugar is dissolved.
3. Reduce heat; add sweet potatoes, arranging in a single layer. Baste well with syrup; cook, covered, over very low heat 15 minutes, turning once. Wash apples; cut each into eight slices; remove core. Toss with lemon juice.
4. Remove cover; add apple; cook, basting occasionally, 15 minutes longer, or until potatoes are well glazed. *Makes 8 servings.*

Note: Vacuum-packed sweet potatoes need less time for glazing.

MOLDED CRANBERRY SAUCE

4 cups sugar
4 cups water
2 lb fresh cranberries (8 cups)
2 tablespoons grated orange peel
Dash salt

1. In a 6-quart kettle, combine sugar with water; bring to boiling, stirring to dissolve sugar. Let boil, uncovered, 10 minutes, to form a syrup.
2. Meanwhile, wash and drain cranberries, removing any stems.
3. Add cranberries, orange peel and salt to syrup. Bring back to boiling; boil, uncovered, 10 to 20 minutes, or until thickened and cranberries are clear.
4. Pour into a 2-quart mold. Let cool at room temperature 1 hour. Refrigerate until well chilled and firm—5 hours or overnight.
5. To unmold: Loosen edge of mold with sharp knife. Invert on serving plate; shake out. Refrigerate. *Makes 2 quarts; about 16 servings.*

PARSNIPS AU GRATIN

2 lb parsnips
Salt

SAUCE
2 tablespoons butter or margarine
2 tablespoons all-purpose flour
½ teaspoon salt
⅛ teaspoon pepper
1½ cups milk

2 tablespoons butter or margarine
¼ cup packaged dry bread crumbs
⅓ cup grated sharp Cheddar cheese

1. Wash parsnips; pare. Cut lengthwise into quarters. Remove core; cut crosswise into 1½-inch pieces.
2. In 1 inch boiling, salted water in 3-quart saucepan, simmer parsnip, covered, 10 to 15 minutes, or just until tender. Drain.
3. Meanwhile, preheat oven to 350F. Grease a 1½-quart casserole.
4. Make Sauce: Melt 2 tablespoons butter in small saucepan. Remove from heat. Stir in flour, salt and pepper to make a smooth mixture. Gradually add milk, stirring.
5. Over medium heat, bring to boiling, stirring constantly. Reduce heat; simmer 1 minute.
6. Combine sauce with parsnip in prepared casserole.
7. In 2 tablespoons butter in a small skillet, brown bread crumbs, stirring.
8. Remove from heat. Add cheese, mixing well. Sprinkle over parsnip mixture.
9. Bake, uncovered, 20 to 25 minutes, or until bubbly and golden. *Makes 4 to 6 servings.*

SWEET-POTATO-AND-PINEAPPLE CASSEROLE

2 cans (1-lb, 1-oz size) vacuum-packed sweet potatoes, undrained
1 can (8¾ oz) crushed pineapple, undrained
⅛ teaspoon ground nutmeg
½ teaspoon salt
2 tablespoons light-brown sugar
¼ cup (½ stick) butter or margarine, melted

CRUNCHY TOPPING
⅓ cup light-brown sugar, firmly packed
½ cup (1 stick) butter or margarine, melted
2 cups cornflakes

1. Preheat oven to 325F.
2. Turn potatoes into a large bowl; mash until smooth. Add pineapple, nutmeg, salt, 2 tablespoons sugar and ¼ cup butter; mix with fork until well combined.
3. Turn into a 1½-quart shallow baking dish, spreading evenly.
4. Make Crunchy Topping: In a medium bowl, mix sugar with butter. Add

cornflakes; toss until cereal is well coated. Sprinkle evenly over sweet-potato mixture.

5. Bake, uncovered, 40 minutes, or until topping is brown and crisp. *Makes 8 to 10 servings.*

CRANBERRY-ORANGE-APPLE RELISH

2 large navel oranges
1 large red apple
1 lb fresh cranberries (4 cups)
1½ cups sugar

1. Grate peel of 1 orange into a large bowl. Remove peel and white pulp from both oranges.

2. Quarter and core unpeeled apple. Cut into ½-inch pieces. Wash and drain cranberries, removing any stems. Coarsely chop cranberries and oranges. Add fruits to grated peel.

3. Add sugar, stirring gently until dissolved. Refrigerate, covered, several hours or overnight. *Makes about 5 cups.*

CRANBERRY-TANGERINE RELISH

3 medium tangerines, or 2 large navel oranges
1 lb fresh cranberries (4 cups)
1½ cups sugar

1. Peel tangerines; reserve half of peel. Remove white membrane and seeds. Chop tangerines coarsely.

2. Wash and drain cranberries, removing any stems. Put cranberries and reserved peel through coarse blade of food chopper. .

3. Add tangerine and sugar; mix well.

4. Refrigerate, covered, several hours. Mix well just before serving. *Makes about 1 quart.*

CRANBERRY-APPLE PIE
(pictured)

Pastry for 2-crust pie
½ lb fresh cranberries (2 cups)
Sugar
¼ cup all-purpose flour
¼ teaspoon salt
6 large tart apples, pared, cored and cut into eighths (2½ lb)
¼ cup maple or maple-flavored syrup
3 tablespoons butter or margarine
1 egg yolk
1 tablespoon water

1. On lightly floured surface, roll out half of pastry into an 11-inch circle. Use to line 9-inch pie plate; trim. Refrigerate,

with rest of pastry, until ready to use.

2. Wash cranberries, removing stems.

3. In 3½-quart saucepan, combine 1¼ cups sugar, the flour and salt; mix well. Add apples, cranberries and maple syrup.

4. Cook, covered, over medium heat, stirring occasionally, until cranberries start to pop and mixture is thickened—8 to 10 minutes. Remove from heat.

5. Add butter; place saucepan in bowl of ice cubes 20 minutes to cool quickly.

6. Preheat oven to 400F.

7. Meanwhile, roll out other half of pastry into an 11-inch circle. With knife or pastry wheel, cut ten ½-inch-wide strips.

8. Turn cranberry-apple filling into pie shell. Moisten edge of shell slightly with cold water. Arrange 5 pastry strips, 1 inch apart, across filling; press ends to rim of pastry. Place 5 pastry strips across first ones at right angle, to make lattice. Press ends to rim of shell.

9. Fold overhang of lower crust over ends of strips, to make a rim. Crimp rim decoratively. Lightly brush lattice, not edge, with egg yolk mixed with water. Sprinkle lattice lightly with sugar.

10. Bake 30 to 35 minutes, or until crust is nicely browned. Cool partially on wire rack; serve slightly warm. Nice served with vanilla ice cream. *Makes 8 servings.*

<hr />

FINALES FOR THE FEAST

PUMPKIN CAKE
(pictured)

4 eggs
2 cups sifted all-purpose flour
2 teaspoons baking soda
½ teaspoon salt
1 teaspoon ground cloves
2 teaspoons ground cinnamon
½ teaspoon ground ginger
¼ teaspoon ground nutmeg
2 cups sugar
1 cup salad oil
1 can (1 lb) pumpkin
Cream-Cheese Frosting, recipe follows
Pecan or walnut halves

1. In large bowl of electric mixer, let eggs warm to room temperature—about 30 minutes.

2. Preheat oven to 350F. Sift flour with baking soda, salt, cloves, cinnamon, ginger and nutmeg.

3. At high speed, beat eggs with sugar until light and fluffy. Beat in oil and pumpkin to blend well. At low speed, beat in flour mixture just until combined.

4. Pour into an ungreased 9-inch tube pan. Bake about 1 hour, or until surface springs back when gently pressed with fingertip.

5. Cool cake completely in pan. With spatula, carefully loosen cake from pan; remove. Place on cake plate; frost with Cream-Cheese Frosting. Decorate with nuts, as pictured. *Makes 12 servings.*

CREAM-CHEESE FROSTING

2 pkg (3-oz size) cream cheese, softened
1 tablespoon rum or 1 teaspoon vanilla extract
3 cups confectioners' sugar

1. In medium bowl, with electric mixer at medium speed, beat cheese with rum until creamy.

2. Gradually beat in sugar, beating until light and fluffy.

3. Spread over Pumpkin Cake, making swirls with knife.

CLOVE CAKE WITH CARAMEL FROSTING
(pictured)

3 cups sifted all-purpose flour
1 tablespoon ground cloves
1 tablespoon ground cinnamon
1 teaspoon baking powder
½ teaspoon baking soda
⅛ teaspoon salt
1 cup seedless raisins
1 cup shortening, butter or margarine, softened
2¼ cups sugar
5 eggs
1 cup buttermilk
Easy Caramel Frosting, recipe follows
1 cup coarsely chopped walnuts

1. Preheat oven to 350F. Lightly grease 10-by-4-inch tube pan.

2. Sift 2¾ cups flour with the cloves, cinnamon, baking powder, soda and salt. Toss raisins with remaining flour.

3. In large bowl of electric mixer, at medium speed, beat shortening until creamy. Gradually add sugar, beating until mixture is light and fluffy—about 5 minutes.

4. In small bowl, beat eggs until very light and fluffy. Blend into sugar mixture at medium speed, using rubber spatula to clean side of bowl.

5. At low speed, alternately blend flour mixture (in thirds) and buttermilk (in halves) into sugar-egg mixture, beginning and ending with flour mixture. Beat only until blended. Stir in floured raisins.

6. Pour batter into tube pan; bake 60 to 65 minutes, or until cake tester inserted in center of cake comes out clean.

7. Cool in pan on wire rack 20 minutes. Gently loosen with a spatula; turn

continued on page 38

continued from page 37

out of pan onto rack. Cool completely—about 1 hour.

8. Frost with Easy Caramel Frosting; decorate side with nuts, as pictured. *Makes 16 servings.*

EASY CARAMEL FROSTING

½ cup (1 stick) butter or margarine
1 cup light-brown sugar, firmly packed
⅓ cup light cream or evaporated milk, undiluted
2 cups unsifted confectioners' sugar
1 teaspoon vanilla extract or ½ teaspoon maple extract

1. In small saucepan, over low heat, melt butter; remove from heat.

2. Add brown sugar, stirring until smooth. Over low heat, bring to boiling, stirring; boil, stirring, 1 minute. Remove from heat.

3. Add cream; over low heat, return just to boiling. Remove from heat; let cool to 110F on candy thermometer, or until bottom of saucepan feels lukewarm.

4. With portable electric mixer at medium speed, or wooden spoon, beat in confectioners' sugar until frosting is thick. If frosting seems too thin to spread, gradually beat in a little more confectioners' sugar. Add the vanilla extract.

5. Set in bowl of ice water; beat until frosting is thick enough to spread and barely holds its shape. Use at once to frost cake.

PUMPKIN MERINGUE PIE
(pictured)

3 eggs
1 can (1 lb) pumpkin
½ cup light-brown sugar, firmly packed
½ cup granulated sugar
1 teaspoon ground cinnamon
½ teaspoon ground ginger
¼ teaspoon ground nutmeg
⅛ teaspoon ground cloves
½ teaspoon salt
¾ cup milk
½ cup heavy cream
9-inch unbaked pie shell

Meringue Ring, recipe follows

1. Preheat oven to 350F. In large bowl, beat eggs slightly. Add pumpkin, both kinds of sugar, spices and salt; beat until well blended. Slowly add milk and cream.

2. Pour into pie shell; bake 60 or 70 minutes, or until knife inserted in center comes out clean. Cool on rack. Serve pie slightly warm; or refrigerate to chill well.

3. To serve, decorate pie with Meringue Ring. *Makes 6 to 8 servings.*

MERINGUE RING

¼ cup egg whites, at room temperature
¼ teaspoon cream of tartar
Dash salt
¼ cup sugar

1. Several hours before serving, preheat oven to 350F. Lightly grease back of a 9-inch layer cake pan.

2. Make meringue: In medium bowl, with electric mixer at high speed, beat egg whites, cream of tartar and salt until soft peaks form when beaters are slowly raised.

3. Gradually beat in sugar, 2 tablespoons at a time, beating well after each addition.

4. Continue beating until stiff peaks form when beaters are slowly raised.

5. Turn meringue into pastry tube with number-5 star tip. Press out eight rosettes, 1 inch apart, around edge of cake pan. Bake 10 to 12 minutes, or until golden-brown. Cool completely on wire rack.

6. To serve: Use spatula to remove rosettes; arrange around edge of pumpkin pie to form a ring, as shown in picture.

MINCEMEAT-APPLE PIE WITH FLAMING RUM SAUCE
(pictured)

1 pkg (11.25 oz) piecrust mix
FILLING
1 jar (1 lb, 12 oz) prepared mincemeat with brandy and rum (3 cups)
1 cup applesauce
1 cup diced, pared tart apple
1 can (4 oz) walnuts, coarsely chopped

1 egg yolk
1 tablespoon water

Flaming Rum Sauce, recipe follows

1. In medium bowl, prepare piecrust mix as package label directs. Shape into a ball.

2. On lightly floured surface, roll out two-thirds of pastry to ⅛-inch thickness. Fit into a 10-inch pie plate; trim overhang to 1 inch.

3. Roll out remaining pastry to a 12-inch circle. Cut, with pastry wheel or knife, into ten ½-inch-wide strips.

4. Preheat oven to 400F.

5. Make Filling: In large bowl, combine mincemeat, applesauce, diced apple, walnuts. Turn into pie shell.

6. Moisten edge of shell slightly with cold water. Arrange 5 pastry strips, 1 inch apart, across filling; press ends to rim of shell. Place 5 strips diagonally across first ones, to make lattice; press ends to rim of shell. Fold overhang of

lower crust over ends of strips, to make a rim. Flute rim.

7. Beat egg yolk with water. Brush over lattice top, but not on edge of pastry.

8. Bake 30 to 35 minutes, or until crust is nicely browned.

9. Make Flaming Rum Sauce.

10. Let pie cool slightly on wire rack. Serve pie warm, with the rum sauce, or with whipped cream or vanilla ice cream, if desired. *Makes 10 to 12 servings.*

FLAMING RUM SAUCE

⅓ cup granulated sugar
⅓ cup light-brown sugar, firmly packed
1 cup water
1 lemon wedge
1 orange wedge
½ cup dark rum

1. In small saucepan, combine sugars with water; cook over medium heat, stirring, until sugars are dissolved.

2. Add lemon and orange wedges; bring to boiling; boil, uncovered, 20 minutes. Discard fruit.

3. Just before serving: Add rum; heat over very low heat just until vapor rises. Remove from heat. Ignite with match, and take flaming sauce to table. Spoon over each piece of warm pie.

TOASTED-COCONUT-ICE-CREAM MOLD
(pictured)

1 can (14 oz) sweetened condensed milk (1⅓ cups)
3 teaspoons vanilla extract
1 cup cold water
2 cups heavy cream
2 cans (4-oz size) shredded coconut
Fresh orange slices

Dark Chocolate Sauce, recipe follows (optional)

1. In small bowl, combine condensed milk, vanilla and cold water. Pour into an 8- or 9-inch square baking pan. Place in freezer 1 to 1½ hours, or until mixture starts to freeze on bottom and sides.

2. In large chilled bowl, beat cream until stiff. Fold in chilled milk mixture. Return mixture to baking pan; freeze until mushy.

3. Meanwhile, preheat oven to 350F. Place coconut in large, shallow baking pan; bake, stirring once or twice, 15 minutes, or until lightly toasted.

4. Turn milk mixture into large chilled bowl; with electric mixer, beat until smooth. Fold in 2 cups toasted coconut. Set aside remaining coconut.

5. Pour mixture into a 1½-quart mold. Freeze overnight.

6. To unmold: Loosen around edge of mold with small spatula. Invert over serving plate; place a hot, damp cloth over mold; shake to release ice cream. Repeat if needed. Lift off mold.

7. Sprinkle reserved coconut over mold, pressing against ice cream, to cover completely. Garnish with orange slices. Serve with Dark Chocolate Sauce. *Makes 8 servings.*

DARK CHOCOLATE SAUCE

3 squares unsweetened chocolate
½ cup water
¾ cup sugar
¼ teaspoon salt
4½ tablespoons (¼ stick plus ½
tablespoon) butter or margarine
¾ teaspoon vanilla extract

1. In small saucepan, combine chocolate with water. Cook, over low heat and stirring occasionally, until chocolate is melted.

2. Add sugar, salt; cook, stirring, until sugar has dissolved and mixture has thickened—about 5 minutes.

3. Remove from heat. Stir in butter and vanilla. Let cool, or serve warm. *Makes about 1½ cups.*

HARVEST FRUIT BOWL

2 large oranges
2 pink grapefruit
1 red apple
1 ripe pear
½ lb Tokay grapes
½ cup Marsala
½ cup apricot nectar
¼ cup sugar
½ cup pitted dates

1. Peel oranges and grapefruit, removing white membrane. With sharp knife, cut sections into a large bowl, holding fruit over bowl to catch juice.

2. Wash, quarter, and core apple and pear. Cut into ½-inch pieces. Add to orange and grapefruit sections.

3. Halve grapes; remove seeds. Add to fruits in bowl, together with Marsala, apricot nectar and sugar. Toss to mix well. Refrigerate, covered, overnight, or until well chilled.

4. An hour before serving, cut dates in half. Add to fruit mixture. Nice to serve with poundcake. *Makes 10 to 12 servings.*

BRANDY-ALEXANDER FRAPPES

1 quart vanilla ice cream
½ cup brandy
½ cup crème de cacao
Chocolate Curls, recipe follows

1. Refrigerate 8 sherbet glasses several hours, to chill well.

2. Remove ice cream from freezer to refrigerator, to let soften—about ½ hour before using.

3. Just before serving, combine ice cream, brandy and crème de cacao in blender. Blend at high speed until smooth.

4. Turn into chilled sherbet glasses. Decorate each with a Chocolate Curl. *Makes 8 servings.*

PINEAPPLE CLOUD PIE

4 egg whites (½ cup)
1½ cups heavy cream
⅓ cup confectioners' sugar
1 teaspoon vanilla extract
1 can (8 oz) crushed pineapple, drained
¼ cup light rum
Chocolate Crumb Crust, recipe follows
3 tablespoons granulated sugar
Chocolate Curls, recipe follows

1. In large bowl of electric mixer, let egg whites warm to room temperature—about 1 hour.

2. In another large bowl, combine heavy cream, confectioners' sugar and vanilla; refrigerate one hour. In small bowl, combine pineapple and rum.

3. Meanwhile, prepare Chocolate Crumb Crust.

4. With electric mixer at high speed, beat cream mixture until stiff. Gently fold in pineapple-rum mixture.

5. With electric mixer at high speed, beat egg whites until soft peaks form when beaters are slowly raised. Gradu-

ally add granulated sugar, 1 tablespoon at a time; beat until stiff peaks form when beaters are slowly raised.

6. Gently fold whipped-cream mixture into meringue. Turn into prepared crust, mounding in center.

7. Freeze until firm—about 2 hours. Before serving, decorate with Chocolate Curls. *Makes 8 to 10 servings.*

CHOCOLATE CRUMB CRUST

1¼ cups finely crushed chocolate wafers
(use blender or food processor)
¼ cup (½ stick) butter or margarine,
melted

1. Place chocolate crumbs in a 9-inch pie plate. Add melted butter; stir with fork until well combined.

2. Press evenly on bottom and side of pie plate, not on rim. Refrigerate until ready to fill.

CHOCOLATE CURLS

To make Chocolate Curls: Let a 1-ounce square of semisweet chocolate stand in paper wrapper in warm place about 15 minutes, to soften slightly. Unwrap chocolate, and carefully draw vegetable parer across broad, flat surface of square. Lift curls with a wooden toothpick, to avoid breaking.

BUTTERSCOTCH-PECAN PIE

3 eggs
1 cup light corn syrup
⅛ teaspoon salt
1 teaspoon vanilla extract
1 cup sugar
2 tablespoons butter or margarine, melted
1 cup pecan halves
9-inch unbaked pie shell
Whipped cream

1. Preheat oven to 400F.

2. In medium bowl, beat eggs slightly. Add corn syrup, salt, vanilla, sugar and butter; mix well. Stir in pecans. Pour into pie shell.

3. Bake 15 minutes. Reduce heat to 350F; bake 30 to 35 minutes, or until outer edge of filling seems set.

4. Let cool completely on wire rack. Just before serving, decorate with rosettes of whipped cream. *Makes 8 servings.*

continued on page 40

continued from page 39

RICH SQUASH PIE

3 eggs
1 pkg (12 oz) frozen mashed squash, thawed
1 cup sugar
1 teaspoon ground cinnamon
1 teaspoon ground nutmeg
½ teaspoon ground ginger
½ teaspoon salt
1 cup heavy cream
¼ cup Cognac or brandy
9-inch unbaked pie shell with fluted edge

Whipped cream
Crystallized ginger, cut in diamonds

1. Preheat oven to 450F.
2. In large bowl, beat eggs slightly. Add squash, sugar, cinnamon, nutmeg, ginger and salt; beat until well blended. Slowly beat in 1 cup cream and Cognac.
3. Place pie shell on oven rack. Pour in custard mixture.
4. Bake 10 minutes. Reduce heat to 300F, and bake 45 to 50 minutes longer, or until knife inserted in center comes out clean.
5. Let cool completely on wire rack—about 4 hours.
6. Decorate with whipped cream and ginger. *Makes 6 to 8 servings.*

SECOND-DAY SPECTACULARS

TURKEY-AND-VEGETABLE PIE
(pictured)

2 tablespoons butter or margarine
½ lb small white onions, peeled
½ cup chopped celery
6 tablespoons all-purpose flour
1 teaspoon salt
⅛ teaspoon pepper
½ teaspoon dried thyme leaves
1 cup canned chicken broth
1 cup milk
1 can (12 oz) whole-kernel corn or 1 pkg (10 oz) frozen peas
3 cups cooked turkey, in large pieces (see Note)
1 lb potatoes, pared and diced
Pastry for 1-crust pie
1 egg yolk
1 teaspoon water

1. Heat butter in large skillet or Dutch oven. Add onions and celery; cook, covered, 10 minutes; remove from heat.
2. Stir in flour, salt, pepper and thyme until well combined. Gradually add broth and milk. Add corn or peas, turkey and potato.
3. Bring to boiling, stirring constantly. Reduce heat; simmer, stirring occasionally, 10 minutes. Turn into a 2-quart shallow baking dish.
4. Preheat oven to 400F. Make pastry.

5. Roll pastry to fit top of baking dish with a ½-inch overhang. Place over turkey mixture; turn edge under; seal to rim of dish, and crimp. Make several slits in top for steam vents. Beat egg yolk with water; brush over pastry.
6. Bake 30 minutes, or until crust is deep golden. *Makes 8 servings.*
Note: Use leftover turkey from roast turkey.

DELUXE TURKEY PIE
(pictured)

3 cups cooked, cubed turkey (see Note)
1 can (10¾ oz) condensed chicken broth
1 soup can water
¼ cup coarsely chopped onion
¼ cup coarsely chopped carrot
¼ cup coarsely chopped celery
1 small bay leaf
1 pinch dried thyme leaves
2 sprigs parsley
½ cup dry white wine
½ pkg (11 oz) piecrust mix
6 small white onions, peeled
2 medium carrots, pared and quartered
2 large potatoes (¾ lb), peeled, cut into ½-inch cubes
3 slices bacon, quartered
¼ lb pork sausage, formed into 6 (1 inch) balls
Water
1 can (3 oz) sliced mushrooms
3 tablespoons all-purpose flour
1 teaspoon salt
Dash pepper
1 tablespoon chopped parsley
1 egg, slightly beaten

1. Set cubed turkey out of refrigerator; let it come to room temperature.
2. In a medium saucepan, combine broth and the soup can of water. Add onion, carrot, celery, bay leaf, thyme, parsley and white wine.
3. Bring to boiling; reduce heat; simmer, covered, ½ hour.
4. Meanwhile, prepare piecrust mix as package label directs; refrigerate.
5. Strain broth, mashing vegetables, into a bowl. Return broth to saucepan. Add white onions, quartered carrot and potato; bring to boiling; reduce heat and cook until carrot is tender—about 20 minutes.
6. At same time, in large skillet, cook slices of bacon until crisp; drain on paper towels; pour off fat. Crumble bacon.
7. In same skillet, cook sausage balls,

turning until browned all over—about 15 minutes.

8. Drain broth from vegetables into a 2-cup measure. Add enough water to make 1¾ cups liquid. Pour back into saucepan; bring to boiling.

9. Drain liquid from mushrooms into a 1-cup measure; add water to make ½ cup. Combine with flour in small bowl, stirring until smooth. Add slowly to boiling liquid, stirring with wire whisk until smooth and thickened. Add salt and pepper.

10. Turn vegetables into a 1½-quart casserole. Add cut-up turkey, sausage balls, drained mushrooms, chopped parsley and thickened sauce; stir just to combine. Top with bacon. Preheat oven to 400F.

11. On lightly floured surface or pastry cloth, roll out pastry ½ inch larger all around than top of casserole. Place on top of casserole, turning edge under; press to rim of casserole, to seal all around. Cut several steam vents in top. Brush lightly with egg. Bake 30 to 35 minutes, or until crust is golden and mixture is bubbly. *Makes 5 to 6 servings.*

Note: Use leftover turkey from roast turkey.

SWEET-AND-PUNGENT TURKEY
(pictured)

1 egg
½ teaspoon soy sauce
3 cups cooked turkey, in large pieces
Salad oil or shortening
⅓ cup cornstarch

SAUCE
2 tablespoons butter or margarine
1 clove garlic, crushed
½ cup 1-inch pieces green onion
2 onions, peeled and cut into wedges
1 can (15¼ oz) pineapple chunks
1 cup sugar
1 cup cider vinegar
2 tablespoons cornstarch
¼ cup water
1 pkg (7 oz) frozen Chinese pea pods
2 tablespoons catsup
2 teaspoons soy sauce

Green-onion flowers (see Note)
Hot cooked rice

1. In pie plate or shallow dish, beat egg with ½ teaspoon soy sauce. Add turkey; toss to coat well; let stand 10 minutes.

2. Meanwhile, fill 3-quart saucepan or deep-fat fryer one-third full with salad oil; slowly heat to 375F on deep-frying thermometer.

3. Place ⅓ cup cornstarch in a clean paper or plastic bag. Shake turkey pieces, a few at a time, in cornstarch until evenly coated.

4. Drop turkey pieces into hot fat; fry, turning once, about 3 to 5 minutes, or until golden on all sides. With slotted spoon, remove turkey; drain on paper towels. Keep warm in oven set at 200F.

5. Make Sauce: Melt butter in large skillet. Sauté garlic, green onion and onion wedges until golden—about 5 minutes.

6. Drain pineapple liquid into 1-cup measure; add water to make 1 cup. Set chunks aside.

7. Add pineapple liquid, sugar and vinegar to skillet; cook, stirring, until sugar is dissolved.

8. In small bowl, combine cornstarch with water until smooth. Stir into liquid in skillet; bring to boiling, stirring. Add pea pods, catsup and soy sauce; simmer 5 minutes.

9. Add turkey pieces and pineapple chunks; stir gently until heated through. Turn into heated serving dish. Garnish with green-onion flowers. Serve with rice. *Makes 4 to 6 servings.*

Note: To make green-onion flowers: Trim tops of green onions; the white portion should be 3 to 4 inches long. Starting 1 inch from bottom, make several lengthwise slits in onions. Place in ice water, to curl.

CURRIED-TURKEY CREPES

TURKEY FILLING
5 tablespoons (½ stick plus 1 tablespoon) butter or margarine
¼ cup all-purpose flour
Salt
1½ cups milk
1 teaspoon chopped shallot or green onion
2 cups cooked turkey in ¼-inch cubes
½ cup dry white wine
1 teaspoon curry powder
¼ teaspoon Worcestershire sauce
⅛ teaspoon pepper
Dash ground red pepper

CREPES
1 cup milk
¾ cup all-purpose flour
¼ teaspoon salt
2 eggs

Salad oil

TOPPING
1 egg yolk
⅛ teaspoon salt
4 tablespoons (½ stick) butter or margarine, melted
2 teaspoons lemon juice
¼ cup heavy cream, whipped

Grated Parmesan cheese

1. Make Turkey Filling: To make white sauce, melt 4 tablespoons butter in medium saucepan; remove from heat. Stir in ¼ cup flour and ½ teaspoon salt until smooth. Gradually stir in milk; bring to boiling, stirring constantly. Reduce heat, and simmer 5 minutes. Remove from heat, and set aside.

2. In 1 tablespoon hot butter in medium skillet, sauté shallot 1 minute. Add turkey; sauté 2 minutes longer. Add wine, curry, ¼ teaspoon salt, the Worcestershire and peppers; cook over medium heat, stirring, 3 minutes. Stir in 1 cup of the white sauce just until blended. Refrigerate while making crepes. Set aside remaining white sauce for topping.

3. Make Crepes: In medium bowl, with rotary beater, beat milk with flour and salt until smooth. Add eggs; beat until well combined.

4. Slowly heat a 5½-inch skillet until a little water sizzles when dropped on it. Brush pan lightly with salad oil. Pour about 1½ tablespoons batter into skillet, tilting pan so batter covers bottom.

5. Cook until nicely browned on underside. Loosen edge; turn; cook until browned on other side. Remove from pan; cool on wire rack. Repeat with rest of batter, to make 18 crepes. Lightly brush pan with oil before cooking each one. As crepes cool, stack them with waxed paper between.

6. Preheat oven to 350F. Remove filling from refrigerator. Spoon 1 rounded tablespoon onto each crepe; fold two opposite sides over filling. Arrange in shallow baking dish; cover with foil. Bake 20 to 25 minutes, or until heated through.

7. Meanwhile, make Topping: In small bowl, with rotary beater, beat egg yolk with salt until foamy; gradually beat in 2 tablespoons melted butter. Mix remaining butter with lemon juice; gradually beat into egg-yolk mixture. With wire whisk or rubber spatula, fold in remaining white sauce just until combined. Fold in whipped cream.

8. Uncover hot crepes. Spoon topping over them; then sprinkle lightly with grated Parmesan cheese. Broil, 4 to 6 inches from heat, until nicely browned. *Makes 6 servings.*

To prepare ahead of time: Make and fill crepes as directed; cover with foil, and refrigerate. Make topping, but do not add whipped cream. Refrigerate. To serve: Bake crepes as directed. Fold the whipped cream into sauce, ready to spoon over the crepes. Sprinkle with cheese. ∎

GREAT HOLIDAY DINNERS

AN AMERICAN INDIAN THANKSGIVING

If you're thinking of traditional American cooking, what could be more authentic than a dinner from the original Americans—the Indians. Long before the first settlers arrived from Europe, Indians held ceremonies to give thanks to the Great Spirit after a bountiful harvest or a successful hunt, and something very like the food shown on this page was served at these rituals. On page 48 you'll find a menu and recipes for an Iroquois dinner, including Roast Stuffed Pheasant, Pumpkin Soup and Indian Cornbread (both based on Iroquois recipes) and a delicious Apple-Cranberry Relish.

GEORGE RATKAI

GREAT HOLIDAY DINNERS

A NEW ENGLAND THANKSGIVING

The dinner shown here is a specialty of Vermont's Woodstock Inn. The inn is noted for continental, as well as regional New England, cuisine, so it's not surprising that this Thanksgiving dinner (which could, as well, be served at Christmas) is planned around goose, Alsatian style. The crisp, roasted bird is filled with a delicious sausage stuffing, set on a bed of sauerkraut and garnished with browned link sausages and glazed apple slices. A White-Wine Sauce goes over all. Served along with it is Baked Acorn Squash that's flavored with orange juice, lemon juice and sherry. The dessert: rum-flavored Pumpkin Mousse (not pictured). For menu and recipes, turn to page 49.

GREAT HOLIDAY DINNERS
A CREOLE THANKSGIVING

Turkey is the conventional holiday choice, but it's not quite so conventional when served with flaming brandy, in the New Orleans style. Roast Turkey Flambé is the main dish in this sumptuous holiday dinner from the famous Caribbean Room of the Pontchartrain Hotel in New Orleans. The rest of the meal is basically traditional, too, but with Creole touches that make it special: for example, oysters and pecans in the stuffing, as well as sausage, celery, onion. Pictured also are two vegetable dishes: a Yam Soufflé and Cauliflower Polonaise. For complete menus and the recipes, turn to page 50.

GEORGE RATKAI

continued from page 42

AN AMERICAN INDIAN THANKSGIVING MENU
(Planned for 6)
CLAMS ON HALF SHELL
PUMPKIN SOUP*
ROAST STUFFED PHEASANT AND WILD-RICE CASSEROLE*
SUCCOTASH
APPLE-CRANBERRY RELISH*
INDIAN CORNBREAD*
BUFFALO-DANCE PUDDING OR MAPLE-SQUASH PIE
CIDER   COFFEE
Recipes given for starred dishes.

PUMPKIN SOUP
(pictured)

2 tablespoons butter or margarine
½ lb yellow onions, thinly sliced
½ tablespoon all-purpose flour
1 can (10¾ oz) condensed chicken broth, undiluted
1 can (1 lb) pumpkin
2 cups milk
1 cup light cream or half-and-half
2 cups water
½ teaspoon salt
⅛ teaspoon pepper
⅛ teaspoon ground ginger
⅛ teaspoon ground cinnamon

1. In hot butter in 6-quart Dutch oven, sauté onion, stirring occasionally, 10 minutes, or until tender. Remove from heat.

2. Stir flour into onion; gradually stir in chicken broth. Bring to boiling; reduce heat; simmer, covered, 10 minutes.

3. Ladle mixture into electric blender. Blend, covered, at high speed one minute, or until completely smooth.

4. Return to Dutch oven; blend in pumpkin with wire whisk. Add milk, cream, water, the seasonings and spices; beat with wire whisk to blend.

5. Heat soup slowly over medium heat just to boiling; reduce heat, and simmer, covered, 15 minutes, stirring occasionally. Serve hot. *Makes 2 quarts; 6 to 8 servings.*

Note: You may make this the day before, and reheat just before serving.

ROAST STUFFED PHEASANT AND WILD-RICE CASSEROLE
(pictured)

1 pkg (6 oz) long-grain-and-wild-rice mix
3 (2-lb size) ready-to-cook pheasants (see Note)
¾ cup (1½ sticks) butter or margarine, melted
½ teaspoon dried thyme leaves
1 tablespoon salt
3 tablespoons dried juniper berries, crushed
⅛ teaspoon pepper
2 lb seedless green grapes, washed
1 cup coarsely chopped walnuts
2 tablespoons all-purpose flour
1 can (10¾ oz) condensed chicken broth, undiluted
1 tablespoon currant jelly

1. Preheat oven to 425F. Prepare rice as package label directs, but omit packet of seasoning.

2. Wash pheasants under cold running water; pat dry with paper towels.

3. To melted butter, add thyme, salt, juniper berries and pepper. Brush birds well, inside and out, with some of seasoned butter.

4. In large bowl, mash half of grapes. Add remaining grapes, the nuts, cooked rice and remaining seasoned butter. Toss gently with fork to combine.

5. Spoon stuffing lightly into neck and body cavities of pheasants, filling only two-thirds full. Turn leftover stuffing into a casserole dish with cover. Fasten skin of neck to back with poultry pin. Fold wing tips under body; then close body cavity with poultry pins. Lace with twine, if necessary. Tie ends of legs together.

6. Place pheasants in shallow roasting pan. Roast, uncovered, 15 minutes; reduce oven temperature to 350F. Continue roasting pheasants, basting frequently, 45 minutes longer, or until birds are tender.

7. About 20 minutes before birds are done, place stuffing casserole in oven. Bake, covered, 25 minutes.

8. Remove pheasants from oven. Lift to heated platter; cover with foil to keep warm.

9. Pour off drippings from roasting pan; discard fat. Return 2 tablespoons drippings to pan.

10. Stir in flour, to make a smooth mixture; brown it slightly over low heat, stirring to loosen browned bits in pan.

11. Gradually stir in chicken broth; add currant jelly. Heat, stirring, until smooth and bubbly. If sauce is too thick, add a little broth, wine or water. Serve with pheasants and stuffing. *Makes 6 servings.*

Note: Or use small whole chickens or Cornish game hens. Cook giblets separately; chop, and add to sauce.

APPLE-CRANBERRY RELISH
(pictured)

1 pkg (8 oz) dried-apple slices
Water
2 cups fresh whole cranberries
1 cup light-brown sugar, firmly packed

1. In 2-quart saucepan, combine apple slices with 2½ cups water. Bring to boiling; reduce heat; simmer, covered, 5 to 10 minutes, or until apples are tender but still hold shape.

2. Remove from heat, and spoon into a medium bowl.

3. In same 2-quart saucepan, combine cranberries, sugar and 1¼ cups water. Bring to boiling, stirring until sugar is dissolved. Cook, stirring occasionally, 2 minutes, or until all cranberries have popped.

4. Stir cooked apples into cranberry mixture. Bring to boiling; reduce heat; simmer, covered and stirring occasionally, 10 minutes.

5. Turn into serving bowl; refrigerate until well chilled. *Makes 6 cups.*

INDIAN CORNBREAD
(pictured)

1½ cups all-purpose flour
3 teaspoons baking powder
1 teaspoon salt
½ cup sugar
¼ cup (½ stick) butter or margarine, softened
2 eggs
1 cup canned pumpkin
½ cup milk
1 cup yellow cornmeal
1 cup blueberries (see Note)
½ cup coarsely chopped walnuts

1. Preheat oven to 350F. Lightly grease a 9-by-5-by-2¾-inch loaf pan.

2. Sift flour with baking powder and salt; set aside.

3. In large bowl, with rotary beater, beat sugar, butter and eggs until smooth. Add pumpkin, milk and cornmeal; beat until smooth.

4. With wooden spoon, stir in flour mixture, mixing just until combined. Gently stir in blueberries and nuts.

5. Turn batter into prepared pan, spreading evenly. Bake 1 hour, or until cake tester inserted in center comes out clean.

6. Let cool in pan on rack 10 minutes. Remove from pan. Serve slightly warm. *Makes 1 loaf.*

Note: Use frozen blueberries (without sugar), thawed and drained.

A NEW ENGLAND THANKSGIVING
MENU FROM THE
WOODSTOCK INN
(Planned for 8)
ASSORTED RELISHES AND NUTS
CRANBERRY SHRUB
ROAST STUFFED GOOSE*
SAUERKRAUT WITH SAUSAGE*
GLAZED APPLES*
POTATOES MOUSSELINE
BAKED ACORN SQUASH*
TOSSED GREEN SALAD
ASSORTED HOT ROLLS
PUMPKIN MOUSSE*
COFFEE   CHILLED WHITE WINE
*Recipes given for starred dishes.

ROAST STUFFED GOOSE
(pictured)

SAUSAGE STUFFING
1 lb sausage meat
2 cups finely chopped onion
1 pkg (8 oz) herb-seasoned-stuffing mix
1 teaspoon salt
¼ teaspoon pepper

10-lb ready-to-cook goose
1 tablespoon lemon juice
1 teaspoon salt
⅛ teaspoon pepper
White-Wine Sauce, recipe follows
Sauerkraut With Sausage, recipe follows
Glazed Apples, recipe follows

1. Make Stuffing: In large skillet, cook sausage about 5 minutes, breaking up with fork into 1-inch chunks. As sausage is cooked, remove it to a large bowl. Pour fat from skillet, reserving 2 tablespoons.

2. In the 2 tablespoons hot fat, sauté onion until tender—5 minutes.

3. Add to sausage with stuffing, salt and pepper, tossing lightly to mix well.

4. Preheat oven to 325F. Remove giblets and neck from goose; reserve for White-Wine Sauce. Wash goose inside and out; dry well with paper towels. Remove all fat from inside, and discard. Rub cavity with lemon juice, salt and pepper.

5. Spoon stuffing lightly into neck cavity; bring skin of neck over back, and fasten with poultry pins. Spoon stuffing lightly into body cavity; close with poultry pins, and lace with twine. Bend wing tips under body; tie ends of legs together.

6. Prick skin only (not meat) over thighs, back and breast very well. Place, breast side up, on rack in large roasting pan.

7. Roast, uncovered, 2 hours. Remove goose from oven.

8. Pour fat from pan, and discard. Roast goose, uncovered, 1 hour longer. Remove goose to platter; keep warm. Make White-Wine Sauce.

9. To serve, spoon the sauerkraut around goose. Garnish with sausage and Glazed Apples. Pass White-Wine Sauce. *Makes 8 to 10 servings.*

WHITE-WINE SAUCE

Goose giblets and neck
2½ cups water
1 celery stalk, cut up
1 medium onion, peeled and quartered
1 medium carrot, pared and cut up
1 teaspoon salt
4 black peppercorns
1 bay leaf
Dry white wine
2 tablespoons all-purpose flour

1. While goose is roasting, wash giblets and neck well. Refrigerate liver until ready to use. Place rest of giblets and neck in 2-quart saucepan; add water, the celery, onion, carrot, salt, peppercorns and bay leaf.

2. Bring to boiling. Reduce heat; simmer, covered, 2½ hours, or until giblets are tender. Add liver; simmer 15 minutes. Discard neck. Chop giblets coarsely; set aside.

3. Strain cooking broth, pressing vegetables through sieve with broth. Measure broth; add enough dry white wine to make 3 cups; set aside.

4. Remove goose to platter; pour drippings into 1-cup measure. Skim fat from surface, and discard. Return 2 tablespoons drippings to roasting pan.

5. Stir in flour until smooth. Over very low heat, stir to brown flour slightly. Remove from heat; gradually stir in broth.

6. Bring to boiling, stirring. Reduce heat; simmer, stirring, 5 minutes, or till thick and smooth. Add chopped giblets, salt to taste; simmer 5 minutes. *Makes about 3 cups.*

SAUERKRAUT WITH SAUSAGE
(pictured)

2 cans (1-lb, 1-oz size) sauerkraut, undrained
¼ lb thick-sliced bacon
½ teaspoon salt
¼ teaspoon pepper
1 lb link sausages

1. Turn 1 can sauerkraut into a 3-quart saucepan; arrange half of bacon slices over sauerkraut. Top with remaining can of sauerkraut, then bacon slices. Sprinkle with salt and pepper.

2. Bring to boiling; reduce heat; simmer, covered, 30 minutes; drain.

3. Meanwhile, prick sausages all over with a fork; arrange in single layer in cold skillet; cook over medium heat 10 to 12 minutes, turning frequently to brown evenly. Drain on paper towels. *Makes 8 servings.*

GLAZED APPLES
(pictured)

¼ cup (½ stick) butter or margarine
¼ cup lemon juice
½ cup sugar
¼ teaspoon salt
½ cup water
2 large red apples

1. In large skillet, melt butter; stir in lemon juice, sugar, salt and water. Bring to boiling, stirring, until sugar is dissolved. Reduce heat; simmer, uncovered, 3 minutes.

2. Wash apples; cut crosswise into ½-inch-thick slices, leaving skin on; remove cores. Place in simmering syrup, turning to coat both sides.

3. Cook apple slices, uncovered, 1 to 2 minutes on each side, or just until tender. Remove from syrup. Use as garnish around goose.

BAKED ACORN SQUASH
(pictured)

4 (1-lb size) acorn squash
4 tablespoons (½ stick) butter or margarine
2 tablespoons coarsely grated orange peel
2 tablespoons coarsely grated lemon peel
2 tablespoons orange juice
2 tablespoons lemon juice
2 tablespoons sherry
Salt

1. Preheat oven to 350F. Cut squash in half; with a spoon, remove seeds and strings. Place, skin side up, on buttered 15-by-10-by-1-inch baking pan.

2. Bake until tender—40 minutes; remove from oven. Turn each squash half over, and prick flesh with fork. Dot each with ½ tablespoon butter. Sprinkle each with ¾ teaspoon mixed orange and lemon peel.

3. In small bowl, combine orange juice, lemon juice and sherry. Spoon mixture over squash and into holes in center. Sprinkle each with a little salt.

4. Return to oven, and bake 15 to 20 minutes longer, basting once or twice with liquid in center. *Makes 8 servings.*

continued on page 50

continued from page 49

PUMPKIN MOUSSE

1 env unflavored gelatine
¼ cup rum or brandy
4 eggs
⅔ cup sugar
1 cup canned pumpkin
½ teaspoon ground cinnamon
½ teaspoon ground ginger
¼ teaspoon ground mace
¼ teaspoon ground cloves
1 cup heavy cream, whipped

DECORATION
½ cup heavy cream, whipped
Walnut halves

1. Fold a 24-inch piece of waxed paper lengthwise in thirds. Form 2-inch collar around 1-quart straight-sided soufflé dish. Tie with string to hold in place.

2. Sprinkle gelatine over rum in small bowl; set bowl in a pan of hot water; simmer to dissolve gelatine. Remove from hot water; cool slightly.

3. In large bowl, with electric mixer at high speed, beat eggs until thick and light. Gradually beat in sugar; continue beating 5 minutes, or until very thick and light.

4. In small bowl, combine pumpkin, cinnamon, ginger, mace and cloves. Stir into egg mixture along with cooled gelatine mixture, blending well.

5. With rubber spatula, gently fold 1 cup cream, whipped, into gelatine mixture until well combined.

6. Turn into prepared soufflé dish, smoothing surface with spatula.

7. Refrigerate until firm—4 hours or overnight.

8. To serve, gently remove paper collar. Decorate top with rosettes of whipped cream; place walnut half on each rosette. *Makes 8 servings.*

**A CREOLE THANKSGIVING
AT THE PONTCHARTRAIN,
NEW ORLEANS**
(Planned for 6 to 8)

OYSTERS ODETTE
ROAST TURKEY FLAMBE
WITH OYSTER-AND-PECAN DRESSING*
GIBLET GRAVY
COMPOTE OF FRESH ORANGES AND
CRANBERRIES
YAM SOUFFLE*
CAULIFLOWER POLONAISE*
TOSSED GREEN SALAD
HOT BUTTERED ROLLS
MILE-HIGH PIE WITH CHOCOLATE
SAUCE
HOT MINCEMEAT PIE WITH HARD
SAUCE*
COFFEE   CHAMPAGNE
*Recipes given for starred dishes.

ROAST TURKEY FLAMBE WITH OYSTER-AND-PECAN DRESSING
(pictured)

12- to 14-lb ready-to-cook turkey, with
   giblets and neck
Oyster-and-Pecan Dressing, recipe follows
¼ cup (½ stick) butter or margarine,
   melted
1½ teaspoons seasoned salt
1 celery stalk, cut up
1 large onion, peeled and halved
1 bay leaf
4 black peppercorns
⅓ cup all-purpose flour
½ cup canned condensed chicken broth,
   undiluted
2 or 3 chicken-bouillon cubes
½ teaspoon liquid gravy seasoning
Watercress (optional)
Orange slices (optional)
½ cup brandy (for flaming)

1. Remove giblets and neck from turkey; wash; set aside. Wash turkey inside and out; pat dry with paper towels. Remove and discard excess fat.

2. Make Oyster-and-Pecan Dressing. Preheat oven to 350F.

3. Spoon some of dressing into neck cavity of turkey. Bring skin of neck over back; fasten with poultry pin.

4. Spoon rest of dressing into body cavity; do not pack. Insert 3 or 4 poultry pins at regular intervals; lace cavity closed with twine, bootlace fashion; tie. Bend wing tips under body. Tie ends of legs together. Brush skin all over with butter; sprinkle with salt.

5. Place turkey inside a brown-in-bag (17 by 22 inches), along with celery, onion, bay leaf, black peppercorns, neck and giblets. Place turkey in bag on rack in large, shallow roasting pan.

6. Insert meat thermometer, right through bag, in inside of thigh at thickest part. Close bag with twist tie, placing tie near turkey. Cut off excess bag. With tip of paring knife or fork, puncture six holes in top of bag (see brown-in-bag package instructions).

7. Roast about 3 hours, or until meat thermometer registers 185F; leg joint should move freely.

8. Remove turkey from oven. Let stand 20 minutes in bag; then slit bag; remove turkey to a warm, large serving platter. Remove twine, poultry pins.

9. Make gravy: Remove giblets; chop coarsely. Discard neck. Strain broth left in pan and bag; pour into medium saucepan. Bring to boiling; boil, uncovered, to reduce broth to 2½ cups—about 20 minutes.

10. In small bowl, combine flour with chicken broth, mixing until smooth. Stir flour mixture into broth mixture in saucepan, along with bouillon cubes. Bring to boiling, stirring until smooth. Add chopped giblets and gravy seasoning; simmer 5 minutes.

11. To serve: If desired, garnish with watercress and orange slices. Flame turkey at table just before serving: In saucepan, warm brandy. Ignite with match; pour, blazing, over turkey. *Makes 12 to 14 servings.*

PONTCHARTRAIN'S OYSTER-AND-PECAN DRESSING

½ lb pork-sausage meat
½ cup (1 stick) butter or margarine
1 cup chopped onion
1 cup chopped celery
2 tablespoons chopped parsley
1 teaspoon salt
¼ teaspoon ground white pepper
½ tablespoon Worcestershire sauce
3 cups fresh oysters, drained; or 3 cans (8-oz size) oysters, drained; or 3 cans (7-oz size) frozen oysters, thawed, drained
1 cup coarsely chopped pecans
6 cups day-old bread cubes, crusts removed

1. In 6-quart Dutch oven or kettle, sauté sausage until golden—about 5 minutes. Remove sausage; add butter to sausage fat. In hot fat, sauté onion, celery, parsley until onion is golden—about 5 minutes. Remove from heat.

2. Add salt, pepper, Worcestershire, oysters, cooked sausage, pecans and bread cubes to Dutch oven. Toss lightly to mix well. Use to fill turkey. *Makes 10 cups,* enough to fill a 12- to 14-pound turkey.

YAM SOUFFLE
(pictured)

6 egg whites
½ teaspoon salt
¼ cup sugar
1 can (1 lb, 8 oz) yams or sweet potatoes, drained (see Note)
¼ cup sugar
¼ teaspoon ground cinnamon
¼ teaspoon ground mace
1 tablespoon grated orange peel
1 cup light cream or half-and-half

1. In large bowl, let egg whites warm to room temperature—about 1 hour. Also, preheat oven to 375F.

2. With electric mixer at high speed, beat egg whites with salt just until soft peaks form when beaters are slowly raised. Gradually add ¼ cup sugar, beating until stiff peaks form when beaters are slowly raised.

3. In another large bowl, using same beaters, combine yams, ¼ cup sugar, the cinnamon, mace and orange peel. Beat at high speed until mixture is smooth—2 minutes.

4. Meanwhile, in small saucepan, heat cream to boiling. Slowly add to yam mixture, beating until combined.

5. With wire whisk or rubber spatula, using an under-and-over motion, fold yam mixture into egg whites just until combined.

6. Gently turn into a 1½-quart, straight-sided soufflé dish. Bake 45 minutes, or until puffy and golden-brown. Serve at once, with butter, if desired. *Makes 8 servings.*

Note: Or use 2 cups mashed, cooked fresh yams or sweet potatoes.

CAULIFLOWER POLONAISE
(pictured)

1 large cauliflower (about 2½ lb)
Boiling water
1½ teaspoons salt
3 slices lemon
1 hard-cooked egg, coarsely chopped
1 tablespoon chopped parsley
½ cup (1 stick) butter or margarine, melted
3 tablespoons lemon juice
½ cup packaged prepared croutons

1. Trim leaves and stem from cauliflower. Place, stem side down, in large kettle. Cover with boiling water. Add salt and lemon slices. Bring to boiling; reduce heat; simmer, covered, 20 to 25 minutes, or until tender. Drain.

2. To serve: Place whole cauliflower in warm serving dish. Sprinkle with hard-cooked egg and parsley. Combine butter with lemon juice and croutons. Pour over cauliflower. *Makes 6 to 8 servings.*

PONTCHARTRAIN'S HOT MINCEMEAT PIE

2 jars (1-lb, 2-oz size) prepared mincemeat
2 tablespoons brandy
¼ cup sherry
1 pkg (11 oz) piecrust mix
1 egg yolk
1 tablespoon light cream

HARD SAUCE
⅔ cup (1⅓ sticks) butter or margarine, softened
1 or 2 tablespoons brandy
2 cups unsifted confectioners' sugar

1. In medium bowl, combine mincemeat, brandy and sherry; mix well.

2. Prepare piecrust mix as package label directs. Form into a ball.

3. On lightly floured surface, roll out half of pastry to form a 12-inch circle. Fit into a 9-inch pie plate. Preheat oven to 425F.

4. Turn mincemeat filling into pie shell; trim pastry to the edge of the pie plate.

5. Roll out remaining pastry to form a 12-inch circle. Make several slits near center for steam vents; adjust pastry over filling. Trim pastry evenly, leaving a ½-inch overhang all around.

6. Fold edge of top crust under bottom crust; press together to seal. Crimp edge decoratively. Lightly brush top, but not edge, with egg yolk beaten with light cream.

7. Bake 30 to 35 minutes, or until crust is golden-brown.

8. Meanwhile, make Hard Sauce: In small bowl, with electric mixer, combine all ingredients; beat at medium speed until smooth and fluffy—2 minutes. Store in refrigerator, covered.

9. Cool pie partially on wire rack. Serve warm with Hard Sauce. *Makes 8 or 9 servings.*

Note: If desired, make pie day before through Step 6. Bake in 425F oven 45 minutes to 1 hour before serving. Make Hard Sauce the day before, also. ∎

THANKSGIVING
WITH A LIGHT TOUCH

A Thanksgiving dinner of turkey, gravy, cranberries, bread stuffing, creamed vegetables, candied sweet potatoes, pumpkin pie and ice cream all add up to a wonderful traditional celebration…and, unfortunately, can also add up to more than 2,000 calories for each of us. Why not start a new tradition by serving these same foods in a new, lighter way, without the heavy sauces and rich creams. You can still stuff the turkey, but here are some luscious, eye-filling ways to keep from stuffing yourself and your guests as well.

TRIM 'N' TASTY TRIMMINGS

You don't need heavy sauces to dress up vegetables! Clockwise, from top: Brussels sprouts, chestnuts and parsnips cooked with a touch of paprika and herbs; baked-potato shells stuffed with golden mashed sweet potatoes; sliced acorn squash topped with a lemony caramel sauce; enoki mushrooms, snow peas, artichokes, hearts of palm and red-pepper rings in a dazzling display; and a make-ahead layered Cranberry-Apple Salad. For recipes, see page 55.

LIGHTER-THAN-AIR DESSERTS

Most desserts are laden with butter or whipped cream, but our cakes are based on air that is beaten into the eggs. Clockwise, from top: Pumpkin Spice Cake has a lattice of soft cream cheese instead of whipped cream; the Mint Madeleines use a light ladyfinger batter; the Orange Cake Rolls, sprinkled with almonds, surround a light spirited filling; kiwi slices and mandarin oranges adorn a Lemon Chiffon Cake glistening with apricot preserves; and the Chocolate-Raspberry Layer Cake is actually a thin cake cut and layered with raspberry sherbet. Recipes start on page 56.

continued from page 53

TRIM 'N' TASTY TRIMMINGS

PARSNIPS WITH BRUSSELS SPROUTS
(pictured)

2 lb parsnips
1 carton (10 oz) fresh Brussels sprouts or
** 1 pkg (10 oz) frozen Brussels sprouts**
½ cup cooked chestnuts (see Note)
¼ teaspoon salt-free herb-and-spice blend
1 tablespoon unsalted butter or margarine
Paprika

1. Wash parsnips; pare. Cut into 3-inch-long pieces. If some pieces are thick, split or quarter them lengthwise.
2. In large skillet, heat ½ inch water to boiling. Add parsnips. Simmer over low heat, covered, 15 minutes, until tender.
3. Meanwhile, wash fresh sprouts. If some are large, cut them into halves. In medium saucepan, heat ½ inch water to boiling. Add sprouts; simmer over low heat, covered, 10 minutes, or just until tender. (If using frozen sprouts, cook as package label directs.) Add chestnuts to sprouts; cook to heat through. Drain; toss with herb-and-spice blend.
4. Drain parsnips; toss with butter; arrange on serving platter; sprinkle with paprika. Top with sprout mixture. *Makes 8 servings.*

Note: To prepare fresh chestnuts, preheat oven to 500F. With sharp knife, make a slit in flat side of shell. Bake for 15 minutes, or until tender. Remove shells and skins.

GOLDEN STUFFED BAKED POTATOES
(pictured)

5 large baking potatoes (3½ lb)
2 sweet potatoes (1½ lb)
Salad oil
2 tablespoons butter or margarine,
** softened**
1 egg
½ teaspoon salt
¼ teaspoon ground white pepper
Parsley sprigs

1. Preheat oven to 425F. Scrub baking and sweet potatoes well; pat dry with paper towels. With fork, prick them several times. Rub with oil; place in baking pan.
2. Bake 1 hour, or until potatoes are tender. Cool until they are easy to handle. Cut four of the baking potatoes in half horizontally. Scoop pulp from potatoes into large bowl of electric mixer, leaving ½-inch-thick shells. Return shells to pan.
3. Peel sweet potatoes and remaining baking potato. Cut into chunks. Or cut potatoes in half, and scoop out pulp. Add sweet- and baking-potato pulp to large bowl with potato.
4. With electric mixer, beat potato pulp with butter, egg, salt and pepper until fluffy, occasionally scraping side of bowl with rubber spatula.

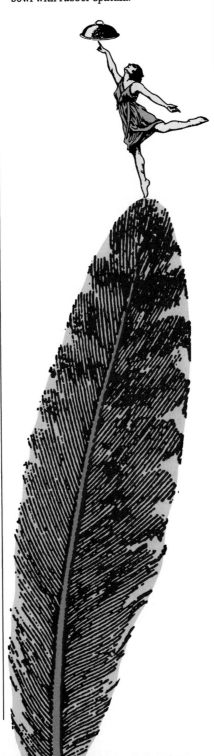

5. Fill each potato shell with mixture. Or spoon mixture into pastry bag with number-4 star tip; pipe mixture in a decorative design to fill shells. (Potatoes may be prepared ahead up to this point, covered and refrigerated overnight.)
6. Rebake potatoes in 425F oven 10 minutes, or until lightly browned. If potatoes are cold, bake 20 minutes. Transfer to serving plate; garnish with parsley. *Makes 8 servings.*

LEMONY ACORN-SQUASH SLICES
(pictured)

2 large acorn squash (1¼ lb each)
½ cup sugar
2 tablespoons water
2 tablespoons lemon juice
1 tablespoon butter or margarine
¼ teaspoon salt
⅛ teaspoon ground white pepper
Lemon wedges
Watercress sprigs

1. Scrub squash. Cut in half lengthwise; remove seeds and stringy fibers. Place squash, cut side down, on cutting board; cut each half crosswise into ½-inch-thick slices, discarding stem and pointed ends. Using a pancake turner, place squash in large skillet.
2. Add 1 cup water to squash; bring to boiling over high heat. Reduce heat; simmer, covered, just until slices are fork-tender—about 20 minutes.
3. Meanwhile, in heavy, medium saucepan, over medium heat, bring sugar and 2 tablespoons water to boiling. Continue to cook, stirring occasionally to dissolve sugar, until sugar crystallizes, then begins to melt into a golden syrup. Remove from heat; add lemon juice, butter, salt and pepper—will sizzle a little. Stir over low heat until mixed.
4. When squash is done, lift from skillet with pancake turner, and arrange on warm platter. Spoon syrup over slices. Garnish with lemon wedges and watercress. *Makes 6 servings.*

continued on page 56

continued from page 55

VEGETABLE STUFFING FOR TURKEY

1 lb carrots, pared and chopped
1 lb mushrooms, sliced
1 lb zucchini, diced
2 large onions, diced
2 cups chopped celery
2 cups water
2 chicken-bouillon cubes
6 cups day-old or toasted white- or whole-wheat bread cubes
2 teaspoons poultry seasoning
Salt and pepper to taste

1. In 8-quart saucepot, combine carrots, mushrooms, zucchini, onion, celery, water and bouillon cubes. Over high heat, bring to boiling; simmer over low heat, covered, 15 minutes, or until vegetables are tender. Drain. Remove from heat. (Use liquid to make gravy, if desired.)

2. Stir in bread cubes and seasonings. Mix well. Stuff into neck and body cavities of turkey just before roasting. *Makes about 11 cups* (enough for a 16-pound turkey).

FESTIVE MUSHROOM SALAD
(pictured)

¾ lb fresh snow peas
1 can (14 oz) hearts of palm, chilled
1 can (14 or 15 oz) hearts of artichokes, chilled
1 pkg (3.5 or 4 oz) fresh enoki mushrooms or ¼ lb small fresh mushrooms
1 head romaine
1 small red pepper
Soy-Vinaigrette Dressing, recipe follows

1. Wash snow peas; remove strings and stem ends. Bring 2 cups water to boiling in saucepan. Add snow peas; blanch for 1 minute; drain; rinse with cold water; pat dry on paper towels; chill.

2. Drain hearts of palm; cut each lengthwise into ⅓-inch strips. Drain artichokes; with fork, pull up the leaves of each to resemble a flower.

3. Wash mushrooms; pat dry. Trim off stem ends. If using regular mushrooms, slice them. Cut off root end of romaine; separate leaves. Wash leaves, and pat dry. Stem, seed and cut red pepper into thin rings; cut rings into halves.

4. On large round serving platter, arrange about six romaine leaves in a fan shape, overlapping slightly. Tear remaining leaves over the whole leaves. Arrange snow peas, hearts of palm, artichokes and mushrooms, as pictured. Rim with halved pepper rings. (Can be assembled ahead.)

5. Make Soy-Vinaigrette Dressing. Pass dressing with salad. *Makes 8 servings.*

SOY-VINAIGRETTE DRESSING

⅓ cup peanut or corn oil
⅓ cup cider vinegar
⅓ cup water
2 tablespoons low-sodium soy sauce
2 tablespoons minced green onion
1 tablespoon honey
½ teaspoon dry mustard

Combine all ingredients in jar with tight-fitting lid. Shake vigorously. Refrigerate dressing until ready to use. Shake again before using. *Makes about 1¼ cups.*

CRANBERRY-APPLE SALAD
(pictured)

1 env unflavored gelatine
1¼ cups apple juice
1 cup low-fat cottage cheese
½ cup diced celery
1 pkg (0.3 oz) sugar-free strawberry-flavor gelatin
1 cup boiling water
1 can (1 lb) whole-berry cranberry sauce
1 tablespoon lime juice
1 tablespoon water
½ teaspoon Dijon-style mustard
3 tablespoons salad oil
¼ cup walnut pieces or halves
2 Granny Smith or Golden Delicious apples, cored and cubed
½ small Red Delicious apple, cored and thinly sliced

1. Into small saucepan, sprinkle unflavored gelatine over ¼ cup apple juice; let stand 5 minutes to soften. Heat over low heat, stirring, until gelatin dissolves. Remove from heat; stir in remaining apple juice. Set pan in large bowl filled with ice, stirring occasionally, just until consistency of unbeaten egg white—10 minutes.

2. In food processor, process cottage cheese until smooth, occasionally stopping to scrape down side of container. Gradually beat in thickened gelatine mixture. With spoon, stir in celery. Pour mixture into 2-quart straight-sided glass bowl. Refrigerate until set—1 hour.

3. In medium bowl, dissolve flavored gelatin in boiling water. Stir in cranberry sauce. Set bowl in large bowl filled with ice, stirring occasionally, until consistency of unbeaten egg white—15 minutes. Spoon cranberry gelatin over cheese layer in glass bowl. Refrigerate until firm—several hours or overnight.

4. Just before serving, in medium bowl, combine lime juice, water and mustard. Whisk in oil; fold in walnuts and cubed apple; spoon over cranberry layer. Arrange apple slices on top of salad. *Makes 16 (½-cup) servings.*

PUMPKIN SPICE CAKE
(pictured)

2 cups sifted cake flour
1¼ cups sugar
1 tablespoon baking powder
1 teaspoon salt
1 teaspoon ground cinnamon
½ teaspoon ground cloves
½ teaspoon ground nutmeg
7 eggs, separated, at room temperature
¾ cup canned pumpkin
½ cup salad oil
½ cup water
½ teaspoon cream of tartar
Soft cream cheese (optional)

1. Preheat oven to 325F. Sift cake flour, sugar, baking powder, salt and spices into medium bowl. With wire whisk, whisk in egg yolks, pumpkin, oil and water until very smooth.

2. Add cream of tartar to egg whites in large bowl of electric mixer; beat at high speed until stiff peaks form. Pour pumpkin mixture over whites; with rubber spatula, using an under-and-over motion, fold in gently until well combined. Pour batter into ungreased 10-inch tube pan with removable bottom.

3. Bake 1 hour and 20 minutes, or until cake tester inserted in center of cake comes out clean. Invert pan on its metal legs, if present, or on wire rack to cool. Cool completely. When cool, loosen cake from side of pan with metal spatula; remove side of pan. Loosen cake from tube and bottom of pan; invert onto plate. Serve plain, or pipe cream cheese in lattice design on top. *Makes 20 servings.*

MINT MADELEINES
(pictured)

4 eggs, separated, at room temperature
⅛ teaspoon salt
¾ cup granulated sugar
2 teaspoons peppermint extract
8 to 10 drops green food color
¾ cup all-purpose flour
3 tablespoons confectioners' sugar
1 tablespoon unsweetened cocoa

1. Preheat oven to 350F. Lightly grease and flour three or four madeleine pans. (If you have only one pan, wash, dry, grease and flour it each time.)

2. In large bowl of electric mixer, at high speed, beat egg whites and salt just until soft peaks form when beaters are slowly raised. Gradually beat in ¼ cup granulated sugar, beating until stiff peaks form.

3. With same beaters, at high speed, beat egg yolks in small bowl with rest of

granulated sugar until thick and lemon-colored—about 5 minutes. At low speed, beat in peppermint extract and food color. With rubber spatula, stir in flour.

4. With rubber spatula, using an under-and-over motion, gently fold yolk mixture into egg whites just until combined.

5. Spoon tablespoon of batter into each madeleine mold. Bake 8 to 10 minutes, or just until surface springs back when gently pressed with fingertip. Remove from molds; cool on wire rack. Repeat.

6. Meanwhile, in small bowl, combine confectioners' sugar and cocoa. To serve, sift cocoa mixture over curved, decorative side of each madeleine. *Makes about 4 dozen.*

ORANGE-CAKE ROLLS
(pictured)

¾ cup sifted cake flour
1 teaspoon baking powder
½ teaspoon salt
4 eggs, at room temperature
¾ cup sugar
Orange Filling, recipe follows
2 tablespoons sliced natural almonds, chopped
Orange slices and leaves for garnish (optional)

1. Preheat oven to 400F. Lightly spray bottom of 15½-by-10½-by-1-inch jelly-roll pan with nonstick cooking spray. Line bottom of pan with waxed paper; spray paper with nonstick cooking spray.

2. Sift flour, baking powder and salt onto waxed paper; set aside.

3. In small bowl of electric mixer, at high speed, beat eggs until very thick and lemon-colored. Beat in granulated sugar, 2 tablespoons at a time; continue beating 5 minutes longer, or until very thick.

4. With rubber spatula, using an under-and-over motion, gently fold in flour mixture just until combined. Spread evenly in prepared pan.

5. Bake 9 minutes, or just until surface springs back when pressed with fingertip.

6. Meanwhile, spray a clean towel (not terry cloth) with nonstick cooking spray to form a 15-by-10-inch rectangle. Invert cake onto sprayed area of towel; gently peel off waxed paper.

7. With rolling pin, lightly roll cake, to flatten slightly. Cut cake lengthwise in half. Starting with a long, uncut edge, roll up cake with towel toward cut edge. Repeat with other half of cake. You will have two long cake rolls.

8. Make Orange Filling. Reserve 2 tablespoons filling for later use. Gently unroll cakes; spread each with half the remaining filling to within ½ inch of edges. Reroll cakes as before but without the towel. Cut each cake roll crosswise into 5 pieces, each about 3 inches long.

9. Brush about a half inch of the outer top edges of each roll with some reserved Orange Filling; sprinkle with some chopped almonds, as pictured. Arrange on plate; garnish with orange slices and leaves, if desired. Refrigerate until serving time. *Makes 10 servings.*

ORANGE FILLING

¼ cup sugar
2 tablespoons cornstarch
⅛ teaspoon salt
1 tablespoon grated orange peel
1 cup orange juice
1 tablespoon lemon juice
1 tablespoon butter or margarine
2 tablespoons orange-flavored liqueur

In small saucepan, combine sugar, cornstarch and salt. Gradually stir in orange peel and orange juice. Over medium heat, bring to boiling, stirring constantly. Boil 1 minute. Remove from heat. Stir in remaining ingredients. Cool to room temperature.

KIWI-MANDARIN ORANGE CAKE
(pictured)

Lemon Chiffon Cake, recipe follows
Lemon Filling, recipe follows
½ cup apricot preserves
2 kiwi fruit
1 can (11 oz) mandarin oranges, drained

1. Make Lemon Chiffon Cake and Lemon Filling.

2. In small saucepan, heat preserves until melted. Strain into small bowl.

3. To assemble cake: Spread Lemon Filling in center indentation of cake. Peel kiwi fruit; trim off ends. Cut each kiwi crosswise into four equal slices. Cut each slice in half. Arrange kiwi half-slices, alternating with orange segments, around edge of cake. Arrange remaining orange segments in center, as pictured. Brush side of cake and fruit topping with strained preserves. Refrigerate cake until serving time. *Makes 12 servings.*

LEMON CHIFFON CAKE

1 cup sifted cake flour
¾ cup sugar
1½ teaspoons baking powder
½ teaspoon salt
¼ cup salad oil
2 egg yolks
1 tablespoon grated lemon peel
¼ cup lemon juice
¼ teaspoon cream of tartar
⅓ cup egg whites (about 3), at room temperature

1. Preheat oven to 350F. Into a small bowl, sift flour, sugar, baking powder and salt; make well in center. Add oil, egg yolks, lemon peel and lemon juice; beat batter with wire whisk until smooth.

2. Add cream of tartar to egg whites in small bowl of electric mixer. At high speed, beat egg whites until very stiff peaks form. With wire whisk or rubber spatula, using an under-and-over motion, gradually and gently fold batter into egg whites just until combined. Do not stir.

3. Pour into ungreased 9-by-1½-inch round flan pan. Bake 25 minutes, or until cake tester inserted in center comes out clean.

4. Invert pan, setting rim on two other cake pans; let cool completely—about 1 hour. With spatula, carefully loosen cake from side of pan; remove cake from pan. Place, bottom side up, on serving plate.

continued on page 63

FEASTS
for a few

Thanksgiving tradition in your family may call for a big turkey. But if it doesn't, we have a gallery of delectable smaller birds—goose, Cornish hens, capon and duck—to give that festive touch to a smaller-scale celebration. Recipes begin on page 60.

ROAST GOOSE

Smaller but traditional, the roast goose of our Plymouth forefathers: stuffed with chestnut-sausage dressing, strung with a necklace of chestnuts and cranberries. For added elegance, it's ringed with raisin-berry-relish-filled pear halves.

CORNISH HENS

Just for the two of you: Cornish hens with wild- and white-rice stuffing. They're crowned with bracelets of spicy capers, festooned with julienne turnips and carrots tied (with scallion strips) into charming vegetable bouquets.

continued from page 59

ROAST GOOSE WITH CHESTNUT-SAUSAGE STUFFING
(pictured)

Chestnut-Sausage Stuffing, recipe follows
10- to 12-lb ready-to-cook goose
2 tablespoons lemon juice
1 teaspoon salt
1/8 teaspoon pepper
Goose Giblet Gravy, recipe follows
Chestnut-Cranberry String, recipe follows
1 can (1 lb, 13 oz) pear halves, drained
Raisin-Berry Relish, recipe follows
Parsley

1. Preheat oven to 400F. Make Chestnut-Sausage Stuffing. Remove giblets and neck from goose, and set aside; discard liver. Wash goose under cold running water; dry well with paper towels. Remove and discard all fat from inside. Rub cavity with lemon juice, salt and pepper.

2. Spoon stuffing into neck cavity; bring skin of neck over back, and fasten with poultry pins. Spoon dressing lightly into body cavity; close with poultry pins, and lace with twine. Bend wing tips under body; tie ends of legs together. (Bake any leftover stuffing in a 1-quart casserole during the last 45 minutes.) Insert meat thermometer in inside of thigh at thickest part.

3. Prick skin only over thighs, back and breast very well. Place, breast side up, on rack in large roasting pan.

4. Roast, uncovered, 1 hour. Remove goose from oven.

5. Pour off and discard fat from pan. Roast goose, uncovered, 2 hours longer. Pour off all fat. Roast 1/2 hour longer, or until skin is nicely browned and crisp. Meaty part of leg should feel soft and meat thermometer register 185F.

6. Place goose on heated platter. Meanwhile, make Goose Giblet Gravy. Garnish roast goose with Chestnut-Cranberry String; pear halves, each filled with 1 tablespoon Raisin-Berry Relish; and parsley. *Makes 8 servings.*

CHESTNUT-SAUSAGE STUFFING

1 lb sausage meat
1 cup chopped onion
1 cup chopped celery
1/4 cup chopped parsley
1 pkg (8 oz) herb-seasoned stuffing mix
2 cans (about 2-lb size) water-packed chestnuts (see Note), well drained and broken into pieces
1/2 teaspoon salt
1/4 teaspoon pepper
1 cup chicken broth

1. In large skillet, sauté sausage meat, stirring until lightly browned. Add onion, celery and parsley; sauté 8 to 10 minutes.

2. In large kettle, combine stuffing mix, chestnuts, salt and pepper; toss to mix well.

3. Add broth along with sausage mixture. Toss lightly, using two large forks. *Makes 8 cups.*

Note: Or use 2 pounds fresh chestnuts: To roast, make a slit in flat side of each shell with a sharp knife. Bake at 500F for 15 minutes. Remove shells and skins. Chop coarsely.

GOOSE GIBLET GRAVY

Giblets and neck from goose
1 1/2 cups water
2 celery stalks, cut up
2 carrots, pared and cut up
1 can (13 3/4 oz) chicken broth
Dash salt
Dash pepper
Goose drippings
1/4 cup all-purpose flour
1/2 cup white wine

1. While goose roasts, place giblets and neck in medium saucepan with water, celery, carrot, broth, salt and pepper.

2. Bring to boiling; reduce heat, and simmer, covered, 2 hours, or until giblets are tender.

3. Remove giblets; discard neck. Chop giblets finely; set aside. Strain broth, and reserve.

4. When goose is done, pour drippings into 1-cup measure; return 1/4 cup of the drippings to roasting pan. Stir in flour, to make a smooth mixture; gradually stir in 2 cups reserved broth and the white wine.

5. Bring to boiling, stirring. Reduce heat; simmer, stirring, 5 minutes, or until thickened and smooth. Add giblets and more salt and pepper, if needed. Serve with goose. *Makes 2 1/2 cups.*

CHESTNUT-CRANBERRY STRING

Thread washed cranberries and roasted chestnuts, as pictured, using a large darning needle and heavy-duty thread.

RAISIN-BERRY RELISH

3 cups (12 oz) fresh or frozen cranberries
1 pkg (15 oz) golden raisins
2 cups orange juice
1 cup water
1/4 cup lemon juice
2/3 cup sugar
1 tablespoon grated orange peel

1. Wash cranberries, removing stems.

2. In 3-quart saucepan, combine raisins, orange juice, water, lemon juice and sugar. Over high heat, bring to boiling, stirring to dissolve sugar. Reduce heat; simmer 10 minutes.

3. Add cranberries. Return to boiling; simmer, uncovered, 5 minutes. Add orange peel; continue simmering about 5 minutes, or until most of the liquid is evaporated.

4. Remove from heat. Cool completely. Store in covered jar in refrigerator. *Makes about 5 cups.*

CORNISH HENS WITH CAPER SAUCE
(pictured)

Water
¼ cup wild rice
Salt
⅓ cup long-grain white rice
2 fresh Cornish hens (1½ lb each) or
   2 frozen Cornish hens, thawed
½ cup white wine
¼ cup lemon juice
Large capers
4 large scallions
4 large mushrooms
1 tablespoon butter or margarine
2 medium carrots
1 turnip
1 tablespoon all-purpose flour

1. Bring 3 cups water to boiling. Add wild rice and ½ teaspoon salt. Simmer, uncovered, 30 minutes. Add white rice; simmer 20 minutes longer, adding a little water if necessary to keep it from boiling dry.

2. Remove giblets from hens. Wash; wrap and freeze or refrigerate for another use. Rinse hens; drain well. Tuck wing tips under backs, and set, breast down, in a glass baking dish. Pour wine and lemon juice over hens; sprinkle with ¼ teaspoon salt and 1 tablespoon capers. Cover; set aside at room temperature no longer than 30 minutes.

3. Wash scallions; cut off 12 6-inch pieces of the green ends. Large pieces may be split lengthwise, if necessary, to make enough. Chop remainder of scallions. Wash and coarsely chop mushrooms.

4. Melt butter in a small skillet. Sauté chopped scallion and mushrooms until golden. Allow rice to just cook dry, being careful not to let it stick to pan. Fold in scallion mixture.

5. Preheat oven to 350F. Turn hens, breast up, in baking dish. Spoon rice mixture into body cavities of hens. Tie legs together. Roast, uncovered, 45 to 50 minutes, basting occasionally with lemon-wine mixture.

6. Peel carrots and turnip. Slice into julienne strips ¼ inch thick. Cut strips into pieces about 2 inches long. Arrange into 6 carrot bundles and 6 turnip bundles.

7. Bring an inch of water to boiling in a large heavy skillet. Add reserved scallion strips. Remove as soon as they are flexible. Cool; then tie one strip around each vegetable bundle. Place bundles in skillet. Cover tightly, and simmer until just tender—6 to 8 minutes.

8. If desired, with needle and thread, make three 6-inch strings of capers. Tie each at ends to make a ring.

9. Arrange hens on serving platter. Keep warm. Stir flour into 2 tablespoons water in a small saucepan. Pour in drippings from baking dish. Cook, stirring, over high heat until thick. Spoon some sauce over hens.

10. Drain vegetable bundles; arrange around hens. Place a ring of capers on each hen, if desired. Pass remaining sauce. *Makes 4 servings.*

ROAST CAPON WITH HERBS

6-lb capon
Salt
Pepper
½ cup (1 stick) butter or margarine,
   softened
1 tablespoon lemon juice
1 tablespoon chopped chives
1 tablespoon chopped parsley
1 clove garlic, minced
1½ teaspoons chopped fresh tarragon or
   ½ teaspoon dried tarragon leaves
¾ teaspoon chopped fresh rosemary or
   ¼ teaspoon dried rosemary leaves
¾ teaspoon chopped fresh thyme or
   ¼ teaspoon dried thyme leaves
1 onion, sliced
2 carrots, pared and sliced
1 stalk celery, sliced
1 can (10¾ oz) condensed chicken broth,
   undiluted
½ cup dry white wine
3 tablespoons all-purpose flour
Fresh tarragon sprigs (optional)

1. Preheat oven to 400F.

2. Wash capon well, inside and out, under cold water. Pat dry, inside and out, with paper towels. Sprinkle inside with 1 teaspoon salt and ¼ teaspoon pepper. Rinse giblets; set aside.

3. In small bowl, with electric mixer or wooden spoon, beat butter with lemon juice, chives, parsley, garlic, chopped tarragon, rosemary, thyme, ½ teaspoon salt and ⅛ teaspoon pepper until well blended.

4. With fingers, carefully loosen skin from breast meat. Spread 2 tablespoons butter mixture over breast meat, under skin, on each side. Tie legs together; fold wing tips under back. Spread 1 tablespoon butter mixture over capon. Insert meat thermometer in inside of thigh at thickest part.

5. Place onion, carrot, celery and giblets (except liver) in shallow roasting pan. Set capon on vegetables.

6. Roast, uncovered, 1 hour. Reduce oven temperature to 325F; roast 1¼ to 1½ hours, basting occasionally with remaining butter mixture, until meat thermometer registers 185F and leg moves easily at joint.

7. Remove capon to heated platter. Remove string. Let stand 20 minutes.

8. Meanwhile, make gravy: Pour undiluted chicken broth into roasting pan; bring to boiling, stirring to dissolve brown bits. Strain into 4-cup measure; skim off fat, and discard.

9. In small saucepan, stir wine into flour until flour is dissolved. Stir in chicken broth. Bring to boiling, stirring constantly, until mixture thickens; reduce heat, and simmer 5 minutes. Add salt and pepper, if necessary.

10. Garnish capon with tarragon sprigs, if desired. Pass gravy. *Makes 8 servings.*

continued on page 62

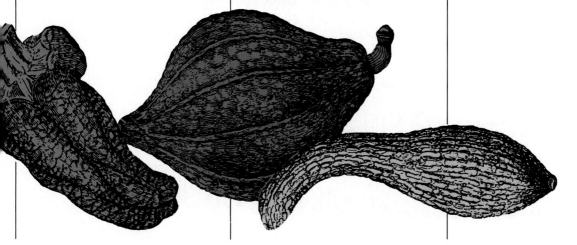

continued from page 61

ROAST STUFFED CAPON WITH PECAN-HERB STUFFING

5½- to 6-lb ready-to-cook capon
Salt
Pepper
Pecan-Herb Stuffing, recipe follows
½ cup (1 stick) butter or margarine, softened
1 tablespoon chopped parsley
½ teaspoon dried thyme leaves
1 can (10¾ oz) condensed chicken broth, undiluted
½ cup dry white wine
3 tablespoons all-purpose flour
Watercress

1. Preheat oven to 325F.
2. Wash capon well, inside and out, under cold water. Pat dry with paper towels. Sprinkle inside with 1 teaspoon salt and ¼ teaspoon pepper. Rinse giblets; reserve for another use.
3. Make Pecan Stuffing.
4. In small bowl, with electric mixer or wooden spoon, beat butter with parsley, thyme, ½ teaspoon salt and ⅛ teaspoon pepper until well blended.
5. With fingers, carefully loosen skin from breast meat. Spread 2 tablespoons butter mixture over breast meat, under skin, on each side.
6. Fill body and neck cavities with stuffing. Tie legs together; fold wing tips under back. Skewer skin at neck. Spread 1 tablespoon of butter mixture over capon. Insert meat thermometer in inside of thigh at thickest part. (Place any remaining stuffing in small baking dish; bake, covered, last 45 minutes of roasting time.)
7. Cover capon loosely with foil.
8. Roast 2½ hours, or until meat thermometer registers 185F, and leg moves easily at joint. Remove foil last half hour, basting occasionally with butter mixture.
9. Remove capon to heated platter. Remove string. Let stand 20 minutes.
10. Meanwhile, make gravy: Pour undiluted chicken broth into roasting pan; bring to boiling, stirring to dissolve brown bits. Strain into a 4-cup measure; skim off fat and discard.
11. In small saucepan, stir wine into flour until flour is dissolved. Stir in chicken broth. Bring to boiling, stirring constantly, until thickened; reduce heat; simmer 5 minutes. Add salt and pepper, if necessary.
12. Garnish with watercress. Pass gravy. *Makes 8 servings.*

PECAN-HERB STUFFING

6 cups fresh white-bread cubes
1 cup coarsely chopped pecans
¼ cup chopped parsley
1 teaspoon dried thyme leaves
½ teaspoon salt
½ teaspoon pepper
½ cup (1 stick) butter or margarine
1 cup chopped celery
1 cup chopped onion

1. In large bowl, combine bread cubes, pecans, parsley, thyme, salt and pepper; toss to mix well.
2. In hot butter in medium skillet, sauté celery and onion until golden—7 to 10 minutes.
3. Add to bread mixture; toss lightly until well mixed.
4. Use to fill prepared capon. *Makes 7 cups.*
Note: Ready-to-cook roasting chicken may be substituted for capon.

DUCKLING WITH TURNIPS

5-lb ready-to-cook duckling
1 teaspoon salt
3 tablespoons butter or margarine
1 medium onion, sliced
1 small white turnip, pared and diced
1 sprig parsley
1 can (10¾ oz) condensed chicken broth, undiluted
½ cup white wine
¼ teaspoon dried thyme leaves
3 tablespoons all-purpose flour
Glazed Vegetables, recipe follows
Chopped parsley

1. Preheat oven to 425F. Sprinkle duckling inside and out with salt. Tie ends of legs together. Prick skin all over with fork. Place, breast side up, on a rack in shallow roasting pan.
2. Roast, uncovered, 45 minutes, or until nicely browned.
3. Meanwhile, in 1 tablespoon hot butter, sauté onion, turnip and parsley sprig until onion is golden—about 10 minutes.
4. Remove duckling from oven. Prick skin all over again. Reduce oven temperature to 350F. Pour all fat from pan, and discard. Arrange sautéed vegetables around duckling. Add 1 cup chicken broth, the wine and thyme. Cover pan with foil.
5. Roast, covered, 1 hour longer, or until tender. Pour off all pan juices, and strain into a 4-cup measure; skim off fat. Add rest of chicken broth and more wine to juices, if necessary, to make 1½ cups. Raise oven temperature to 400F. Return duckling to oven, uncovered, for 15 minutes, to crisp skin.
6. Melt 2 tablespoons butter in saucepan; remove from heat. Stir in flour until smooth. Gradually stir in pan juices; bring to boiling, stirring constantly. Reduce heat, and simmer 3 minutes.
7. To serve: Arrange duckling and Glazed Vegetables on heated platter. Garnish with chopped parsley. Pass sauce. *Makes 4 servings.*

GLAZED VEGETABLES

20 small white onions, peeled
4 white turnips, pared and cut into eighths
2 tablespoons butter or margarine
2 teaspoons sugar

1. Cook onions and turnips separately in 1 inch boiling salted water just until tender—15 to 25 minutes for onions, about 10 minutes for turnips. Drain each well.
2. Heat 1 tablespoon butter in large skillet; add onions, and sprinkle with 1 teaspoon sugar. Cook over medium heat, shaking pan often, until onions are golden and glazed—5 minutes. Keep warm.
3. Heat remaining butter in same skillet. Add turnips, and sprinkle with 1 teaspoon sugar. Cook until golden and glazed. Keep warm. *Makes 4 servings.* ■

continued from page 57

LEMON FILLING

1 egg
1 egg yolk
½ cup sugar
3 tablespoons lemon juice
¼ cup water
2 teaspoons grated lemon peel
1 teaspoon butter

Combine all ingredients in small, heavy saucepan. Over medium heat, whisk constantly until mixture boils; boil 1 minute. Cover surface with plastic wrap. Refrigerate until cold.

CHOCOLATE-RASPBERRY LAYER CAKE
(pictured)

4 eggs, separated and at room temperature
¾ cup granulated sugar
½ cup all-purpose flour
⅓ cup unsweetened cocoa
½ teaspoon baking powder
¼ teaspoon baking soda
⅛ teaspoon salt
¼ cup water
1 teaspoon vanilla extract
1½ pints raspberry sherbet
Confectioners' sugar

1. Preheat oven to 350F. Lightly grease a 15½-by-10½-by-1-inch jelly-roll pan; line bottom with waxed paper; grease paper.
2. In large bowl of electric mixer, at high speed, beat egg whites until soft peaks form when beaters are slowly raised. Gradually beat in ½ cup of the granulated sugar, beating until stiff peaks form.
3. With same beaters, at high speed, beat egg yolks in small bowl with rest of sugar until thick and lemon-colored—about 5 minutes. Meanwhile, sift flour, cocoa, baking powder, soda and salt onto waxed paper. At low speed, beat water, vanilla, then flour mixture into egg-yolk mixture until combined, scraping side of bowl with rubber spatula. With rubber spatula, using an under-and-over motion,

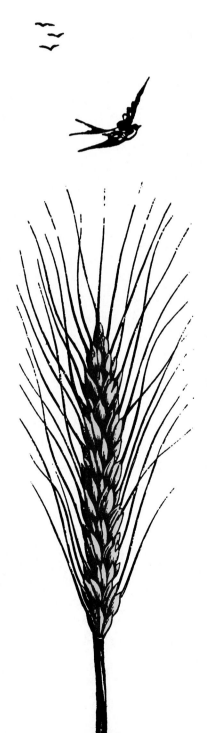

gently fold egg-yolk mixture into beaten egg whites; spread evenly in prepared pan.
4. Bake 12 to 15 minutes, or just until surface springs back when gently pressed with fingertip. Cool cake in pan on wire rack 10 minutes; invert cake onto large wire rack; gently peel off waxed paper; turn cake top side up; cool completely. With serrated knife, cut cake crosswise into quarters to form four 10-by-3¾-inch layers.

5. Line jelly-roll pan with foil. Bring up one short edge of foil to form an 11¼-by-10-inch rectangle. Soften sherbet slightly, and spread in foil-lined pan; refreeze until firm. When firm, cut sherbet crosswise into three pieces, right through the foil.
6. Place one cake layer on serving plate; invert raspberry sherbet over cake layer; peel off foil. Repeat with remaining cake and sherbet layers, ending with cake layer, placed top side up. Loosely wrap cake with plastic wrap; freeze until firm.
7. Just before serving, cut a rectangle of waxed paper ½ inch smaller all around than top of cake layer. Place on top of cake; dust edges heavily with confectioners' sugar. Remove paper; dust center lightly with more sugar, as pictured. *Makes 16 servings.*

LOW-CALORIE SPONGECAKE

1 cup skim milk
2 cups sifted all-purpose flour
1 tablespoon baking powder
Dash salt
6 eggs, at room temperature
1½ cups sugar
4 teaspoons grated lemon peel

1. In small saucepan, heat milk until bubbles form around edge of pan. Remove from heat; set aside.
2. Preheat oven to 350F. Sift flour, baking powder and salt onto waxed paper; set aside.
3. In large bowl of electric mixer, at high speed, beat eggs until thick and lemon-colored. Gradually add sugar, beating until mixture is smooth and well blended—about 10 minutes.
4. At low speed, blend in flour mixture just until smooth. Add warm milk and lemon peel, beating just until combined.
5. Immediately pour batter into ungreased 10-inch tube pan with removable bottom. Bake 35 to 40 minutes, or until cake tester inserted in center of cake comes out clean. Invert pan, placing center opening over neck of bottle; let cool completely. Remove from pan. Serve plain. *Makes 20 servings.* ∎

Make-It-Yourself Thanksgiving Centerpieces

The next few pages feature a trio of glorious floral arrangements that anyone can make at home in no time—no green thumb necessary! The materials can be purchased from your local crafts store or flower shop, and the easy, illustrated, step-by-step directions on the opposite page show you how to create a beautiful centerpiece to proudly grace your holiday table.

Thanksgiving Flower Basket

An ordinary basket is transformed into a stunning burst of warm autumn colors, below. Orange silk flowers, cattails, wheat shafts and clusters of nuts mingle with German statice to produce this lovely dried arrangement that can be preserved for years to come.

Floral design by Ann Page, Page's Flower and Plant Shop, Durham, Conn.
Photographed at Town Farms Inn, Middletown, Conn.

Thanksgiving Flower Basket

DAVID VIENS

1. Place dry floral foam in basket. Secure block to basket with tape. Fill basket with Spanish moss to completely cover the block and tape. Pack moss tightly.

2. Bend each piece of wire into a hairpin shape. Anchor the "hairpins" in the block by placing one pin on each of four sides and one in the top, centered.

3. Insert 12 pieces of statice in block around rim of basket so points of statice bend toward bottom of basket. With 8 pieces of statice, make a second circle inside first circle, placing each piece at a 45-degree angle. Fill center with remaining pieces of statice, placing them upright.

4. Insert 12″ cattail in top center of arrangement, about 2″ into block. Insert two 10″ cattails at 2 o'clock and 8 o'clock positions, about 2″ into block. Insert two 8″ cattails at 4 o'clock and 10 o'clock positions, about 2″ into block.

5. Insert one nut pick in between two cattails. Insert remaining nut picks to form a triangle. Insert 8″ flower in center; insert 7″ flower to the right. Insert remaining flowers as shown above.

6. Insert wheat randomly in the arrangement to fill spaces between flowers and nut picks. Do not water. To preserve arrangement, store in a plastic bag with one moth ball. Tie bag securely.

Materials

1 block of dry floral foam, 4″ × 3″
1 basket, about 8″ in diameter and 3″ deep
2 strips of adhesive tape, each 5″ × ¼″
1 small bag of Spanish moss (you will have some left over)
5 pieces of floral wire, each 4″ long

26 pieces of German statice, about 6″ long, each end cut to a point
1 pencil cattail, 12″ long
2 pencil cattails, each 10″ long
2 pencil cattails, each 8″ long
3 nut picks (cluster of artificial nuts and leaves on a pick)

1 orange silk flower, about 8″ long and 2½″ in diameter
1 orange silk flower, about 7″ long and 2½″ in diameter
5 orange silk flowers, each about 6″ long and 2½″ in diameter
9 pieces of wheat, each about 8″ long

Pumpkin-In-Bloom

Here's a clever idea: A small hollowed-out pumpkin becomes the "vase" for a delicate arrangement of fresh yellow pompom chrysanthemums, German statice and cattails, all beautifully nestled in vibrant forest-green fern tips. You can create similar arrangements in miniature, using hollowed-out gourds.

Floral design by Ann Page, Page's Flower and Plant Shop, Durham, C
Photographed at Town Farms Inn, Middletown, Conn.

Pumpkin-In-Bloom

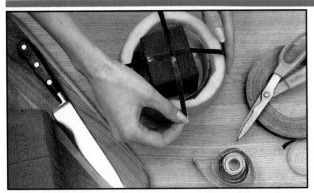

1. Place container in pumpkin. Soak cut floral foam in water; place soaked block in container. Secure block and container to pumpkin with tape.

2. Insert eight fern tips in sides of block to form a circle around rim of pumpkin. Insert remaining 16 fern tips upright in top of block to completely cover the block.

3. Insert the 10″ chrysanthemums in top center of block, about 1″ apart. Insert four 6″ chrysanthemums, equally spaced, in sides of block at rim of pumpkin.

4. Insert remaining 6″ flowers in a circle above bottom flowers, placing them in between bottom ones. Insert the statice in a circle just below, as shown.

5. Insert cattails at top of arrangement to form a triangle. Fill the container with water. Check daily; water should remain just below rim of container. Place pumpkin in a small dish or on a mat so it does not mark furniture.

6. Gourd Arrangements: Prepare container and floral foam as in Step 1 above. Place Spanish moss on top. Insert flowers in moss-covered block. Arrange cattails as shown. Fill container with water.

Materials
1 container to fit into pumpkin (such as cream-cheese or margarine plastic tub)
1 small pumpkin, about 6″ in diameter, top removed and insides scooped out
1 block of dry floral foam, cut to fit container and to extend 1″ above top of container
2 strips of adhesive tape, each 8″ × ¼″
24 leather-leaf fern tips, each 5″ to 6″ long

3 yellow pompom chrysanthemums, about 10″ long, each stem cut to a point
8 yellow pompom chrysanthemums, about 6″ long, each stem cut to a point
5 pieces of German statice, each about 6″ long
3 pencil cattails, each 8″ long

Gourd Materials
Assorted gourds, tops removed and insides scooped out

Small containers to fit inside of gourds (such as small paper cups, cut to size)
Dry floral foam, cut to fit containers
Strips of adhesive tape, cut to fit gourds
Spanish moss
Hybrid lilies, or similar flowers, with ½″ to 1″ stems
Pencil cattails, 8″ to 10″ long

Autumn Glory Arrangement

Your table will be aglow with the gorgeous colors and heavenly scent of the bountiful arrangement of fresh yellow, bronze and gold pompom chrysanthemums studded with fragrant dried bronze eucalyptus. Two 12″ candles stand majestically above, ready to cast their light over your sumptuous banquet.

Floral design by Jeanne Parker, Cedar Mountain Florist, Newington, Conn.
Photographed at Town Farms Inn, Middletown, Conn.

Autumn Glory Arrangement

1. Soak cut block of dry floral foam in water; place soaked block in bowl. Secure block to bowl with tape.

2. Insert fern tips in sides of block to form a circle around rim of bowl. Break remaining fern branches into smaller branches and fill in the center of block, leaving two spaces for candles.

3. Insert the candles in the center of the arrangement, 1″ deep in the block and about 1″ apart.

4. Insert six of the daisy pompoms in an evenly spaced circle around the rim of the bowl. Insert the remaining daisy pompoms above and in between the bottom ones as shown.

5. Insert the bronze pompoms in the spaces between the daisy pompoms. Insert the gold button pompom clusters evenly in the arrangement as shown.

6. Insert the bronze eucalyptus pieces evenly in the sides of the arrangement. Fill the bowl with water. Check daily; water should remain just below rim of bowl.

Materials

1 block of dry floral foam, 4½″ square, cut to extend 1″ above top of bowl
1 glass bowl, about 6″ in diameter and 2½″ high
2 strips of adhesive tape, each 10″ × ¼″

8 leather-leaf fern tips, each about 6″ long (save remaining parts to fill spaces)
2 yellow dripless candles, 12″ long (see Note)
12 yellow daisy pompom chrysanthemums, each about 6″ long

10 bronze pompom chrysanthemums, each about 5″ long
12 gold button pompom chrysanthemum clusters, each about 6″ long
5 pieces of dried bronze eucalyptus, each about 10″ long

Note: Use extreme caution when burning candles; do not leave candles in this arrangement unattended.

TWO

'TIS THE SEASON FOR PARTIES

Perhaps no other time of the year lends itself so well to parties as does the holiday season. There's a wonderful spirit of sharing that draws us closer to our families and friends in celebrations that range from elaborate, formal affairs to simple afternoon teas with the neighbors…and *everything* in between. How about a cookie-baking party? A cookie swap with neighbors can be a scrumptious party in itself. Plan an easy-on-the-feet party after a long day shopping with friends, then gather them later to share present-wrapping tricks. A tree-trimming party can be lots of fun, and the children will love getting together to make their own special ornaments. Have a warm-up party after a brisk evening of caroling. And don't forget, there may be birthdays and anniversaries to celebrate, too.

In this section you'll find our best recipes and ideas for party hors d'oeuvres, buffets and desserts. There's even a party menu for children and a selection of fast 'n' fabulous 30-minute meals that give you time to catch your breath before the next round of parties begins!

SAVORY WAYS TO SAY 'WELCOME'

It's not a minute too soon to start planning those festive parties that are so much a part of the joyous holiday season. In the pages that follow, we have assembled our best ideas for getting things off to a sensational start: luscious, out-of-the-ordinary hors d'oeuvres. Top left, creamy quiche Lorraine; then, clockwise, velvety chicken-liver pâté en croûte; a molded loaf made of three cheeses, iced with soft Cheddar; stuffed green olives baked in feathery puff pastry; an oversize egg roll to slice and serve with mustard and plum sauce; bite-size balls of Parmesan and bread crumbs—as well as chicken and tofu—deep-fried and served with soy sauce. Recipes for all these delectable hors d'oeuvres are on the following pages.

age 73

I

PUFF-PASTRY OLIVES*
THREE-CHEESE LOAF*
BASKET OF ASSORTED CRACKERS
CHINESE EGG ROLLS*
HOT MUSTARD   PLUM SAUCE
SAVORY STEAK SLICES
HERB-BUTTERED FRENCH BREAD
BOWL OF ASSORTED CRISP
VEGETABLES ON CRUSHED ICE

II

HOT CHEESE BALLS*
CHICKEN-TOFU BALLS*
TERIYAKI SAUCE
COLD RATATOUILLE ON GARLIC BREAD
PATE EN CROUTE*
WARM TOAST SQUARES
PUFF-PASTRY OLIVES*
BOWL OF ASSORTED CRISP
VEGETABLES ON CRUSHED ICE

III

OUR BEST QUICHE LORRAINE*
COLD RATATOUILLE ON GARLIC TOAST
BEEF BALLS BOURGUIGNON
IN CHAFING DISH
CHINESE EGG ROLLS*
HOT MUSTARD   PLUM SAUCE
BOWL OF CRISP ASSORTED
VEGETABLES ON CRUSHED ICE

Recipes given for starred dishes.

PUFF-PASTRY OLIVES
(pictured)

1 pkg (17.4 oz) prepared puff pastry
1 egg yolk
1 tablespoon water
2 jars (3¼-oz size) medium-size stuffed
   olives, well drained

1. Remove frozen pastry from package. Let stand at room temperature 20 minutes to thaw.
2. Preheat oven to 400F.
3. Unfold one sheet of pastry (two in a package). Using a 3-inch leaf-shape cookie cutter, cut 26 leaves from each sheet.
4. In small bowl, beat egg yolk with water.
5. Brush puff-pastry leaves with half of egg-yolk mixture. Wrap a leaf around each olive; overlap tip of dough; press firmly to seal. Brush with rest of yolk.
6. Place on cookie sheet, 1 inch apart. Bake 15 minutes, or until golden-brown. Remove to rack. Serve warm. *Makes 52.*

THREE-CHEESE LOAF
(pictured)

2 pkg (8-oz size) cream cheese, softened
8 oz blue cheese, softened
2 pkg (10-oz size) sharp Cheddar cheese,
   grated
2 tablespoons grated onion
1 teaspoon Worcestershire sauce
½ cup chopped stuffed olives
½ cup finely chopped parsley

CHEESE FROSTING
1 pkg (10 oz) processed sharp Cheddar-
   cheese spread
2 tablespoons milk
3 large stuffed olives, sliced
Parsley sprigs

1. Line a 9-by-5-by-2¾-inch loaf pan with plastic wrap. In large bowl, combine cheeses, onion and Worcestershire. Knead with hands until well blended.
2. Work in chopped olives and parsley. Turn into pan, spreading evenly.
3. Refrigerate, covered, overnight.
4. Next day, about 1 hour before serving, unmold by inverting loaf on plate. Remove pan and plastic wrap.
5. Make Cheese Frosting: In small bowl of electric mixer, combine cheese spread and milk; beat until smooth.
6. With spatula, spread entire surface of loaf smoothly with cheese spread. Turn rest of spread into pastry bag with number-5 star tip. Make ruching on loaf. Arrange olives in center, overlapping slightly. Garnish with parsley. Refrigerate. *Makes 40 servings.*

CHINESE EGG ROLLS
(Trader Vic's)
(pictured)

FILLING
¼ lb boiled ham
¼ lb cooked chicken
¼ lb sugar peas or snow peas
4 scallions
4 sprigs parsley
1 lb bean sprouts
1 can (8 oz) bamboo shoots
1 can (8 oz) water chestnuts
2 tablespoons salad oil
½ teaspoon salt
½ teaspoon pepper
1 tablespoon soy sauce
1 teaspoon finely grated fresh ginger

EGG-ROLL SKINS
6 eggs
¼ cup cornstarch
¼ teaspoon salt
¼ cup water
Salad oil

BATTER
⅓ cup all-purpose flour
⅓ cup cornstarch
1½ teaspoons baking powder
¼ teaspoon salt
½ cup water
1 egg

Butter
Salad oil for frying
Prepared plum sauce
Prepared hot mustard

1. Make Filling: Finely chop ham, chicken, peas, scallions, parsley, bean sprouts, bamboo shoots and water chestnuts. Heat 2 tablespoons oil in a large heavy skillet or wok. Add vegetables; sauté 2 minutes. Drain well in colander. Add ½ teaspoon salt, the pepper, soy sauce and grated ginger; refrigerate to chill.
2. Make Egg-Roll Skins: In medium bowl, with wire whisk or rotary beater, beat 6 eggs until frothy. In a 1-cup measure, combine ¼ cup cornstarch, ¼ teaspoon salt and ¼ cup water; mix well. Add to eggs, and beat until well combined.
3. Slowly heat skillet with 10-inch bottom until a little water sizzles when dropped on it. Brush pan lightly with salad oil. Pour ⅓ cup batter into skillet, tilting pan so batter covers bottom completely.
4. Cook until nicely browned on underside and firm on top. Turn out onto waxed paper. Repeat to make 6 egg-roll skins in all. Lightly brush pan with oil before making each one.
5. Make Batter: In a medium bowl, combine flour, cornstarch, baking powder and salt; mix well. Gradually beat in ½ cup water, beating until mixture is smooth. Add egg; beat until well combined. Set aside.
6. Spoon filling into centers of egg-roll skins, dividing evenly. Spread to make a long narrow mound, leaving about 1 inch of skin on either end.
7. Fold ends of egg-roll skins over filling. Roll up, and seal with a dot of butter. Repeat to make 6 large egg rolls.
8. Heat salad oil (1½ inches deep) in a medium skillet to 325F. Stir batter. Dip the egg rolls in batter to coat completely. Using a slotted spoon or spatula, lift out and allow excess to drip back into bowl.
9. Place two of the rolls in hot fat, and fry until golden on one side. Turn, and fry until golden on the other side—about 5 minutes in all. Drain on paper towels. Fry two at a time until all are done. Slice into 1-inch-thick pieces. Serve hot with plum sauce and hot mustard. *Makes 6 egg rolls, 24 servings.*

Note: These may be made and cooked ahead and refrigerated. Reheat in a 450F oven, uncovered, 10 minutes before serving.

HOT CHEESE BALLS
(Trader Vic's)
(pictured)

½ lb (2 cups) grated Parmesan cheese
1 pkg (8 oz) cream cheese, softened
2 eggs
Dash ground red pepper
1 cup Japanese-style bread crumbs (see Note, Chicken-Tofu Balls)
Peanut or salad oil for deep frying

1. In medium bowl, combine both kinds of cheese, the eggs and pepper. Beat with wooden spoon until smooth. Form into 1¼-inch balls.
2. Roll each lightly in bread crumbs on waxed paper. Refrigerate.
3. In a deep skillet or deep-fat fryer, slowly heat oil (about 2 inches) to 350F on deep-frying thermometer. Fry cheese balls, turning once, 1 minute, or until golden-brown. Drain on paper towels. Serve hot. *Makes 24.*

CHICKEN-TOFU BALLS
(Trader Vic's)
(pictured)

½ lb boneless raw chicken
½ lb firm tofu
1 medium onion
1 egg
2¼ cups Japanese-style bread crumbs (see Note)
½ teaspoon salt
¼ teaspoon ground white pepper
2 tablespoons sherry
¼ cup finely chopped scallion
Salad oil for deep-fat frying
Bottled teriyaki sauce

1. Cut chicken, tofu and onion into ½-inch pieces. Place in blender or processor along with the egg, 1½ cups bread crumbs, salt and pepper. Blend until smooth.
2. Fold in sherry and scallion. Shape mixture into balls 1¼ inches in diameter. Roll them in the remaining bread crumbs. Refrigerate at least 2 hours.
3. In a medium saucepan, heat 2 inches of oil to 325F. Fry balls, several at a time, until golden-brown—about 4 minutes.
4. Serve hot with toothpicks and teriyaki sauce for dipping. *Makes 20 balls.*

Note: Japanese-style bread crumbs may be purchased in Japanese food shops, or made by removing crusts from a loaf of firm white bread, grating it and spreading the crumbs on cookie sheets, uncovered, to dry at room temperature for several days. Or dry out in 150F oven several hours.

PATE EN CROUTE
(pictured)

3 lb chicken livers
6 tablespoons (¾ stick) butter or margarine
⅓ cup chopped onion
1 tablespoon dried savory leaves
1 tablespoon dried tarragon leaves
6 tablespoons cognac or brandy
½ cup light cream or half-and-half
5 eggs
1 tablespoon salt
¼ teaspoon pepper
8 slices bacon
2 bay leaves
1 pkg (17¼ oz) frozen puff pastry
1 egg yolk
1 tablespoon water

1. Trim any white part from chicken livers; wash livers, and dry on paper towels. Cut in half.
2. In hot butter in skillet, sauté onion and dried herbs until onion is golden. Add chicken livers; sauté, stirring, about 5 minutes.
3. In bowl, combine livers, cognac, cream, eggs, salt and pepper; mix well. Put mixture through blender or food processor, about one-third at a time, to make a smooth purée.
4. Preheat oven to 400F. Line a 1¾-quart oval or round casserole (7¾ inches in diameter) with bacon slices. Arrange bay leaves in bottom of casserole.
5. Pour liver mixture into casserole; place in pan of very hot water (water should measure 1 inch). Bake 1 hour.
6. Remove casserole from hot water; let cool on wire rack 1 hour.
7. Meanwhile, remove frozen pastry from package. Let stand at room temperature 20 minutes to thaw.
8. Unfold one sheet of pastry (two in package).
9. Using a 3-inch leaf-shape cookie cutter, cut 18 leaves.
10. Cut an oval or round from remaining sheet of frozen puff pastry, making it the same size as top of casserole. Place on top of cooled pâté. Moisten edge of dish with cold water. Press pastry to edge to seal all around. Cut a 1-inch hole in center.
11. Arrange leaves around edge, overlapping slightly. Brush with egg yolk, beaten with water.
12. Bake 20 to 25 minutes, or until golden-brown and puffy. Remove to rack to cool 1 hour; serve slightly warm or cooled completely. Serve with toast rounds. *Makes 40 servings.*

OUR BEST QUICHE LORRAINE
(pictured)

PIE SHELL
1 pkg (10 oz) piecrust mix
Water
1 egg white, slightly beaten

FILLING
½ lb sliced bacon
¾ lb natural Swiss cheese, grated (3 cups)
6 whole eggs
1 egg yolk
1¼ teaspoons salt
⅛ teaspoon ground nutmeg
⅛ teaspoon black pepper
Dash ground red pepper
3 cups light cream or half-and-half
3 slices bacon, crisp-cooked

1. Make piecrust as label directs, sprinkling some water over all of pastry mix; toss lightly with fork after each addition, pushing dampened portion to side. Shape three-fourths of the pastry into a ball; flatten to make a 6-inch round. Freeze the remaining dough.
2. On lightly floured pastry cloth or surface, with light strokes, roll pastry from center to edge, alternating directions, to form a 14-inch circle. Trim edge to make 13-inch circle. Fold pastry in half; place, with fold in center, in bottom of 9-inch springform pan.
3. Unfold pastry; fit carefully into pan. Pastry will measure 2 inches high on side of pan. Pat pastry to fit snugly and evenly in pan. Brush bottom and side of pastry lightly with egg white. Refrigerate to chill slightly, until ready to use. Preheat oven to 375F.
4. Make Filling: Fry ½ pound bacon until crisp; drain; crumble. Sprinkle over bottom of pie shell. Sprinkle cheese over bacon. In bowl, with wire whisk or rotary beater, beat eggs and egg yolk, salt, nutmeg and peppers slightly. Gradually beat in half-and-half.
5. Beat mixture just until well combined, not frothy. Slowly pour over bacon and cheese in pie shell. Bake 50 to 55 minutes, or until top is golden-brown and puffy and the center seems firm when it is gently pressed with fingertip. Remove to wire rack.
6. Let cool 15 minutes on wire rack. With sharp knife, loosen edge of pastry from side of pan; gently remove side of springform pan. Place, still on bottom of springform pan, on plate. Garnish with bacon slices, as pictured. Serve warm. *Makes 12 hors-d'oeuvre servings.* ∎

O TIDINGS OF COMFORT AND JOY

For most of us, the greatest joy this season offers is the chance for families to get together and for friends to be reunited. Here are some buffet ideas to make this year's gatherings even more memorable. The main course is a simple but delicious *boeuf Bourguignon* (center): beef and vegetables in the French manner, cooked in Burgundy wine. With it, a salad of vegetables marinated in a vinaigrette sauce and arranged in rows on a tray. For dessert, a light, delicious fruit supreme: lemon sherbet ringed with fresh fruit, and pink champagne poured over all. Recipes for these and other holiday buffet specials, which serve up to 24 guests, begin on page 78.

continued from page 77

HOLIDAY BUFFET MENU
(Planned for 24)

LIVER PATE EN GELEE*
OR CRABMEAT BISQUE*
BEEF BOURGUIGNON* WITH NEW
POTATOES
OR BEEF STROGANOFF* WITH
WILD AND WHITE RICE
OR COQ AU VIN WITH MUSHROOMS*
AND FLUFFY WHITE RICE
VEGETABLE-SALAD PLATTER*
GREEN MAYONNAISE*
CRISP FRENCH BREAD   BUTTER
CARAFES OF RED AND WHITE WINES

DESSERT TABLE:
FRUIT SUPREME WITH PINK
CHAMPAGNE*
WITH A TRAY OF CHRISTMAS COOKIES
OR SLICED FRUITCAKE
OR AUSTRIAN BUTTER CAKE
OR FROSTED DAIQUIRI PIE*
COFFEE

Recipes given for starred dishes.

LIVER PATE EN GELEE

1½ teaspoons unflavored gelatine
1 cup canned condensed beef broth
4 canned whole mushrooms
1 can (4¾ oz) liver pâté
1 tablespoon butter or margarine, softened
1 teaspoon brandy
Thin slices toast

1. In small saucepan, sprinkle gelatine over ¼ cup undiluted broth; let stand 5 minutes to soften. Heat over low heat, stirring constantly, until gelatine dissolves. Remove from heat. Add remaining broth.

2. Place 1½-cup decorative mold in pan of ice and water. Spoon about 2 tablespoons gelatine mixture into mold. Let stand a few minutes, until almost set.

3. Cut mushrooms in half. Arrange in a pattern on set gelatine in mold. Add enough additional gelatine mixture to cover mushrooms.

4. In small bowl, combine liver pâté, butter and brandy. With electric mixer or fork, beat until combined.

5. Turn out mixture into empty liver-pâté can, making top even; invert onto waxed paper. With can opener, remove end of can. Lift can, and carefully push pâté through can onto center of set gelatine in mold, being careful to keep its shape.

6. Spoon remaining chilled gelatine mixture around and over pâté. Refrigerate, covered, 3 hours, or until firm.

7. To unmold: Run sharp knife around edge of mold. Invert over serving plate. Place hot damp dishcloth over mold; shake gently to release. Life off mold.

8. Remove crusts from toast; cut toast diagonally in quarters. Arrange triangles around mold. Or serve mold with crackers, if you wish. *Makes 8 servings.*

CRABMEAT BISQUE

5 cans (11-oz size) tomato bisque
4 cups light cream or half-and-half
½ cup milk
Ground nutmeg
1 cup very dry sherry
1 can (5 oz) crabmeat, drained

1. In large saucepan or kettle, combine soup, cream, milk, ½ teaspoon nutmeg. Stir to combine. Heat slowly just to boiling—about 10 minutes.

2. Add sherry and crabmeat, stirring; heat until thoroughly hot; do not boil.

3. Serve in individual soup cups. Sprinkle top of each with a little nutmeg. *Makes 24 (½-cup) servings.*

BEEF BOURGUIGNON
(pictured)

Butter or margarine
5 lb boneless beef chuck, cut into 1½-inch cubes
6 tablespoons brandy
1 lb small white onions, peeled (24)
1 lb small fresh mushrooms
½ cup potato flour
5 teaspoons meat-extract paste
¼ cup tomato paste
3 cups Burgundy
1½ cups dry sherry
1½ cups ruby port
1 can (10½ oz) condensed beef broth, undiluted
¼ teaspoon pepper
5 bay leaves
24 small new potatoes
Chopped parsley

1. Day before: Slowly heat an 8-quart Dutch oven with tight-fitting lid. Add 4 tablespoons butter; heat—do not burn.

2. In hot butter, over high heat, brown beef cubes well all over (about a fourth at a time—just enough to cover bottom of Dutch oven).

3. Lift out beef as it browns. Continue until all beef is browned, adding more butter as needed. Then return beef to Dutch oven.

4. In small saucepan, heat 4 tablespoons brandy just until vapor rises. Ignite and pour over beef. As flame dies, remove beef cubes; set aside.

5. Add 2 tablespoons butter to Dutch oven; heat slightly. Add onions; cook over low heat, covered, until onions brown slightly. Then add mushrooms; cook, stirring, 3 minutes. Remove from heat.

6. Stir in flour, meat-extract paste and tomato paste until well blended. Stir in Burgundy, sherry, port and beef broth.

7. Preheat oven to 350F.

8. Bring wine mixture just to boiling, stirring; remove from heat. Add beef, pepper and 2 bay leaves; mix well.

9. Bake, covered and stirring occasionally, 45 minutes, adding remaining brandy little by little. Bake with sheet of waxed paper placed over Dutch oven and lid placed on top. Discard any liquid collecting on top of paper.

10. Meanwhile, scrub potatoes, leaving skins on. Cook, covered, in small amount of lightly salted, boiling water 10 minutes. Drain. Add potatoes to beef mixture, spooning liquid over potatoes.

11. Let cool; refrigerate, covered, overnight.

12. To serve: Heat gently, covered, about 1 hour, stirring in a little more wine, if necessary, to thin sauce. Sprinkle with chopped parsley and garnish with 3 bay leaves. *Makes 12 servings.*

Note: For 24 servings, you will need to make this recipe twice. This is easier than doubling the recipe and making it all at once.

BEEF STROGANOFF

2 (2-lb size) flank steaks or 4 lb boneless beef sirloin, ½ inch thick
Instant unseasoned meat tenderizer
¼ to ⅓ cup (½ to ⅔ stick) butter or margarine
2 cups chopped onion
2 cloves garlic, finely chopped
1 lb fresh mushrooms, sliced ¼ inch thick
¼ cup all-purpose flour
2 tablespoons tomato paste
4 teaspoons meat-extract paste
1 teaspoon salt
⅛ teaspoon pepper
1 can (10½ oz) condensed beef broth, undiluted
⅓ cup dry white wine
1½ tablespoons snipped fresh dill
3 cups sour cream
¼ cup snipped fresh dill or parsley (optional)

1. Day before: Wipe beef with damp paper towels. Place in freezer 15 minutes; it will be easier to slice. With sharp knife, slice steak ¼ inch thick, across the grain. Sprinkle cut surface lightly with meat tenderizer.

2. Slowly heat a large heavy skillet. Melt 2 tablespoons butter. Add just enough beef strips to cover skillet bottom. Over high heat, sear quickly on all sides. With tongs, remove beef as it browns. Brown rest of beef, adding more butter as needed.

3. Pour drippings from skillet into 5-quart Dutch oven. Add onion, garlic and mushrooms; sauté until onion is golden —about 5 minutes. Remove from heat.

4. Stir in flour, tomato paste, meat-extract paste, salt and pepper until well blended. Gradually stir in broth; bring to boiling, stirring constantly. Reduce heat and simmer 5 minutes.

5. Stir in wine and 1½ tablespoons dill until well combined. Remove from heat; stir in meat. Refrigerate, covered, overnight.

6. About 1 hour before serving, bring beef mixture to boiling over medium heat. Remove from heat. Gradually stir in sour cream; cook over low heat until hot but not boiling.

7. Keep warm in chafing dish. Garnish with snipped fresh dill. Serve with wild and white rice, cooked according to package directions. *Makes 12 servings.*

Note: For 24 servings, make recipe twice.

COQ AU VIN WITH MUSHROOMS

12 whole chicken breasts (12-oz size)
¾ lb bacon, chopped coarsely, or ¾ lb salt pork, cut up (see Notes)
20 small white onions, peeled
6 tablespoons cognac
6 shallots, peeled
Bouquet garni (see Notes)
1 clove garlic, pressed
¾ lb fresh mushrooms, sliced
1 bottle dry red wine (about 3⅓ cups)
2 teaspoons salt
¾ teaspoon pepper
2 teaspoons sugar
½ teaspoon ground nutmeg
6 tablespoons all-purpose flour
¼ cup dry sherry
3 tablespoons chopped parsley

1. Day before: Cut chicken breasts in half; wipe well with damp paper towels.

2. In large skillet, heat bacon. Add onions; sauté over medium heat until golden. Lift out onions and bacon with slotted spoon.

3. Add chicken breasts, skin side down; sauté, turning, until golden-brown on each side—about 5 minutes.

4. Heat cognac slightly; pour over chicken; ignite. Remove chicken with liquid to 6-quart Dutch oven.

5. Add shallots, bouquet garni, garlic and mushrooms to skillet. Simmer, covered, over low heat 20 minutes.

6. Meanwhile, in large saucepan, reheat bacon; add ¾ of the red wine; bring to boiling; pour over chicken. Add salt, pepper, sugar and nutmeg; stir to mix well. Bring to boiling; reduce heat and simmer, covered, 30 minutes. Add onions during last 20 to 25 minutes of cooking.

7. Combine rest of wine with flour, to make a smooth mixture; stir into liquid in Dutch oven; bring to boiling; sauce will be slightly thickened. Remove and discard bouquet garni. Refrigerate, covered, overnight.

8. To serve: Add sherry and reheat gently, covered, 30 minutes; if sauce seems too thick, add a little more wine. Arrange the Coq au Vin on a serving platter, and sprinkle with chopped parsley. Serve with fluffy white rice. *Makes 12 servings.*

Notes: For 24 servings, make recipe twice.

If you are using bacon, you may want to use half the amount of salt called for in recipe.

To make a bouquet garni, tie a large sprig of fresh parsley, ½ teaspoon dried thyme leaves and a bay leaf in a square of cheesecloth to make a small bag.

continued on page 103

PARTIES TO PUT YOU ON THE MAP

Give your holiday spreads festive flavors from all four corners of the country with this treasury of the very best regional recipes. Celebrate with salmon from the Pacific Northwest or a genuine New England Yankee Pot Roast Dinner. Our Southwestern Fiesta will please even finicky eaters, and the spicy, exotic flavors of Louisiana Cajun cuisine will bring everyone back for more. Recipes begin on page 87.

Tex-Mex Fiesta

Enthusiasm for Tex-Mex foods has spread all across the country. Here's our selection of zesty Southwestern favorites to create and enjoy as part of a make-your-own buffet. At top, center: Deep-Dish Picadillo Pie of ground beef, tomatoes, corn and chiles in a golden cornmeal crust. Moving clockwise: Barbecued Chicken served over savory Mexican Rice; Stuffed Zucchini; Beef Empanadas (pastries plump with meat, tomatoes, onions and olives) served with a fiery Salsa; Beef Enchiladas; and Meatballs Mole in a satiny smooth sauce touched with chocolate. Start the festivities with Guacamole Dip, then cool down with Caramel-Custard Mold and icy cold Sangria.

Cajun Dinner

GUS FRANCISCO

The fish and fowl that thrive in Louisiana bayous are the mainstay of our Cajun meal. Wine-braised Duck Fricassee and zesty Shrimp Étouffée, wreathed in rice, are complemented by oyster-stuffed artichokes, a triple-squash sauté and ever popular Cornbread. Cajun cuisine, with its roots in country-French cooking, also caters to a sweet tooth: At bottom left, fried pastries drizzled with syrup and dotted with pecans are made to resemble pigs' ears. And the Sweet-Potato-Pecan Pie is heavenly when served with molasses-and-rum-laced coffee to crown a Deep South celebration.

Nantucket Supper

Savory, hearty fare is what makes Northeastern suppers special. Our Nantucket spread starts with the clam chowder so famous in New England. For the main dish: Yankee Pot Roast, oven-braised with onions and served with glazed carrots and Corn Pudding. With a round loaf of Portuguese Bread and fluffy Cranberry Whip topped with Custard Sauce, this meal is a culinary classic.

Pacific Northwest Dinner

Salmon abounds in the Pacific Northwest. Lightly broiled and lemon-buttered, it's our choice for an elegant entrée when the dinner is formal. On the side: sautéed fresh vegetables, baked-potato ovals and, for the finale, a tantalizing apple tart.

GUS FRANCISCO

continued from page 80

TEX-MEX FIESTA

(Planned for 6)

SANGRIA
GUACAMOLE DIP WITH CRISP
VEGETABLES*
BARBECUED CHICKEN*
DEEP-DISH PICADILLO PIE*
MEATBALLS MOLE*
BEEF ENCHILADAS*
OR
BEEF EMPANADAS*
MEXICAN RICE*   SALSA*
MEXICAN STUFFED ZUCCHINI*
CARAMEL-CUSTARD MOLD*

*Recipes given for starred dishes.

GUACAMOLE DIP WITH CRISP VEGETABLES

1 medium tomato, peeled
2 ripe avocados (about 1½ lb)
¼ cup finely chopped onion
2 tablespoons finely chopped canned chili
    peppers
1½ tablespoons white vinegar
1 teaspoon salt
Chilled cauliflowerets
Crisp celery sticks
Green onions
Radishes
Cucumber sticks

1. In medium bowl, crush tomato with potato masher.
2. Halve avocados lengthwise; remove pits and peel. Slice avocados into crushed tomato; then mash until well blended.
3. Add onion, chili pepper, vinegar and salt; mix well.
4. Place guacamole in bowl. Surround with vegetables. *Makes about 2 cups.*

BARBECUED CHICKEN WITH MEXICAN RICE

(pictured)

BARBECUE SAUCE
½ cup cider vinegar
¼ cup brown sugar, firmly packed
2 tablespoons prepared mustard
2 teaspoons salt
¼ teaspoon crushed red pepper
½ teaspoon black pepper
Dash hot red-pepper sauce
1 cup chopped onion
1 small lemon, sliced
1 tablespoon Worcestershire sauce
¼ cup water
¼ cup chili sauce
1 cup catsup

3 (2-lb size) broiler-fryers, cut up
Mexican Rice, recipe follows

1. Make Barbecue Sauce: In large saucepan, combine vinegar, sugar, mustard, salt, red and black pepper, pepper sauce, chopped onion, sliced lemon, Worcestershire and water; mix well. Bring to boiling; reduce heat, and simmer, uncovered, 20 minutes.
2. Add chili sauce and catsup; bring just to boiling.
3. Preheat oven to 400F. Wash chicken; pat dry with paper towels.
4. Place chicken, skin side down, in large shallow roasting pan.
5. Spoon some Barbecue Sauce over chicken; bake 30 minutes; turn chicken, skin side up. Meanwhile, make Mexican Rice.
6. Brush chicken liberally with Barbecue Sauce; bake 30 minutes longer, basting frequently. Serve barbecued chicken with more of the sauce, if desired, and with the Mexican Rice. *Makes 6 servings.*

MEXICAN RICE

⅔ cup chopped onion
3 tablespoons bacon fat
1½ cups raw converted white rice
1 cup chopped green pepper
1 teaspoon chili powder
1 cup tomato juice
½ cup catsup
2 teaspoons salt
3 cups water
Chopped fresh tomato and chopped green
    pepper (optional)

1. In heavy 5-quart Dutch oven with a tight-fitting cover, sauté onion in hot bacon fat. Stir in rice, 1 cup chopped green pepper, the chili powder, tomato juice, catsup and salt.
2. Add water. Bring to boiling; reduce heat; simmer, covered, 20 minutes, or until liquid is absorbed and rice is cooked. Garnish with chopped tomato and green pepper. *Makes 6 servings.*

DEEP-DISH PICADILLO PIE

(pictured)

1 lb ground beef chuck or round
½ cup finely chopped onion
1 clove garlic, pressed
1 can (1 lb) tomatoes, undrained
1 can (16 oz) whole-kernel corn, drained
1 can (3 oz) chopped green chiles, drained
¼ cup tomato paste
½ teaspoon dried oregano leaves
½ teaspoon dried basil leaves
1 teaspoon salt
¼ teaspoon pepper
Cornmeal Crust, recipe follows
1 egg yolk, beaten slightly
1 tablespoon water

1. In a large heavy skillet, sauté beef, stirring until red color disappears. Add onion and garlic; cook, stirring, about 5 minutes. Drain off excess fat.
2. Add tomatoes, corn, chiles, tomato paste, oregano, basil, salt and pepper; mix well. Turn into a 2-quart casserole.
3. Make Cornmeal Crust. Preheat oven to 425F. Carefully place cornmeal dough on top of beef mixture; pinch edge to seal all around. Brush top lightly with egg yolk combined with water.
4. Bake 15 minutes, or until golden-brown and bubbly. *Makes 6 servings.*

CORNMEAL CRUST

¾ cup yellow cornmeal
¾ cup all-purpose flour
2½ teaspoons baking powder
1 teaspoon salt
⅓ cup shortening
About ½ cup milk

1. Into medium bowl, sift cornmeal with flour, baking powder and salt.
2. Cut shortening into flour mixture, with a pastry blender or 2 knives (used scissors fashion), until mixture resembles coarse cornmeal.
3. Make a well in the center. Pour in ½ cup milk all at once. Stir quickly around the bowl with a fork. If mixture seems dry, add a little more milk to form dough just moist enough (but not wet) to leave side of bowl and form ball.
4. Turn out dough onto a lightly floured surface, to knead. Gently pick up dough from side away from you; fold over toward you; press out lightly with palm of hand. Give the dough a quarter turn. Repeat ten times.
5. Gently roll out dough from center to ½-inch thickness into a circle 9 inches in diameter. Cut out circle, about 1½ inches in diameter, from center. Cut 8 diamonds all around circle, as pictured.

continued on page 88

continued from page 87

MEATBALLS MOLE
(pictured)

1 lb ground chuck
1 egg, slightly beaten
½ cup milk
¾ cup crushed corn chips
2½ teaspoons salt
2½ tablespoons all-purpose flour
2 tablespoons shortening
2 cups sliced onion
1 clove garlic, crushed
2 tablespoons sugar
1 tablespoon chili powder
1 teaspoon ground cumin
1 teaspoon ground coriander
1 teaspoon dried oregano leaves
1 can (1 lb) tomatoes, undrained
1 square (1 oz) unsweetened chocolate
1 cup water
Toasted seasame seeds (see Note)
3 cups cooked white rice

1. In large bowl, lightly toss chuck with egg, milk, corn chips and 1 teaspoon salt to combine. Refrigerate, covered, 1 hour.

2. Gently shape into 20 meatballs, using 2 tablespoons meat mixture for each. Roll meatballs lightly in 2 tablespoons flour, coating completely.

3. Slowly heat shortening in large, heavy skillet with tight-fitting lid. Then sauté meatballs, a few at a time, until nicely browned all over. Remove meatballs from skillet as they are browned.

4. In same skillet, cook onion and garlic, stirring occasionally, about 5 minutes, or until tender. Remove the skillet from the heat.

5. Combine sugar, chili powder, cumin, coriander, oregano and rest of salt and flour. Stir into skillet along with tomatoes, chocolate and water, mixing well.

6. Bring mixture to boiling, stirring constantly. Reduce heat; simmer, covered and stirring occasionally, 45 minutes.

7. Add meatballs to skillet; simmer, covered, 15 minutes. Uncover; simmer 15 minutes.

8. Turn meatballs and sauce into dish. Garnish meatballs with toasted sesame seeds. Serve with rice. *Makes 6 servings.*

Note: To toast sesame seeds, place in shallow pan and bake in 325F oven about 5 minutes.

BEEF ENCHILADAS
(pictured)

MEAT FILLING
1 lb ground chuck
1 clove garlic, finely chopped
2 teaspoons salt
1 tablespoon tequila, cognac or water
1 tablespoon chili powder
1 can (1 lb) kidney beans, undrained

TOMATO SAUCE
3 tablespoons salad oil
1 clove garlic, very finely chopped
½ cup chopped onion
¼ cup chopped green pepper
3 tablespoons flour
2 cans (1-lb size) tomatoes, undrained
1 beef-bouillon cube
1 cup boiling water
2 tablespoons chopped canned green chiles
Dash ground cumin
½ teaspoon salt
Dash pepper

ENCHILADAS
8 tortillas
1 cup grated sharp Cheddar cheese

1. Prepare Meat Filling: In medium skillet, over low heat, sauté chuck with 1 clove garlic, 2 teaspoons salt, the tequila and chili powder until chuck is browned. Stir in kidney beans.

2. Make Tomato Sauce: In hot oil in skillet, sauté garlic, onion and green pepper until golden.

3. Remove from heat. Stir in flour until smooth; stir in tomatoes and bouillon cube dissolved in boiling water.

4. Over medium heat, bring mixture to boiling, stirring.

5. Add chiles, cumin, salt and pepper; simmer, uncovered and stirring occasionally, about 10 minutes.

6. To assemble Enchiladas: Preheat oven to 350F.

7. Place about ½ cup filling in center of each tortilla; roll up. Arrange, seam side down, in a 13-by-9-by-2-inch baking dish. Pour Tomato Sauce over all; sprinkle with cheese.

8. Bake 25 minutes. *Makes 8 servings.*

Note: Meat Filling and Tomato Sauce may be made ahead of time and refrigerated. Reheat slightly when ready to use.

BEEF EMPANADAS
(pictured)

FILLING
2 tablespoons butter or margarine
½ cup chopped onion
1 lb ground beef
2 large ripe tomatoes (1 lb), chopped
1 can (3 oz) green chiles, drained, chopped
1 teaspoon salt
1 bay leaf
2 tablespoons chopped black olives

PASTRY (see Note)
1½ cups all-purpose flour
¾ teaspoon salt
½ cup shortening
4 to 4½ tablespoons ice water
1 egg yolk
1 tablespoon water

Salsa, recipe follows

1. Make Filling: In hot butter in large skillet, sauté onion until tender. Add beef, and sauté until no longer red.

2. Add tomato, chiles, 1 teaspoon salt and the bay leaf; simmer, stirring occasionally, 30 to 35 minutes, or until most of liquid has evaporated. Remove from heat; discard bay leaf. Stir in olives.

3. Preheat oven to 400F.

4. Meanwhile, make Pastry: In medium bowl, combine flour and salt. With pastry blender, cut in shortening until well blended. Sprinkle with ice water; stir with fork until mixture holds together. Shape into a ball.

5. Divide pastry into 12 pieces. On lightly floured surface, roll each piece into a 6-inch round. Place about 3 tablespoons filling in one-half of each round; fold over other half.

6. Press edges together with fingers to seal; flute edges. Cut slits on top of each empanada. Brush with egg yolk beaten with the tablespoon water.

7. Bake 20 to 25 minutes, or until golden-brown. Serve hot with Salsa. *Makes 6 servings.*

Note: Or use packaged pastry mix; prepare as label directs. Continue recipe as in Step 5.

SALSA
(pictured)

1 can (1 lb, 12 oz) tomatoes, drained and chopped
1 cup finely chopped onion
1 can (3 oz) green chiles, drained and finely chopped
1 tablespoon canned jalapeño pepper, finely chopped
1 clove garlic, crushed
2 tablespoons peanut or salad oil
½ teaspoon salt
¼ teaspoon pepper
¼ teaspoon chili powder

1. Make Salsa one or two days ahead: In medium saucepan, combine all ingredients; stir to mix well. Bring to boiling, stirring. Reduce heat, and simmer 20 minutes, stirring occasionally. Refrigerate, covered, overnight or longer.

2. To serve, reheat gently, or serve cold, if desired. Serve with Beef Empanadas. *Makes 2½ cups.*

MEXICAN STUFFED ZUCCHINI
(pictured)

4 medium zucchini (1½ to 2 lb)
Salt
2 slices bacon, cut up
1 cup chopped mushrooms
½ cup chopped green pepper
1 can (4 oz) chopped green chiles
½ cup chopped onion
1 clove garlic, crushed
1 can (8 oz) whole-kernel corn, drained
1 can (8 oz) tomato sauce
¼ cup sliced black olives
1½ cups cooked rice
Dash pepper
1 egg, slightly beaten
1 cup grated Cheddar cheese

1. Preheat oven to 350F.
2. Wash zucchini; cut off and discard stems. Cut each in half lengthwise. Scoop out and discard seeds.
3. In medium skillet with tight-fitting cover, bring 2 cups water and 1 teaspoon salt to boiling.
4. Add zucchini, cut side down; cook, covered, over medium heat 5 minutes, or until tender, not mushy. Drain well.
5. In medium skillet, sauté bacon until crisp; drain, discarding fat.
6. Stir in mushrooms, green pepper, chiles, onion and garlic. Sauté, stirring, until onion is tender—about 5 minutes.
7. Remove from heat; add corn, tomato sauce, olives, rice, ¼ teaspoon salt, the pepper and egg; mix well.
8. Fill zucchini halves with rice mixture, dividing evenly. Sprinkle with cheese.
9. Arrange in bottom of roasting pan. Bake 15 to 20 minutes, or until heated through. *Makes 8 servings.*

CARAMEL-CUSTARD MOLD

CARAMELIZED SUGAR
1 cup sugar

CUSTARD
1 quart milk
6 eggs
½ cup sugar
⅛ teaspoon salt
1 teaspoon vanilla extract

1. Preheat oven to 325F.
2. Make Caramelized Sugar: Place 1 cup sugar in heavy skillet; cook over low to medium heat, without stirring, until sugar has melted and begins to form light-brown syrup. Stir to blend. Use at once to coat 1½-quart casserole: Hold with pot holder, and slowly pour in hot syrup. Turn and rotate until bottom and side are thoroughly coated.
3. Make Custard: In medium saucepan, over medium heat, heat milk just until bubbles form around edge of pan.
4. In large bowl, with rotary beater, beat eggs slightly. Stir in ½ cup sugar,

the salt and vanilla. Gradually add hot milk, stirring constantly. Pour into prepared dish.
5. Place in shallow pan; pour hot water to ½-inch depth around dish.
6. Bake 1 hour and 15 minutes, or until knife blade inserted deep into center of custard comes out clean. Cool; refrigerate overnight.
7. To serve: Run small spatula around edge of dish to loosen. Invert onto shallow serving dish; shake gently to release. The caramel will serve as a sauce. *Makes 8 servings.*

CAJUN DINNER
(Planned for 12)

OYSTER-FILLED ARTICHOKES*
SHRIMP ETOUFFEE WITH RICE*
DUCK FRICASSEE*
SAUTEED SQUASH SLICES*
CORNBREAD*
SWEET-POTATO-PECAN PIE*
PIG'S-EAR TWISTS*
CAJUN COFFEE*

*Recipes given for starred dishes.

OYSTER-FILLED ARTICHOKES
(pictured)

12 medium artichokes (4½-5 lb in all)
1 tablespoon olive or salad oil
6 slices lemon
1 clove garlic, split
1 teaspoon salt
⅛ teaspoon pepper

OYSTER FILLING
2 pints raw oysters, with liquor
Water
1 cup (2 sticks) unsalted butter or
**   margarine**
1 cup chopped green onion
2 cloves garlic, minced
1 teaspoon salt
1 teaspoon ground red pepper
½ teaspoon white pepper
½ teaspoon dried thyme leaves
2 pkg (9-oz size) frozen artichoke hearts,
**   thawed, sliced**
½ cup all-purpose flour
1 cup heavy cream

½ cup grated Parmesan cheese

1. Trim stalk from base of each artichoke; cut a ½-inch slice from top. Remove discolored leaves; snip off spike ends. Wash artichokes in cold water; drain.
2. In large, 8-quart kettle, bring 3 inches of water to boiling. Add olive oil, lemon slices, split clove of garlic, 1 teaspoon salt and ⅛ teaspoon pepper.

3. Add artichokes to boiling water. Simmer over low heat, covered, 30 to 40 minutes, or until artichoke bases can be pierced with a fork. Drain artichokes; cool.
4. Spread artichokes to reveal centers. Scoop out and discard prickly choke; set artichokes aside.
5. Make Oyster Filling: Drain and pick over oysters, discarding any bits of shell; set oysters aside. Add water to oyster liquor to make 6 cups.
6. In large saucepan, melt butter. Add green onion, garlic, salt, red and white pepper, thyme and sliced artichoke hearts; sauté, stirring constantly, about 2 minutes. Add flour, stirring until mixed.
7. Slowly add cream and reserved oyster liquor, stirring until blended. Over medium heat, bring to boiling, stirring constantly. Reduce heat; simmer 5 minutes, stirring constantly. Add oysters; simmer 3 minutes. Remove from heat.
8. Spoon oyster mixture into centers of artichokes, dividing evenly. Sprinkle with Parmesan cheese. Place artichokes in broiler pan without its rack or in a shallow baking pan. Broil 6 inches from heat just until cheese turns golden. *Makes 12 servings.*

SHRIMP ETOUFFEE WITH RICE
(pictured)

Rice Ring, recipe follows
1 teaspoon salt
1 teaspoon ground red pepper
½ teaspoon black pepper
1 teaspoon dried basil leaves
½ teaspoon dried thyme leaves
⅓ cup salad oil
¾ cup all-purpose flour
½ cup chopped onion
½ cup chopped celery
½ cup chopped green pepper
1 clove garlic, minced
Water
1 can (13¾ or 14½ oz) chicken broth
½ cup chopped green onion
¼ cup (½ stick) butter or margarine
2 lb raw medium-size shrimp, shelled and
**   deveined**

1. Make Rice Ring.
2. In small bowl, combine salt, red and black pepper, basil and thyme; set aside.
3. In heavy, 5-quart Dutch oven, over medium-high heat, heat oil until very hot. Stir in flour, and cook, stirring constantly, until roux is dark brown—about 5 to 7 minutes. Remove from heat. Add onion, celery, green pepper, garlic and reserved spice mixture. Continue cooking over medium-high heat, stirring constantly, until vegetables are tender-crisp—2 to 3 minutes.

continued on page 90

continued from page 89

4. Add water to chicken broth to make 2 cups. Gradually stir broth mixture into cooked vegetables until well mixed. Simmer over low heat, stirring constantly, about 2 minutes. Stir in green onion. Remove from heat.

5. In large skillet, over medium heat, melt butter; stir in shrimp; sauté until tender—2 to 3 minutes. Remove from heat.

6. To serve: Run a small spatula around edge of Rice Ring; turn out onto warm, rimmed serving platter. Spoon some of the sauce in center of and around Rice Ring. With slotted spoon, arrange shrimp in center of and around Rice Ring. Stir shrimp juices remaining in skillet into sauce. Serve sauce separately. *Makes 8 servings.*

RICE RING

5 cups cooked white rice
2 tablespoons finely chopped green onion
2 tablespoons finely chopped celery
2 tablespoons finely chopped green pepper
¼ cup (½ stick) butter or margarine, melted
Salt to taste
Dash ground red pepper
Dash black pepper

1. Grease very well a 1½-quart ring mold. In large bowl, combine all ingredients. Pack lightly into mold, smoothing top. Cover with foil; set aside.

2. About 20 minutes before serving, preheat oven to 350F. Bake Rice Ring 15 minutes, or until heated. Remove foil just before serving.

DUCK FRICASSEE

(pictured)

2 (5-lb size) ducklings, quartered (if frozen, thaw completely)
1 teaspoon salt
¼ teaspoon pepper

MARINADE
1½ cups dry red wine
¼ cup brandy
1 cup chopped onion
1 teaspoon dried thyme leaves
½ teaspoon dried marjoram leaves
½ teaspoon crushed bay leaf
¼ teaspoon ground allspice

1 can (13¾ or 14½ oz) chicken broth
1 clove garlic, pressed or minced
1 lb fresh mushrooms, halved
¼ cup all-purpose flour

1. Day ahead: Wipe duckling quarters with damp paper towels. Sprinkle with salt and pepper.

2. Make Marinade: In large bowl, mix marinade ingredients. Add duckling quarters, turning in marinade until all pieces are well coated. Cover tightly with foil; refrigerate overnight (occasionally turn the pieces).

3. Next day: With tongs, remove duckling quarters from the marinade, allowing excess liquid to drip back into the bowl; drain on paper towels. Strain marinade, and reserve.

4. In 8-quart Dutch oven, over medium heat, place four duckling quarters, skin side down, in pan. Cook, turning often, until browned all over—about 15 minutes; remove to paper towels. Repeat to brown other pieces. Pour off fat, reserving ¼ cup.

5. Return duckling to Dutch oven; add 1½ cups strained marinade and the chicken broth. Bring to boiling; reduce heat to low; cover; simmer 1½ hours, or until duckling is tender.

6. Remove duckling to platter; keep warm. Strain cooking liquid into 4-cup measuring cup or bowl; skim off fat. If necessary, add water to make 2½ cups. In Dutch oven, heat the reserved ¼ cup fat. Sauté the garlic and mushrooms just until tender; stir in flour. Gradually stir in the 2½ cups cooking liquid. Bring to boiling, stirring until thickened. Pour some mushroom gravy over the duck, and pass the remaining gravy. *Makes 8 servings.*

SAUTEED SQUASH SLICES

(pictured)

3 medium zucchini (1½ lb)
3 medium yellow squash (1½ lb)
1 chayote (see Note)
2 tablespoons butter or margarine
2 tablespoons olive or salad oil
Salt
Pepper

1. Cut zucchini and yellow squash into ¼-inch-thick diagonal slices. Cut chayote lengthwise into quarters, then crosswise into ⅛-inch-thick slices.

2. In large skillet, heat butter and 1 tablespoon olive oil; add zucchini. Sauté over medium heat, turning occasionally with slotted spoon, just until zucchini is tender-crisp—3 to 5 minutes. Sprinkle lightly with salt and pepper. Arrange zucchini on warm platter; keep warm.

3. Add remaining oil to fat remaining in skillet. Sauté yellow squash over medium heat, turning occasionally just until squash is tender-crisp—3 to 5 minutes. Sprinkle with salt and pepper. Arrange yellow squash over zucchini; keep warm.

4. In fat remaining in skillet, sauté chayote, stirring occasionally, until tender—5 to 8 minutes; sprinkle with salt and pepper. Arrange chayote over yellow squash. Serve immediately. *Makes 12 servings.*

Note: Chayote is a pale-green, pear-shape squash. Commonly found in Latin American markets and in the Gulf States, it's also called christophine, mirliton and vegetable pear. If not available, use another zucchini.

CORNBREAD

(pictured)

1⅓ cups all-purpose flour
½ cup sugar
5 teaspoons baking powder
½ teaspoon salt
1 cup yellow cornmeal
1 egg
1⅓ cups milk
5 tablespoons (½ stick plus 1 tablespoon) butter or margarine, melted

1. Preheat oven to 350F. Grease an 8-by-8-by-2-inch baking pan.

2. Onto sheet of waxed paper, sift together flour, sugar, baking powder and salt; add cornmeal.

3. In medium bowl, combine egg, milk and butter, mixing well. Add flour mixture, stirring only until flour mixture is moistened.

4. Spoon batter into prepared pan; bake 50 to 55 minutes, or until golden-brown. Cut into small squares. *Makes 16 servings.*

SWEET-POTATO-PECAN PIE

(pictured)

9-inch unbaked pie shell

SWEET-POTATO FILLING
1 egg
1½ cups mashed, cooked fresh sweet potato
¼ cup sugar
2 tablespoons unsalted butter or margarine, softened
1 teaspoon vanilla extract
¼ teaspoon salt
¼ teaspoon ground cinnamon
⅛ teaspoon ground allspice
⅛ teaspoon ground nutmeg

PECAN TOPPING
2 eggs
½ cup sugar
½ cup dark corn syrup
2 tablespoons unsalted butter or margarine, melted
1 teaspoon vanilla extract
Dash ground cinnamon
1 cup pecan halves

½ cup heavy cream, whipped

1. Prepare pie shell; set aside.
2. Make Sweet-Potato Filling: In medium bowl, with portable electric mixer, beat 1 egg until frothy. Add remaining filling ingredients; beat at medium speed until mixture is smooth—about 2 minutes.
3. Make Pecan Topping: In medium bowl, with portable electric mixer, beat eggs until frothy. Add sugar, corn syrup, melted butter, vanilla and cinnamon. Beat at low speed just until the mixture is well blended—about 1 minute. Stir in pecans.
4. Preheat oven to 350F.
5. To assemble: Turn Sweet-Potato Filling into bottom of unbaked pie shell, spreading evenly. Pour Pecan Topping over top. Bake 60 to 70 minutes, until set and knife inserted in center comes out clean.
6. Remove pie to rack; cool completely. Just before serving, decorate with whipped cream, as pictured. *Makes 12 servings.*

PIG'S-EAR TWISTS
(pictured)

3 eggs
¼ cup (½ stick) butter or margarine, melted
2 cups all-purpose flour
¼ teaspoon salt
Salad oil or shortening for frying

GLAZE
1⅓ cups dark corn syrup
½ cup chopped pecans

1. In large bowl, with wooden spoon, beat eggs lightly. Stir in melted butter. Add the flour and salt, mixing until blended.
2. Turn dough out onto lightly floured pastry cloth or board; knead until smooth—about 3 minutes. Pinch off 1-inch pieces of dough (about the size of a walnut). On lightly floured pastry cloth or board, roll each piece into a 3- to 3½-inch circle, about ⅛ inch thick.
3. To form the "ear": Put the tines of a fork in the center of each circle, piercing the dough; twist the dough a quarter turn.
4. Meanwhile, in deep-fat fryer or heavy Dutch oven, slowly heat 2 inches salad oil to 360F on deep-frying thermometer.
5. Fry twists, three or four at a time, in hot oil, turning until golden-brown on both sides. Lift out; drain on paper towels. Place in single layer on sheets of foil.
6. Make Glaze: In a small saucepan, over high heat, bring corn syrup to boiling. Reduce heat to low; simmer 5 minutes. Spoon syrup over twists; sprinkle quickly with chopped pecans. Let syrup set; transfer twists to serving plate. *Makes about 2½ dozen.*

CAJUN COFFEE
(pictured)

6 cups hot strong black coffee (see Note)
½ cup dark molasses
12 tablespoons dark rum
1 cup heavy cream, whipped
Ground nutmeg

1. In large saucepan, over medium heat, heat coffee and molasses, stirring constantly until molasses is dissolved. Do not boil.
2. Spoon 1 tablespoon rum into each of 12 cups. Divide coffee mixture evenly among the cups.
3. Top each with a dollop of whipped cream. Sprinkle with nutmeg. *Makes 12 servings.*
Note: Coffee made with finely ground, dark-roast Italian coffee in a special espresso pot is preferred. Or make instant espresso coffee according to label directions.

NANTUCKET SUPPER
(Planned for 12)

NEW ENGLAND CLAM CHOWDER*
YANKEE POT ROAST WITH ONIONS*
MAPLE-GLAZED CARROTS*
CORN PUDDING*
PORTUGUESE BREAD*
CRANBERRY WHIP WITH CUSTARD SAUCE*

Recipes given for starred dishes.

NEW ENGLAND CLAM CHOWDER
(pictured)

3 slices bacon, coarsely chopped
1½ cups finely chopped onion
2 cans (7½- or 10½-oz size) minced clams
3 cups cubed peeled potato
½ teaspoon salt
¼ teaspoon pepper
3 cups light cream or half-and-half

1. In 5-quart Dutch oven, sauté bacon until almost crisp. Add onion; cook, stirring occasionally, about 5 minutes.
2. Drain clams, reserving clam liquid.
3. Add potato, salt, pepper and reserved clam liquid to Dutch oven. Cook over medium heat, covered, 15 minutes, or until potato cubes are fork-tender.
4. Add clams and cream to Dutch oven; mix well. Heat about 3 minutes; do not boil. *Makes 12 servings.*
Note: One pint shucked fresh clams may be used in place of canned clams. Chop clams coarsely; use 1 bottle (8 ounces) clam juice or broth for the liquid.

YANKEE POT ROAST WITH ONIONS
(pictured)

2 tablespoons bacon fat or salad oil
5-to-5½-lb beef rump or round roast
½ cup chopped onion
½ cup chopped carrot
1 clove garlic, minced
½ bay leaf, crumbled
Water
1 can (10½ oz) condensed beef broth, undiluted
1 can (8 oz) tomato sauce
½ teaspoon salt
¼ teaspoon pepper
1 lb small white boiling onions, peeled
2 tablespoons all-purpose flour

1. In hot bacon fat in 6-quart oven-proof Dutch oven, brown meat, turning with two wooden spoons, until well browned on all sides—about 20 minutes in all.
2. Preheat oven to 350F.
3. Push roast to one side of pan; add chopped onion, carrot, garlic and bay leaf; sauté 5 minutes. Add water to beef broth to make 1½ cups; pour over meat, along with tomato sauce. Add salt and pepper.
4. Bake, covered, 1½ hours, or until meat is almost fork-tender; add boiling onions. Bake 20 minutes longer, or until meat is fork-tender. Remove roast and onions to warm serving platter.
5. Strain pan liquid, discarding particles. Skim fat off liquid. In small bowl, combine flour and ½ cup water, stirring until smooth.
6. Return strained liquid to Dutch oven; stir in flour mixture. Bring to boiling, stirring until slightly thickened. Pass sauce with the meat. *(Makes 2⅔ to 3 cups.) Makes 20 servings.*

MAPLE-GLAZED CARROTS
(pictured)

3 lb carrots, pared
½ teaspoon salt
¼ cup (½ stick) butter or margarine
¼ cup maple syrup
¼ teaspoon ground nutmeg

1. Cut carrots crosswise into halves. Cut the thick carrot halves lengthwise into quarters. In large skillet, bring 1½ cups water to boiling; add carrots and salt. Simmer, covered, 10 to 15 minutes, or until tender. Drain in colander.
2. Return carrots to skillet. Add butter, maple syrup and nutmeg. Cook over medium heat, stirring occasionally, until carrots are glazed. *Makes 12 servings.*

continued on page 92

continued from page 91

CORN PUDDING
(pictured)

4 eggs
2 pkg (10-oz size) frozen whole-kernel
  corn, thawed and drained
½ cup plain cracker crumbs
1 tablespoon sugar
1 teaspoon salt
¼ teaspoon white pepper
Dash ground nutmeg
3 cups light cream or half-and-half
2 tablespoons butter or margarine, melted

1. Preheat oven to 350F. Lightly grease a deep 1½-quart casserole.
2. In large bowl, beat eggs; stir in corn, crumbs, sugar, salt, pepper and nutmeg.
3. Add cream and butter; mix well. Pour into prepared casserole. Set casserole in baking pan; pour hot tap water to 1-inch depth around casserole.
4. Bake, uncovered, 1½ hours, or until pudding is firm and knife inserted in center comes out clean. Serve corn pudding hot. *Makes 12 servings.*
   Note: If using a shallow 1½-quart casserole, bake 1 hour and 10 minutes.

PORTUGUESE BREAD
(pictured)

2 cups warm water (105 to 115F)
2 pkg fast-rising yeast
2 tablespoons sugar
1½ teaspoons salt
¼ cup (½ stick) butter or margarine,
  softened
5½ to 6 cups all-purpose flour
1 egg white, beaten with 1 teaspoon water

1. If possible, check temperature of water with thermometer. Sprinkle yeast and sugar over water in large bowl; stir until dissolved.
2. Add salt, butter and 3 cups flour. With wooden spoon, beat vigorously until smooth—about 2 minutes.
3. Gradually add remaining flour, mixing in last of it with hands until dough is stiff enough to leave side of bowl.
4. Turn out dough onto lightly floured pastry cloth or board. Knead until smooth—about 10 minutes.
5. Place in lightly greased large bowl; turn dough over to bring greased side up. Cover with towel; let rise in warm place (85F), free from drafts, until double in bulk—about 30 minutes.
6. Turn dough out onto lightly floured pastry cloth or board; divide in half.
7. Shape each half into a smooth, 6-inch ball; tuck edge under; place in two lightly greased 8-by-1½-inch layer cake pans.

8. Cover with towel; let rise in warm place (85F), free from drafts, until double in bulk—30 to 40 minutes.
9. Preheat oven to 375F.
10. Before baking, lightly brush tops of loaves with beaten egg-white mixture.
11. Bake loaves about 30 minutes, or until they sound hollow when tapped with knuckle. Remove from pans to wire rack. Serve slightly warm, or cool completely. *Makes 2 loaves (8 slices each).*

CRANBERRY WHIP WITH CUSTARD SAUCE
(pictured)

3 cups fresh cranberries
2 cups cold water
2 env unflavored gelatine
1¼ cups sugar
6 egg whites (⅔ cup), at room
  temperature
Custard Sauce, recipe follows
Lemon Zest Glacé, recipe follows (optional)

1. Wash the cranberries and remove stems.
2. In medium saucepan, bring cranberries and 1½ cups water to boiling. Cook over medium heat, covered, until cranberries pop—about 8 minutes.
3. Meanwhile, in medium bowl, sprinkle gelatine over remaining ½ cup water; let stand for 5 minutes, to soften. Place food mill or large sieve over the gelatine in bowl; press cranberries and their liquid through to remove skins; discard skins. With wooden spoon, stir ¾ cup sugar into cranberry-gelatine mixture until dissolved.
4. Set the bowl in a large bowl of ice water, stirring occasionally, until gelatine mixture begins to thicken and is the consistency of unbeaten egg white—about 10 minutes.
5. In large bowl, with electric mixer at high speed, beat egg whites until foamy. Gradually add remaining ½ cup sugar, beating until moist, stiff peaks form when beaters are slowly raised.
6. With same beaters, beat gelatine mixture until light; fold into beaten egg whites until well blended. Spoon into 12 (6-oz) oiled custard cups. Refrigerate until firm—about 3 hours.
7. Meanwhile, make Custard Sauce and Lemon Zest Glacé.
8. To serve: Run a small spatula around the inside edge of each cup; turn out into individual dishes. Spoon 2 to 3 tablespoons Custard Sauce over each dessert; garnish with lemon zest. *Makes 12 servings.*

CUSTARD SAUCE

1½ cups milk
3 egg yolks
¼ cup sugar
Dash salt
½ teaspoon vanilla extract

1. In top of double boiler, directly over low heat, heat milk until tiny bubbles appear around edge of pan; remove from heat.
2. In small bowl, with wire whisk, beat yolks, sugar and salt. Very slowly pour hot milk into egg-yolk mixture, beating constantly.
3. Return mixture to double-boiler top; place over hot, not boiling, water (water in lower part of double boiler should not touch upper part).
4. Cook, stirring constantly, until the custard thinly coats a metal spoon—10 to 12 minutes.
5. Immediately pour custard into a bowl; stir in vanilla; cover surface directly with waxed paper. Refrigerate until very cold. *Makes about 1⅔ cups.*

LEMON ZEST GLACE

In small saucepan, bring ½ cup sugar and ¾ cup water to boiling. Cut zest, or yellow part of the rind, off ½ lemon in long strips. Cut zest to make twelve 2½-by-⅛-inch strips. Add to sugar syrup; simmer over low heat, uncovered, 15 minutes. Cool and drain.

PACIFIC NORTHWEST DINNER

(Planned for 6)

SALMON WITH LEMON BUTTER*
JULIENNE VEGETABLES*
SAUTEED POTATO OVALS*
TOSSED GREEN SALAD WITH
HAZELNUT DRESSING*
GLAZED APPLE TART*

Recipes given for starred dishes.

SALMON WITH LEMON BUTTER

(pictured)

4 pkg (8-oz size) fresh or frozen boned and
  butterflied silver coho salmon
¼ cup (½ stick) butter or margarine
2 tablespoons lemon juice
4 slices lemon, halved
Watercress sprigs

1. Unwrap salmon; if frozen, thaw. Rinse salmon well under running cold water; pat dry with paper towels. Cut each in half lengthwise to separate into two fillets; cut off tail.
2. Place salmon, skin side down, on greased rack over broiler pan. In small saucepan, melt butter. Brush salmon with half of the melted butter.
3. Broil, 4 inches from heat, 2 to 3 minutes, or until fish flakes easily when tested with a fork. (No need to turn salmon.)
4. Meanwhile, reheat butter and stir in lemon juice; keep warm.
5. Remove salmon fillets to heated serving plates. Spoon lemon butter over salmon. Garnish, as pictured, with lemon and watercress. *Makes 8 servings.*

JULIENNE VEGETABLES

(pictured)

½ lb fresh Brussels sprouts
2 medium carrots, pared
2 small zucchini (¾ lb)
2 small yellow squash (¾ lb)
1 medium red pepper (6 oz)
2 fresh chanterelle, shiitake or other
  mushrooms
¼ cup (½ stick) butter or margarine
½ teaspoon salt
Dash pepper

1. Cut off stem end from each Brussels sprout; cut each sprout in half lengthwise. Cut carrots, zucchini and yellow squash into julienne strips, about 3 inches long and ⅛ to ¼ inch wide. Cut red pepper in half lengthwise; discard stem, ribs and seeds. Slice into strips ⅛ to ¼ inch wide. Thinly slice mushrooms.

2. In large skillet, over medium heat, melt butter. Add Brussels sprouts and carrots; sauté 1 minute. Cover, and cook over low heat 3 minutes, stirring occasionally. Add remaining vegetables, and cook over medium heat, uncovered and stirring occasionally, 3 to 5 minutes, or until vegetables are tender-crisp.
3. Season with salt and pepper. Serve immediately. *Makes 6 servings.*

SAUTEED POTATO OVALS

(pictured)

3 large baking potatoes (1½ lb)
Boiling water
¼ cup salad oil
2 tablespoons butter or margarine
¼ teaspoon salt
Dash pepper

1. Pare the potatoes; cut each lengthwise into quarters to form thick wedges; then cut each potato in half crosswise.
2. With sharp, swivel-blade vegetable parer, shape each piece by paring into an oval, 1½ inches long. As each is shaped, drop into a bowl of water to keep from discoloring.
3. Drain potatoes; pour boiling water over them. Let stand 1 minute. Drain potatoes again; pat dry with paper towels.
4. In medium skillet, over medium heat, heat oil and butter. Add potatoes; cook, stirring occasionally, until they are tender and lightly browned—about 10 minutes. Sprinkle with salt and pepper. *Makes 6 servings.*

Note: The trimmings from shaping the potatoes may be cooked in soups or used to make mashed potato. Refrigerate in bowl of water until needed; drain; use within a day.

TOSSED GREEN SALAD WITH HAZELNUT DRESSING

½ clove garlic
1 small head Boston lettuce
1 head Bibb lettuce
½ head red-leaf lettuce
2 Belgian endives
½ cup hazelnuts or filberts, toasted and
  coarsely chopped
⅓ cup olive or salad oil
¼ cup tarragon-flavored vinegar
½ teaspoon salt
Freshly ground pepper

1. Rub inside of salad bowl with garlic; discard. Tear greens into bite-size pieces into bowl; leave small leaves whole.
2. In jar with tight-fitting lid, shake hazelnuts, oil, vinegar and salt. Pour dressing over greens.
3. With salad spoon and fork, toss greens until coated. Add pepper to taste and serve immediately. *Makes 6 servings.*

GLAZED APPLE TART

(pictured)

1 pkg (10 or 11 oz) piecrust mix
1½ lb (about 5) Granny Smith or other tart
  cooking apples
½ cup sugar
¼ cup all-purpose flour
2 teaspoons ground cinnamon
Dash salt
½ cup apricot preserves

1. Preheat oven to 425F.
2. Prepare pastry as package label directs; shape into a ball.
3. On lightly floured pastry cloth or board, roll two-thirds of the pastry into a 12-inch circle. (Refrigerate remaining third of pastry for later use.) With rolled pastry, line a fluted 10-inch tart pan with removable bottom; trim pastry even with edge of pan; refrigerate trimmings.
4. Line pastry in pan with a sheet of foil, extending up side; weight down pastry with dried beans or aluminum pie weights. Bake shell 15 minutes. Remove to rack; remove foil and beans. Reduce temperature to 375F.
5. Pare apples; core and thinly slice into large bowl. In small bowl, combine sugar, flour, cinnamon and salt; add to apples, tossing lightly to combine.
6. Cover bottom of tart shell with one layer of apples. Arrange remaining apples, overlapping, over apple layer. Pour any liquid remaining in bowl over apples.
7. Roll out dough trimmings and remaining pastry into an oval, about 11 inches long and 5 inches wide. With knife or pastry wheel, cut into ten 11-by-½-inch strips.
8. Place four strips on top of tart at right angles to one another, forming a 5-inch square in center of tart. Lay one strip across center of tart, intersecting two corners of square. Lay one strip on each side, parallel to center strip, with center of strip intersecting a corner of the square. Lay a strip at right angle to center strip, intersecting at center; lay remaining two strips on top, on each side, parallel to center strip. Trim strips even with edge.
9. Bake 40 to 45 mintues, or until apples are tender and crust is golden-brown.
10. Meanwhile, in small skillet, melt apricot preserves; strain.
11. Remove tart to wire rack; brush with strained apricot preserves, to glaze top. Cool partially. Serve warm. *Makes 8 servings.* ∎

KIDS' STUFF

Youngsters will cheer over a holiday party that features fare like this: pizza—loaded with cheese, pepperoni, mushrooms and peppers; Mulled Cranberry-Apple Cider; and Molasses Cutout Cookies, each iced with a child's name. Recipes, page 96.

continued from page 94

CHRISTMAS PARTY MENU FOR CHILDREN

**CHRISTMAS PIZZA* OR
SWEET AND HOT SAUSAGE IN PITA
BREAD***
CARROT AND CUCUMBER STICKS
**CELERY HEARTS, RADISHES, BLACK
AND GREEN OLIVES**
MAKE-YOUR-OWN SUNDAES:
BOWL OF ASSORTED ICE-CREAM BALLS
STRAWBERRY OR RASPBERRY,
QUICK CHOCOLATE OR HOT FUDGE
AND HOT BUTTERSCOTCH SAUCES*
WHIPPED CREAM, CHOPPED NUTS,
MARSHMALLOW, CHERRIES
MOLASSES CUTOUT COOKIES*
MULLED CRANBERRY-APPLE CIDER*

*Recipes given for starred dishes.

CHRISTMAS PIZZA

(pictured)

PIZZA CRUST
1⅓ cups warm water (105 to 115F)
1 pkg active dry yeast
Salad oil
2 teaspoons salt
4⅓ cups sifted all-purpose flour

PIZZA SAUCE
¼ cup salad or olive oil
1 cup chopped onion
2 cloves garlic, crushed
1 can (1 lb) Italian tomatoes, undrained
2 cans (8-oz size) tomato sauce
1 tablespoon sugar
1½ teaspoons salt
½ teaspoon dried oregano leaves
½ teaspoon dried basil leaves
¼ teaspoon pepper

TOPPING FOR PIZZA
1 lb mozzarella cheese, grated
1 large green pepper, thinly sliced
1 large red pepper, thinly sliced
1 lb pepperoni, thinly sliced
½ lb small mushrooms, washed and sliced
4 pimiento-stuffed olives, sliced
6 large pitted black olives
Grated Parmesan (optional)

1. Day before, prepare Pizza Crust: If possible, check temperature of warm water with thermometer. Sprinkle yeast over water in large bowl, stirring until dissolved.

2. Add 2 tablespoons salad oil, the salt and 4 cups flour; stir with wooden spoon until all flour is moistened.

3. Turn out on lightly floured surface. Knead in remaining flour until smooth—takes about 10 minutes.

4. Place in medium bowl; brush very lightly with salad oil. Cover with towel; let rise in warm place (85F), free from drafts, until double in bulk—about 2 hours. (Or, if desired, refrigerate dough, covered, to rise overnight.)

5. Make Pizza Sauce: In hot oil in medium saucepan, sauté onion and garlic until golden-brown—about 5 minutes. Add the undrained tomatoes, tomato sauce, sugar, salt, oregano, basil and pepper; mix well, mashing tomatoes with fork.

6. Bring to boiling; reduce heat; simmer, uncovered, 25 minutes, stirring. Makes 3 cups.

7. Remove dough from refrigerator; let stand at room temperature 30 minutes.

8. Punch down dough; knead five times on unfloured surface. Oil a 17¾-by-14-by-1-inch baking pan or metal tray. Pat and stretch dough to fit pan. Brush top lightly with oil. (See Note.)

9. Preheat oven to 450F. Move oven rack to lowest position; bake crust 15 minutes, or until bottom is golden.

10. Over baked crust, spread pizza sauce. Sprinkle grated mozzarella cheese over top.

11. Arrange green- and red-pepper slices, pepperoni, mushrooms and olives on top, as pictured. Brush mushrooms and peppers with oil. If desired, sprinkle with grated Parmesan.

12. Bake 15 to 20 minutes, or until cheese melts and pizza is hot. Remove from oven. Cool. Cut into squares or triangles. *Makes 12 servings.*

Note: If desired, bake in two 14-inch round pizza pans.

SWEET AND HOT SAUSAGE IN PITA BREAD

1½ lb hot Italian sausages
1½ lb sweet Italian sausages
¼ cup water
3 green peppers (1 lb)
3 red peppers (1 lb)
3 large yellow onions (1 lb)
2 cans (8-oz size) tomato sauce
8 pita breads or 16 hero rolls (6 inches long)

1. In 6-quart Dutch oven, combine sausages with water. Cook over medium heat, covered, 30 minutes.

2. Remove cover; continue cooking until liquid evaporates and sausage is well browned—about 15 minutes. Drain excess fat from pan, reserving ¼ cup. Remove to tray to cool; slice on diagonal into ½-inch-thick slices.

3. Cut peppers in half lengthwise; remove ribs and seeds. Cut lengthwise into ½-inch strips. Peel onions; slice into ¼-inch-thick slices.

4. In ¼ cup reserved drippings, sauté pepper and onion until tender—about 5 minutes.

5. Return sausage to Dutch oven. Add tomato sauce. Bring to boiling; simmer, covered, 20 minutes.

6. Serve inside pita bread, halved across, then slit to form a pocket, or in hero rolls. *Makes 16 servings.*

STRAWBERRY SAUCE

1 pkg (10 oz) frozen sliced strawberries, thawed
Water
¼ cup sugar
1 tablespoon cornstarch
2 tablespoons strawberry preserves

1. Drain berries; reserve syrup. Add water to syrup to measure 1 cup.

2. In small saucepan, combine sugar and cornstarch. Gradually add strawberry syrup, stirring until smooth.

3. Over low heat, slowly bring to boiling, stirring, until mixture is thickened and translucent.

4. Remove from heat. Stir in strawberries and strawberry preserves.

5. Stir until preserves are melted. Refrigerate until cold. *Makes 1⅓ cups.*

RASPBERRY SAUCE

2 pkg (10-oz size) frozen raspberries, thawed
Water
2 tablespoons cornstarch
½ cup currant jelly

1. Drain raspberries, reserving liquid. Add enough water to liquid to make 2 cups.
2. In small saucepan, blend liquid with cornstarch. Bring to boiling over medium heat, stirring constantly; boil 5 minutes. Stir in jelly until melted. Remove from heat; add raspberries. Refrigerate, covered, until cold. *Makes 2 cups.*

QUICK CHOCOLATE SAUCE

1 pkg (6 oz) semisweet chocolate pieces
⅔ cup light cream or half-and-half

1. Combine chocolate pieces and cream in medium saucepan. Stir constantly, over low heat, just until chocolate is melted.
2. Serve warm. *Makes about 1 cup.*

HOT FUDGE SAUCE

¼ cup sugar
⅓ cup light cream or half-and-half
1 pkg (4 oz) sweet cooking chocolate
1 square (1 oz) unsweetened chocolate

1. In top of double boiler, combine sugar and 2 tablespoons cream; cook, over boiling water, until sugar is dissolved.
2. Cut up both kinds of chocolate. Remove double boiler from heat, but leave top over bottom. Add chocolate to cream mixture, stirring until melted.
3. With spoon, beat in remaining cream. Serve warm. *Makes 1 cup.*

HOT BUTTERSCOTCH SAUCE

⅓ cup (⅔ stick) butter or margarine
1 cup light-brown sugar, firmly packed
2 tablespoons light corn syrup
⅓ cup heavy cream

Melt butter in saucepan over low heat. Stir in brown sugar, corn syrup and cream; cook to boiling point. Then remove from heat, and cool slightly. Serve warm or cold. *Makes 1¼ cups.*

Mary Cero's
MOLASSES CUTOUT COOKIES
(pictured)

1 cup sugar
1 cup shortening
1 cup light molasses
2 tablespoons vinegar
2 eggs
5½ cups sifted all-purpose flour
½ teaspoon salt
1½ teaspoons baking soda
2 teaspoons ground ginger
1 teaspoon ground cinnamon
½ teaspoon ground cloves
Frosting, recipe follows

1. Combine sugar, shortening, molasses and vinegar in saucepan. Bring to boil. Cook 2 minutes, and cool. Turn into large bowl.
2. Beat eggs into cooled molasses mixture.
3. Sift together dry ingredients; add to molasses mixture. Chill dough overnight.
4. Then roll out in portions, one-fourth at a time, on lightly floured surface to ⅛-inch thickness.
5. Cut with assorted cookie cutters. Place 1 inch apart on greased cookie sheet. Bake, at 375F, 6 to 8 minutes. *Makes 6 to 7 dozen cookies.*

FROSTING

½ cup egg whites (4 eggs)
3¼ cups sifted confectioners' sugar

1. In medium bowl, with portable electric mixer at medium speed, beat the egg whites with the confectioners' sugar to make a smooth, stiff frosting. Cover with a damp cloth until ready to use, to prevent drying out.
2. To decorate: Fill pastry bag with a number-3 or -4 small tip for writing with frosting. Pipe on frosting following outline of cookies. Decorate cookies as desired. Let frosting dry. Store in covered tin at room temperature.

MULLED CRANBERRY-APPLE CIDER
(pictured)

2 quarts apple cider
1½ quarts cranberry or cranberry-apple juice
½ cup light-brown sugar, firmly packed
8 to 10 (3-inch) cinnamon sticks, broken into pieces
10 to 15 whole allspice
20 to 25 whole cloves

1. In 6-quart kettle, bring all ingredients to boiling; simmer, uncovered, 30 minutes. Strain; discard spices.
2. Refrigerate cider until needed. Reheat for serving. Place a cinnamon-stick stirrer in each mug if desired. Nice served warm; or serve well chilled. *Makes 12 cups.* ∎

TERRIFIC TARTS & TORTES

Spoil your family and guests with desserts that tantalize the eye as well as the taste buds. Clockwise from top: custard-filled Marzipan Torte topped with cherry preserves and almonds; spirited Chocolate-Raspberry Torte swirled with Chocolate-Sour-Cream Frosting; spiced Cranberry-Raisin Tart brimming with apples, raisins and walnuts; creamy Frozen Cranberry Bavarian garnished with frosted cranberries; jelly-glazed Apple Custard Tarts. For recipes, turn to page 100.

continued from page 98

MARZIPAN TORTE
(pictured)

TORTE
6 eggs
½ cup all-purpose flour
1 teaspoon baking powder
¼ teaspoon salt
½ cup sugar
1 can (8 oz) almond paste
1 teaspoon vanilla extract
½ teaspoon almond extract

Custard Filling, recipe follows
1 jar (12 oz) cherry preserves, melted
½ cup chopped toasted blanched almonds
10 whole toasted blanched almonds

1. Separate eggs, putting whites in large bowl of electric mixer, yolks in small bowl. Let whites stand at room temperature 1 hour.

2. Preheat oven to 350F. Butter and flour a 9-inch Turk's-head or tube pan. Sift together the flour and baking powder.

3. In large bowl of electric mixer, beat egg whites with salt until soft peaks form when beaters are slowly raised. Add sugar, 2 tablespoons at a time, beating well after each addition; continue beating until moist stiff peaks form when beaters are slowly raised.

4. Using the same beaters, beat egg yolks until thick and lemon-colored. In small bowl, break almond paste into small pieces with a fork. Add almond paste, vanilla and almond extracts to egg yolks; beat until smooth.

5. At low speed, blend in flour mixture, guiding into beaters with rubber spatula.

6. With rubber spatula or wire whisk, using an under-and-over motion, gently fold egg-yolk mixture into egg whites just until blended.

7. Pour batter into prepared pan; bake 30 to 35 minutes, or until cake tester inserted in center comes out clean; cool completely on wire rack. Cake will fall slightly.

8. Meanwhile, make Custard Filling.

9. To assemble: Cut cake crosswise into three layers. Place bottom layer, cut side up, on plate; spread with half the filling. Repeat with second layer. Top with last layer, cut side down.

10. Brush entire cake with preserves. Sprinkle side, as pictured, with chopped almonds. Arrange whole almonds on top. *Makes 10 servings.*

CUSTARD FILLING
⅓ cup sugar
2 tablespoons cornstarch
2 cups hot milk
2 egg yolks, beaten
½ teaspoon almond extract

1. In small saucepan, combine sugar and cornstarch; mix well. Slowly add hot milk, stirring constantly.

2. With wooden spoon, stir over medium heat until mixture starts to boil; remove from heat.

3. Add ½ cup hot mixture to egg yolks; mix well. Return to saucepan; continue cooking, stirring, until filling is thick. Remove from heat; add almond extract.

4. Place pan in bowl of ice water to cool completely—about 30 minutes. *Makes 2 cups.*

CHOCOLATE-RASPBERRY TORTE
(pictured)

CAKE
2 cups sifted all-purpose flour
2 teaspoons baking soda
½ teaspoon salt
½ teaspoon baking powder
3 squares (1-oz size) unsweetened chocolate
½ cup (1 stick) butter or margarine
2 cups light-brown sugar, firmly packed
3 eggs
1½ teaspoons vanilla extract
¾ cup sour cream
½ cup strong coffee
⅓ cup coffee-flavored liqueur

¾ cup heavy cream
2 tablespoons confectioners' sugar
1 jar (12 oz) raspberry or strawberry preserves
Chocolate-Sour-Cream Frosting, recipe follows
Fresh raspberries or strawberries

1. Make Cake: Sift flour with baking soda, salt and baking powder. Preheat oven to 350F. Grease well and lightly flour two 9-by-1½-inch layer cake pans.

2. Melt chocolate in custard cup placed in hot, not boiling, water; let cool.

3. In large bowl of electric mixer, at high speed, beat butter, brown sugar, eggs and vanilla, scraping bowl occasionally, until light—about 5 minutes; beat in melted chocolate and the vanilla.

4. At low speed, beat in flour mixture (in fourths), alternating with sour cream (in thirds), beginning and ending with flour mixture. Add coffee and liqueur, blending until smooth.

5. Pour batter into pans, dividing evenly; smooth top. Bake 30 to 35 minutes, or until surface springs back when gently pressed with fingertip.

6. Cool in pans 10 minutes. Carefully loosen sides with spatula; remove from pans; cool on wire racks.

7. Beat cream with confectioners' sugar until stiff; refrigerate. Slice layers in half horizontally, to make four layers.

8. To assemble: Place a layer, cut side up, on cake plate. Spread with ⅓ cup raspberry preserves and ½ cup whipped cream. Repeat with remaining layers, ending with top layer, cut side down.

9. Frost top and side with Chocolate-Sour-Cream Frosting, swirling it as you spread. Arrange whole berries around edge. *Makes 12 servings.*

CHOCOLATE-SOUR-CREAM FROSTING

1½ pkg (6-oz size) semisweet chocolate pieces
¾ cup sour cream
Dash salt

1. Melt chocolate pieces in top of double boiler over hot water. Remove top of double boiler from hot water.

2. Add sour cream and salt. With portable mixer at medium speed, or rotary beater, beat frosting until creamy and of spreading consistency.

CRANBERRY-RAISIN TART
(pictured)

1 pkg (11 oz) piecrust mix

FILLING
1 cup whole cranberries, chopped
1 cup chopped pared tart apple
1 cup raisins
½ cup chopped walnuts
⅓ cup (⅔ stick) butter or margarine
⅓ cup light-brown sugar, firmly packed
⅓ cup granulated sugar
1 teaspoon ground cinnamon
¼ teaspoon ground nutmeg
¼ teaspoon salt
½ cup water
¼ cup light or dark rum
1 tablespoon cornstarch

1 egg yolk
2 teaspoons water
1 tablespoon granulated sugar

1. Prepare pastry as package label directs. Shape into a ball; divide in half.

2. Make Filling: In a 3-quart saucepan, combine cranberries, apple, raisins, walnuts, butter, brown sugar, granulated sugar, cinnamon, nutmeg, salt and ½ cup water.

3. Bring to boiling; reduce heat, and cook, covered and stirring occasionally, 10 to 15 minutes.

4. Mix rum with cornstarch until smooth. Add to filling; bring to boiling, stirring constantly, about 2 minutes, or until thickened. Simmer 2 minutes. Remove from heat. Place saucepan in bowl of ice water to cool completely. Makes 3½ cups.

5. Preheat oven to 400F.

6. On lightly floured pastry cloth or board, roll half of pastry to a 12-inch circle. Use to line a fluted 9-inch pan with removable bottom; trim edge.

7. Roll out second half of pastry 12 inches long and 6 inches wide.

8. With pastry wheel, cut 8 strips ½ inch wide and 10 inches long.

9. Turn filling into pastry-lined pan. Place 2 strips, 1 inch apart, across each side of pie, as pictured. Brush strips with egg yolk mixed with 2 teaspoons water. Sprinkle strips with granulated sugar.

10. Bake 40 to 45 minutes, or until pastry is golden. (Cover with foil after 30 minutes.) Remove to wire rack. Serve warm with vanilla ice cream. *Makes 8 servings.*

FROZEN CRANBERRY BAVARIAN
(Guy Savoy)
(pictured)

4 cups fresh cranberries (1 lb)
½ cup honey
2 env unflavored gelatine
⅓ cup cold water
3 cups milk
10 egg yolks
1⅓ cups granulated sugar
1 teaspoon vanilla extract
2½ cups heavy cream
3 egg whites
2 tablespoons kirsch
2 tablespoons confectioners' sugar
Frosted Cranberries, recipe follows

1. Wash cranberries, removing stems. In medium saucepan, combine cranberries with honey. Simmer, covered, until cranberries are soft—6 to 8 minutes. Set aside to cool.

2. In small bowl, sprinkle gelatine over cold water; let stand 5 minutes to soften.

3. Heat milk in top of double boiler, over direct heat, until tiny bubbles appear around edge of pan. In medium bowl, beat egg yolks and granulated sugar until well blended.

4. Slowly pour hot milk into egg mixture, beating constantly. Return mixture to double-boiler top; place over hot, not boiling, water. Water in lower part of double boiler should not touch upper part.

5. Cook, stirring constantly, until thin coating forms on metal spoon—8 to 10 minutes. Add gelatine mixture, stirring until gelatine is dissolved. Add vanilla.

6. Set double-boiler top in bowl of ice, stirring occasionally, until custard mixture thickens and mounds slightly.

7. Meanwhile, in large bowl, with electric mixer, beat 1½ cups cream until stiff; refrigerate.

8. In small bowl of electric mixer, with clean beaters, beat egg whites until stiff peaks form when beaters are slowly raised.

9. With wire whisk or rubber spatula, fold chilled gelatine mixture, egg whites and kirsch into cream until well combined. Fold in cranberries and their juices.

10. Turn mixture into a 9-cup decorative mold or bowl; freeze until firm—4 hours or overnight.

11. To serve: Invert mold over chilled serving platter. Place hot, damp cloth over mold; shake to release Bavarian. In medium bowl, combine remaining cup of heavy cream and confectioners' sugar; beat until stiff. Turn into pastry bag with number-5 tip; decorate as pictured. Garnish with Frosted Cranberries. *Makes 16 servings.*

FROSTED CRANBERRIES

1 egg white
1 cup fresh cranberries
¼ cup granulated sugar

In medium bowl, beat egg white until stiff. Coat cranberries with egg white. Toss, a few at a time, in sugar. Let dry in shallow pan at room temperature 1 hour.

APPLE CUSTARD TARTS
(pictured)

TART SHELLS
½ cup (1 stick) butter or margarine, softened
¼ cup sugar
¼ teaspoon salt
1 egg white
1½ cups sifted all-purpose flour

4 (1½ lb) small tart apples (Granny Smith)
1 cup sugar
1 cup water
2 tablespoons lemon juice
¼ cup almond paste
2 eggs
¼ cup sugar
¾ cup heavy cream
½ cup currant jelly
1 tablespoon light corn syrup
¼ cup chopped pistachio nuts or walnuts

1. Make Tart Shells: In medium bowl, with fork, blend butter, ¼ cup sugar, the salt and egg white until smooth and well combined.

2. Gradually stir in flour, mixing until smooth and well combined.

3. On waxed paper, with palms of hands, roll pastry into a roll 10 inches long; refrigerate 30 minutes. Divide into ten 1-inch pieces.

4. On lightly floured pastry cloth or work surface, roll each part into a 5-inch circle. Press pastry evenly to bottom and side of ten 4-by-1½-inch pans; trim edges.

5. Preheat oven to 375F.

6. Meanwhile, pare and core apples; cut each into 8 wedges. In large skillet, combine 1 cup sugar, the water and lemon juice; bring to boiling. Add 30 apple wedges, cut side up, in a single layer; simmer gently, covered, 5 minutes. (Save 2 apple wedges for a snack.)

7. Turn apples; simmer 2 minutes, or just until tender but not mushy. With slotted utensil, remove apples; drain on paper towels; cool.

8. Bake tart shells on large cookie sheet 10 to 12 minutes, or until golden-brown. Cool completely on wire rack.

9. Place 1 teaspoon almond paste in bottom of each baked tart shell. Top with 3 apple wedges, cut side down.

10. In small bowl, beat together eggs, sugar and heavy cream until combined. Pour 2½ tablespoons over each apple.

11. Bake on large cookie sheet 20 to 25 minutes, or just until custard is set. Cool on rack 15 minutes.

12. Remove tarts from pans. Brush apple with melted jelly combined with corn syrup. Sprinkle edges with chopped nuts. *Makes 10.*

TRADER VIC'S NUT RUM PIE

9-inch unbaked pie shell

FILLING
4 eggs
½ cup sugar
1 cup light corn syrup
¼ cup (½ stick) butter or margarine, melted
1 teaspoon vanilla extract
2 tablespoons dark rum
1 cup coarsely chopped pecans
1 cup chopped dates
Whipped cream

1. Prepare pie shell and refrigerate.

2. Preheat oven to 375F.

3. Make Filling: In a medium bowl, with a rotary beater, beat eggs well.

4. Add sugar, corn syrup, butter, vanilla and rum; beat until well combined.

5. Stir in pecans and dates; mix well.

6. Turn into unbaked pie shell. Bake about 40 minutes, or until filling is set in center when pie is shaken gently.

7. Cool pie completely on wire rack; chill slightly before serving. Serve with whipped cream. *Makes 8 servings.*

continued on page 102

continued from page 101

BLUM'S COFFEE-TOFFEE PIE

PASTRY SHELL
½ pkg (11-oz size) piecrust mix or pastry
    for a 1-crust pie
¼ cup light-brown sugar, firmly packed
¾ cup finely chopped walnuts
1 square unsweetened chocolate, grated
1 tablespoon water
1 teaspoon vanilla extract

FILLING
½ cup (1 stick) butter or margarine,
    softened
¾ cup granulated sugar
1 square unsweetened chocolate, melted,
    cooled
2 teaspoons instant coffee granules
2 eggs

TOPPING
2 cups heavy cream
2 tablespoons instant coffee granules
½ cup confectioners' sugar
Chocolate curls

1. Preheat oven to 375F.
2. Make Pastry Shell: In medium
bowl, combine piecrust mix with brown
sugar, walnuts and grated chocolate. Add
1 tablespoon water and the vanilla; using
fork, mix until well blended. Turn into
well-greased 9-inch pie plate; press firmly
against bottom and side of pie plate. Bake
for 15 minutes. Cool pastry in pie plate
on wire rack.
3. Meanwhile, make Filling: In small
bowl, with electric mixer at medium speed,
beat butter until creamy.
4. Gradually add granulated sugar,
beating until light. Blend in cool melted
chocolate and 2 teaspoons instant coffee
granules.
5. Add 1 egg; beat 5 minutes. Add
remaining egg; beat 5 minutes longer.
6. Turn filling into baked pie shell.
Refrigerate pie, covered, overnight.
7. Next day, make Topping: In large
bowl, combine cream with instant coffee
granules and confectioners' sugar. Refrigerate, covered, 1 hour.
8. Beat cream mixture until stiff.
Decorate pie with topping, using pastry
bag with number-6 decorating tip, if desired. Garnish with chocolate curls. Refrigerate the pie at least 2 hours. *Makes
8 servings.*

BUTTERNUT-SQUASH PIE

FILLING
3 eggs, slightly beaten
½ cup sugar
½ cup maple or maple-flavored syrup
½ teaspoon ground cinnamon
½ teaspoon ground ginger
½ teaspoon salt
2 pkg (12-oz size) thawed frozen winter
    squash, undrained (see Note)
1 cup light cream or half-and-half

9-inch unbaked pie shell
½ cup heavy cream, whipped
Maple syrup

1. Preheat oven to 400F. Make Filling: In large bowl, combine eggs, sugar,
maple syrup, spices, salt, squash and light
cream. Beat, with rotary beater, until
smooth.
2. Turn most of filling into unbaked
pie shell. Place on lowest shelf of oven;
pour in rest of filling. Bake 55 to 60
minutes, or until filling is set in center
when pie is gently shaken.
3. Let cool on wire rack. Garnish with
whipped-cream rosettes drizzled with
maple syrup. Serve pie slightly warm or
cold. *Makes 8 servings.*
Note: Or substitute 3 cups canned
pumpkin.

AMBROSIA

4 large navel oranges
1 can (1 lb, 4 oz) pineapple chunks
2 tablespoons Cointreau or orange juice
4 medium bananas (1½ lb)
4 tablespoons confectioners' sugar
1 can (3½ oz) flaked coconut

1. Peel oranges; remove white membrane. Cut oranges crosswise into ⅛-inch-
thick slices.
2. Drain pineapple, combining syrup
and Cointreau.
3. Peel bananas. Cut diagonally into
⅛-inch-thick slices.
4. In attractive serving bowl, layer
half the orange slices; sprinkle with 2
tablespoons confectioners' sugar. Layer
half the banana slices and half the pineapple; sprinkle with half the coconut.
5. Repeat layers of fruit and sugar.
Pour syrup mixture over fruit. Sprinkle
with remaining coconut.
6. Refrigerate several hours, or until
well chilled. *Makes 10 servings.*

PEAR PIE WITH STREUSEL TOPPING

9-inch unbaked pie shell

STREUSEL TOPPING
⅔ cup sifted all-purpose flour
⅓ cup light-brown sugar, firmly packed
⅓ cup (⅔ stick) butter or margarine

FILLING
¼ cup granulated sugar
¼ teaspoon ground ginger
4 teaspoons all-purpose flour
5 ripe Bartlett or Anjou pears (2 lb)
4 teaspoons lemon juice
¼ cup light corn syrup

1. Prepare pie shell.
2. Make Streusel Topping: In small
bowl, combine ⅔ cup flour and the brown
sugar. Cut in butter with pastry blender
or 2 knives until mixture resembles coarse
cornmeal. Refrigerate.
3. Preheat oven to 450F.
4. Make Filling: Combine granulated
sugar, ginger and flour; sprinkle about a
third of mixture over bottom of pie shell.
5. Peel and core pears; slice thinly
into bowl. Arrange half of pears in shell;
sprinkle with a third of sugar mixture.
Add remaining pears; sprinkle with remaining sugar mixture. Drizzle lemon
juice and corn syrup over top.
6. Cover with Streusel Topping. Bake
15 minutes. Reduce oven temperature to
350F and bake 30 minutes longer. *Makes
8 servings.* ■

continued from page 79

VEGETABLE-SALAD PLATTER
(pictured)

MARINADE
3 cups salad oil
1 cup white-wine vinegar
1 tablespoon salt
1 tablespoon sugar
1 teaspoon cracked black pepper

1 lb fresh young green beans
Salt
Boiling water
1 head cauliflower (2½ to 3 lb)
1½ lb zucchini
2 lb small, thin carrots
3 pkg (10-oz size) frozen broccoli spears
2 cans (15-oz size) white asparagus, drained
6 medium-size ripe tomatoes, cut in half with scallop cutter (see Note)
3 heads Boston lettuce, washed and crisped
Green Mayonnaise, recipe follows

1. Day before, marinate vegetables. For Marinade: Combine oil, vinegar, 1 tablespoon salt, the sugar and black pepper in large jar with a tight-fitting cover. Shake to mix well. Refrigerate until ready to use.

2. Prepare vegetables: Wash beans under cold, running water; drain. Trim ends of beans. Place in a 2½-quart saucepan. Add 1 teaspoon salt and boiling water to measure 1 inch. Bring to boiling; boil green beans gently, covered, 12 minutes, or just until tender-crisp; drain. Arrange in shallow baking dish or roasting pan. Pour some of marinade over hot beans, to coat well.

3. Wash cauliflower thoroughly; cut into flowerets. Cook, covered, in 1 inch lightly salted boiling water just until tender—about 10 minutes; drain well. Arrange in baking dish with beans; pour some of marinade over hot cauliflower.

4. Wash zucchini; cut into 3-inch fingers. In medium skillet with tight-fitting cover, bring ⅓ cup water with ½ teaspoon salt to boiling. Add zucchini; cook, covered, over medium heat 6 to 8 minutes, or just until tender, not mushy. Drain well. Arrange in baking dish with other vegetables. Pour some of marinade over hot zucchini.

5. Wash carrots; pare. Cut in half lengthwise; pare each half to look like a small whole carrot. Place in large saucepan; add 1 teaspoon salt and enough boiling water to cover. Bring to boiling; simmer gently, covered, 15 minutes, or until tender. Drain. Arrange in baking dish with other vegetables; pour some of marinade over hot carrots.

6. Cook broccoli as package label directs; drain; cool. Remove stems, leaving flowerets. Add to baking dish. Pour some of marinade over broccoli flowerets.

7. Arrange drained asparagus and tomato halves, cut again into quarters, in baking dish. Pour marinade over them.

8. Turn vegetables to coat well with marinade. Refrigerate, covered, overnight.

9. Several hours before serving, arrange drained vegetables, as pictured, on two large platters, lined with crisp lettuce leaves. Refrigerate until serving time. Serve very well chilled, with Green Mayonnaise. *Makes 24 servings.*

Note: A scallop cutter is a special knife designed for use with fruits and vegetables. A plain slicing knife may be used.

GREEN MAYONNAISE

3 cups mayonnaise
6 tablespoons lemon juice
6 tablespoons chopped parsley
3 tablespoons chopped chives
3 tablespoons chopped watercress

1. Day before: In a large bowl, combine mayonnaise, lemon juice, parsley, chives and watercress; mix well.

2. Refrigerate, covered, overnight. Mix well before serving. *Makes 3¾ cups; 24 servings.*

FRUIT SUPREME WITH PINK CHAMPAGNE
(pictured)

3 pints lemon sherbet
4 large grapefruit
6 large navel oranges
2 pkg (8-oz size) pitted dates or 1 lb fresh dates, pitted and halved
1½ lb green grapes, washed and stems removed, halved
2 pint boxes strawberries or 2 pkg (16-oz size) frozen whole strawberries
1 bottle (1 pt, 10 oz) pink champagne

1. Day ahead: Pack sherbet into a 1½-quart mold; freeze until firm—at least 4 hours or overnight.

2. Peel and section grapefruit and oranges, catching any juices. In large bowl, combine grapefruit and orange sections with juice, dates and grapes. Refrigerate, covered.

3. Before serving: Wash strawberries; drain. Remove hulls; cut any large berries in half. (If using frozen strawberries, thaw and drain.) Also refrigerate champagne until ready to use.

4. To serve: Combine strawberries with fruit mixture; toss gently. Turn into chilled serving bowl. Unmold sherbet: Loosen edge with sharp knife; dip bottom quickly in hot water; invert into center of dish, on top of fruit.

5. Pour champagne over fruit. *Makes 24 servings.*

FROSTED DAIQUIRI PIE

1 pkg (8 oz) cream cheese, softened
1 can (14 oz) sweetened condensed milk
1 tablespoon grated lime peel
½ cup fresh lime juice
⅓ cup light rum
9-inch graham-cracker crust (see Notes)
1 cup heavy cream
1 tablespoon light rum
1 teaspoon grated lime peel

1. In medium bowl, with portable electric mixer, beat cream cheese until soft and fluffy. Beat in condensed milk gradually. Add 1 tablespoon lime peel, the lime juice and ⅓ cup rum, stirring until well combined. Pour into pie shell. Refrigerate 3 hours or overnight, or until stiff.

2. To serve: Beat cream until stiff. Gradually add 1 tablespoon rum. Spread over top of pie; sprinkle surface with grated lime peel. *Makes 8 servings.*

Notes: For 24 servings, you will need to make three pies; make them one at a time the day before. Garnish with whipped cream just before serving.

You may buy prepared graham-cracker crusts. ∎

Sweet Finishes

They Won't Forget

GEORGE RATKAI

The grand finale to a fabulous evening: an eye-boggling dessert—or two or three. Top right, mile-high ice-cream pie crowned with meringue; then, clockwise, Sour-Cream Apple Pie with latticework crust; melt-in-your-mouth Nesselrode Pie strewn with chocolate shavings; creamy, Old-Fashioned Pumpkin Custard Pie; and, finally, Scotch Apple Tart, a delicious mélange of apples, currants, cinnamon and rum. For these recipes and more, see page 106.

continued from page 105

MILE-HIGH MINCEMEAT GLACE PIE
(pictured)

2 quarts vanilla ice cream
2 cups prepared mincemeat
½ cup slivered toasted almonds
5 egg whites
½ teaspoon vanilla extract
½ teaspoon cream of tartar
½ cup sugar
10-inch baked pie shell

1. Let ice cream stand at room temperature to soften slightly. Meanwhile, line a 10-inch pie plate with foil. Combine mincemeat and almonds; mix well.

2. Into foil-lined pie plate, spoon ice cream in alternate layers with mincemeat mixture, ending with ice cream. Freeze until ready to use—several hours.

3. To serve: In large bowl of electric mixer, let egg whites warm to room temperature—about 1 hour. At high speed, beat egg whites, vanilla and cream of tartar just until frothy.

4. Add sugar, 2 tablespoons at a time, beating well after each addition. Continue beating until meringue is shiny and stiff peaks form. Preheat oven to 425F.

5. Remove foil from bottom of frozen ice-cream-mincemeat layer; place in baked pie shell. With metal spatula, spread meringue over pie, covering ice cream and edge of crust completely. Make swirls on top.

6. Bake, on lowest shelf of oven, 7 to 8 minutes, or just until meringue is golden-brown. Serve at once. *Makes 10 servings.*

SOUR-CREAM APPLE PIE
(pictured)

Pastry for 2-crust pie
3 lb (about 7) tart cooking apples, such as Granny Smith, Rome Beauty or greening
2 tablespoons lemon juice
1 cup sour cream
1 cup granulated sugar
2 tablespoons flour
1 teaspoon ground cinnamon
⅛ teaspoon ground nutmeg
¼ teaspoon salt

TOPPING
3 tablespoons dark-brown sugar
3 tablespoons granulated sugar
1 teaspoon ground cinnamon
1 cup chopped walnuts

2 tablespoons butter or margarine
Milk
Granulated sugar

1. Shape pastry into a ball; divide in half.

2. On lightly floured surface, roll out half of pastry into a 12-inch circle. Use to line 9-inch pie plate. Refrigerate, along with remaining pastry, until ready to use.

3. Peel, core and thinly slice apples into large bowl. Sprinkle with lemon juice. Toss with sour cream. In small bowl, combine 1 cup granulated sugar, the flour, 1 teaspoon cinnamon, the nutmeg and salt; mix well. Add to apples; toss lightly to combine.

4. Make Topping: Combine brown sugar, 3 tablespoons granulated sugar, the cinnamon and walnuts; mix well.

5. Roll out remaining half of pastry into a 10-inch circle. With knife or pastry wheel, cut into 9 (1-inch-wide) strips.

6. Preheat oven to 400F. Turn apple mixture into pastry-lined pie plate. Dot top with butter. Sprinkle topping evenly over apple mixture.

7. Moisten rim of pastry slightly with cold water. Arrange 5 pastry strips, ½ inch apart, over filling; press ends to pastry rim. Place remaining strips across first ones at right angles, to make a lattice, and press to rim. Fold overhang of bottom crust over ends of strips, and crimp decoratively. Brush lattice top, but not rim, lightly with milk, and sprinkle with granulated sugar.

8. Bake 50 minutes, or until crust is golden and juice bubbles through lattice. (After 30 minutes, place a foil tent loosely over top to prevent overbrowning.)

9. Cool on wire rack. Serve warm, with ice cream, if desired. *Makes 8 servings.*

NESSELRODE PIE
(pictured)

2 eggs
1½ env unflavored gelatine
¼ cup cold water
2 cups light cream or half-and-half
⅔ cup sugar
Dash salt
3 tablespoons golden rum
¾ cup bottled Nesselrode sauce (see Note)
1 cup heavy cream, whipped
9-inch baked pie shell
1 square (1 oz) semisweet chocolate

1. Make pie day before: Separate eggs, placing yolks in small bowl and whites in a large bowl. Let whites warm to room temperature.

2. In small bowl, sprinkle gelatine over ¼ cup cold water to soften.

3. In top of double boiler, heat cream slightly (do not boil); add ⅓ cup sugar, the salt and softened gelatine; heat, stirring, to dissolve gelatine.

4. In medium bowl, beat egg yolks until thick; stir in some of cream mixture, mixing well. Return to rest of cream mixture in top of double boiler.

5. Place over boiling water; cook, stirring, until thickened—about 5 minutes. Set double-boiler top in bowl of ice, stirring occasionally, until gelatine mixture just begins to set—20 to 25 minutes. Stir in rum and ½ cup Nesselrode. Remove from ice.

6. Meanwhile, beat egg whites just until soft peaks form. Gradually beat in remaining ⅓ cup sugar, 2 tablespoons at a time. Continue beating until stiff peaks form when beaters are slowly raised.

7. With wire whisk or rubber spatula, gently fold thickened egg-yolk mixture into whites, to combine well. With rubber spatula, gently fold in half of whipped cream. Turn into pie shell, mounding high and smoothing top with metal spatula. Refrigerate until well chilled and firm enough to cut—4 hours or overnight. Cover and refrigerate remaining cream.

8. To serve, spread with rest of whipped cream. With vegetable parer, shave chocolate over top. Decorate around edge with ¼ cup Nesselrode. *Makes 8 servings.*

Note: If Nesselrode sauce is not available, use ¾ cup finely chopped mixed candied fruits.

OLD-FASHIONED PUMPKIN CUSTARD PIE
(pictured)

9-inch unbaked pie shell, with high edge
3 eggs
¾ cup sugar
½ teaspoon salt
½ teaspoon ground cinnamon
½ teaspoon ground ginger
¼ teaspoon ground allspice
¼ teaspoon ground cloves
1 can (1 lb) pumpkin
2 cans (6-oz size) evaporated milk, undiluted
3 tablespoons molasses
1 egg white, slightly beaten
½ cup heavy cream, whipped
Chopped walnuts

1. Refrigerate pie shell until ready to fill.

2. Preheat oven to 400F.

3. In medium bowl, with rotary beater, beat eggs until frothy.

4. Combine sugar, salt, cinnamon, ginger, allspice and cloves; mix well. Add to eggs with pumpkin, milk and molasses; beat until smooth and well combined. Let stand ½ hour to dissolve sugar.

5. Brush pie shell with egg white. Stir filling to mix well; pour most of filling into pie shell. Place on lowest rack of oven; pour in rest of filling; bake 30 minutes. Place foil collar lightly over edge of crust to prevent overbrowning. Bake 25 to 30 minutes longer, or until a silver knife inserted in custard comes out clean and it is set in center when gently shaken.

6. Cool on wire rack. To serve: Beat heavy cream with rotary beater until stiff. Turn into pastry bag with a number-4 or -5 tip. Force cream through tip to form a decorative edge. Sprinkle with chopped nuts. *Makes 8 servings.*

SCOTCH APPLE TART
(pictured)

1 pkg (11 oz) piecrust mix
FILLING
3 cups diced, pared, tart green apple (4), such as Granny Smith or Rome Beauty
⅓ cup (⅔ stick) butter or margarine
1¾ cups currants
⅓ cup light-brown sugar, firmly packed
⅓ cup granulated sugar
1 teaspoon ground cinnamon
¼ teaspoon ground nutmeg
¼ teaspoon salt
½ cup water
¼ cup light or dark rum
2 teaspoons cornstarch

1 egg yolk
2 teaspoons water

1. Prepare pastry as package label directs. Shape into a ball; divide in half. Wrap in waxed paper and refrigerate until ready to use.

2. Preheat oven to 400F.

3. Make Filling: In a 3-quart saucepan, combine apple, butter, currants, brown sugar, granulated sugar, cinnamon, nutmeg, salt and ½ cup water.

4. Bring to boiling; reduce heat, and cook, covered and stirring occasionally, until apple is tender but not mushy—takes 10 to 15 minutes.

5. Mix rum with cornstarch until smooth. Add to filling; bring to boiling, stirring constantly. Remove from heat; cool completely.

6. On lightly floured pastry cloth or board, roll half of pastry to a 12-inch circle. Use to line a 9-inch tart pan with removable bottom. Trim edge.

7. Roll out second half of pastry to a 9-inch circle. Place tart pan on pastry. Using edge of pan as guide, with pastry wheel or sharp knife, cut around pan. Remove pan.

8. With pastry wheel, cut circle into eight triangles. From center, cut out and remove a circle 2 inches in diameter; discard along with one triangle.

9. Turn filling into pastry-lined pan, mounding slightly in center. On top, place seven pastry triangles, spoke fashion. Brush pastry triangles with egg yolk mixed with 2 teaspoons water.

10. Bake 40 to 45 minutes, or until pastry is golden. Serve warm. If not serving at once, cool completely on wire rack. Refrigerate, wrapped in foil.

11. To serve: preheat oven to 400F. Remove foil from pie; heat in oven 20 minutes. Serve warm with vanilla ice cream or hard sauce, if desired. *Makes 8 servings.*

PEPPERMINT-ICE-CREAM-SUNDAE PIE
(A Holiday Pie for Children)

3 pints vanilla ice cream, slightly softened
¼ lb peppermint-stick candy, crushed
2 cups chocolate-wafer crumbs
⅓ cup (⅔ stick) butter or margarine, softened
Fudge Sauce, recipe follows
1 cup heavy cream, whipped
¼ cup chopped walnuts

1. Turn ice cream into large bowl. With spoon, swirl crushed candy into ice cream just enough to give a marbled effect—do not overmix. Return ice cream to containers; freeze.

2. Combine wafer crumbs with butter; mix with fork until thoroughly combined.

3. Press crumb mixture evenly on bottom and side of a 9-inch pie plate. Refrigerate until well chilled—about 1 hour.

4. Meanwhile, make Fudge Sauce.

5. Fill cookie shell with scoops of ice cream, mounding in center.

6. Pour ½ cup Fudge Sauce over the top. Store in freezer until serving time.

7. Just before serving, garnish with mounds of whipped cream; sprinkle with nuts. Pass rest of Fudge Sauce, if desired. *Makes 8 servings.*

FUDGE SAUCE

3 squares unsweetened chocolate
½ cup water
¾ cup sugar
¼ teaspoon salt
4 tablespoons (½ stick) butter or margarine
¾ teaspoon vanilla extract

1. In small saucepan, combine chocolate with ½ cup water. Cook over low heat, stirring occasionally, until chocolate is melted.

2. Add sugar and salt; cook, stirring, until sugar is dissolved and mixture thickens—about 5 minutes.

3. Remove from heat; stir in butter and vanilla. Let cool. *Makes about 1½ cups.*

DEEP-DISH CRANBERRY-PEAR PIE

3 fresh pears (see Note)
1 cup fresh cranberries
¾ cup light-brown sugar, firmly packed
3 tablespoons flour
⅛ teaspoon salt
Dash ground cloves
Dash ground nutmeg
⅓ cup heavy cream
2 tablespoons lemon juice
2 tablespoons butter or margarine
Pastry for 1-crust pie
1 egg yolk
1 tablespoon water
Heavy cream or vanilla ice cream

1. Halve pears lengthwise; scoop out cores; cut a *V* shape to remove stems. Pare and slice to make 7 cups. Wash cranberries; cut in half.

2. In small bowl, combine brown sugar, flour, salt, cloves and nutmeg. Stir in ⅓ cup cream.

3. Place sliced pears and cranberries in an 8¼-inch round, shallow baking dish or 9-inch deep-dish pie plate (about 1¾ inches deep). Sprinkle with lemon juice; add cream mixture. With wooden spoon, stir gently until well mixed. Dot with butter.

4. Preheat oven to 400F.

5. On lightly floured surface, roll out pastry to an 11-inch circle. Fold in half; make slits for steam vents.

6. Place over fruit in baking dish, and unfold. Press pastry to edge of dish. For decorative edge, press firmly all around with thumb.

7. Lightly beat egg yolk with water. Brush over pastry.

8. Place a piece of foil, a little larger than baking dish, on oven rack below the one on which pie bakes, to catch any juices that may bubble over edge of dish. Bake pie 35 to 40 minutes, or until crust is golden and juice bubbles through steam vents.

9. Let pie cool on wire rack about 30 minutes. Serve warm, with heavy cream or ice cream. *Makes 8 servings.*

Note: To make pie with canned pears, use 2 cans (1-pound, 13-ounce size) sliced pears. Drain, reserving 2 tablespoons syrup. Make as above, reducing sugar to ½ cup and decreasing flour to 2 tablespoons. Add reserved syrup with heavy cream. ∎

Getting together for a relaxing family meal isn't easy during this season with so much to do and seemingly so little time to do it. But if you've got just half an hour to spare, we can show you how to prepare nine splendid homemade meals that let you catch your breath…and also catch your family for a delicious "time out" from the hustle and bustle. There are quick-and-easy menus that can lead off an evening of cookie baking, or fast, but festive, dinners for the end of a busy shopping day. The Rush-Hour Supper, opposite, is perfect for a special mid-week family celebration…or impromptu entertaining. Menus, market orders and timed preparation steps for each meal help make each half hour count!

30-Minute Menus For the Holiday Season

GEORGE RATKAI

Rush-Hour Supper

(Planned for 6)

TOMATO BISQUE

♦

CHICKEN, HAM AND BROCCOLI
HOLLANDAISE

♦

WARM POPPY-SEED ROLLS

♦

HOT MINCEMEAT PASTRIES

♦

COFFEE

♦

ROSE OR WHITE WINE

YOU WILL NEED:
6 tablespoons (¾ stick) butter or
  margarine for cooking, plus ¼ lb
  (1 stick) for serving
3 cups natural-type cereal
1 jar (28 oz) mincemeat
6 boned and skinned chicken-breast
  halves (about 1½ lb)
Prepared mustard
6 slices boiled ham (½ lb)
6 slices Swiss cheese (6 oz)
2 pkg (10-oz size) frozen broccoli with
  hollandaise sauce (in separate packet)
2 cans (11-oz size) tomato bisque
Dried basil leaves
2 or 3 lemons
1 pkg baked poppy-seed rolls
1 pint vanilla ice cream or 1 jar prepared
  hard sauce
Coffee
Milk, sugar (optional)
Rosé or white wine

☕ 6:00 to 6:10 P.M.

1. Preheat oven to 400F.

2. With 1 tablespoon butter, lightly grease bottom of a 10-by-6-inch baking dish. Spread 1½ cups cereal evenly over bottom of dish. Spoon mincemeat evenly over cereal. Dot surface with 1 tablespoon butter. Sprinkle evenly with 1½ cups cereal. Bake 15 minutes.

3. Meanwhile, wipe chicken breasts with damp paper towels. Pound with mallet or back of a large, heavy knife to flatten into scallops.

☕ 6:10 to 6:20 P.M.

1. In 1 tablespoon hot butter in large skillet, sauté chicken breasts (three scallops at a time) until golden on each side. Remove to a heatproof serving platter.

2. Spread each chicken breast with mustard (about ¼ teaspoon for each). Top each with 1 slice ham and 1 slice Swiss cheese. Place in oven 10 minutes.

3. Thaw the hollandaise sauce in warm water, as package directs. In large saucepan, bring 1 cup lightly salted water to boil, for cooking broccoli.

☕ 6:20 to 6:30 P.M.

1. Heat tomato bisque in saucepan with 1 can water, ½ teaspoon dried basil leaves, 1 teaspoon grated lemon peel and ½ teaspoon lemon juice.

2. Cook broccoli in boiling water, as package directs.

3. Remove dessert from oven. Heat rolls in oven.

4. Spread chicken and ham with hollandaise. Run under broiler after removing rolls from oven.

5. Turn tomato bisque into soup bowls; top each with a lemon slice.

6. Arrange the broccoli around edge of chicken platter as pictured. Pour 3 tablespoons melted butter, mixed with 1 teaspoon lemon juice, over broccoli.

7. To serve dessert, cut into 8 squares. Serve with ice cream or hard sauce.

JOHN UHER

A Trim-The-Tree Favorite

(Planned for 8)

HEARTY BEAN-SAUSAGE SOUP

◆

HERBED ONION PITA ROUNDS

◆

NECTARINE TART

◆

BEER

◆

COFFEE

◆

TEA

YOU WILL NEED:
1 pkg (12 oz) frozen chopped onions
⅛ teaspoon dried thyme leaves
¼ cup (½ stick) butter or margarine
1 lb Swiss chard or spinach, washed
3 cans (19-oz size) white kidney beans
   (cannellini), drained
2 cans (6-oz size) sliced mushrooms
   broiled in butter, undrained
1 lb smoked sausage, sliced diagonally
1 pkg (8 oz) mini pita bread or ⅔ pkg
   (12-oz size) pita bread
10-inch spongecake layer or 8 (4-inch
   diameter) shortcake dessert cups
⅓ cup orange juice
½ pkg (1-lb size) refrigerated ready-to-
   serve vanilla pudding (4 individual
   cups per package)
4 ripe medium nectarines
¼ cup apple jelly, melted
Chopped parsley (optional)
Beer
Coffee or tea
Milk, sugar, lemon (optional)

6:00 to 6:10 P.M.

1. In medium skillet, over medium-high heat, sauté onions and thyme in butter until onions are golden—about 15 minutes.

2. Cut Swiss-chard stems into 1-inch pieces (if using spinach, discard stems); cut up leaves coarsely; set aside. In blender or food processor, purée 1 can beans and ½ cup water; turn into 5- or 6-quart Dutch oven. Repeat with another can of beans and ½ cup water. Add Swiss-chard stems, undrained mushrooms and sausage to puréed beans. Over high heat, bring to boiling; reduce heat; simmer, covered, 10 minutes.

6:10 to 6:20 P.M.

1. With scissors, cut around edge of each pita to make 2 round halves; place, crust sides down, on large cookie sheet. Spoon onion mixture onto center of each pita half, spreading slightly.

2. Stir Swiss-chard leaves and the remaining can of beans into the soup. Cook 10 minutes.

3. Place cake or dessert cups on plate; drizzle with orange juice. Spread pudding evenly on cake, or divide among dessert cups.

6:20 to 6:30 P.M.

1. Preheat broiler. Cut nectarines in half; discard pits. Cut into thin slices, and arrange on pudding, lengthwise toward center and overlapping slightly, around edge of cake. In center, place slices, ends overlapping, to make a floral pattern. (Fan slices on pudding if using dessert cups.) Brush nectarine slices with the melted jelly.

2. Broil pita, 5 inches from heat, until toasted—about 1 minute. Garnish with chopped parsley, if desired. Arrange in towel-lined bread basket.

GEORGE RATKAI

Before-The-Pageant Dinner

(Planned for 4)

CHICKEN EGG-DROP SOUP

◆

ORIENTAL BEEF WITH CASHEWS

◆

HOT BUTTERED RICE

◆

MELON AND GRAPES WITH LIME SHERBET

◆

FORTUNE COOKIES

◆

GREEN TEA

YOU WILL NEED:
1¼ cups raw long-grain white rice
Salt
1 tablespoon butter or margarine
1 red pepper
1 green pepper
4 large mushrooms
1 large onion
¾ lb boneless beef sirloin
½ lb fresh bean sprouts or 1 can (16 oz) bean sprouts
2 scallions
2 cans (13¾-oz size) clear chicken broth
1 honeydew melon
½ lb seedless green grapes
1 garlic clove
2 tablespoons vegetable oil
2½ tablespoons cornstarch
Sugar
Pepper
2 eggs
¼ cup soy sauce
⅓ cup dry sherry
⅓ cup salted cashew nuts
1 pint lime sherbet
Fortune cookies
Green tea

❧ 6:00 to 6:10 P.M.

1. Measure 2¾ cups cold water into heavy saucepan with tight-fitting lid. Stir in 1¼ cups rice, ¾ teaspoon salt and 1 tablespoon butter. Bring to boiling, uncovered. Reduce heat; cover; simmer 15 to 20 minutes, until tender.

2. Wash and slice peppers and mushrooms. Peel and slice onion. Cut beef into slices ⅛ inch thick. Rinse and drain bean sprouts.

3. Chop 2 scallions. Pour chicken broth into medium saucepan. Bring to boiling.

❧ 6:10 to 6:20 P.M.

1. Cut four 3-inch-wide slices from honeydew. Place on individual dessert plates. Wash and drain grapes. Arrange on and around melon.

2. Peel and split 1 clove garlic. Heat 2 tablespoons oil in a large heavy skillet. Add beef slices and garlic; sauté over high heat until well browned on one side. Remove meat; keep warm.

3. Add peppers, mushrooms and onion to skillet. Cook, stirring, over high heat 3 minutes. Discard garlic.

❧ 6:20 to 6:30 P.M.

1. Combine 1½ tablespoons cornstarch with ¼ cup water; mix well. Stir ¼ teaspoon salt, ¼ teaspoon sugar and ⅛ teaspoon pepper into boiling broth. Continue stirring, and add cornstarch mixture gradually. Return to boiling; reduce heat. Beat eggs slightly. Pour very slowly into the boiling soup, stirring to separate eggs into shreds. Pour into 4 bowls; top with scallion.

2. Stir together ¼ cup soy sauce, ⅓ cup sherry and 1 tablespoon cornstarch. Stir into vegetable mixture. Fold in bean sprouts and ⅓ cup cashews. Cook, stirring, until thickened and sprouts are crisp-tender. Fold in beef.

3. Fluff up rice with a fork; turn into serving bowl. Garnish with fresh scallions, if desired. Spoon lime sherbet onto melon wedges. Place in freezer until dessert time—no more than 30 minutes.

GEORGE RATKAI

Gift-Wrappers' Buffet

(Planned for 4 to 6)

EGGPLANT NEAPOLITAN

◆

GREEN NOODLES

◆

ROMAINE-AND-ENDIVE SALAD

◆

ITALIAN BREAD STICKS

◆

FLOATING CREAM PUFFS

◆

COFFEE

◆

RED WINE

YOU WILL NEED:
2 medium-size eggplants
1 pkg (8 oz) green noodles
2 squares unsweetened chocolate
½ cup milk
1 cup Italian-flavor bread crumbs
¼ cup (½ stick) butter or margarine for cooking, plus ¼ lb (1 stick) for serving
½ lb mozzarella cheese
1 head romaine, washed and crisped
2 or 3 endive, washed and crisped
2 jars (15-oz size) prepared spaghetti sauce
1 can (14 oz) sweetened condensed milk
12 bread sticks
Prepared Italian salad dressing
Chopped parsley
Watercress, washed and crisped
1 bag (5 oz) anginetti (tiny Italian cream puffs)
Confectioners' sugar
Coffee
Milk, sugar (optional)
Red wine

🕕 6:00 to 6:10 P.M.

1. Wash eggplants, and slice crosswise into "steaks" ¾ inch thick. In 1 cup boiling salted water in a large skillet, cook eggplant, covered, just until tender when pierced with a fork—6 to 8 minutes.

2. In medium saucepan, bring 1 quart salted water to boiling, for cooking noodles.

3. Over very low heat, melt chocolate in ½ cup milk, stirring occasionally.

🕕 6:10 to 6:20 P.M.

1. Thoroughly drain eggplant slices. Dry the skillet. Spread 1 cup bread crumbs on waxed paper. Roll eggplant slices in crumbs, to coat completely on all sides. Sauté the slices in 1 tablespoon butter until golden.

2. If necessary, add 1 more tablespoon butter to the skillet; turn eggplant slices. Slice mozzarella; place on eggplant. Cover, lower heat, and sauté until cheese melts.

3. Break romaine and endive into salad bowl; toss to combine. Refrigerate until serving time.

4. Add noodles to boiling water. Boil 8 minutes, uncovered, according to directions on package label.

🕕 6:20 to 6:30 P.M.

1. Heat spaghetti sauce, stirring occasionally.

2. Fold chocolate mixture into sweetened condensed milk. Pour some of chocolate sauce into serving dish, and chill until serving time. (Place in freezer to chill quickly.)

3. Arrange bread sticks in serving dish. Drain and butter the noodles. Toss salad with Italian dressing.

4. Turn some of spaghetti sauce onto platter. Stack eggplant slices in pairs and arrange in sauce, as pictured. Sprinkle with chopped parsley. Garnish with watercress. Pass remaining sauce.

5. To serve dessert, arrange puffs on chocolate sauce, mounding them high. Sprinkle liberally with confectioners' sugar. Serve with rest of chocolate sauce.

GEORGE RATKAI

Carolers' Delight

(Planned for 8)

CHILI FOR A CROWD

◆

CAULIFLOWER-AND-AVOCADO
SALAD

◆

WARM FRENCH BREAD
BUTTER

◆

WARM BANANA-PINEAPPLE
CAKE
WHIPPED CREAM

◆

COFFEE

◆

RED WINE

YOU WILL NEED:
1 can (8 oz) crushed pineapple
1 pkg (18.5 oz) banana-flavored cake
   mix
½ cup dark raisins
4 cans (16-oz size) red kidney beans
Red wine
2 cans (16-oz size) tomato sauce
1½ lb ground chuck
2 large green peppers
2 onions
Salt
Chili powder
Ground cumin
2 cloves garlic
1 pkg (4 oz) shredded Cheddar cheese
1 large bag tortilla chips
Dill pickles
1 small cauliflower
1 ripe avocado
2 tablespoons lemon juice
1 head romaine, washed and crisped
½ cup pitted black olives
2 scallions, washed
Prepared salad dressing
Cornmeal
½ pint heavy cream
(continued next column)

Vanilla
Confectioners' sugar
Coffee
Milk, sugar (optional)

⏱ 6:00 to 6:10 P.M.

1. Preheat oven to 350F. Grease two (9-by-13-by-2-inch) baking pans.

2. Drain liquid from pineapple into measuring cup. Add water to make amount of liquid called for in cake mix. Prepare mix as package directs. Stir in pineapple and ½ cup raisins. Divide into prepared pans, and bake 20 minutes.

3. In large, heavy pan, combine undrained beans, ½ cup red wine and the tomato sauce. Stir; cover; bring to boiling. Cook over medium heat 15 minutes.

⏱ 6:10 to 6:20 P.M.

1. In large skillet, sauté ground beef until browned—5 minutes. Spoon off fat.

2. Wash and slice green peppers. Peel and thinly slice onions. Add to beef with ½ teaspoon salt, 4 teaspoons chili powder, 1½ teaspoons cumin and 2 cloves garlic, pressed. Mix well; cover; sauté 5 minutes.

3. Put the cheese, tortilla chips, dill pickles in dishes.

4. Wash cauliflower; remove stem and leaves. Thinly slice through whole head. Peel and thinly slice avocado; toss with 2 tablespoons lemon juice.

⏱ 6:20 to 6:30 P.M.

1. Arrange romaine, cauliflower, avocado and drained olives on platter. Chop scallions; sprinkle over cauliflower. Serve with dressing.

2. Stir 1 tablespoon corn meal into ¼ cup red wine. Add to bean mixture, stirring until thickened. Fold in meat mixture; simmer 5 minutes.

3. Whip cream with ½ teaspoon vanilla and 2 tablespoons confectioners' sugar. Let cakes cool slightly; cut each into eighths; dust with confectioners' sugar. Serve with whipped cream.

GEORGE RATKAI

Decorate-The-House Special

(Planned for 4)

CREAM-OF-CAULIFLOWER SOUP

◆

GLAZED HAM STEAK WITH
CORNBREAD STUFFING

◆

BUTTERED GREEN BEANS

◆

SPICED PEACHES

◆

PRALINE PARFAITS

◆

COFFEE

◆

TEA

◆

MILK

YOU WILL NEED:
6 tablespoons (¾ stick) butter or
   margarine for cooking
1 fully-cooked ham steak, ¾ inch thick
   (1¼ lb)
1 medium onion
1 pkg (10 oz) frozen corn
1 pkg (8 oz) cornbread stuffing mix
¼ cup apricot jam
Prepared mustard
1 can (1 lb, 12 oz) peach halves
Cinnamon stick
8 whole cloves
½ cup light-brown sugar, firmly packed
1 tablespoon light corn syrup
3 tablespoons light cream or half-and-half
1 pkg (10 oz) frozen cauliflower
2 pkg (9-oz size) frozen whole green
   beans
1 cup milk
1 can (10¾ oz) condensed cream-of-
   celery soup
1 pkg (4 oz) grated Cheddar cheese
Chopped parsley
1 pint vanilla ice cream
Pecan halves
Coffee or tea
Milk, sugar, lemon (optional)

🐦 6:00 to 6:10 P.M.

1. Preheat oven to 375F. In medium skillet, melt 2 tablespoons butter. Add ham steak; sauté to brown on both sides. Remove to heatproof platter.

2. Coarsely chop 1 medium onion. Add to skillet; sauté 2 minutes. Add 1 cup frozen corn and ¾ cup water. Simmer 3 minutes. Add 2 cups stuffing mix; mix with fork. Spoon around ham.

3. Combine ¼ cup apricot jam and 1 tablespoon prepared mustard. Spread over ham steak; place in oven.

🐦 6:10 to 6:20 P.M.

1. In medium saucepan bring undrained peaches to boiling with 1 broken cinnamon stick and 8 cloves. Reduce heat; simmer 10 minutes. Turn into serving dish.

2. Prepare praline sauce: Melt 3 tablespoons butter in saucepan over low heat. Stir in ½ cup light-brown sugar, 1 tablespoon light corn syrup and 3 tablespoons light cream; bring to boiling. Remove from heat; cool.

3. In saucepan, heat ½ cup water to boiling. Cook cauliflower as label directs.

🐦 6:20 to 6:30 P.M.

1. In ½ cup boiling water in large saucepan, cook green beans as label directs.

2. In medium bowl, combine 1 cup milk with cream-of-celery soup; mix well. Add to undrained cauliflower in saucepan with the grated cheese. Bring to boiling. Blend in blender to make a purée. Serve with parsley.

3. Turn green beans, tossed with 1 tablespoon butter, into serving dish.

4. At dessert time, layer vanilla ice cream in parfait glasses with praline sauce and pecans.

GEORGE RATKAI

A Before-The-Theater Treat

(Planned for 4)

SCALLOPS AND BACON EN
BROCHETTE

◆

SHOESTRING POTATOES

◆

PEAS AND LETTUCE

◆

TOMATO SALAD

◆

WARM ROLLS AND BUTTER

◆

PEACH-AND-BLUEBERRY
SHORTCAKE

◆

COFFEE

◆

WHITE WINE

YOU WILL NEED:
8 leaves romaine, washed and crisped
2 large tomatoes
Chopped parsley (optional)
Prepared salad dressing
1 lb sea scallops
2 or 3 lemons
Salt
1 bag (20 oz) frozen shoestring potatoes
Salad oil
2 pkg (10-oz size) frozen sliced peaches
½ pint heavy cream
Confectioners' sugar
Almond extract
½ lb bacon
1 pkg (10 oz) frozen peas
Ready-to-serve rolls
4 large Boston lettuce leaves, washed
  and crisped
1 tablespoon butter or margarine for
  cooking, plus ¼ lb (1 stick) for
  serving
1 pkg (9½ oz) frozen blueberry muffins
Coffee
Milk, sugar (optional)
White wine

❧ 6:00 to 6:10 P.M.

1. Preheat oven to 450F. Arrange romaine on salad platter. Wash and slice tomatoes; arrange on romaine. Sprinkle with chopped parsley. Refrigerate. At serving time, pass dressing.

2. Rinse scallops; drain well. Toss with 2 tablespoons lemon juice, ¼ teaspoon salt.

3. Arrange ¾ bag of potatoes on cookie sheet. Drizzle with ½ tablespoon salad oil. Bake, stirring occasionally, until lightly browned—about 10 to 15 minutes.

❧ 6:10 to 6:20 P.M.

1. Thaw peaches according to package directions. Drain, reserving 2 tablespoons syrup. Add to peaches and toss. Set aside. Whip cream with 2 tablespoons confectioners' sugar and ¼ teaspoon almond extract. Refrigerate.

2. Bring ½ cup salted water to boiling.

3. Arrange 8 slices bacon on broiler pan. Place under broiler until just browned—2 to 3 minutes; turn; broil 1 minute longer.

❧ 6:20 to 6:30 P.M.

1. Add peas to boiling water; return to boiling and cook, covered, 3 minutes.

2. Thread bacon and scallops on four skewers. Place under broiler until lightly browned—3 or 4 minutes. Turn and broil other side until browned. Serve immediately, with lemon wedges.

3. Warm the rolls in oven. Break Boston lettuce leaves into quarters. Add to peas; cover and remove from heat. Set aside 5 minutes. Then drain, and toss with 1 tablespoon butter.

4. Remove potatoes from the oven, and toss with ½ teaspoon salt.

5. Place muffins in oven, with heat off, and allow to warm while eating dinner. To serve: Cut muffins into quarters from top. Place on individual serving plates. Top with peaches and whipped cream. Serve immediately.

GEORGE RATKAI

Shoppers' Night Special

(Planned for 6)

COLESLAW-STUFFED CABBAGE

◆

CORNED-BEEF-AND-SWISS-CHEESE ROLLS

◆

HOT POTATO SALAD

◆

PUMPERNICKEL LOAF
BUTTER

◆

WARM PLUM KUCHEN A LA MODE

◆

ICED COFFEE

◆

TEA

YOU WILL NEED:

4 Italian plums
1 pkg (10.5 oz) crumb-cake mix with pan
3 baking potatoes (1¾ lb)
1 medium onion
1 tablespoon butter or margarine for
    cooking, plus ¼ lb (1 stick) for
    serving
1 medium cabbage with outer leaves
1 large carrot
1 medium red pepper
1 medium green pepper
1 bottle (8 oz) coleslaw dressing
1 loaf unsliced pumpernickel
½ lb (6 or 8 slices) Swiss cheese
¾ lb delicatessen corned beef, thinly
    sliced
2 large tomatoes
Granulated sugar
Salt
Pepper
¼ cup cider vinegar
1 quart vanilla ice cream
Confectioners' sugar
Coffee or tea
Milk, sugar, lemon (optional)

🫖 6:00 to 6:10 P.M.

1. Preheat oven to 375F. Wash plums, and cut into quarters. Prepare crumb-cake batter as directed on package. Turn into foil pan.

2. Arrange plums in two rows on top. Sprinkle with topping from mix. Bake 25 minutes, until top feels firm.

3. Scrub potatoes. Slice into thin rounds. Slice onion thinly. Melt 1 tablespoon butter in a large skillet; add potato and onion. Sauté, stirring occasionally, over medium heat 5 minutes.

🫖 6:10 to 6:20 P.M.

1. Wash cabbage. Turn back several rows of outer leaves. With a paring knife, reach inside leaves to base of cabbage, and cut stem, to release center, leaving outer leaves attached to stem, to form a bowl.

2. Drain outer leaves well. Place on serving platter or board. With knife, shredder or processor, shred center of cabbage. Place in a bowl.

3. Stir potato, to loosen from pan. Cover, reduce heat and simmer 10 minutes longer, stirring occasionally.

4. Pare and shred carrot; wash and thinly slice ½ red pepper and ½ green pepper. Add to cabbage. Toss with coleslaw dressing. Spoon into cabbage-leaf bowl.

🫖 6:20 to 6:30 P.M.

1. Place bread in oven to warm. Separate the cheese slices. Top each with one or two slices corned beef. Roll each into a cone, and arrange around cabbage.

2. Wash tomatoes; cut into wedges and place between cones, as pictured.

3. Mix together 2 tablespoons granulated sugar, 1 teaspoon salt, dash pepper and ¼ cup cider vinegar. Pour over hot potato. Toss well, to coat. Turn into serving dish.

4. Let ice cream soften. Remove kuchen to wire rack. Sift a little confectioners' sugar over the top. Remove from pan at serving time. Serve with soft ice cream.

GEORGE RATKAI

Christmas Eve Supper

(Planned for 2)

SHRIMP SOUFFLES

◆

PETITS POIS

◆

BUTTERED RICE

◆

AVOCADO AND ORANGE SALAD

◆

BUTTERED HOT ROLLS

◆

LEMON SHERBET WITH
PINEAPPLE-MINT SAUCE

◆

FRUITCAKE

◆

CHILLED WHITE WINE
OR CHAMPAGNE

YOU WILL NEED:
½ cup raw, converted white rice
Salt
About 4 tablespoons (½ stick) butter or
   margarine for cooking, plus ⅛ lb (½
   stick) for serving
4 lettuce leaves, washed and crisped
1 ripe avocado (see Note)
1 orange
1 small onion
1 green pepper
Curry powder
Lemon juice
½ lb raw shrimp, shelled and deveined
1 egg white
½ cup mayonnaise
1 can (8 oz) crushed pineapple in juice
Green crème de menthe
½ pint lemon sherbet
1 pkg (10 oz) frozen small peas
1 pkg baked rolls
Chutney
Prepared oil-and-vinegar dressing
Fruitcake, purchased or homemade
Chilled white wine or champagne

🍴 6:00 to 6:10 P.M.

1. In medium saucepan, combine ½ cup rice, 1¼ cups water, ½ teaspoon salt and 2 teaspoons butter. Bring to boiling; reduce heat and simmer, covered, until rice is tender and water is absorbed—about 20 minutes.

2. Preheat oven to 350F.

3. Arrange lettuce leaves on two salad plates. Peel ½ avocado; slice. Peel and slice orange; quarter slices. Gently toss orange and avocado in bowl; arrange on lettuce; refrigerate.

4. Chop together onion and ¼ green pepper. In small skillet, in 1 tablespoon butter, with 1 teaspoon curry powder, sauté until tender—several minutes. Stir in 1 tablespoon lemon juice.

🍴 6:10 to 6:20 P.M.

1. Rinse shrimp; split lengthwise and cut crosswise. Toss with onion-and-pepper mixture in skillet.

2. In medium bowl, with rotary beater, beat 1 egg white with ¼ teaspoon salt just until stiff. With rubber spatula, fold in ½ cup mayonnaise and the shrimp mixture just to combine. Turn into 2 scallop shells or small casseroles. Bake 15 minutes, or until puffed and golden.

3. In small saucepan, bring ½ cup salted water to boiling.

4. Combine ½ cup crushed pineapple and 1 tablespoon crème de menthe; mix well. Refrigerate until serving.

🍴 6:20 to 6:30 P.M.

1. Make 2 scoops of sherbet; refreeze.

2. Cook peas in boiling water as package directs.

3. Heat rolls in oven. Spoon chutney into dish.

4. Drain peas; add 2 tablespoons butter; turn peas and rice into serving dishes.

5. Drizzle each salad with 1 tablespoon prepared dressing.

6. Serve soufflés at once.

7. At dessert time, spoon pineapple sauce over sherbet. Serve with fruitcake.

Note: Buy avocado several days ahead; store at room temperature until ripe. ∎

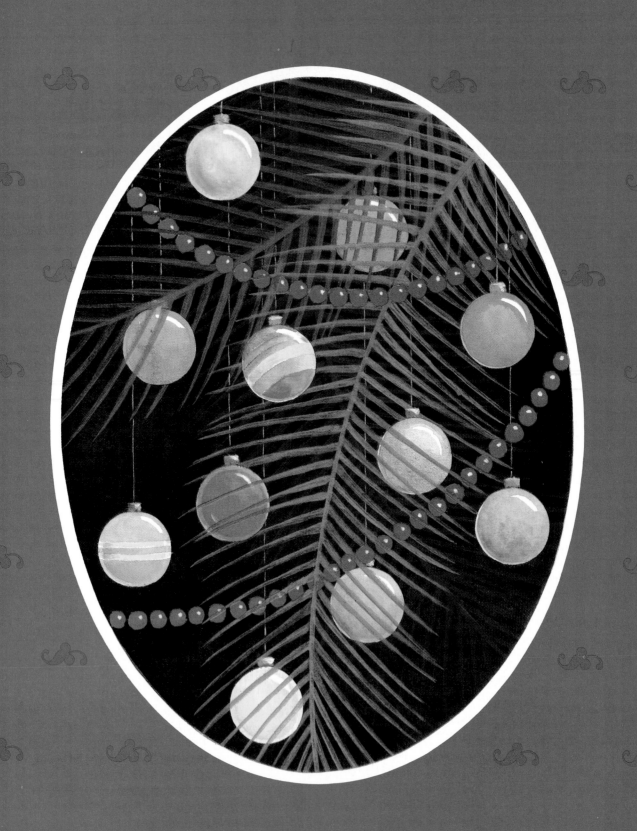

THREE

DECK THE HALLS

According to a popular Christmas song, boughs of holly make jolly decorations. And so do our festive, creative adornments that capture all the excitement and joyous spirit of the season.

Picture last year's Christmas decorations. Could the mantel use more flourish? Do the tree ornaments need sprucing-up? How about new ideas for the front-door wreath? Whether this picture requires just a few minor touches or a major make-over, you'll find all the inspiration (and directions) you need in this section. We've crisscrossed America to let you sample the unique beauty and distinctive flavor of the yuletide decor from various regions of the country. In keeping with one of the tenets of interior decorating—make the most of what you already have—we show you imaginative ways to turn cherished keepsakes and collections into charming holiday displays. If it's a wreath you'd like, we have more than twenty delightfully different designs to dress up the front door, a window or any room in the house. There are step-by-step directions for creating your own elegant table or mantelpiece arrangements, plus patterns and instructions for a treasury of enchanting handmade tree ornaments. With inspiration such as this, your Christmas decorations this year are sure to be picture-perfect!

America's Most Enchanting Decorations

MITCH KEZAR

To inspire
your artistry: a treasury
of trees, wreaths, ornaments
and more from all parts
of the country.

Design by Minnesota Landscape Arboretum

$\mathcal{F}$rom New Hampshire to Minnesota, Georgia to New Mexico, come these eight pages of unique, imaginative decorations that perfectly capture the holiday flavor of their own regions. You can re-create them beautifully wherever you live or let them guide you in designing your own enchanting originals. The wreath, opposite, made of artemisia and dried flowers, is from the Midwest.

Northeast

The two holiday trees on this page—made of dried flowers— hail from hearty New Hampshire. Both are as light, soft and lovely as newly fallen snow.

1. A tabletop tree of artemisia, statice, joe-pye weed and tiny white lights

2. A heavenly hydrangea tree, accented by nosegays and red clay cherries

1

2

Design by Christmas in October Volunteers.

1

Midwest

All things bright and beautiful: ornaments from Minnesota, made with dried flowers, wreaths, baskets and pods. Pick the flowers from your own garden and dry them—or call on your local florist. Collect the pinecones yourself for the topiary (sculptured) pinecone tree, opposite, bottom right.

1. On a doily, a big strawflower amid tiny buds
2. Artichokes and chestnut leaves on a grapevine wreath
3. A basket of baby's breath with a delicate bouquet
4. A milkweed pod cradles purple statice and princess pine
5. A profusion of color in a wicker bed
6. Flower-filled milkweed pods, the tree's crowning star
7. A wreath of straw with squirrel and rabbit-tail grasses
8. A shapely larch-and-spruce cone tree, tied with a bow

2

3

4

5

6

7

8

1

South

Relish the romance and charm of these grand holiday decorations from Georgia. Among them: a Victorian tree festooned with ribbons and lace; an elegant wreath of peaches, pecans and magnolia leaves; even a Southern-hospitality tree from which birds can feed.

1. Fans, ribbons and potpourri-covered birds
2. Christmas Victoriana: pink partridges and plaid ribbons (see detail, below)
3. Silver and red Georgian dazzle
4. Magnolia leaves gracing a banister
5. Governor's wreath of peaches and pecans
6. Outdoor tree with fruits and nuts for birds and animals

2

2

Design by David A. De Angelis.

5

Design by Dennis Schuhart.

3

Design by Currier's Flowers, Inc.

4

Design by Primrose Garden Club.

6

Southwest

These Mexican- and Indian-inspired creations from New Mexico decorate the season in lively fashion. On Christmas Eve, magical *luminarias* (painted lanterns made of ordinary brown paper bags), right, line adobe rooftops, forming ribbons of light across the sky. Opposite, possibly America's most charming Christmas crèche—enchanting clay folk-art figures sing out hymns before a glowing fire.

1. *Colorful ears of Indian corn fan out on this wreath. Pinecones, chiles and flowers cluster at its center.*
2. *An adorable adobe gingerbread house in holiday attire is crowned with tiny luminarias made with birthday candles.*
3. *Hand-painted luminarias frame a Santa Fe-blue door, adorned with a wreath of Ojo de Dios (Eye of God) yarn ornaments.*
4. *A wreath of pinecones comes alive with exuberant clay carolers.*
5. *A tree is festooned with straw ornaments and satin chiles.* ∎

Design by Nona Wesley and Anne Forbes.

1

Design by Lorreta Valdez.

4

Design by The Shop, Inn at Loretto.

2

Design by Mary Hannifin.

5

Design by Ed Berry.

Stand-up clay carolers add enchantment to your family's Christmas.

Design by Juan Sandoval.

COLLECT YOUR OWN
CHRISTMAS MAGIC

Christmas is the time to let your collections shine. Gather together those cherished family keepsakes, treasures and toys. Then add some holiday flourish to create your own personal decorations—and bring a warm, spirited feeling to your home.

Choose a spot to be extravagant. The mantel, above, becomes an elegant focal point with garlands of greenery, lace-trimmed velvet ribbon and favorite dolls dressed in holiday finery.

A vine wreath, left, of bleached pinecones and dried flowers in seasonal soft pastels draws attention to a prized collection of antique china and glass.

The sweet songs of the season begin in this family music corner, at right. Fresh carnations and baby's breath add special charm to a Christmas tree trimmed with miniature musical instruments. Treasured songbooks stand ready to guide the carolers.

Designed by Michael Cannarozzi.

At left, a heartwarming grouping of old family photographs and beloved stuffed animals in Santa suits provide a link to Christmases past. Miniature toys on an evergreen wreath add to the nostalgia.

Glass, silver and brass candlesticks gathered from all around the house create a glowing display. We put ours on the parlor organ, right, under Uncle Maurice's portrait, next to an old family album. Boughs of spruce and pine fill cachepots.

This treasured ceramic crèche, below, a reminder of the true meaning of the holiday, is displayed on a bookshelf throughout the year. At Christmastime, boxwood highlights its delicate, handcrafted details and neutral tones. ■

WREATHS THAT

These easy-to-do Christmas decorations make the most imaginative use of some traditional, and some very surprising, materials.

1. Clusters of orange-red mountain-ash berries nestle in a circle of arborvitae greens for a sophisticated, yet traditional, look.

2. Exquisite wood carvings in natural tones form a striking Della Robbia wreath (a round plaque set with fruits and nuts).

3. Closeup of 2: Multiple bows and flowing green ribbons call attention to the pineapple, a symbol of hospitality the world over.

4. As delicately woven as a real bird's nest is this vine wreath of dried wildflowers. Strips of jute and cranberries decorate the windows.

5. Pungent scent for a pretty wreath: Rich green laurel is intertwined with narrow yellow ribbon and surprised with fresh lemons and limes.

6. Festoons of fragrant laurel—nothing more—decorate the window. The laurel wreath is tied with yellow ribbon.

SAY 'WELCOME'

7. A snowshoe forms the base of this fanciful wreath of red pine and spruce with pinecones and sparkling pearly everlasting.

8. Folk-art tin farm animals frolic in an evergreen wreath and prance in a row above antique glass at the top of this doorway.

9. A country-style wreath with fragrant greens celebrates the hunt. The old wooden yoke sports a carved horse and hunting whip.

10. Pieces of fabric, calico stars and an antique wooden house fashion a personal, and quite extraordinary, straw wreath.

11. A menagerie of jolly, tiny cloth toys peeks out of straw baskets. A bed of evergreens on a board binds it all together.

12. This summer straw bonnet makes a gorgeous Christmas wreath, brimming with velvet ribbon, cinnamon sticks and eucalyptus.

*F*or the front door:
Clusters of pecans,
crab apples and pome-
granates adorn a
Williamsburg wreath
of boxwood and
evergreen.

Wreaths That Say 'Welcome' In Every Room

These wonderful, often whimsical, wreaths are sure to enliven your holiday decor. Instructions can be found on page 154.

Perfection for a paneled bar, above: Wine and champagne corks are fastened into straw with toothpicks.

Below is a small, silken quicksilver wreath of folded ribbons for a young girl's fancy.

For a child's room, top of page: Colorful bubblegum and jaw-breakers are glued onto a Styrofoam wreath for nonedible cheer.

For a Christmas kitchen, left: Air-dried herbs and flowers entwine with a pungent mixture of heather and lavender on a straw base.

Dining-room decor, left: Dried green and red chili peppers are wired into a twig wreath.

WONDERFUL WREATHS

Plain wreaths of straw, Styrofoam, grapevine and evergreen become these spectacular holiday decorations with just some glue, floral wire and simple materials available from any arts-and-crafts store or florist shop...or even your own home. Our easy-to-follow directions guide you every step of the way in creating your own uniquely original wreath to deck the halls (doors and walls, too).

Statice Spice Wreath

Swirls of statice; tiny bundles of dried flowers; and fragrant eucalyptus, dill and cinnamon create this lush and lovely wreath. For step-by-step directions, turn to page 139.

Grapevine Wreath

Red silk flowers and delicate baby's breath nestle in the greenery of this festive bow-tied wreath, above. For step-by-step directions, turn to page 138.

Della Robbia Wreath

Simply gather a squirrel's cache of acorns, cones, herbs and nuts to create this traditional all-natural wreath and candleholder, opposite. Directions begin on page 155.

Tiny Toy Wreath

Furry little toy animals and bright plaid ribbon make a charming miniature display—in grand holiday style. Directions are on page 155.

Grapevine Wreath *(pictured, page 137)*

1. Use wire cutters to cut floral wire into two pieces, each 16″ long (see Note). Wire floral foam to the wreath, crisscrossing block as shown. Twist wire tightly at back several times. Trim off the ends with wire cutters.

2. Cover the floral-foam block with Spanish moss, molding the moss around the base of the block.

3. Cut off each silk flower from the bunches at an angle at the base of the stem. Insert flowers in the block as shown.

4. Cut off individual stems of baby's breath and insert in the block as shown, spreading little blossoms.

5. Cut white branches into random 4″ to 6″ lengths. Insert the branches in the block.

6. Add a 6-loop bow at the top of the wreath. Spread wires and twist tightly at back. Make a loop for hanging the wreath. Cut off extra wire.

Materials

Wire cutters
32″ of floral wire (22 gauge)
1 block of dry floral foam, 2″ x 3½″
1 12″ oval or round grapevine wreath
Spanish moss
4 bunches of red silk flowers, each flower
    2″ in diameter

1 stem of baby's breath
3 thin white branches (you can spray-paint
    your own)
1 6-loop bow (see page 145)

Note: You may use 2 pieces of adhesive tape, each 16″ long.

DAVID VIENS

Statice Spice Wreath *(pictured, page 137)*

1. Break the statice into small bunches, each approximately 6″ to 8″ long. Starting on the outer edge of the wreath, secure each statice bunch to the wreath with two S pins. Continue around the perimeter of wreath to complete the first row.

2. Use utility scissors to trim stems evenly on the inside edge of the wreath.

3. Place statice bunches around the wreath to make a second row, securing each bunch with two S pins. Attach each bunch at an angle as shown above. Tuck the stem end of the last bunch under so it doesn't show. Complete the last row in the same manner as the second row, tucking in the last stems.

4. Dip the stem end of each eucalyptus piece into craft glue, then insert in the wreath; position as shown.

5. Dip each white yarrow stem into glue and place randomly around the wreath. Separate the olive and pink star flowers into 6 bunches each; cut into 5″ lengths. Separate the rust star flowers into 12 tiny bunches, each about 5″ long. Dip stems of each flower bunch into glue and place randomly around wreath.

6. Dip each dill stem into glue and place evenly around the outer edge of the wreath. Dip each cinnamon stick into glue and place on the wreath as shown above. To store the wreath, wrap in tissue and keep in a dry place.

Materials
1 16 oz bunch of German statice
1 14″ straw wreath
Approximately 75 S pins or fern pins
Utility scissors
5 pieces of blue eucalyptus, each 6″ to 8″
   long

White craft glue
6 stems of bleached yarrow
1 pkg of olive star flowers
1 pkg of pink star flowers
1 pkg of rust star flowers

3 dill stems, each 10″ to 12″ long
5 cinnamon sticks, each 6″ to 10″ long
   (vary the lengths)

Note: **If there is no wire loop for hanging, attach one to the back of the wreath.**

DAVID VIENS

Home-For-The-Holiday Arrangements

Nothing is quite as festive as a holiday table or mantel crowned with a stunning arrangement of flowers, candles and bows artfully positioned in a perfect balance of color and design. And nothing is quite as satisfying as doing it all by yourself. It's easy. Our step-by-step directions show you how to create these three glorious arrangements. And we even show you how to master the art of making bows (page 145). You'll be an expert in no time!

CHRISTMAS CANDLE WREATH

Small votive candles and elegant tapers cast their glow in this evergreen-wreath centerpiece studded with apples, berries and festive ribbon. For directions, turn to page 142.

Candle wreath designed by Jeanne Parker, Cedar Mountain Florist, Newington, Conn.

CHRISTMAS CARNATION CENTERPIECE

Lovely fresh carnations and velvet bows nestle in a sprawling candlelit bed of juniper, white pine and andromeda. For directions, turn to page 143.

SILKY POINSETTIA MANTELPIECE

The wicker basket on the mantel overflows with a colorful display of traditional holiday favorites—poinsettias, pinecones, berries and evergreens—all done up with a velvet bow. For directions, turn to page 144.

Mantelpiece designed by Cynthia Gorsky, Cedar Mountain Florist, Newington, Conn.
Photographed at Town Farms Inn, Middletown, Conn.

Christmas Candle Wreath *(pictured, page 140)*

1. Separate and spread the stems and branches of the wreath to increase fullness. Cut ribbon into 6 pieces, each 1 yard long. Make 6 bows. (Follow directions on page 145, Steps 1 and 2; measure off 18″ of ribbon; leave an 8″ tail.)

2. For each bow, bend a piece of floral wire in half around the middle of the bow, twisting the two pieces of wire at the back of the bow very tightly. Wrap the wires tightly around a floral pick. Trim the ends. Cut a V into each ribbon end.

3. Insert two bows in the wreath at the same point. Place the other four bows in pairs as shown above, for three groups of two bows each.

4. Tightly wrap the wires on each holly stem around a floral pick. Trim the ends of holly stems. Insert the holly on either side of the bow groupings as shown.

5. Tightly wrap the wires of each apple, crab-apple-bunch and berry stem around a pick. Trim the ends. Arrange the apples, crab apples and berries as shown.

6. Place a small lump of florist's clay on the bottom of each votive candleholder. Insert the candles and place on the wreath in between each bow arrangement. Insert the 12″ candles in the candlesticks and place in the center of the wreath.

Materials

1 18″ evergreen wreath (real or artificial)
6 yards of 1¼″- or 1½″-wide ribbon
6 pieces of floral wire, each 8″ long (see Note)
21 floral picks, each about 3″ long

Wire cutters
6 wired stems of holly, each 8″ long
3 2″ plastic apples on wired stems
6 bunches of 1″ plastic crab apples on wired stems
6 wired stems of small red berries
Florist's clay

3 red votive candles and candleholders
3 red candles, each 12″ long
3 candlesticks, 4″ to 6″ in height (brass, pewter, etc.)

Note: If the apples, crab apples and berries you purchase are not wired, cut an 8″ piece of floral wire, bend in half and twist tightly onto each of the plastic stems.

Christmas Carnation Centerpiece *(pictured, page 140)*

1. Place soaked floral-foam block in the container. Secure block to the container with adhesive tape. Insert the candle about 3 inches into the center of the block.

2. Using a knife, scrape 1 inch of needles from the ends of two 15″ and two 8″ pieces of juniper. Insert each 15″ piece at an angle into the short sides of the block, so that the juniper tips touch the table. Insert each 8″ piece at the same angle into the long sides of the block.

3. Using a knife, scrape 1 inch of needles from the end of eight 6″ and the remaining twelve 8″ pieces of juniper. Insert the 8″ pieces around the sides of the block, evenly spacing them between the four main pieces of juniper. Insert the 6″ pieces into the top of the block at about a 45-degree angle.

4. Using a knife, scrape 1 inch of needles from the ends of two 12″ and ten 8″ white-pine tips. Cut stems to a sharp point. Insert the 12″ pine tips into the short sides of the block. Insert the 8″ pine tips into the sides and top of the block to fill in spaces. Insert the andromeda tips into the block to fill remaining spaces.

5. Using a knife, cut each carnation stem to a sharp point. Insert the 13″ stems into the short sides of the block above the 15″ pieces of juniper. Insert the 5″ stems into the long sides. Then insert the 7″ carnation stems at a 45-degree angle between the 5″ and 13″ carnations so that the 7″ carnations are opposite each other.

6. Insert each bow into the block next to the candle on the opposite corners with no carnations. Fill the container with water. Check daily; the water level should remain just below the rim of the container.

Materials

- 1 block of dry floral foam, 4¼″ × 2¼″, soaked in water and cut to extend 2″ above rim of container
- 1 container, about 6″ in diameter and 2″ high
- 2 strips of adhesive tape, each 8″ × ¼″
- 1 red candle, 15″ long
- 2 pieces of juniper greens, each 15″ long
- 14 pieces of juniper greens, each 8″ long
- 8 pieces of juniper greens, each 6″ long
- 2 white-pine tips, each 12″ long
- 10 white-pine tips, each 8″ long
- 10 andromeda or mountain-laurel tips, each 4″ to 5″ long (stems cut to a sharp point)
- 2 peppermint, red or white carnations, each 13″ long
- 2 peppermint, red or white carnations, each 5″ long
- 2 peppermint, red or white carnations, each 7″ long
- 2 8-loop bows, each made from 1½ yards of ½″-wide red-velvet ribbon (see page 145 for directions: leave 4″ tails; use 5″ of ribbon for each loop; wire each bow to a 2½″ floral pick)

Notes: Do not leave the lit candle unattended. You can easily make this a Thanksgiving centerpiece by changing the colors of the candle, flowers and bows to yellow or orange.

Silky Poinsettia Mantelpiece *(pictured, page 141)*

1. Place a ½″ lump of floral clay on the bottom of a plastic anchor pin. Place pin, prong side up, on center of basket so that clay fastens the pin to the basket. Cover the foam block with Spanish moss. Anchor with 4″ wires bent into hairpin shape.

2. Cut needles from 4″ of each stem of the evergreen branches. Insert a branch in the bottom of each of three corners of the block. Insert the fourth branch at an angle in the fourth corner at the top of the block. Spread the branches apart.

3. Insert the three branches of red berries as shown. Spread the small branches of the berries apart.

4. Spray the pinecones lightly with flat white paint. Attach a 5″ piece of wire around the base petals of each pinecone; wrap tightly around a floral pick. Insert the wired cones in the arrangement as shown.

5. Insert the 13″ poinsettia stem in front of the upright evergreen branch. Insert one 10″ poinsettia stem in front and to the right of the first stem, on the right side of the basket handle. Insert one 10″ poinsettia stem on the other side of the handle. Insert the last 10″ poinsettia stem at right angles to the middle evergreen branch. Insert the three 8″ poinsettias as shown.

6. Tightly wrap an 8″ wire around one end of each 10″ ribbon. Wrap wires tightly around a floral pick. Cut a V into the ribbon ends. Tightly wrap the bow wires around a floral pick. Insert the bow and tails as shown. To dust your arrangement, use a hair dryer. To store, place it in a plastic bag with a mothball and tie securely. Keep bag in a cool, dark place.

Materials

Floral clay
1 plastic anchor pin
1 wicker miniature fireside basket, about 8″ in diameter
1 block of dry floral foam or Styrofoam, 3″ × 2½″
1 small bag of Spanish moss (you will have some left over)

Floral wire
4 silk evergreen branches, each 15″ long
3 branches of red berries, each 12″ long
4 medium pinecones, each about 4″ long
Spray can of flat white paint
7 floral picks
1 silk red poinsettia "flower," 5″ in diameter and stem 13″ long
3 silk red poinsettia "flowers," each 5″ in diameter and stem 10″ long

3 silk red poinsettia "flowers," each 5″ in diameter and stem 8″ long
2 pieces of 2½- to 3″-wide lace-trimmed #40 velvet ribbon, each 10″ long
1 6-loop bow made from 2½ yards of same velvet ribbon (see page 145 for directions)

Tie Your Own Bow

1. Measure off 22″ of ribbon; *do not cut.* Fold back to make a 5″ loop, using 10″ of ribbon. Leave a 12″ tail. Gather the middle tightly between your fingers.

2. Keep the tail toward your body. From the remaining ribbon, use an additional 10″ to bring a second 5″ loop up and over. Pinch at the middle again.

3. Make a third 5″ loop by bringing 10″ of ribbon over and under, gathering in the middle again.

4. Make a fourth 5″ loop by bringing 10″ of ribbon under and over to the middle; pinch again. Repeat Steps 3 and 4 if you wish to make a 6-loop bow.

5. Holding the gathered ribbon in your left hand, take 4″ of ribbon and make a small loop in the center as shown. Make sure the second tail falls in the direction opposite the first tail.

6. Insert floral wire halfway through the center loop as shown. Twist two pieces of wire at the back of the bow *very* tightly several times. Cut the second tail at 12″. Trim tail ends at an angle if you wish.

Bow by Jeanne Parker, Cedar Mountain Florist, Newington, Conn.

Materials

For a 4-loop bow: approximately 2 yards of ribbon
For a 6-loop bow: approximately 2½ yards of ribbon
1 piece of floral wire, 18″ long
Wire cutters or old scissors

O TANNENBAUM, O TANNENBAUM,

THOU TREE MOST FAIR AND LOVELY!

A
richly
ornament-
ed tree, glow-
ing and green,
epitomizes the joy
of the holiday season.
The handmade decora-
tions on these pages will
add a touch of whimsy and
sparkle to your Christmases for
years to come. A merry menagerie
of colorful felt animals frolics on the
branches of the tree below. Directions
for making these charming creatures begin on page 148. A rainbow of ribbons—velvet, satin, metallic—wraps around Styrofoam
balls to create the vibrant ornaments at left. The
technique is surprisingly simple; directions can be
found on
page 154.

continued from page 147

Ornaments are pictured on pages 146 and 147.

FELT ANIMALS

Materials listed below are for a dozen animals (two of each kind).

MATERIALS

12-by-9-inch rectangles of felt in the following colors: light brown (bears); red (beavers and trims); light gold (lions); tan (camels); white (lambs and trims); lavender (hippos)

Large scraps of dark gold (lions' manes) and bright green (holly, trims)

Small scraps of beige, pink, black, magenta, blue and yellow

Four inches gold braid (lions)

Eight green sequins (lions)

Two small artificial trees (bears)

OTHER MATERIALS AND TOOLS

Sewing thread, black carpet thread, polyester fiberfill or cotton batting for stuffing, white household glue, pipe cleaners, nutpick, small sharp scissors, black ballpoint pen, black felt-tip pen and sewing machine. Pinking shears and a paper punch are useful tools but not essential.

GENERAL DIRECTIONS

Patterns: Enlarge patterns, below, and transfer to light cardboard, following solid lines and broken outer lines (which indicate openings to be left for stuffing). Include any facial features and inner leg lines that will be outlined with stitching and the words "Cut" and "Stitch." Pieces marked "Cut" are trimming parts. They are marked on a single layer of felt, cut out on the marked line and glued to the stitched animal. Pieces marked "Stitch" are major body pieces, which must be marked on a single layer of felt, pinned to a second layer of felt and stitched *before* they are cut out. The marked line on these pieces is the stitching line—all of the cutting is done outside this line.

Layout: One piece of 12-by-9-inch felt, cut in half crosswise, will make two of most animals, with leftovers. Using a fine-ballpoint pen, draw around cardboard pattern on one half of the felt (single thickness), sketching inner leg lines and facial features that will be stitched. Pin marked half securely to remaining felt.

Stitching: Sewing through both layers, slowly stitch outlines of animal with sewing machine, starting and stopping with backstitch to prevent raveling. Be sure *not* to stitch areas marked by broken lines, or you will be unable to stuff the animal.

Cutting: Using small sharp scissors, cut stitched pieces 1/16 inch *outside* of stitching *except* at openings left for stuffing; leave 1/4 inch of excess at those openings.

Stuffing: Wrap small amounts of cotton batting or polyester fiberfill around point of nutpick, and insert in narrow spots first. Then poke in larger pieces of filler to make firm legs and necks, but never so much that lines are distorted. After stuffing is completed, pin opening, making sure no filler will be caught in seam. Machine-stitch opening, and cut to match rest of body.

Gluing and marking features: Use glue sparingly, as felt will not stick if saturated. Squeeze out a little glue, and apply to felt with toothpick. Glue is also used to prepare surface for marking fea-

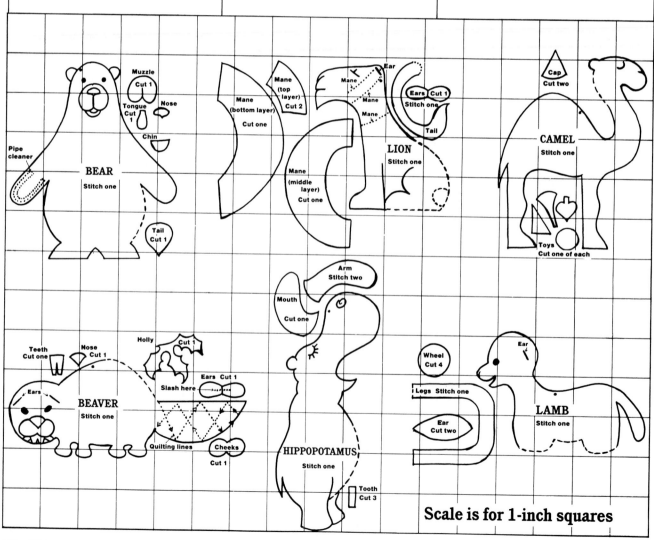

Scale is for 1-inch squares

tures. Sketch features with pencil or ballpoint, coat area lightly with glue and let dry. Then mark clearly in black with a fine-felt-tip pen. (Should you prefer to work features with black embroidery thread, do not coat with glue.) Beavers' teeth and holly may be coated with glue to stiffen them if the felt used is a bit limp.

Hangers: A dot on the back or head of each animal marks the place where its hanger should be. Using heavy black thread, insert needle an inch away from dot, draw up through dot until end of thread disappears, and make a catch stitch. Then form a 2½-inch loop, knot thread around base of loop, take another catch stitch; reinsert needle and come out again an inch away from hanger. Cut thread so loose end disappears inside the animal.

SPECIFIC DIRECTIONS

Bear: Mark body on light-brown (alternate colors: tan, dull gold or white) felt, with muzzle of beige (or pink), nose black and tongue red. Stitch outline of body with red thread, leaving ears free. Cut out the body, cutting around the ears as you go. Then cut off both ears on the front piece, so only ears of back half remain. Form a two-inch length of pipe cleaner into a U-shape, and insert in hand that will hold the tree. Do not stuff this hand. Stuff rest of body. Pin opening and machine-stitch. Trim. For face, cut out muzzle and machine-stitch just inside the outer edge and up the center line. Glue to tongue so red shows through. Glue over chin. Glue nose to muzzle so point is just over red stitching at center. Glue unit to face. Mark eyes as described in general directions. Glue small artificial Christmas tree to hand, bending pipe cleaner around to hold. (If tree has no pot, make one by spreading glue on one side of strip of red felt, 2 inches long by ½ inch wide, and winding it around stem of tree. Glue so seam is against body.) Bear might carry peppermint stick or flower instead of tree. Glue tail, point down, to back of bear. Add hanger.

Lion: Mark body and tail on light-gold felt, mane on darker gold. (Or use two shades of some other color, such as pink.) Stitch tail with red thread, leaving rounded end open. Cut out. Stuff with 4-inch length of pipe cleaner. Smooth and reshape if necessary. Stitch body in red, cut out and stuff. Pin bottom of hind foot so that stuffing won't fall out. Pin tail in place and finish stuffing body. Stitch opening and trim. Cut ears apart, and glue in small slots cut in either side of head, forcing in with nutpick. Mark eyes. Add hanger. For mane, cut one bottom layer, one middle layer and two top layers. Fringe each from wider edge to narrow edge, making cuts roughly ⅛ inch apart. Slant cuts so individual fringes are tapered to remain parallel with ends. Spread uncut edge of bottom layer with glue and fasten around neck at line indicated on pattern, overlapping at chest if necessary. Repeat with middle layer, gluing center just behind ears and bringing ends together under chin. Glue one top layer of mane to either side of face, beginning at base of ear and ending at cheek. For crown, glue two inches of gold braid, preferably with loops on upper edge, into ring a little more than half an inch in diameter. Pull looped edge outward to make crown shape. Flatten ring to narrow oval, and glue to lion's head between ears. Glue two green sequins to each side of crown for "crown jewels."

Camel: Mark body on tan (or peach, gold or yellow) felt. Stitch in red. Cut out. Stuff face and neck through opening. Stitch closed and trim. Make cut through top thickness only at hump, where it will be covered by blanket. Stuff legs and body through here. For saddlebag, cut green blanket 3 inches long and 1½ inches wide. Fold crosswise, spread inside with glue and place over hump, pinching corners that extend beyond hump. When dry, trim to follow curve of hump. Fringe bottom edge and glue narrow black belt around stomach, if desired. Cut second green rectangle of same width but 2½ inches long; round the ends. Fold crosswise, and cut shallow semicircle from fold. Slip this opening over hump, and glue edges of resultant saddlebag to blanket. Cut four simple toys, and glue two in either side of bag (red ball, yellow horn, blue top, white sailboat). Mark eyes. Add hanger.

Santa cap is optional. To make, cut two red triangles and glue to either side of head and to each other. Cut white strip ⅜ inch by 2 inches, and glue around head for cuff. Press ends together, and trim to shape when dry. Punch out two white circles, and glue to either side of point for pompom.

Beaver: Mark body pattern on red (or brown) felt, sketching in quilting lines on tail as shown. Stitch with red thread. Cut out. Stuff, using very little filler in tail. Stitch opening, starting at top of back and continuing across tail on quilting lines, following arrows. Trim. Cut ears apart and slash straight edges. Overlap, spread with glue and force into diagonal cuts above eyes. Trim, if necessary, to make same size and shape. Mark eyes. Cut cheeks from light pink felt and teeth from white felt. Glue cheeks over top edge of teeth. Cut and glue on black nose, centering carefully. Cut holly from bright-green felt and glue a green wire stem (about 2 inches long) to back of center leaf. Glue small red-felt dots to holly for berries. Glue stem to beaver's chin. Then glue cheeks and teeth to face, with teeth overlapping holly stem. Add hanger.

Hippo: Mark body and arms on lavender (or gray or light blue) felt. Trim inside edge of mouth, and glue pink inner mouth to back side of marked felt. Glue one tooth at upper end of pink and another at either side of it in lower jaw. Pin to backing felt. Stitch, using red thread on gray, purple on either of the other colors. Stitch around lavender part of mouth, leaving outer edge of pink mouth free. Cut out, being careful not to extract any teeth. Stuff. Stitch opening. Stitch two arms. Cut out. Make small cut through one layer only at shoulder and stuff arms. Glue to body so cut is hidden. Make songbook of gold cardboard from old greeting card: Cut a rectangle of cardboard 2 by 1½ inches, and fold crosswise. (Scoring first makes a neater crease.) Glue hands to book. Wipe off excess glue. Mark eyes and nostrils. Add hanger. Cut scarf of magenta felt 7 inches by ½ inch, and tie around neck with single knot at back.

Lamb: Mark body on white felt, legs on black (use chalk or dressmaker's white marking pencil). Stitch with white thread. Cut out body and back of head with pinking shears, keeping inner points ⅛ inch from stitching. With regular scissors, cut face, front of neck and legs 1/16 inch outside of stitching. Snip off points of pinking for woolly look. (If you have no pinking shears, cut small scallops with regular scissors.) Stuff legs with 6-inch pipe cleaner, cutting off any excess. Make an extra line of white stitching on legs to hold pipe cleaner in place. Place curved section of legs inside body and pin at stomach. Finish stuffing body, inserting filler from both sides so black does not show through. Stitch. Cut out ears, and fold in half lengthwise. Crease. Make a tiny cut on either side of head, spread pointed end of ear with glue and push into slot with nutpick, folded edge up. Mark eye. Cut red collar 2 inches by ¼ inch, and glue around neck. Add hanger. For base, cut a piece of bright-green felt 4½ by 1½ inches. Fold lengthwise, and press or crease firmly. Place 4-inch pipe cleaner in fold, and insert lamb's feet inside base next to pipe cleaner. Pin securely, making sure legs are straight, parallel and equidistant from ends of base. Stitch around four sides of base, ¼ inch from ends and from fold. Trim base to 1/16 inch outside stitching. Cut four wheels from red felt, and glue to base. Punch out four black circles, and glue to centers of wheels.

continued on page 154

Handmade Treasures

For Your Tree

Lovely to look at, quick and easy to make, these darling ornaments radiate a festive, whimsical spirit. Each one will add its own special touch of charm and beauty to your Christmas tree and become a delightful addition to your collection of cherished ornaments.

Bright holiday fabrics are used for the colorful collection of ornaments above. The stocking can hold candy canes or small toys. The heart, tree and balloon are lightly stuffed. Turn to page 152 for patterns and directions.

Delicate lace "hats," above, decorate the tree in elegant style. For the easy directions, see page 155.

Design by P. Jane Sterry, Patches & Patchwork, Portland, Conn.

Design by Maryla Gelland, La Fleur, Middletown, Conn.

DAVID VIENS

These darling minibaskets are bursting with Christmas cheer. Starting at the top, then clockwise: Cinnamon-Sticks Basket, White-Rose Basket, Berry-Pine Basket, Teddy Bear Basket and Golden-Cones Basket. Directions begin on page 152.

continued from page 150

Ornaments are pictured on pages 150 and 151.

STOCKING FOR STUFFING

MATERIALS
¼ yard holiday fabric (face)
¼ yard muslin
Thread to match holiday fabric
Nylon thread for hanger
Lace trim (optional)

DIRECTIONS

1. Cut 2 holiday-fabric stockings and 2 muslin stockings from pattern.

2. With right sides together, sew one face piece and one muslin piece along top edge. Repeat with other face and muslin pieces. Press seams open.

3. With right sides together, pin the two pieces face to face and muslin to muslin. Sew all around edges, leaving an opening between X's. Clip curves.

4. Turn completely right side out and press. Sew opening closed. Push muslin liner inside face stocking.

5. Use nylon thread to string a loop at *; knot.

6. Lace can be sewn on or glued on top edge.

Note: You can sew strips of fabric together for one or both face pieces.

CINNAMON-STICKS BASKET

MATERIALS
Red-and-white-dot ribbon, ⅜" wide
1 basket, about 2" in diameter
White craft glue
2 stems caspia
7 cinnamon sticks, each about 3" long
3 wired red berries

DIRECTIONS

1. Cut length of ribbon to go around basket; glue in place. Make a tiny 6-loop bow (see page 145 for directions). Glue on side by handle.

2. Cut caspia into pieces 3" long. Make a bunch the size of the basket opening; place in basket.

3. Insert cinnamon sticks, one at top by the handle and the other six evenly spaced around edge at an angle.

4. Place berries between cinnamon sticks at top.

TEDDY BEAR BASKET

MATERIALS
Red-and-white-check ribbon, ⅜" wide
1 basket, about 2" in diameter
White craft glue
2 stems glycerined baby's breath
1 teddy bear, about 1¼" long
1 floral pick, about 2" long

DIRECTIONS

1. Cut length of ribbon to go around basket; glue in place. Make a small bow and glue to basket where ribbon ends overlap.

2. Cut baby's breath into pieces 3" long. Make a bunch the size of the basket opening; place in basket.

3. Put teddy bear on a pick (if it does not come on one) by pushing pointed end of pick through bottom of bear. Insert teddy bear in middle of baby's breath in basket.

HOLIDAY HEART

MATERIALS
⅛ yard holiday fabric
Thread to match holiday fabric
Lace
Stuffing
Nylon thread for hanger
¼ yard of ¼"-wide ribbon

DIRECTIONS

1. Cut 2 hearts from pattern.

2. Sew lace along edge of right side of one heart.

3. With right sides together, pin second heart to heart with lace. Sew around edge, leaving an opening between X's.

4. Clip curves and turn right side out. Press.

5. *Stuff lightly* and sew opening closed.

6. Use nylon thread to string a loop at *; knot. Tack a ribbon bow at *.

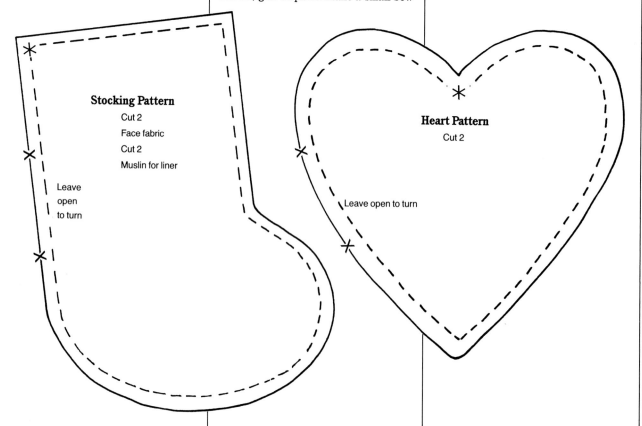

Stocking Pattern

Cut 2

Face fabric

Cut 2

Muslin for liner

Leave open to turn

Heart Pattern

Cut 2

Leave open to turn

HANDMADE TREASURES FOR YOUR TREE

RIBBON-TAIL BALLOON

MATERIALS
⅛ yard holiday fabric
Thread to match holiday fabric
Stuffing
¼ yard of ⅛"-wide ribbon
Nylon thread for hanger

DIRECTIONS
1. Cut 2 balloons from pattern.
2. With right sides together, sew balloon pieces all around edge, leaving an opening between X's.
3. Carefully clip all around. Turn right side out and press.
4. *Stuff lightly* and sew opening closed.
5. At base of balloon, tie ribbon into a bow, leaving one end long.
6. Use nylon thread to string a loop at *. Knot and hang.

BERRY-PINE BASKET

MATERIALS
White craft glue
1 piece dry floral foam, 1" square
1 basket, about 2" in diameter, sprayed white
3 silk pine-spray picks
7 wired red berries
Green-and-white-dot ribbon, ⅜" wide

DIRECTIONS
1. Glue floral-foam block to bottom of basket.
2. Cut pine into pieces 1½" long. Insert in block, filling the basket.

3. Insert red berries in block between pine pieces.
4. Make a tiny 6-loop bow (see page 145 for directions). Insert on side by handle.

WHITE-ROSE BASKET

MATERIALS
2 stems glycerined baby's breath
1 basket, about 2" in diameter, sprayed red
5 white silk roses, each ½" in diameter
3 wired red berries
Red velvet ribbon, ⅜" wide
White craft glue

DIRECTIONS
1. Cut baby's breath into pieces 3" long. Make a bunch the size of the basket opening; place in basket.
2. Cut rose stems 2½" long. Place one in the middle of basket and the other four evenly spaced around edge.
3. Place berries between roses at top.
4. Cut 4" length of ribbon; glue ends together under handle to make hanger.
5. Make a tiny 4-loop bow (see page 145 for directions). Glue to hanger where ends overlap.

CALICO CHRISTMAS TREE

MATERIALS
¼ yard holiday fabric
Thread to match holiday fabric
Stuffing
Nylon thread for hanger

DIRECTIONS
1. Cut 4 trees from pattern.
2. With right sides together, sew two tree pieces all around edge, leaving an opening between X's.
3. Clip points, and turn right side out. Press.
4. *Stuff lightly* and sew opening closed.
5. Repeat Steps 2 through 4 for other two pieces.
6. Place one stuffed tree on top of the other and sew a seam line down the middle.
7. Use nylon thread to string a loop at *. Knot and hang.

continued on page 155

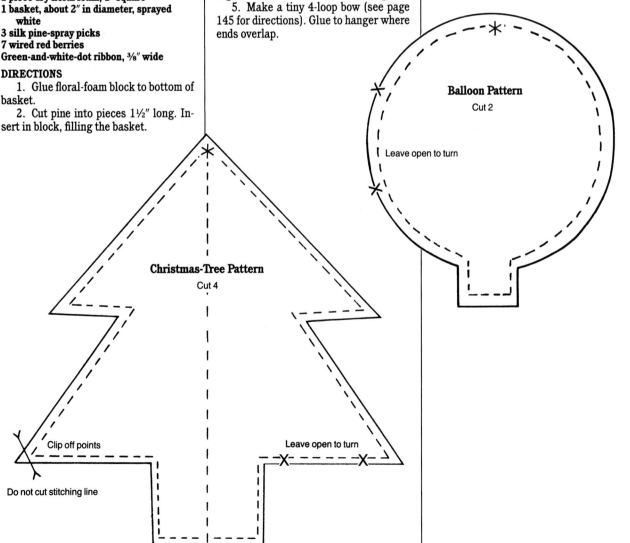

Balloon Pattern — Cut 2 — Leave open to turn

Christmas-Tree Pattern — Cut 4 — Clip off points — Leave open to turn — Do not cut stitching line

continued from page 135
Wreaths are pictured on pages 134 and 135.

The bases we used for our various wreaths—evergreens, straw, Styrofoam, twigs—are all available at garden centers and nurseries.

DRIED-HERB WREATH
(designed by Ruth Katz)

MATERIALS
Dried field flowers, such as statice, clover and heather; herbs, such as lavender and thyme (these should be hung upside down in a dry place for approximately five days to air-dry); weeds such as Queen Anne's lace or goldenrod
Straw wreath base (ours measures 19 inches across)
Hairpins (*not* bobby pins)

Simply affix clusters of herbs or flowers to wreath with hairpins as desired, in a random pattern.

CHILI-PEPPER WREATH
(designed by Susan Cameron, A.S.I.D.)

MATERIALS
Red and green chili peppers
Lemon juice
Water
Florist's wire
Twig wreath base (ours measures 16 inches across)

First, prepare the peppers: Soak in a strong solution of lemon juice and water (about 3 parts lemon juice to one part water), for approximately one hour. (This will help peppers retain their color when dried.) Remove from solution, pat thoroughly dry and spread the peppers out on an oven rack. Place in a very slow oven (about 150 degrees) until thoroughly dry.

Cut lengths of florist's wire into approximately 8-inch lengths. Alternating red peppers with green, string four peppers at a time on each piece of wire, beginning about halfway up the wire. (Thread wire through the top part of the pepper, just below the stem, not through the stem itself.) Twist the tops of two of the strung wires as you would the twist-tie on a plastic bag, just above the top pepper on each wire; then push the bare parts of wires through twigs of wreath base; tie in back. To save time, you might want to thread several bunches of peppers together before securing any to the base.

WILLIAMSBURG WREATH
(designed by Susan Cameron, A.S.I.D.)

MATERIALS
Florist's wire
Pomegranates
Boxwood or evergreen wreath to use as base (ours is about 20 inches across)
Pecans or walnuts
White all-purpose quick-setting glue
Crab apples or lady apples

Cut florist's wire into lengths that will fit through pomegranates, allowing about 3 extra inches at each end. Then bend wire into a *U* shape, and tie the ends of the wire around to the back of wreath base, spacing the fruits symmetrically around the entire wreath. Glue five of the pecans or walnuts together in a cluster; add an additional nut at center. Put a dab of glue at the base of each nut cluster, and insert a length of wire. Wrap and tie these clusters around wreath base, spaced as you like them. Wire five or six of the apples together in the same manner as the pomegranates, and attach these to wreath base. Depending upon the wreath diameter, use as many pomegranates and apples as necessary.

CORK WREATH
(designed by Betty Jo Jones)

MATERIALS
As many assorted corks as you can find: wine, champagne, liqueurs, etc.
Round wooden toothpicks
Straw wreath base (ours is 22 inches across)

Simply spear corks with toothpicks, and push into the straw base as close together as possible. We added a knotted piece of fabric rather than a bow.

RIBBON WREATH
(designed by Ruth Katz)

MATERIALS
An assortment of ⅝- to 1-inch-wide ribbon (we used taffeta, satin and grosgrain in different shades of pink)
Styrofoam wreath base (ours measures 8 inches across)
Straight pins

Cut the ribbons into 3-inch lengths, and fold each length in half, right side out. Slightly gather the two loose ends, and secure through wreath base with a straight pin. Continue in rows, starting at outer edge and working inward, slightly overlapping each loop of ribbon. Secure one large bow (we used a candy-stripe pattern for contrast) at center.

All ribbon by Wrights.

BUBBLE-GUM WREATH
(designed by Ruth Katz)

MATERIALS
White all-purpose, quick-setting glue
Assorted-color bubble-gum balls and jawbreakers
Styrofoam wreath base (ours is 12 inches across)

Starting at outside edge and working inward, begin by gluing gum balls and jawbreakers in a random color arrangement very close together on wreath base. When you have an even layer, begin to glue the candies on top of one another and in between until wreath is built up to a thickness of about two inches. (The surface will not be level—it is the bumpy texture you want to achieve.) ∎

O TANNENBAUM, O TANNENBAUM

continued from page 149

RIBBON ORNAMENTS

Materials needed for each ornament: 1 Styrofoam ball, 3 inches in diameter; two different colors of ⅝-inch ribbon (42 inches of each color); 24 inches of ¼-inch ribbon (this is enough to wrap the ornament *once*, tie a bow and make a hanger loop; you will have to add 10 inches to the length of the ribbon for each additional wrap); straight pins; scissors

Beginning with one color of ⅝-inch ribbon, wrap the ribbon once around the ball so that the ends meet at the top. Cut the ribbon, and pin the piece to the Styrofoam with straight pins in four different places. Continue wrapping, cutting and pinning this color until you have used all the ribbon. Then repeat the process with the second color, allowing sections of the first color to show through. Be sure that you cut and pin each layer of ribbon—if you try to twist the ribbon instead of cutting it, the resultant ornament will be lumpy.

To complete the ornament, wrap it once around with the ¼-inch ribbon, tying a bow at the top to cover the place where the cut ribbons meet. Use remaining ¼-inch ribbon to make a hanger loop, and pin it in place under the bow. ∎

continued from page 137

TINY TOY WREATH

(pictured)

MATERIALS
Floral wire
Assorted small toys—stuffed, wooden, ceramic, etc.
1 evergreen wreath
Wire cutters
Ribbon, ½" to 1" wide (enough length to wrap around the wreath plus make a bow)
6-loop bow (see page 145)

DIRECTIONS
1. Wire each toy to the wreath in a pleasing arrangement, twisting the wire tightly at back several times. Trim off the ends with wire cutters.

2. Starting at the top of the wreath, wrap the ribbon several times around the wreath, carefully going in between the toys as pictured. At the top, tie the ribbon ends together at back.

3. Add a 6-loop bow at the top: Spread wires and twist tightly at back. Make a loop for hanging the wreath. Cut off extra wire.

DELLA ROBBIA CANDLEHOLDER

(pictured)

MATERIALS
White craft glue
1 large candle
1 heavy cardboard circle, 7" in diameter
3 large white-pine cones
Utility knife
Small cones, acorns and other nuts of various sizes
Dried flowers, herbs and spices (see wreath)
Small red bow (optional)

DIRECTIONS
1. Glue the candle to the center of the cardboard ring. (To make it really secure, push a nail up through the cardboard into the candle.)

2. Hold a white-pine cone by the top petals; carefully split the cone in half, down the center, with the utility knife. Pluck off the petals. Repeat with the remaining white-pine cones.

3. Glue one row of white-pine-cone petals along the edge of the cardboard circle, with the rounded edge of each petal extending ½" over the outer edge of the circle. Glue a second row of petals ½" in from the first row.

4. Glue small cones in a circle around the candle. Fill in with acorns and nuts, building up several inches from the cardboard base. Glue on the flowers, herbs and spices last.

5. If desired, attach a small red bow.

DELLA ROBBIA WREATH

(pictured)

MATERIALS
White craft glue
1½ yards of 2"-wide red velvet or satin ribbon
1 Styrofoam ring, about 9" in diameter and 2" wide (see Note)
5 large white-pine cones (an easy way to recognize a white pine: The needles grow in clusters of five)
Utility knife
Assorted cones and nuts: red-pine cones, acorns, hemlock cones, peanuts, filberts, walnuts, chestnuts, hazelnuts, horse chestnuts, etc.
Dried flowers, herbs and spices: cardamom, ginger root, cinnamon sticks, nutmeg, bay leaves, whole cloves, goldenrod, wormwood, lilacs, strawflowers, statice, yellow yarrow, rosemary, etc.

DIRECTIONS
1. Glue ribbon to outer and inner edges of ring for a finished look.

2. Hold a white-pine cone by the top petals; carefully split the cone in half, down the center, with the utility knife. Pluck off the petals. Repeat with the remaining white-pine cones.

3. Glue one row of white-pine-cone petals along the inner edge of the ring, with the rounded edge of each petal extending ½" over the inner edge of the ring.

4. Repeat Step 3 for the outer edge of the ring.

5. Glue the assorted cones and nuts to the ring in a pleasing arrangement. Start with the larger cones; then fill in with smaller nuts. Glue on the flowers, herbs and spices last. Be sure to fill in all spaces. Build up the arrangement so that the wreath takes on a rounded shape.

Note: You may use a heavy cardboard ring, 9" in diameter. Omit ribbon. ∎

HANDMADE TREASURES FOR YOUR TREE

continued from page 153

LACE 'HATS'

MATERIALS
(Makes 2 hats)
1 Styrofoam ball, 1½" in diameter
1¼ yards of wedding lace, 2¾" wide
1 yard of double-faced satin ribbon, ⅛" wide
White craft glue
Thread to match ribbon
Nylon thread for hanger

DIRECTIONS
1. Use a knife to cut Styrofoam ball in half.

2. Cut two 5½" pieces of lace and two 5½" pieces of ribbon. Weave one ribbon through each piece of lace, creating your own design (see photo).

3. Cover each Styrofoam ball half with lace, gluing the ends underneath, on flat side of ball.

4. Cut remaining lace in half into two 17" pieces. Knot thread and baste along one long edge of each piece of lace. Pull thread tightly to gather lace into a circle. Knot to secure.

5. Glue flat part of each ball onto a lace circle.

6. Cut remaining ribbon in half. Glue a ribbon around the base of each ball, then tie a bow.

7. Use nylon thread to string a loop through back of lace circle; knot.

GOLDEN-CONES BASKET

MATERIALS
White craft glue
1 piece dry floral foam, 1" square
1 basket, about 2" in diameter
Spanish moss
2 stems bleached baby's breath
Floral wire
5 hemlock cones
3 pieces golden yarrow
Gold velvet ribbon, ⅜" wide

DIRECTIONS
1. Glue floral-foam block to bottom of basket. Cover block with small amount of Spanish moss.

2. Cut baby's breath into pieces 1½" long. Insert in block, filling the basket.

3. Attach a piece of wire around the base of each cone; twist to secure. Insert in block through baby's breath, one in middle and the other four evenly spaced around edge.

4. Insert yarrow pieces between cones.

5. Make a tiny 6-loop bow (see page 145 for directions). Insert between cones.

6. Cut 4" length of ribbon; glue ends together under handle to make hanger. ∎

FOUR

HOLIDAY GIFTS WITH A HOMEMADE TOUCH

Homemade holiday gifts are always among the most treasured because they are much more than presents: They are gifts of your time, imagination and thoughtfulness that whisper to the receiver, "I really care about you." Take a good look at your holiday list. Surely there's someone who would really appreciate one of our fabulous fruitcakes or prettily packaged preserves. Our freeze-ahead breads make delightful last-minute presents, and one taste from our candy counter will send your favorite sweet-tooth owner into seventh heaven. There are great hors-d'oeuvres gifts for the holiday party host or hostess...plus unique food-basket ideas that can solve your can't-find-the-perfect-present problems.

Turning from foods to crafts...is there anyone on your list, young or just young at heart, who loves teddy bears? We have a family of seven adorable bears to crochet. There are also easy-to-follow instructions for a colorful wall hanging and a cross-stitch design, plus six whimsical stockings that will give Santa a big chuckle. Kids and nonsewers can easily create our stunningly simple ornaments, decorations and gifts with just some glue, ribbon, lace...and imagination.

Finally, we show you more than 40 clever ways to make the wrappings as special and personalized as the homemade gifts within. To paraphrase an old saying, "'Tis just as wonderful to give as it is to receive."

FABULOUS FRUITCAKES

GEORGE RATKAI

Who wouldn't love to receive one of these, our very best collection of fruitcakes! Clockwise, from top left: Sour-Cream Fruitcake dribbled with frosting and fruit; a frosted sherry-soaked loaf with stripes of fruit; Grandma's Fruitcake laced with coconut and bedecked with nuts and cherries; White Fruitcake with a wreath of marzipan; an almond-trimmed Dundee Cake; the Dearborn Inn's spicy variation; and the traditional moist, frosted English Fruitcake. Recipes for these delights, including smaller versions of the latter two cakes, begin on page 160.

continued from page 159

All recipes are pictured on pages 158 and 159.

SOUR-CREAM FRUITCAKE

6 egg whites (¾ cup)
3 cups sifted all-purpose flour
¼ teaspoon baking soda
⅛ teaspoon salt
2 cups sugar
1 cup (2 sticks) butter or margarine
6 egg yolks
1 cup sour cream
1 teaspoon vanilla extract
1 teaspoon almond extract
1 jar (8 oz) mixed candied fruit, coarsely chopped
1 cup walnuts, coarsely chopped
Frosting Glaze, recipe follows
1 jar (3½ oz) mixed candied peel

1. In medium bowl of electric mixer, let egg whites warm to room temperature—about 1 hour.
2. Preheat oven to 350F. Grease and flour a 10-inch bundt pan or tube pan.
3. Sift together flour, baking soda and salt.
4. With electric mixer at high speed, beat egg whites until foamy. Gradually beat in 1 cup sugar, beating after each addition. Continue beating until soft peaks form when beaters are slowly raised.
5. In large bowl of electric mixer, using the same beaters, beat butter with remaining sugar until light. Beat in egg yolks, one at a time. Then beat until mixture is light and fluffy.
6. At low speed, beat in flour mixture (in thirds) alternately with sour cream (in halves), beginning and ending with flour.
7. Add vanilla and almond extracts, chopped candied fruit and the walnuts; mix until well combined.
8. With wooden spoon, fold in egg-white mixture just until blended.
9. Turn into prepared pan; bake 1 hour and 15 minutes, or until a cake tester inserted in center comes out clean.
10. Cool on wire rack 30 minutes. Remove from pan; cool completely.
11. Before serving, make Frosting Glaze. With teaspoon, drizzle over top of cake, letting it run down side. Decorate with candied peel, as pictured. *Makes 20 servings.*

FROSTING GLAZE

¾ cup confectioners' sugar
1½ to 2 tablespoons milk
⅛ teaspoon almond extract

In small bowl, combine confectioners' sugar, milk and almond extract; beat until smooth. Makes a thin glaze.

MRS. HALKS' FRUITCAKE

1 lb diced mixed candied fruit
½ lb candied cherries, halved
½ lb cubed candied pineapple, halved
1 pkg (15 oz) white raisins
1 cup sherry
2 cups (4 sticks) butter, softened
2 cups sugar
10 eggs
4 cups all-purpose flour
Sherry
Mrs. Halks' Frosting Glaze, recipe follows
Candied green and red cherries, chopped

1. Day before, prepare fruit mixture: In large bowl, combine mixed fruit, cherries, pineapple, raisins and 1 cup sherry; mix well. Let stand at room temperature, covered, overnight.
2. Next day, prepare pans. Line three (8½-by-4½-by-2⅝-inch) greased loaf pans with strips of greased brown paper.
3. Preheat oven to 275F.
4. In large bowl, with electric mixer at high speed, beat butter, sugar and 1 egg until smooth and fluffy. Add remaining eggs, beating well after each addition until smooth and light.
5. At low speed, beat in flour. Add batter to fruit mixture; mix until well combined. Turn batter into prepared pans, dividing evenly.
6. Bake 2 hours and 20 minutes, or until cake tester inserted in center comes out clean.
7. Cool completely in pans on wire rack. Turn out of pans; gently peel off paper. Wrap each of the cooled cakes in a piece of cheesecloth that has been soaked in ½ cup sherry; wrap in foil. Store in refrigerator two to three weeks, to develop flavor.
8. To decorate before serving or giving as gift, make Mrs. Halks' Frosting Glaze. Spread over tops of cakes, letting it run down sides. Decorate as desired with green and red candied cherries. *Makes 3 (2½-pound) loaves.*

MRS HALKS' FROSTING GLAZE

2¼ cups confectioners' sugar
2½ to 3 tablespoons milk

In medium bowl, combine sugar and milk; mix well.

GRANDMA'S FRUITCAKE

1 jar (8 oz) mixed candied fruit
1 jar (8 oz) candied pineapple chunks
1 jar (3½ oz) candied red cherries, halved
1 jar (4 oz) candied green cherries, halved
1 cup white raisins
1 cup chopped pecans
1 cup chopped walnuts
½ cup sliced almonds
½ cup flaked coconut
⅓ cup unsweetened pineapple juice
1 teaspoon rum flavoring
1¼ cups all-purpose flour
¾ teaspoon baking powder
½ teaspoon salt
½ cup (1 stick) butter or margarine, softened
½ cup sugar
3 eggs

DECORATION
1 tablespoon light corn syrup
2 tablespoons candied red cherries, halved
2 tablespoons candied green cherries, halved
½ cup whole pecans

1. Lightly grease and line with brown paper a 9¾-inch ring mold (9-cup size). Grease paper as well.
2. In large bowl, combine candied fruit, pineapple, cherries, raisins, pecans, walnuts, almonds, coconut, pineapple juice and rum flavoring; mix well.
3. Sift flour with baking powder and salt; set aside. Preheat oven to 275F.
4. In large bowl of electric mixer, at high speed, beat butter with sugar and eggs until light and fluffy—about 2 minutes. At low speed, blend in flour mixture just until combined.
5. Pour batter over fruit mixture; mix thoroughly. Turn into prepared ring mold. Bake 2 hours, or until cake tester inserted in cake comes out clean.
6. Let cake cool in pan 30 minutes on rack. Loosen edge from pan with spatula. Turn out on rack to cool 1 hour before removing paper (or ring may break).
7. To store: Put cake in waxed-paper-lined tin box with a tight cover; place ½ apple in the hole. Cover top of cake with waxed paper. Keep cake in a cool place to mellow for 2 weeks; occasionally replace apple with fresh piece.
8. Before serving, decorate cake: Brush top of cake with corn syrup; decorate with red and green candied cherries and whole pecans, as pictured, to look like a wreath. *Makes one 4-pound fruitcake.*

WHITE FRUITCAKE

FRUIT MIXTURE
1½ cups blanched almonds, coarsely chopped
1 cup light raisins
1 jar (4 oz) diced candied citron
1 jar (3½ oz) candied red cherries, halved
1 jar (4 oz) candied pineapple slices, cut into strips
¼ cup rum or sherry

CAKE BATTER
¾ cup (1½ sticks) butter or margarine, softened
1 cup sugar
½ teaspoon almond extract
3 eggs
2 cups all-purpose flour
⅓ cup orange juice

Rum or sherry
White Fruitcake Frosting, recipe follows
Marzipan fruits (optional)
Pecans (optional)

1. Day before, prepare Fruit Mixture: In large bowl, combine almonds, raisins, citron, cherries, pineapple and ¼ cup rum; mix well. Let stand at room temperature, covered, overnight.

2. Next day, line a 9-inch tube pan: On heavy brown paper, draw a 14½-inch circle and cut out. Set pan in center of circle; draw around base of pan and tube. With pencil lines outside, fold paper into eighths; snip off tip. Unfold circle; cut along folds to circle drawn around base of pan. Grease both tube pan and paper well; fit paper, greased side up, into pan.

3. Make Cake Batter: Preheat oven to 275F.

4. In large bowl, with electric mixer at high speed, beat butter, sugar and almond extract until smooth and fluffy. Add eggs, one at a time, beating after each addition until light and fluffy.

5. At low speed, beat in flour (in fourths) alternately with orange juice (in thirds), beginning and ending with flour.

6. Add batter to fruit mixture; mix until well combined. Turn the batter into the prepared pan, packing lightly.

7. Bake 2½ hours, or until cake tester inserted in cake comes out clean. Let cool completely in pan on wire rack. Turn out of pan; peel off paper.

8. Wrap cooled cake in cheesecloth that has been soaked in ⅓ cup rum. Then wrap very tightly in plastic wrap or foil. Store in refrigerator. Resoak cheesecloth with rum as it dries out—about once a week. Store cake four to five weeks, to develop flavor.

9. To decorate before serving: Make White Fruitcake Frosting and spread over top of cake. If desired, arrange marzipan fruits, alternating with pecans, around the hole in the center of the cake, to look like a wreath. *Makes one 3¼-pound tube cake.*

WHITE FRUITCAKE FROSTING

1½ cups confectioners' sugar
1½ to 2 tablespoons milk

In small bowl, combine sugar and milk; beat until smooth.

DUNDEE CAKE

3 cups all-purpose flour
1½ teaspoons baking powder
¾ teaspoon salt
¼ teaspoon ground nutmeg
1½ cups dried currants
1 cup mixed candied fruits and peels
1 cup seedless raisins
¾ cup light raisins
½ cup candied red cherries, halved
1¼ cups (2½ sticks) butter or margarine, softened
1 cup sugar
5 eggs
¾ cup whole blanched almonds

1. Preheat oven to 325F. Grease well a 9-inch tube pan.

2. Sift flour with baking powder, salt and nutmeg.

3. In large bowl, combine currants, candied fruits and peels, raisins and cherries; mix well.

4. In large bowl, with electric mixer at medium speed, beat butter with sugar until light and fluffy. Add eggs, one at a time, beating well after each addition.

5. At low speed, gradually add flour mixture, beating until well combined.

6. With wooden spoon, stir fruit mixture into batter until combined. Turn into prepared pan; smooth top with spatula. Arrange almonds around edge and around opening of tube, as pictured.

7. Bake 1 hour and 20 minutes, or until cake tester inserted in cake comes out clean. If top of cake seems too brown, cover pan with a square of brown paper for last 30 minutes of baking.

8. Let cool in pan on wire rack 30 minutes. Remove from pan; let cool completely. Wrap in transparent wrap and foil; store in cool place. *Makes one 9-inch tube cake.*

continued on page 179

PRESERVED PRESENTS

Give gleaming glass jars filled with Red-Pepper Jelly; an Italian favorite, Antipasto Medley; easy-to-make Preserved Kumquats; Dilled Mustard Sauce; Onion Marmalade, wonderful as a sauce with cold meats; Pickled Dried Fruit in a rum-flavored, spicy syrup; or tangy Cranberry Chutney.

HOMEMADE
FOR THE HOLIDAYS

Here is a dazzling array of food gifts to make and package prettily. They cost less, and mean more, than similar store-bought delicacies. One more personal touch: Attach a recipe card with serving suggestions. Recipes begin on page 168.

SNACKS AND NIBBLES

Give a box of delectable White- or Dark-Chocolate-Dipped Dried Fruits; a jar of crunchy Spiced Sugar Peanuts or Oriental Pecans for "nutty" friends; a combination of two all-time favorites: Pizza-Flavored Popcorn.

FESTIVE SPREADS

Succulent spreads for cheese lovers: Garlic-Herb Cheese presented on a pretty plate (given for keeps); Low-Calorie Cheese Spread with crisp vegetables; Piquant Cheese Logs studded with assorted nuts (these can be made ahead).

SWEET
TREATS
Get a head start on
the holidays with
these mini-treats that
you bake and freeze
now…to give later on.

Five fabulous holiday breads

Apricot-glazed individual babas au rhum

Mouth-watering Danish pastry wreaths

A perfect plum of a pudding

A treasure chest of tiny fruitcakes

PARTY PANACHE

These gifts from the hearth make fabulous take-alongs for the next party you're invited to. They're great looking, great tasting and made inexpensively in your own kitchen. Clockwise from the top: Crisp Breadflats in a napkin holder; a tin of Savory Cheddar Crackers; a jar of Marinated Goat Cheese; Jalapeño Cheese Bell on a serving platter; Turkey Terrine on a wooden cutting board; Speedy Soft Pretzels stacked on a wooden mallet; bagged Party Popcorn Mix.

THE SWEETEST GIFT

GEORGE RATKAI

Homemade Christmas candy is always welcome, and the array above includes something for every taste. At top, Christmas Popcorn Balls with red and green cherries; center, Old-Fashioned Hard Candy flavored with anise and peppermint; bottom left, Candied Pineapple Rings. For chocolate lovers, feast your eyes on the Chocolate-Date Yule Log, bottom right; to the left, a crystal dish with caramel-centered chocolate Turtles (pecans form the head and feet), Chocolate Surprises and Holiday Chocolate Clusters, among other treats. Make an extra batch of these confections for the family's sweet tooth, too! Recipes begin on page 175.

continued from page 163

All recipes are pictured on pages 162 to 166.

PRESERVED PRESENTS

RED-PEPPER JELLY

4 medium red peppers (1½ lb)
3¼ cups sugar
½ cup cider vinegar
1 teaspoon hot red-pepper sauce
1 pouch (3 oz) liquid pectin

1. Wash peppers. Cut in half; remove and discard stems, ribs and seeds. Cube peppers. In food processor or blender, process or blend the peppers until very finely chopped.
2. Strain peppers to get 1 cup juice. (Discard pepper solids, or reserve for other recipes.)
3. In 5-quart Dutch oven, combine red-pepper juice, sugar, vinegar and red-pepper sauce; over high heat, bring to boiling, stirring constantly. Quickly stir in pectin; then bring to a full, rolling boil; boil hard 1 minute, stirring constantly.
4. Remove from heat; skim off foam with a metal spoon. Quickly ladle into four hot, sterilized half-pint jars. Cover at once with ⅛-inch hot paraffin. Seal jars with lids. Cool; label. *Makes 4 jars.*

ANTIPASTO MEDLEY

3 large red peppers (1½ lb)
2 large yellow peppers (1 lb)
2 large green peppers (1 lb)
2 pkg (9-oz size) frozen artichoke hearts

DRESSING
2 cups olive oil
½ cup lemon juice
1 teaspoon salt
4 small cloves garlic, minced

2 cups pitted black olives
1 can (2 oz) flat anchovies, drained

1. Wash peppers; drain well.
2. Place peppers on rack over broiler pan; broil, 4 inches from heat, until peppers become blistered and charred—about 15 minutes. With tongs, turn peppers every 3 to 5 minutes.
3. Place hot peppers in a large plastic bag. Let stand 15 minutes.
4. Meanwhile, cook artichokes according to package directions; drain. Cool completely.
5. With sharp knife, peel off charred skin of peppers. Cut each pepper into eighths. Remove stems, ribs and seeds.
6. Make Dressing: In large bowl, combine oil, lemon juice, salt and garlic.
7. In each of two 1-quart jars, layer

vegetables, olives and anchovies, as pictured. Pour dressing into jars, dividing evenly. Cover; label. Refrigerate overnight to develop flavor. Keeps well up to 1 week. Delicious served as an appetizer or used in a tossed salad. *Makes 2 jars.*

PRESERVED KUMQUATS

1 quart fresh kumquats
2 cups sugar
1 cup water
2 tablespoons Cointreau or Grand Marnier

1. Prepare kumquats: Remove stem ends and leaves; discard. Wash; drain well. Prick each kumquat several times with a small metal skewer.
2. In medium saucepan, combine sugar and water; over high heat, bring to boiling, stirring just until sugar is dissolved. Reduce heat; simmer, uncovered, 5 minutes.
3. Add Cointreau and kumquats; cook gently, uncovered, 30 to 40 minutes, or just until kumquats are tender.
4. Remove from heat. Ladle into two hot, sterilized 1-pint jars. Cover; cool completely. Label. Store in refrigerator. *Makes 2 jars.*

DILLED MUSTARD SAUCE

½ cup Dijon-style mustard
2 tablespoons dry mustard
¼ cup tarragon-flavored vinegar
⅓ cup salad oil
¼ cup chopped fresh dill or 1 tablespoon dried dill

1. In small bowl, combine mustards, vinegar and salad oil; mix well with wire whisk or wooden spoon.
2. Add dill; beat well.
3. Fill two clean small jars, dividing evenly. Cover; label. *Makes 1¼ cups or 2 small jars.*

ONION MARMALADE

2 lb small white onions
2 tablespoons butter or margarine
1 teaspoon salt
1 teaspoon pepper
½ cup sugar
½ cup red-wine vinegar
1 cup white wine
2 tablespoons grenadine syrup

1. Peel and quarter onions (very small onions can be left whole).
2. In a 10-inch skillet, melt butter. Add onions, salt, pepper and sugar. Cook, covered, over medium-high heat, stirring occasionally, until moisture evaporates—about 25 minutes.

3. Add vinegar, wine and grenadine. Continue cooking, uncovered and stirring occasionally, until liquid evaporates—about 30 minutes.
4. Remove from heat. Spoon into a 1-pint jar. Cover; cool completely. Label. Store in refrigerator. Nice to serve cold as a sauce or condiment with meat or pâté. *Makes 1 jar.*

PICKLED DRIED FRUIT

2 cups assorted dried fruit (apricots, raisins, figs, pears, peaches and apple slices)
1 cup light-brown sugar, firmly packed
1 cup granulated sugar
1½ cups cider vinegar
¼ cup light rum
2 cinnamon sticks, 2 inches long
4 whole allspice
2 whole cloves
½ cup fresh cranberries

1. Place dried fruits (except apple slices, if using) in 3-quart saucepan; cover with 2 cups cold water. Bring to boiling; simmer, covered, 5 to 6 minutes, or just until fruit softens. Add apple slices at the last minute. Drain fruit in colander.
2. In same saucepan, combine both kinds of sugar, vinegar, rum and spices tied in cheesecloth. Bring to boiling, stirring until sugar is dissolved. Return dried fruit to saucepan; simmer, covered and stirring occasionally, until fruit is almost plump—10 minutes. Add cranberries; cook 5 minutes. Remove and discard spices.
3. Ladle fruit and syrup into a 1-quart jar. Cover; cool completely. Label. Store in refrigerator at least 1 week before gift-giving, to allow flavors to blend. *Makes 1 jar.*

CRANBERRY CHUTNEY

1½ cups fresh or frozen cranberries
1½ cups distilled white vinegar
1½ cups sugar
¼ cup slivered, peeled fresh ginger
1 clove garlic, minced
1 teaspoon mustard seed
¾ teaspoon salt
⅛ teaspoon red-pepper flakes
2½ cups cubed, peeled tart apple
½ cup golden raisins
1 cup walnut pieces

1. Wash cranberries; remove stems.
2. In 5-quart Dutch oven, combine vinegar, sugar, ginger, garlic, mustard seed, salt and red-pepper flakes. Over high heat, bring to boiling, stirring to dissolve sugar. Reduce heat; simmer, uncovered, 5 minutes.
3. Add apple and raisins; continue

simmering 5 minutes, or just until apple cubes are tender but still hold their shape. Add nuts and cranberries; simmer 2 minutes.

4. Remove from heat. Ladle into 1-quart jar. Cover; cool completely. Label, and store in refrigerator. *Makes 1 jar.*

SNACKS AND NIBBLES

WHITE- OR DARK-CHOCOLATE-DIPPED DRIED FRUITS

8 oz white chocolate
½ pkg (16-oz size) pitted dates
½ pkg (15-oz size) pitted prunes
½ cup semisweet chocolate pieces
2 teaspoons shortening
8 oz dried apricots

1. In top of double boiler over hot, not boiling, water, melt white chocolate until smooth enough to coat dates and prunes.
2. Remove top of double boiler from hot water. Cool slightly.
3. Dip dates and prunes, one at a time, into coating, covering halfway; let excess drip off. Place on tray lined with waxed paper. Repeat to dip all dates and prunes. Refrigerate until set—about 1 hour.
4. In top of double boiler, over hot, not boiling, water, melt semisweet chocolate with shortening. Dip apricots, as in Step 3, in dark chocolate; refrigerate.
5. Keep dipped fruits refrigerated between layers of waxed paper until ready to box or package for gifts. *Makes about 1½ pounds.*

SPICED SUGAR PEANUTS

3 cups unsalted peanuts
¼ cup (½ stick) butter or margarine
1 cup sugar
¼ cup light corn syrup
1 teaspoon vanilla extract
½ teaspoon ground cinnamon
¼ teaspoon ground cloves

1. Preheat oven to 250F.
2. Place peanuts in a jelly-roll pan; warm in oven 10 minutes.
3. Meanwhile, melt butter in medium saucepan; stir in sugar and corn syrup. Bring to boiling, stirring constantly. Cook over low heat, without stirring, 5 minutes.
4. Remove from heat; stir in vanilla, cinnamon and cloves. Pour over warm peanuts; toss until well combined.
5. Return to oven. Bake 1 hour, tossing occasionally.
6. Spread peanuts on waxed paper, to cool completely. Break up any large clusters. Pack in a 1-quart jar. Cover; label. *Makes 1 jar.*

ORIENTAL PECANS

¼ cup (½ stick) butter or margarine
4 cups (1lb) pecan halves
1 tablespoon light soy sauce
½ teaspoon crushed red-pepper flakes

1. Preheat oven to 300F.
2. In shallow roasting·pan, melt butter. Add pecans; toss until well coated.
3. Toast pecans in oven 30 minutes, stirring occasionally.
4. Remove from oven; stir in soy sauce and red-pepper flakes.
5. Cool completely at room temperature before packing in two 1-pint jars. *Makes 2 jars.*

PIZZA-FLAVORED POPCORN

2 tablespoons grated Parmesan cheese
1 teaspoon garlic powder
1 teaspoon Italian herb seasoning
1 teaspoon paprika
½ teaspoon salt
Dash pepper
2 quarts freshly popped or hot popcorn (about ½ cup unpopped)

1. In blender, blend Parmesan cheese, garlic powder, Italian herb seasoning, paprika, salt and pepper until finely ground—about 3 minutes.
2. Place popcorn in large bowl; sprinkle with cheese mixture. Toss to coat evenly.
3. Package in decorative tin lined with waxed paper. Cover; label. *Makes 3 quarts.*

FESTIVE SPREADS

GARLIC-HERB CHEESE

2 pkg (8-oz size) cream cheese, softened
½ cup (1 stick) butter (not margarine), softened
2 teaspoons Worcestershire sauce
¼ teaspoon hot red-pepper sauce
1 small clove garlic, minced
1 teaspoon dried thyme leaves
Dried tarragon, thyme and parsley leaves
1 pkg (10 oz) sesame crackers

1. Line a straight-sided, decorative 2½- or 3-cup mold with plastic wrap, extending it up the side of the mold.
2. In medium bowl, with electric mixer, beat cream cheese, butter, Worcestershire, red-pepper sauce, garlic and 1 teaspoon thyme until well mixed.
3. Pack cheese mixture into mold. Wrap with plastic; refrigerate until firm—several hours or overnight.
4. Lift out of mold onto plate for gift-giving. Remove plastic wrap. Sprinkle side of cheese with dried herbs. Cover with plastic wrap; refrigerate until gift-giving time.

5. For gift-giving, add a ribbon bow to cheese plate; give it with the package of crackers. *Makes about 2½ cups.*

LOW-CALORIE CHEESE SPREAD

1 can (8 oz) crushed pineapple packed in juice, drained
2 pkg (7½-oz size) farmer's cheese
½ cup chopped green pepper
¼ cup chopped green onion
1 very large red or green pepper
Fresh vegetables: celery chunks, carrot sticks, zucchini slices, cauliflowerets

1. In medium bowl, with fork, mix pineapple, cheese, chopped green pepper and green onion until well blended. Refrigerate, covered, several hours, to blend flavors.
2. Wash red pepper. Remove and discard stem, ribs and seeds. Cut thin slice off bottom so pepper will stand upright.
3. For gift-giving: Spoon some cheese mixture into red pepper. Place in napkin-lined basket. Surround with vegetables. *Makes 3 cups.*

PIQUANT CHEESE LOGS

½ cup light beer
1½ lb natural sharp Cheddar cheese, cubed
6 oz blue cheese, softened
3 tablespoons butter or margarine
1 teaspoon dry mustard
1 teaspoon Worcestershire sauce
1 teaspoon onion powder
Dash hot red-pepper sauce
⅓ cup chopped walnuts
⅓ cup chopped pistachios
¼ cup chopped pecans
5 pecan halves
¼ cup chopped unblanched almonds
5 unblanched almond slices

1. In food processor, place beer and half the Cheddar cheese; process until smooth, occasionally scraping side of container with rubber spatula. Add remaining Cheddar and continue to process until well mixed.
2. Add blue cheese, butter, mustard, Worcestershire, onion powder and red-pepper sauce; process until mixture is smooth. Divide mixture into four equal parts, and place each on a sheet of foil or plastic·wrap. Shape each into a 4-inch log. Wrap logs, and refrigerate them several hours, or until firm.
3. Press chopped walnuts onto sides of one cheese log; wrap in plastic wrap, allowing 4 inches of wrap at each end to tie with narrow ribbon. Coat another log with pistachios; wrap, and tie with ribbon.

continued on page 170

...ued from page 169

4. Press chopped pecans onto ends of a cheese log; decorate sides with pecan halves. Wrap in plastic wrap. Coat ends of remaining log with chopped almonds and decorate sides with sliced almonds; wrap.

5. Refrigerate logs; they keep well up to 2 weeks. *Makes 4 logs.*

SWEET TREATS

MINIATURE BABAS AU RHUM

¼ cup warm water (105 to 115F)
1 pkg active dry yeast
2 tablespoons sugar
½ teaspoon salt
3 eggs
1¾ cups sifted all-purpose flour
¼ cup (½ stick) butter or margarine, softened

RUM SYRUP
2½ cups sugar
2 cups water
1 unpeeled medium-size orange, sliced crosswise
½ unpeeled lemon, sliced crosswise
1½ cups light rum

Apricot Glaze, recipe follows
Red candied cherries
Angelica
Sweetened whipped cream (optional)

1. Lightly grease 16 (2½-inch) muffin-pan cups. Check temperature of warm water with thermometer.

2. Sprinkle yeast over water in small bowl of electric mixer, stirring until dissolved.

3. Add 2 tablespoons sugar, the salt, eggs and 1¼ cups flour. At medium speed, beat 4 minutes, or until smooth, scraping side of bowl and guiding mixture into beaters with rubber spatula.

4. Add butter; beat 2 minutes, or until very well blended.

5. At low speed, beat in rest of flour; beat until smooth—about 2 minutes. Batter will be thick.

6. Turn batter into prepared muffin cups, using 1 rounded tablespoon batter for each cup; cover with towel.

7. Let rise in warm place (85F), free from drafts, 1 hour, or until babas have risen to rims of muffin cups—more than double in bulk.

8. Meanwhile, make Rum Syrup: In medium saucepan, combine sugar with water; bring to boiling, stirring until sugar is dissolved. Boil, uncovered, 10 minutes.

9. Reduce heat. Add orange and lemon slices; simmer 10 minutes. Remove from heat. Add rum.

10. Preheat oven to 375F. Bake babas 15 to 18 minutes, or until golden-brown.

11. Turn out babas; arrange in a 13-by-9-by-2-inch pan, tops up. Poke holes in babas, at ½-inch intervals, with cake tester.

12. Pour hot syrup over babas; let stand, basting occasionally, at least 1 hour, or until all syrup is absorbed. (Turn babas upside down in syrup several times.)

13. Meanwhile, make Apricot Glaze. Brush tops and sides with glaze. Decorate with candied cherries and angelica, as pictured.

14. Serve slightly warm, with sweetened whipped cream, if desired. *Makes 16 servings.*

Note: For gift-giving, babas may be baked, soaked in syrup, then cooled completely. Freezer-wrap, pan and all; freeze. To gift-wrap: Let stand at room temperature 1 hour; glaze and decorate. To serve: Reheat, foil-wrapped, 20 minutes at 350F. Serve as above.

APRICOT GLAZE

1 cup apricot preserves
1 teaspoon grated lemon peel
2 teaspoons lemon juice

In small saucepan, over low heat, melt apricot preserves. Stir in lemon peel and juice; strain. Refrigerate until ready to use.

LEMON TEA BREAD

2 cups all-purpose flour
1½ teaspoons baking powder
¼ teaspoon salt
½ cup (1 stick) butter or margarine
1 cup sugar
2 eggs
⅓ cup milk
½ cup chopped walnuts
2 teaspoons grated lemon peel

SYRUP
¼ cup lemon juice
⅓ cup sugar
Candied lemon or orange peel (optional, for garnish)

1. Lightly grease two foil loaf pans, 7 by 3½ by 2 inches. Preheat oven to 350F.

2. Sift flour with baking powder and salt; set aside.

3. In large bowl of electric mixer, at medium speed, beat butter with 1 cup sugar until light and fluffy. Add eggs, one at a time, beating well after each addition; beat until very light and fluffy.

4. At low speed, beat in flour mixture alternately with milk, beginning and ending with flour mixture; beat just until combined.

5. Stir in nuts and lemon peel. Turn batter into prepared pans. Place on cookie

sheet. Bake 45 minutes, or until cake tester inserted in center comes out clean.

6. Make Syrup: In small saucepan, combine lemon juice and sugar; cook, stirring, 1 minute, or until syrupy. Pour evenly over breads as soon as they are removed from oven.

7. Let cool in pans 10 minutes. Remove to wire rack; let cool completely.

8. To store: Wrap each loaf in foil, plastic wrap or moisture-vapor-proof freezer paper; seal and label. Freeze.

9. Remove number of loaves desired from freezer. Let thaw, still in wrapping, at room temperature several hours, or until loaves reach room temperature. If desired, decorate, as pictured, with candied lemon or orange peel. *Makes 2 loaves.*

PINEAPPLE-APRICOT-NUT LOAF

2¾ cups sifted all-purpose flour
3 teaspoons baking powder
¼ teaspoon baking soda
¼ teaspoon salt
¾ cup sugar
⅓ cup (⅔ stick) butter, melted
1 egg
⅓ cup milk
1 can (8 oz) crushed pineapple, in juice, undrained
⅓ cup chopped dried apricots
¼ cup light raisins
1 tablespoon chopped candied green cherries or citron
1 cup chopped walnuts
Candied pineapple and diced apricots (optional, for garnish)

1. Preheat oven to 375F. Grease three foil loaf pans, 7 by 3½ by 2 inches. Sift flour with baking powder, soda and salt; set aside.

2. In large bowl, combine sugar, melted butter and egg; using wooden spoon, beat until ingredients are well blended.

3. Add milk, undrained pineapple, apricots, raisins and cherries; blend well.

4. Add flour mixture; beat just until combined. Stir in nuts. Turn into prepared pans. Place on cookie sheet.

5. Bake 45 minutes, or until cake tester inserted in center comes out clean.

6. Let cool in the pans 10 minutes. Remove from pans; let cool completely on wire rack.

7. To store: Wrap each loaf in foil, plastic wrap or moisture-vapor-proof freezer paper; seal and label. Freeze.

8. Remove number of loaves desired from freezer. Let thaw, still in wrapping, at room temperature several hours, or until loaves reach room temperature. If desired, decorate, as pictured, with candied pineapple and diced apricots. *Makes 3 loaves.*

PUMPKIN LOAVES

2 cups all-purpose flour
½ teaspoon salt
½ teaspoon baking powder
1 teaspoon baking soda
1 teaspoon ground cloves
1 teaspoon ground cinnamon
1 teaspoon ground nutmeg
2 cups sugar
¾ cup (1½ sticks) butter or margarine,
    softened
2 eggs
1 can (1 lb) pumpkin
Confectioners' sugar (optional, for garnish)

1. Lightly grease three foil loaf pans, 7 by 3½ by 2 inches. Preheat oven to 350F.

2. Sift flour with salt, baking powder, soda and spices; set aside.

3. In large bowl of electric mixer, at medium speed, beat sugar with butter just until blended. Add eggs, one at a time, beating well after each addition; continue beating until very light and fluffy. Beat in pumpkin. At low speed, beat in flour mixture until combined.

4. Turn batter into prepared pans, dividing evenly. Place on cookie sheet. Bake 50 to 55 minutes, or until cake tester inserted in center comes out clean.

5. Let cool in pans 10 minutes. Turn out onto wire racks to cool completely.

6. To store: Wrap each loaf in foil, plastic wrap or moisture-vapor-proof freezer paper; seal and label. Freeze.

7. Remove number of loaves desired from freezer. Let thaw, still in wrapping, at room temeperature several hours, or until loaves reach room temperature. If desired, decorate, as pictured, with confectioners' sugar. *Makes 3 loaves.*

DATE-NUT BREAD

1 pkg (8 oz) pitted dates, coarsely chopped
1½ cups boiling water
2¾ cups sifted all-purpose flour
1 teaspoon baking powder
1½ teaspoons baking soda
1 teaspoon salt
1 egg, beaten
1 cup sugar
2 tablespoons butter or margarine, melted
1 teaspoon vanilla extract
1 cup coarsely chopped walnuts
Dates and walnut halves (optional, for
    garnish)

1. In small bowl, combine dates with boiling water; let cool to room temperature.

2. Meanwhile, preheat oven to 350F. Grease two foil loaf pans, 7 by 3½ by 2 inches.

3. Sift flour with baking powder, soda and salt; set aside.

4. In medium bowl, with wooden spoon or rotary beater, beat egg, sugar, butter and vanilla until smooth.

5. Add cooled date mixture, mixing well. Then add flour mixture, beating with wooden spoon until well combined. Stir in nuts.

6. Turn batter into prepared pans. Place on cookie sheet. Bake 45 to 50 minutes, or until cake tester inserted in center comes out clean.

7. Let cool in pans 10 minutes. Remove from pans; cool completely on wire rack.

8. To store: Wrap each loaf in foil, plastic wrap or moisture-vapor-proof freezer paper; seal and label. Freeze.

9. Remove number of loaves desired from freezer. Let thaw, still in wrapping, at room temperature several hours, or until loaves reach room temperature. If desired, decorate, as pictured, with dates and walnut halves. *Makes 2 loaves.*

CRANBERRY-NUT BREAD

1 cup fresh cranberries
2 cups sifted all-purpose flour
¾ cup sugar
3 teaspoons baking powder
¼ teaspoon salt
½ cup walnuts, chopped
2 eggs
1 cup milk
¼ cup (½ stick) butter or margarine,
    melted
1 teaspoon vanilla extract
Cranberries and walnut halves (optional,
    for garnish)

1. Preheat oven to 350F. Grease two foil loaf pans, 7 by 3½ by 2 inches. Wash cranberries, removing stems; chop coarsely.

2. Sift flour with sugar, baking powder and salt into large bowl. Stir in cranberries and walnuts.

3. In small bowl, with rotary beater, beat eggs with milk, butter and vanilla.

4. Make well in center of cranberry mixture. Pour in egg mixture; with fork, stir just until dry ingredients are moistened.

5. Turn into prepared pans. Place on cookie sheet. Bake 40 to 45 minutes, or until golden-brown on top and cake tester inserted in center comes out clean.

6. Cool in pan 10 minutes. Remove from pan; cool on wire rack.

7. To store: Wrap each loaf in foil, plastic wrap or moisture-vapor-proof freezer paper; seal and label. Freeze.

8. Remove number of loaves desired from freezer. Let thaw, still in wrapping, at room temperature several hours, or until loaves reach room temperature. If desired, decorate, as pictured, with a few cranberries and walnut halves. *Makes 2 loaves.*

STEAMED PLUM PUDDINGS

1 jar (8 oz) diced mixed candied peel
¼ lb suet, finely chopped
⅓ cup finely chopped walnuts or pecans
1½ cups raisins
1 cup currants
1 tablespoon ground cinnamon
1½ teaspoons ground ginger
½ teaspoon ground allspice
¼ teaspoon ground nutmeg
¼ teaspoon salt
1 cup sugar
½ cup strawberry or cherry preserves
2 cups packaged dry bread crumbs
4 eggs
2 tablespoons milk
⅓ cup rum or brandy
⅓ cup sherry
Hard Sauce, recipe follows

1. Chop candied peel very fine.

2. In large bowl, combine peel, suet, nuts, raisins, currants, spices, salt, sugar, preserves and bread crumbs.

3. In medium bowl, beat eggs until very thick. Beat in milk.

4. To fruit-spice mixture, add beaten egg mixture, along with rum and sherry. Mix well with large spoon.

5. Turn batter into two well-greased 3- or 4-cup pudding molds, or two 3-cup Pyrex bowls. Wrap molds completely in several thicknesses of cheesecloth. Secure cheesecloth at tops with string. Place molds on trivet in kettle; pour in boiling water to come halfway up sides of molds; cover kettle; steam puddings 3 hours. (Water should boil gently; add water as needed.) Let cool right in mold.

6. To store: Refrigerate puddings, still in molds wrapped in cheesecloth, several weeks.

7. Gift-wrap, still in cheesecloth, along with half of Hard Sauce. (Include directions for resteaming pudding, below.)

8. To serve: Steam pudding, still in mold and covered with cheesecloth, on trivet in kettle as directed in Step 3. Steam pudding 30 minutes, or until heated through. Remove cheesecloth; loosen edge of pudding from mold with spatula; turn out on serving tray. Serve with Hard Sauce. *Each pudding makes 6 to 8 servings.*

continued on page 172

continued from page 171

HARD SAUCE

⅔ cup (1⅓ sticks) butter or margarine,
softened
2 teaspoons vanilla extract
2 cups confectioners' sugar

1. Day or two before serving or giving
as a gift: In small bowl, with electric
mixer at high speed, cream butter until
light.

2. Add vanilla and confectioners'
sugar; beat until fluffy. Divide in half.
Refrigerate in gift containers. *Makes 2
cups.*

SMALL FRUITCAKES

1 cup golden raisins
½ cup dark raisins
¼ cup dark rum or brandy
¼ lb candied pineapple
¼ lb candied red cherries
1 jar (8 oz) mixed candied peel
1 cup all-purpose flour
¼ teaspoon ground mace
¼ teaspoon ground cinnamon
¼ teaspoon baking soda
½ cup blanched whole almonds, coarsely
chopped
½ cup walnuts or pecans, coarsely chopped
¼ cup (½ stick) butter or margarine,
softened
½ cup granulated sugar
½ cup light-brown sugar, firmly packed
2 eggs, slightly beaten
1½ teaspoons milk
½ teaspoon almond extract
Rum or brandy
Unpeeled raw apple
Light corn syrup
Candied red and green cherries
Blanched whole almonds

1. In large bowl, combine golden and
dark raisins. Add rum; toss to combine.
Let stand, covered, overnight.

2. Prepare fruits: With sharp knife,
cut pineapple in thin wedges; cut ¼ pound
cherries in half; add to raisins with mixed
candied peel; mix well.

3. On sheet of waxed paper, sift ¾
cup flour with spices and baking soda; set
aside. Preheat oven to 325F.

4. Combine remaining ¼ cup flour
with nuts and fruits; toss lightly.

5. In large bowl of electric mixer, at
medium speed, beat butter until light.
Gradually beat in granulated sugar, then
brown sugar, beating until very light and
fluffy.

6. Beat in eggs, milk and almond extract until thoroughly combined.

7. At low speed, beat in flour mixture,
mixing just until combined. Turn batter
into fruits and nuts. Mix well with hands.

8. Turn into midget (2-inch) foil cups;
use one slightly rounded tablespoon batter per cup.

9. Bake 40 minutes, or until a cake
tester inserted near center comes out dry.

10. Let stand on wire rack to cool.

11. To store: Wrap cakes in cheesecloth soaked in rum or brandy. Place in a
cake tin with a tight-fitting cover. Add a
few pieces of unpeeled raw apple. (As
cheesecloth dries out, resoak in rum or
brandy.) Store in a cool place several
weeks.

12. To decorate cakes for giving:
Brush with corn syrup. Cut cherries in
half. Decorate cakes with almonds and
cherries, as pictured. *Makes 30.*

DANISH PASTRY WREATHS

1½ cups (3 sticks) butter or margarine,
softened
4 cups all-purpose flour
¾ cup milk
⅓ cup granulated sugar
1 teaspoon salt
½ cup warm water (105 to 115F)
2 pkg active dry yeast
1 egg

FILLING
1 can (8 oz) almond paste (1 cup)
¾ cup crushed zwieback (8)
½ cup (1 stick) butter, melted
1 egg
½ teaspoon almond extract

2 cups confectioners' sugar
2½ tablespoons milk
Candied red cherries
Angelica bits

1. In bowl, with wooden spoon, beat
butter and ¼ cup flour until smooth.
Spread on waxed paper (on wet surface)
to 12-by-8-inch rectangle. Refrigerate on
cookie sheet.

2. Heat ¾ cup milk slightly. Add
granulated sugar and salt; stir to dissolve. Cool to lukewarm.

3. If possible, check temperature of
warm water with thermometer. Pour into
large bowl; sprinkle with yeast; stir to
dissolve. Stir in milk mixture, egg and 3
cups flour; beat with wooden spoon until
smooth. Mix in rest of flour with hand
until dough leaves side of bowl.

4. Refrigerate, covered, ½ hour. Turn
out onto lightly floured pastry cloth. With
covered rolling pin, roll into 16-by-12-
inch rectangle.

5. Place chilled butter mixture on half
of dough; remove paper. Fold other half
of dough over butter; pinch the edges to
seal.

6. With fold at right, roll out from
center to a 16-by-8-inch rectangle. From
short side, fold dough into thirds, making
three layers; seal edges; chill 1 hour.

7. Repeat rolling and folding (if butter breaks through, brush with flour); seal
edges; chill ½ hour.

8. Roll, fold again and seal edges;
chill, wrapped in foil, 3 hours or overnight. Roll half of dough into a 22-by-8-
inch strip. (Chill other half.) Cut into thirds
lengthwise.

9. Mix Filling ingredients. Fill center
of each strip with ⅓ cup; close edges over
filling, pinching edges together tightly.

10. Cut in half crosswise. With hands,
roll each rope on lightly floured pastry
cloth to 14-inch length. Place 3 ropes
side by side; pinch tops together. Braid
into a strip.

11. Form wreath, 4 inches across in
center, on brown paper on cookie sheet;
pinch ends together to seal. Repeat with
other three ropes to form second wreath
on same cookie sheet. Repeat with other
half of chilled dough, to make four wreaths
in all.

12. Let rise in warm place 1 hour—
until double in bulk.

13. Preheat oven to 375F. Bake 25 to
30 minutes. Cool on rack; freezer-wrap
and freeze.

14. To serve or give as gift: Thaw ½
hour, still wrapped. Mix confectioners'
sugar and milk (if glaze seems thick, add
more milk); spread one-fourth over each
pastry. Decorate with red cherries and
angelica bits, as pictured. Wrap in plastic
wrap. *Makes 4 wreaths.*

PARTY PANACHE

CRISP BREADFLATS

1 pkg (1 lb) hot-roll mix
3 tablespoons butter or margarine
Salad oil
1 cup finely chopped onion
4 teaspoons dried thyme leaves

1. Prepare hot-roll mix as package
label directs, but omit butter or margarine in the dough. Knead as directed; place
in greased bowl. Cover, and let rise in
warm place (85F), free from drafts, until
almost double in bulk—30 minutes.

2. Punch dough down; cut into 8
pieces; shape each into a ball. Place on
lightly floured pastry cloth or board. Cover
with towel; let rise in warm place 30
minutes.

3. Meanwhile, in medium skillet, melt
butter. Pour 2 tablespoons melted butter
into small cup; keep warm. Add 1 tablespoon oil and the onion to skillet. Over

medium-low heat, sauté onion until soft and translucent—about 15 minutes. Remove from heat; set aside.

4. Preheat oven to 400F. Lightly oil two or three small cookie sheets. Directly on a cookie sheet, roll one ball of dough to an 11-inch circle. Sprinkle one-fourth of the onion over rolled dough.

5. Bake on bottom oven rack 4 minutes. Meanwhile, roll another ball of dough on another cookie sheet. When ready to bake, move first sheet to top oven rack; bake second sheet on bottom rack. Bake first sheet 4 to 5 minutes longer, or until breadflat is crisp and brown around edge. Remove breadflat to wire rack to cool.

6. Make two more balls of dough with onion, letting cookie sheets cool before rolling dough on them.

7. With remaining four balls of dough, roll out as above; brush each with 1 teaspoon melted butter, and sprinkle each with 1 teaspoon thyme.

8. Store breadflats in airtight container or in large plastic bag. Store at room temperature, or freeze if made several weeks ahead. To reheat, unwrap and loosely stack on cookie sheet; heat in 300F oven about 10 minutes to crisp. *Makes 8 breadflats.*

SAVORY CHEDDAR CRACKERS

2 cups all-purpose flour
½ teaspoon dry mustard
Dash ground red pepper
¾ cup (1½ sticks) butter or margarine, softened
1½ cups (6 oz) finely shredded Cheddar cheese
1 large egg, lightly beaten
Poppy seeds or paprika (optional)

1. In medium bowl, combine flour, mustard and pepper; mix well. With pastry blender or two knives, cut butter into flour mixture until it resembles coarse cornmeal. Stir in Cheddar. With hands, press mixture together to form a ball; divide in half. Wrap dough; refrigerate at least 30 minutes.

2. Preheat oven to 375F. Line two large cookie sheets with parchment or brown paper. On dampened surface, between two sheets of waxed paper, roll half of dough into 9-inch square. Remove top sheet of paper. With pastry wheel or knife, cut into diamonds 1½ inches on each side.

3. Place diamonds on a prepared cookie sheet, ½ inch apart; lightly brush with beaten egg. Sprinkle diamonds with poppy seeds or paprika, or leave plain. Bake 12 to 15 minutes, or till firm; remove to wire rack to cool. Repeat with

remaining dough. Reroll all dough trimmings; cut and bake. Store crackers in airtight container. *Makes about 5 dozen crackers.*

MARINATED GOAT CHEESE

2 cups salad oil
4 cloves garlic, halved lengthwise
20 black peppercorns
8 small dried hot red peppers
4 bay leaves
2 (10- or 11-oz size) or 3 (8-oz size) log-shape, uncoated, rindless goat cheeses (chèvre)

1. In small saucepan, over medium-high heat, heat ½ cup oil and the garlic until garlic begins to brown; add peppercorns, red peppers and bay leaves. Cook 30 seconds longer; remove from heat; let stand 10 minutes.

2. Meanwhile, cut each 10- or 11-ounce cheese log crosswise into 9 slices; if using 8-ounce logs, cut each into 6 slices. Arrange cheese slices in two 1-pint or one 1-quart wide-mouth jar.

3. Add remaining oil to saucepan. Pour oil and spices into jar over cheese. (If necessary, add more oil to cover cheese.) Cover jar; refrigerate several days to marinate. (Marinated cheese may be stored in refrigerator up to two or three weeks.)

4. To serve: Carefully lift cheese from oil. If desired, place on lettuce-lined plate; let cheese warm to room temperature. Or serve cheese warm: Place cheese in single layer in baking dish; bake cheese at 300F 5 minutes, or microwave at HIGH 30 seconds, until cheese is warm and very soft. Drizzle with some oil from the jar before serving. *Makes 18 slices.*

JALAPENO CHEESE BELL

1 lb Monterey Jack cheese, shredded
1 pkg (8 oz) cream cheese, softened
4 to 6 canned jalapeño peppers, drained, seeded and chopped (¼ cup)
½ cup chili sauce
¼ cup finely chopped green onion
Green-onion tops for garnish
Paprika
Chopped parsley

1. In food processor or large bowl of electric mixer, process or beat cheeses until well blended. Add peppers, chili sauce and onion; process or mix until well blended.

2. Turn cheese mixture onto serving plate or paper plate for gift-giving. Using a knife or metal spatula, form cheese into a bell 8½ inches long, 5½ inches wide at the base and about 1½ inches high.

3. To decorate, cut green-onion tops lengthwise into ⅛-inch strips; cut strips crosswise into ¾-inch lengths. Arrange in zigzag pattern across bell, making five rows. Cut foil or waxed paper into five 6-by-1-inch strips, or use 1-inch-wide masking tape. Place strips or tape, sticky side up, over onion pattern.

4. Dust top of bell with paprika. Remove strips or tape. Pat chopped parsley around top and bottom edges of bell. *Makes about 24 servings.*

continued on page 174

continued from page 173

TURKEY TERRINE

¼ cup (½ stick) butter or margarine
1 large onion, chopped
½ cup chopped green pepper
2 lb fresh or thawed frozen ground raw
    turkey
½ lb sweet Italian sausage, casings
    removed
½ cup chopped parsley
1 cup fresh white-bread crumbs (2 slices)
1 large egg
1 teaspoon salt
¼ teaspoon pepper
4 medium carrots, pared
1 cup pitted large ripe olives, halved
    lengthwise
1 jar (4 oz) whole pimientos, drained and
    cut into ½-inch strips
Watercress and pimiento

1. In medium skillet, melt butter; sauté onion and green pepper 5 minutes. Transfer to large bowl; cool. With fork, stir in turkey, sausage, parsley, bread crumbs, egg, salt and pepper; mix well.

2. Cut each carrot in half crosswise. Leaving narrow end of carrot whole, cut wide end in half or quarters lengthwise, according to thickness. In small saucepan, cover carrots with water, and bring to boiling. Simmer, covered, until tender. Drain; pat dry with paper towels; set aside. Butter four 5-by-3-by-2¼-inch disposable foil loaf pans. Preheat oven to 350F.

3. Spread ¾ cup turkey mixture into bottom of each loaf pan. Arrange about 7 olive halves, 2 carrot lengths and pimiento strips lengthwise over turkey mixture; layer each with ¾ cup turkey mixture, the remaining olives, carrots and pimiento, dividing evenly. Top each with remaining turkey mixture. Place loaf pans on cookie sheet.

4. Bake 20 to 30 minutes, or until terrine is firm and pulls away from side of pan. Cool; cover with plastic wrap; refrigerate overnight. (Juices will be reabsorbed.)

5. For gift-giving, unmold terrine, and garnish with watercress and pimiento. Cover with plastic wrap. *Makes 4 terrines (18 slices each).*

SPEEDY SOFT PRETZELS

3 to 3½ cups all-purpose flour
1 pkg fast-rising yeast
1 tablespoon sugar
1 teaspoon salt
1 cup very hot water (125 to 130F)
¼ cup salad oil
1 large egg, beaten with 1 teaspoon water
Coarse salt or sesame seeds

1. In large bowl, combine 1½ cups flour, the yeast, sugar and salt; mix well. With wooden spoon, stir water and oil into flour mixture until smooth. Gradually stir in enough remaining flour to make dough stiff enough to leave side of bowl.

2. Turn dough out onto lightly floured pastry cloth. Knead until smooth and elastic—about 5 minutes. Place in lightly greased bowl; turn dough over to bring up greased side. Cover with towel. Let rise in warm place (85F), free from drafts, until almost double in bulk—30 minutes.

3. On lightly floured pastry cloth or board, divide dough in half (cover one half until ready to use). Cut other half into 12 equal pieces. With palms of hands, roll each piece into an 18-inch rope.

4. To shape each rope into a pretzel, bring ends together, crossing 1½ inches from ends and making a circle. Twist ends once; place twisted part of rope in center of circle; place tip of ends on lower part of circle, 1 inch apart. Press tips onto pretzel, to seal.

5. Repeat with remaining half of dough. Place pretzels on ungreased cookie sheets, 1 inch apart. Cover with towel; let rise in warm place 15 minutes.

6. Preheat oven to 400F. Brush pretzels with egg mixture; sprinkle with coarse salt or sesame seeds. Bake 15 to 20 minutes, or until golden-brown. Remove to wire racks to cool. Store in airtight container. (Soft pretzels are best eaten the same day they are made. However, if made ahead, they can be baked, cooled, wrapped and frozen. *Makes 24 soft pretzels.*

PARTY POPCORN MIX

3 quarts freshly popped popcorn (about ½
    cup unpopped)
2 cups bite-size crisp bran-cereal squares
2 cups small pretzel sticks (unsalted if
    available)
1 cup unsalted dry-roasted mixed nuts
6 tablespoons unsalted margarine
2 teaspoons salt-free herb-and-spice blend

1. In large bowl, mix popcorn, cereal squares, pretzel sticks and nuts.

2. In small saucepan, melt margarine; stir in herb-and-spice blend. Drizzle seasoned margarine over popcorn mixture; toss until well blended. Store popcorn mixture in plastic bag or airtight container. *Makes about 16 cups.* ∎

continued from page 167

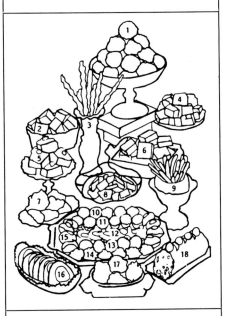

1. *Christmas Popcorn Balls.* 2. *Chocolate-Crunch Squares.* 3. *Barley-Sugar Twists.* 4. *Rocky Roads.* 5. *Divinity Fudge.* 6. *Holiday Chocolate Fudge.* 7. *California Popcorn Brittle.* 8. *Old-Fashioned Hard Candy.* 9. *Chocolate-Dipped Orange and Grapefruit Peel.* 10. *Chocolate Surprises.* 11. *Hazelnut Caramels.* 12. *Turtles.* 13. *Coconut Bonbons.* 14. *Holiday Chocolate Clusters.* 15. *Sugarplums.* 16. *Candied Pineapple Rings.* 17. *Seafoam.* 18. *Chocolate-Date Yule Log.*

CHRISTMAS POPCORN BALLS

6 tablespoons salad oil
½ cup unpopped popcorn (see Note)
1½ cups salted peanuts, coarsely chopped
¼ cup candied red cherries, quartered
¼ cup candied green cherries, quartered
1 cup light corn syrup
½ cup sugar
1 pkg (3 oz) strawberry or lime gelatine

1. To pop popcorn: Heat oil in heavy, 4-quart saucepan over medium heat. To test temperature of pan, add 1 kernel of corn; cover pan and shake often. When kernel pops, add ½ cup popcorn in a single layer; cover; shake pan often. Continue until all corn in pan is popped. Turn into large bowl.

2. Add peanuts and candied cherries to popcorn; toss to combine.

3. In a 1-quart saucepan, combine corn syrup and sugar. Cook, stirring with a wooden spoon, over medium heat, until sugar is dissolved. Without stirring, bring mixture to a full, rolling boil. Remove from heat.

4. Add gelatine; stir until dissolved.

5. Pour syrup mixture over popcorn mixture; toss to coat well.

6. Drop mixture onto waxed paper, to make about 1½ dozen mounds. With lightly buttered hands, form popcorn mixture into balls. Place on waxed-paper-lined tray, to dry at room temperature. *Makes about 1½ dozen.*

To store: When popcorn balls are thoroughly dry, wrap individually in plastic wrap or colored foil. Will keep several weeks at room temperature.

Note: Or use 1 bag (3½ ounces or about 12 cups) ready-to-eat popcorn.

CHOCOLATE-CRUNCH SQUARES

1 pkg (11 oz) social tea biscuits
2 tablespoons light corn syrup
2 tablespoons unsweetened cocoa
½ cup (1 stick) plus 3 tablespoons butter or margarine, melted
5 squares (1-oz size) semisweet chocolate
½ tablespoon butter or margarine

1. With rolling pin, crush tea biscuits to make 4 cups coarse crumbs.

2. In medium bowl, combine corn syrup and cocoa; mix well. Stir in melted butter; mix well. Add crumbs; mix well until thoroughly combined.

3. Line a metal ice-cube tray or a 9-by-5-by-3-inch loaf pan with waxed paper. Pack crumb mixture into tray, pressing in firmly. Refrigerate until firm—at least 1 hour.

4. In top of double boiler, over hot, not boiling, water, melt chocolate with ½ tablespoon butter. Spread over crumb mixture, making a smooth layer. Refrigerate until firm enough to cut.

5. Cut into 1½-inch squares. *Makes 18.*

BARLEY-SUGAR TWISTS

2 cups sugar
1 cup water
1 tablespoon cider vinegar
1 teaspoon peppermint extract
Red and green food colors

1. In a 2-quart saucepan, mix sugar, water and vinegar; cook over low heat, stirring, until sugar is dissolved.

2. Increase heat to medium; cook, covered, a few minutes, to let steam wash down sugar crystals. Cook, uncovered, without stirring, to 300F on candy thermometer, or until a few drops of syrup tested in cold water form hard, brittle threads. Add peppermint extract.

3. Turn half into another pan. To one half add a few drops red color. To other half add a few drops green color.

4. Pour onto two lightly greased cookie sheets. Cut into strips 6 inches long, ¾ inch wide.

5. Place in warm oven (250F). Remove one strip at a time, and twist into spirals. Place on tray. *Makes 24.*

ROCKY ROADS

18 large marshmallows
½ cup coarsely chopped walnuts
8 squares (1-oz size) semisweet chocolate

1. Line a 9-by-5-by-3-inch loaf pan with waxed paper. Lightly butter waxed paper.

2. Arrange marshmallows over bottom of prepared pan. Sprinkle walnuts on and around marshmallows.

3. In top of double boiler, over hot, not boiling, water, melt chocolate, stirring occasionally.

4. Remove from heat. Pour melted chocolate over marshmallows and nuts, smoothing with spatula. Let cool.

5. When firm, cut into rough squares with a sharp knife. *Makes about 1 pound.*

To store: Wrap each piece individually in waxed paper or plastic wrap. Will keep several weeks at room temperature.

DIVINITY FUDGE

3 egg whites (⅓ cup)
3 cups sugar
⅔ cup light corn syrup
¾ cup water
¼ teaspoon salt
1 teaspoon vanilla extract
1 cup coarsely chopped pecans or walnuts
6 candied cherries, quartered
6 candied cherries, halved
12 pecan or walnut halves

1. Turn egg whites into large bowl of electric mixer; let warm to room temperature—about 1 hour. Line an 11-by-7-by-1½-inch pan with waxed paper.

2. In a heavy 3-quart saucepan, combine sugar and corn syrup with the water. Cook, stirring, over low heat, to dissolve sugar. Cover; cook 1 minute longer to dissolve sugar crystals on side of pan.

3. Uncover; bring to boiling, without stirring; cook to 260F on candy thermometer, or until a small amount in cold water forms a ball hard enough to hold its shape. Let cool slightly.

4. When candy thermometer goes down to 250F, beat egg whites with salt until stiff peaks form when beaters are slowly raised.

5. Gradually pour hot syrup over egg whites in a thin stream, beating constantly at high speed until stiff peaks

continued on page 176

continued from page 175

form when beaters are raised—5 minutes.

6. Using wooden spoon, beat in vanilla, chopped pecans and quartered cherries; continue beating until mixture is stiff enough to hold its shape and looks dull.

7. Turn into prepared pan. Do not scrape saucepan. Let stand until firm. With sharp knife, cut into 24 pieces. Top each with a cherry half or pecan. *Makes 24 pieces.*

Note: Divinity may be kept for at least a week if wrapped in waxed paper and stored in a closed container.

HOLIDAY CHOCOLATE FUDGE

2 pkg (6-oz size) or 1 pkg (12 oz)
   semisweet chocolate pieces
1 can (14 oz) sweetened condensed milk
1 cup coarsely chopped walnuts
¼ cup coarsely chopped candied cherries

1. Line a 9-by-5-by-3-inch loaf pan with waxed paper. Let paper hang over sides slightly; butter lightly.

2. In top of double boiler, over hot, not boiling, water, melt chocolate. Add condensed milk, nuts and cherries; mix well.

3. Turn into prepared pan. Refrigerate several hours, or until firm. To turn out of pan, grasp paper and remove fudge in one block. Cut into squares. *Makes 2 pounds.*

CALIFORNIA POPCORN BRITTLE

1 cup light-brown sugar, firmly packed
1 cup granulated sugar
¾ cup light corn syrup
¾ cup water
½ teaspoon salt
6 tablespoons (¾ stick) butter or
   margarine
1⅓ cups already-popped popcorn
⅔ cup whole blanched almonds
⅔ cup pecans
½ teaspoon vanilla extract

1. Combine both kinds of sugar, corn syrup, water and the salt in a large saucepan. Stir with wooden spoon to mix well.

2. Heat, stirring, just until sugar is dissolved; then cook to 260F on candy thermometer, or until a few drops tested in cold water form a firm ball. Stir in butter, and continue cooking until candy thermometer reaches 270F, or until a few drops tested in cold water separate into hard, but not brittle, threads.

3. Remove from heat and stir in popcorn, almonds, pecans and vanilla.

4. Pour onto a lightly buttered cookie sheet. When cool and firm, break into pieces. *Makes about 1½ pounds.*

OLD-FASHIONED HARD CANDY

2 cups granulated sugar
1 cup water
¾ cup light corn syrup
Green and red food colors
1½ teaspoons anise extract
1½ teaspoons peppermint extract
Confectioners' sugar

1. In a heavy 2-quart saucepan, combine granulated sugar, water and corn syrup. Cook, stirring, until sugar is dissolved.

2. Cook, uncovered and without stirring, to 300F on candy thermometer, or until a few drops of syrup tested in cold water form hard, brittle threads.

3. Remove from heat; divide in half. To one half add 2 drops green color and 1½ teaspoons anise extract. To other half add 2 drops red color and 1½ teaspoons peppermint extract.

4. Pour each into a well-greased pan (about 8 by 8 by 2 inches). Just as soon as candy is cool, working quickly, cut into ½-inch strips with scissors; then cut strips into 1-inch pieces (you may need two people to do this).

5. Place candies in single layer on greased cookie sheet. When hard and brittle, sprinkle lightly with confectioners' sugar. *Makes 1 pound; about 60 pieces.*

CHOCOLATE-DIPPED ORANGE AND GRAPEFRUIT PEEL

1 large grapefruit
3 large navel oranges
1 cup honey
⅔ cup water
About 1 cup sugar
2 pkg (8-oz size) semisweet chocolate
   squares (16 1-oz squares)

1. With sharp knife, remove peel from grapefruit and oranges in quarters. With scissors or sharp knife, cut peel into ¼-inch-wide strips. Place in a 5-quart saucepan; cover with cold water; bring to a full boil; then drain. Repeat four times.

2. Transfer drained peel to a large skillet; add honey and ⅔ cup water. Cook slowly until all syrup is gone—about 60 minutes. Cook 15 minutes longer over very low heat, being careful not to scorch fruit.

3. Drain thoroughly; cool; then roll each strip in sugar. Spread out on cookie sheets in single layer; dry overnight. Next day, roll again in sugar.

4. In top of double boiler, over hot, not boiling, water, melt chocolate. Holding with tongs or impaled on a toothpick, dip each strip in the chocolate; drain off excess chocolate. Place on waxed paper on tray. Cool. Store in refrigerator. *Makes 2½ pounds.*

CHOCOLATE SURPRISES

1 pkg (6 oz) semisweet chocolate pieces
½ cup sour cream
Salt
1 cup vanilla-wafer crumbs (see Note)
2½ tablespoons rum
3 tablespoons butter or margarine, melted
2 tablespoons unsweetened cocoa
½ cup confectioners' sugar
½ cup finely chopped pecans or walnuts
1 jar (2¾ oz) chocolate sprinkles

1. Melt chocolate pieces in top of double boiler, over hot, not boiling, water. Remove from heat, and stir in sour cream and dash salt. Refrigerate overnight.

2. Next day: In small bowl, mix vanilla-wafer crumbs with rum, butter, cocoa, confectioners' sugar, chopped nuts and dash salt with a fork until mixture holds shape easily.

3. Form chilled chocolate mixture into balls the size of a grape. Cover each chocolate ball with some of vanilla-wafer-crumb mixture—at this point they are the size of a walnut. Roll each in chocolate sprinkles. Store in an airtight container in refrigerator for 24 hours to mellow. *Makes 2 to 2½ dozen.*

Note: Roll about 24 vanilla wafers with rolling pin to make 1 cup fine crumbs.

HAZELNUT CARAMELS

1¼ cups sugar
¾ cup light corn syrup
¼ cup dark corn syrup
1 cup heavy cream
1 tablespoon butter or margarine
½ cup chopped hazelnuts or filberts

1. In heavy 3-quart saucepan, combine sugar, light and dark corn syrups and heavy cream. Stir to mix well.

2. Cook over medium heat, uncovered, to 240F on candy thermometer, or until a little syrup dropped in cold water forms a hard ball—about 45 minutes. Add butter and nuts.

3. Pour into foil bonbon cups; place on tray. Or pour into an 8-by-8-by-2-inch

pan lined with foil that has been buttered lightly. Cool; cut into ½-inch squares. Store in refrigerator. *Makes about 70.*

TURTLES

CARAMEL
1 cup granulated sugar
½ cup light-brown sugar, firmly packed
½ cup light corn syrup
½ cup heavy cream
1 cup milk
¼ cup (½ stick) butter or margarine
1 teaspoon vanilla extract

1 can (6 oz) pecan halves
2 bars (4-oz size) German sweet chocolate

1. Make Caramel: Line an 8-by-8-by-2-inch baking pan with foil. Lightly butter foil.

2. In a heavy 2½-quart saucepan, combine all ingredients except vanilla, nuts and chocolate.

3. Cook, stirring with wooden spoon, over low heat until sugar is dissolved.

4. Over medium heat, cook, stirring occasionally, to 244F on candy thermometer, or until a little syrup in cold water forms a firm ball.

5. Remove from heat; stir in vanilla. Turn into prepared pan; let cool 30 minutes.

6. With sharp knife, cut into 26 pieces.

7. Roll each piece into a ball; place on buttered cookie sheet about ½ inch apart. To make feet and head: Press 5 pecan halves into each ball, equidistant around edge, lengthwise, with half of each pecan overhanging edge.

8. Melt chocolate in double-boiler top, over hot, not boiling, water. Spoon 1 teaspoon melted chocolate over each caramel, covering surface, but leaving part of the pecans showing. Refrigerate to let the chocolate harden slightly. *Makes 26.*

COCONUT BONBONS

3 cans (3½-oz size) flaked coconut
¾ cup raisins
½ cup coarsely chopped candied red cherries
½ cup coarsely chopped candied green cherries
1 can (14 oz) sweetened condensed milk
¼ teaspoon salt
1 teaspoon vanilla extract
Granulated sugar

1. Preheat oven to 350F.

2. Spread coconut evenly on a cookie sheet. Toast, stirring occasionally, 8 to 10 minutes, or until light golden.

3. In large bowl, combine toasted coconut, raisins, cherries, condensed milk, salt and vanilla; mix well.

4. With moistened hands, form mixture into small balls, about 1½ inches in diameter.

5. Roll in granulated sugar. Place on tray lined with waxed paper to dry. *Makes about 4 dozen.*

To store: Store in tightly covered container at room temperature. Will keep several weeks.

HOLIDAY CHOCOLATE CLUSTERS

1 pkg (6 oz) semisweet chocolate pieces or 1 cup semisweet chocolate-flavor pieces
¼ cup light corn syrup
1 tablespoon water
2 cups raisins or salted peanuts (or use 1 cup of each)
Red cinnamon candies
Angelica

1. In top of double boiler, combine chocolate pieces, corn syrup and 1 tablespoon water. Over hot, not boiling, water, melt chocolate.

2. Remove from heat; add raisins and/or nuts; mix well.

3. Drop by teaspoonfuls onto cookie sheet covered with waxed paper. Top each with 3 red candies and 3 angelica slivers, to make a flower.

4. Refrigerate to harden chocolate slightly—1 hour. *Makes about 2½ dozen.*

SUGARPLUMS

1 can (8 oz) almond paste, crumbled
1 cup flaked coconut
¼ cup light corn syrup
¼ cup chopped candied cherries
2 containers (7-oz size) pitted dates
Granulated sugar

1. In small bowl, combine almond paste, coconut, corn syrup and cherries; mix well.

2. With a sharp knife, make a lengthwise slit in each date. Force open and fill each with about 1½ teaspoons almond-paste mixture. Close dates partially, leaving about ½ inch of filling showing.

3. Roll each stuffed date in sugar. Pack in a tightly covered container, and refrigerate. Dates will keep several weeks. Reroll in sugar before serving. *Makes 50 to 60.*

CANDIED PINEAPPLE RINGS

3 cups sugar
⅓ cup light corn syrup
1 cup water
2 cans (20-oz size) sliced pineapple in sugar syrup

1. Combine 2 cups of the sugar, the corn syrup and water in large, heavy skillet; cook over medium heat, stirring constantly, until sugar is dissolved. Continue cooking, without stirring, to 232F on candy thermometer, or until a little syrup dropped from spoon spins a 2-inch thread.

2. Meanwhile, drain pineapple very well on paper towels. Drop 6 or 7 rings at a time into syrup; simmer slowly 5 minutes. Turn; then simmer until translucent—about 7 more minutes. Drain on wire rack placed on waxed-paper-lined tray. Continue until all pineapple is candied.

3. Let pineapple stand, uncovered, 24 hours. Sprinkle all sides with ½ cup sugar. Let stand 24 hours longer; then sprinkle with rest of sugar. Refrigerate, covered. (Keeps about two weeks.) *Makes 20 rings, or about 2 pounds.*

Note: Serve on tray with other candied fruit, such as apricots or cherries.

continued on page 178

continued from page 177

SEAFOAM

2 egg whites (¼ cup)
1 cup light-brown sugar, firmly packed
1 cup granulated sugar
2 tablespoons light corn syrup
½ cup water
¼ teaspoon salt
1 teaspoon vanilla extract
½ cup coarsely chopped walnuts or pecans

1. In small bowl of electric mixer, let egg whites warm to room temperature—about 1 hour.

2. In heavy 2-quart saucepan, combine both kinds of sugar, the corn syrup and water. Cook, stirring with wooden spoon, over low heat until sugar is dissolved.

3. Continue cooking over medium heat, without stirring, to 255F on candy thermometer, or until a little syrup in cold water forms a hard ball. Set aside to cool slightly.

4. Meanwhile, at high speed, beat egg whites with salt until stiff peaks form when beaters are slowly raised.

5. When thermometer goes down to 250F, gradually pour hot syrup in a thin stream over egg whites, beating constantly at high speed. Continue beating until mixture is stiff enough to hold its shape when beaters are raised.

6. With wooden spoon, beat in vanilla and nuts.

7. Drop by rounded teaspoonfuls, 2½ inches apart, onto a tray lined with waxed paper, swirling each candy into a peak. Let dry at room temperature. *Makes about 1 pound (22 pieces).*

To store: Store at room temperature in a covered container. Will keep several weeks.

CHOCOLATE-DATE YULE LOG

1 lb pitted dates
⅔ cup coarsely chopped walnuts
5 pieces candied ginger, finely chopped
   (about 3 tablespoons)
2 tablespoons sugar
4 squares (1-oz size) semisweet chocolate
Candied red cherries
Angelica or green gumdrops

1. Grind dates through finest blade of meat grinder, or chop very fine in blender.

2. Combine dates, nuts and ginger. Turn out on breadboard sprinkled with sugar. Knead with hands to blend thoroughly.

3. Form into a roll 2 inches thick and about 9 inches long. Wrap in waxed paper; refrigerate at least 1 hour before coating with chocolate.

4. In top of double boiler, melt chocolate over hot, not boiling, water. Pour over date roll, spreading to coat evenly all over. Refrigerate until chocolate is hard.

5. Decorate with candied cherries and bits of angelica for green leaves, as pictured.

6. To serve, cut into thin slices. *Makes 1 log, about 1½ pounds.* ∎

continued from page 161

DEARBORN INN FRUITCAKE

1½ cups light raisins
1½ cups dark raisins
1½ cups currants
1 cup coarsely chopped pitted dates
1 jar (8 oz) diced mixed candied peel
¾ cup coarsely chopped blanched almonds
¾ cup coarsely chopped walnuts
½ cup candied red cherries, quartered
½ cup candied green cherries, quartered
¾ cup finely chopped, pared, cored tart apple
½ cup finely chopped whole unpeeled orange
3 cups sifted all-purpose flour
½ teaspoon salt
1 teaspoon baking powder
1 teaspoon ground cinnamon
1 teaspoon ground ginger
1 teaspoon ground mace
¾ teaspoon ground cloves
1 cup (2 sticks) butter or margarine
1 cup light-brown sugar, firmly packed
6 eggs, beaten
2 tablespoons light or dark molasses
3 tablespoons dark rum
Dark rum or brandy

1. Lightly grease a 10-inch tube pan. Line bottom and side with heavy brown paper; then lightly grease paper.

2. In very large bowl, combine raisins, currants, dates, candied peel, nuts, candied cherries, apple and orange. Sift ¼ cup flour over mixture; toss to mix well.

3. Sift rest of flour with salt, baking powder, cinnamon, ginger, mace and cloves; set aside. Preheat oven to 275F.

4. In large bowl of electric mixer, at medium speed, beat butter with brown sugar until light and fluffy. Beat in eggs until well combined; then beat in molasses and 3 tablespoons rum.

5. With wooden spoon, stir fruit-nut mixture into egg mixture until well combined. Then add flour mixture, combining well.

6. Turn into prepared pan. Press batter with spatula to spread evenly.

7. Bake about 2½ hours, or until cake tester inserted in cake comes out clean. Let cool completely in pan on wire rack. Then remove from pan; peel off paper.

8. To age cake: Wrap cake in cheesecloth soaked in ⅓ cup dark rum or brandy. Then wrap cake in foil and store in airtight tin container or refrigerator at least two weeks. Resoak cheesecloth from time to time as it dries out. *Makes one 6-pound cake.*

To make three (8½-by-4½-by-2⅝-inch) loaves: Line greased pans with strips of brown paper; then lightly grease paper. Turn batter into prepared pans, dividing evenly. Bake 1¾ to 2 hours, or until cake tester inserted in cake comes out clean. *Makes 3 (2-pound) cakes.*

ENGLISH FRUITCAKE

1 box (10 oz) currants
1 box (15 oz) raisins
2 jars (4-oz size) citron, chopped
2 jars (3½-oz size) candied cherries, halved
1 can (8 oz) walnuts, chopped
1 cup brandy or rum, plus more brandy for soaking cheesecloth wrap
2 cups all-purpose flour
½ teaspoon ground nutmeg
½ teaspoon ground cinnamon
1 cup (2 sticks) butter, softened
1 cup sugar
5 eggs
¼ cup apricot preserves, melted and strained
1 can (8 oz) almond paste
Royal Icing, recipe follows

1. Prepare a 9-by-3-inch springform pan (see Note).

2. In a large bowl, toss currants, raisins, citron, cherries and walnuts with ½ cup brandy until well mixed.

3. Preheat oven to 275F. Sift together flour, nutmeg and cinnamon; set aside.

4. In large bowl, with electric mixer at medium speed, beat butter and sugar until light and fluffy. Add eggs, one at a time, beating well after each addition; beat until very light and fluffy.

5. At low speed, beat in flour mixture (in fourths) alternately with remaining ½ cup brandy (in thirds), beginning and ending with flour mixture.

6. Pour batter over fruit mixture; mix until well combined. Turn into prepared pan.

7. On low rack in oven, bake 2½ to 3 hours, or until cake tester inserted near center comes out clean.

8. Cool cake completely in pan on wire rack. Remove from pan, and peel off paper. Wrap fruitcake in brandy-soaked cheesecloth, then in foil; store for several weeks. (Resoak the cheesecloth in brandy several times, as necessary.)

9. Before serving: Brush top of cake with apricot preserves. Roll almond paste between two sheets of waxed paper into a 9-inch circle. Remove top sheet of paper. Invert paste onto cake; remove paper. With sharp knife, trim edge of paste; then press paste to cake.

10. Make Royal Icing. With spatula, spread an even layer smoothly on top and side of cake. Fill pastry bag with icing, using number-1 writing tip. Pipe diagonal lines ½ inch apart all around the cake. Then starting at the top of each line, pipe another line diagonally in other direction to form diamonds, as pictured.

11. For top and bottom edge: Fill pastry bag with icing, using number-4 star tip. Pipe rosettes all around the bottom. Using the same pastry bag, make ruching around top edge of cake. *Makes one 7-pound fruitcake.*

For individual cakes: Prepare pans: Line five (5¾-by-3-by-2-inch) greased loaf pans with strips of greased brown paper. Turn batter into prepared pans, dividing evenly. Bake 2 to 2¼ hours at 275F, or until cake tester inserted in cake comes out clean. *Makes 5 (1¼-pound) cakes.*

Note: To line a 9-by-3-inch springform pan: On heavy brown paper, draw an 18-inch circle and cut out. Draw around base of pan. With pencil lines outside, fold paper into eighths. Unfold circle; make cuts 3 inches long on each fold. Grease the pan and unpenciled side of paper well. Fit paper, greased side up, into pan.

ROYAL ICING

4 egg whites (½ cup)
6 cups confectioners' sugar

1. In large bowl of electric mixer, let egg whites warm to room temperature—about 1 hour.

2. Gradually add confectioners' sugar to egg whites, beating at medium speed until smooth. Cover icing with damp cloth, to prevent drying out. Beat again, if necessary. *Makes 4 cups.* ∎

BOUNTIFUL BASKETS TO MAKE AND TAKE

The quickest way to anyone's heart is through the stomach — so why not solve your can't-find-the-perfect-present problem with food baskets this year? Not necessarily the prepackaged assortments from catalogs or specialty shops, but delightfully distinctive baskets you can put together yourself, often for less money. Here is a variety of ideas for creating special packages for everybody from joggers to pet lovers to new parents.

The Outdoor Chef
For barbecue enthusiasts, fill a basket with the essentials: a long-handled fork, spatula, tongs and basting brush all tied together with ribbon. Tuck in a jar of barbecue sauce and a bottle of Italian dressing for marinating.

Ice-Cream Delight
Give the makings for the ultimate sundae: a glass bowl or goblet nestled in a basket along with a jar of topping, a bottle of liqueur or brandied fruit (for adults), a package of nuts for crunch and a jar of cherries to top it off. If your budget allows, include a gift certificate for a quart of ice cream from a favorite ice-cream shop.

Setting Up House
For singles or newlyweds moving into that first apartment, fill a skillet with recipes for a week's worth of tasty, quick-to-fix, inexpensive skillet dinners for one or two. Include some of the ingredients to get them started, plus a measuring cup filled with a few basic utensils: wooden spoon, rubber spatula, measuring spoons, paring knife (cover the blade!), can opener and vegetable peeler. Tie it all up in a colorful dish towel.

Colossal Cookie
Bake one giant cookie (chocolate chip, oatmeal, sugar cookie, etc.) in a 12-inch pizza pan, then place in a foil-lined take-out pizza box decorated on the outside with holiday wrappings. Include a recipe for homemade pizza to put the pan to good use once the cookie is gobbled up.

Lunch-Box Treats
To end boring brown-bag meals, start with an inexpensive lunch box and pile it up with raisins, sunflower seeds, granola bars, a small jar of peanut butter, fruit and juice in aseptic containers.

Bundle of Joy
For new or expectant parents, pack a diaper bag or tote with bibs, jars of baby food, boxes of baby cereal, teething biscuits and some tiny T-shirts.

The Cookie Monster
Arrange an assortment of home-baked cookies in a whimsical cookie jar. Or use a molded-plastic kitchen-drawer organizer, fill each section with different cookies and wrap in clear plastic with a festive napkin as a bow.

BOUNTIFUL BASKETS TO MAKE AND TAKE

Pack a Punch
Good cheer will flow when you give a plastic punch bowl filled with fixings: oranges, lemons, limes, a bottle of rum or brandy, a jar of spice mix for hot mulled cider or apple juice. Tie a holiday bow on each cup handle.

Holiday Brew-Ha-Ha
Stock a small Styrofoam cooler with several varieties of bottled beer wrapped in foil and tied with ribbon at the neck; drop in bags of pretzels, peanuts or beer nuts.

Say Cheese!
Smiles are what you'll get in return when you give a wooden cheese board piled with a selection of fine cheeses—Havarti, Pré Monde (with reduced salt and cholesterol), Brie and fontina, for example. Cover each piece in plastic wrap and add a decorative label. Top it off with a cheese slicer.

Fiesta Fare
For those who like it hot, fill a basket with the makings of a Mexican meal. Most supermarkets carry salsa, refried beans, jalapeño peppers, taco shells, hot sauce and canned tortillas.

From the Far East
Fans of Chinese and Japanese cooking will be delighted with this basketful of oriental favorites, such as duck sauce, mustard, soy sauce, cans of sprouts and water chestnuts, canned wonton soup, oyster sauce, sweet rice and seaweed for sushi. Add some chopsticks.

Nibbles From the North
To Yankees who can't get home for the holidays, send a box filled with New England goodies like clam chowder, baked beans, canned Boston brown bread, maple syrup, Vermont cheese and canned succotash.

Southern Jamboree
For displaced Southerners, pack a basket with the fixings for a down-home feast: black-eyed peas, grits, cornbread mix, canned greens and jars of chitlins, ham hocks and pigs' knuckles.

Rations for Runners
Since most runners like to "carbo-load" before a race, load a box with starchy foods such as rice, spaghetti or noodles, pancake mix, cereal, crackers and cookies. Trim the box with a pair of shoelaces and a sweatband.

A Lift for Skiers
At high altitudes, skiers need high-energy foods such as candy bars, packets of dried-fruit-and-nut mix and individually wrapped cookies and pastries. For après ski, add a spiced-tea mix to the basket. Decorate with boot laces.

Doggie Bag
Whether the pet is a poodle, Persian or parakeet, give your favorite animal lover a bag filled with cans or small packages of food, a pet toy—and a box of animal crackers for the owner.

The Fruit and Nutsnacker
Here's an arrangement that makes a charming centerpiece—until someone gets hungry! In a high-handled basket, place apples, small oranges or other citrus fruits, unshelled walnuts, chestnuts (which must be roasted before they're eaten) and grapes.

Dieter's Delight
There's little to gain but good taste and good health from a basket stuffed with cans of water-packed tuna or salmon, low-calorie crackers, low-fat cheese, fresh fruits and vegetables and sugar-free soda. Tie it up with a tape-measure bow.

Lotsa Pasta
Pack all the ingredients for an Italian feast into a colander—a jar of spaghetti sauce, pesto sauce, anchovies, Parmesan or Romano cheese, a small bottle of olive oil, a can of clams, a variety of dried or fresh pasta and bread sticks.

Coffee Break in a Bag
Co-workers will go beans over this midmorning-pick-me-up present. In a brown-paper bag decorated with ribbons, place boxes of crackers, packets of instant soup, individually wrapped pastries and a bag of freshly ground coffee. Perhaps add a cute mug.

Everything's Kosher
To make a delightful Hanukkah gift, arrange kosher delicacies like matzo-ball soup, matzo meal, gefillte fish and beet borsch in a basket.

Chock-Full of Chocolate
Give a chocoholic what he or she craves most: a glossy brown-paper gift bag (available at stationery stores and card shops) packed with chocolate cookies, brownies, boxes of pudding, chocolate bars, chocolate truffles, chocolate liqueur—and maybe even add a chocolate-lovers' cookbook.

Winter-Picnic Pouch
Who says picnics are just for warm weather? Stuff a Christmas stocking with a bottle of wine, a box of wheat crackers, some foil-wrapped cheese and apples.

Primed for a Party
What a hostess needs the mostest—an ice bucket (they come in a range of prices) packed with "entertaining" staples: nuts, olives, after-dinner mints, a can of anchovies, sardines or smoked oysters, fancy crackers, cocktail napkins, decorative toothpicks and so on.

Down-on-the-Farm Charm
A-tisket, a-tasket, a special country basket: Fill several one-quart canning jars with grains and beans—rice, oats, barley, split peas, lentils. Glue a calico or gingham square to the lid and tie a grosgrain ribbon around the rim.

Tea Timer
For afternoon-tea devotees, arrange several varieties of tea biscuits, a jar of marmalade, a jar of strawberry preserves and an assortment of teas in a doily-lined basket.

A Batch of Baker's Goodies
Arrange all the things a baker needs for kneading in a large plastic mixing bowl: a variety of flours—such as whole wheat, rye or buckwheat—chocolate chips, walnuts, pecans, oats, packages of yeast, baking soda and a bottle of vanilla extract. ∎

SWEET AND SPICY
HOLIDAY BASKETS

A-tisket, a-tasket, a do-it-yourself holiday basket. Here are two kinds of unique containers to hold small, thoughtful presents for special people…or to use as your own family centerpiece. They're assembled from ordinary household items—custard cups, supermarket mushroom baskets and plastic food containers—artfully transformed with sticks of cinnamon or peppermint and a little glue. The cinnamon baskets on the left have a textured, rough-hewn look and a spicy fragrance that summons all the joys of the season. And what could be sweeter than the bright red-and-white peppermint group above? After the holidays, these baskets can hold potpourri, soaps or dried flowers. For full instructions, please turn to page 209.

ONCE
UPON A TIME

Once upon a time there was a family of seven bears who were crocheted in Christmas stripes. From the smallest bear to his medium-size brothers and sisters to Mama and Papa Bear, they enchanted everyone who saw them—children, teens and adults. And, of course, they lived happily ever after. Instructions begin on page 186.

continued from page 185

STRIPED TEDDY BEARS
(pictured)

Bears are adapted by Laura Gilberg from a design by Talon American. Seated, bears approximately measure, from left to right, 30″, 70″, 51″, 12″, 24″, 36″ and 19″. Pattern directions are for all bears. Yarn and hook size determine size of bear.

Materials, hook size and type of yarn:
   12″ bear: #9 steel, #5 Pearl Cotton or 2 strands of Bedspread crochet
   19″: C2, 1 strand of Sport yarn
   24″: E4, 1 strand of Knitting Worsted
   30″: G6, 2 strands of Knitting Worsted
   36″: H8, 1 strand of Rug Yarn
   51″: J10, 2 strands of Rug Yarn
   70″: Q, 4 strands of Rug Yarn

ABBREVIATIONS

beg	begin(ning)
ch	chain
dc	double crochet
dec	decrease
hdc	half double crochet
inc	increase
lp	loop
pat	pattern
rem	remain(ing)
rep	repeat
rnd	round
sc	single crochet
sl	slip
sl st	slip stitch
st	stitch
tr	treble
yo	yarn over
*	repeat whatever follows * as indicated

GAUGE: Bears require a very tight gauge, and you may have to switch to a smaller hook if you crochet loosely. To test (7 hdc = 2″): With G hook, ch 20; hdc in 2nd ch from hook and in each ch across; ch 2, turn. Work 4 rows in hdc. Finish off. Place work on flat surface, and measure sts in center of piece. If it's larger than needed, a smaller hook has to be used. Remember: A very tight gauge is needed so stuffing doesn't show. Suggested gauge guide per 2″: #9 = 12 hdc; C2 = 11 hdc; E4 = 9 hdc; G6 = 8 hdc; H8 = 7 hdc; J10 = 6 hdc; Q = 3 hdc.

All bears (except 70″, which is solid) are worked with legs and body in a multitude of colors, creating a rainbow effect. Use about 1 skein of each color (14 in all) and 4 skeins of brown, adding several yards of dark brown or black for eyes and nose tip.

Colors used, from bottom to top, range from purple to lilac; blues, dark to light; greens, dark to light; reds; orange; and yellow.

Color names of Aunt Lydia's Rug Yarn are: Lilac 010, Pink 110, National Blue 715, True Blue 317, Medium Blue 710, Lt. Blue 705, Hemlock 620, Grass Green 615, Spring Green 605, Red 120, Phantom Red 140, Tangerine 315, Sunset 550, Yellow 510, Brown 420 and Wood Brown 425.

Color names of Dawn Sayelle Knitting Worsted are: Purple 335A, Lilac 335, Blue 317A, True Blue 317, Bluebell 316, Baby Blue 312, Forest Green 356, Grass Green 357, Lt. Green 338, Flame 325A, Country Red 329, Watermelon 325, Orange 347, Lemon 331.

Note: Not all colors may be available for the Sport or # 5 Pearl Cotton Bears. Experiment with your own color combinations. Excess yarns from other projects may be used. Double or triple strands, if necessary.

Fewer colors may be used for the stripes by following the suggested guide below:

NUMBER OF ROUNDS PER COLOR
BODY (42 Rnds)
14 colors, 3 rnds of each
12 colors, 4 rnds of 9; 2 rnds of 3
10 colors, 4 rnds of 8; 5 rnds of 2
9 colors, 5 rnds of 6; 4 rnds of 3
8 colors, 5 rnds of 6; 6 rnds of 2
7 colors, 6 rnds of each
LEGS (28 Rnds)
14 colors, 2 rnds of each
12 colors, 2 rnds of 10; 4 rnds of 2
10 colors, 3 rnds of 8; 2 rnds of 2
9 colors, 4 rnds of 5; 2 rnds of 4
8 colors, 4 rnds of 6; 2 rnds of 2
7 colors, 4 rnds of each

Start the neck and head with directions that begin with **Rnd 50.**

Large solid-color bear requires 64 skeins of Aunt Lydia's Rug Yarn Brown 420 (70 yards), 2 skeins Wood Brown 425. Follow directions, using 4 strands as one, but disregard color-stripe information.

Approximate amounts of Fiberfil needed for stuffing: 12″, 3 lbs.; 19″, 5 lbs.; 24″, 6 lbs.; 30″, 8 lbs.; 36″, 9 lbs.; 51″, 12 lbs.; 70″, 18 lbs. (Old socks and hosiery can also be used along with the Fiberfil.)

BODY: With Brown, ch 2. **Rnd 1:** 9 sc in 2nd ch from hook. Mark first st of rnd with a st marker. (Entire bear is worked in rnds that are not joined. Mark beg of each rnd, and move marker up as you work.) **Rnd 2:** 2 hdc in each sc: 18 hdc. **Rnd 3:** 2 hdc in each hdc: 36 hdc. **Rnd 4:** * Hdc in each of next 2 sts, 2 hdc in next st; rep from * around: 48 hdc. **Rnd 5:** * 2 hdc in next st, hdc in each of next 3 sts; rep from * around: 60 hdc. **Rnd 6:** * Hdc in each of next 5 sts, 2 hdc in next st; rep from * around: 70 hdc. **Rnd 7:** Hdc in each of next 4 sts, 2 hdc in next st: 84 hdc. **Rnd 8:** For striped bears, work colors as established. Working in back lp only (lp away from you) of each st, * hdc in each of next 2 sts, 2 hdc in next st; rep from * around: 112 hdc. *(Note:* At this point, bottom piece will not lie flat, but it will when bear is stuffed.) **Rnds 9 through 30:** Work even in hdc. **Rnd 31:** Beg dec in hdc. To dec: Yo hook and draw up a lp in next st; draw up a lp in next st: 4 lps on hook; yo and draw through all 4 lps. (With contrasting yarn, mark first st of this rnd for center back.) Hdc in first 18 sts; * dec, hdc in each of next 3 hdc; rep from * to last 18 sts, hdc in each rem st: 93 hdc. **Rnds 32 through 38:** Work even in hdc. **Rnd 39:** Hdc around, dec 6 sts evenly spaced: 87 hdc. **Rnds 40 through 43:** Work even in hdc. **Rnd 44:** Hdc around, dec 4 sts evenly spaced: 83 hdc. **Rnd 45:** Work even in hdc. **Rnds 46 and 47:** Rep rnds 44 and 45: 79 hdc. **Rnd 48:** Hdc around, dec one st. **Rnd 49:** Work even in hdc. Stuff body full and smooth into shape.

NECK AND HEAD: Rnd 50: * Change to Brown. Hdc in next 4 sts, dec; rep from * around: 65 hdc. **Rnd 51:** * Hdc in next 3 sts, dec; rep from * around. **Rnd 52:** Work even in hdc. **Rnd 53:** * Hdc in each of next 3 sts, 2 hdc in next st; rep from * around: 65 hdc. **Rnd 54:** * Hdc in each of next 4 sts, 2 hdc in next st; rep from * around: 78 hdc.

SHAPE CHEEKS: Back of head should be placed directly over center back, so beg this rnd directly above the marked center back. (If necessary, adjust position of beg of next rnd so it will start directly above marked st.) **Rnd 55:** Hdc in 12 sts, 2 hdc in next st; (hdc in each of next 2 sts, 2 hdc in next st) 7 times; hdc in next 12 sts; (2 hdc in next st, hdc in each of next 2 sts) 7 times; hdc in rem 11 sts: 93 hdc. **Rnd 56:** Hdc in 43 sts, dec; hdc in 3 sts, dec; hdc in rem 43 sts: 91 hdc. **Rnds 57 through 62:** Work even in hdc. **Rnd 63:** (Be sure rnd beg directly above marker for center back.) Hdc in first 12 hdc, dec; hdc in next 22 hdc, dec; hdc in next 16 hdc, dec; hdc in next 22 hdc, dec; hdc in last 11 hdc: 87 hdc. **Rnd 64:** Hdc in first 11 hdc, dec; (hdc in next 6 hdc, dec) twice; hdc in next 5 hdc, dec; hdc in next 15 hdc, dec; hdc in next 5 hdc, dec; (hdc in next 6 hdc, dec) twice; hdc in last 11 hdc: 79 hdc. At this point, stuff head firmly, filling out cheeks on each side. Continue to stuff every few rnds. **Rnd 65:** Hdc in next 12 hdc, dec; (hdc in next 6 hdc, dec) twice; hdc in next 21 hdc; (dec, hdc in next 6 hdc) twice; dec, hdc in next 10 hdc: 73 hdc. **Rnd 66:** Hdc in next 10 sts; (dec, hdc in next st) 6 times; hdc in next 19 sts; (dec, hdc in next st) 6 times; hdc in last 8 hdc: 61 hdc. **Rnd 67:** Work even in hdc. **Rnd 68:** Work in hdc, dec 6 sts evenly spaced around: 55 hdc. **Rnd 69:** Work in hdc, dec 4 sts evenly spaced: 51 hdc. **Rnd 70:** Rep rnd 69, but do not work decs directly above those of previous rnd: 47 hdc. **Rnds 71 and 72:** Rep rnd 70: 39 hdc. **Rnd 73:** * Hdc in next 4 sts, dec; rep from * around, ending with 3 hdc: 33 hdc. **Rnd 74:** Dec in each st around, and stuff head completely to this point. **Rnd 75:** Rep rnd 74. **Rnd 76:** Working in sc, dec around. Finish off. Add any extra stuffing; sew opening together tightly.

LEGS (make 2): With Brown, starting at sole center, ch 4. **Rnd 1:** 3 sc in 2nd ch from hook, 2 sc in next ch, 3 sc in end ch; working in opposite side of chain, 2 sc in middle ch: 10 sc; do not join, mark beg of rnds as before. **Rnd 2:** 2 sc in first sc; (2 sc in next sc) twice; sc in next 2 sts; (2 sc in next sc) 3 times; sc in last 2 sts: 16 sc. **Rnd 3:** Work now in hdc. (2 hdc in each of next 6 sc, hdc in each of next 2 sc) twice: 28 hdc. **Rnd 4:** Hdc in first 2 hdc; (2 hdc in next hdc) 8 times; hdc in next 6 hdc; (2 hdc in next hdc) 8 times; hdc in last 4 sts: 44 hdc. **Rnd 5:** Hdc in first 7 sts; 2 hdc in each of next 8 sts; hdc in each of next 14 sts; 2 hdc in each of next 8 sts; hdc in each of last 7 sts: 60 hdc. **Rnd 6:** Hdc in first 10 hdc; (2 hdc in next st, hdc in next st) 6 times; mark this section for toe; hdc in next 19 sts; (2 hdc in next st, hdc in next st) 4 times; hdc in each of next 10 sts, sc in last st: 70 sts. **Rnd 7:** Working in back lp only of each st (lp away from you), hdc in each st around.

This completes sole. Now begin foot and leg. Change to stripe colors. **Rnd 8:** Working in both lps again, hdc first 9 sts; (dec, hdc in next st) 7 times; hdc in each st around: 63 hdc. **Rnd 9:** Hdc in first 7 sts; (dec, hdc in next st) 6 times; hdc in each st around: 57 hdc. **Rnds 10 through 13:** Work even in hdc. **Rnd 14:** Work in hdc, dec 2 sts over toe section: 55 hdc. **Rnds 15 and 16:** Work even in hdc. **Rnd 17:** Rep rnd 14: 53 hdc. **Rnds 18 and 19:** Work even in hdc. **Rnd 20:** Work in hdc, dec 4 sts evenly spaced: 49 hdc. **Rnds 21 through 23:** Work even in hdc. **Rnd 24:** Rep rnd 20: 45 hdc. **Rnds 25 through 27:** Work even in hdc. **Rnd 28:** Rep rnd 20: 41 hdc. **Rnds 29 through 35:** Work even in hdc. **Rnds 36 through 39:** Work 4 more rnds. Finish off, leaving an 18″ end.

ARMS (make 2): With Brown, starting at bottom of paw, ch 2. **Rnd 1:** 7 sc in 2nd ch from hook; do not join, mark beg of rnds as before. **Rnd 2:** 2 sc in each sc: 14 sc. **Rnd 3:** * Hdc in first sc, 2 hdc in next sc; rep from * around: 21 hdc. **Rnd 4:** * 2 hdc in first hdc, hdc in each of next 2 hdc; rep from * around: 28 hdc. **Rnds 5 and 6:** Work even in hdc. **Rnd 7:** Hdc in first 14 hdc, 3 hdc in next st; hdc in rem 13 hdc: 30 hdc. **Rnd 8:** Hdc in first st, 2 hdc in next st; hdc in each of next 12 sts; 2 hdc in each of next 3 sts, hdc in each st to last 2 sts, 2 hdc in each of these sts: 36 hdc. **Rnd 9:** Hdc in first 15 sts, 2 hdc in each of next 6 sts; hdc in each of rem 15 sts: 41 hdc. **Rnd 10:** Work even in hdc. **Rnd 11:** Hdc in first 18 sts, dec 3 sts, hdc in rem sts: 38 hdc. **Rnds 12 through 18:** Work even in hdc. **Rnd 19:** Dec, hdc in next 17 sts; dec, hdc in next 17 sts: 36 hdc. **Rnds 20 and 21:** Work even in hdc. **Rnd 22:** Rep rnd 19: 34 hdc. **Rnds 23 and 24:** Work even in hdc. **Rnd 25:** Rep rnd 19: 32 hdc. **Rnds 26 through 32:** Work even in hdc. Finish off, leaving a 24″ end for sewing.

SNOUT: With Brown, ch 2. **Rnd 1:** 7 sc in 2nd ch from hook; do not join, mark beg of rnds as before. **Rnd 2:** 2 hdc in each sc around: 14 hdc. **Rnd 3:** * Hdc in next hdc,

2 hdc in next hdc; rep from * around: 21 hdc. **Rnd 4:** Hdc in first hdc; * hdc in next hdc, 2 hdc in next hdc, rep from * around: 31 hdc. **Rnds 5 and 6:** Work even in hdc. **Rnd 7:** Hdc in next hdc; * hdc in next 2 hdc, 2 hdc in next hdc; rep from * around: 41 hdc. **Rnd 8:** (Hdc in next 3 hdc, 2 hdc in next hdc) 9 times; hdc in last 5 hdc: 50 hdc. Finish by working sc in next hdc, sl st in next hdc. Finish off, leaving an 18″ end for sewing.

EARS (make 2): With Brown, ch 6. **Row 1:** 2 hdc in 3rd ch from hook and two hdc in each of 3 rem chs: 8 hdc; ch 2, turn (turning ch does not count as first st of next row). **Row 2:** Hdc in first st, (hdc, dc) in next st; 2 dc in each of next 3 sts; (dc, hdc) in next st; 2 hdc in next st, sc in last st; ch 1, turn. **Row 3:** Sc in first st, 2 hdc in next st; (hdc, dc) in next st; 2 dc in next st; (dc, tr) in next st; 2 tr in each of next 5 sts; (tr, dc) in next st; 2 dc in next st; (dc, hdc) in next st; sc in last st. Finish off, leaving a 12″ end.

NOSE TIP: Rnd 1: With Dark Brown, ch 2, 7 sc in 2nd ch from hook. **Rnd 2:** 2 sc in each sc around: 14 sc; sl st in next st. Finish off, leaving a 12″ end for sewing. Sew to snout, positioned slightly above center.

EYES (make 2): **Rnd 1:** With Dark Brown, ch 2, 7 sc in 2nd ch from hook, join with sl st. Finish off, leaving a 12″ end for sewing. Sew eyes above snout, separated in middle by about 6 hdc.

ASSEMBLY: With double strands of thread, sew ears to each side of head at top. Stuff snout firmly, and sew at center of face between cheeks. Stuff arms firmly, carefully poking stuffing into thumbs. Leave last 4 rows at top of arm stuffed lightly so arms can hang down. Sew top of arm closed, then sew to body at shoulder. Stuff legs firmly, again using less stuffing at last 4 top rows; sew legs closed, and sew to body.

CROCHETED SCARF: Aunt Lydia's Rug Yarn, or 2 strands of knitting worsted weight yarn, with a "K" crochet hook. Ch to measure 7½″. Work * hdc in each st across, ch 1, turn. Rep from * across. (Ch 1 is not a st.) Work for 3″, change color and continue in pat, working 3″ stripes, until there are 40 stripes. Length, 120″. ∎

These Are a Few of Our Favorite
THINGS

And they're sure to be yours, too, because they let you say "Happy Holidays" in the most beautiful ways. Say it sweetly with potpourri and lace in decorative hoops or on a wreath. Say it lovingly with graceful winged angels in needlework. Say it simply with foil ornaments that shine with the lights of the Christmas tree. Say it all with these fabulous gifts…that speak for themselves.

Design by Petra B. Jenkinson, PJ's Almost Heirlooms, Berlin, Conn.

Design by Maureen Lo Presti, Durham, Conn.

Lace Sachet Hoops— wonderfully fragrant, lovely and amazingly quick and easy. Directions begin on page 192; potpourri recipes, page 197.

'Joy' Angel Counted Cross-Stitch—a treasured heirloom to herald the glorious message of the season. Directions begin on page 197.

Scented 'Victorian' Wreath—tiny bundles of potpourri, delicate baby's breath and ribbon beautifully adorn a grapevine wreath. Directions begin on page 193; potpourri recipes, page 197.

Angel Wall Hanging—an adorable quilted cherub designed to capture your holiday heart. Directions begin on page 194.

Design by Maureen Lo Presti, Durham, Conn.

Design by Petra B. Jenkinson, PJ's Almost Heirlooms, Berlin, Conn.

Simple, Shiny Ornaments—your tree will shine with this festive trio of ornaments made from aluminum foil and other simple, inexpensive materials. They're easy enough for kids to make—and special enough for gift-giving. They can also double as attractive package decorations.

STOCKING

STAR

CANDLE

SIMPLE SHINY ORNAMENTS

Folk-Art Ornaments

1. Pop cardboard insert out of plastic craft/photo frame. Trace insert on aluminum pan (we used Reynolds Redi-Pan cookie pan) and on a piece of paper.

2. Draw candle, stocking or star on paper; tape to aluminum circle. Carefully pierce outline of design with sharp pin. Remove paper design; cut out circle.

3. Spread craft glue on inside back edge of frame. Center punched aluminum design in frame, smooth side facing out. Make ribbon bow; glue to top of frame.

Materials

Round plastic craft/photo frames
Aluminum pan with smooth bottom
Tape
Sharp pin (straight pin or pushpin)
Craft glue
Ribbon

Cookie-Cutter Ornaments

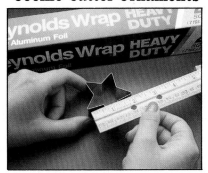

1. Measure longest side of cookie cutter. Cut a strip of heavy-duty aluminum foil four times as long as this measurement and 4 inches wide.

2. Fold in half lengthwise and then into thirds. Starting at the top, mold foil band around outer edge of cookie cutter.

3. Overlap ½ inch; trim excess and secure with tape. Remove cutter; punch hole through center of overlap. Tie with yarn.

Materials

Cookie cutters
Heavy-duty aluminum foil
Tape
Hole punch
Yarn

Pinwheel Ornaments

1. Press a 1-inch cardboard circle to the center of a 3-inch square of self-adhesive shelf paper. Press paper and cardboard to dull side of heavy-duty aluminum foil.

2. Trim foil to the size of shelf paper. Starting at each corner, make 4 cuts toward center of square, stopping at the edge of the cardboard circle.

3. Turn the left point of each corner toward the center. Secure with scrap of shelf paper. Pierce one corner with a sharp pin; tie with ribbon.

Materials

Small piece of cardboard
Self-adhesive shelf paper
Heavy-duty aluminum foil
Sharp pin
Ribbon

Lace Sachet Hoops *(pictured, page 188)*

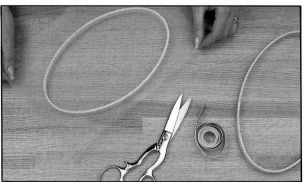

DAVID VIENS

1. Unscrew the wooden embroidery hoop and separate. Place the inner ring (without the clasp) down on the work surface. Center two pieces of illusion veil over the hoop.

2. Spoon the potpourri onto the illusion veil and arrange it evenly in the inner ring, keeping about ¾″ away from the ring edges. Place the third piece of illusion veil over the potpourri; then place the flowered/textured veil on top, face up, making sure all edges are even.

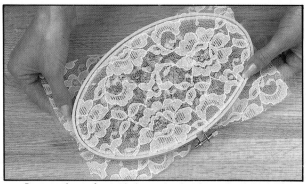

3. Loosen clasp of outside hoop ring but keep ring intact. Place this ring, with clasp at the top, over all layers of bridal veil and potpourri. Tighten clasp slowly and pull veil gently from edges (alternate these steps) to make the veil/potpourri sandwich "tight as a drum." Tighten clasp completely.

4. Turn the hoop over and carefully cut off all the excess veil from the back as close to the wood as possible. Run a line of thick glue (Tacky, Sobo or Elmer's Craft) all around the back inside edge of the hoop.

5. Starting at the top clasp, press the gathered lace down (ruffle facing out) on the glue. Pins can be inserted every few inches, straight down on the hoop edges to temporarily hold the lace in place. In 10 to 15 minutes the glue will set; remove the pins and press lace down again.

6. Cut off an 8″ piece of ribbon. With the remainder, make a 4″ S loop (a 2″ loop for the round hoops). Double knot the 8″ ribbon tightly around the loop's center and then knot it around the clasp. Tie a slip knot 1″ from clasp to hang sachet. Trim excess ribbon.

Materials

OVAL HOOP
1 wooden embroidery hoop, 5″ × 9″
3 pieces of white or ecru illusion bridal veil, each 7″ × 11″
5 to 6 tablespoons potpourri
1 piece of white or ecru flowered/textured bridal veil, 7″ × 11″

White craft glue
1 piece of 1½″-wide white or ecru gathered net lace, 24″ long
1 piece of ¼″- or ⅜″-wide fabric ribbon, 1 to 1½ yards long

ROUND HOOP
1 3″ (4″) wooden embroidery hoop
3 pieces of white or ecru illusion bridal veil, each 5″ (6″) square

3 to 4 tablespoons potpourri
1 piece of white or ecru flowered/textured bridal veil, 5″ (6″) square

White craft glue
1 piece of ⅜″- or ½″-wide white or ecru gathered net lace, 12″ (16″) long
1 piece of ¼″- or ⅜″-wide fabric ribbon, 27″ long

Scented 'Victorian' Wreath *(pictured, page 188)*

1. Using pinking shears, cut six 8″ squares of flowered/textured veil and six 9″ squares of illusion veil. Using regular scissors, cut the ribbons into 4″ lengths.

2. For each sachet bag, lay a flowered/textured-veil square face down on the work surface. Lay an illusion-veil square down over the flowered/textured-veil square so that it is centered, leaving a ½″ overlap on all sides.

3. Place 3 to 4 tablespoons of the potpourri in the center of the square.

4. Grasp the four corners of the veils and hold in one hand. With the other hand, take two contrasting ribbons and wrap around the veils, close to the potpourri, forming a little bag. Tie the ribbons in a double knot, trimming ends with a diagonal cut.

5. Insert a piece of floral wire under the ribbon in the back of each sachet bag. Run the wire around a piece of grapevine and twist to attach each bag to the wreath. Attach all the sachet bags to the wreath in the same manner, spacing them evenly and leaving extra room between the two bags nearest the bottom of the wreath for a space to attach the ribbon.

6. Cut a 10″ piece from the 50″ ribbon. Loop both 40″ ribbons together in a 6″ S loop. Double knot the 10″ ribbon around the loop's center; trim ends to ½″. Run a wire through the back of the knot and attach the ribbon to the bottom center of wreath. Insert the baby's breath between the grapevines, filling entire top of wreath. Attach wire to top (back) of wreath for a hanger.

Materials

⅓ yard of white or ecru flowered/textured bridal veil (see Note)

⅓ yard of white or ecru illusion bridal veil

2 contrasting-colored pieces of ¼″- or ⅜″-wide fabric ribbon, each 24″ long

18 to 24 tablespoons potpourri

8 pieces of fine floral wire, each 4″ long

1 18″ grapevine wreath

1 piece of ¼″- or ⅜″-wide fabric ribbon, 50″ long

1 contrasting-colored piece of ¼″- or ⅜″-wide fabric ribbon, 40″ long

1 bundle of preserved baby's breath or white phlox (broken into 2″ or 3″ pieces)

Note: ⅓ yard is sufficient for bridal veil if available only in 60″ widths. If it can be purchased in 36″ or 45″ widths, ½ yard will suffice.

continued from page 189

ANGEL WALL HANGING
(pictured)
Finished size 39″ × 47″

FABRIC (43″ to 44″ wide)
Color A: dark green—2 yards (for backing, strips, hearts)
Color B: rose/green print—1⅓ yards (for strips, hearts, bodice, sleeves, small heart on bib, skirt band)
Color C: unbleached muslin—¾ yard (for center panel)
Color D: burgundy print—⅓ yard (for wings)
Color E: pink print—⅓ yard (for skirt, bib, cuffs, small hearts on skirt band)
Color F: brown print—scrap (for hair)
Color G: flesh—scrap (for face and hands)
Color H: yellow print—scrap (for halo)
Color I: pink—scrap (for cheeks)
6 strands 2-ply embroidery floss—brown (for eyes); pink (for nose, mouth)
¼″ velvet ribbons: wine—1 yard; green— 1 yard
Quilt batt—39″ × 47″

CUTTING DIRECTIONS

Prewash and press all fabrics.

Note: Pattern pieces for angel and hearts do not include seam allowance. Add ¼″ all around each piece if you plan to hand appliqué, and baste under seam allowance on all edges except those that will be overlapped.

From Color A: Cut one piece for backing and binding (backing is brought around to front of quilt and folded over 1″ with a ½″ hem) 42″ × 50″. From remaining green, cut two strips (each 6½″ × 29½″) and eight large hearts. If a casing for hanging is desired, cut a strip 4½″ × 38″.

From Color B: Cut two strips 5¼″ × 47″ and two strips 5¼″ × 29½″. Then, from enlarged pattern, cut two sleeves, bodice, skirt band, small heart for bib and ten large hearts.

From Color C: Cut a rectangle 25½″ × 29½″.

From Color D: Cut two wings.

From Color E: Cut skirt, bib, cuffs and five small hearts.

From Color F: Cut hair.

From Color G: Cut face and two hands.

From Color H: Cut halo.

From Color I: Cut two cheeks.

CONSTRUCTION

1. Appliqué five small hearts to skirt band, spacing evenly. Blindstitch band to skirt. Cut lengths of wine ribbon to fit above and below skirt band and along top of skirt, folding ribbon ¼″ over back of skirt. Cut lengths of green ribbon to fit above and below wine ribbon on skirt band, also folding ¼″ over back. Blindstitch all ribbons to skirt.

Appliqué heart to bib and cheeks to face. Embroider features. Pin skirt to muslin square, with center bottom of skirt 3¾″ from lower edge of muslin and lower side edges of skirt 8¾″ from side edges of muslin. Using photograph and pattern as guides, position remaining pieces of angel. Baste. Blindstitch all pieces (or machine appliqué).

2. Find center of dark green strips by folding in half lengthwise and crosswise. Fold one rose/green print heart in quarters to find its center and position on center of strip. Place remaining hearts on strip (two to either side of center heart) 3½″ apart. Appliqué. Repeat for other strip.

Place dark green hearts on rose/green strips (5¼″ × 29½″), having two outer hearts 5″ in from ends of strip and 2″ above lower raw edge of bottom strip (2″ below upper raw edge of top strip). Place remaining two center hearts on each strip 3½″ from outer hearts. Appliqué.

3. To piece quilt: All seams are ¼″ wide. Stitch dark green strips above and below appliquéd panel. Stitch 5¼″ × 29½″ rose/green strips above and below dark green strips. Press all seams toward outer edges. Stitch 5¼″ × 47″ strips to both sides of center panel. Press seams toward outer edges.

4. To assemble quilt: Lay dark green backing/border piece down, wrong side up. Center quilt batt on backing. Place completed top piece, right side up, on batt, adjusting carefully to center on backing. Pin. Baste all three layers together, starting from center and radiating out to edges.

5. Quilting: Begin quilting stitches in center of quilt and work outward, using diagram as a guide for location of stitches. Mark quilting lines, radiating out from angel. Four of these lines go from points on the angel to within ¼″ of all four muslin corners. The lines adjacent to these go from the angel to a point 7″ on either side of corner line. Use photograph to determine the point at which each line radiates from angel.

Quilting is done on both sides of all long seams and on short edges of dark green strips. Quilt rose/green and dark green hearts.

Mark heart quilting pattern on long rose/green strips, having the motif 1¾″ in from each end. The remaining seven hearts are marked at a distance of 2¾″ from each other. Repeat for other strip. Quilt.

6. Finishing: Fold 1½″ of backing over front of quilt on all four sides. Fold under a ½″ hem. This leaves a 1″ binding. Pin; miter corners. Blindstitch in place.

Cut a length of green ribbon 11″ long. Make a bow and tack to angel's neckline.

7. To hang quilt: Fold under short ends of casing strip ¼″ twice; stitch. With right sides together, stitch long edges with a ¼″ seam. Turn right side out; press. Blindstitch casing along top back edge of quilt (leaving an opening to slip through a decorative rod for hanging), placing casing 1″ in from each long side of quilt.

continued on page 197

THESE ARE A FEW OF OUR FAVORITE THINGS

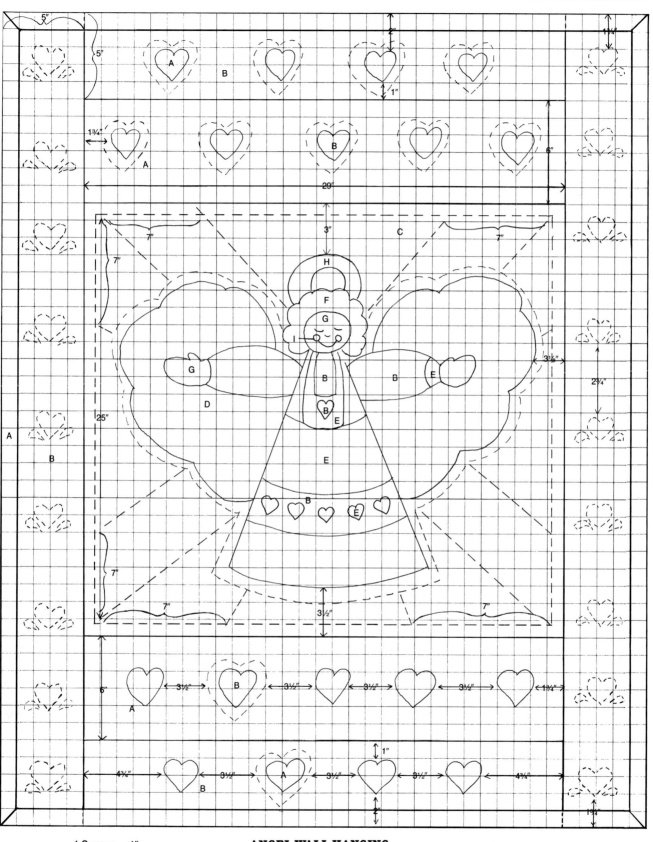

1 Square = 1"
(angel not drawn to scale)

ANGEL WALL HANGING
39"W × 47"L

Inked letters = Color code
(see yardage requirements)

Binding folded over 1"

Broken lines = Quilting lines

'JOY' ANGEL COUNTED CROSS-STITCH
73″W x 115″L

continued from page 194

'JOY' ANGEL
COUNTED CROSS-STITCH
(pictured)
Design area 73″W × 115″L

MATERIALS
9½″ × 11½″ off-white hardanger (22 count)
Tapestry needle
Embroidery hoop
DMC embroidery floss, as indicated on color chart below

COLOR CODES

Symbol	DMC thread #	Color
‘	310	Black
∧	318	Steel gray, light
S	400	Mahogany, dark
+	739	Tan, ultra very light
●	754	Peach flesh, light
O	3362	Loden green, dark
X	3364	Loden green, light
/	3685	Mauve, dark
—	3688	Mauve, medium
G	–	Fil D'or* (metallic gold thread)

* If Fil D'or is unavailable, you may use DMC 676, Old Gold, light.

LARGE STITCHING AREAS:
1 X Fill in sleeves with 3364
2 ∧ Fill in wings with 318
3 — Fill in skirt top with 3688
4 X Fill in skirt bottom with 3364

GENERAL INSTRUCTIONS
1. Whipstitch raw edges of hardanger to prevent fraying.
2. Fold fabric in half, lengthwise and crosswise, to find center. Follow arrows on coded diagram, opposite, to locate center of design. This is the starting point for the stitching.
3. Use 1 strand of embroidery floss or 1 strand of metallic gold thread throughout, both for cross-stitches and for backstitches.
4. Use a hoop for embroidery.
5. Do not tie knots. Leave a ½″ tail on the underside each time a new color is started; anchor this tail with the first five or six stitches. When the thread is almost finished, run the needle through five or six stitches on the underside to secure the thread. Cut excess.
6. Make sure the top stitches of all the X's are going in the same direction.

BACKSTITCHING
After all cross-stitching is completed, backstitch the following areas (solid lines on chart indicate backstitching lines):
   wings—Fil D'or or DMC 676, Old Gold, light
   hair—with 400
   hands, cuffs, sleeves, collar, bodice, skirt—with 3362
   mouth—with 3685
   eyes (bottom and inside edges)—with 310

HOW TO BACKSTITCH
Backstitching is done after all cross-stitches are worked. It may be used to accent and/or outline. Each backstitch is the same length as the stitches comprising the cross-stitches: that is, they extend from one hole in the fabric to an adjacent hole.

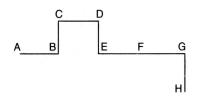

Run floss through a few previously worked cross-stitches to anchor the thread. Start the backstitching by coming up at A and going down at B; come up at C and go down at B; come up at D and go down at C; come up at E and go down at D, and so on. Anchor floss by running through a few previously worked stitches on the underside.

LAVENDER-ROSE POTPOURRI
INGREDIENTS
1¼ cups dried rose petals (see Note 1)
½ cup dried lavender petals
¼ cup cinnamon stick, broken into small pieces
1 teaspoon crumbled bay leaf
2 teaspoons orris-root powder*
1½ tablespoons dried orange peel
3 to 4 drops rose oil (see Note 2)

* Orris-root powder is a potpourri preservative, available in some drugstores and craft stores.

   Mix all the dry ingredients together. Add the rose oil one drop at a time and mix well after each drop. Place in a tin or covered container and let cure for five to six weeks, stirring occasionally. *Makes about 2 cups potpourri.*
   Note 1: If you have your own garden, the rose and lavender flower petals should be picked in the morning after the dew evaporates or in the evening before the dew arrives. Spread the petals out to dry for eight to ten days, until they no longer feel moist. The quantity of flowers picked will be reduced approximately 50 to 60 percent in the drying process.
   Note 2: Potpourri Refresher: After two to four months, when the potpourri scent starts to fade, several drops of the scented oil (either rose, clove or other complementary scent) will refresh the potpourri for another two to four months. A potpourri can last many years, if the scent is refreshed as needed.

CLOVE-AND-SPICE POTPOURRI
INGREDIENTS
½ cup whole cloves
¼ cup cinnamon stick, broken into small pieces
4 tablespoons anise seed
1 teaspoon crumbled bay leaf
1 tablespoon orange peel
1 teaspoon orris-root powder
3 to 4 drops clove oil (see Note 2 above)

   Mix all the dry ingredients together. Add the clove oil one drop at a time, mixing well after each drop. Place in a tin or covered container and let cure for five to six weeks, stirring or shaking occasionally. *Makes about 1 cup potpourri.* ■

A little glue, an assortment of decorative ribbons and a touch of imagination are all you need to turn ordinary, inexpensive picture frames, mirrors, desk accessories and wooden boxes into expensive-looking gifts similar to those found in exclusive boutiques. And the best news: You don't have to know how to sew at all! Easy-to-follow instructions begin on page 200.

All Done Up In
RIBBON

continued from page 198

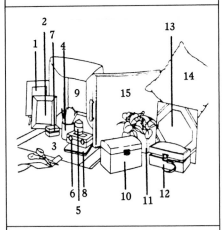

1. *Mat* 2. *Shadow-box frame* 3. *Blotter* 4. *Pencil holder* 5. *Paper-clip holder* 6. *Mitered box* 7. *Lattice box* 8. *Address book* 9. *Padded frame* 10. *Diagonal box* 11. *Planter* 12. *Sewing box* 13. *Mirror* 14. *Pillow* 15. *Breakfast tray*

GENERAL INSTRUCTIONS

MATERIALS
Glue
12-inch aluminum ruler
Single-edge razor blades
Steel triangle
Ribbons

GENERAL NOTES

Razor blades should be changed after 2 cuts to assure a clean edge. If a dull blade is used, the ribbons will fray.

Several types of glues can be used. Glues such as Sobo and Elmer's should be watered down. Glue should be brushed on the ribbons for even distribution. Always do a sample test first, since there is a tendency for some glues to stain the ribbons. Starting at one end, press ribbon down slowly across to the other end. Be certain to follow manufacturer's directions before using any glue.

Double-faced masking tape can be used for covering boxes with ribbons.

Individual designs are not given for the items shown. Instead, work out your ribbon designs by placing them on a white sheet of paper. Ribbons with a picot edge might be used as a border and a narrower one placed on top. Work with the ribbons, changing them around until you come up with the effect that suits you. Colors that might clash normally can work well if separated by a neutral color. Layering and overlapping ribbons can create endless varieties.

When working with velvet ribbons, do not place other ribbons on top of them since nap of velvet ribbon may cause ribbon on top to move.

Mitering is a neat and professional way of finishing off corners. To miter is to achieve a right angle. After gluing a corner, place a straightedge at a 45-degree angle at corner, and cut, using a very sharp razor blade. Peel away excess. See corner in diagram below.

Box openings should be taped closed with paper tape—such as masking tape—before gluing on any ribbons. By doing this, the ribbons line up with one another when the box is opened. When ribbons have been glued in place and if hinges are needed, feel along for opening edge with your finger, and cut that side with a razor blade. Then attach hinges. If a clasp is to be used, follow the same method. Then open up the side edges. For a more professional look, edges as well as inside can be lined.

MAT

MATERIALS
1 yard 1⅜-inch ribbon by Century
1 picture-frame mat, 8″ × 10″

DIRECTIONS

Cut 4 strips of ribbon slightly larger than needed for each side. Glue on ribbons. Starting at one side, press ribbon onto mat to secure. Continue around mat, mitering each corner as you go.

SHADOW-BOX FRAME

MATERIALS
1 yard each of two ⅞-inch solid-color ribbons
1 frame, 7″ × 9″
1 yard of ¼-inch floral ribbon by Century

DIRECTIONS

Glue the outside-edge ribbon to frame, then the inside-edge ribbon. Center floral ribbon on top. Miter each corner as you go.

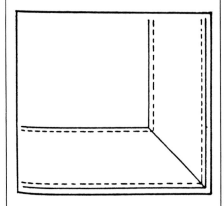

BLOTTER

MATERIALS
1 piece of cardboard, 18″ × 30″
1½ yards of ¹⁵⁄₁₆-inch solid-color ribbon
3 yards of ¼-inch solid-color ribbon
1 piece of cardboard slightly smaller than 18″ × 24″, for back
1 piece of blotting paper, 18″ × 24″
1½ yards of ¼-inch solid ribbon
1½ yards of 2-inch floral ribbon by Century

DIRECTIONS

Score back of larger piece of cardboard on each of the 18-inch sides 3 inches from edge, and fold to the front to make cuffs. (Finished size is 18 by 24 inches.) Glue ribbons on the 3-inch bands with an overhang on back of blotter of at least an inch on all sides. Attach smaller piece of cardboard to the back with glue. Insert blotting paper on front, slipping it under cuffs on either side.

PENCIL HOLDER

MATERIALS
2 empty cardboard rolls from 1½-inch-wide masking tape
1½ yards of 2-inch floral ribbon by Century
1½ yards each of ¹⁵⁄₁₆-inch ribbon (2 colors) and ¼-inch ribbon (2 colors) (see Note)
1 cardboard base cut to fit dimensions of the tape rolls

DIRECTIONS

Tape together two tape rolls to form a tube. Put a dab of glue on ends of all ribbons, and wrap ribbons around the tube, starting at the bottom inner edge, over the top and down the outside edge of the tube and over again into the inside of the tube. Attach cardboard base to bottom of tube.

Note: All ribbons should be cut approximately 4½ times length of tube.

PAPER-CLIP HOLDER

MATERIALS
⅓ yard of 2-inch floral ribbon by Century
⅓ yard each of ¼-inch ribbon and ¹⁵⁄₁₆-inch ribbon
1 standard-size clip holder

DIRECTIONS

Glue ribbons around the circumference of the holder, having them meet in back of holder to form a seam.

ALL DONE UP IN RIBBON

MITERED BOX

MATERIALS
⅔ yard of ¾-inch floral ribbon by Wright's
⅔ yard of 1-inch picot-edge ribbon
⅔ yard each of ¹⁵⁄₁₆-inch solid-color ribbon
   and ¼-inch ribbon
1 wooden box (with cover), 5½″ × 4″ × 2″
   or any size desired
Lining for inside of box, optional

DIRECTIONS
Work out ribbon design on paper first. Place small piece of ribbon horizontally across center of box cover. Work on one side at a time, from the outside in, cutting the ribbon lengths slightly longer than needed. Work in toward center until reaching center ribbon; miter corner. Continue until all corners have been done. Follow general directions for finishing box. Wrap ribbons along the side of the box, with seam on back corner.

LATTICE BOX

MATERIALS
⅔ yard each of ½-inch floral and dot
   ribbons by Century (3 different types)
⅔ yard each of ¼-inch solid-color ribbons
   (5 colors)
1 wooden box (with cover), 3″ × 2¼″ × 2″
   or any size desired

DIRECTIONS
Lay out ribbon design on paper. Ribbons are woven together using 7-inch-length strips for the horizontal weave and 8-inch-length strips for the vertical weave. Weave ribbons wrong side up, weaving only to fit the measurements of the top of the box (in this case, 3 by 2¼ inches). Leave ends free. Apply glue to top of box and attach to wrong side of ribbons, centering box on woven section. Glue ribbon strips to sides of box. Slit opening edge with razor. Finish off with a thin ribbon around opening edge of box.

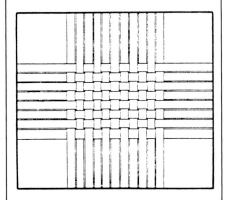

ADDRESS BOOK

MATERIALS
1 address book with removable pages
3 yards of ¹⁵⁄₁₆-inch solid-color ribbon
2 ½ yards each of ½-inch floral ribbons by
   Century (3 colors)
2 yards of 1-inch gingham ribbon by
   Burlington
2 ½ yards of ¹⁵⁄₁₆-inch stripe ribbon by
   Burlington

DIRECTIONS
Take out pages of address book, and work only with outer cover. Apply glue to wrong side of solid-color ribbon, and fold in half to form a casing around entire perimeter of book. Working from inside back seam, glue ribbons horizontally around outside of book and back again to the inside seam. Continue until book is covered.

PADDED FRAME

MATERIALS
1 piece of plywood, 18″ × 20″
Two pieces of foam sheeting, 22″ × 24″
Approximately 6 yards of 1½-inch floral
   ribbon by Wiener Laces
2 yards of ½-inch floral ribbon by Wiener
   Laces
2 yards of ¾-inch floral ribbon by Century
4 yards each of 2-inch and 1-inch solid-
   color ribbon (2 colors in each width)
2 strips of muslin, each 40″ × 10″
One 12-inch square mirror
Felt or muslin to finish back (optional)

DIRECTIONS
Cut an 8-by-10-inch opening in 18-by-20-inch piece of plywood (5 inches in from each side). Stretch 2 layers of foam sheeting onto frame, allowing a 2-inch overhang in back. Cut opening in center of foam and tack or staple to back. Glue ribbons according to your design to one of the muslin strips (this creates a ribbon fabric). Follow the same design for the other strip. Cut the ribbon fabric slightly larger than needed to cover the foam. With right sides together and ribbons all going in the same direction, sew a 45-degree angle, making a little curve at the outside corners. Place fabric wrong side up on the foam side. Tuck and pull the fabric to achieve a taut surface. Tack down the top and bottom with either staples or tacks. Glue corners of mirror, and place in back of frame. Finally, cut a piece of felt or muslin and use it to finish the back, if you desire.

DIAGONAL BOX

MATERIALS
1 wooden box (with cover), 8¼″ × 5¼″ ×
   5⅝″ or any size desired
1½ yards of 1⅜-inch floral ribbon by
   Century
1½ yards each of 1-inch picot-edge ribbons
   (2 colors)
1½ yards of 1-inch solid-color ribbon
1½ yards of ¼-inch solid-color ribbon
1½ yards of 1½-inch solid-color ribbon

DIRECTIONS
Follow general box directions above. Take the floral ribbon in your design, and glue across top of box diagonally. Proceed to wrap and glue box diagonally with ribbons, as if wrapping Christmas presents. After the first ribbon is attached, continue gluing the rest, one by one, until box is completely covered. Proceed with hinges and locks as described above.

PLANTER

MATERIALS
1 can, 6″ × 6″ or any size desired
1 yard each of 1-inch plaid ribbon by
   Century and 1½-inch stripe ribbon by
   Century
1 yard of 1½-inch solid-color ribbon
1 yard of 1-inch solid-color ribbons
   (3 colors) and ¼-inch solid-color
   ribbons (2 colors)
Felt for bottom of can

DIRECTIONS
Work out design on paper first. Alternating patterns, work 2 sides horizontally and 2 sides vertically. Leave a 1-inch overhang on inside of can. To finish, cover bottom with felt.

SEWING BOX

MATERIALS
3 pieces of foam sheeting (one should be
   exact size of box top, one slightly
   smaller, one slightly larger)
1 wooden box with shadow-box lid, 4⅞″ ×
   8¼″ × 3⅜″ or any size desired
½ yard of A.E. Nathan's White Rose
   Gingham fabric
2 yards each of ¼-inch solid-color ribbon
   and 1½-inch solid-color ribbon
2 yards of 1-inch picot-edge solid-color
   ribbon
2 yards of 1-inch floral ribbon by Lowenthal
Felt for bottom of box

DIRECTIONS
Place foam sheeting on top of shadow-box lid, with a smaller piece on bottom, medium piece in middle and larger one on top. Tack foam to lid. Cover with gingham.

continued on page 209

FOOTWORK

E ven Santa will get a kick out of these stockings that you can knit or crochet to fit each family member's personality. From left: a pink slipper for the aspiring ballerina; a cowboy boot for your "pardner"; a penny loafer for the preppie; a sneaker for the athlete; a high-buttoned shoe for the lover of nostalgia; a hiking boot for the outdoorsman. For instructions, see page 204.

continued from page 202

All patterns for tracing are found on pages 204, 207 and 208.

GENERAL DIRECTIONS

MATERIALS

Paternayan Persian Yarn (full strand) is used throughout (see individual directions for colors and amounts). Worsted-weight yarn, or any yarn that will obtain gauge, may be substituted. Aluminum crochet hook, size G (6). Cardboard for soles and heels. Knitting needles (if required). Fiberfil stuffing.

Gauge: 4 sc = 1"; 5 rows = 1" (11 rnds = 2") on size G hook.

ABBREVIATIONS

sc	single crochet
dc	double crochet
sl st	slip stitch
ch	chain
st (s)	stitch (es)
dec (s)	decrease (s)
inc (s)	increase (s)
rnd (s)	round (s)
rem	remain (ing)
rep	repeat
cont	continue
sk	skip
lp (s)	loop (s)
St st	Stockinette stitch (knit one row, purl one row)
k	knit
p	purl
dp	double-pointed
beg	begin (ning)
yo	yarn over
pat	pattern
rs	right side
ws	wrong side
tog	together
psso	pass slip stitch over
"	inch (es)
*	repeat whatever follows as indicated

CROCHETED SLIPPER WITH KNITTED LEG

MATERIALS

3 oz #354 bright pink; 3 oz #946 pale pink; ½ yard red marabou; cardboard and stuffing. No. 8 straight knitting needles; 1 set No. 8 dp needles. Stitch holder. Size G crochet hook. 2 stitch markers.

Slipper: Beg at toe edge, with bright pink, ch 2. **Rnd 1:** Work 9 sc in ch 1. Join with sl st to first sc to form circle. Do not turn rnds. **Rnd 2:** Ch 1, *sc in 2 sc; work 2 sc in next sc (inc made), rep from* around (12 sc). Join. **Rnd 3:** Ch 1, * sc in 3 sc, inc in next sc, rep from * around. Join. **Rnds 4-13:** Work as for Rnd 3, having 1 more sc between incs than on previous rnd. (There will be 3 incs on each rnd and 45 sc at the end of Rnd 13.) **Rnd 14:** Ch

1, sc in each sc around. Join. **Rnds 15-22:** Rep Rnd 14 (45 sc). At end of last rnd, ch 1, turn. **Back sole. Row 1:** Sc in first 15 sc. Do not work over rem sts. Ch 1, turn. **Rows 2-27:** Work even over 15 sc. **Row 28:** Ch 1, draw up a lp in each of next 2 sc, yo and draw through all 3 lps on hook (dec made); sc in each sc to last 2 sc, dec over 2 sc (13 sc). Ch 1, turn. **Row 29:** Work even. **Row 30:** Rep row 28 (11 sc). Fasten off.

Heel bottom: With bright pink, ch 6. **Row 1:** Beg at inner bottom edge of heel. Sc in 2nd ch from hook and in each ch across (5 sc). Ch 1, turn. **Row 2:** Sc in each sc across. Ch 1 turn. **Rows 3-4:** Rep Row 2. **Row 5:** Dec over first 2 sc, sc in next sc, dec over last 2 sc. Ch 1, turn. **Rnd 1:** Work 20 sc around entire edge of heel bottom. Join with sl st to first sc. Do not turn rnds. **Rnd 2:** Ch 1, working in back lps only, sc in each sc around. Join. **Rnd 3:** Ch 1, working under both lps hereafter, sc in each sc around, dec 2 sc around back curved edge of heel. Join. **Rnd 4:** Ch 1, sc in each sc around, inc 1 sc at center back of heel (19 sc). Join. **Rnds 5-10:** Rep Rnd 4 (25 sc). **Rnd 11:** Ch 1, sc around back edge of heel for 6 sts. Ch 1, turn. **Rnd 12:** Ch 1, sc in each sc around. Join. Fasten off.

Sole edging: Join bright pink at rs edge of sole, just behind last rnd of toe. **Row 1:** Draw up a lp, ch 1, sc in joining, sc evenly around back edge of sole, ending at corresponding place on left edge. Fasten off.

Leg: With light pink and No. 8 knitting needles, cast on 50 sts. Work in rib of k 1, p 1 for 6 rows. K 2 rows for hem. Change to St st, and work for 9½", dec 1 st at each end every 4", 2 times; end with a p row (46 sts).

Heel and instep. Row 1 (rs): With dp needle, k 10; with 2nd dp needle, k 26, and slip to stitch holder; with straight needle, k 10 sts; on same needle, k 10 from first dp needle (20 sts for heel are joined at center back). **Row 2:** P. **Row 3 (rs):** *K 1, slip 1, rep from * across, end k 2. Rep these 2 rows for 1½". Bind off. (Back of heel is complete.)

With rs facing and dp needles, pick up and k 10 along left side edge of heel, place marker on needle, k 26 from holder, place marker on needle, pick up and k 10 along rs edge of heel (46 sts). **Row 1 (ws):** P to 3 sts before marker, p next st, return to left needle, pass next st over the purled st; with point of right needle, slip rem st back to right needle, p 1, slip

COWBOY BOOT

marker, p 26, slip marker, p1, p 2 tog, p rem sts. **Row 2:** K to 3 sts before marker, k 2 tog, k 1, slip marker, k 26, slip marker, k 1, slip 1, k 1, psso, k rem st. **Rows 3-6:** Rep Rows 1 and 2. **Row 7:** Rep Row 1 (32 sts). Cont in St st for 4½". Bind off. Sew back seam. Stuff slipper heel. Sew leg in place around top edge of slipper. Cut cardboard for sole, using pat as guide, and place inside slipper. Stuff slipper and leg.

Garter: With bright pink, ch 5. **Row 1:** Sc in 2nd ch from hook and in each ch across (4 sc). Ch 1, turn. Work even over 4 sc until strip reaches around stuffed leg. At end of last row, ch 1; do not turn.

Ruffled edging. Row 1: Sc evenly along one long edge of strip to opposite corner. Ch 3, turn. **Row 2:** Work 2 dc in first sc (ch 3 counts as 1 dc), *work 3 dc in next sc. Rep from * across. Fasten off. With same side facing, join yarn in top corner of opposite long side of strip. Work Rows 1 and 2 of edging to correspond. Sew garter around top of leg. Cut 6" of marabou, and form a circle; sew to garter where short edges meet. Form a circle with remaining marabou, and sew to vamp of slipper.

CROCHETED COWBOY BOOT

MATERIALS

5 oz (5 skeins) #972 red; 1 oz #202 black; 1 oz #204 gray. Tapestry needle for embroidery. Size G crochet hook. Cardboard and stuffing.

Foot: Beg at toe with red, ch 2. **Rnd 1:** Work 9 sc in ch 1. Join with sl st to first sc to form circle. Do not turn rnds. **Rnd 2:** Ch 1, * sc in 2 sc; work 2 sc in next sc (inc made). Rep from * around (12 sc). Join. **Rnd 3:** Ch 1, * sc in 3 sc, inc in next sc. Rep from * around. Join. **Rnds 4-13:** Work as for Rnd 3, having one more sc between inc than on previous rnd. (There will be 3 incs on each rnd and 45 sc at the end of Rnd 13.) **Rnd 14:** Ch 1, sc in each sc around. Join. **Rnds 15-19:** Rep Rnd 14 (45 sc). **Rnd 20:** Ch 1, draw up a lp in each of next 2 sc, yo and draw through all 3 lps on hook (dec made); sc in next 18 sc, dec over next 2 sc, complete rnd (43 sc). Join. **Rnd 21:** Ch 1, dec over first 2 sc, sc in 17 sc, dec over next 2 sc, complete rnd (41 sc). Join. **Rnd 22:** Ch 1 (sc in 5 sc, inc in next sc) twice (instep); sc in each rem sc (43 sc). Join. **Rnd 23:** Ch 1 (sc in 6 sc, inc in next sc) twice; complete rnd (45 sc). **Rnd 24:** Sc in 25 sc, dec 1 sc, sc in 7 sc, dec 1 sc, complete rnd (43 sc). **Rnd 25:** Ch 1 (sc in 7 sc, inc in next sc) twice; sc in 9 sc, dec 1 sc, sc in 6 sc, dec 1 sc, complete rnd (43 sc).

SLIPPER

Rnd 26: Work even (43 sc). **Rnd 27:** Ch 1, sc in 7 sc, inc in next sc, sc in 9 sc, inc in next sc, complete rnd (45 sc). **Rnd 28:** Ch 1, sc in 28 sc, dec 1 sc, sc in 4 sc, dec in next sc, complete rnd (43 sc). **Rnd 29:** Ch 1, sc in 8 sc, inc in next sc, sc in 9 sc, inc in next sc, complete rnd (45 sc). Join and fasten off.

Sole and sides: Sk next 14 sc, join yarn in following st. **Row 1:** Draw up a lp, ch 1, sc in joining and in next 30 sc, ending in previous joining (31 sc). Do not work over rem sts. Ch 1, turn. **Row 2:** Sc in each sc across (31 sc). Ch 1, turn. **Rows 3-25:** Rep Row 2. Fasten off and turn.

Back of heel: Sk 10 sc, join yarn in following sc. **Row 1:** Draw up a lp, ch 1, sc in joining and in next 10 sc. Do not work over rem sts. Ch 1, turn. **Rows 2-10:** Work even over 10 sc. Fasten off. Sew side edges of rows just worked to 10 sk sts at each side, forming back of upper heel.

Top of boot: Join yarn in 6th st of 10 sc at back of heel. **Row 1:** Work 28 sc along edge of side rows to instep, work 13 sc across instep sc, work 28 sc along opposite side edge of boot, ending at back of heel. Do not join. Ch 1, turn. **Row 2:** Sc in 28 sc, dec over next 2 sc, sc in 9 instep sc, dec over next 2 sc, sc in rem 28 sc. Ch 1, turn. **Row 3:** Sc in 26 sc, dec over next 2 sc, sc in 11 instep sc, dec over next 2

sc, sc in rem 26 sc. **Row 4:** Sc in 27 sc, dec over next 2 sc, sc in 7 instep sc, dec over next 2 sc, sc in rem 27 sc. **Row 5:** Sc in 25 sc, dec over next 2 sc, sc in 9 instep sc, dec over next 2 sc, sc in rem 25 sc. **Row 6:** Sc in 26 sc, dec over next 2 sc, sc in 5 instep sc, dec over next 2 sc, sc in rem 26 sc. **Row 7:** Sc in 24 sc, dec over next 2 sc, sc in 7 instep sc, dec over next 2 sc, sc in rem 24 sc. **Row 8:** Sc in 25 sc, dec over next 2 sc, sc in 3 instep sc, dec over next 2 sc, sc in rem 25 sc. **Row 9:** Sc in 23 sc, dec over next 2 sc, sc in 5 instep sc, dec over next 2 sc, sc in rem 23 sc. **Row 10:** Sc in 24 sc, dec over next 2 sc, sc in one instep sc, dec over next 2 sc, sc in rem 24 sc (51 sc). Work even for 23 rows. Do not ch 1 at end of last row. Turn.

Left boot top. Row 1: Sl st in first 2 sts, ch 1, sc in 22 sc. Do not work over rem sts. Ch 1, turn. **Row 2:** Dec over first 2 sc, sc in each sc to last 2 sc, dec over last 2 sc. Ch 1, turn. **Rows 3-8:** Rep Row 2. Fasten off.

Right boot top: Sk 1 sc on last long row worked, join yarn in next sc and work Rows 1-8 to correspond to opposite top of boot. Sew back edges together.

Embroidery: Following diagram on page 178 for embroidery, with gray and tapestry needle, embroider design in ch st.

Top edging: Join yarn at top center back edge. **Rnd 1:** Sc evenly around top edge. Join. Fasten off.

Heel: With black, beg at inner bottom edge of heel, ch 10. **Row 1:** Sc in 2nd ch from hook and in each ch across (9 sc). Ch 1, turn. **Rows 2-6:** Work even. **Row 7:** Dec one sc at each end of row. **Row 8:** Work even. **Rows 9-10:** Rep Rows 7 and 8. Do not turn at end of last row.

Side of heel. Rnd 1: Working in back lps only, sc evenly around entire edge, working 3 sc in each inner corner. Join. Ch 1, turn. **Rnd 2:** Working through both lps hereafter, sc in each sc around. Join. Ch 1, turn. **Rnd 3:** Sc in each sc around, inc 2 sc around back (curved) edge of heel. Join. Ch 1, turn. **Rnds 4-7:** Rep Rnd 3. Fasten off.

Using pat as guide, cut sole and heel from cardboard, and place cardboard inside heel. Stuff heel, and sew to boot. Place cardboard inside sole of boot. Join black yarn at rs edge of boot just in front of heel. **Toe edging:** Sc evenly around edge of boot where cardboard sole ends, ending at opposite front edge of heel. Fasten off.

Top tabs (make 2): With black, ch 6. **Row 1:** Sc in 2nd ch from hook and in each ch across (5 sc). Ch 1, turn. Work even over 5 sc for 4″. Fasten off. Fold tab in half, and sew inside side edge of boot. Stuff boot.

continued on page 206

COWBOY BOOT

EMBROIDERY FOR TIP OF TOE

(DIAGRAMS ARE HALF ACTUAL SIZE)

EMBROIDERY FOR RIGHT SIDE OF BOOT
REVERSE FOR LEFT SIDE

continued from page 205

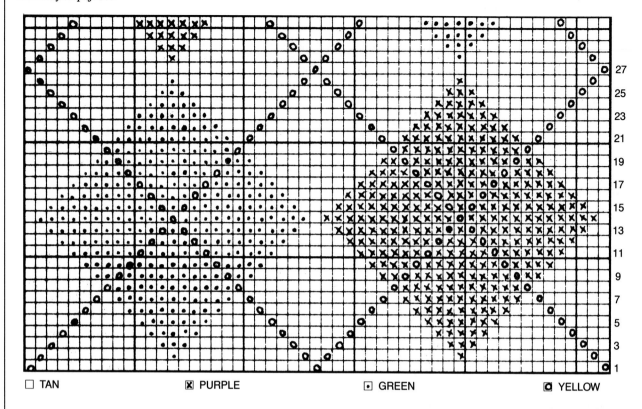

☐ TAN   ☒ PURPLE   ⊡ GREEN   ◖ YELLOW

CROCHETED PENNY LOAFER WITH ARGYLE SOCK

MATERIALS

3 oz brown; 2 oz #406 tan; 1 oz #631 green; 1 oz #331 purple; 1 oz #202 black; 1 oz #712 yellow. Size G crochet hook. No. 7 knitting needles; 1 set No. 7 dp needles. Bobbins. Cardboard and stuffing. Stitch holder.

Charts: Each square equals one st and each line equals one row. Read each chart from right to left for knit rows (rs); from left to right for purl rows (ws). To change colors, pick up new strand from under old strand. Carry unused yarn, loosely twisting yarn after every 3rd st.

Sole: Beg at toe edge with brown, ch 6. **Row 1 (rs):** Sc in 2nd ch from hook and in each ch across (5 sc). Ch1, turn. **Row 2:** Work 2 sc in first sc, sc in each sc to last sc, inc in last sc (7 sc). Ch 1, turn. **Rows 3-4:** Rep Row 2 (11 sc). **Row 5:** Sc in each sc across. Ch 1, turn. **Row 6:** Rep Row 2 (13 sc). **Rows 7-9:** Rep row 5. **Row 10:** Rep Row 2 (15 sc). **Row 11-12:** Rep Row 5. **Row 13:** Rep Row 2 (17 sc). **Rows 14-21:** Rep Row 5. **Row 22:** Draw up a lp in first sc, draw up a lp in next sc, yo and draw through all 3 lps on hook (dec made), sc in each sc to last 2 sc, dec over last 2 sc (15 sc). Ch 1, turn. **Rows 23-27:** Rep Row 5. **Row 28:** Rep Row 22 (13 sc). **Rows 29-47:** Rep Row 5. **Rows 48-51:** Rep Row 22 (5 sc). At end of Row 51, ch 1, do not turn.

Edge rnd (rs): (Work 1 sc in every row of sole.) Sc in same sc as ch 1; keeping edge flat, sc evenly around entire outer edge. Join with sl st to first sc. Fasten off.

Vertical edge of toe: Starting at center of toe on edge rnd, count 28 sts along rs of toe on edge rnd. Join yarn in this (28th) sc. **Row 1:** With rs facing, draw up a lp, ch 1, working in *front* lps only, sc in each sc around toe edge, ending in 28th sc from center on left side of toe. Ch 1, turn. **Row 2:** Working under both lps, sc in each sc across (56 sc). Ch 1, turn. **Rows 3-7:** Rep Row 2. At end of Row 7, do not ch 1. Fasten off.

Vertical edge of heel: Join yarn on left side edge next to first row of vertical edge of toe. **Row 1:** With rs facing, draw up a lp, ch 1, sc in front lp of each sc to corresponding place on right edge. Ch 1, turn. **Rows 2-9:** Work same as for Row 2 of vertical edge of toe. Fasten off. Sew edges of vertical front and back tog at sides, leaving extra row on back free at top of seams.

Top of toe and tongue: Beg at toe edge with brown, ch 6. **Row 1 (rs):** Sc in 2nd ch from hook and in each ch across (5 sc). Ch 1, turn. **Row 2:** Work 2 sc in first sc (inc made), sc in each sc to last sc, inc in last sc (7 sc). Ch 1, turn. **Rows 3-4:** Rep Row 2 (11 sc). **Row 5:** Sc in each sc across. Ch 1, turn. **Row 6:** Rep Row 2 (13 sc). **Rows 7-9:** Rep Row 5. **Row 10:** Rep Row 2 (15 sc). **Rows 11-**
12: Rep Row 5. **Row 13:** Rep Row 2 (17 sc). **Rows 14-21:** Rep Row 5. **Row 22:** Draw up a lp in first sc, draw up a lp in next sc, yo and draw through all 3 lps on hook (dec made), sc in each sc to last 2 sc, dec over last 2 sc (15 sc). Ch 1, turn. **Rows 23-27:** Rep Row 5. **Row 28:** Rep Row 22 (13 sc). **Rows 29-31:** Rep Row 5. **Rows 32-34:** Rep Row 22 (7 sc). At end of Row 34, ch 1; do not turn.

Top of toe and tongue edge. Rnd 1 (rs): Sc in same place as ch 1, keeping edge flat, sc evenly around entire outer edge. Join. Fasten off. With Row 1 at front edge, pin top of toe and tongue inside top edge of vertical edge of toe, with beg of tongue meeting free top row of vertical edge of back. With top of shoe facing, join yarn in rs edge where tongue meets free top row of back. Working through both top of toe and vertical edge, sc around entire toe edge, joining top to edge. Fasten off.

Instep strap with opening for penny: Beg at side edge, ch 9. **Row 1 (rs):** Sc in 2nd ch from hook and in each ch across (8 sc). **Rows 2-12:** Sc in each sc across. Ch 1, turn. **Row 13:** Sc in first 2 sc, dec over next 2 sc. Do not work over rem sts. Ch 1, turn. **Row 14:** Rep Row 2 (3 sc). **Row 15:** Sc in first sc, dec over next 2 sc. **Rows 16-17:** Rep Row 2 (2 sc). **Row 18 (ws):** Inc in first sc, sc in last sc (3 sc). Ch 1, turn. **Row 19:** Rep Row 2. **Row 20:** Inc in first sc, sc in rem 2 sc (4 sc). Ch 1, turn. **Row 21:** Rep Row 2. Fasten off. Right half of diamond opening is completed. With rs facing, join yarn in first free sc (5th st) on Row 13. Draw up a lp, ch 1, dec over this and next sc, sc in last 2 sc (3 sc). Ch 1, turn. Complete Rows 14-21 to correspond to right half of diamond opening, reversing all shaping (4 sc). Ch 1, turn. **Row 22 (ws):** Sc in each of next 4 sc, sc in each of 4 sc on right half of opening (8 sc). Ch 1, turn. **Rows 23-34:** Rep Row 2. Fasten off. Sew strap across top of shoe where free top row of vertical edge of back meets tongue.

Heel: Beg at bottom with black, ch 6. **Row 1 (rs):** Sc in 2nd ch from hook and in each ch across (5 sc). **Rows 2-5:** Work 2 sc in first sc (inc made), sc in each sc to last sc, inc in last sc (13 sc). Ch 1, turn. **Rows 6-17:** Sc in each sc across. Ch 1, turn. At end of Row 17, ch 1, do not turn.

Side edge of heel. Rnd 1: Sc in same place as ch 1, keeping edge flat, sc evenly around entire outer edge. Join. Do not turn. **Rnd 2:** Ch 1, sc in joining and in each sc around through back lps only, to form ridge. Join. **Rnds 3-6:** Work even in sc through both lps. Fasten off.

Argyle sock: Beg at top with No. 8 straight needles and tan, cast on 52 sts. **Row 1:** Work in rib of k 2, p 2 for 6 rows, inc 1 st at end of last row. Following chart (page 206) for Argyle pat and color key, work 2 reps of chart. When chart is complete, cont with tan only, working 2 rows in St st, end with a rs row. **Next row:** P, dec 7 sts evenly spaced (46 sts).

Heel and instep. Row 1 (rs): With dp needle, k 10 sts; with 2nd dp needle, k 26 sts, and slip to stitch holder; with straight needle, k rem 10 sts; on same needle, k 10 from first dp needle (20 sts for heel are joined at center back). Work as follows: **Row 2:** P. **Row 3 (rs):** *K 1, slip 1, rep from * across, end k 2. Rep these 2 rows for 1½". Bind off. (Back of heel is complete.) With rs facing and dp needles, pick up and k 10 along left side edge of heel, place marker on needle, k 26 from holder, place marker on needle; pick up and k 10 along rs edge of heel (46 sts). **Row 1 (ws):** P to 3 sts before marker, p next st, return to left needle, pass next st over the purled st with point of right needle, slip the rem st back to right needle, p 1, slip marker, p 26, slip marker, p 1, p 2 tog, p rem sts. **Row 2:** K to 3 sts before marker, k 2 tog, k 1, slip marker, k 26, slip marker, slip 1, k 1, psso, k rem st. **Rows 3-6:** Rep Rows 1 and 2. **Row 7:** Rep Row 1 (32 sts). Cont in St st for 4½". Bind off. Sew back tog.

Using pat as guide, cut cardboard for heel and sole. Place inside heel, stuff and sew in place. Sew sock in place around top edge of shoe. Stuff the sock.

PENNY LOAFER

CROCHETED RUNNING SHOE

MATERIALS
3 oz (3 skeins) #204 gray; 2 oz #541 blue; 1 oz #972 red. Size G crochet hook. One tube sock. Cardboard and stuffing.

Toe: Beg at toe edge, with gray, ch 2. **Rnd 1:** Work 8 sc in ch 1. Join with sl st to first sc to form circle. Do not turn rnds. **Rnd 2:** Ch 1, work 2 sc in first sc (inc made), *2 sc in next sc. Rep from * around (16 sc). Join. **Rnd 3:** Ch 1, sc in each sc around. Join. **Rnd 4:** Ch 1, *sc in 1 sc, 2 sc in next sc. Rep from * around (24 sc). Join. **Rnds 5-6:** Rep Rnd 3. **Rnd 7:** Ch 1, *sc in 3 sc, 2 sc in next sc. Rep from * around (30 sc). Join. **Rnd 8:** Rep Rnd 3. **Rnd 9:** Ch 1, *sc in 4 sc, 2 sc in next sc. Rep from * around (36 sc). Join. **Rnd 10:** Rep Rnd 3. **Rnd 11:** Ch 1, *sc in 5 sc, 2 sc in next sc. Rep from * around (42 sc). Join. **Rnds 12-15:** Rep Rnd 3.

Sole and sides. Row 1: Ch 1, sc in 38 sc. Do not work over rem 4 sts. Ch 1, turn. **Row 2:** Sc in each sc across. Ch 1, turn. **Rows 3-5:** Rep Row 2. **Row 6:** Inc in first sc, sc in each sc to last sc, inc in last sc. Ch 1, turn. **Rows 7-11:** Rep Row 2. **Row 12:** Rep Row 6. **Rows 13-17:** Rep Row 2. **Row 18:** Rep Row 6 (44 sc). **Rows 19-24:** Rep Row 2. At end of last row, do not ch 1. Turn. **Row 25:** Sl st in first 9 sts, ch 1, sc in 9th st and in next 27 sc. Do not work over rem 8 sts. Ch 1, turn. **Row 26:** Sc in each sc across (28 sc). Ch 1, turn. **Rows 27-45:** Rep Row 26. Fasten off. Turn.

Back of upper heel. Row 1: Sk first 9 sts, join yarn in next st, draw up a lp, ch 1, sc in same sc and in next 9 sc. Do not work over rem 9 sts. Ch 1, turn. Work even over 10 sc for 11 more rows. Fasten off. Sew side edges of rows just worked to 9 skipped sts at sides, forming heel, with 1 row of heel sts extending above side edges.

Tongue. Row 1: With gray, ch 4, sc in 4 unworked sts on last rnd worked (front of shoe). Ch 5, turn. **Row 2:** Sc in 2nd ch from hook, sc in rem 3 ch, sc in 4 sc, sc in each ch at end of row (12 sc). Ch 1, turn. **Row 3:** Sc in each sc across. Ch 1, turn. Rep Row 3 to top edge of shoe. **Next row:** Dec one sc over first 2 sts, sc to last 2 sts, dec over last 2 sts. Ch 1, turn. Rep last row twice (6 sc). Fasten off. Sew 4 sts at each side of tongue inside shoe opening.

Edging: With toe facing you, join gray at left top edge of front opening. Sc evenly around ankle edge to opposite front corner of opening. Fasten off. **Toe trim:** With blue, ch 41. **Row 1:** Sc in 2nd ch from hook and in each ch across (40 sc). Ch 1, turn. **Row 2:** Sc in each sc across. Ch 1, turn. **Row 3:** Dec 1 sc each side of row. **Row 4:** Rep Row 3. Fasten off. Sew around front of toe.

Front opening trim: With blue, ch 7. **Row 1:** Sc in 2nd ch from hook and in each ch across (6 sc). Ch 1, turn. **Row 2:** Sc in each sc across, inc 1 sc each side of row. **Rows 3-4:** Rep Row 2 (12 sc). Ch 1, turn. **Row 5:** Sc in first 4 sc. Do not work rem sts. Ch 1, turn. Work even over 4 sc until trim measures same as front opening. Fasten off. Sk next 4 unworked sts on Row 4, join yarn in next st. Draw up a lp, ch 1, sc in same sc and in last 3 sc (4 sc). Ch 1, turn. Work to correspond to other side. Sew trim around front opening of shoe, aligning edges. With gray, work a ch to measure 40" long. Lace through front and trim opening, as shown in photograph. Knot each end of ch.

Heel trim: With blue, ch 37. **Row 1:** Sc in 2nd ch from hook and in each ch across (36 sc). **Rows 2-12:** Dec 1 sc each side of row (14 sc). Fasten off. Sew around back of shoe at lower edge.

Side trim: With red, ch 4. **Row 1:** Sc in 2nd ch from hook and in each ch across (3 sc). **Rows 2-4:** Sc in each sc across, inc 1 sc each side of row (9 sc). **Row 5:** Sc in first 5 sc only. Ch 1, turn. **Row 6:** Work even on 5 sc. **Row 7:** Sc in first 4 sc only. Ch 1, turn. **Row 8:** Work even on 4 sc. **Row 9:** Sc in first 3 sc only. Ch 1, turn. Work even over 3 sc until trim reaches from center of side edge to center of back heel sts. Fasten off. Work other side to correspond, reversing shaping. Sew short edges of trim tog. Sew trim around shoe, with lower edge of side trim meeting upper edge of heel trim.

Using pat as guide, cut cardboard for sole; place inside shoe. Stuff tube sock, and place inside shoe. Sew sock to shoe.

CROCHETED HIGH-BUTTON SHOE

MATERIALS
2 oz (2 skeins) #341 purple; 3 oz (3 skeins) #344 gray. Six small round buttons. Size G crochet hook. Cardboard and stuffing.

Foot: Beg at toe with purple, ch 2. **Rnd 1:** Work 9 sc in ch 1. Join with sl st to first sc to form circle. Do not turn rnds. **Rnd 2:** Ch 1, * sc in 2 sc; work 2 sc in next sc (inc made). Rep from * around (12 sc). Join. **Rnd 3:** Ch 1, * sc in 3 sc, inc in next sc. Rep from * around. Join. **Rnds 4-13:** Work as for Rnd 3, having one more sc between incs than on previous rnd. (There will be 3 incs on each rnd 45 sc at the end of Rnd 13.) **Rnd 14:** Ch 1, sc in each sc around. Join. **Rnds 15-18:** Rep Rnd 14 (45 sc).

continued on page 208

RUNNING SHOE

continued from page 207

Sole and side edges: Sk next 24 sts; join yarn in next st. **Row 1:** Draw up a lp, ch 1, sc in same sc and next 29 sc. Do not work over rem sts. Ch 1, turn. **Row 2:** Sc in each sc across (30 sc). Ch 1, turn. **Rows 3-8:** Rep Row 2. **Row 9:** Sc in 8 sc, dec over next 2 sc, sc in 10 sc, dec over next 2 sc, sc in rem 8 sc (28 sc). Ch 1, turn. **Rows 10-11:** Work same as for Row 9, having 2 less sc between dec than on previous row—24 sc at end of Row 11. **Rows 12-44:** Rep Row 2 (24 sc). Fasten off. Turn.

Upper back heel: Sk first 8 sc, join yarn in next sc. **Row 1:** Draw up a lp, ch 1, sc in same sc and in next 7 sc. Do not work over rem 8 sc. Ch 1, turn. **Rows 2-10:** Work even. Fasten off. Sew sides of rows just worked to 8 skipped sts, forming back of heel.

Edging: With purple, join yarn at center back of top edge. **Rnd 1:** Draw up a lp, ch 1; drawing edge in slightly, work 30 sc to front instep corner, draw up a lp in each of next 3 sc, yo and draw through all 4 lps on hook, work 5 sc to center front of instep, ch 3 for front picot, sc in same place, work 4 sc to last 3 sc, draw up a lp in each of next 3 sc, yo and draw through all 4 lps on hook, work 30 sc to center back of heel (72 sc). Join with sl st to first sc. Fasten off.

Boot top: Join gray in back lp of first sc after ch 3 picot. **Row 1:** Ch 1; working in back lps only, sc to first front corner sc, dec 1 sc at corner, sc in each sc around side and back edges, dec 2 sc around back of heel, dec 1 sc at opposite front corner, sc in each sc to ch 3 picot (68 sc). Do not join (front opening). Ch 1, turn. **Row 2:** Working under both lps hereafter, sc in 4 sc, dec 1 sc in corner, sc in each sc to back of heel, dec 1 sc, sc in each sc to last 6 sc, dec 1 sc over next 2 sc, sc in rem 4 sc. Ch 1, turn. **Row 3:** Rep Row 2 (62 sc). **Row 4:** Sc in 4 sc, dec 1 sc, sc in each sc to last 6 sc, dec 1 sc, sc rem 4 sc. Ch 1, turn. **Rows 5-12:** Rep Row 4. **Row 13:** Rep Row 2. **Rows 14-15:** Rep Rows 4 and 2. **Row 16:** Sc in each sc across. Ch 1, turn. **Rows 17-35:** Rep Row 16. Fasten off.

Front edging: Join gray in lower edge of right front opening. **Row 1:** Draw up a lp, ch 1, work 25 sc along edge, ending in right top corner. Ch 1, turn. **Row 2:** Sc in each sc across. Ch 1, turn. **Rows 3-6:** Rep Row 2. **Row 7 (rs):** Sc in first sc, * sk 1 sc, work 5 dc in next sc, sk 1 sc, sc in next sc; rep from * across (6 shells). Fasten off.

Heel bottom: With purple, ch 6. **Row 1:** Beg at inner bottom edge of heel, sc in 2nd ch from hook and in each ch across

(5 sc). Ch 1, turn. **Row 2:** Sc in each sc across. Ch 1, turn. **Rows 3-4:** Rep Row 2. **Row 5:** Dec over first 2 sc, sc in next sc, dec over last 2 sc. Ch 1, turn. **Rnd 1:** Work 20 sc around entire edge of heel bottom. Join with sl st to first sc. Do not turn rnds. **Rnd 2:** Ch 1; working in back lps only, sc in each sc around. Join. **Rnd 3:** Ch 1; working under both lps hereafter, sc in each sc around, dec 2 sc around back curved edge of heel. Join. **Rnd 4:** Ch 1, sc in each sc around, inc 1 sc at center back of heel (19 sc). Join. **Rnds 5-10:** Rep Rnd 4 (25 sc). **Rnd 11:** Ch 1, sc around back edge of heel for 6 sts. Ch 1, turn. **Rnd 12:** Ch 1, sc in each sc around. Join. Fasten off.

Using pat as guide, cut cardboard for sole, and slip inside shoe. Overlap front edges to close shoe, and sew a button in the center of each shell, sewing through both thicknesses. Stuff heel, and sew to shoe. Stuff shoe.

CROCHETED HIKING BOOT WITH KNITTED SOCK

MATERIALS

3 oz #712 yellow; 5 oz #612 green; 2 oz #204 gray; 1 oz #972 red. Cardboard and stuffing. One set No. 8 dp knitting needles. Size G crochet hook.

Boot: Beg at heel edge with yellow, ch 6. **Row 1 (rs):** Sc in 2nd ch from hook and in each ch across (5 sc). Ch 1, turn. **Row 2:** Work 2 sc in first sc (inc made), sc in each sc to last sc, inc in last sc (7 sc). Ch 1, turn. **Rows 3-5:** same as Row 2 (13 sc). **Rows 6-28:** Ch 1, sc in each sc across.

Shape arch. Row 29: Inc 1 sc at arch side (14 sc). **Row 30:** Rep Row 6. **Row 31:** Rep Row 2 (16 sc). **Rows 32-33:** Rep Row 29 (18 sc). **Rows 34-43:** Rep Row 6.

Opposite side shaping. Row 44: Ch 1, draw up a lp in each of next 2 sc, yo and draw through all 3 lps on hook (dec made); sc in rem sts (17 sc). **Row 45:** Rep Row 6. **Row 46:** Dec 1 st each end (15 sc). **Row 47:** Rep Row 6. **Row 48:** Rep Row 46 (13 sc). **Row 49:** Rep Row 6. **Row 50:** Rep Row 46 (11 sc). **Row 51:** Rep Row 6. **Row 52:** Rep Row 46 (9 sc). **Row 53:** Rep Row 6. **Row 54:** Rep Row 46 (7 sc). **Row 55:** Rep Row 6. **Row 56:** Rep Row 46 (5 sc). Ch 1. Sc evenly around entire sole, making sure to keep flat. Sl st into ch 1, ch 1, do not turn. Work 3 rows sc, 1 sc in each st. Fasten off.

Toe uppers: Beg at toe with green, ch 9. **Row 1 (rs):** Sc in 2nd ch from hook and

in each ch across (8 sc). Ch 1, turn. **Row 2:** Work 2 sc in first sc (inc made), sc in each sc to last sc, inc in last sc (10 sc). **Rows 3-5:** Rep Row 2. **Rows 6-9:** Ch 1, sc in each sc across. **Row 10:** Same as Row 2 (18 sc). **Rows 11-20:** Same as Row 6. **Row 21:** Sc in first st, inc 1 in next sc, sc in each sc to 2 sc from end, inc 1, sc in last sc (20 sc). **Row 22:** Rep Row 6. **Row 23:** Rep Row 21 (22 sc). **Row 24:** Rep Row 6. **Row 25:** Rep Row 21 (24 sc). **Row 26:** Rep Row 6. **Row 27:** Rep Row 21 (26 sc). **Row 28:** Rep Row 6. **Row 29:** Rep Row 21 (28 sc). **Row 30:** Rep Row 6. Ch 1. Sc evenly around curved edge of toe, making sure to keep it flat. Fasten off. With green, sew upper to sole, matching toe ends and picking up inside lps of sole (yellow).

Vertical edge of shoe: Beg at corner where upper meets sole, with green, pick up inside lps (yellow). Sc in each sc around heel to meet other corner. Ch 1, turn. Cont in sc for 10 rows. Fasten off. Sew vertical edge of shoe to upper.

Boot shaft: With green, starting at corner, work sc, dec 1 st in each corner for 4 rows. Do not turn. Work even for 30 rows. Change to yellow, and work 2 rows more. Fasten off. Starting at back of heel with top facing you, with yellow, work 1 row of sc around yellow edge. **Heel:** With yellow, ch 5. **Row 1 (rs):** Sc in 2nd ch from hook in each ch across (4 sc). Ch 1, turn. **Row 2:** Work 2 sc in first sc (inc made), sc in each sc to last sc, inc in last sc (6 sc). Ch 1, turn. **Rows 3-5:** Same as Row 2 (12 sc). **Rows 6-15:** Ch 1, sc in each sc around. At end of Row 15, ch 1, do not turn.

Side edge of heel. Rnd 1: Sc in same place as ch 1; keeping edge flat, sc evenly around entire outer edge. Join. Do not turn. **Rnd 2:** Ch 1, sc in joining and in each sc around through back lps only, to form ridge. Join. **Rnds 3-5:** Work even in sc through both lps. Fasten off.

Using pat as guide, cut cardboard for heel, and place in bottom of heel. Stuff heel, and sew to sole.

Shoelace: With yellow, make a chain 60″ long. Fasten off. Cut cardboard for sole, and slip inside boot.

Gray sock for boot: With No. 8 dp needles and gray, cast on 48 sts. Work in rib of k2, p2 for 4 rnds. Change to red, and work in rib for 4 rnds. Change to gray, and work rib for 2 rnds. Change to red, and work rib for 2 rnds. Change to gray, and cont in rib for 3″ from beg. Beg St st, and work even until sock measures 6½″ from beg. Bind off. Begin lacing boot where decs end at instep, and end 4″ below the top edge of boot, using photograph as guide. Sew sock to inside of boot. Stuff boot. ∎

HIKING BOOT

HIGH BUTTON SHOE

SWEET AND SPICY HOLIDAY BASKETS

continued from page 183

PEPPERMINT-STICK BASKETS

To make baskets from peppermint sticks, you can use the glue method described above or simply secure sticks to the containers with bits of florist's clay (also available at florists or garden-supply centers).

We used plastic food-storage containers to make the baskets pictured. Should the peppermints become tacky to the touch, they can be sprayed with a clear fixative, obtainable at any art-supply store. Kept in the cold, however, peppermints should remain smooth. Tie rickrack or other decorative trim around the baskets, knotting or tying into small bows. To make "handles" as shown, you will need longer peppermint sticks: two for the uprights, two for the horizontal grips. After securing the upright sticks with glue or clay, place one horizontally on each side about an inch from the top and secure; or simply secure one stick straight across the top. Wrap and tie ribbon around the "joints" to cover spaces between sticks.

CINNAMON-STICK BASKETS

To make cinnamon-stick baskets, use ordinary household items as bases: individual-size ramekins or custard cups, a supermarket mushroom basket, plastic storage or freezer containers, baking tins.

You will need garden shears or heavy-duty clippers to cut the lengths of cinnamon to size. To cover small containers, cut sticks to the height of the container; then run a thick band of white glue around inside of container. Allow the glue to become slightly tacky (about ten minutes); then begin to apply cinnamon sticks around the inside, butting them closely together as you go. Repeat this procedure on the outside of container. This will leave a space between the two layers of cinnamon sticks that can be filled with moss, raffia, straw or similar substance to enhance the textural appearance. To finish, knot a length of silk cord or ribbon around the outside.

To cover a larger object, such as the mushroom basket shown, you will need florist's wire (available at any florist or garden-supply center). We used longer lengths of cinnamon to give added depth, interweaving the sticks with the wire (alternating one over, one under, about one inch from top and bottom edges of sticks) on a flat surface to equal the circumference of the basket. Here, too, butt the sticks as closely together as possible while interweaving with the wire. When the flat "mat" of sticks is complete, simply wrap around the basket and secure the ends with wire. Glue smaller sticks of cinnamon around the top of handle and, if desired, give the basket a flourish with a lavish bow. ∎

ALL DONE UP IN RIBBON

continued from page 201

Line inside of box with gingham. Wrap ribbons around the circumference of the box, ending at back edge. Place a 1-inch floral ribbon along shadow-box edge, mitering corners. Glue ribbons to bottom half of box sides. Cut piece of felt to finish bottom.

MIRROR

MATERIALS
One 12-inch square mirror
2 yards of ½-inch floral ribbon by Century
2 yards of 1-inch solid-color ribbon
⅔ yard of 2¼-inch solid-color ribbon
1½ yards of 1-inch solid-color ribbon

DIRECTIONS
At the center point of each side of mirror, center a 2¼-inch strip of ribbon, and attach with glue. Again at this center point, lay ribbons, one at a time, diagonally across corners and working toward corners, and glue down.

PILLOW

MATERIALS
2 yards each of 1½-inch floral and 1¾-inch floral ribbons by Wright's
2½ yards each of 1-inch solid-color ribbons (2 colors) and 1½-inch solid-color ribbon
2½ yards of 2-inch solid-color picot-edge ribbon
One 16-inch-square stretcher frame
One 16-inch-square piece of muslin
Pillow form or stuffing
Fabric for backing pillow

DIRECTIONS
Cut 16-inch lengths of ribbon, and tack or staple them to stretcher frame vertically. Then tack 16-inch ribbon lengths to one side, and weave them horizontally across. Brush piece of muslin and wrong sides of ribbons with glue. Place glue side of muslin on wrong side of ribbons. Pat muslin side down. Take ribbons off the stretcher, and proceed to finish off pillow. Ribbons and muslin are treated as if they were a piece of fabric.

BREAKFAST TRAY

MATERIALS
1 piece of paper, 18″ × 24″
2 pieces of glass, 18″ × 24″
6 yards of 1⅜-inch floral ribbon by Read & Harding
1 yard of ¹⁵⁄₁₆-inch gingham ribbon by Century
½ yard of floral trim (about 1 inch) by Wright's
6 yards of 2-inch solid-color ribbon
1¼ yards of ¾-inch solid-color ribbon
3 yards each of ¼-inch solid-color ribbons (3 colors)
1 frame, 18″ × 24″
2 handles

DIRECTIONS
On a piece of paper the exact size of the glass, sketch out design. Put tracing of this sketch under one sheet of glass, and attach ribbons with glue, placing them so that the 1⅜-inch floral ribbon is glued down last, after the ¼-inch and 2-inch solids are glued down. Miter all corners. After the entire ribbon design is glued down, take second sheet of glass and place it on top of ribbons, sandwiching the ribbons between the two pieces of glass. (Plywood can be used in back of tray for added strength instead of one of the pieces of glass.) On the back of the tray, insert thin pieces of wood the dimensions of the frame, to act as a brace and make the tray sturdy. Attach handles to frame; center on each 18-inch end.

All items designed by D. & D. Studio Workshop. ∎

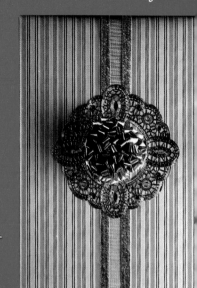

IT'S A WRAP

Shooting Stars

Lacy & Lovely

Package your gifts to give pleasure even before they're opened.

Silver Sack

Horn of Holly

Wrap it up in tantalizing fashion. Embellish with lacy doilies, shiny silver bags, cornucopias or decorative stickers. (Books, records, hard-to-wrap gifts receive our special attention.) Dress up every package in the season's newest hues: frothy pink and blue spruce, as well as traditional Christmas colors. All are easy to do, even the handmade lace snowflake and the print-your-own wrapping paper (made with ordinary buttons). Directions begin on page 212.

Strips and Stripes

Record Wrap

Buttons & Bows

Read All Over

Fit To Be Tied

continued from page 211

GENERAL DIRECTIONS

1. The step-by-step wrapping directions and the patterns that follow will help you make perfect, foolproof gift wraps.

2. Listed under materials for each gift wrap are the materials you will need *in addition to* the basic materials listed here.

3. The amount of wrapping paper and ribbon needed will depend on the size of the package you are wrapping.

Note: If you cannot find the wrapping paper specified, substitute a similar type of paper.

To Wrap: Center box, top down, on wrapping paper. Bring one side of paper over box, and tape. Fold remaining side over about an inch, to make a neat seam (see Diagram 1). Bring up over box and over taped-down edge. Tape in place. (Use double-faced tape if you don't want tape to show.) To wrap ends, fold top down (see Diagram 2). Tape edge in place. To make neatly mitered corners, fold sides toward center, creasing paper along edges of box as you do (see Diagram 3). Tape sides together at bottom edge. Fold bottom flap over about an inch (see detail). Tape in place. Repeat on opposite end of box.

TO WRAP

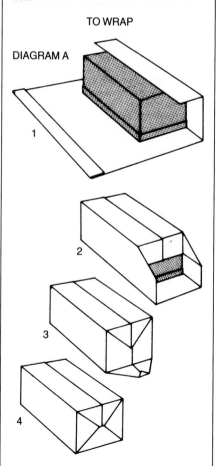

DIAGRAM A

To Use Patterns:

Enlarge them to fit your package size. Solid lines on pattern indicate cut lines; use metal ruler held firmly in place and X-acto knife for cutting. Dotted lines on pattern indicate folded lines; folded lines must be scored.

Basic Materials Needed: Gift wrap, ribbons, stickers as specified; lightweight cardboard (posterboard, shirt cardboard, Bristol board, etc.); scissors; metal ruler; X-acto knife; stapler; small hole punch; rubber cement or spray adhesive; pencil; white glue; straight pins; double-faced sticky tape.

To Score: Place a metal ruler on dotted line, and hold firmly in place. Using X-acto knife, score a line lightly against edge of ruler, to get a clean, straight line. Do not cut all the way through.

To Laminate: Cut cardboard and gift-wrap paper slightly larger than pattern shape you are making. Spread spray adhesive (following manufacturer's directions) or thin coat of rubber cement on one side of cardboard and wrong side of gift-wrap paper. Let dry. Press cemented sides together. Proceed with pattern directions.

GOLDEN HOLLY LEAVES

MATERIALS
Wrapping paper
Florists' wire
12 gold leaves
1 sprig red berries
Flat gold cord

DIRECTIONS

Wrap box following directions in Diagram A. Wire gold leaves together, placing sprig of berries in center as shown in photograph. Tape flat gold cord on package. With tape, secure bunch of leaves to center of package by the stems. Flatten leaves to cover tape.

CREDITS
Paper: Designed by Heather Cooper for Ruby Street, Inc., 131 Seventh Ave., Brooklyn, NY 11215. Gold leaves: Dennison Products, 390 Fifth Ave., New York, NY 10018

SILVER SACK

DIRECTIONS

Secure bag tightly around gift with wire tie or ribbon. Roll bag down from top, folding loosely, to form "collar." Attach bow with tape or glue in center of collar.

CREDITS
Wrapsac™, The Glemby Company, Inc., 120 E. 16 St., New York, NY 10003. Silver bow: Dennison Products.

DECORATIVE DOILY

MATERIALS
Wrapping paper
Ribbon
Glitter ribbon
Doily
Ready-made or homemade bow

DIRECTIONS

Wrap box following directions in Diagram A. Tape plain ribbon lengthwise to package. Then tape 1 length of glitter ribbon on each side of plain ribbon (see photograph). With double-faced tape, secure doily to package. Add bow.

CREDITS
Paper: Stephen Lawrence Company, 150 Louis St., P.O. Box 2324, South Hackensack, NJ 07606. Glitter ribbon: Stribbons, Roslyn Heights, NY 11577. Doily and bow: Dennison Products.

LACY & LOVELY

DIRECTIONS

Cut 40 inches of 1½-inch-wide lace ribbon into eight 5-inch lengths. Trim ends of each piece at an angle (see Diagram 5). With wrong side of ribbon facing you, curve ends around and up until the two points meet (Diagrams 6 and 7). Glue ends together. Let dry. Repeat for seven remaining pieces. Arrange the eight folded pieces into "Snowflake," as shown in photograph, on cardboard, and pin in place to hold shape. Glue sides of each section to sides of adjoining sections. Let dry. Remove pins. If desired, attach thin string or wire to end of one point for hanging later as an ornament. (Reprinted by permission of Lion Ribbon Company.)

CREDITS
Paper: Hallmark, Inc. Ribbon: Lion Ribbon Company, 225 Fifth Ave., New York, NY 10010.

LACY & LOVELY

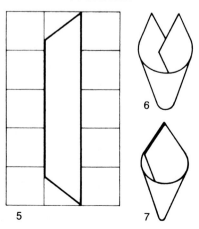

BUTTONS & BOWS

MATERIALS
Masking tape
Classified or real-estate sections of
  newspaper
White tissue paper
Straightedge or T-square
Marking pen
Iron
Hairpins or plastic-bag wire ties
Buttons with interesting front surfaces
Foam-type stamp pad
Stamp-pad ink
Plastic gloves (optional)

DIRECTIONS

Tape six layers of newspaper pages, with columns running horizontally, to table or drawing board (layers are for padding; columns are for grid guides). Lay pieces of tissue paper squarely over the newspaper and tape into place (this tissue will become pattern guide). Using straightedge, trace horizontal lines of columns onto tissue with a marking pen.

Draw vertical lines at even intervals with straightedge; or, if you need a guide, untape newspaper, turn columns to vertical position, replace tissue and trace vertical lines to form a grid. This grid will assure even placement of button design, but freehand placement is also attractive. Press tissue paper to be decorated with cool iron to remove wrinkles. Lay tissue over newspaper and grid guide, taping in place at corners. Attach wire tie or hairpin to button shank from back to form a handle for printing (front surface of button is used as stamp). Press button onto stamp pad, then print on tissue, using grid to aid in forming design. Dries immediately. (Buttons with ornately carved fronts may require additional layers of newspaper for clear imprint.) Accent color may be added with colored marking pens.

CREDITS
Paper: Helen Raffels. "Pequot" ribbon: Stephen Lawrence Company.

HORN OF HOLLY

DIRECTIONS

Enlarge pattern. Trace onto cardboard or laminated gift-wrap paper, indicating hole marks and fold lines. Fold to form cornucopia, as shown in photograph. Overlap ends, and staple in back. Punch holes. Pull cord through holes and tie knots at each end to form handle. Fill with small pinecones or holly berries. Secure cornucopia and handle to package with double-faced tape.

CREDITS
Paper: Stephen Lawrence Company. Striped paper: Sample House. Ribbon: Offray Ribbon Company.

HORN OF HOLLY

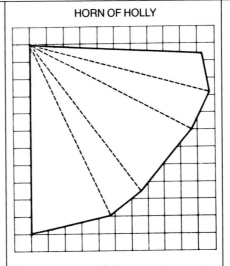

SHOOTING STARS

DIRECTIONS

Wrap gift, and tie with "Flair" ribbon bow. Cut extra lengths of ribbon five inches and six inches long to create "shooting stars." Fold in half. Slip one end under ribbon tie on package, and pull up. Hold cut ends together with star stickers placed back to back. "Flair" ribbon is stiff.

CREDITS
Paper, "Flair" ribbon: Stephen Lawrence Company; "Star" foil stickers: Dennison Products.

RECORD WRAP

DIRECTIONS

Tree wrap: Cut 17½-inch square of gift-wrap paper. Place record on the diagonal on reverse side of paper (see Diagram). Fold points of paper over album toward center. Secure with sticker.

Ribbon wrap: Cut gift wrap to 16¼-by-31-inch rectangle. Fold short sides together, wrong sides facing. Place record album in paper wrap ¾ inch up from center fold and equidistant from both sides (about 2 inches). Run thumb and index finger around the four edges of album to mark paper and aid in folding sides and top. Fold sides forward and in toward album ½ inch and then ½ inch again. Repeat at top. Mark centers of the four sides. Punch hole at marks. Fold 2 yards of ribbon in half. Tie a single knot at fold; this will serve as anchor for ribbon. Starting at back of package, draw both ends of ribbon through bottom hole until knot stops passage. Take one ribbon and draw it through one side hole front to back; draw other end through opposite side front to back. Draw both ends through top hole, back to front. Tie in bow.

Hole-punch wrap: Cut gift wrap to 16¼-by-29-inch rectangle. Fold short sides together, wrong sides of paper facing. Place record album in paper wrap against fold, equidistant from sides. Fold front sides of paper over top of album. Fold back side against front fold. Secure with spray adhesive. Run thumb and index finger along album edge to use as guide for side folds. Fold each side in half lengthwise, toward back of package. Cut two strips of solid-color wrap 13¼ inches by 2 inches. Fold in half lengthwise. Spray reverse side with adhesive. Place edge of package sides onto adhesive, leaving ½-inch excess at each end. Close sides of package with strips by placing package on fold line of strip and pressing strip over package sides. Trim excess from ends. Punch holes at ¾-inch intervals along side strips of package.

CREDITS
"Tree" paper: Stephen Lawrence Company. "Tree" sticker: Mrs. Grossman Paper Company. Green paper: Sample House. Ribbon: Offray Ribbon Company. "Dot" paper: Accord Publications, Inc.

RECORD WRAP

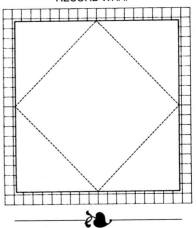

READ ALL OVER

DIRECTIONS

Cut piece of scrap cardboard to book size and place on cover of book. Wrap book in wrapping paper. Cut rectangle (ours was 1 inch by 6 inches) from laminated gift-wrap paper to coordinate with wrapped book. Place sticker at top. Back sticker with paper cut to shape, so it will not stick to book wrapping. Make two parallel slits in book wrapping (ours are 1⅛ inches wide) ¼ inch apart. (Cardboard under wrapping will protect cover.) Slip bookmark through slits as shown. Message may be written on back.

CREDITS
Papers: Accord Publications, Inc. Bow sticker: Gordon Fraser Gallery, Ltd., 225 Fifth Ave., New York, NY 10010.

continued on page 221

SURPRISE
PACKAGES

Even the gift that's impossible to wrap can be cleverly and festively packaged. All you have to do is cut and fold in just the right places!

Upper left: A colorful cube can disguise any mind-twisting game or toy. Below it: Bag a bit of jewelry, a batch of hair ribbons—almost anything—in a handmade tote. Bottom left (and second from top at right): Our "double-torpedo" package (the ends are slit and gathered with cheerful bows) can hold gloves, a bottle of fragrance—any small surprise. Top right: A perky basket for candy, cookies, baubles or what-have-you. Center right: A tiny house to hold miniature dolls, a set of cocktail napkins, a pouch of potpourri. Bottom right: Stash a small stuffed animal, a scented candle—any little thing—in a pretty version of a carry-out container.

SURPRISE PACKAGES

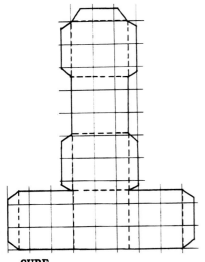

CUBE
CUT 9 SQUARES OF COLORED PAPER FOR
EACH EXPOSED SURFACE; GLUE IN PLACE.

MATERIALS: Light-weight cardboard (posterboard, Bristol board, mat board, shirt cardboard, etc.) that is flexible but still firm enough to use in constructing a box to hold your gift (Oaktag is ideal); metal ruler; a good cutting tool: paper shears, mat knife or X-acto knife; small trimming scissors (whatever you use should be sharp and pointed enough to get into tiny areas and make clean, crisp cuts); spray adhesive; rubber cement; glue stick; gift-wrap paper; an assortment of ribbons, yarns, trims, etc., for making closures.

GENERAL INFORMATION

Patterns are shown to scale: one square equals one inch. Enlarge to appropriate size for your gift.

Once you have traced your pattern onto the cardboard, remember to *fold* on the dotted lines and *cut* on the solid lines, as indicated on the pattern. If the cardboard is thick and doesn't fold easily, you will have to score all the fold lines with a sharp knife. Place a metal ruler against the dotted line to be scored, and hold it firmly in place. Then cut lightly against the edge of the ruler to get a clean, straight line. Do *not* cut all the way through the cardboard.

Cut and fold all the appropriate lines on each box.

To cover the box with gift-wrap paper, first use your box pattern to measure the approximate amount of paper you will need. Spread the cardboard evenly with glue, and work the paper carefully around the box form, smoothing it over curves and folds. (Spray adhesive is ideal for an even, thin mist of glue.) Trim away any excess paper from the edges of the box.

Once the entire box is covered with the gift-wrap paper, assemble it, using rubber cement to glue the tabs and closures together. Touch up edges with a glue stick.

Be sure to have plenty of newspaper on your work surface and change it often, since spray adhesive tends to be messy.

Trim finished boxes to suit your fancy. ■

1 SQUARE = 1″

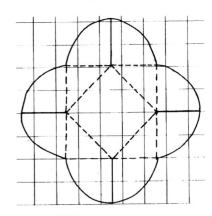

BASKET
CUT STRIP OF PAPER-COVERED CARDBOARD FOR HANDLE; GLUE IN PLACE. OURS IS PAPERED INSIDE AS WELL.

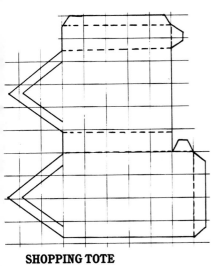

SHOPPING TOTE

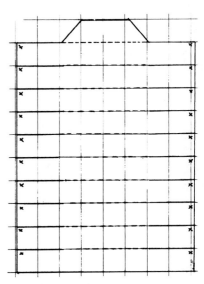

DOUBLE TORPEDO
PUNCH HOLES AT X; THREAD RIBBON THROUGH HOLES.

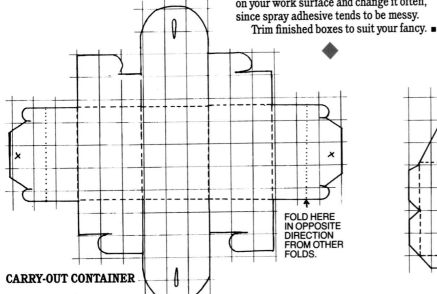

CARRY-OUT CONTAINER

FOLD HERE
IN OPPOSITE
DIRECTION
FROM OTHER
FOLDS.

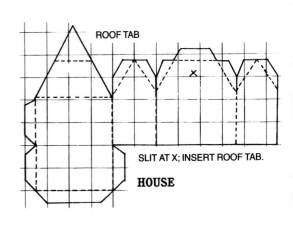

ROOF TAB

SLIT AT X; INSERT ROOF TAB.

HOUSE

WRAPPED WITH IMAGINATION... AND ALMOST NO MONEY

Half the fun of a gift is its package, and here are some ideas for original and inexpensive (sometimes free) gift wraps. A big DECEMBER 25 from a calendar makes a handsome seal. Newspaper stock-market pages make a clever wrap for Wall Street buffs: For a note of optimism tape a cord that zigzags up. Heavy-duty wrapping paper, spiraled into a cone with top point tucked in, can hold all sorts of goodies. We've stuffed it with ice-cream-color towels. Re-use beautifully designed shopping bags for gift wraps, as we've done in the deep blue package below the cone, the Christmas-tile package behind it and the Christmas-tree package at right. For shirts or ties, make a shirt-front package of brown wrapping paper, foil and glue-on buttons. Paste tracings of your own hands to hold the gift card on a personal package. Tie the gift you sewed yourself with dressmaker's tape; paste FRAGILE stickers on a box that holds breakables. The oversize pencil is made from two oatmeal boxes. Directions are on page 221.

GIFT WRAPS

THAT GO EVERYWHERE

Over the river and through the woods (or even longer journeys on train or plane) needn't wreak havoc on your beautifully wrapped gifts. These easy-to-make packages will also retain their good looks though sent through the mail, packed into suitcases or piled under the tree. Just cut, paste or fold, using simple materials like shelf paper and doilies, gift wrap and ribbon. Then let everyone admire the results of your ingenuity! Instructions begin on page 220.

continued from page 219

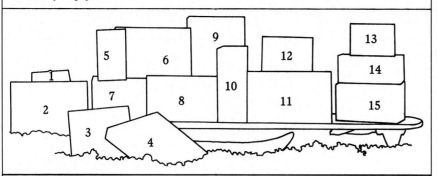

1. *Crushed-foil package.* 2. *Cutout paper snowflake.* 3. *Photo hang tag.* 4. *Trivet trim.* 5. *Calendar gift wrap.* 6. *Cutout-trees overwrap.* 7. *Cutout-trees stencil.* 8, 11 & 14. *Fold-and-cut decorations.* 9, 10, 12 & 15. *Border wraps.* 13. *Christmas-card decal.*

DIRECTIONS FOR CUTOUTS

The "paper doll" cutting method (cutting shapes to form a continuous chain of one design): Evenly pleat a piece of paper accordion style to form a packet. The number of folded sections should be enough to make the chain your desired length; the size of the sections is determined by the design (use the widest part of design as a guide; e.g., since the snowman is 2 inches at the base, folded sections should be 2 inches wide). Center and outline the design onto the first section of the folded packet, making sure that some point on both sides of the design touches the folded edges. (The finished chain will be attached where each side touches the folds.) Cookie cutters may be used for the design, or you can draw your own freehand design, using ours as an example. After drawing design on the packet, cut out with sharp scissors, taking care to leave sides touching. Unfold the packet, and glue on package, decorating as desired.

Sled from Faces of Time, N.Y.C. All unglazed white shelf paper: Royalace Division, Millen Industries, Inc., N.Y.C. All trim stickers: Mrs. Grossman's Paper Co., 1933 S. Broadway, Los Angeles, CA 90007.

1. Crushed-foil package. Cut length of aluminum foil slightly larger than needed to wrap package. Crush loosely into a ball. Carefully open foil, and flatten it slightly, but do not smooth bumps. Wrap package. We used 6 strands of yarn twisted together to tie and knot package.
Yarn: Hallmark Cards, Inc.

2. Cutout paper snowflake. Materials: white 8½-by-8½-inch paper; pencil; scissors or X-acto knife; white glue. Fold paper once diagonally to form a triangle. Fold triangle in half again. Fold triangle in half once more. Sketch design on triangle, remembering that the corner made by all the folded edges will become the center of the snowflake. Sketch lines should start at one edge and end at the same edge. The more interesting the cuts at this stage, the more intricate the design will be when it is unfolded. Cut out design; unfold snowflake very carefully. Refold and recut if more cuts are needed. When completed, cover with paper for protection of cutouts, and press with warm iron. Glue to package.
Green paper: Family Line, Inc., Westmont, IL 60559.

3. Photo hang tag. Cut photograph to desired size. Attach to a piece of colored paper, using double-faced tape. Cut colored paper to form a frame, and fashion a point at the top. Punch a hole in the point; add yarn tie to hang. *Note:* If using instant prints, only Kodak TrimPrint camera prints can be cut.

4. Trivet trim. Materials: wrapping paper; double-faced tape; straw trivet. This wrapping is a gift in itself. Straw trivet is held in place on wrapped gift with double-faced tape. Wood trivets may also be used.
Straw trivet: Woolworth & Co.

5. Calendar gift wrap. Use attractive December calendar page as giftwrap. Tips: Mark December 25th prominently on the package, and use a bow to emphasize the date. (Photocopy calendar page to make more wrapping paper, if desired.)
Ribbon: C.M. Offray & Son, Inc., Chester, N.J.

6. Cutout-trees overwrap. Materials: white unglazed shelf paper; solid-color wrapping paper; scissors or X-acto knife; pencil; tree-shape cookie cutter (or trace or draw tree freehand); transparent tape; narrow ribbon, if desired. Make decorative overwrap with white shelf paper folded accordion style as in the paper-doll method. Size of overwrap is determined by size of package. (Ours was 5 inches high with 1-inch segments.) Sketch half of tree pattern onto folded edge of packet. Pattern should not touch both edges. Cut out tree shape from packet. If slits are desired, fold packet again, and cut out small rectangles on fold above and below tree. Make angled cuts at top and bottom of packet, or round each end in a scallop to make overwrap more decorative. Open packet, lay it on a flat surface, cover it with plain paper (for protection of cutouts) and iron it with a warm iron to smooth. Wrap gift with solid-color wrapping paper. Secure overwrap on package with transparent tape. If you choose to make slits as shown, narrow ribbon can be run through the overwrap for a more colorful look.
Green paper: Hallmark Cards, Inc.
Ribbon: C.M. Offray & Son, Inc.

7. Cutout-trees stencil. Materials: all materials needed for No. 6, plus two small shallow dishes; red and green tempera or poster paint; ½-inch-deep new sponge; repositionable spray adhesive (optional); gold-star sticker (optional). Proceed as for No. 6 overwrap, using glazed wrapping paper or other medium-weight paper and cutting out design by overwrap method described above. Add rows of slits at top and bottom of trees by cutting in from both edges of packet, taking care not to cut all the way through. Press as in No. 6. Wrap package in shelf paper or other absorbent paper. Place overwrap on top of package, and use as a stencil: Hold in place at the corners with small pieces of tape or a light misting of spray adhesive used according to manufacturer's directions. Pour small amounts of paint into separate shallow dishes. Cut sponge into rectangles about 2 by 1½ inches. Dip end of dry sponge into paint, and dab lightly onto package through the cutouts and the slits on stencil. Use one sponge for each color. Do not try to cover cutouts completely; let sponge texture remain. When paint is completely dry, remove stencil. (Paint dries quickly.) If desired, place gold-star sticker on top of one of the trees.

8, 11 and 14. Fold-and-cut decorations. Materials: shelf paper; brown kraft paper or large paper bag; scissors; white glue; stickers (to decorate snowman, Teddy bear and bell shapes cut from cookie cutters, or drawn freehand); wrapping paper. Wrap gift as desired. Make decorative border of snowman, bear or bell, using paper-doll method. Glue border to wrapped package, and decorate with stickers. We used thin green string on bells package.

Red and green paper, kraft mailing paper: Hallmark Cards, Inc.

9, 10, 12 and 15. Border wraps. Materials: wrapping papers; transparent tape; scissors. Wrap packages with solid-color wrapping paper. Cut borders from wrapping paper with border designs. Tape borders in place over wrapped packages.

Red and green paper, "Country Fare," "Rainbow Noel," "Alpine Ribbon,"

"Cathy's Christmas" patterned papers: Family Line, Inc.

13. Christmas-card decal. Materials: Christmas card; white glue; wrapping paper; scissors. Cut out Christmas-card scene, and glue corners to wrapped gift.

Paper: Hallmark Cards, Inc. Framed scene: Cape Shore Paper Products, Inc., Yarmouth, Maine.

Note: Other inexpensive gift-wrap suggestions: newspapers (e.g., comics, classified, editorials, foreign); brown kraft

paper; plain newsprint paper from art-supply stores; paper tablecloths; maps; clear corsage bags from florists, lined with tissue paper.

Numbers 1 and 3 were designed by Michael Cannarozzi; number 6 was designed by Butch Krutchik; and all other packages were designed by Helen Raffels. ∎

IT'S A WRAP

continued from page 213

STRIPS AND STRIPES

DIRECTIONS

Enlarge pattern. Trace onto green cardboard or laminated gift-wrap paper, indicating holes. Cut. Punch holes. Knot end of cord or ribbon. With right side of tree facing you, draw cord through first hole on left side at base of tree. Using photograph as guide, continue lacing cord through all holes, leaving remaining cord at top for hanging. If desired, place foil star at top.

CREDITS
Papers: Stephen Lawrence Company. "Star" sticker: Dennison Products. "Rattail" cord: Ruby Street.

STRIPS AND STRIPES

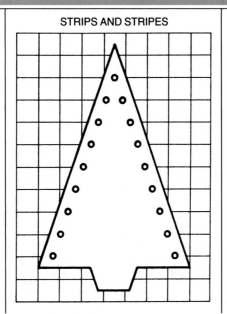

FIT TO BE TIED
DIRECTIONS

Wrap gift in wrapping paper. Cut length of wide ribbon 9 inches longer than package girth. Bring ribbon around package and up to top. Pinch together with thumb and forefinger, holding tightly against package. Punch two holes through both thicknesses of ribbon ½ inch apart as close to package as possible. Draw narrow ribbon through holes, and tie tightly in bow. Cut tops of wide ribbon at angles. Tension of ribbons holds wide ribbon upright.

CREDITS
Paper, ribbon: Stephen Lawrence Company. ∎

WRAPPED WITH IMAGINATION...

continued from page 217

BIG PENCIL

MATERIALS
Two oatmeal boxes
Clear Scotch tape
Brown wrapping paper
Pink and black tempera paints
Library paste
Shiny yellow gift-wrap paper
Watercolor paper
Silver or aluminum foil

DIRECTIONS

The Big Pencil is sure to be a hit with the kids and is a snap to put together. Get two empty oatmeal boxes, cut out the bottom of one oatmeal box and tape the two boxes together so that you have a long cylinder. Put your gift(s) inside; then make a cone out of brown wrapping paper, and tape to the open end of the package. Paint on a "lead" point. Paste yellow

paper around the body of the pencil. To make the eraser, cover the bottom of the box with watercolor paper and paint pink. Use strips of silver or aluminum foil for the little "metal" part of the pencil; tape seams with clear tape, and you're done. To open, just pull off the point of the pencil. You can get materials at art-supply or variety stores. ∎

DIXON'S SECRETARY №3

FIVE

VISIONS OF GINGERBREAD

Of all the holiday adornments, nothing evokes the wide-eyed, excited child in each of us quite like a homemade gingerbread house. There's something wonderfully nostalgic about baking, building and decorating your own miniature work of art to proudly display as the table or mantel centerpiece.

We've captured a sweet bit of that yesteryear spirit with our neighborhood of traditional—and not-so-traditional—cookie houses. By following our easy directions, recipes and "blueprints," you can construct an exquisite Victorian mansion, a cozy cottage, an authentic-looking Swiss chalet, an impressive chapel, even a little village…all from gingerbread. For a change in architecture and flavor, our neighborhood also has a Spanish adobe ranch made from peanut-butter-cookie dough, an almond-speculaas-cookie windmill, a cocoa-shortbread log cabin and a spectacular candy house made from sugar-cookie dough.

Choose your favorite house, or group several together to form "Cookie House Lane," a place built on the spirit of the holiday season.

CLASSIC COOKIE HOUSES

Here are eight fabulous Christmas centerpieces, each one adorably and authentically detailed. Gather the family to share in all the fun of baking and building your own holiday masterpiece. Directions begin on page 232.

Fingerprints make the "tile" roof, cinnamon sticks form the canopied entrance and a peanut-butter dough becomes the walls of our Spanish adobe ranch. Real chiles dry near the door, as gum-candy cacti bloom in the front yard.

This elaborate Victorian manse, built from traditional gingerbread, is modeled after an actual house, right down to the front porch supported by peppermint-stick columns and the bay window adorned with lace curtains. The trees are molded from lollipop syrup, and a dusting of confectioners'-sugar "snow" clings to the vanilla-cookie-shingled roof.

Santa hangs out on a blade of this Dutch-inspired windmill, made from spicy almond-studded speculaas-cookie dough. The blade trim and door wreath are white frosting with red and green sugars. Make Santa from our pattern on page 235.

IRWIN HOROWITZ

This cozy cabin in the woods is made of cocoa-shortbread logs and thatched with shredded whole-wheat biscuits. The chimney is built from chocolate drops and caramels; the winding path is chocolate-covered raisins; the tree, spearmint candy leaves.

A path of chopped pecans leads through the snow-covered yard and up to the frosted front door of our festive cottage. The walls, shutters, fence and weather vane are gingerbread (as is the visiting cat). The roof is overlapping rows of chocolate wafers; the chimney, caramels mortared with icing.

Our gingerbread Swiss chalet swings open its red frosted shutters to welcome the holidays. The curtains are cut from red-striped gum, the roof is overlapping tea cookies and the evergreen trees are actually inverted ice-cream cones piped with green-colored frosting. Broken chocolate and licorice become the rocky path, and nougat candies stack up for a wonderful chimney. The finishing touch: generous dollops of snow frosting.

Here's a sweet fantasy-come-true for kids of all ages: a candyland house that adults can put together (using a simple sugar-cookie dough) and children can decorate with mini-marshmallows, jelly beans, gumdrops, mints, peppermint candies and sticks, and licorice candies and laces. A little dab of snow frosting "glues" each piece of candy in place to create the doors, windows, rooftop and yard of this enchanting house that before existed only in our fondest dreams.

A colorful angel trumpets the glad tidings of the season in front of this exquisite gingerbread chapel, complete with stained-glass windows (red sugar syrup) and a clock tower. The roof, clocks, doors and churchyard bricks (as well as the angel) are all gingerbread; snow frosting is swirled along the sides for a stucco effect.

VISIONS OF GINGERBREAD 231

continued from page 224

ADOBE RANCH
(pictured)

3 recipes Peanut-Butter-Cookie Dough,
   recipe follows
Paper for patterns
Corrugated cardboard
Masking tape
Brown thread
1 egg white
1 teaspoon water
9 (3-inch) cinnamon sticks
2 recipes Decorator Frosting, recipe
   follows
10 to 20 green 1½-by-1-inch gumdrops
4 to 8 green gumdrop rings
Toothpicks
Granulated sugar
2 red 1½-by-1-inch gumdrops
Green food color
Dried red peppers (optional)

1. Make Peanut-Butter-Cookie Dough. Wrap each recipe of dough separately; refrigerate until ready to use.

2. Make paper patterns: For front-back, draw and cut a 14-by-6-inch rectangle from paper. Measure several points 2½ inches in from each end; draw a line connecting the points. Make a 2½-by-2-inch rectangle from paper; fold in half crosswise to make a 2-by-1¼-inch rectangle. Draw and cut a line rounding off one pair of cut corners. Open for window pattern. Place on one side of front-back pattern, 1½ inches up from bottom edge and ½ inch toward center from the line you drew (i.e., 3 inches from edge). Draw around window pattern. Fold front-back pattern in half crosswise; cut out window through double thickness of paper. Open; label "front-back."

3. For side pattern, draw and cut a 7-by-6-inch rectangle. Label the 7-inch sides top and bottom. Mark several points 1 inch in from a side edge; draw a line connecting them. At the same side of the pattern, mark a point 1½ inches up from the bottom and ½ inch in from the side edge; draw a straight line from the top of the 1-inch line to the point ½ inch in from the edge. Continue the line, curving to meet the bottom corner. Cut along line. Place window pattern 1½ inches up from bottom and 2 inches in from straight edge of side pattern. Draw around window; cut out. Label pattern "side." Trace curved end of pattern to the 1-inch line. Cut out; label "extension side."

4. Draw, cut out and label a 14-by-6-inch rectangle for the roof, a 4½-by-¾-inch rectangle for roof-elevation sides, a 3-by-¾-inch rectangle for roof-elevation ends, a 4½-by-3-inch rectangle for roof elevation tops, an 8½-by-1½-inch rectangle for veranda and a 3¼-by-1¼-inch rectangle for door canopy. Draw and cut a 3½-by-2½-inch rectangle. Fold in half

lengthwise, and round off one pair of cut corners for door pattern.

5. Make cardboard pieces: Using front-back pattern, trace and cut 2 rectangles from cardboard. Trace and cut windows only on front. Trace patterns, and cut two sides, one roof, four roof-elevation sides, four roof-elevation ends, two roof-elevation tops, two extension sides and one door canopy. Measure and cut one 14-by-7-inch rectangle for base and two 6-by-2½-inch rectangles for extension front. Cut a hole in center of base for lighting, if desired.

6. Assemble cardboard frame: Lay back piece on a flat surface. Lay a side piece with straight end touching back on each side of back piece; tape securely together. Lay the roof piece above back; tape securely to back. Lay base piece below back, and tape securely to back. Raise side and roof pieces; tape together. Raise bottom piece; tape to sides. Set frame on bottom. Slip front in place, touching edge of roof and 1 inch back from edge of base. Tape securely.

7. Tape fronts of extension onto sides of frame, curving cardboard to meet exactly. Tape remaining piece of extension into place on each side. To make roof-elevation frames, arrange cardboard pieces on a flat surface, side, end, side, end, with short edges touching. Tape securely. Set up and form into a rectangle; tape remaining corner; repeat. Tape a roof-elevation top onto each rectangle.

8. Preheat oven to 350F. With lightly floured rolling pin, roll out half of one recipe of dough on a large well-greased cookie sheet to make a 14-by-6-inch rectangle. Place front-back pattern on dough; cut around it with a sharp knife. Do not cut out windows. Remove trimmings.

9. Bake 8 to 10 minutes, or until edges just start to brown. Cool 5 minutes on cookie sheet. While still warm, place pattern on cookie, and trim areas that have expanded more than ⅛ inch beyond pattern. Remove to wire rack, and cool completely.

10. Roll out another half recipe dough; cut around front-back pattern. This time cut around windows and remove dough. Make a cut all the way through dough at the lines 2½ inches in from the edge. Bake as above. Trim around windows if dough has spread. Separate end pieces of dough. Lay frame on its back, and place the 2½-inch end pieces of cookie on the extensions while still warm. Press gently to curve to fit the frame. Gently carve three holes in each extension, as pictured, for cinnamon sticks. Cool completely on the frame.

11. Roll out another half recipe dough. Cut out four sides and four ends, for the roof elevation. Cut out one extension side. Trim ¼ inch from the straight side, and

remove. Turn pattern over and repeat, so you have an extension side facing in each direction. Cut door, using pattern; remove trimmings.

12. Roll out another half recipe dough. Cut out two sides. Be sure to turn pattern over for second side so they are opposites. Using a 1-inch cookie or doughnut-hole cutter, cut out four circles. Cut each in half. Press ends of a 3-inch piece of thread, ½ inch apart, into one half-circle, with center of thread extending above straight edge. Moisten dough, and top with another half-circle to make a hanging basket. Repeat to make remaining baskets. Bake and cool as above.

13. Roll out and trim half of remaining recipe of dough to make a 16½-by-6½-inch rectangle. With finger, press a row of indentations along one edge. Press another row just behind the first one, with each indentation centered behind the point on the first row where two meet, to resemble roof tiles. Repeat to make three more rows. Turn piece around, and repeat, working in from the other long edge and meeting the finished section at the center. Beat egg white with 1 teaspoon water, and brush over dough to glaze. Bake and cool as above.

14. Roll out remaining dough. Cut out two roof-elevation tops, a door canopy and the veranda. Remove trimmings. Press indentations into roof pieces as above. With a knife, score veranda diagonally in two directions to resemble tile. Glaze roof pieces and veranda. Score cinnamon sticks with a knife, and break to make four 1½-inch pieces. Place pieces ½ inch apart on cookie sheet. Carefully remove dough piece for canopy from tray; place on top of pieces of cinnamon even with one end of sticks and allowing other end of sticks to extend beyond dough. Gently press dough part way into the spaces between the sticks. Glaze. Bake and cool remaining pieces as above.

15. Assemble Adobe Ranch: Carefully remove cookies from front of extension. Edge windows with masking tape to make a smooth finish. Securely tape string of one hanging basket above center of each window. Make one recipe Decorator Frosting. Spread over back; press back piece into place. Spread frosting over sides and center front of frame. Press sides and front into place. Frost back of door; press onto center of front, ¼ inch above base.

16. Frost sides and fronts of extensions; press sides into place. If they extend beyond edge of frame, gently carve off excess cookie. Press fronts in place. Trim veranda to fit on cardboard frame. Frost into place. Frost cardboard roof; press cookie roof into place. Frost roof elevations, and press cookie pieces into place. Trim cardboard canopy to fit cinnamon-stick-and-cookie canopy. Turn

cookie canopy upside down. Frost one side and the edges of the cardboard canopy. Press onto cookie piece. Frost bottom. Set ranch and canopy aside several hours to dry completely.

17. Meanwhile, make desired number of cacti: For small cactus, round off top or trim away a piece about ½ inch long and ¼ inch wide from a long green gumdrop. Cut ½-inch pieces from a green gumdrop ring. Fasten pieces of gumdrop ring onto large gumdrop with toothpicks. Dip any cut edges into granulated sugar to coat. Trim a tiny chunk from the red gumdrop. Cut crosswise in two directions to make four flower petals. Stick onto one of the branches of the cactus.

18. For medium cactus, proceed as above but trim a slice off bottom and a slice from one end of another green gumdrop. Toothpick the two cut ends together; add more arms to bottom of cactus.

19. For largest cactus, trim one end from two gumdrops and both ends from one candy. Assemble with the one with both ends trimmed in the middle. Use toothpicks or a wooden skewer to hold together. Add arms and flowers as above.

20. Prepare the second batch of Decorator Frosting without the cocoa and yellow color. Remove ¼ cup. Add the cocoa and food color to remainder, and beat until well combined. Stir some green food color into the reserved ¼ cup frosting.

21. Spoon Decorator Frosting into a pastry bag with a medium writing tip. Make a shell border (see Note) at all edges and around windows. Pipe some frosting onto bottom of roof elevations. Set in place, centered on roof 1 inch in from each end.

22. Pipe some frosting on the straight edge of the canopy. Dip both ends of a cinnamon stick into frosting. Press canopy into place above door. Set cinnamon stick in place, holding one edge of canopy. Repeat with another cinnamon stick at other edge. Hold canopy in place several minutes, until it adheres.

23. Make six ¾-inch pieces of cinnamon stick. Frost into holes at top of extension. With a pastry bag and leaf tip, pipe green frosting onto hanging basket. Gently set small pieces of red gum candy into place for flowers. Let ranch dry overnight before moving.

24. To set up, place ranch on red or rust-colored felt or tablecloth. Arrange cacti around it. If large cacti are unstable, prop them with a toothpick. If desired, cut ½-inch pieces from pointed end of 10 to 12 dried red peppers. Using needle and thread, make a string of peppers. Hang from one cinnamon stick on canopy.

25. If desired, a Christmas-tree bulb in a standing socket may be placed inside ranch to illuminate it. To preserve ranch, spray it lightly with semi-gloss polyurethane spray; let dry completely; cover tightly, and store in a cool dry place.

Note: To make shell border, hold tip near surface to be decorated; squeeze tube, raise tip ¼ inch, then ease off pressure and pull forward. Repeat.

PEANUT-BUTTER-COOKIE DOUGH

⅓ cup (⅔ stick) butter or margarine, softened
½ cup peanut butter
½ cup light-brown sugar, firmly packed
1 egg
1¾ cups all-purpose flour
1 teaspoon vanilla extract

1. In bowl of electric mixer, combine butter, peanut butter and brown sugar. Beat until fluffy.

2. Scrape sides of bowl. Add egg, and beat until well combined.

3. Add flour and vanilla. Mix just until combined.

DECORATOR FROSTING

3 egg whites (at room temperature)
1 pkg (1 lb) confectioners' sugar
2 tablespoons unsweetened cocoa
½ teaspoon cream of tartar
15 drops yellow food color

1. Place egg whites, confectioners' sugar, cocoa, cream of tartar and yellow food color in large bowl. With mixer at medium speed, beat 7 to 10 minutes, or until the mixture is very stiff.

2. Cover bowl with damp cloth. *Makes about 2 cups.*

GINGERBREAD VICTORIAN HOUSE
(pictured)

2 recipes Gingerbread Dough, recipe follows
Paper for patterns
Corrugated cardboard
Masking tape
Cellophane or plastic wrap
Wide lace hem binding
Aluminum foil
3 pkg fruit-flavored Life-Savers
Small plastic bags
3 recipes Snow Frosting, recipe follows
1 box (12 oz) vanilla cookies
1 rectangular sesame-seed candy
3 (5-inch size) peppermint candy sticks
Red thread or yarn
2 tricolor nougats
Green food color
Salad oil
1 recipe Lollipop Syrup, recipe follows
Confectioners' sugar

1. Make Gingerbread Dough. Refrigerate until firm enough to roll out—several hours.

2. Make paper patterns: For front and back, draw and cut a 14-by-11-inch rectangle from paper; fold in half lengthwise to make a 14-by-5½-inch rectangle. Label one narrow end "top" and the other "bottom." Mark a point on cut side 10½ inches up from bottom. Draw and cut a diagonal line from the top folded corner to the point. Open pattern. It should measure 14 inches from point to bottom and 11 inches across widest part.

3. For downstairs bay, draw and cut an 8-by-5½-inch rectangle from paper. Label one long side "top" and the other "bottom." Measure and mark points 2 inches in from each 5½-inch side. Draw a line on each side. Make a 3-by-1¾-inch rectangle for window pattern. Measure and mark points ½ inch from one 3-inch side. Fold over ½ inch of the pattern. Center pattern, still folded, 1½ inches above bottom of one of the 2-inch sides of downstairs bay pattern; trace. Repeat on other side. Open window pattern to full size, and trace, centered, in middle section 1½ inches above bottom. Cut out the three windows.

4. Make upstairs bay: Cut an 8½-by-7-inch rectangle. Fold it in half lengthwise to make an 8½-by-3½-inch rectangle. Label one narrow end "top" and the other "bottom." Mark a point on cut side 5 inches up from bottom. Draw and cut a diagonal line from top folded corner to 5-inch point. Open pattern. It should be 8½ inches from point to bottom and 7 inches across widest part. Center window pattern 1¼ inches above bottom of bay pattern. Trace and cut out. With compass, cookie cutter or jar lid, make a 2-inch circle; fold and cut in half. Center a half-circle 1¾ inches down from peak; trace and cut out. Draw and cut a 27-by-1½-inch rectangle. Measure and mark points 5 inches in from one end and 10 inches in from the same end. Repeat on other end. On one end only, label 5-inch section first in from end "bay roof." Label second 5-inch section "bay side."

5. For side pattern, draw and cut a 10½-by-8-inch rectangle. Center window pattern on side pattern 2 inches up from bottom edge; draw around it. Cut out window. For roof pattern, draw and cut an 8-by-6½-inch rectangle.

6. For porch-gable front, draw and cut a 5¾-by-3¾-inch rectangle from paper. Fold in half crosswise to make a 3¾-by-2⅞-inch rectangle. Label one narrow end "top" and the other "bottom." Draw and cut a diagonal line from top folded corner

continued on page 234

continued from page 233

to bottom cut corner. Open pattern. It should measure 5¾ inches across widest part and 3¾ inches from point to bottom. Label.

7. Make cardboard pieces: Using paper patterns, trace and cut two front-back pieces, two side pieces, one downstairs bay, one upstairs bay front, one 27-inch strip for upstairs bay sides and roof, one porch gable and two roof pieces. Trace window pattern 2 inches up from bottom and 2 inches in from side on one front-back piece. Cut out. Repeat from other side of same piece. Label piece "back."

8. On remaining front-back piece, measure and draw a 6-by-3½-inch rectangle 1½ inches from bottom and ½ inch in from left side. Cut out. Center a 4-by-2½-inch rectangle vertically 1¾ inches above the 6-by-3½-inch rectangle you just cut. Cut it out. These will allow light to come through the bays.

9. Measure and cut one 16¼-by-11-inch rectangle for base, one 11-by-3½-inch rectangle for porch roof and one 9-by-3½-inch rectangle for roof of porch gable. On porch roof, draw and cut off a 7-by-1½-inch rectangle from one corner so roof will fit around bay. On roof of porch gable, label one 9-inch side "front" and the other "back." Draw and cut off a 1¾-inch-lengthwise-by-2-inch-crosswise rectangle from left back corner. Fold piece in half crosswise to make a 4½-by-3½-inch rectangle. Measure and mark a point ½ inch in from front folded corner. Draw and cut a diagonal line from that point to front cut corners. On right end of pattern, mark a point 1 inch up on back edge from cut corners. Draw a diagonal line to front cut corners. Cut on line through right side and what remains of left side.

10. Fit masking tape over rough edges around all windows. Cut eight 4-by-2½-inch rectangles of cellophane or plastic wrap. Place over window holes on outside of house pieces, and tape edges securely. Turn pieces over. Cut eight 4-inch strips of lace. Tape one on inside of each window, using one piece of tape above and one below.

11. Assemble cardboard frame: Lay cardboard front on flat surface. Lay a side piece on each side of the front. Tape together securely. Lay back pattern beside right side; tape securely. Set up to form house. Tape remaining back edge. Tape inside corners, and tape all the way around house above windows, using one piece of tape. Fit roof pieces onto house. Tape securely in place.

12. Measure and mark several points 7 inches in from lower left side of the front. Tape downstairs bay securely at left corner of front. Tape other side of bay

at 7-inch marks. Using pattern, fold 27-inch strip at marks. Starting at point of upstairs bay front, tape roof, side, bottom, side and roof to upstairs bay front, to make a 3-dimensional piece. Tape securely to house above downstairs bay. Back of bay will be open above house roof.

13. To make porch and base, label one 11-inch side of cardboard base piece "porch" and the other "base." Slide "porch" side under front of downstairs bay until edge touches house front. Make sure cardboard is lined up evenly with front of house. Trace around downstairs bay. Remove cardboard piece, and cut on traced line. Discard bay-shape piece of cardboard. Starting from "base" end of cardboard, measure and mark several points 11¾ inches and 12½ inches in from end. Score a line across cardboard at each of these points. Fold cardboard on scored lines. If you wish to light the house, cut a 3-inch square centered 3 inches in from "base" edge.

14. Lay house frame on its back. Tape "base" end of cardboard to back of house. Securely tape sides of base to sides of house. Set house up. Tape front of house to base. Fold porch over, and fit around bay. Cut two 3¾-by-¾-inch rectangles of cardboard. Tape in place for sides of porch. Tape porch securely to front of house.

15. Fit roof of porch gable onto front of porch gable with cut-off side to the left back, and tape securely.

16. Preheat oven to 350F. Place half of one Gingerbread Dough recipe on greased cookie sheet. With lightly floured rolling pin, roll out to ⅛-inch thickness. Lay paper pattern for back on dough; cut with a sharp knife. Cut out and carefully remove windows. With long knife, score crosswise, as pictured. Bake 8 to 10 minutes, or until edges just start to brown. Cool 5 minutes on cookie sheet. While still warm, place pattern on gingerbread, and trim areas that have expanded more than ⅛ inch beyond the pattern. Remove gingerbread to wire rack, and cool completely.

17. Roll out another half recipe of Gingerbread Dough. Using paper patterns, cut out one side piece and its windows for right side; score. Cut out porch-gable front. Bake and cool as above.

18. Roll out half of second recipe of Gingerbread Dough. Place pattern for remaining side on dough. Cut pattern for top bay side from 27-inch strip. Discard rest of strip. Place top bay side at top right edge of house side. Cut out side, including top extension for bay; cut out windows; score. Cut out downstairs bay with windows; score. Score heavily at lines on pattern, dividing bay into sections. Bake. Cut bay into three sections at scored lines; cool as above.

19. Roll out remaining piece of dough on foil, shiny side up. Measure and draw a line 7 inches in from the left side of the front-back pattern. Extend line 10½ inches up from bottom. Place upstairs-bay-front pattern so that roof angle is at the 10½-inch point. Trace roof line onto front pattern. Cut along this line. Discard left side of pattern. Fit the pattern you have made onto the house frame to make sure it covers right side of house front but not bays. Place pattern on dough; cut out. Cut out upstairs-bay front and one top-bay side. Make two thin rolls of dough, and place in semi-circular window, to make wedge-shape panes, as pictured. Score dough as pictured. Cut out a 5-by-3-inch rectangle for door. Cut off some ⅛-inch-thick strips from dough scraps. Moisten door. Press strips in place on door to make framed panels, as pictured. Make a tiny ball of dough for door knob. Bake 6 minutes. Remove from oven. Meanwhile, crack one red and one green candy in separate plastic bags. Use to fill open spaces in stained-glass window. Bake 2 minutes longer, or until candy has melted.

20. Knead together scraps of dough. Roll out on foil, shiny side up. Using window pattern, cut out 6 windows. Trim dough, leaving ¼-inch frame and ¼-inch-thick separation through center, as pictured. Bake 6 minutes. Meanwhile, in separate plastic bags, crack more red and green hard candies. Remove windows from oven. Fill open spaces with cracked candy. Return to oven just until candy has melted—2 to 3 minutes. Cool on a flat surface. Trim foil around windows, leaving foil on back of window in place. Roll out a little piece of dough ⅛ inch thick. Cut out a 1-inch square. Roll up to resemble rolled newspaper. Bake until edges just start to brown—about 8 minutes.

21. Make one recipe Snow Frosting. Spread one side of house with frosting. Press a gingerbread side in place; hold until it sticks. Repeat with second side; then add front and back. Spread some frosting on downstairs bay. Press gingerbread pieces into place. Frost upstairs bay, and press gingerbread into place with foil back still in place. Frost back of door, and press into place ¼ inch above porch, as pictured. Press stained-glass windows into place on top floor of sides and back. Frost gingerbread to front of porch gable. Set all aside at least 1 hour to dry.

22. Prepare second batch of Snow Frosting. Generously frost roof and roof of upstairs bay. Starting at bottom of each side of roof, press vanilla cookies into place, overlapping rows and alternating spaces, shingle fashion. Arrange a row of cookies at top center. Repeat on upstairs bay roof. Make a swirl of frosting at top

center. Fill in open space at back of bay with frosting. Frost roof of porch gable. Cover with cookies, being careful to trim them to exact dimensions of back and cut-out areas of cardboard piece.

23. Frost front porch. Unwrap sesame candy, and set into place for doormat. Fit cardboard porch roof into place over gingerbread front; trim, if necessary; dimensions vary once gingerbread is on frame. Unwrap peppermint sticks. Lightly frost underside of porch roof. Generously frost back edge. Press porch roof into place just below upstairs bay window and slanting down toward edge of porch. Still holding porch roof with one hand, dip top of a peppermint stick in frosting. Fit into place, holding up one end of roof. Repeat with remaining sticks, placing them as pictured. Hold roof in place several minutes, until it seems secure. Tie red yarn or thread around newspaper. Place on porch. Let house dry, untouched, several hours or overnight. (It is possible for one person to do this step, but it is much easier with help.)

24. Prepare third batch of Snow Frosting. Fit porch gable onto porch roof. Trim if necessary. Frost into place. Frost porch roof, and cover with cookies. Put white frosting into a pastry bag with adapter and small star tip. Pipe a shell border (see Note) along eaves of house at front, back, top bay and porch-gable roof, along corners where gingerbread pieces meet and at lines where porch roof and bays meet house. Frost nougats in place for chimney. Pipe a star border around windows, across lower windows for separation and for decoration on gables, as pictured. Change to a writing tip, and pipe dots for decoration on porch gable and on house front, as pictured.

25. Color a little frosting green. With pastry bag and leaf tip, pipe a garland of greens along edge of porch. Allow to dry several hours beore moving.

26. To make trees, place a double thickness of foil on a flat surface, shiny side up. Set a tree-shape cookie cutter (or a tree shape cut from cardboard) on foil. Gently mold foil around form until it fits tightly and has sides at least ½ inch high. Slip out form without changing shape of foil mold; oil mold lightly. Make six tree molds. Place six 3-inch squares of foil on a cookie sheet, shiny side up.

27. Prepare Lollipop Syrup. Pour into molds—about ¼ inch deep. Pour remaining syrup on the squares of foil into six 1½- to 2-inch rounds. Let cool until trees are firm—about 1 hour.

28. Preheat oven to 350F. Remove trees from foil. Place rounds in oven on cookie sheet until melted enough to be just tacky. Be careful not to make them too soft. Remove from oven, and press a tree upright into the candy. If they do not stay upright when pressed in, candy is too soft. Press remaining trees into bases when candy has cooled a little. Let cool completely before removing foil from bottom. Trees will stay pretty for several weeks if kept in a dry place; humidity will cloud them. They may be brushed with corn syrup to restore shine, but transparency will not return.

29. To set up, place house on a white tablecloth or piece of white cardboard. Place trees around house. Sift some confectioners' sugar over house to look like snow. If desired, a Christmas-tree bulb in a standing socket may be placed inside house, to illuminate it. To preserve house, spray lightly with semi-gloss polyurethane spray; let dry completely; cover tightly; store in cool dry place. Trees will not store well.

Note: To make a shell border, hold tip near surface to be decorated; squeeze tube, raise tip ¼ inch, then ease off pressure and pull forward. Repeat.

GINGERBREAD DOUGH

3½ cups all-purpose flour
¼ teaspoon salt
1½ teaspoons ground ginger
1 teaspoon ground cloves
½ cup (1 stick) butter or margarine, softened
¾ cup light-brown sugar, firmly packed
1 egg
¾ cup light molasses

1. Sift flour, salt, ginger and cloves onto sheet of waxed paper. Set aside.

2. In large bowl of electric mixer, at high speed, beat butter, brown sugar and egg until light and fluffy. Add molasses; beat until well blended. With wooden spoon, stir in flour mixture; mix with hands until dough is well blended and smooth.

3. Divide dough in half; flatten into squares. Wrap each part separately in foil or waxed paper; refrigerate several hours.

SNOW FROSTING

3 egg whites (at room temperature)
1 pkg (1 lb) confectioners' sugar
½ teaspoon cream of tartar

1. Place egg whites, sugar and cream of tartar in large bowl. With mixer at medium speed, beat 7 to 10 minutes, until stiff.

2. Cover bowl with damp cloth. *Makes about 2 cups.*

LOLLIPOP SYRUP

1 cup sugar
¼ cup water
⅓ cup light corn syrup
Green food color

1. In a small, heavy saucepan, combine sugar, water and corn syrup. Cook over high heat, stirring constantly with a wooden spoon, until sugar is dissolved. With a pastry brush dipped in hot water, wash down side of pan to remove any sugar crystals.

2. Place candy thermometer in mixture, and continue boiling, without stirring, until thermometer registers 280F. Remove from heat, and stir in 4 or 5 drops of food color.

WINDMILL
(pictured)

2 recipes Speculaas Dough, recipe follows
Paper for patterns
Corrugated cardboard
22-inch-square foam-core board or other very strong warp-resistant cardboard
Masking tape
18-inch dowel rod, ¼ inch in diameter
Brown thread
1 recipe Decorator Frosting, page 233
Red and green sugar
Green food color
Spiral-design peppermint candy

1. Prepare Speculaas dough. Refrigerate until ready to use.

2. Meanwhile, prepare paper patterns: For windmill side, draw and cut a 10-by-4-inch rectangle from paper. Fold in half lengthwise to make a 10-by-2-inch

continued on page 236

continued from page 235

rectangle. Mark one narrow end "top" and the other "bottom." On top end, mark a point 1 inch in from cut corners. Draw and cut a diagonal line from that point to the lower cut corners. Draw and cut a 1¼-by-1-inch rectangle for windows. Center pattern on side pattern 2 inches down from top. Trace around pattern; cut out. Trace and cut another window ¼ inch below the one you just cut. Measure several points 3 inches up from wide end; draw a line. Label top section "blade pattern." Entire pattern is windmill-side pattern.

3. For top, cut a 3-by-2-inch rectangle. Fold in half crosswise. Draw and cut a diagonal line from one folded corner to the opposite pair of cut corners. Open triangular pattern. Draw and cut a 2½-by-1¼-inch rectangle for door. Trace Santa pattern on page 235.

4. Make cardboard frame: Using paper patterns, trace and cut 5 cardboard sides. Trace and cut out top window on two pieces and lower window on another piece. (No windows on two cardboard pieces.) Trace and cut 5 triangular pieces for windmill top. Draw a 2-inch square in center of foam-core board. Trace blade pattern onto each side of square. Cut out in one piece. Cut a ¼-inch hole in center.

5. Assemble frame: Place two plain side pieces on a flat surface, long sides touching, with narrow ends in same direction. Tape together. Place pieces with upper windows on either side of plain pieces; tape together. Tape remaining piece to one side. Set up to form a pentagonal tower; tape together.

6. Place the triangular top pieces side by side, with edges touching and points at the same side. Tape together. Set up and tape remaining side.

7. Cutting down from the top edge of the side section with low window, remove a ¼-inch square of cardboard from center. Trim ¼ inch from top corner of pieces with no windows at spot where they meet. Cut off a 5-inch section of dowel rod. Push in place on windmill, using grooves where cardboard was removed. Set top on pentagonal tower, with each triangle piece centered above a side piece. Tape securely together.

8. Preheat oven to 350F. On a well-greased cookie sheet, roll out half of one recipe of Speculaas Dough. Place paper pattern for sides on dough. Trace around pattern to make the two sides without windows. Using a 3-inch round cookie cutter, cut out two rounds of dough; cut a ¼-inch hole in center of each, for wheel. Cut out several top triangles. Remove trimmings. Bake 12 to 15 minutes, or until edges are golden-brown. Cool 5 min-

utes on cookie sheet; then carefully remove to cooling rack, and cool completely.

9. Roll out another half recipe of dough. Cut out two sides with upper windows, a 2-inch square and remaining triangular top pieces. Cut a ¼-inch hole in center of square. Remove trimmings, and bake as above.

10. Roll out half of second dough recipe. Cut out windmill side with low window. Trim off bottom of side pattern to make blade pattern. Cut out one or two blades. Remove trimmings, and bake.

11. Roll out remaining dough. Cut out remaining blades and door. Remove trimmings, and bake.

12. Knead together trimmings, and roll out ⅛ inch thick. Place Santa pattern on dough; cut around pattern. Trim toy bag from pattern at dotted line. Cut out another Santa without the bag. Remove trimmings. Cut two 12-inch pieces of brown thread. Fold in half, and place folded end of each on center of Santa with bag. Run one double thickness of thread up each arm, staying away from bag area of cutout. Moisten Santa (but not bag). Carefully remove Santa without bag from cookie sheet, and place on top of Santa with bag, matching arms and legs. Press together. Bake as above.

13. Make Decorator Frosting without cocoa or yellow color. Remove ¼ cup. Add cocoa and color to remaining frosting; beat until evenly colored. Spread a little white frosting on suit and hat area; sprinkle with red sugar. Spread toy bag with frosting; sprinkle with green sugar. Set aside to dry.

14. Spread windmill with frosting. Gently press each cookie piece into frosting, holding until it has adhered. Lay foam-core-board blade frame on a flat surface. Place Santa below one blade, about 1 inch in from end. Separate each double string, and tie securely to blade. Frost whole blade frame generously, and press cookie pieces onto form-core board, with square in center. Remove any frosting from hole in center. Gently twist dowel rod into hole, to make sure if will fit.

15. Place a writing tip with a ¼-inch opening on a pastry bag. Fill with Decorator Frosting. Pipe a shell border (see Note) along each edge where cookies meet, around windows and door and at edges of windmill blades.

16. Frost backs of the two round cookies together. Cut off a 12-inch piece of dowel rod. Prop one end of this rod just below back end of upper dowel rod, removing frosting if necessary to make a place for it; set cookie wheel on edge, and fit other end of dowel rod into center, gently carving away cookie to make a ridge for it. With Decorator Frosting and pastry bag, frost dowel rod securely into wheel. Allow other end to lean unat-

tached to the mill for ease in moving.

17. Place some white frosting in a pastry bag with small writing tip. Pipe beard, fur borders and eyes on Santa. Carefully place a bit of green sugar on each eye.

18. Remove white frosting from pastry bag. Color green, and place in pastry bag with a leaf tip. Pipe wreath on front door. Place some pieces of red sugar on wreath. Frost peppermint candy onto center of blade covering front of hole. Do not allow frosting to fill hole. Pipe a wreath around it. Pipe one small leaf at intersection of each shell in border. Pipe on 5 or 6 leaves; then place a bit of red sugar on each one before it dries. Continue working 5 or 6 at a time until all are completed. Allow all pieces to dry overnight before moving.

19. Next day, move windmill to place where it will be displayed. Push dowel rod at top of mill so that at least ½ inch extends out at front. Carefully slide blade onto dowel rod, being careful not to push peppermint off front. Set wheel in place.

20. If desired, a Christmas-tree bulb in a standing socket may be placed inside windmill to illuminate it. To preserve windmill, spray it with semi-gloss polyurethane spray; let dry completely; cover tightly, and store in a cool dry place.

Note: To make shell border, hold tip near surface to be decorated; squeeze tube, raise tip ¼ inch, then ease off pressure and pull forward. Repeat.

SPECULAAS DOUGH

3 cups all-purpose flour
1½ teaspoons ground cinnamon
1 teaspoon ground cloves
1 teaspoon ground ginger
⅛ teaspoon salt
1 cup (2 sticks) butter or margarine, softened
1¼ cups light-brown sugar, firmly packed
1 egg
½ cup sliced blanched almonds

1. On sheet of waxed paper, sift flour with spices and salt. Set aside.

2. In large bowl of electric mixer, at high speed, beat butter with brown sugar and egg until mixture is very light and fluffy.

3. With wooden spoon, stir in half of flour mixture; then beat in rest of flour mixture and the almonds, mixing with hands if necessary.

LOG CABIN
(pictured)

2 recipes Cocoa-Shortbread Dough, recipe
  follows
Paper for patterns
Corrugated cardboard
Masking tape
Plastic wrap
2 recipes Snow Frosting, page 235
½ lb chocolate drops
½ lb chocolate-coated caramels
½ lb chocolate-coated raisins
1 box (10 oz) large shredded whole-wheat
  biscuits
Green food color
½ lb spearmint-gum leaves
Toothpicks

1. Prepare Cocoa-Shortbread Dough. Refrigerate 1 hour.

2. Make paper patterns: Draw and cut a 10-by-6-inch rectangle. Fold lengthwise to make a 10-by-3-inch rectangle. Label one 3-inch end "top" and the other "bottom." Mark a point 6 inches up from bottom on cut sides. Draw a diagonal line from the point you marked to the top folded corner. Cut on line. Open to make side pattern. Draw and cut a 2-by-1½-inch rectangle for window pattern. Center pattern vertically 1½ inches above bottom of side pattern. Trace and cut out window.

3. For front-back pattern, draw and cut out a 10-by-6-inch rectangle. Trace window pattern 1½ inches in from one 6-inch side and 1½ inches up from bottom. Fold pattern in half crosswise. Cut out window through double thickness. Open pattern. Trace and cut out another window 1½ inches up from bottom and centered over fold line. The two outer windows are for front. The one center window is for back.

4. Make cardboard frame: Trace and cut side pattern twice, to make cardboard side pieces. Cut window on only one piece. Trace and cut front-back pattern twice, making two side windows on one piece, for front, and one center window on other piece, for back. Cut one 10-by-6-inch rectangle for base. Cut a 2-inch square in center if lighting is desired. Cut two 10-by-5-inch rectangles for roof.

5. Assemble frame: Lay cardboard pieces on a flat surface with edges touching. Place windowed side to left of front and plain side to right. Place back next to either side. Tape securely together. Set up and tape remaining side. Tape roof pieces together at a 10-inch side. Place on cabin. Tape securely to cabin. Tape base on cabin. Tape edges of windows to make a smooth finish.

6. Preheat oven to 350F. With a lightly floured rolling pin, roll out half of one recipe of dough, ⅛ inch thick, on a greased cookie sheet. Cut into strips ¾ to 1 inch wide. Score to look like wood. Bake 8 to 12 minutes, or until cookie feels firm when gently touched. Remove from oven. Cut "boards" apart while warm. Cool on rack. Repeat with another two pieces of dough.

7. Roll out part of remaining dough. Cut out a 3½-by-2-inch rectangle for door. Score as pictured. Bake and cool as above. (Rest of dough may be made into cookies.)

8. Cut four 3-by-2½-inch pieces of plastic wrap. Place one over a window on cardboard frame. Tape securely at top. Pull tight, and tape bottom and sides. Repeat with remaining windows.

9. Prepare one recipe of Snow Frosting. Lay house frame on front. Generously frost back of house. With sharp knife, carefully cut boards to fit house, meeting evenly at corners. Press into frosting. Repeat on sides. Lay house on back, and frost front. Fit boards onto front. Frost back of door. Press into place in center.

10. Set house on windowed side. Make a 6-by-3-by-¾-inch box from cardboard (or use candy box). Frost to lower center of plain side of house. Cut 12 chocolate drops and 12 caramels in half vertically. Frost box generously. Press candies into frosting, as pictured, to make chimney. Press chocolate-coated raisins into spaces between candies. Spread a thick layer of frosting, about 2 inches wide, from top of box to top of roof, centered over bottom of chimney. Set a whole chocolate drop on each side of top of box. Fill in with whole caramels. Complete chimney with whole candies, as pictured, filling in spaces with chocolate-covered raisins. Let dry several hours.

11. Set house on its base. Prepare another recipe of Snow Frosting. Frost roof generously. Split shredded-wheat biscuits, and press onto roof, as pictured, starting at bottom. Start second row with ½ biscuit, and proceed so seams will be centered over biscuits in first row. The third row will be like the first. Repeat, to make three rows on the other side.

12. Spoon 1 cup frosting into a pastry bag with adapter and writing tip with ¼-inch opening. Pipe a shell border just under roof on sides and down each corner of the log cabin. Pipe a puff of frosting, and pull down gently to a point, for icicles, about every 1½ inches along border of the roof. Pipe a cluster of icicles at

corners of roof. Pipe a shell border (see Note) of frosting along top of roof, ending in an icicle at the windowed side. Pipe some frosting on top of chimney and adjacent roof, and set 4 whole candies on top of chimney.

13. Change to small writing tip. Pipe a border around windows, and divide into panes, as pictured. Pipe hinges and latch on door.

14. Color some frosting green. Place in pastry bag with leaf tip, and pipe garland over the door. Let house dry several hours.

15. Make spearmint trees: Place one spearmint leaf flat, and place 2 toothpicks in the center. Push 2 spearmint leaves, backs together, on end, onto toothpicks. For taller trees, toothpick a single spearmint leaf, on end, on top of double ones. Split 10 spearmint leaves for small trees and 15 for large ones. Working from bottom, fasten split leaves to base with bits of toothpick. Work in concentric circles, ending with three leaves at top, as pictured. Make desired number of trees.

16. To set up, set cabin on green felt, as pictured, or on a white tablecloth or piece of white cardboard, to look like snow. If desired, place a Christmas-tree bulb in a standing socket inside cabin, to illuminate it. Set trees around cabin, and make a path with remaining chocolate-coated raisins.

17. To preserve cabin, spray it lightly with semi-gloss polyurethane spray; let dry completely; cover tightly and store in a cool dry place.

Note: To make shell border, hold tip near surface to be decorated; squeeze tube, raise tip ¼ inch, then ease off pressure and pull forward. Repeat.

COCOA-SHORTBREAD DOUGH

¾ cup (1½ sticks) butter or margarine,
  softened
⅔ cup sugar
¼ teaspoon salt
1 egg
1 teaspoon vanilla extract
1¾ cups all-purpose flour
⅓ cup unsweetened cocoa

1. Measure butter, sugar and salt into bowl. With electric mixer at medium speed, beat until mixture is smooth.

2. Add egg and vanilla. Beat until fluffy—2 minutes.

3. Gradually add flour and cocoa, stirring until well combined and smooth.

4. With hands or spoon, shape dough into a ball. Place on waxed paper, plastic wrap or foil. Flatten dough, wrap and refrigerate until needed.

continued on page 238

continued from page 237

GINGERBREAD COTTAGE
(pictured)

1 recipe Gingerbread-Cottage Dough,
   recipe follows
Paper for patterns
Corrugated cardboard
Masking tape
Household glue or rubber cement
Colored cellophane or plastic wrap
3 recipes Snow Frosting, page 235
1 box (8½ oz) 2½-inch chocolate wafers
12 red cinnamon candies
Toothpicks
1 roll (1.74 oz) chocolate-covered caramel
   rounds
1 pkg (7½ oz) spearmint leaves
2 pkg (1⅞-oz size) colored gumdrops
1 large red gumdrop
2 tablespoons finely chopped pecans or
   walnuts
Green-color sugar
5 peppermint sticks
2 pkg (14-oz size) caramels
Confectioners' sugar

1. Make Gingerbread-Cottage-Dough recipe. Refrigerate until dough is manageable—several hours or overnight.

2. Make paper patterns: For windows, draw a 1½-by-1-inch rectangle; cut out and label. For front, make a 10-by-8½-inch rectangle. Fold in half to mark vertical center. Label one end of fold "top" and the other "bottom." Measure a point 4½ inches up from the bottom corner of the open side. Draw a diagonal line from this point to the top of the folded edge. Cut on the diagonal line, and open pattern. Place window pattern 2 inches from the side and 1½ inches from bottom left (as you face pattern) of front pattern. Trace around window, and cut out. Use a cookie cutter or small lid to draw a 1½-inch circle centered 2¾ inches below top point; cut out. Label pattern "front." For back, trace outside of front pattern, and cut out. Center the window pattern 1½ inches up from the bottom. Trace and cut out. Label.

3. For sides, make a 7½-by-4½-inch rectangle. Place window pattern 1¼ inches in from one side and 1½ inches up from the bottom. Trace window, and cut out. Repeat at other side of pattern for second window. Label pattern. For roof, make a 15-by-8½-inch rectangle. Fold in half crosswise to mark center of roof. Each side will measure 8½ by 7½ inches. Label.

4. For door, make a 3¾-by-2-inch rectangle. Fold in half lengthwise; trim to round top corners. Label. For shutters, draw, cut out and label a 1½-by-¾-inch rectangle. For cat, draw a ¾-inch circle. At its top, slightly overlapping, draw a ½-inch circle. Draw two ears and a tail. Cut out. Trace rooster weather-vane pattern on this page. Cut out and label.

5. To make cardboard pieces, place patterns for front, back and roof on cardboard. Trace and cut out. Place side pattern on cardboard. Trace and cut out one piece according to the pattern, to make right side of house. Trace again, omitting left window to make left side of house; cut out.

6. To assemble cardboard house: Lay cardboard front on flat surface. Lay right side piece on the right of the front. Lay left side piece on the left of the front. Tape together securely. Lay back pattern beside right side; tape securely. Set up to form house. Tape remaining back edge. Tape inside corners, and tape all the way around house just above windows, using one piece of tape.

7. Score roof along center line on pattern; fold on line. Generously spread glue or cement along top of house pieces. Fit roof onto house. Tape securely in place. Cut six 3-by-2-inch rectangles of cellophane or plastic wrap. Place over window holes, and tape edges securely. Set house aside to dry.

8. Several hours later or next day, preheat oven to 350F. Place one-third of gingerbread dough on greased cookie sheet. With lightly floured rolling pin, roll out to ⅛-inch thickness. Lay paper patterns for front and door on dough; cut around each with sharp knife. Cut out and remove windows. Score front crosswise with a long knife, to resemble boards. Using shutter pattern, cut out four shutters. Use scalloped pastry cutter, if desired. Lift off dough trimmings. Make sure there is at least ½ inch between pieces.

9. Bake cutouts 8 to 10 minutes, or until edges just start to brown. Cool 5 minutes on cookie sheet. While still warm, place pattern on cookie and trim areas of gingerbread that have expanded more than ⅛ inch beyond the pattern. Remove gingerbread to wire rack, and cool completely.

10. Meanwhile, place another one-third of the dough on a greased cookie sheet. Cut out the two sides. Remove windows, and score as above, remembering not to cut the left window on the left side. Bake and cool. Repeat with remaining dough to make back,

six shutters, cat and rooster weather vane.

11. Knead together trimmings, and roll out ⅛ inch thick. Cut into strips ⅜ inch wide. Cut the strips into six pieces 2 inches long, two pieces 3 inches long and two pieces 6 inches long, to make the fence. Lay four of the 2-inch strips, side by side on a cookie sheet, leaving 1¼ inches between them. Fold down the second and fourth strips. Place one of the 6-inch strips over the first and third strips ⅜ inch down from the top. Replace folded strips. Fold up bottoms of first and third strips. Place second 6-inch strip ⅜ inch below first. Replace folded strips. Repeat with two remaining 2-inch strips and the two 3-inch strips, to make smaller portion of fence. Trim tops of all fence posts at an angle, as pictured. Bake and cool as for house pieces.

12. Assemble gingerbread cottage: Make one recipe Snow Frosting. Spread one side of house with frosting. Place a gingerbread side in place; hold until it sticks. Repeat with second side; then add front and back. There will be about ¼ inch at each corner not covered with gingerbread.

13. Shingle roof: Spread frosting on one side of roof. Place cookies on roof, row by row, starting at lower edge. Cut cookies as necessary, so they overlap and edges alternate to give shingle effect. Cut cookies in half for top row. Repeat with other side. Set aside to dry thoroughly.

14. Meanwhile, frost door with Snow Frosting. Arrange red cinnamon candies on door, as pictured. Set aside to dry. Using a pastry bag and writing tip, decorate shutters with a border of Snow-Frosting dots ⅛ inch in from edge. Set aside to dry. Pipe eyes and mouth on cat. Pipe molding on each window to divide it into four panes. Pipe a row of dots just inside window holes to outline windows.

15. For yard, cut a 14-inch square of cardboard; cut a 1½-inch square from the center to insert light, if desired.

16. Assemble flowerpots and evergreen tree: For each flowerpot, stick a toothpick into the center of a chocolate-covered caramel round. Push bottom tip of a spearmint leaf onto toothpick; slide down and push to one side. Repeat with another spearmint leaf; push to the other side. Top with a red flower-shape gumdrop, as pictured. Make five flowerpots. For evergreen tree, push a toothpick into the center of a large red gumdrop. Split six green spearmint leaves to make 12 thin leaves. Place in layers on toothpick, sugared side up and points out. Press tips of leaves down to resemble an evergreen tree.

17. Prepare two recipes of Snow Frosting. Lightly frost yard to within 3 inches of each side of hole. Center house in yard. Spread some frosting on backs of door and shutters. Press door into place on right side of front. Press a shutter in place on each side of windows. Cut a chocolate wafer

in half. Place in front of door for step. Spoon chopped nuts onto frosting to make a path 1 inch wide, leading from front step to front edge of yard. Press the nuts into the frosting.

18. Using a pastry bag and a number-32 star tip, pipe a shell (see Note) border along top of roof and along each side of path. Sprinkle sides of path with green-color sugar. Pipe a double shell border to fill in each corner of house. Using scissors, trim 4 peppermint sticks to fit corners; press into place. Pipe a double shell border along "eaves" at front and back of the house. Press 9 gumdrops into border at front, alternating red and green, as pictured. Hold each candy until it seems securely attached. Set rooster weather vane in place.

19. Cut a 2-inch piece from a candy stick. Set the two sections of fence into Snow Frosting in front left side of yard, as pictured. Set piece of candy stick at corner. Hold until firm. If necessary, pipe a little more frosting at bottom of posts to hold them securely. Set cat in yard.

20. Build chimney. With Snow Frosting as mortar, stack caramels, one deep, brick fashion, against left side of house, 1½ inches from the back. Use three candies for first row. Slice one in half for beginning and end of second row. Repeat to edge of roof. Trim caramels to fill in as roof tapers until chimney is two candies deep. When chimney is 12 layers high, taper front caramels, and continue with a stack two wide and two deep for the next three rows. Top with a "drift" of frosting. For smokestack, cut one piece of peppermint stick, 1½ inches long. Set peppermint stick into frosting at top.

21. Pipe some frosting on the yard in front of each window. Set a flowerpot in place at each spot. Pipe a dot of frosting in the yard at left front of house. Press evergreen tree into place. Sift some confectioners' sugar on roof and yard to look like snow. Let dry thoroughly and use as table centerpiece or mantle decoration.

22. To preserve cottage, spray it lightly with semi-gloss polyurethane spray; let dry completely; cover tightly and store in a cool dry place.

Note: To make shell border, hold tip near surface to be decorated; squeeze tube; raise tip ¼ inch; then ease off pressure and pull forward. Repeat.

GINGERBREAD-COTTAGE DOUGH

4 cups sifted all-purpose flour
2 tablespoons sugar
1½ teaspoons ground ginger
1½ teaspoons baking powder
½ teaspoon baking soda
½ teaspoon salt
1 cup light molasses
½ cup (1 stick) butter or margarine
¼ cup milk

1. In large bowl, combine flour with sugar, ginger, baking powder, soda and salt.

2. In small saucepan, heat molasses with butter just until mixture boils. Stir in milk.

3. Add molasses mixture to flour mixture; stir, with wooden spoon, until smooth.

4. Wrap gingerbread dough in foil or plastic wrap. Refrigerate overnight.

GINGERBREAD SWISS CHALET
(pictured)

Gingerbread-Cottage Dough, this page
Heavy brown paper
Illustration board or cardboard
Masking tape
Marshmallow whip or household cement
1 box (11 oz) tea cookies
3 recipes Snow Frosting, page 235
Unsweetened cocoa
Red and green food color
1 oval vanilla-sandwich cookie
1 chocolate caramel
2 pkg fruit-striped chewing gum
½ lb nougat candies (see Note)
1 peppermint stick
5 rolled sugar ice-cream cones
1 pkg (1⅛ oz) assorted candy wafers
4 red-hot candies

Allow several days to make house, so parts can dry properly.

1. Make Gingerbread-Cottage Dough, and refrigerate overnight.

2. Make paper patterns (see Diagram A): For front of house, draw an 8½-by-8-inch rectangle on paper; cut out. Fold in half lengthwise; then cut a triangle from one end (see dotted line). For side window, cut out 1½-by-1-inch rectangle 1¾ inches from bottom and from right side. For top window, cut out 1-inch square 1½ inches from peak.

3. For back of house, make pattern like the front; omit windows.

4. For sides, draw two 6¼-by-5-inch rectangles; cut out.

5. For door, draw a 3¼-by-2-inch rectangle; cut out. Trim at one end, to round top of door, as pictured. For window, cut out a ½-inch square 1½ inches from rounded top.

6. For shutters, draw two 1-by-⅝-inch rectangles and two 1¼-by-¾-inch rectangles; cut out.

7. For scalloped roof trim, trace top of house front on paper, extending each

side 1¼ inches. Starting from center, draw scallops, about ¾ inch deep; cut out.

8. Make illustration-board house: Trace paper patterns for front, back and sides on illustration board; cut out. Save paper patterns.

9. For roof, cut two 5¾-inch squares (see Diagram B). Make chimney cutout on one square.

10. For canopy over door, cut two 2-by-1½-inch rectangles.

11. For yard, cut a rectangle 14 by 12 inches.

12. Assemble the illustration-board house: Tape two sides to front securely. Tape back of house in place. Reinforce inside with tape. Place on yard, with 2 inches of yard at back of house and equal space at sides; tape in place. Tape the two roof squares together, so chimney cutout will be on right side of house toward back. Place on house; tape securely. Set aside house and paper patterns.

13. Next day, preheat oven to 350F. Place one-third of gingerbread dough on greased and floured cookie sheet. With lightly floured rolling pin, roll out to ⅛-inch thickness. Lay paper patterns for door, shutters and scalloped roof trim on dough; cut around each with sharp knife. Lift off dough trimmings.

14. Bake cutouts 5 to 8 minutes, or until edges just start to brown. Cool on cookie sheet on wire rack.

15. Meanwhile, place remaining dough on greased and floured 17-by-14-inch cookie sheet. With lightly floured rolling pin, roll out until dough covers cookie sheet.

16. Bake 15 minutes, or until center of dough feels firm when gently pressed with fingertip. Let cool on cookie sheet on wire rack 10 minutes.

17. Carefully fit paper patterns for front, back and sides of house on warm dough. Cut around side patterns. Cut around front and back patterns, cutting sides, but not tops and bottoms, ¼ inch wider than patterns. Remove all trimmings.

18. Decorate the illustration-board house: Spread one side with marshmallow whip. Place a gingerbread side in place; hold until it sticks. Repeat with second side; then add front and back.

19. Shingle roof: Spread marshmallow whip on roof and on backs of tea cookies as they are needed. Place cookies on roof, row by row, starting at lower edge. Cut cookies as necessary, so they join and overlap, to give shingle effect. If desired, slightly soften three cookies over boiling water; place over roof ridge where shingles meet, and mold to fit roof.

continued on page 240

continued from page 239

20. Make one recipe of Snow Frosting. Spread top half of house front with frosting. Place ½ cup frosting in small bowl; stir in 2 to 3 tablespoons cocoa, or enough for desired color. (Add several drops of water if frosting becomes too thick.) Pipe chocolate latticework over frosting on house, as pictured (we used number-44 decorating tip).

21. Place ¼ cup frosting in small bowl; stir in about 1 teaspoon red food color. Spread on gingerbread door and shutters; let stand about 10 minutes, or until dry. Then cement to house.

22. Separate sandwich cookie; cement one half, filling side down, over large front window. Decorate center with red frosting. Cut caramel in half lengthwise; cement under window, for window box.

23. Cut curtains from red-striped gum. Cement in place.

24. Tape cardboard door-canopy rectangles together. Bend and cement over door, as pictured. Cover with white frosting.

25. Build chimney: With marshmallow whip as mortar, stack nougat candies, brick fashion, against side of house. Use two candies at base; taper to one when chimney is 4½ inches high. For smokestacks, push two pieces of peppermint stick into top nougat before placing on chimney.

26. For trees, trim ice-cream cones to desired heights. Add 3 teaspoons green food color to remaining frosting. Spread on cones, covering completely. Or, with number-67 leaf tip, pipe frosting onto cones in slightly overlapping rows.

27. Let house and trees dry overnight.

28. Next day, make recipe for Snow Frosting twice. Spread on yard, and pile it to resemble snowdrifts. For path, spread frosting smoothly, and pave with broken chocolate and licorice candy wafers. Set trees in place, and frost tops. Add frosting to house, for snow effect. Place red-hot candies in snow in window box.

29. Let dry, and use as table centerpiece or mantel decoration or under the Christmas tree.

30. To preserve chalet, spray it lightly with semi-gloss polyurethane spray; let dry completely; cover tightly and store in a cool dry place.

Note: We used 14 pieces (1¾ by 1 inch) individually boxed Italian torrone.

CANDYLAND HOUSE
(pictured)

Heavy brown paper
Illustration board or cardboard
Corrugated cardboard
Masking or cellophane tape
Spiced Cookie Dough, recipe follows
Snow Frosting, page 235
1 pkg (6¼ oz) miniature marshmallows
(see Note)
½ lb assorted jelly slices
½ lb gumdrops
½ lb jelly beans
½ lb round peppermint candies
½ lb pink and striped pillow mints
12 peppermint sticks
1 lb assorted licorice candies
2 red licorice twists
36 inches red licorice laces
4 red lollipops

1. Allow several days for making this house. Because candy decorations are heavy, it is necessary to construct a sturdy, illustration-board house frame and allow ample drying time for each assembly step.

2. Make paper patterns: For walls, draw a 12-by-6-inch rectangle on heavy brown paper. Cut out. Mark center of each long side and center of one end. Draw a line between each side point and end point. Cut on lines. For gables, cut out an 8½-by-4-inch rectangle; divide on diagonal. Then cut along diagonal. You use only one piece for pattern. For chimney, cut out a 2¼-by-4½-inch rectangle. On long sides, make mark 2 inches from one end. Draw line between points; mark center of line. Draw lines from center mark to nearest corners. Cut along these two lines. For roof (see Diagram B), draw a 17-by-8-inch rectangle. On 17-inch sides, mark off 2½ inches from both ends. Draw lines across width to connect marks. On these 2 lines, mark 1⅛ inches from both sides toward center. Join marks as in diagram. Cut out.

3. To construct: Trace pattern for wall of house on illustration board 4 times, with sides touching. Cut out in one piece. Score between sections. Trace pattern for gable on illustration board twice, wide ends touching, as in Diagram B. Repeat. Cut out; score on dotted line. (Chimney is made of cookie pieces and does not need reinforcement.) Trace pattern for roof on

GINGERBREAD SWISS CHALET

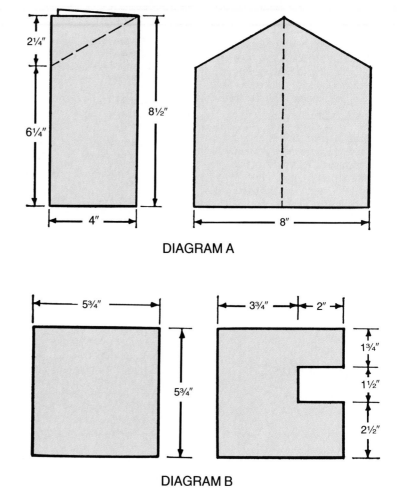

DIAGRAM A

DIAGRAM B

illustration board. Cut out; score on dotted line. Draw a 12½-inch square on illustration board for base of house. Mark sides 3 inches from all corners. Join points, as in Diagram A. Score on dotted lines (see diagram). Cut out a 12-inch square of corrugated cardboard. Slash base from each corner to inner dotted-line square (see Diagram A). Cut a wedge, tapering from ⅝ inch wide, from each corner. Bend along scored lines; tape corners together. Mount base on corrugated-cardboard square, and secure with tape. Fold house walls on scored lines, to make right-angle corners. Tape open corner together. Set house walls on base; tape in place. Fold roof and both gables on dotted lines. Tape a gable to each side of roof (see Diagram C). Do not set illustration-board roof on walls at this point.

4. Make and bake Spiced Cookie Dough. Cut out cookie walls, gables and chimney as directed in recipe. When all cookie pieces are ready, make Snow Frosting.

5. To assemble and decorate house: Decorate cookie walls with candies, as pictured. (Front and back walls are identical; side walls are the same.) Put a dab of frosting on each candy; set in place. With candies, make doors for front and back walls, windows for side walls. Let dry overnight.

6. Spread frosting on undecorated side of one wall. Press against illustration-board framework; hold 1 or 2 minutes. Repeat with other 3 walls. Decorate the house base with candies, using dabs of frosting as glue. Let set overnight.

7. Set illustration-board gabled roof on walls (see Diagram C). Spread each cookie gable piece with frosting; set in place. Let dry 1 hour.

8. Spread all except top edges of cookie chimney pieces with frosting. Place on roof (Diagram C). Let dry overnight.

9. Frost and decorate gabled roof and chimney.

Note: The candies in the ingredient list are ones we used; you may decorate the house to suit your fancy.

SPICED COOKIE DOUGH

5 pkg (13-oz size) sugar-cookie mix
Ground cinnamon
Ground nutmeg
5 eggs

1. Preheat oven to 375F. Lightly grease 15½-by-12-inch cookie sheet.

2. In large bowl, combine 1 package cookie mix with 1½ tablespoons cinnamon, 1½ teaspoons nutmeg, 1 egg. Mix well with spoon; knead 3 to 5 minutes until dough is smooth.

CANDYLAND HOUSE

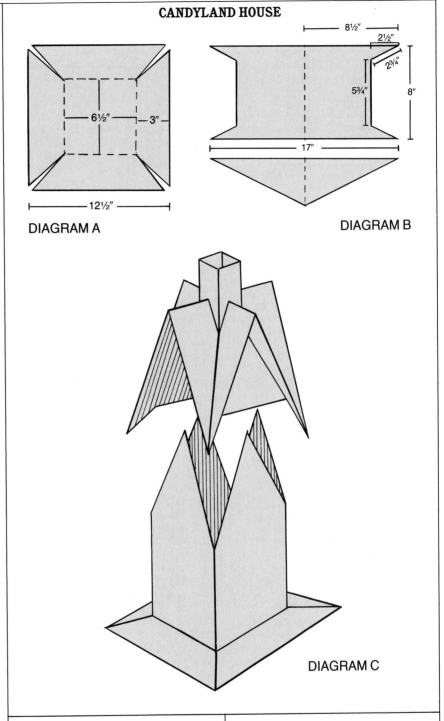

DIAGRAM A

DIAGRAM B

DIAGRAM C

3. Roll out dough on cookie sheet to about ⅜-inch thickness, leaving 1-inch border around dough.

4. Bake 8 to 10 minutes, or until cake tester inserted in center comes out clean.

5. Cool on cookie sheet on wire rack until cool enough to touch—about 10 minutes.

6. Lay paper-pattern pieces for wall of house, chimney and gable on warm dough. Cut around each with sharp, pointed knife. Cut out as many pieces as possible. (You will need 4 walls, 4 chimney pieces, 8 gable pieces.) Remove trimmings.

7. With spatula, remove pieces to waxed-paper-lined tray. Let cool. Cover loosely until ready to decorate and assemble house.

8. Repeat with remaining packages of cookie mix until all house sections are cut out.

continued on page 242

continued from page 241

GINGERBREAD CHAPEL
(pictured)

3 recipes Gingerbread-Cottage Dough, page 239
Heavy brown paper
Illustration board or cardboard
Masking tape
Household cement
Almond paste
Aluminum foil
Stained-Glass Windows, recipe follows
3 recipes Snow Frosting, page 235
Red, blue, green and yellow food color
1 torrone or nougat (1¾ by 1 inch)

1. Make Gingerbread-Cottage Dough; refrigerate overnight.

2. Make paper patterns: For left side, draw and cut a 15-by-4½-inch rectangle from brown paper. For right side, draw and cut an 8-by-4½-inch rectangle and a 4½-by-1¼- inch rectangle. For window, draw and cut a 2¼-by-1-inch rectangle; fold in half lengthwise and round off the corner at one end. Using this, draw five windows, evenly spaced, 1¼ inches from bottom on pattern for the left side; cut out. Repeat to make three windows on the larger right-side pattern.

3. For front, draw and cut an 11½-by-8-inch rectangle. Fold in half lengthwise; measure a point 4½ inches from one cut edge. Draw and cut an 8-inch diagonal line from this point to the folded corner farthest away. Copy this pattern for back. Draw and cut a 5-by-2¾-inch rectangle. Fold in half lengthwise. Measure a point 3 inches from one cut edge. Draw and cut a 2½-inch diagonal line from the point to the nearest folded corner. Center this on the bottom of the front pattern, leaving about 2½ inches on each side. Trace and cut this out; save small pattern for front of entry. On large front pattern, draw a circle, using a nickel, centered above the point of the entry. Draw and cut a 1¾-by-3-inch rectangle for the sides of the entry. Label "cut 2." Draw and cut a 5½-inch square. Fold in half lengthwise. Measure a point 2 inches from one cut edge. Measure and cut a 3½-inch diagonal line from this point to the nearest folded corner. Center this on the bottom of the back pattern, so there will be about 1¼ inches on each side. Trace and cut out. Discard the small pattern. Draw and cut a 3½-by-2½-inch rectangle for the sides of the apse. Label "cut 3."

4. For tower and right-side extension, see diagrams *A* through *F*. (All diagrams appear on page 243.) For third wall of extension, draw and cut a 2¾-by-3⅛-inch rectangle. Draw and cut out a ¾-inch square, centered 1½ inches from the bottom of this rectangle. Discard small square. For clock faces, draw and cut a 1½-inch circle; label "cut 4." For doors, draw and cut a 2-by-1¼-inch rectangle. Fold in half lengthwise, and round off the top; label "cut 2."

5. For tower top, draw and cut a 3½-by-2½-inch rectangle. Cut ½ inch from the bottom of the window pattern. Center the pattern 1 inch from the bottom of this pattern. Trace and cut out window. Label pattern "cut 4." Discard window pattern.

6. For left roof, draw and cut a 15-by-8-inch rectangle. For right roof, see diagram *G*. For entry roof, draw and cut a 2½-by-1¾-inch rectangle. Label "cut 2." For tower roof, see diagram *H*. Also cut a 2½-inch square for top. For apse roof, draw and cut a 3-by-2½-inch rectangle. Fold in half lengthwise, and cut a 3¼-inch diagonal line from a cut corner to the opposite folded corner. Label "cut 3." You should have 24 patterns.

7. Assemble the illustration-board base: Cut a 15-by-22-inch churchyard. If you wish to illuminate your chapel, as pictured, cut a 4-inch square in the center of the yard. Trace all patterns, except those made from diagrams *B*, *C* and *D*, onto the illustration board. If patterns are labeled to be used more than once, trace them as often as called for. Trace the pattern from diagram *A* four times. Cut out all pieces. Cut out a square slightly less than 3 inches. Reserve patterns.

8. To assemble the illustration-board chapel: Tape front and back to the left side. Tape the small section of the right side to the front and the large section to the back. Tape together the three apse sides, the four tower sides and the two sides and front of the entry. Set up chapel, centered on churchyard. Place the tower next to the large section of the right side so that 1½ inches of it extend outside the left side. Tape the sides and window wall of the extension into place in front of the tower. Reinforce all taped areas with household cement on the inside. Attach the 3-inch square ¼ inch below the straight top edge of the tower. Reinforce securely. Allow to dry several hours; then tape and glue roof sections and tower top into place.

9. To make angel: Knead almond paste; form a ¾-inch ball and cut in half. Flatten some of almond paste to make a 5-inch square. Cut out angel, using patterns *I*, *J*, *K* and *L*. For trumpet, mold a 1-inch tapered roll about ⅛ inch in diameter at the most. Pinch large end to flare. Let all pieces dry overnight.

10. Next day, preheat oven to 350F. Place two-thirds of one recipe of Gingerbread-Cottage Dough on a greased 17-by-14-inch cookie sheet. With floured rolling pin, roll out to ⅛-inch thickness. Lay patterns on the gingerbread, starting with the largest, and cut around them with a sharp knife. Remove trimmings and set aside. Cut the two large roof pieces ¼ inch larger than the pattern on each end and the bottom to form an overhang; score, as pictured, with a large knife or the edge of a cookie sheet. Bake 12 to 15 minutes, or until dough feels firm when gently pressed and has started to brown at the edges. Place patterns on the baked gingerbread, and trim to original size. Let cool on cookie sheets 10 minutes; then remove to wire rack. If possible, use several cookie sheets. Repeat until all pieces have been baked. (Use pieces *A, B, C* and *D* once only.) Roll out all remaining dough, and cut into rectangles about ¾ by 1¼ inches for churchyard bricks.

11. Place side pieces, front and window wall of extension on foil (shiny side up). Make red sugar syrup (Stained-Glass Windows, page 243), and pour into the window openings. Allow to cool.

12. Make one recipe of Snow Frosting. Spread on illustration-board base, to attach all side, front and tower pieces, including sides of entry and apse. Hold each piece in place until it has adhered. Make another recipe of frosting, and frost sides, swirling to make stucco effect. Attach doors and clock circles as pictured. Color small portions of frosting pink, blue and yellow. Thin with water to consistency of cream. Use to paint the angel, as pictured. Let dry several hours.

13. Prepare third recipe of Snow Frosting; spread over roof surfaces and install roof sections, one at a time, trimming to make fit, if necessary.

14. Place ¼ cup frosting in pastry bag with writing tip. Outline clock faces, and draw hands at the desired time. Draw center line on each door. Pipe frosting onto the back of the angel, and attach to the front of the chapel. Hold in place until it is secure. Color a little frosting red and a little green. Using a leaf tip, make a wreath on the door, as pictured. Add red berries with writing tip.

15. Using remaining frosting, cover yard, and lay gingerbread bricks. Cut nougat in half lengthwise, and use for steps at each door. Let dry completely before moving.

16. To preserve chapel, spray it lightly with semi-gloss polyurethane spray; let dry completely; cover tightly and store in a cool dry place.

CLASSIC COOKIE HOUSES

STAINED-GLASS WINDOWS

1 cup sugar
¼ cup corn syrup
¼ cup water
Red food color

1. Combine sugar, corn syrup and ¼ cup water in small saucepan. Cook, without stirring, until mixture reaches 300F on candy thermometer. Stir in several drops food color, and pour carefully into window holes, filling slightly less than to top of gingerbread. Cool completely before moving; then peel off foil and use as directed. (Any excess syrup may be dropped in dots on extra foil to be used as hard candy.) ■

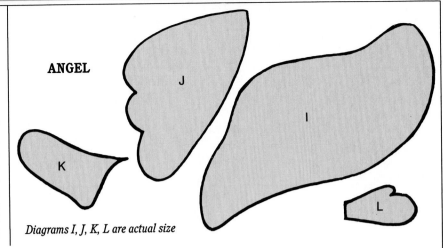

ANGEL

Diagrams I, J, K, L are actual size

GINGERBREAD CHAPEL

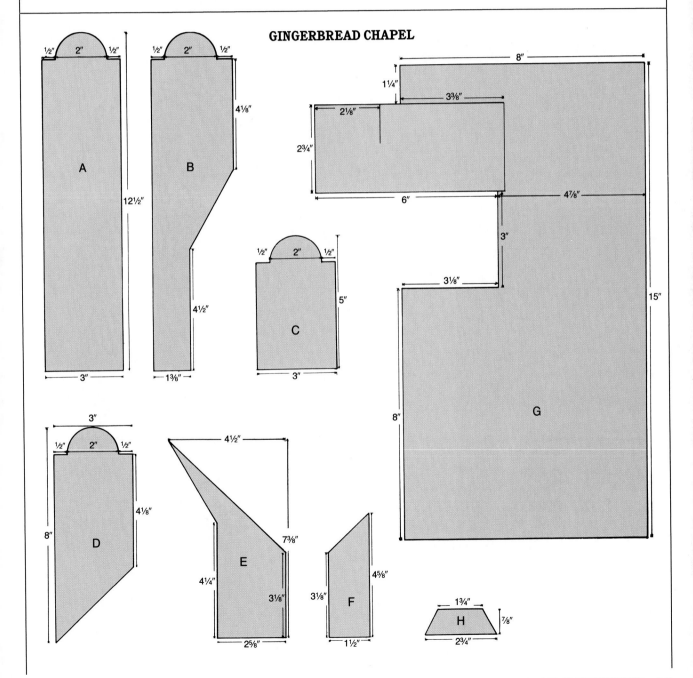

BAKE YOUR OWN
VICTORIAN VILLAGE

Grace your table all through the holidays with a bake-it-yourself gingerbread barn, house and railroad depot. Add marzipan horses, a pretzel corral, a candy-cane lamppost, blue-mint-candy pond, frosted ice-cream-cone trees, a chocolate train on gingerbread tracks, a marzipan sleigh on candy-cane runners...and lots of gingerbread people. Surround it all with fluffy icing. Directions and patterns begin on page 246.

continued from page 245

VICTORIAN VILLAGE
(pictured)

2 recipes Gingerbread-Village Dough, recipe follows
Paper or thin cardboard for patterns or backing
Mint-Candy Pond, directions follow
About 5 recipes Snow Frosting, recipe follows
Green, red and yellow food colors
Wreaths and Trees, directions follow
Lamp Post, directions follow
Marzipan Horses and Sleigh, directions follow
½-inch-thick Styrofoam or foam-core board for inside bases; heavy cardboard for buildings
Unsweetened cocoa
Assorted candies: 14 red and 14 green jelly beans; silver dragées; green-pea candies; eight flat, round red jelly candies; four 3¾-inch peppermint sticks; chocolate train (optional) (check individual recipes below for other candies needed)
Pretzel Corral, directions follow
Confectioners' sugar

1. Make Gingerbread-Village Dough up to a week ahead, and bake as needed. (Or bake cookies ahead; store flat with waxed paper between layers in airtight containers.)

2. Draw pattern pieces to scale on paper (patterns start on opposite page; all patterns are half actual size); mark all pieces to identify them, and keep each building's pieces together; cut out with scissors. If you wish to preserve buildings, using thin cardboard, cut out building fronts, backs, sides and roofs ¼ inch smaller than patterns. Glue to back of cookies before assembling.

3. *To cut out house:* On floured 15-by-12-inch sheet of parchment paper or foil (or one large enough to cover cookie sheet), with floured rolling pin, roll out one piece of dough to between ⅛- to ¼-inch thickness. Flour reverse sides of patterns; lay as many patterns of house as possible on dough, ½ inch apart. With pizza wheel or X-acto knife, cut around patterns, using a ruler as a guide for the straight edges. Carefully remove patterns and all excess dough. (Save dough trimmings in plastic bag; chill to reroll later.) Place parchment paper of cut gingerbread dough on cookie sheet. Chill 15 minutes; meanwhile, roll and cut more dough. (Chilling dough makes it easier to cut out details like windows.) With X-acto knife, cut out all dark areas or areas marked "cut out" on patterns, such as windows, doors, rails. Of the cutouts, save and bake only the window shutter. Cut out balcony doors, backstair door and side top windows; remove and place on another part of the parchment or foil.

(These will be baked.) Reshape pieces, if necessary, after moving them. With tip of knife, lightly score dough to mark windows or doors that have *not* been removed. (Be careful not to cut through the dough.) Score lattice design on doors as marked. With cupola, you can cut out windows, bake and glue on later, or just score to mark them. If you have a small star cutter, use it to cut star rather than using pattern. Patterns are marked as to how many cookies need to be cut.

4. Preheat oven to 350F. Bake cookies 10 to 15 minutes, or until firm and browned. Remove smaller pieces first, since they bake faster. Remove cookie sheet to wire rack. While cookies are still hot, place pattern on cookies, and trim or straighten edges that may have expanded more than ⅛ inch beyond pattern. Cool cookies before removing from paper.

5. *To cut out barn:* Roll out dough as in Step 3. When cutting out barn back, do not cut out hayloft window or doors; it should be a solid wall. With the barn front, cut out dark areas of hayloft windows; add these cutouts to bag of dough trimmings. Cut and remove windows and top half of Dutch doors to bake separately. Lightly score dough on barn sides to mark window shutters. Score walls of barn and tower vertically to resemble siding. (If desired, use a small animal cookie cutter to cut animal for top of weather vane rather than using pattern.) Bake cookies as in Step 4.

6. *To cut out railroad depot:* Roll out dough as in Step 3. When cutting out depot back, do not cut out windows or doors; it should be a solid wall. With front, cut out doors; bake separately. Cut out all dark areas of windows, doors and rails. Add these cutouts to bag of dough trimmings. Half-inch (miniature) heart- and crescent-shape cutters were used to cut out design in rails quickly; if you do not have them, use knife to cut out a design. Lightly score dough for the chimney to get a brick effect. Bake cookies as in Step 4.

7. Knead together all dough trimmings; roll to ³⁄₁₆-inch thickness. Using cookie cutters or patterns, cut out reindeer and gingerbread boys and girls. To personalize boys and girls, add bits of dough for hair, muffs, hats or clothing, as pictured. Bake as in Step 4. Using dough, make Mint-Candy Pond.

8. Make one batch of Snow Frosting. Remove 1 cup to small bowl; tint green with food color. Remove ½ cup to another bowl or paper cup; tint dark pink. Spoon green and pink icing into separate pastry bags, each fitted with a coupler and a leaf tip or number-3 writing tip. Keep remaining white icing covered with plastic wrap.

Use icing to make wreaths, trees and lamp post. Decorate reindeer cookies, if desired, to give away to village visitors. To keep icing at tip of bag from drying out, insert round toothpick into tip, or wrap with plastic. Make the horses and sleigh.

9. Using Styrofoam, cut out three rectangles to use as inside bases or floors of buildings. Sizes are approximate, depending on how you join buildings at the corners. House is 5½ by 3⅛ inches; barn is 5¾ by 5¼ inches; depot is 5¼ by 5 inches. Cut heavy cardboard or Styrofoam into three 10-by-8-inch pieces for building bases. If desired, a Christmas-tree bulb in a standing socket may be placed inside house to illuminate it; be sure to cut a hole in outer base and inside base or floor before assembling house so bulb can be inserted.

10. *To assemble house:* Make one batch of Snow Frosting, and stir in about six tablespoons cocoa to tint dark brown, adding drops of water if too stiff. Spoon into pastry bag fitted with small writing tip. (If all icing does not fit into bag, keep leftover in bowl covered with plastic wrap.) Use brown icing to join or "glue" all pieces. Pipe brown icing along outer wall edges of house sides and back wall edges of front. Using Styrofoam base as the floor, hold front upright against floor, and press sides into back edges of front. (See photograph on page 251 for front and bay-window side of house.) Hold in place until icing dries, or sets. Repeat to glue back wall to sides, to complete house frame. (Back of house and shuttered side are pictured on page 244.) For added support, pipe a line of icing along inside corners. For the long back bay windows, pipe icing along bottom and two long edges of bay front and bottom of the two bay sides; press onto bay floor; let set. Pipe icing along top edge of window sides; press side supports into sides so that shortest edge goes to the back of the window; let set. When set, pipe icing on top edges, and press roof onto bay window; let set. Assemble side bay window the same as back bay window, but roof will go on top without any side supports. For stairs, pipe icing along top edge of stair sides; press top stair into place; let set. (Use Styrofoam between stair sides to brace.) Put dot of icing on top of step supports; glue on steps; glue last step vertically at bottom. Glue rails to each side of top step; let set. For stair roof, pipe icing on back of stair-roof eave along straight edges. Press stair-roof pieces in place; where they meet at peak, pipe icing to join. Make balcony roof as above. For balcony, glue on side and front rails; let set. For cupola, pipe icing along edges of sides, front and

continued on page 248

VICTORIAN-VILLAGE PATTERNS
(All Patterns Are Half Actual Size)

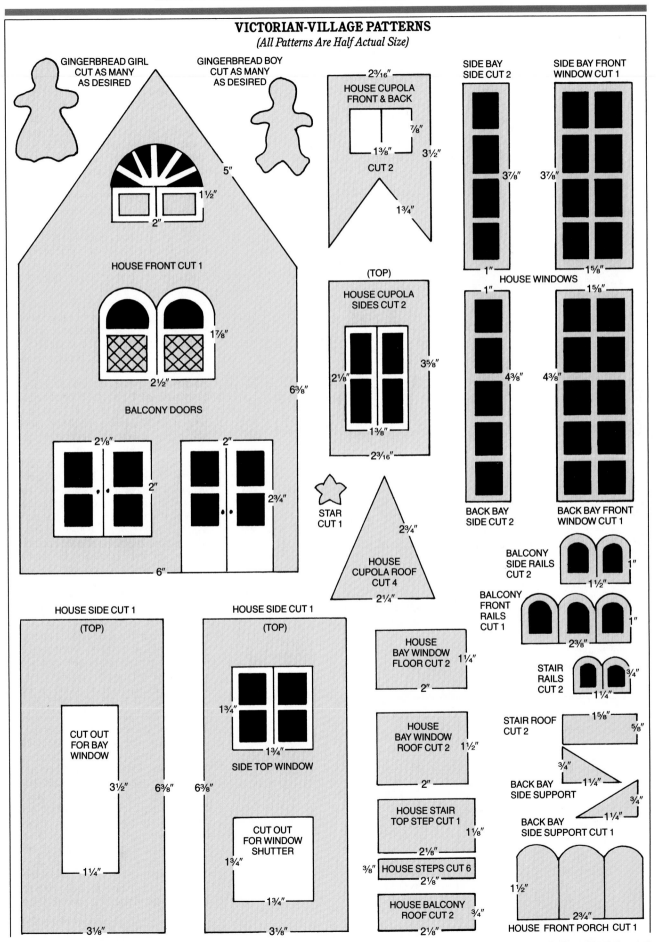

GINGERBREAD GIRL CUT AS MANY AS DESIRED

GINGERBREAD BOY CUT AS MANY AS DESIRED

HOUSE CUPOLA FRONT & BACK

2³⁄₁₆″

⁷⁄₈″

1³⁄₈″

3½″

CUT 2

1³⁄₄″

SIDE BAY SIDE CUT 2

SIDE BAY FRONT WINDOW CUT 1

3⁷⁄₈″

3⁷⁄₈″

1″

1⁵⁄₈″

HOUSE WINDOWS

HOUSE FRONT CUT 1

5″

1½″

2″

6³⁄₈″

(TOP)

HOUSE CUPOLA SIDES CUT 2

3⁵⁄₈″

2¹⁄₈″

1³⁄₈″

2³⁄₁₆″

1⁷⁄₈″

2½″

BALCONY DOORS

2¹⁄₈″

2″

2″

2″

2³⁄₄″

STAR CUT 1

HOUSE CUPOLA ROOF CUT 4

2³⁄₄″

2¼″

6″

1″

1⁵⁄₈″

4³⁄₈″

4³⁄₈″

BACK BAY SIDE CUT 2

BACK BAY FRONT WINDOW CUT 1

BALCONY SIDE RAILS CUT 2

1″

1½″

BALCONY FRONT RAILS CUT 1

1″

2³⁄₈″

STAIR RAILS CUT 2

¾″

1¼″

HOUSE SIDE CUT 1

(TOP)

HOUSE SIDE CUT 1

(TOP)

1³⁄₄″

1³⁄₄″

SIDE TOP WINDOW

CUT OUT FOR BAY WINDOW

3½″

6³⁄₈″

6³⁄₈″

CUT OUT FOR WINDOW SHUTTER

1³⁄₄″

1¼″

1³⁄₄″

3¹⁄₈″

3¹⁄₈″

HOUSE BAY WINDOW FLOOR CUT 2

1¼″

2″

HOUSE BAY WINDOW ROOF CUT 2

1½″

2″

HOUSE STAIR TOP STEP CUT 1

1¹⁄₈″

2¹⁄₈″

³⁄₈″ HOUSE STEPS CUT 6

2¹⁄₈″

HOUSE BALCONY ROOF CUT 2

¾″

2¹⁄₈″

STAIR ROOF CUT 2

1⁵⁄₈″

⁵⁄₈″

BACK BAY SIDE SUPPORT

¾″

1¼″

¾″

1¼″

BACK BAY SIDE SUPPORT CUT 1

1½″

2³⁄₄″

HOUSE FRONT PORCH CUT 1

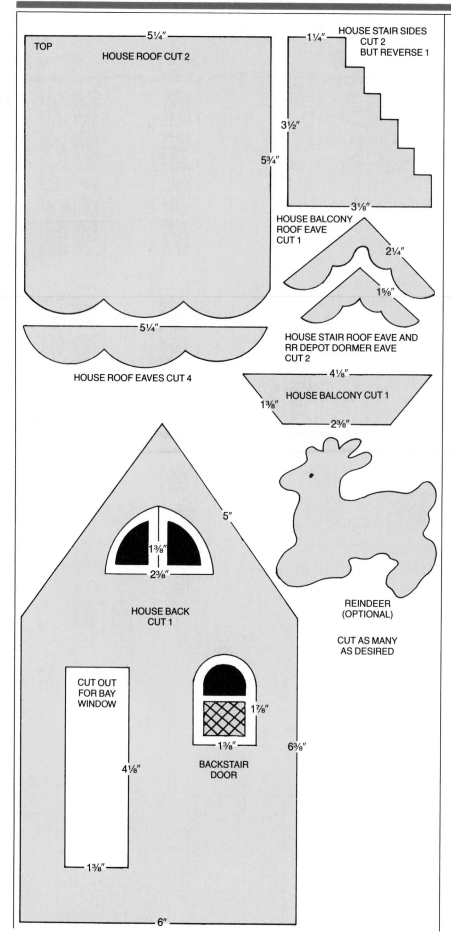

TOP

HOUSE ROOF CUT 2

5¼"

5¾"

HOUSE STAIR SIDES
CUT 2
BUT REVERSE 1

1¼"

3½"

3⅛"

HOUSE BALCONY
ROOF EAVE
CUT 1

2¼"

1⅝"

HOUSE STAIR ROOF EAVE AND
RR DEPOT DORMER EAVE
CUT 2

HOUSE ROOF EAVES CUT 4

5¼"

4⅛"

HOUSE BALCONY CUT 1

1⅜"

2⅜"

5"

1⅜"

2⅜"

HOUSE BACK
CUT 1

CUT OUT
FOR BAY
WINDOW

4⅛"

1⅜"

1⅞"

1⅜"

6⅜"

BACKSTAIR
DOOR

6"

REINDEER
(OPTIONAL)

CUT AS MANY
AS DESIRED

continued from page 246

back; join; let set. Pipe icing along long sides of each roof piece; join all pieces for roof; let set. Pipe icing along top edge of cupola sides; press roof onto cupola. Glue on any cutout windows; let set. Before attaching all pieces to house, place house frame on heavy cardboard. Pipe icing along top edges of house frame; press roof into place; hold until set. Reinforce seam at peak of roof with icing; glue eaves to roof edges on front and back of house. Pipe icing onto backs of bay windows; attach to house back and side (put a piece of Styrofoam underneath window to support until icing dries). Pipe icing onto back of balcony; attach to house front, supporting it until icing dries. Attach balcony doors; let dry. Glue on balcony roof; let set. Pipe icing onto back of stairs; attach to back of house. Glue on stair roof, door, side top windows and side shutters. Glue the cupola onto the roof.

11. *To decorate house:* Make another batch of Snow Frosting; remove ½ cup to small bowl or paper cup, and tint yellow; cover with plastic wrap. With remaining white icing, frost house roof around cupola on top. While icing is still wet, apply jelly beans, as pictured. Ice roofs of cupola, bay windows, balcony and stairs. With yellow icing, frost star on both sides; let dry. Attach to top of cupola. Spoon remaining yellow icing into pastry bag fitted with small writing tip; cover tip; use icing later. Spoon white icing into pastry bag fitted with a coupler and small writing tip; pipe onto windows, door and shutter to decorate; attach dragées and wreaths to decorate. Decorate bay windows with string of green and pink icing dots. Change tip on green icing bag to a small star tip; pipe swag on house roof eaves and over front door; decorate with pink icing dots. Decorate cupola roof with green icing and dragées. Decorate balcony and stair rails as pictured. Change tip on white icing bag to a small star tip, and pipe a shell design on top of roof, the cupola's corners and its roof. With white icing, glue front porch to cardboard below doors.

12. *To assemble barn:* Make barn frame like the house frame, with the Styrofoam base inside as the floor; let set. Reinforce inside and outside corners of walls with brown icing. Place barn frame on heavy cardboard. Pipe brown icing on each side and bottom of hayloft windows; attach cutout windows and window ledge. When barn frame is secure, pipe brown icing on top edge of barn front and back and along one long edge of each top roof piece. Press iced edges of roof together on top of barn frame; let set. Attach bottom roof pieces

continued on page 250

BAKE YOUR OWN VICTORIAN VILLAGE

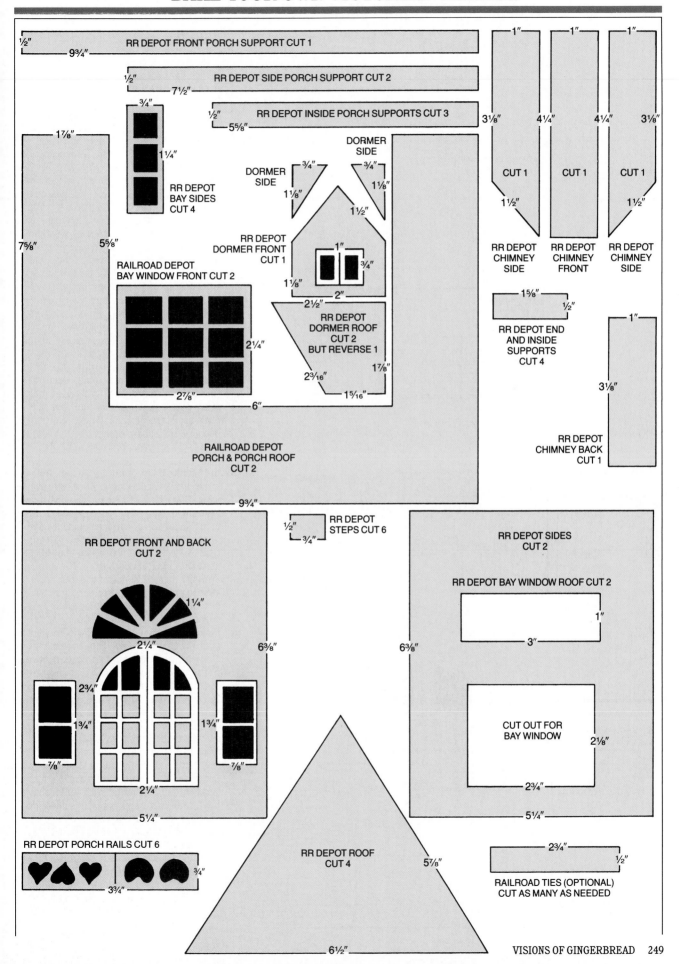

RR DEPOT FRONT PORCH SUPPORT CUT 1

RR DEPOT SIDE PORCH SUPPORT CUT 2

RR DEPOT INSIDE PORCH SUPPORTS CUT 3

RR DEPOT BAY SIDES CUT 4

RAILROAD DEPOT BAY WINDOW FRONT CUT 2

DORMER SIDE

DORMER SIDE

DORMER SIDE

RR DEPOT DORMER FRONT CUT 1

RR DEPOT DORMER ROOF CUT 2 BUT REVERSE 1

RAILROAD DEPOT PORCH & PORCH ROOF CUT 2

RR DEPOT STEPS CUT 6

RR DEPOT CHIMNEY SIDE

RR DEPOT CHIMNEY FRONT

RR DEPOT CHIMNEY SIDE

CUT 1

RR DEPOT END AND INSIDE SUPPORTS CUT 4

RR DEPOT CHIMNEY BACK CUT 1

RR DEPOT FRONT AND BACK CUT 2

RR DEPOT SIDES CUT 2

RR DEPOT BAY WINDOW ROOF CUT 2

CUT OUT FOR BAY WINDOW

RR DEPOT PORCH RAILS CUT 6

RR DEPOT ROOF CUT 4

RAILROAD TIES (OPTIONAL) CUT AS MANY AS NEEDED

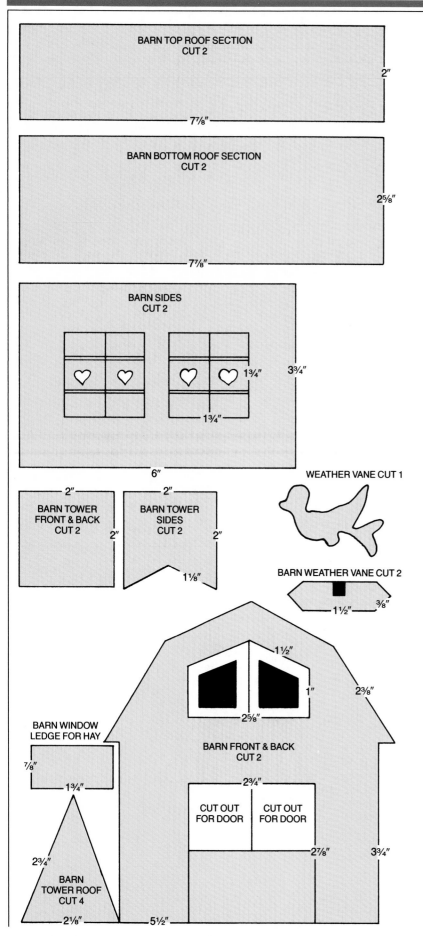

BARN TOP ROOF SECTION
CUT 2
2"
7⅞"

BARN BOTTOM ROOF SECTION
CUT 2
2⅝"
7⅞"

BARN SIDES
CUT 2
1¾"
3¾"
1¾"
6"

WEATHER VANE CUT 1

BARN TOWER
FRONT & BACK
CUT 2
2"
2"

BARN TOWER
SIDES
CUT 2
2"
2"
1⅛"

BARN WEATHER VANE CUT 2
1½"
⅜"

BARN WINDOW
LEDGE FOR HAY
⅞"
1¾"

BARN FRONT & BACK
CUT 2
1½"
1"
2⅜"
2⅝"
2¾"

CUT OUT
FOR DOOR
CUT OUT
FOR DOOR
2⅞"
3¾"

BARN
TOWER ROOF
CUT 4
2¾"
2⅛"
5½"

continued from page 248

as above, but glue long edges to top roof; let set. For tower, glue sides to front; glue back to sides; let set. For tower roof, glue long edges of sections together; let set. Pipe brown icing on top edge of tower sides, and glue on roof section. Glue top half of doors to barn; let set.

13. *To decorate barn:* If necessary, make one batch of Snow Frosting. Frost tower and barn roofs; place tower on top of barn. While icing is wet, put pea candies on barn roof to resemble a wreath; decorate with pink icing dots. Pipe dot of brown icing in center cuts of weathervane pieces; insert into each other to cross in center; let set. With white icing, pipe one letter—N, S, E and W—on the points. Glue to top of tower. Outline bird with icing; glue to weather vane. Using white icing, outline windows, doors and shutters on side of barn. Pipe yellow icing on window ledge to make hay. Change tip of white-icing bag to star tip, and pipe shell design on barn roof; decorate with dragées and dots of green icing. Decorate tower sides with dots of green and pink icing; pipe pink-icing swag on roof; add dragées. Make pink hearts on shutters; decorate top of barn doors.

14. *To assemble railroad depot:* Make depot frame like the house frame, with the Styrofoam base inside; let set. Reinforce inside corners of walls with brown icing. Place depot frame on cardboard or Styrofoam base. For porch, pipe icing along underside of porch edges, one edge at a time, placing support pieces on icing. Glue between supports since they connect. Let dry until very secure. Turn porch upright, and slide next to depot front; glue to wall of depot. For each bay window of depot, pipe brown icing along long edges of bay front; attach sides; let set. Pipe icing along top edges of window, and glue on bay roof; let set. Pipe brown icing along top outer edges of porch, except in front of doors; press on rails, connecting sections with icing. Glue doors open to front of depot. Glue dragées for doorknobs. Glue a red jelly candy to each corner of porch. Dot center of each candy with white icing; insert a long peppermint stick to use for porch-roof supports; let dry, straightening the sticks if necessary. Cut a piece of thin cardboard ¼ inch smaller than porch roof. With white icing, frost cardboard, and press to underside of porch roof. Dot tops of peppermint sticks with icing; add another jelly candy and more icing. Rest porch roof, cardboard side down, on candy supports. Pipe white icing between depot and porch roof to attach; let set. When set, frost porch roof. For depot roof, glue short edges of

roof pieces together; let set until very firm. Pipe brown icing along top edges of depot frame, and place roof on top; let set. For dormer, glue the 1⅛-inch edge of each dormer side to back edges of dormer front. Glue dormer onto depot roof. Glue roof pieces onto dormer; reinforce center roof seam. Glue eaves to dormer roof. For chimney, glue sides to front; let set. Glue chimney onto depot roof; let set.

15. *To decorate depot:* If necessary, make last batch of Snow Frosting. Using white-icing bag with writing tip, pipe lattice design onto porch bottom; outline windows; insert dragées for knobs. Change tip of pastry bag to star tip; use to decorate depot and dormer roofs, chimney top, porch-rail base and porch roof. Pipe pink and green icing dots on top of rails. Using white icing, frost cardboard in front of depot; insert steps in front. Decorate windows with wreaths. Decorate dormer eaves with green icing and dragées.

16. Make pretzel corral.

17. *To set up village:* With white icing, frost cardboard or Styrofoam all around buildings. Place trees, lamp post, sleigh and pond around the buildings. Frost Styrofoam base of corral, and put horse in corral; insert stick horses in open barn doors. Using white icing, glue gingerbread boys and girls onto pond, steps and around buildings. Let icing dry. If desired, arrange railroad ties and chocolate train on top as pictured. Sift confectioners' sugar over village to look like snow.

18. To preserve buildings, spray them lightly with semi-gloss polyurethane spray; let dry completely; cover tightly and store in a cool dry place.

To make mint-candy pond: Using

about a 12-by-¾-inch strip of leftover rolled gingerbread dough, place it on a greased small sheet of foil, and shape into an oval, pressing ends to join. Place foil on cookie sheet. Press dough around inner edge to flatten. Bake in preheated 350F oven 9 minutes. Meanwhile, finely crush hard blue mint candy to get 2 tablespoons. Sprinkle in center of partially baked oval; bake a few minutes longer just to melt the candy. Leave on cookie sheet; cool on wire rack; peel off foil.

To make wreaths: Onto waxed paper, using pastry bag fitted with leaf tip, pipe green icing into 1-inch or smaller circles. Decorate with dots of pink icing. Let dry, and peel off paper. (Make about 11.)

To make trees: Using pastry bag fitted with leaf tip, pipe green icing into leaves to cover ice-cream sugar cones. Let dry. (Make about 6.)

To make lamp post: Insert a 3½-inch red peppermint stick into a ½-inch ball of plain marzipan (below) for base; cover with white icing. With same icing, glue a red candy on top of peppermint stick. (Make 1 or more.)

To make marzipan horses and sleigh: In bowl with fork, mix ½ cup almond paste with 1 egg white and ¼ teaspoon vanilla extract. Gradually work in 2 to 2½ cups confectioners' sugar until mixture is stiff and not sticky. Use hands to work in sugar, if necessary. Break off about ½-inch piece of marzipan; keep remainder wrapped in plastic wrap. Knead unsweetened cocoa into small piece of marzipan to make a dark-brown color. Make two stick horses for the barn: For each, take 1-inch plain marzipan, and shape into horse's head and neck; insert toothpick halfway into neck. Using brown marzipan, shape small pieces into horses' manes, forelocks and eyes. Using light corn syrup or egg white, glue mane, forelock and eyes onto each head. Let them dry until firm. To make one horse for corral, shape 3-by-1-by-1-inch plain marzipan into a horse's body with head; apply small flat pieces to each back side to resemble rump of horse. Using brown marzipan, shape small pieces into tail, mane, forelock and eyes; attach to horse; let dry. For the sleigh, press ⅛-inch-thick rolled-out marzipan inside a confectioners'-sugar-dusted 2½-by-1½-inch toy sleigh (use as a mold, or shape sleigh free form). Trim marzipan even with sides of sleigh; remove sleigh from mold; let dry until firm. Decorate with icing, as pictured, and attach four tiny candy canes on bottom for the runners. Use leftover marzipan for lamp base and more horses or decorations.

To make pretzel corral: Using brown icing, ice two pretzel sticks on half of one side; place them 1 inch apart, and lay three pretzel sticks across frosted sticks. Let dry. Make about five of these fence sections (make more for a larger corral). For the gate, using scissors, cut three pretzel sticks to ¾ of their length. Glue them together lengthwise. Glue a whole stick parallel to each side of three short sticks. Cut a pretzel in half crosswise; glue to gate at right angles to resemble a fence post. From ½-inch-thick Styrofoam, cut out a 6-by-4-inch rectangle. Using a thick skewer, punch holes around top edge of rectangle to insert fence sections along three sides, gate at one short end; glue in place with white icing.

GINGERBREAD-VILLAGE DOUGH

8½ to 9 cups all-purpose flour
1 tablespoon ground ginger
2 teaspoons ground cinnamon
½ teaspoon salt
1¼ cups (2½ sticks) margarine
1 bottle (16 oz) dark corn syrup
1½ cups dark-brown sugar, firmly packed

1. In large bowl, mix together 4 cups flour, the ginger, cinnamon and salt.

2. In medium saucepan, over low heat, melt margarine; stir in corn syrup and the dark-brown sugar until ingredients are well mixed. Remove from heat.

3. With electric mixer, at low speed, gradually beat syrup mixture into flour mixture. At medium speed, beat in 2 cups flour. With wooden spoon or hands, mix in remaining 2½ to 3 cups flour until stiff dough forms. Dough should be firm, not sticky. Divide dough into four parts; place each on plastic wrap; flatten into ½-inch-thick rectangles; wrap, and refrigerate at least 1 hour, or up to a week.

SNOW FROSTING

3 egg whites (⅓ cup), at room temperature
1 pkg (1 lb) confectioners' sugar
½ teaspoon cream of tartar

In small bowl of electric mixer, combine egg whites, sugar and cream of tartar. Beat at high speed until icing is stiff enough to hold its shape. Place a sheet of plastic wrap on icing surface, to keep from drying out. *Makes about 2 cups* ∎

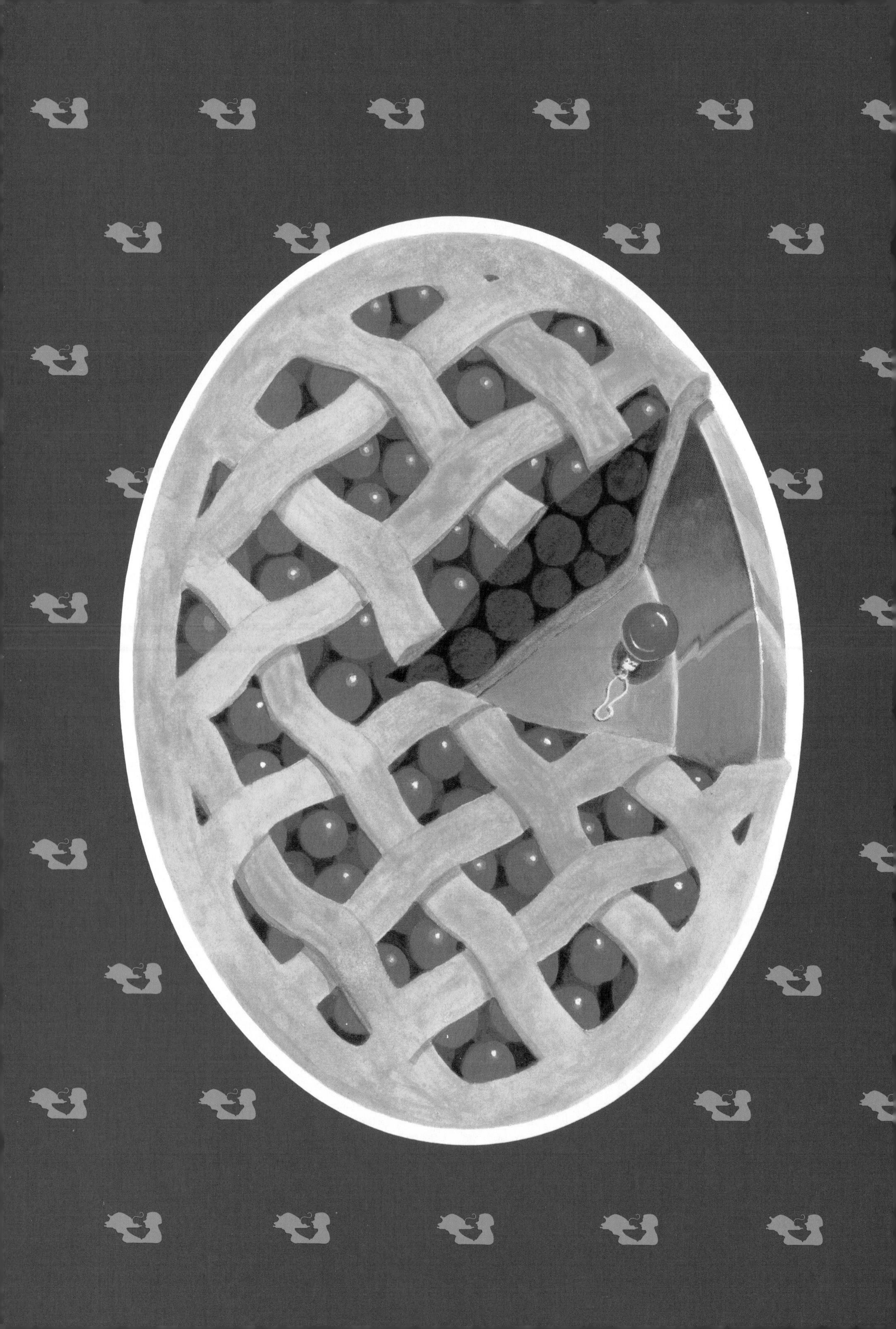

SIX

FESTIVE FOODS FOR JOYOUS CELEBRATIONS

This is it: All of the season's preparations and special efforts culminate in these exciting, precious few days when families and friends come together in the ultimate celebration of joy. Such a cherished once-a-year occasion deserves no less than the very best of everything, especially when it comes to food. And that's just what you'll find in the following pages: our very best recipes and menu ideas that help you capture all the flavors of the festive spirit to lovingly share with others. For a taste of tradition we present two Hanukkah menus that celebrate the Festival of Lights. There's also a Colonial Christmas menu similar to one that might have been put before some of our Revolutionary War forebears and a trio of classic Christmas meals taken from the pages of history and literature. To send your tastebuds on a holiday travel, we baked an international collection of sweet breads and assembled a typical British feast fit for regal dining. Closer to home: a real Southern-style dinner; plus, from all over America, the yuletide favorites of some of the most creative cooks: your own friends and neighbors. And do we have sweets! Cakes, cookies, pies, tortes and candies from simple to spectacular. Enough said.... Bon appétit!

LUSCIOUS FEASTS FOR THE FESTIVAL OF LIGHTS

A FAVORITE POT ROAST DINNER

Hanukkah is one of the most festive and happy of the Jewish holidays. During the eight-day celebration, homes glow with the light of the Menorah's candles, and traditional foods are lovingly prepared and served. Here we have some favorites: a Fruited Pot Roast, foreground, cooked tender in a mixture of prunes, apricots and raisins; to the left, golden-fried potato *latkes,* or pancakes (they're served with applesauce); at top, a molded Honey Cake, distinctively flavored with black coffee. Recipes for these and many other classics begin on page 258.

This hearty celebration meal contains more traditional Hanukkah favorites. Clockwise from top center: Kapusta, or Hot Cabbage Soup; Vegetable-Stuffed Breast of Veal served with yams; fruited Noodle Pudding; Sweet-And-Sour Jellied Fish; Apple-Cranberry Sauce; Potato Pancakes; Mandel Bread rolled around a filling of raisin-nut-preserves; delicious Chicken Fricassee with seasoned chicken balls. Recipes begin on page 260.

A CLASSIC HANUKKAH MEAL

continued from page 254

FAVORITE POT ROAST DINNER

FRUITED POT ROAST
(pictured)

5-lb chuck roast
2 teaspoons salt
¼ teaspoon pepper
2 tablespoons shortening
1 cup chopped carrot
1 cup chopped onion
1 clove garlic, crushed
1 can (1 lb) tomatoes, undrained
1 cup pitted prunes
½ cup dried apricots
½ cup raisins
Water
3 tablespoons all-purpose flour

1. Wipe roast with damp paper towel. Trim excess fat from roast.
2. Rub salt and pepper into surface of meat.
3. In hot shortening, in 6-quart oven-proof Dutch oven, brown meat with carrot, onion and garlic over high heat, turning to brown on all sides—about 20 minutes.
4. Meanwhile, preheat oven to 350F.
5. Pour tomatoes over roast. Bake, covered, about 2 hours.
6. Add prunes, apricots and raisins to Dutch oven. Bake, covered, ½ hour, or until beef is tender.
7. Remove roast and dried fruits to warm serving platter; keep warm.
8. Pour pan drippings into 2-cup measure. Skim off and discard fat. Add water to make 2 cups. Return to Dutch oven.
9. In small bowl, stir flour with ½ cup cold water until smooth. Stir into pan juices in Dutch oven; bring to boiling, stirring. Reduce heat, and simmer 3 minutes; strain. Serve with roast. *Makes 8 servings.*

GOLDEN POTATO PANCAKES
(pictured)

4 large potatoes (2 lb)
½ cup grated carrot
¼ cup grated onion
2 tablespoons matzo meal
Pinch of baking powder
1 teaspoon salt
¼ teaspoon pepper
2 eggs
½ cup shortening or butter for frying

Chilled applesauce

1. Peel potatoes and soak one hour in ice water.
2. Using medium grater, grate potatoes into a colander; drain thoroughly.

3. While potato is draining, combine carrot and onion in a medium bowl.
4. Add thoroughly drained potato (if necessary, squeeze out any excess moisture between folds of a clean dish towel) to onion and carrot.
5. Sprinkle matzo meal, baking powder, salt and pepper over vegetables.
6. In a small bowl, beat eggs well. Pour over vegetables and stir with a wooden spoon to thoroughly combine ingredients.
7. Heat half the shortening in a heavy skillet; for each pancake, drop two tablespoons of potato mixture into hot fat. Flatten with a spatula to make 3-inch cakes. Fry about 3 minutes on each side or until golden-brown.
8. Drain fried cakes on paper towels; keep hot while frying remaining cakes. Add more shortening as needed.
9. Serve hot with chilled applesauce. *Makes 14.*

HONEY CAKE
(pictured)

3 cups sifted cake flour
2 teaspoons baking powder
1¼ teaspoons ground cinnamon
½ teaspoon ground ginger
½ teaspoon ground nutmeg
2 tablespoons salad oil
1 cup sugar
3 eggs
1 cup cold black coffee
1 cup honey
Confectioners' sugar (optional)

1. Preheat oven to 350F.
2. Sift together flour, baking powder, cinnamon, ginger and nutmeg; set aside. Grease and flour a 10-inch bundt or 10-inch tube pan.
3. In the large bowl of electric mixer, combine oil, sugar and eggs; beat, at high speed, until thick and fluffy—about 2 minutes.
4. In small bowl, combine coffee and honey; mix well.
5. At low speed, add flour mixture (in fourths) to sugar mixture alternately with honey mixture (in thirds), beginning and ending with flour mixture. Beat just until combined. Turn into prepared pan.
6. Bake 55 to 60 minutes, or until cake tester inserted in center comes out clean.
7. Cool in pan on wire rack—5 minutes. With spatula, carefully loosen cake from pan. Let stand until completely cool.
8. Serve plain; or sprinkle with confectioners' sugar before serving. *Makes 16 servings.*

POTATO PUDDING (KUGEL)

3 lb Idaho potatoes
4 eggs
⅓ cup potato flour
1½ teaspoons salt
¾ teaspoon baking powder
⅛ teaspoon pepper
¼ cup grated onion
About ½ cup (1 stick) butter or margarine, melted

1. Wash and pare potatoes. Grate potatoes on coarse grater into large bowl filled with ice water. Let stand 15 minutes.
2. Preheat oven to 350F. Grease inside of 1½-quart baking dish.
3. Drain potato; pat dry with a clean dish towel. Measure about 5½ cups.
4. In large bowl, with electric mixer, beat eggs until thick and light. Stir in the potato, potato flour, salt, baking powder, pepper, onion and ¼ cup melted butter; mix well.
5. Turn into prepared baking dish. Bake, uncovered, ½ hour; brush top with some of melted butter. Bake 45 minutes longer, brushing every 10 minutes with butter, until top is crusty and golden-brown. *Makes 8 servings.*

KASHA VARNISHKES

1 cup uncooked kasha
1 egg
½ cup chopped onion
2 tablespoons butter or margarine
1 teaspoon salt
⅛ teaspoon pepper
Boiling water
1½ cups bow-tie noodles
Chopped parsley

1. In medium bowl, combine kasha and egg; mix until well blended.
2. In medium skillet, over medium heat, heat kasha mixture, stirring, until grains become dry and separated (about 3 minutes). Remove from heat.
3. In small skillet, sauté onion in butter until golden.
4. Add onion, salt, pepper and 2 cups boiling water to kasha mixture; mix well.
5. Cook, covered, over medium heat 15 minutes, stirring occasionally so kasha doesn't stick to bottom of pan.
6. Meanwhile, cook bow-tie noodles according to the package directions; drain.
7. Add noodles to kasha; toss lightly to combine. Sprinkle with chopped parsley. Serve while hot. *Makes 8 servings.*

Note: Sautéed sliced mushrooms may be added, if desired.

CHALLAH (SABBATH TWIST)

1¼ cups warm water (105 to 115F)
1 pkg active dry yeast
¼ cup sugar
1½ teaspoons salt
¼ cup salad oil
2 eggs, slightly beaten
5½ cups all-purpose flour
1 egg yolk
2 tablespoons water
2 tablespoons sesame seed

1. If possible, check temperature of water with thermometer. In large bowl, sprinkle yeast and sugar over water, stirring until dissolved.

2. Add salt, oil, eggs and 3 cups flour; beat with electric mixer until smooth—about 2 minutes. Gradually add remaining flour, mixing in flour with hand until dough is stiff enough to leave side of bowl.

3. Turn out dough onto lightly floured pastry cloth or board. Knead until smooth and elastic—about 5 minutes.

4. Place in lightly greased large bowl; turn dough over to bring up greased side. Cover with towel; let rise in warm place (85F), free from drafts, about 1 hour, or until double in bulk.

5. Turn out dough onto lightly floured pastry cloth or board. Divide two-thirds into 3 equal parts. Using palms of hands, roll each part into 20-inch-long strips. Braid 3 strips; pinch ends together. Place on large greased cookie sheet.

6. Divide remaining one-third of the dough into 3 equal parts. Roll each part into 18-inch-long strips; braid 3 strips together; pinch ends together. Place on top of the larger braid.

7. Cover with a clean dish towel; let rise in warm place (85F), free from drafts, until double in bulk—50 to 60 minutes.

8. Preheat oven to 375F.

9. Brush surface of loaf with egg yolk mixed with 2 tablespoons water. Sprinkle with sesame seed.

10. Bake 35 to 40 minutes, or until a rich golden-brown. (If crust seems too brown after 25 minutes of baking, cover with foil or brown paper.) Remove to wire rack to cool. Serve warm or cold. *Makes 1 braid.*

APRICOT-GLAZED NOODLE PUDDING

½ pkg (8-oz size) wide egg noodles (4 oz)
1 pkg (8 oz) cream cheese, at room temperature
½ cup (1 stick) butter or margarine, softened
2 cups sour cream
1 cup sugar
8 eggs
1 tart apple, pared and grated
2 teaspoons vanilla extract
½ cup raisins
¼ cup apricot preserves, melted
4 red candied cherries, halved

1. Cook noodles in boiling salted water as package label directs; drain well.

2. Preheat oven to 350F. Lightly butter a 2-quart baking dish.

3. In large bowl of electric mixer, combine cheese, butter, sour cream and sugar. Beat until well combined. Add eggs, grated apple and vanilla; blend until smooth. Stir in raisins and noodles.

4. Turn into prepared dish. Bake 45 minutes, or until knife inserted 1 inch from edge comes out clean. Remove to rack.

5. Brush with apricot preserves; decorate with cherries. Serve warm; or let cool, and refrigerate, covered, until serving. *Makes 10 servings.*

CHOPPED CHICKEN LIVERS

¾ cup chicken fat
2½ cups thinly sliced onion
1 lb chicken livers, rinsed and drained
2 hard-cooked eggs
¾ cup white-bread cubes
1½ teaspoons salt
¼ teaspoon pepper
Crisp lettuce leaves
2 tablespoons finely chopped parsley
Crackers or white toast

1. In large skillet, heat ¼ cup chicken fat. Add onion; sauté, stirring, until golden—takes about 10 minutes. Remove onion with slotted spoon; set aside.

2. Add ¼ cup chicken fat to same skillet; heat. Add chicken livers; sauté just until they are cooked but still slightly pink in center—about 8 minutes. Reserve pan drippings.

3. Using medium blade of meat grinder, grind eggs, then onion and livers into medium bowl. Grind bread cubes. Toss liver mixture with pan drippings, 3 tablespoons chicken fat, salt and pepper. Mix well; refrigerate, covered, to chill well.

4. To serve, mound chicken livers on crisp lettuce on chilled serving plate. Spoon remaining 1 tablespoon chicken fat over top; sprinkle with parsley. Serve with crackers. *Makes 2½ cups.*

RATNER'S FAMOUS MARBLE CHEESECAKE
(by James Zolatas of Ratner's)

COOKIE CRUST
¾ cup sugar
½ cup soft shortening
1¼ cups plus 2 tablespoons cake flour
1 tablespoon beaten egg
1½ teaspoons water
⅛ teaspoon salt
⅛ teaspoon grated lemon peel
2 tablespoons packaged dry bread crumbs

CHEESE FILLING
3½ pkg (8-oz size) cream cheese
1 container (8 oz) skim-milk cottage cheese (see Note)
1¼ cups sugar
3 eggs
2 tablespoons heavy cream
2 teaspoons vanilla extract
3 squares semisweet chocolate, melted

1. Make Cookie Crust: Preheat oven to 350F.

2. In large bowl, combine ¾ cup sugar, the shortening, cake flour, egg, water, the salt and lemon peel. With electric mixer, beat at medium speed until well combined and dough leaves side of bowl.

3. Form dough into a ball. Fit onto bottom of a 9-inch springform pan, rolling lightly with rolling pin to make a smooth surface. Trim pastry ⅛ inch from edge all around. Prick with fork to prevent shrinkage.

4. Bake 10 minutes. Remove from oven; cool on wire rack 15 minutes. Then lightly grease inside of side of springform pan. Sprinkle lightly with bread crumbs, and attach side to bottom of pan with cookie crust. Retrim crust, if necessary.

5. Meanwhile, make Cheese Filling: Increase oven temperature to 400F.

6. In large bowl, with electric mixer, combine cream cheese, cottage cheese and sugar. Beat at medium speed until mixture is smooth and creamy.

7. Beat in eggs, one at a time, beating well after each addition. Beat in cream and vanilla.

8. Pour half of batter into prepared springform pan. Drizzle 2 tablespoons melted chocolate over batter. With finger, lightly swirl chocolate over surface.

9. Repeat with rest of batter and chocolate.

10. Bake 15 minutes. Remove to wire rack. Let cake cool 45 minutes. Heat oven to 350F.

11. Bake cake 25 minutes longer. Let cool completely on wire rack. Refrigerate several hours or overnight, if possible, before serving.

12. Gently remove side of springform pan before serving. *Makes 8 to 10 servings.*

Note: If cottage cheese is moist, drain very well before using.

continued on page 260

continued from page 259

CLASSIC HANUKKAH MEAL

KAPUSTA
(Hot Cabbage Soup)
(pictured)

2-lb head of cabbage, shredded (10 cups)
⅓ cup kosher salt
½ teaspoon white pepper
1 cup chopped onion
1½ quarts water
1½ lb beef chuck (flanken-style ribs)
1 large soup bone (2½ lb)
2 cans (1-lb size) tomato purée
1 large potato, pared and cubed (1½ cups)
1 teaspoon sour salt
1 cup sugar
2 cloves garlic, crushed

1. In large 6-quart kettle, combine cabbage, kosher salt, pepper, onion and water. Bring to boiling, covered. Add beef, soup bone and tomato purée. Bring to boiling; reduce heat and simmer, covered, 1 hour.

2. Add potato; simmer, covered, 1 hour.

3. Twenty minutes before end of cooking time, add sour salt and sugar.

4. Five minutes before serving, add garlic.

5. To serve: Pour into tureen or individual bowls. Beef can be served separately, or cut up and added to soup. *Makes 2½ quarts.*

STUFFED BREAST OF VEAL
(pictured)

STUFFING
½ cup grated potato
½ cup chopped onion
⅓ cup finely chopped green pepper
1 large carrot, grated (½ cup)
1 small parsnip, grated
¼ lb green beans, finely chopped
1 tablespoon farina
1 tablespoon matzo meal
1 teaspoon salt
⅛ teaspoon pepper
½ teaspoon dried oregano leaves
1 egg
2 tablespoons chicken fat, melted

5-lb breast of veal, with pocket for stuffing
2 cloves garlic, crushed
1 teaspoon salt
¼ teaspoon paprika
⅛ teaspoon pepper
½ cup coarsely chopped onion
½ cup coarsely chopped celery
2 cups water

Boiled yams (optional)

1. Preheat oven to 350F.
2. Make Stuffing: In medium bowl, combine all stuffing ingredients; mix well.

3. Spoon mixture into veal pocket, pushing mixture well into cavity. Sew open side of veal to hold in stuffing.

4. Place veal, meat side up, in 15-by-10-by-2-inch roasting pan. Cut 6 slits, ½ inch long and ¼ inch deep, in top.

5. Spread garlic over top; sprinkle with salt, paprika and pepper.

6. Place onion and celery around veal. Add the water to bottom of pan.

7. Bake, uncovered, 2 hours; bake, covered with foil, 30 minutes more.

8. Remove veal to platter. Press vegetables with liquid through strainer; heat to boiling. Pour over veal.

9. Serve sliced, with yams, if desired. *Makes 6 to 8 servings.*

NOODLE PUDDING
(pictured)

1 pkg (8 oz) medium noodles
2 tablespoons margarine, melted
1 large tart apple, pared and grated
1 teaspoon kosher salt
¼ teaspoon white pepper
2 eggs
½ cup white raisins
1 teaspoon ground cinnamon
½ cup sugar

4 candied red cherries, quartered

1. Preheat oven to 350F. Grease well an 8-by-8-by-2-inch or 1½-quart shallow oval baking dish.

2. Cook noodles according to package directions; drain well.

3. In large mixing bowl, combine the noodles, margarine, grated apple, salt, pepper, eggs, raisins, cinnamon and sugar; mix well.

4. Turn into prepared baking dish, spreading evenly.

5. Bake one hour, or until top is crisp and richly browned. Serve warm or cold with meat, or as a dessert. For dessert, decorate with candied cherries. *Makes 8 servings.*

SWEET-AND-SOUR JELLIED FISH
(pictured)

3-lb striped bass, head and tail removed
2 medium onions, coarsely chopped
1 large carrot, pared and sliced
1 teaspoon salt
⅛ teaspoon pepper
1½ teaspoons mixed pickling spice
2 bay leaves
⅓ cup sugar
4 cups water
1 cup white vinegar

1. Wipe fish with damp paper towels. Cut into 2-inch slices.

2. In 10-inch skillet, combine onion, carrot, salt, pepper, pickling spice, bay leaves and sugar with water.

3. Bring to boiling; simmer, covered, 30 minutes. Add vinegar.

4. Arrange fish on top; simmer, covered, 1 hour, basting occasionally, until fish flakes easily with fork.

5. Remove from heat. Cool to room temperature in marinade—½ hour. Arrange fish on serving platter with sauce spooned over. Refrigerate, covered, 4 hours, until sauce has jelled.

6. Serve as an appetizer or entrée. *Makes 4 to 6 servings.*

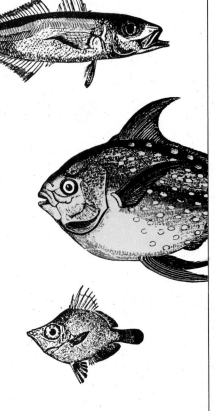

APPLE-CRANBERRY SAUCE
(pictured)

1 lb cranberries (4 cups)
Water
3 lb Winesap apples, pared, cored and
    quartered
½ cup sugar

1. Wash cranberries; drain and remove stems.
2. Turn into 3½-quart saucepan; add 1½ cups water; cook, covered, over medium heat, until soft—15 to 20 minutes.
3. Press cranberries and liquid through sieve, to remove skins and seeds.
4. In 5-quart Dutch oven, combine cranberry purée, apple, 3 cups water and sugar. Bring to boiling; reduce heat; simmer, covered, 30 minutes, or until apple is soft but not mushy.
5. Cool; serve cold with meat. *Makes 6½ cups.*

POTATO PANCAKES
(pictured)

4 large potatoes (2 lb), pared
¼ cup grated onion
2 eggs, slightly beaten
2 tablespoons all-purpose flour
¾ teaspoon salt
Dash ground nutmeg
Dash pepper
Salad oil or shortening for frying

Chilled applesauce or sour cream

1. On medium grater, grate potatoes. Drain very well; pat dry with dish towel; measure 3 cups.
2. In large bowl, combine grated potato with onion, eggs, flour, salt, nutmeg and pepper.
3. In large, heavy skillet, slowly heat oil, ⅛ inch deep, until very hot but not smoking.
4. For each pancake, drop potato mixture, 2 tablespoons at a time, into hot fat. With spatula, flatten against bottom of skillet to make a pancake 4 inches in diameter. Fry 2 or 3 minutes on each side, or until golden-brown.
5. Drain pancakes well on paper towels. Serve hot with applesauce or sour cream. *Makes 12.*

FANNIE'S MANDEL BREAD
(pictured)

6 eggs
1 cup granulated sugar
1 cup salad oil
6 cups all-purpose flour
4 teaspoons baking powder
FILLING
1 can (6 oz) pecans or walnuts, coarsely
    chopped (2 cups)
⅓ cup granulated sugar
2 teaspoons ground cinnamon
1 cup white raisins

Salad oil
1 jar (1 lb, 2 oz) strawberry or cherry
    preserves
Confectioners' sugar (optional)

1. In medium bowl, combine eggs and 1 cup each granulated sugar and salad oil; beat with rotary beater just until well combined.
2. Sift flour with baking powder into large bowl.
3. Make a well in the center; pour in egg mixture all at once. Stir around the bowl, using a wooden spoon, until mixture is well blended.
4. Turn the dough out onto lightly floured pastry cloth. Coat lightly with flour; knead until it is smooth—about 5 minutes.
5. Preheat oven to 350F. Grease lightly two roasting pans, 15½ by 10½ by 2¼ inches. In small bowl, mix together all ingredients for filling.
6. Divide dough into 5 equal parts.
7. On lightly floured pastry cloth, roll each fifth of dough into a 12-by-10-inch rectangle.
8. Brush lightly with one teaspoon oil. Spread 5 tablespoons preserves over surface; sprinkle with ½ cup filling. From long side, roll tightly as for jelly roll; pinch ends to seal.
9. Place three rolls, seam side down, ½ inch apart, into prepared pan. Place two rolls, ½ inch apart, into other pan.
10. Bake 45 to 50 minutes, or until golden-brown.
11. Remove pans to wire rack; cool 10 minutes before taking bread from pan. Cool completely.
12. To serve: Cut each loaf into 12 diagonal slices. If desired, sprinkle with confectioners' sugar. *Makes 5 loaves (60 servings).*

Note: This mellows with storage. Slice; store, covered, in cool, dry place.

CHICKEN FRICASSEE
(pictured)

5-lb roasting chicken, cut in serving pieces
1½ cups coarsely chopped onion
1 medium tomato, chopped
1½ teaspoons paprika
1 teaspoon salt
⅛ teaspoon pepper
¼ cup grated onion
½ cup grated carrot
2 eggs
2 tablespoons matzo meal
1½ teaspoons sour salt
½ cup sugar
Water

1. Wash chicken; pat dry with paper towels. (Use all parts of chicken except liver, heart and gizzard.)
2. Remove skin from all pieces of chicken except wings; set breast meat aside. Cut remaining pieces of chicken into smaller pieces.
3. In 5-quart Dutch oven, over medium heat, brown chicken pieces (except breast meat), turning often, along with the chopped onion, tomato, paprika, salt and pepper—about 20 minutes. Cover; cook 20 minutes.
4. Meanwhile, remove bones from chicken breasts; chop finely.
5. In medium bowl, combine chopped chicken breast, grated onion, grated carrot, eggs and matzo meal. Shape into 1-inch balls.
6. Add to chicken mixture in Dutch oven, along with sour salt and sugar. Add water (about ½ cup) if needed.
7. Bring to boiling; simmer, covered, 1 hour.
8. Serve chicken balls with chicken-sauce mixture in pan. *Makes 6 servings.*

GRANDPA'S DESSERT

2 pkg (11-oz size) dried mixed fruit
¼ lb dried apples
½ cup light raisins
6 cups hot water
½ cup sugar

1. Place all dried fruits in 5-quart Dutch oven or saucepan. Add hot water to cover fruit. Refrigerate, covered, several hours or overnight.
2. Next day, bring to boiling; simmer, covered, ½ hour, until soft, not mushy. Add sugar the last 5 minutes.
3. Turn into serving dish; refrigerate, covered, until well chilled—several hours or overnight. *Makes 10 to 12 servings.* ■

A World of Sweet Seasonal BREADS

The flavorings of Christmas—lemon, cardamom, cinnamon, nutmeg, ginger and almond—envelop these traditional holiday breads made from sweet yeast dough. At center, a Ukrainian Kolach Wreath. Clockwise from top right: Italian Panettone, Norwegian Christmas Bread with sugar icing, Finnish Christmas Dolls, Scandinavian Christmas Bread, pretzel-shaped Danish Kringles and a German Kugelhopf. Recipes begin on page 264.

continued from page 263

KOLACH WREATH
(pictured)

1½ cups milk
Sugar
1½ teaspoons salt
½ cup warm water (105 to 115F)
1 pkg active dry yeast
6½ cups all-purpose flour
3 tablespoons grated lemon peel
¼ cup (½ stick) butter or margarine,
    softened
3 whole eggs
1 egg yolk
1 tablespoon water

1. In small saucepan, heat milk until bubbles form around edge of pan; remove from heat. Stir in 1 tablespoon sugar and the salt; let cool to lukewarm.

2. If possible, check temperature of warm water with thermometer. Sprinkle yeast over water in large bowl; stir until dissolved. Stir in lukewarm milk mixture, 2½ cups flour and the lemon peel; with wooden spoon, beat until smooth—about 2 minutes.

3. Cover bowl with towel; let rise in warm place (85F), free from drafts, until double in bulk—about 1 hour. Batter will be light and spongy.

4. In large bowl, with electric mixer at medium speed, beat butter with ½ cup sugar until light and fluffy. Beat in whole eggs, one at a time, beating after each addition; beat until smooth.

5. At low speed, beat in 1 cup flour and risen batter until smooth and well blended.

6. With wooden spoon, stir in remaining flour; mix in with hand until dough leaves side of bowl. Turn out on lightly floured pastry cloth; knead until dough is smooth—about 5 minutes.

7. Place in lightly greased large bowl; turn to bring greased side up. Cover with towel; let rise in warm place (85F), free from drafts, until double in bulk—1 to 1½ hours.

8. Punch down dough. Turn out on lightly floured surface; divide into six equal parts. With hands, roll each part into a long roll, about 24 inches. Arrange two rolls side by side. Starting at center, twist rolls together, rope fashion, working toward each end. There will be three ropes.

9. Line up the three ropes side by side. Braid together, starting at center and working toward each end. Trim off the narrow ends, about 2½ inches from each end.

10. On a large greased cookie sheet, shape braid into a circle, pressing ends together to join neatly.

11. Divide the trimmed dough in half. Roll each into a 30-inch length. Twist together to make a rope, as directed above. Place on top of braid around outer edge. Place a greased tin in center of wreath, to keep wreath shape. Cover; let rise in warm place until almost double in bulk—1 hour.

12. Preheat oven to 400F. Beat egg yolk with 1 tablespoon water; use to brush top of wreath. Bake 15 minutes; reduce heat to 350F; bake 25 minutes longer, or until nicely browned and bread sounds hollow when tapped with knuckle.

13. Cool on wire rack or serve slightly warm. *Makes 1 large wreath.*

ITALIAN PANETTONE
(pictured)

1 cup warm water (105 to 115F)
2 pkg active dry yeast
½ cup sugar
2 teaspoons salt
½ cup (1 stick) butter or margarine,
    softened
3 eggs, beaten
1 egg, separated
5½ to 6 cups sifted all-purpose flour
1 cup raisins
1 cup (8 oz) mixed candied peel
½ cup (4 oz) red candied cherries, halved
1 tablespoon butter or margarine, melted
2 tablespoons water
2 tablespoons sugar

1. If possible, check temperature of warm water with thermometer. Sprinkle yeast over water in large bowl, stirring until dissolved.

2. Add ½ cup sugar, the salt, ½ cup butter, 3 eggs, the egg yolk and 3 cups flour; beat with wooden spoon or electric mixer until smooth—about 2 minutes.

3. Gradually add remaining flour; mix in last part with hand until dough leaves side of bowl.

4. Turn onto lightly floured board or pastry cloth. Knead until smooth—5 minutes. (Dough is soft.)

5. Place in lightly greased large bowl; turn to bring greased side up. Cover with towel; let rise in warm place (85F), free from drafts, until double in bulk—about 1 hour.

6. Grease well and line inside of an 8-inch springform pan with a 4-inch-wide strip of buttered brown paper.

7. Punch down dough; turn out onto lightly floured pastry cloth or board. Knead in raisins and candied fruits until well distributed—about 5 minutes.

8. Place dough in prepared pan. Brush

top with 1 tablespoon melted butter. Cover with towel; let rise in warm place (85F), free from drafts, until more than double in bulk—about 2 hours.

9. Preheat oven to 350F.

10. With sharp knife, cut a deep cross on top of bread. Brush with egg white combined with 2 tablespoons water. Bake 30 minutes.

11. Remove bread from oven. Brush again with egg white, and sprinkle with sugar. Continue baking 30 minutes, or until golden-brown.

12. Remove from pan; cool on rack. *Makes 1 loaf.*

NORWEGIAN CHRISTMAS BREAD
(pictured)

1½ cups milk
1 cup sugar
1 cup (2 sticks) butter or margarine
1 teaspoon salt
1/2 cup warm water (105 to 115F)
2 pkg active dry yeast
8½ to 9 cups all-purpose flour
2 teaspoons ground cardamom
3 eggs, beaten
1 jar (8 oz) diced mixed candied fruit, chopped
1 cup light raisins
Confectioners'-Sugar Icing, recipe follows
Red and green candied cherries

1. In a small saucepan, heat milk just until bubbles form around edge of pan; remove from heat. Add sugar, butter and salt, stirring until sugar is dissolved and butter melted. Let cool to lukewarm (a drop on wrist won't feel warm).

2. If possible, check temperature of warm water with thermometer. Sprinkle yeast over water in large bowl, stirring until dissolved.

3. Stir in lukewarm milk mixture, 4 cups flour, the cardamom and eggs; beat with wooden spoon or electric beater until smooth—about 2 minutes.

4. Gradually add remaining flour, mixing in with hand until dough is stiff enough to leave side of bowl.

5. Turn out dough onto lightly floured pastry cloth or board. Knead until smooth—about 5 minutes.

6. Place in lightly greased bowl; turn dough over to bring greased side up. Cover with towel; let rise in warm place (85F), free from drafts, until double in bulk—about 1 hour.

7. Turn out dough onto lightly floured pastry cloth or board. Knead in candied fruit and raisins.

8. Grease two cookie sheets. Divide dough in half. Shape each half into a smooth ball—8 inches in diameter; tuck edges under.

9. Place on prepared cookie sheets. Cover with towel; let rise in warm place, free from drafts, until double in bulk—1 to 1½ hours.

10. Preheat oven to 350F.

11. Bake 40 minutes, or until golden-brown. Remove to wire rack to cool slightly.

12. Spread warm breads with Confectioners'-Sugar Icing, letting it run down sides. Decorate with candied red and green cherries, as pictured. *Makes 2 loaves.*

CONFECTIONERS'-SUGAR ICING

2 cups confectioners' sugar
3 tablespoons milk

In small bowl, combine confectioners' sugar with milk; mix well. *Makes 1 cup.*

FINNISH CHRISTMAS DOLLS
(pictured)

1 cup milk
¾ cup sugar
1 teaspoon salt
¾ cup (1½ sticks) butter or margarine, softened
¾ cup warm water (105 to 115F)
2 pkg active dry yeast
6½ cups sifted all-purpose flour
1½ teaspoons crushed cardamom
2 whole eggs
1¼ cups raisins
2 egg yolks
2 tablespoons water
Raisins

1. In small saucepan, heat milk until bubbles form around edge of pan; remove from heat.

2. Add sugar, salt and butter, stirring until butter is melted. Cool to lukewarm.

3. If possible, check temperature of warm water with thermometer. Sprinkle yeast over water in large bowl; stir to dissolve. Add lukewarm milk mixture.

4. Add 3½ cups flour and the cardamom; beat with wooden spoon until smooth—about 2 minutes.

5. Beat in whole eggs; add 1¼ cups raisins. Gradually add remaining flour, mixing in last of it with hand until dough leaves side of bowl (dough is soft).

6. Turn out dough onto lightly floured pastry cloth. Cover with bowl; let rest 10 minutes.

7. Turn dough to coat with flour; knead until smooth—about 5 minutes.

8. Place in lightly greased large bowl; turn to bring greased side up. Cover with towel; let rise in warm place (85F), free from drafts, until double in bulk—1 to 1½ hours. Punch down. Turn out onto lightly floured pastry cloth.

9. Divide and shape: For girl, cut a 1½-inch circle of dough for head. Place on lightly greased large cookie sheet. With picture as guide, use two strips, 8 inches long by ⅛ inch thick, for hair. Arrange around head, curling up at ends. Place a 10-by-½-inch strip for neck, shoulder and arms under head. Cut a triangle (2¾ inches on sides, 3 inches at base and ½ inch thick) for top of body; place under neck. Then cut a triangle (3¾ inches on sides, 4½ inches at base and ½ inch thick). Place below top for skirt. For legs, cut two strips 2¼ inches long, ¾ inch wide. Attach to skirt. For feet, cut a circle 1½ inches in diameter; cut in half. Attach each half to a leg.

10. Brush lightly with 2 egg yolks beaten with 2 tablespoons water. Place raisins for eyes, mouth and buttons on front. Let rise, covered, in warm place until almost double in bulk—about 1 hour. Preheat oven to 375F.

11. Bake, on upper shelf of oven, 15 minutes. Let cool on wire rack.

12. To shape boy, cut a 1½-inch circle of dough for head. Place on lightly greased large cookie sheet. For beret, cut a 1½-inch circle; cut in half; flatten slightly; place on head. Pinch small pieces from other half of circle to use for ears. Curve a 10-by-½-inch strip for neck, shoulder and arms under head. Cut a triangle (2¾ inches on sides, 2 inches at base and ½ inch thick) for vest; place under neck. For pants, cut a 4-by-2-inch rectangle, ½ inch thick; place under vest. Cut a line down center, starting 1 inch below top of pants. Separate two halves slightly to make legs. For feet, cut a 1½-inch round; cut in half; place at bottom of each leg. Decorate face and vest with raisins. Brush and let rise as in Step 10. Bake as in Step 11. *Makes about 8 dolls.*

continued on page 266

continued from page 265

SCANDINAVIAN CHRISTMAS BREAD

(pictured)

¾ cup warm water (105 to 115F)
2 pkg active dry yeast
½ cup granulated sugar
1 teaspoon salt
½ cup (1 stick) butter or margarine, softened
3 eggs
4½ cups all-purpose flour
1½ teaspoons crushed cardamom
½ cup finely cut-up candied citron
½ cup candied red cherries, halved
½ cup light raisins
1 egg yolk
2 teaspoons water
6 sugar cubes, coarsely crushed
½ cup coarsely chopped unblanched almonds

1. If possible, check temperature of warm water with thermometer. Sprinkle yeast over water in large warm bowl; stir until dissolved. Add granulated sugar and salt; stir until dissolved.

2. Add butter, 3 eggs, 3 cups flour and the cardamom. Beat vigorously with wooden spoon, or with electric mixer at medium speed, until smooth—about 2 minutes.

3. Gradually add remaining flour, mixing with a wooden spoon, then with hands, until dough is smooth and stiff enough to leave side of bowl.

4. Turn out dough onto lightly floured surface. Knead until smooth—about 5 minutes.

5. Place in lightly greased large bowl; turn to bring greased side up. Cover with towel; let rise in warm place (85F), free from drafts, until double in bulk—about 1½ hours.

6. Punch down dough. Add citron, cherries and raisins, working them in with hands until thoroughly combined. Turn out onto lightly floured surface.

7. To shape: Divide into six parts. With hands, roll each part into an 18-inch-long strip.

8. Braid three strips together. Place on a large greased cookie sheet; pinch ends together to seal. Braid remaining three strips; pinch ends together to seal. Place braid directly on top of first braid.

9. Cover with towel; let rise in warm place (85F), free from drafts, until double in bulk—about 1½ hours.

10. Preheat oven to 375F. In small bowl, using fork, beat egg yolk with water. Brush egg-yolk glaze on braid. Combine crushed sugar and nuts; sprinkle over bread.

11. Bake 30 to 35 minutes, or until nicely browned and bread sounds hollow when tapped with knuckle. Remove to wire rack, and let cool completely.

12. To store: Wrap in foil; seal. Place in freezer for several weeks.

13. To serve: Preheat oven to 400F. Heat foil-wrapped frozen braid 30 to 35 minutes, or just until heated through. *Makes 1 loaf.*

DANISH KRINGLES

(pictured)

1¾ cups milk
3 tablespoons sugar
1 cup (2 sticks) butter or margarine
6 cups all-purpose flour
1 teaspoon ground cardamom
1 teaspoon salt
¼ cup warm water (105 to 115F)
1 pkg active dry yeast

FILLING

2 tablespoons sugar
2 teaspoons ground cinnamon
1 cup raisins
½ cup chopped citron
¾ cup (1½ sticks) butter or margarine, softened

1 egg yolk
2 tablespoons water
⅓ cup sliced almonds
2 tablespoons sugar

1. In small saucepan, heat milk until bubbles form around edge of pan; remove from heat. Add 3 tablespoons sugar and 1 cup butter; stir until butter is melted; let cool to lukewarm.

2. Sift together flour, cardamom and salt. Grease two large cookie sheets.

3. If possible, check temperature of warm water with thermometer. Sprinkle yeast over water in large bowl; stir until dissolved. Stir in lukewarm milk mixture and 3 cups flour mixture; beat vigorously with wooden spoon, or electric mixer on medium speed, until smooth—about 2 minutes.

4. Gradually add remaining flour mixture; mix in last of flour mixture with hand until dough is stiff enough to leave side of bowl.

5. Turn out dough onto lightly floured pastry cloth or board. Knead until smooth and elastic—about 5 minutes.

6. Place in lightly greased large bowl; turn dough over to bring greased side up. Cover with towel; let rise in warm place (85F), free from drafts, until double in bulk—about 1½ hours.

7. Prepare Filling: In small bowl, combine 2 tablespoons sugar, the cinnamon, raisins and citron.

8. Turn dough out onto lightly floured pastry cloth or board. Divide in half. Roll each part into a long piece, 40 inches long and 6 inches wide.

9. Spread each with half of softened butter; sprinkle each with half of raisin mixture. Roll up jelly-roll fashion. Pinch edges together to seal.

10. Shape each into a pretzel shape on prepared cookie sheet, seam side down. Cover with towel.

11. Let rise in warm place free from drafts, until double in bulk—about 1 to 1½ hours.

12. Preheat oven to 350F.

13. Brush each Kringle with egg yolk mixed with water. Bake 20 minutes. Remove from oven.

14. Brush with remaining egg-yolk mixture; sprinkle with sliced almonds, then with sugar. Bake 10 to 15 minutes longer, or until breads are golden-brown. Remove to wire rack. Serve warm. *Makes 2 Kringles.*

KUGELHOPF

(pictured)

1 cup seedless raisins
3 tablespoons brandy
1 tablespoon grated lemon peel
1 cup milk
¾ cup granulated sugar
½ cup warm water (105 to 115F)
1 pkg active dry yeast
4½ cups sifted all-purpose flour
½ cup slivered almonds
14 to 16 whole blanched almonds
¾ cup (1½ sticks) butter or margarine, softened
1 teaspoon salt
4 eggs
¼ cup (½ stick) butter or margarine, melted
Confectioners' sugar

1. In small bowl, combine raisins, brandy and lemon peel; toss lightly to mix well; set aside.

2. In small saucepan, heat milk until bubbles form around edge of pan; remove from heat. Stir in ¼ cup granulated sugar; let cool to lukewarm.

3. If possible, check temperature of warm water with thermometer. Sprinkle yeast over water in large bowl; stir until dissolved. Stir in lukewarm milk mixture and 2½ cups flour; with wooden spoon or electric mixer beat until smooth—about 2 minutes.

4. Cover bowl with towel; let rise in warm place (85F), free from drafts, until double in bulk—about 1 hour. Batter will be light and spongy.

5. Meanwhile, butter generously a 3-quart Turk's-head tube mold, 9 inches in diameter. Sprinkle inside of mold with slivered almonds. Place whole almond in each indentation in bottom of mold.

6. In large bowl, with electric mixer at medium speed, beat softened butter with remaining ½ cup granulated sugar and the salt until light and fluffy. Beat in eggs, one at a time, beating after each addition; beat until smooth.

7. At low speed, beat in 1 cup flour and the risen batter until smooth and well blended.

8. With wooden spoon, stir in remaining flour and the raisin mixture, beating until well combined.

9. Pour batter into prepared mold. Cover with towel; let rise in warm place (85F), free from drafts, 1 hour and 20 minutes, or until batter rises almost to top of pan.

10. Meanwhile, preheat oven to 350F.

11. Bake Kugelhopf 50 to 60 minutes, or until a cake tester inserted near the center comes out clean. Let cool in pan on wire rack about 20 minutes.

12. Run spatula around sides of pan to loosen; turn out on wire rack. Brush with melted butter. Let cool completely.

13. To store: Wrap in waxed paper, then in foil. Store in a cool, dry place or in the refrigerator if storing for a week or two. Store in freezer if keeping longer.

14. To serve: Let warm to room temperature. Sprinkle lightly with confectioners' sugar. Slice thinly; serve, lightly buttered, with coffee. *Makes 1 large Kugelhopf.*

STOLLEN

1 cup milk
½ cup granulated sugar
1 cup (2 sticks) butter or margarine
½ teaspoon salt
2 pkg active dry yeast
½ cup warm water (105 to 115F)
6 cups all-purpose flour
½ teaspoon ground nutmeg or mace
1 tablespoon grated lemon peel
2 eggs
1 cup dark raisins
1 jar (4 oz) candied red cherries, coarsely chopped
1 jar (8 oz) diced mixed candied peel
½ cup finely chopped blanched almonds
¼ cup (½ stick) butter or margarine, melted
Confectioners' sugar

1. In small saucepan, heat milk just until bubbles form around edge of pan; remove from heat. Add granulated sugar, 1 cup butter and the salt, stirring until dissolved. Let cool to lukewarm (a drop on wrist won't feel warm).

2. In large bowl that has been rinsed with hot water, sprinkle yeast over warm water (if possible, check temperature of warm water with thermometer); stir until dissolved.

3. Stir in milk mixture, 3 cups flour, the nutmeg, lemon peel and eggs; beat with wooden spoon or electric mixer until smooth—at least 2 minutes.

4. Gradually add remaining 3 cups flour; mix in last of it with hand until dough is stiff enough to leave side of bowl.

5. Turn out onto lightly floured pastry cloth or board. Knead until smooth and elastic—about 5 minutes.

6. Place in lightly greased large bowl; turn dough over to bring greased side up. Cover with towel; let rise in warm place (85F), free from drafts, until double in bulk—about 1 hour. Grease 2 cookie sheets.

7. Punch down dough. Turn out onto lightly floured pastry cloth or board. Knead in raisins, candied fruit and almonds until well distributed—about 5 minutes.

8. Divide dough in half; shape each half into an oval 10 inches long and 6 inches across at widest part. Brush each with 1 tablespoon melted butter.

9. Fold dough in half lengthwise. Place on prepared cookie sheet. Press folded edge lightly, to crease; then curve into crescent shape. Repeat with other half of dough.

10. Cover Stollen with towels; let rise in warm place (85F) until double in bulk—1½ to 2 hours.

11. Preheat oven to 375F.

12. Bake 25 to 30 minutes, or until nicely browned (if crust seems too brown after 20 minutes of baking, cover with foil or brown paper).

13. Remove to wire rack. Brush each with 1 tablespoon butter; cool.

14. To store: Wrap in plastic wrap, then in foil. Store in refrigerator or freezer several weeks.

15. To serve: Let warm to room temperature. Just before serving, sprinkle with confectioners' sugar. *Makes 2 Stollen.*

■

A Holiday Feast
To Remember

*P*icture a scrumptious holiday roast-goose dinner at your house, served with all the old-fashioned charm and elegance of Christmases past! From one of America's oldest inns— the Beekman Arms in Rhinebeck, New York, where George Washington and Lafayette dined—we present the menu: creamy Pumpkin Bisque ladled from a tureen; Wine-Braised Goose with cranberries, acorn squash and apples; broccoli and cauliflower medley; crisp salad; warm yeast rolls; and for a spectacular finale, moist Coconut-Carrot Cake and flaming steamed Plum Pudding, below. Recipes begin on page 270.

JOHN PAUL ENDRESS

continued from page 269

DINNER AT BEEKMAN ARMS

DUTCHESS COUNTY NATURAL CIDER
OR PUMPKIN BISQUE*
APPLE WINE-BRAISED GOOSE*
STEAMED ACORN SQUASH
WITH CRANBERRIES*
SELECTION OF FRESH VEGETABLES
HOMEMADE YEAST ROLLS
BEEKMAN SALAD
COCONUT-CARROT CAKE* OR
PLUM PUDDING
WITH BRANDY HARD SAUCE*
OR CHOCOLATE PECAN PIE*

Recipes given for starred dishes.

PUMPKIN BISQUE
(pictured)

1 tablespoon butter or margarine
2 tablespoons finely minced shallots or
    white part of green onions
2 cans (10¾-oz size) condensed chicken
    broth, undiluted, or 2½ cups homemade
    chicken or goose broth (see Note 1)
1 can (1 lb) pumpkin
¼ teaspoon dried thyme leaves
⅛ teaspoon pepper
Dash ground nutmeg
Dash ground allspice
1 cup (½ pint) heavy cream

In 3-quart saucepan, over medium heat, melt butter. Add shallots; sauté until tender. Stir in broth, pumpkin, thyme, pepper, nutmeg and allspice; simmer, uncovered, 5 minutes. Add cream; continue cooking until hot but not boiling. (If using homemade broth, add salt to taste.) *Makes 6 servings.*

Note 1: To make goose broth: In large saucepan, heat 1 tablespoon goose fat or salad oil. Add giblets and neck from goose; brown. Add 1 small onion, sliced; a few celery leaves; and 3 cups water. Bring to boiling; simmer, covered, 1 hour; strain.

Note 2: Recipe was doubled for the soup tureen in photograph.

APPLE WINE-BRAISED GOOSE
(pictured)

8 lb fresh or frozen goose (thawed, if frozen)
Salt
Pepper
6 medium (2 lb) cooking apples, cored, cut
    into 2-inch chunks
2 cloves garlic, peeled
1 large carrot, pared, cut into 1-inch pieces
1 large stalk celery, cut into 1-inch pieces
1 medium onion, sliced
Quick Brown Sauce, recipe follows
1 cup dry apple wine (or dry white wine)
¼ cup apple jelly
Sugared lady apples (see Note)
Fresh parsley sprigs

1. Preheat oven to 425F. Remove giblets and neck from goose; rinse under cold water; pat dry with paper towels. Freeze liver to use for pâté or other recipes; use neck and rest of giblets to make broth in Pumpkin Bisque, if desired. Remove fat from neck and body cavities; render and use for other recipes, if desired. Rinse goose under cold water; pat dry with paper towels. Season goose inside and out with salt and pepper.

2. Loosely pack cavities with apple chunks; bring skin of neck over back, and fasten with poultry pins. Close body cavity with poultry pins, and lace with string. Bend wing tips under body; tie ends of legs together.

3. Place goose, breast side up, on rack in large roasting pan. Place garlic, carrot, celery and onion in pan around goose. Roast, uncovered, 1¼ to 1½ hours, or until browned. Meanwhile, prepare Quick Brown Sauce.

4. Remove goose from oven; lift goose onto large sheet of heavy-duty foil; remove rack; pour fat from roasting pan, leaving vegetables. Add brown sauce, 1 cup wine and ¼ cup apple jelly to pan. Return goose to pan, placing it on top of vegetables. Cover pan tightly with heavy-duty foil. Reduce oven temperature to 350F; roast goose, covered, 45 minutes longer, or until instant-reading meat thermometer inserted in meaty part of leg registers 185F. (Thigh juices should run clear when thigh is pierced with a fork.)

5. Transfer goose to warm serving platter; remove pins and string; garnish goose with sugared lady apples, parsley and Steamed Acorn Squash With Cranberries, if desired. Strain pan juices, discarding vegetables. Remove and discard fat from juices. Pass juices with goose. *Makes 8 servings.*

Note: To make sugared lady apples: In small bowl, lightly beat 1 egg white. With a pastry brush, brush each of 6 lady apples with egg white. Over waxed paper, sprinkle granulated sugar over apples until they are evenly coated, reusing sugar on paper. Let sugar coating on apples dry completely before serving.

QUICK BROWN SAUCE

2 tablespoons butter or margarine
1 medium onion, finely chopped
2 tablespoons all-purpose flour
1 can (13¾ or 14½ oz) beef broth
2 tablespoons tomato paste
Pepper

In small saucepan, over medium heat, heat butter. Add onion, and sauté until golden—about 5 minutes. Stir in flour; cook, stirring, until flour begins to brown. Gradually add beef broth and 2 tablespoons tomato paste, stirring until smooth. Bring to boiling, stirring; simmer over medium heat until sauce thickens and is reduced to 1 cup—about 20 minutes. Add pepper to taste. *Makes 1 cup.*

STEAMED ACORN SQUASH WITH CRANBERRIES
(pictured)

1 large acorn squash
1 pkg (12 oz) fresh cranberries
⅔ cup sugar
⅔ cup orange juice
1 tablespoon cornstarch
1 teaspoon grated orange peel

1. Cut acorn squash lengthwise into 6 wedges. Remove and discard seeds and stringy fibers. In large skillet with ½ inch water, place squash, skin side down. Over medium heat, bring to boiling. Reduce heat; simmer, covered, 15 minutes, or until tender when pierced with fork. Drain.

2. Meanwhile, in medium saucepan, combine cranberries, sugar, orange juice, cornstarch and peel; stir to mix. Over medium heat, bring to boiling, stirring; reduce heat, and simmer 3 minutes.

3. To serve: Place squash wedges, skin side down, on platter. With slotted spoon, spoon some of the cranberries into cavity of squash wedges. Serve remaining cranberries and sauce separately. *Makes 6 servings.*

Note: To cook squash in a microwave oven, prepare as directed, adjusting recipe as follows: Lightly brush squash with salad oil. In microwave-safe baking dish, place squash and ¼ inch water. Cover with plastic wrap; turn back one corner to vent. Microwave on HIGH 12 minutes; let stand 5 minutes; drain. To cook cranberries in microwave oven: In medium microwave-safe bowl, combine cranberries and remaining ingredients. Cover with plastic wrap; turn back one corner to vent. Microwave on HIGH 6 minutes, stirring every 2 minutes, until thickened.

COCONUT-CARROT CAKE

(pictured)

CAKE
2 cups granulated sugar
1½ cups salad oil
4 large eggs
2 cups all-purpose flour
2 teaspoons baking soda
2 teaspoons ground cinnamon
1 teaspoon salt
2 cups shredded carrots (2 large or 3 medium)
1 can (8 oz) crushed pineapple, drained
1 cup finely chopped walnuts

FROSTING
1½ pkg (8-oz size) cream cheese, softened
⅓ cup (⅔ stick) butter or margarine, softened
½ teaspoon vanilla extract
2 cups confectioners' sugar
2 tablespoons milk
½ cup flaked coconut
¼ cup currants or chopped raisins
¼ cup finely chopped walnuts

¼ cup flaked coconut
Walnut halves (optional)

1. Make Cake: Grease well and flour a 10-inch springform or 10-by-2½-inch round layer cake pan. Preheat oven to 350F.

2. In large bowl, with electric mixer at medium speed, beat sugar, oil and eggs until well blended—2 minutes.

3. At low speed, gradually add flour, baking soda, cinnamon and salt, beating just until batter is smooth. Stir in shredded carrots, pineapple and 1 cup chopped walnuts. Pour batter into prepared pan. Bake 60 or 70 minutes, or until cake tester inserted in center comes out clean.

4. Cool cake in pan on wire rack 10 minutes. With spatula, carefully loosen side of cake from pan; remove side of springform pan, or remove cake from cake pan, and cool cake completely on rack.

5. Meanwhile, make Frosting: In large bowl, with electric mixer at medium speed, beat cream cheese, butter and vanilla until mixture is smooth and fluffy; add 1 cup confectioners' sugar and the milk; beat until well combined. Gradually beat in enough of remaining sugar until frosting is spreadable. With spoon, stir in coconut, currants and chopped walnuts. Makes about 4 cups.

6. To assemble cake: Split cooled cake in thirds horizontally to make three layers. Place first layer, cut side up, on serving plate; spread with one-fourth of frosting. Place second layer on top of first layer, and spread with one-fourth of frosting. Place third layer, cut side down, on top, and frost with one-fourth of frosting. Frost top and side of cake with remaining frosting. Lightly press ¼ cup flaked coconut into frosting around side of cake. Garnish top of cake with walnut halves. *Makes 16 servings.*

PLUM PUDDING WITH BRANDY HARD SAUCE

(pictured)

PLUM PUDDING
¼ cup (½ stick) unsalted butter or margarine, softened
⅓ cup granulated sugar
3 large eggs, separated
¼ lb ground suet
½ cup dark molasses
2¼ cups all-purpose flour
1 teaspoon salt
½ teaspoon baking powder
½ teaspoon ground cinnamon
¼ teaspoon ground allspice
1½ cups dark seedless raisins
1 cup diced pitted prunes
1 cup diced mixed candied fruit
1 can (8 oz) whole-berry or jellied cranberry sauce

BRANDY HARD SAUCE
1 cup (2 sticks) unsalted butter, softened (do not use margarine)
1 cup confectioners' sugar
Dash ground nutmeg
½ cup brandy

¼ cup brandy

1. Make Plum Pudding: In large bowl, with electric mixer at medium speed, beat ¼ cup butter and the granulated sugar until light. Add egg yolks, one at a time, blending thoroughly after each addition. Add suet and molasses, and continue beating until mixture is light and fluffy.

2. With mixer at low speed, beat in flour, salt, baking powder and spices until batter is well mixed; it will be stiff.

3. In small bowl, with electric mixer at high speed, using clean beaters, beat egg whites until stiff peaks form when beaters are slowly raised; fold into batter.

4. With wooden spoon, stir raisins, prunes, candied fruit and cranberry sauce into batter. Pour into well-greased 2½-quart pudding mold; cover tightly with its lid or foil tied on tightly with string.

5. Place mold on trivet or rack in 10- or 12-quart kettle. Add boiling water to come three-quarters up side of mold. Steam, covered, over medium-low heat 4 hours. Add more boiling water if necessary.

6. While pudding steams, make Brandy Hard Sauce: In small bowl, with electric mixer at medium speed, beat butter and confectioners' sugar until fluffy; add nutmeg. With mixer at high speed, gradually add ½ cup brandy in a thin stream, beating until hard sauce is very light and fluffy—about 3 minutes. Spoon into serving bowl; cover, and refrigerate.

7. Carefully remove mold to wire rack; uncover. Invert serving plate over mold;

hold mold and plate; invert; gently remove mold from pudding.

8. To flame pudding: In small, heavy saucepan, over medium-low heat, heat ¼ cup brandy. When vapor rises, ignite. Carefully ladle flaming brandy over pudding. Serve with Brandy Hard Sauce. *Makes 16 servings.*

Note: To make Plum Pudding ahead: Unmold, and let pudding cool completely. Wrap in plastic wrap, then in foil. May be refrigerated several weeks. Make Hard Sauce day before serving; store in covered container; refrigerate. To serve: Return pudding to mold; cover, and steam as directed above 50 minutes, or until pudding is thoroughly hot. Let Hard Sauce warm to room temperature; spoon into small bowl. With electric mixer at high speed, beat until light and fluffy. Serve with Plum Pudding.

CHOCOLATE PECAN PIE

1 pkg (9½ or 11 oz) piecrust mix

FILLING
3 squares (1-oz size) semisweet chocolate
¼ cup (½ stick) butter or margarine
4 large eggs
½ cup sugar
¾ cup dark corn syrup
⅓ cup light corn syrup
⅓ cup honey
2 cups pecan halves

Whipped cream (optional)

1. Prepare piecrust mix as package label directs for two-crust pie. Shape pastry into a ball; flatten to 1-inch thickness. Roll on lightly floured surface to form a 12½-inch circle. Fit pastry circle loosely into a 10-inch pie plate (do not stretch); fold edge of pastry under ½ inch; crimp or flute edge decoratively. Refrigerate until ready to use.

2. Preheat oven to 350F. Make Filling: In medium saucepan, over low heat, melt chocolate and butter, stirring frequently; remove from heat, and cool slightly.

3. In medium bowl, with rotary beater or portable electric mixer at low speed, beat eggs well; add sugar, corn syrups and honey; continue to beat at low speed until all ingredients are well combined. Stir in melted chocolate mixture; blend well.

4. Spread pecans evenly in bottom of prepared pie shell; pour chocolate mixture evenly over pecans. Bake 50 minutes, or until filling is set in the center when pie is shaken gently.

5. Cool pie completely on wire rack. If desired, chill slightly before serving, and garnish with whipped cream. *Makes 10 servings.* ∎

CLASSIC CHRISTMAS FEASTS

LITTLE WOMEN

The March girls scrimped and saved to prepare a special Christmas breakfast. Then they learned of a poor family nearby with no breakfast at all. So they bundled up in hoods and mittens to carry their own meal to the hungry family. The simple but hearty fare that went into the basket was probably very much like that pictured: cinnamon-poached apples, buckwheat pancakes, sausage, muffins and braided Christmas bread. These and other Classic Christmas Feasts recipes begin on page 278.

CLASSIC CHRISTMAS FEASTS

AMAHL AND THE NIGHT VISITORS

Amahl's shepherd friends had little to offer the three kings on their way to find the Christ Child: "Olives and quinces, apples and raisins... medlars and chestnuts...citrons and lemons...goat cheese and walnuts...honeycombs and cinnamon, thyme, mint and garlic, this is all we shepherds can offer you," they said. But from their humble offerings, we have concocted an array of rich and exotic holiday dishes. Counterclockwise from top: Cocktail Olives, a Chocolate-Chestnut Cake, Honey-Walnut Palmiers, Sugared Nuts, Cinnamon Stars, Three Kings' Cake, Spiced Oranges and (not shown) Cheese Pie.

CLASSIC CHRISTMAS FEASTS

THE WIND IN THE WILLOWS

Rat was entertaining Mr. Mole at a notably frugal Christmas Eve supper— "No bread, no butter, ...no pâté de foie gras, no champagne!"— when the field-mice carolers arrived. So enchanted was Rat by their bright eyes and piping voices that he forgot his parsimonious ways and sent one small mouse off to shop for a suitable feast. At right, set out around the mouse-size table, is our version of Rat's Christmas spread for the little carolers. Counterclockwise from the top: Christmas Pâté, Hot Sardine and Salmon Crescents, Breast of Turkey in Aspic and Mulled Ale with whole roasted apples.

continued from page 272

LITTLE WOMEN

THE MARCHES' CHRISTMAS BREAKFAST

ROSY CINNAMON APPLES* WITH CREAM

BUCKWHEAT CAKES

MAPLE SYRUP OR MOLASSES

COUNTRY SAUSAGE

BROWN-SUGAR MUFFINS*

MEG'S CHRISTMAS BRAID* OR OLD-FASHIONED CHRISTMAS BREAD

TEA   COFFEE

Recipes given for starred dishes.

ROSY CINNAMON APPLES

(pictured)

½ cup sugar
1 cup red cinnamon candies
3 cups hot water
6 medium-size tart apples (2½ lb), such as Winesap
Light cream or half-and-half

1. In medium skillet, dissolve sugar and candies in hot water, stirring; bring to boiling; simmer, uncovered, 5 minutes.
2. Pare and core apples; arrange on side in syrup.
3. Cook, uncovered, over medium heat 10 minutes. Turn apples; cook 10 to 15 minutes longer, covered, or until tender when pierced with cake tester.
4. Serve slightly warm or well chilled in their syrup with cream. *Makes 6 servings.*

BROWN-SUGAR MUFFINS

(pictured)

TOPPING

¼ cup light-brown sugar, firmly packed
¼ cup sifted all-purpose flour
2 tablespoons butter or margarine
2 teaspoons ground cinnamon

BATTER

1⅓ cups sifted all-purpose flour
1½ teaspoons baking powder
½ teaspoon salt
¼ cup (½ stick) butter or margarine, softened
½ cup light-brown sugar, firmly packed
1 egg
½ cup milk

1. Preheat oven to 375F. Lightly grease bottoms of 12 (2½-inch) muffin-pan cups.
2. Make Topping: In small bowl, combine topping ingredients; mix until crumbly.
3. Make Batter: Sift flour with baking powder and salt.
4. In large bowl of electric mixer, at medium speed, beat butter until fluffy. Beat in brown sugar, then egg until very light and fluffy. At low speed, blend in milk, then flour mixture, just until combined. Divide evenly into muffin cups.
5. Sprinkle topping over each muffin. Bake 20 minutes, or until cake tester inserted in center comes out clean.
6. Cool slightly in pan on wire rack. Gently remove from pan. Serve warm. *Makes 12.*

MEG'S CHRISTMAS BRAID

(pictured)

½ cup (1 stick) butter or margarine
1½ cups buttermilk
2 pkg active dry yeast
½ cup granulated sugar
½ teaspoon salt
4 cups sifted all-purpose flour
½ cup strawberry or raspberry jam
1 egg, beaten
Candied red and green cherries, cut up
½ cup confectioners' sugar
1 tablespoon water

1. In medium saucepan over medium heat, heat butter with buttermilk, stirring to melt butter. Turn into large bowl of electric mixer; let cool to lukewarm (105 to 115F). (If possible, check temperature with thermometer.)
2. Sprinkle yeast over lukewarm mixture, stirring to dissolve. Add sugar, salt and half of flour. Beat at medium speed until smooth. With wooden spoon or hands, mix in rest of flour until thoroughly combined.
3. Turn dough out on lightly floured pastry cloth. Roll dough over to coat with flour. Knead by folding dough toward you, then pushing down and away from you with heel of hand. Knead until smooth and blisters form—5 minutes.
4. Place in lightly greased bowl; turn greased side up. Cover with towel; let rise in warm place (85F), free from drafts, until double in bulk—45 to 60 minutes.
5. Knead dough again until smooth. Roll out to form a 20-by-12-inch rectangle. Transfer to lightly greased cookie sheet.

6. With knife, make diagonal cuts 3 inches long at 1-inch intervals on long sides. Spread uncut center part with jam. Overlap cut ends over jam section.
7. Let rise again until double in size—45 to 60 minutes.
8. Preheat oven to 375F. Brush dough with beaten egg. Bake 20 to 25 minutes, or until nicely browned.
9. Remove bread to wire rack to cool slightly, covered with towel.
10. Decorate with pieces of candied cherry. Combine confectioners' sugar with water; drizzle over bread. Serve bread slightly warm. *Makes 1 large loaf.*

Note: This can be made day ahead, reheated in foil and decorated after heating.

AMAHL AND THE NIGHT VISITORS

COCKTAIL OLIVES

(pictured)

2 cups olive, salad or peanut oil
½ cup white vinegar
1 lemon-peel spiral
3 dried red hot chiles
8 whole black peppercorns
1 tablespoon salt
1½ teaspoons dried thyme leaves
2 bay leaves
½ teaspoon dried tarragon leaves
1 teaspoon dried marjoram leaves
2 cans (2-oz size) anchovy fillets
2 jars (4-oz size) pitted large green olives, drained
1 jar (4 oz) pimientos, drained
1 can (5¾ oz) pitted large ripe olives, drained
3 cloves garlic
1 sprig parsley
3 tablespoons capers

1. In large jar (about 2-quart size), combine oil, vinegar, lemon peel, chiles, peppercorns, salt, thyme, bay leaves, tarragon, marjoram; stir to combine.
2. Drain anchovies; add oil from anchovies to above mixture. Cut anchovies in half crosswise; use to fill cavities in green olives.
3. Cut pimientos in strips; use to fill cavities in black olives.
4. Crush 1 clove garlic; sliver other 2 cloves garlic; add garlic and olives to jar, along with parsley and capers.
5. Let stand, covered, at room temperature at least 3 days before serving. *Makes about 2 quarts.*

CHOCOLATE-CHESTNUT CAKE

(pictured)

3 cans (10-oz size) chestnuts, drained
1½ cups light cream
½ cup brandy or amber rum
3 pkg (6-oz size) semisweet chocolate
    pieces
6 tablespoons (¾ stick) butter or
    margarine
4 egg yolks
1½ cups granulated sugar
3 eggs
¼ cup cornstarch
⅛ teaspoon salt
1 cup sifted confectioners' sugar
Glacéed marrons

1. Lightly butter bottom and side of a 10-inch springform pan. (Or use a 9-cup scalloped mold, lightly greased; see picture.) Line bottom of springform pan with waxed paper; grease paper.

2. In electric blender or food processor, combine chestnuts, cream and brandy; blend until smooth. (If using a blender, purée one-third of ingredients at a time.) Pour into a large bowl.

3. In small saucepan over low heat, melt chocolate with butter, stirring constantly. Let cool slightly; stir into chestnut mixture.

4. Preheat oven to 375F.

5. In small bowl of electric mixer, beat egg yolks with granulated sugar until very thick and light. Add whole eggs, one at a time, beating well after each addition, until thick and light colored. Beat in cornstarch and salt.

6. With wire whisk or rubber spatula, fold egg mixture into chestnut mixture until thoroughly combined. Turn into prepared pan (see Note).

7. Bake 1 hour and 10 minutes. Let cool in pan on wire rack. Refrigerate to chill well—several hours.

8. To serve: Remove side of springform pan, or turn out of mold onto serving plate. Sprinkle with confectioners' sugar. Decorate with marrons. *Makes 10 to 12 servings.*

Note: If using the springform pan, you will need to bake 1⅓ cups of the batter separately in a small, buttered loaf pan.

HONEY-WALNUT PALMIERS

(pictured)

2 pkg (10-oz size) frozen patty shells
6 tablespoons sugar
½ cup warm honey
½ cup coarsely chopped walnuts

1. Cover a large cookie sheet with double thickness of brown paper.

2. Let the patty shells stand at room temperature ½ hour, to soften.

3. On lightly floured pastry cloth, overlap patty shells, making three rows of 4 shells each. With rolling pin, roll to make a solid rectangle of pastry, 16 by 8 inches. Push in sides to make even.

4. Starting from short side, fold pastry in thirds; press edges to seal. Turn and roll again, to make a 16-by-8-inch rectangle; fold in thirds. Repeat turning, rolling and folding. Refrigerate, wrapped in foil, 30 minutes.

5. Shape Palmiers: Sprinkle pastry cloth evenly with ¼ cup sugar. On this, roll chilled pastry into a 12-by-10-inch rectangle. Sprinkle with 2 tablespoons sugar.

6. Fold each end toward center to form a 9-by-7-inch rectangle. Fold sides over again to form a 9-by-3½-inch rectangle. Wrap and refrigerate 30 minutes.

7. Preheat oven to 400F.

8. Cut pastry crosswise into eight even slices. Place slices, cut side up, 2 inches apart on paper-covered cookie sheet. With tip of paring knife, separate center of each slice to form a heart shape. With rolling pin, flatten to ¼-inch thickness.

9. Bake 12 minutes; remove from oven. Using broad spatula, turn on other side. Bake 12 minutes longer, or until golden-brown.

10. Remove to wire rack. Brush each with 1 tablespoon warm honey; sprinkle with nuts. Serve slightly warm or cold. *Makes 8.*

SUGARED NUTS

(pictured)

2 cups light-brown sugar, firmly packed
1 cup granulated sugar
1 cup sour cream
2 teaspoons vanilla extract
2 cups walnut halves
1 cup pecans
1 cup unblanched almonds

1. Combine both kinds of sugar and the sour cream in large saucepan. Cook over medium heat, stirring, until sugar is dissolved.

2. Continue cooking without stirring to 238F on candy thermometer, or until a little in cold water forms a soft ball. Remove from heat.

3. Add vanilla and nuts. Stir gently until all nuts are coated.

4. Turn onto waxed paper; with a fork, separate the nuts. Let dry. *Makes about 2 pounds.*

CINNAMON STARS

(pictured)

⅓ cup egg whites
1½ cups granulated sugar
1½ cups unblanched almonds, ground
1½ tablespoons ground cinnamon
½ cup all-purpose flour
1 cup sifted confectioners' sugar
2 tablespoons water

1. Day before: In small bowl of electric mixer, let egg whites warm to room temperature—about 1 hour.

2. With electric mixer at medium speed, beat egg whites until soft peaks form when beaters are slowly raised.

3. At high speed, beat in 1¼ cups granulated sugar, 2 tablespoons at a time; continue beating until mixture is thick and glossy—5 minutes.

4. In medium bowl, combine the almonds and cinnamon, tossing to combine. Add egg-white mixture, mixing until thoroughly combined. Refrigerate, covered, overnight.

5. Next day, sprinkle a pastry cloth or a pastry board with ½ cup flour and ¼ cup granulated sugar, rubbing into cloth evenly. Grease several cookie sheets very well.

6. Roll out one-fourth of dough ¼ inch thick. Keep rest refrigerated.

7. Cut out dough, using a 6-inch star cut from cardboard as a pattern. With wide spatula, carefully remove stars to prepared cookie sheets, placing 1 inch apart. Continue rolling and cutting rest of dough and any trimmings.

8. Let cookies stand, uncovered, at room temperature 3 hours.

9. Preheat oven to 300F. In small bowl, mix confectioners' sugar with 2 tablespoons water; stir until smooth.

10. Bake stars 35 minutes. Remove from oven; brush with glaze; bake 5 minutes longer.

11. With wide spatula, remove cookies to wire rack to cool completely. *Makes about 9 large stars.* (Nice to use as favors on the Christmas table.)

Note: These are best when freshly baked—do not make more than several days ahead.

continued on page 280

continued from page 279

THREE-KINGS' CAKE
(pictured)

5 cups light raisins
2 cups dark raisins
¾ cup Scotch whisky, rum or orange juice
3½ cups sifted all-purpose flour
1 teaspoon baking powder
1 teaspoon salt
½ cup diced candied orange peel
½ cup diced candied citron
½ cup chopped walnuts
½ cup chopped almonds
1½ cups granulated sugar
1 cup (2 sticks) plus 3 tablespoons butter
**   or margarine, melted**
5 eggs (1 cup)
3 tablespoons honey
1 tablespoon sliced almonds

FROSTING
1¼ cups confectioners' sugar
⅓ cup Scotch whisky, rum or orange juice
½ cup light raisins
1 tablespoon diced candied orange peel
1 tablespoon chopped walnuts
Candied cherries for decoration
Candied citron for decoration

1. Lightly grease a 9-by-3½-inch angel-food-cake pan. Line bottom and sides of pan with brown paper; grease again.

2. In medium bowl, combine 5 cups light raisins and the dark raisins with 6 tablespoons whisky; toss to mix well; let stand 5 minutes or longer. Preheat oven to 275F.

3. Sift flour with baking powder and salt into large bowl. Add raisin mixture, candied peel, citron and chopped nuts; toss to mix well. Add granulated sugar; mix well.

4. With wooden spoon, stir in melted butter, mixing until well combined. Beat in eggs, one at a time, beating well after each addition with wooden spoon. Stir in honey.

5. Turn into prepared pan. Sprinkle top of batter with almonds. Bake 2 hours, 30 minutes. (If cake browns too fast on top, cover loosely with foil.)

6. Remove cake from oven; pour 3 tablespoons whisky evenly over top. Cool on wire rack.

7. When cake has cooled, turn out of pan; gently remove paper. Pour remaining 3 tablespoons whisky evenly over top of cake. Wrap cake in cheesecloth moistened with more whisky; store in tightly covered cake tin in cool place. Cake should stand at least 2 days before serving.

8. Make Frosting: In small bowl, combine confectioners' sugar and whisky; stir until smooth. Combine raisins, peel and walnuts; mix well. Sprinkle half of raisin mixture over top of cake.

9. Pour sugar mixture over cake, letting it run down sides. Sprinkle top with rest of raisin mixture. Decorate with cherries and citron, as pictured. *Makes 6-pound cake.*

CHRISTMAS SPICED ORANGES
(pictured)

8 small navel oranges

FILLING
⅔ cup light raisins
½ cup currants
½ cup mixed diced candied fruit
¼ cup chopped walnuts
½ cup golden rum

SYRUP
7 cups sugar
3 cups water
2 (3-inch) cinnamon sticks
2 whole nutmegs
5 whole cloves
5-inch vanilla bean
1 lemon-peel spiral
½ cup golden rum

1. Wash oranges. Remove stems; cut an X at stem end of each orange. Pierce oranges all over with cake tester or metal skewer.

2. In large kettle, bring 6 quarts water to boiling. Add oranges; boil 15 minutes. Then plunge oranges into cold water; let stand 30 minutes, changing water twice.

3. Using spoon, scoop out half of pulp through X in each orange, leaving shells intact. (Serve scooped-out pulp in fruit cup.)

4. Make Filling: In small bowl, combine filling ingredients; mix well; let stand 10 minutes. Use to fill oranges; close openings with wooden skewers.

5. Make Syrup: In 6-quart kettle combine sugar and water. Stir with wooden spoon over low heat until sugar is dissolved. Bring to boiling.

6. Plunge oranges into syrup; bring back to boiling; simmer gently 30 minutes. Remove oranges to bowl with slotted spoon.

7. Add cinnamon sticks, nutmegs, cloves, vanilla bean and lemon spiral to syrup; simmer 15 minutes. Pour syrup over oranges; let cool to lukewarm; add rum.

8. Meanwhile, wash 3 or 4 pint jars in very hot water; let drain.

9. Fill jars with hot oranges and syrup. Let cool completely before covering with jar tops. Store in refrigerator.

10. To serve: Cut in quarters or halves. Serve in syrup. Nice with vanilla ice cream or custard sauce. *Makes 8 oranges.*

GREEK CHEESE PIE

9-inch unbaked pie shell
¾ lb feta cheese, cut into small pieces
1 cup light cream or half-and-half
3 eggs
½ teaspoon dried thyme leaves
1 teaspoon cornstarch
Dash pepper
1 small clove garlic, crushed
8 large pitted ripe olives
8 large pitted green olives
1 pimiento, cut into strips

1. Preheat oven to 425F. Prick crust well with fork; place in freezer 10 minutes.

2. Bake pie shell 10 minutes; cool.

3. Blend cheese in electric blender or food processor with cream and eggs until smooth. Add thyme, cornstarch and pepper; blend. Stir in garlic. Turn into pie shell.

4. Bake pie 10 minutes. Arrange olives over top; bake 25 minutes longer, or until filling is set. Decorate with pimiento strips. Serve warm. *Makes 8 servings.*

Note: This pie may be made early in day and reheated for serving.

THE WIND IN THE WILLOWS

CHRISTMAS SPREAD FOR CAROLERS

CHERRY-TOMATO HORS D'OEUVRES*
HOT SARDINE AND SALMON CRESCENTS*
CHRISTMAS PATE*
BREAST OF TURKEY IN ASPIC*
MELANGE OF CHRISTMAS FRUITS
CHRISTMAS COOKIES
BOWL OF MULLED ALE* OR FROSTED DAIQUIRIS* OR FIELD-MOUSE SPECIAL*
COFFEE
*Recipes given for starred dishes.

CHERRY-TOMATO HORS D'OEUVRES

2 dozen cherry tomatoes
1 pkg (8 oz) cream cheese, softened
2 tablespoons catsup
1 tablespoon lemon juice
1 tablespoon prepared horseradish
1 tablespoon light cream or half-and-half
¼ teaspoon paprika
Parsley
Watercress
½ lemon

1. Wash tomatoes; dry on paper towels. Cut slice from each at stem end.

2. In medium bowl, combine cheese, catsup, lemon juice, horseradish, cream and paprika. Mix well with fork.

3. Press cheese mixture through pastry bag with a number-6 star tip, making rosettes on each tomato. Decorate each with parsley. Arrange on bed of watercress, sprinkled with lemon juice, on tray. Refrigerate at least 30 minutes before serving. *Makes 24.*

HOT SARDINE AND SALMON CRESCENTS
(pictured)

SARDINE FILLING
2 cans (4⅜-oz size) boneless, skinless sardines, drained
⅓ cup catsup
2 tablespoons Dijon-style mustard
12 drops hot red-pepper sauce
Dash pepper
⅓ cup capers
1 tablespoon chopped parsley
1 egg

SALMON FILLING
1 can (7¾ oz) salmon
1 tablespoon butter or margarine
1 teaspoon chopped onion
¼ lb fresh mushrooms, coarsely chopped
1 hard-cooked egg, coarsely chopped
1 tablespoon soy sauce
1 tablespoon Dijon-style mustard
1 teaspoon chopped parsley

3 pkg (8-oz size) refrigerator crescent rolls (see Note)
1 egg
1 tablespoon water

1. Make Sardine Filling: With fork, crush sardines in medium bowl; add rest of filling ingredients; mix well with fork. Refrigerate, covered.

2. Make Salmon Filling: Drain salmon; remove any skin and bones.

3. In hot butter in small skillet, sauté onion until tender; add mushrooms; cook until tender. Remove from heat; add rest of filling ingredients; mix well. Refrigerate, covered.

4. Preheat oven to 375F. Lightly grease several cookie sheets. Unroll crescent dough, as label directs.

5. Fill half of crescent rolls with each mixture; roll up as directed, pinching to seal ends. Place on cookie sheets. Beat egg with water; use to brush crescents.

6. Bake 15 minutes. Serve warm. *Makes 24.*

Note: Keep packages of rolls refrigerated until just before using.

CHRISTMAS PATE
(pictured)

3 lb chicken livers
6 tablespoons (¾ stick) butter or margarine
⅓ cup chopped onion
1 tablespoon dried savory leaves
1 tablespoon dried tarragon leaves
6 tablespoons cognac
½ cup light cream or half-and-half
5 eggs
1 teaspoon salt
¼ teaspoon pepper
8 slices bacon
2 bay leaves

GLAZE
1 env unflavored gelatine
¼ cup water
1 cup dry white wine
½ teaspoon dried tarragon leaves
½ teaspoon chopped parsley

DECORATION
10 ripe olives, 1 green olive
1 jar (4 oz) roasted pimientos
Parsley (optional)

1. Day before: Discard any fat globules from chicken livers; wash livers and dry on paper towels.

2. In hot butter in skillet, sauté onion and dried herbs until onion is golden. Add chicken livers; sauté, stirring, about 5 minutes. Cut up livers.

3. In bowl, combine livers, cognac, cream, eggs, salt and pepper; mix well. Put mixture through blender, about one-third at a time, to make a smooth purée, or process ingredients in a food processor fitted with the steel blade.

4. Preheat oven to 400F. Line a 1¾-quart round casserole with bacon slices. Arrange bay leaves in bottom of casserole.

5. Pour liver mixture into casserole; place in pan of very hot water (water should measure 1 inch). Bake 1 hour.

6. Remove casserole from hot water; let cool completely on wire rack. Refrigerate, covered, overnight. Next day, unmold: Loosen edge with spatula; turn out on a tray. Remove bacon; smooth surface with spatula. Refrigerate.

7. Prepare Glaze: Sprinkle gelatine over ¼ cup water in small saucepan; let stand 5 minutes to soften. Add wine, tarragon and parsley; stir over low heat until mixture is hot and gelatine is dissolved; strain if desired.

8. Set pan in ice water; let stand, stirring occasionally, until mixture starts to jell—15 minutes.

9. Meanwhile, arrange slices of the olives and pimientos around edge and on top of pâté, to form design of cock's head, as pictured. Spoon half of glaze over pâté, covering completely. Refrigerate pâté to set glaze—30 minutes. Reheat remaining glaze; cool and spoon over chilled pâté. Refrigerate until serving time to set glaze. Garnish with parsley, if desired. Serve with thinly sliced pumpernickel and rye bread. *Makes 40 servings.*

continued on page 287

As the British Feast at Christmas

Set before you are some of the almost legendary holiday dishes of Great Britain that will give a British accent to your holiday feasting. Clockwise from left: an imposing ham with a golden crust served with a fruited Cumberland Sauce; an American version of an English partridge pie that substitutes squabs for the British birds; Syllabub, the English forerunner of our eggnog; a Dickensian Roast Goose With Sage Stuffing, a circle of Glazed Apples and a rich Plum Sauce; the Trifle, a mouthwatering, sherry-sprinkled dessert that no holiday table should be without; a Spiced Sirloin Steak marinated in wine; and, finally, a noble Saddle of Lamb garnished with bright strings of cranberries and lavishly covered with a creamy Caper Sauce. For the recipes, please turn the page.

continued from page 283

All recipes are pictured on pages 282 and 283.

BAKED HAM IN CRUST WITH CUMBERLAND SAUCE

PASTRY
2 pkg (11-oz size) piecrust mix
1½ tablespoons dry mustard
1½ teaspoons dried sage leaves
½ cup ice water

12-lb fully cooked bone-in whole ham
1 egg yolk
1 teaspoon water
Cumberland Sauce, recipe follows

1. Preheat oven to 375F.
2. Make Pastry: In medium bowl, combine piecrust mix, mustard and sage; mix well. Blend in the ice water as package label directs. Shape into a ball.
3. On lightly floured surface, roll out pastry to about ⅛-inch thickness. Trim to make a 22-by-17½-inch rectangle. Save trimmings.
4. Remove rind from ham. Place ham near one end of rectangle, covering about one-third of the pastry, and mold short end of pastry to ham. Bring long end of pastry over ham, and mold around top and sides of ham, pressing firmly. Moisten edges with cold water, and press together firmly, to seal.
5. Roll out trimmings, and cut with leaf cookie cutter.
6. Beat egg yolk with 1 teaspoon water; brush some of egg mixture over pastry. Arrange leaf cutouts decoratively on top; brush with egg mixture. Place ham on cookie sheet or in jelly-roll pan.
7. Bake 1½ hours, or until pastry is a deep golden-brown. (If pastry breaks, tuck a piece of foil under ham, to keep it level.)
8. For buffet serving, cut a lengthwise slice from thin underside; then stand ham on cut side. Cut slices from top to bone; serve with Cumberland Sauce. *Makes 24 servings.*

CUMBERLAND SAUCE

2 cups ruby port
⅓ cup grated orange peel
⅔ cup orange juice
2 tablespoons lemon juice
1 cup red-currant jelly
Dash ground red pepper

1. In medium saucepan, combine port and orange peel. Cook over medium heat, uncovered, until reduced to 1⅓ cups—10 to 15 minutes.
2. Stir in orange juice, lemon juice, currant jelly and pepper until well blended.
3. Bring to boiling; reduce heat and simmer, uncovered, 10 minutes, or until jelly is melted and mixture is thickened. Serve hot, with ham. *Makes about 2 cups.*

PARTRIDGE PIE

PASTRY
1 pkg (11 oz) piecrust mix
¼ teaspoon baking powder
¼ cup ice water
3 tablespoons butter or margarine, softened

4 squabs, halved (4 lb in all), with livers
⅓ cup (⅔ stick) butter or margarine
12 small white onions, peeled
½ cup cognac
1 cup diced fully cooked ham
½ cup all-purpose flour
1 teaspoon salt
½ teaspoon dried thyme leaves
⅛ teaspoon pepper
1½ cups Burgundy
1 can (10¾ oz) condensed chicken broth, undiluted
1 tablespoon currant jelly
¾ teaspoon liquid gravy seasoning
¼ cup finely chopped carrot
1 egg yolk
1 teaspoon water

1. Make Pastry: Prepare piecrust mix as package label directs, thoroughly blending baking powder with dry mix before adding water. Shape into a ball.
2. On lightly floured surface, roll out pastry to a 14-by-12-inch rectangle. At one end, spread 3 tablespoons butter over two-thirds of pastry, leaving ½-inch margin. Fold pastry in thirds, starting with unbuttered end.

3. With folded edge at right, carefully roll again to a 14-by-12-inch rectangle. (If butter breaks through, brush spot lightly with flour.) Fold in thirds, and wrap in waxed paper. Refrigerate until ready to use.
4. Wash squabs; pat dry with paper towels. Chop livers; set aside.
5. In hot butter in large skillet or Dutch oven, brown onions. Remove, and set aside.
6. Brown squabs, a few halves at a time, on all sides in drippings in skillet. Remove as browned. Return all squabs to pan. Remove from heat.
7. Heat cognac in a small saucepan; pour over squabs and ignite. When flame dies out, return to heat, and cook, covered, over low heat 10 minutes. Add onions and ham; cook 5 minutes longer. With slotted utensil, remove squabs, onions and ham to a 2½-quart deep baking dish (about 12 by 10 inches); set aside.
8. Remove skillet from heat. Stir flour, salt, thyme and pepper into drippings until well blended. Stir in Burgundy, chicken broth, jelly and gravy seasoning.
9. Bring to boiling, stirring constantly. Boil 1 minute. Stir in the chopped liver and carrot. Pour over squab mixture in baking dish.
10. Preheat oven to 425F.
11. On lightly floured surface, roll out pastry into a 14-by-12-inch rectangle. Trim edges (save trimmings to make pastry decorations).
12. Fold pastry rectangle in half lengthwise. Unfold over filled baking dish; cut several slits for steam vents; crimp edge. Roll out trimmings, and cut as desired.
13. Beat egg yolk with water. Brush over pastry. (If using pastry decorations, gently press in place. Save some of the egg mixture to brush over decorations.)
14. Bake 10 minutes. Reduce oven temperature to 350F; bake 1¼ hours longer. If pastry becomes too brown, cover loosely with foil. *Makes 4 to 6 servings.*

SYLLABUB

3 cups cream sherry or Madeira
2 cups sugar
⅓ cup lemon juice
1 tablespoon grated lemon peel
2 cups heavy cream, chilled

1. In small punch bowl, combine sherry, sugar, lemon juice and peel; stir until sugar is dissolved.
2. Refrigerate, covered, several hours or overnight.
3. Just before serving, whip cream until soft peaks form. Spoon over sherry mixture. Fold together just until combined. *Makes about 16 (4-oz) servings.*

ROAST GOOSE WITH SAGE STUFFING AND PLUM SAUCE

SAGE STUFFING
3 lb large onions, peeled and quartered
2 pkg (7-oz size) cubed herb-seasoned stuffing mix
1 to 1½ tablespoons dried sage leaves, crushed
¼ cup (½ stick) butter or margarine, melted
1 can (10¾ oz) condensed chicken broth, undiluted

12- to 14-lb ready-to-cook goose
1 tablespoon lemon juice
1 teaspoon salt
⅛ teaspoon pepper

Plum Sauce, recipe follows
Brown-Sugar-Glazed Apples, recipe follows
Galax or other green leaves, washed

1. Make Sage Stuffing: Cook onion in lightly salted boiling water to cover until just tender—about 15 minutes. Drain. Chop onion medium fine.
2. In large bowl, with fork, toss stuffing mix with chopped onion, sage, butter and chicken broth until well blended.
3. Preheat oven to 325F. Remove giblets and neck from goose. Discard giblets and neck. Wash goose, inside and out, and dry well with paper towels. Remove all fat from inside, and discard. Rub cavity with lemon juice, salt and pepper.
4. Spoon dressing into neck cavity; bring skin of neck over back, and fasten with poultry pins. Spoon dressing lightly into body cavity; close with poultry pins, and lace with twine. Bend wing tips under body; tie ends of legs together.
5. Prick skin only (not meat) over thighs, back and breast very well. Place, breast side up, on rack in large roasting pan.
6. Roast, uncovered, 2 hours. Remove goose from oven.
7. Pour off fat from pan, and discard. Roast goose, uncovered, 2 hours longer. Pour off all fat, saving 2 tablespoons for Plum Sauce and discarding rest. Roast ½ hour longer, or until skin is nicely browned and crisp.
8. Place goose on heated platter. Garnish with Glazed Apples and the leaves. Pass Plum Sauce. *Makes 8 servings.*

BROWN-SUGAR-GLAZED APPLES

6 small red apples (about 1½ lb)
⅓ cup light-brown sugar, firmly packed
3 tablespoons light corn syrup
3 tablespoons butter or margarine, melted

1. Wash apples; core each, being careful not to cut through the bottom. Remove a thin slice from stem end, and make a decorative sawtooth edge on each apple.
2. Place apples in shallow baking dish. Sprinkle cut surfaces with brown sugar; drizzle with corn syrup and butter.
3. Place in oven with goose during last hour of roasting; baste apples every 20 minutes. *Makes 6.*

PLUM SAUCE

1 can (1 lb, 14 oz) purple plums
2 tablespoons reserved goose fat
1½ tablespoons flour
1 cup ruby port
Dash ground cinnamon
Dash ground red pepper

1. Drain plums well; remove pits, and discard. Mash fruit.
2. In hot goose fat, heat flour, stirring constantly, until flour turns light brown—about 2 or 3 minutes.
3. Gradually stir in port; bring to boiling, stirring constantly. Boil 1 minute, stirring; sauce will thicken.
4. Add plums, cinnamon and red pepper; simmer 5 minutes longer, stirring occasionally. Keep warm. *Makes about 2 cups.*

continued on page 286

continued from page 285

ENGLISH TRIFLE

CUSTARD
1 cup sugar
1 tablespoon cornstarch
½ teaspoon salt
4 cups milk
8 egg yolks
2 teaspoons vanilla extract
1 tablespoon cream sherry

2 (8-inch) bakers' spongecake layers
¾ cup cream sherry
6 tablespoons raspberry preserves
6 tablespoons toasted slivered almonds
½ cup heavy cream, whipped
Candied green and red cherries

1. Make Custard: In a heavy, medium saucepan, combine sugar, cornstarch and salt. Gradually add milk; stir until smooth.

2. Cook over medium heat, stirring constantly, until mixture is thickened and comes to boil. Boil 1 minute. Remove from heat.

3. In medium bowl, slightly beat egg yolks. Gradually add a little hot mixture, beating well.

4. Stir into rest of hot mixture; cook over medium heat, stirring constantly, just until mixture boils. Remove from heat; stir in vanilla and the tablespoon sherry.

5. Strain custard immediately into bowl. Refrigerate, covered, until well chilled—several hours or overnight.

6. Split spongecake layers in half crosswise, to make 4 layers in all. Sprinkle each layer with 3 tablespoons sherry.

7. Spread each of three layers with 2 tablespoons preserves, and sprinkle each with 2 tablespoons almonds. In attractive deep serving bowl, stack prepared layers, jam side up, spreading each with about 1 cup custard. Top with plain layer, then remaining custard.

8. Decorate with whipped cream and candied cherries. Refrigerate until serving time. *Makes 8 to 10 servings.*

SPICED SIRLOIN STEAK WITH MADEIRA SAUCE

MARINADE
1½ cups red-wine vinegar
1 cup catsup
½ cup salad oil
3 tablespoons salt
1½ teaspoons pepper
1½ teaspoons dry mustard
1½ teaspoons celery salt
¾ teaspoon garlic salt
¾ teaspoon dried thyme leaves
¾ teaspoon ground cloves

5- or 6-lb sirloin steak, 2 inches thick

MADEIRA SAUCE
¼ cup all-purpose flour
1 can (10½ oz) condensed beef broth, undiluted
½ cup Madeira

1. Make Marinade: In large, deep roasting pan, combine vinegar, catsup, oil, salt, pepper, mustard, celery salt, garlic salt, thyme and cloves; mix well.

2. Wipe steak with damp paper towels. Place in roasting pan; spoon the marinade over steak until it is well coated.

3. Refrigerate, covered, overnight.

4. Next day, remove beef from marinade, and place on broiler rack. Reserve marinade. Insert meat thermometer into thickest part of meat, away from bone and fat.

5. Broil steak, turning once and brushing with more marinade, about 20 minutes per side—until thermometer registers 140F, for rare. Remove steak to heated serving platter; cover with foil; keep in warm place.

6. Meanwhile, make Madeira Sauce: Combine flour with some of broth, mixing to make a smooth paste. Stir in 1 cup reserved marinade and rest of broth. Bring to boiling, stirring until sauce thickens—about 1 minute. Reduce heat, and simmer 5 minutes. Add Madeira.

7. Serve steak thinly sliced, with Madeira Sauce. *Makes 10 to 12 servings.*

ROAST SADDLE OF LAMB WITH CAPER SAUCE

7-lb saddle of lamb
Salt
3 lb potatoes, pared and quartered lengthwise
2 lamb kidneys
1 cup water

CAPER SAUCE
5 teaspoons butter or margarine
2½ tablespoons all-purpose flour
¼ teaspoon salt
Dash pepper
1 can (10½ oz) condensed beef broth, undiluted
2 teaspoons vinegar
1 teaspoon prepared mustard
¼ cup heavy cream
2 tablespoons capers, drained

Watercress (optional)
Cranberries on a string (optional)

1. Preheat oven to 350F. Wipe lamb with damp paper towels. Rub with ½ teaspoon salt. Place lamb, fat side up, in shallow roasting pan. Insert meat thermometer in thickest part, away from bone or fat.

2. Roast, uncovered, 1½ hours. Arrange potatoes in drippings around lamb, turning to coat evenly. Roast, turning potatoes several times, about 1 hour longer, or until meat thermometer registers 160F.

3. Meanwhile, remove fat and any loose membrane from kidneys; rinse well. Place in small saucepan with water and ½ teaspoon salt; bring to boiling. Reduce heat, and simmer, covered, 30 minutes, or until tender. Keep warm.

4. Also, make Caper Sauce: Melt butter in medium saucepan; remove from heat. Stir in flour, salt and pepper until smooth. Gradually stir in beef broth, vinegar and mustard.

5. Bring to boiling, stirring constantly; boil gently 1 minute. Reduce heat; stir in cream and capers, and cook until very hot. Set pan over hot water, to keep sauce warm.

6. To serve: Place meat on heated platter; pile potatoes in groups around meat. Slice kidneys crosswise; arrange on lamb. Garnish with watercress and a string of cranberries, if desired. Pass Caper Sauce. *Makes 8 servings.* ∎

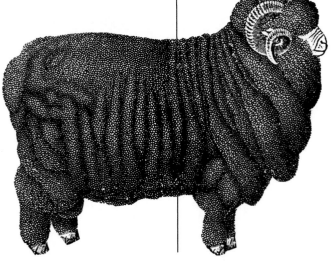

continued from page 281

BREAST OF TURKEY IN ASPIC
(pictured)

6-lb turkey breast
2 cans (10¾-oz size) condensed chicken broth, undiluted
2 cups water
1 cup dry white wine
2 onions, each stuck with 4 cloves
4 celery stalks with leaves, cut up
4 medium carrots, pared and sliced
2 teaspoons salt
10 black peppercorns
1 bay leaf

GLAZE
1½ tablespoons (1½ env) unflavored gelatine
½ cup water
2½ cups broth from turkey
½ cup heavy cream

DECORATION
½ jar (4-oz size) pimientos
3 sprigs parsley
2 bay leaves
Watercress sprig
Whole cloves
Watercress (optional)

1. Day before: Wipe turkey with damp paper towels. Cook turkey: In 6-quart Dutch oven or large kettle, combine chicken broth, water, wine, the onions with cloves, celery, carrot, salt, peppercorns and bay leaf. Bring to boiling; add turkey breast. Bring back to boiling; reduce heat; simmer, covered, just until tender—about 2½ hours. Remove from heat; cool. Remove turkey to large bowl, breast side down; strain liquid; discard vegetables.

2. Pour broth over turkey. Refrigerate, covered, overnight.

3. Next day, remove turkey from broth; refrigerate turkey. Skim fat from surface of broth.

4. Make Glaze: In small saucepan, sprinkle gelatine over ½ cup water; let stand 10 minutes to soften. Add 2½ cups broth.

5. Heat, stirring, over medium heat until gelatine is dissolved. In medium bowl, combine 1½ cups gelatine mixture and the cream. Set bowl in ice water; let gelatine mixture stand about 15 minutes. (Set aside remaining clear gelatine mixture.)

6. Place turkey breast on rack on a tray. Spoon glaze over turkey to cover completely; refrigerate until cream-glaze sets—about 30 minutes.

7. Make Decoration: Cut pimientos in shape of flower petals, as pictured. Arrange over turkey breast, along with parsley, bay leaves, watercress sprig and whole cloves, as pictured. Refrigerate.

8. Set remaining clear gelatine mixture in bowl of ice water until thickened.

Then spoon over turkey, covering completely. Refrigerate until clear glaze sets—about 30 minutes. Remove any clear glaze on tray, and reheat until melted; rechill in ice water. Then spoon over turkey, coating completely. Refrigerate until set.

9. To serve: Arrange turkey on platter. Garnish with watercress, if desired. Slice very thinly. *Makes 10 to 12 servings.*

MULLED ALE
(pictured)

Orange-peel spiral
Whole cloves
6 small red apples
3 bottles (12-oz size) ale
3 cups dark rum
⅔ cup sugar
⅛ teaspoon ground ginger

1. Preheat oven to 350F.
2. Stud orange spiral with cloves ½ inch apart. Place in shallow pan along with apples; bake, uncovered, 20 minutes.
3. In large saucepan, combine ale, rum, sugar and ginger; bring just to boiling, stirring until sugar is dissolved.
4. Place hot orange spiral and roasted apples in heatproof punch bowl; pour hot ale mixture over them. Serve hot in punch cups. *Makes 15 (punch-cup) servings.*

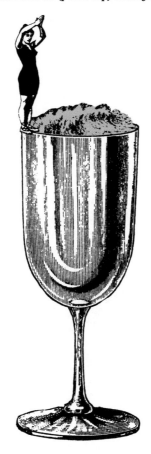

FROSTED DAIQUIRIS

Frosted Punch Bowl, recipe follows
1 bottle (16 oz) daiquiri mix
6 tablespoons superfine sugar
2½ cups light rum
½ cup Curaçao or Cointreau
2 dozen ice cubes
1 bottle (1 pint, 12 oz) club soda, chilled
1 lime, sliced (optional)

1. Day ahead, prepare Frosted Punch Bowl.
2. Next day, in pitcher or bowl, combine daiquiri mix and sugar; stir until sugar is dissolved. Add rum and Curaçao.
3. Refrigerate, stirring occasionally, until well chilled—about 3 hours.
4. To serve: Place half of daiquiri mixture and 1 dozen ice cubes in blender; blend at high speed 15 to 20 seconds. Pour into frosted punch bowl. Repeat with remaining mixture and ice. Stir in club soda. Float lime slices on top. *Makes about 20 (4-ounce) servings.*

Note: You may use 2 cans (6-ounce size) frozen daiquiri mix. If blender is not available, crush ice cubes very fine. Place with daiquiri mixture in jar with tight-fitting lid. Shake vigorously 1 minute.

FROSTED PUNCH BOWL

Beat 1 egg white with 1 tablespoon water. Use to brush a band about 1½ inches wide on outside of punch bowl, at top. Sprinkle sheet of waxed paper with granulated sugar. Roll edge of bowl in sugar, to frost it. Let stand at room temperature about 20 minutes; then roll in sugar again. Set aside to dry—3 to 4 hours or overnight.

FIELD-MOUSE SPECIAL

SUGAR SYRUP
1 cup sugar
½ cup water
12 whole cloves
2 sticks (2-inch pieces) of cinnamon

1 can (46 oz) unsweetened grapefruit juice
1 can (6 oz) frozen orange-juice concentrate, reconstituted
1 quart cider
Orange slices (optional)
Cinnamon sticks (optional)

1. Make Sugar Syrup: In small saucepan, combine sugar, water, the cloves and cinnamon; bring to boiling. Reduce heat; simmer, uncovered, 20 minutes. Strain.
2. In large bowl, combine fruit juices and cider; mix well. Stir in Sugar Syrup.
3. Reheat, and serve hot. (Or serve well chilled.) If desired, garnish with orange slices and cinnamon sticks. *Makes 26 punch-cup servings.* ∎

CHRISTMAS DINNER WITH A SOUTHERN ACCENT

Southern hospitality really shines during the holiday season, and we'd like to share this delightful Dixie meal with you and your family. Here, Roast Loin of Pork ringed with Souffléed Yams in Orange Shells. Continuing counterclockwise: lighter-than-air Butter Rolls and molded cranberry relish; Japanese Fruitcake (rich spice cake and plain layer cake separated by tart lemon filling, all iced with coconut); and Pumpkin Chiffon Pie with the surprise of a gingersnap crust. For these recipes and more, see page 290.

continued from page 288

ANNA HODGE'S CHRISTMAS DINNER

EGGNOG   CHAMPAGNE
ANNA'S CHEESE BISCUITS*
SALTED NUTS
OYSTER PIE*
ROAST TURKEY WITH CORNBREAD STUFFING
BAKED HAM OR
ANNA'S ROAST LOIN OF PORK*
JELLIED CRANBERRY RELISH*
SOUFFLEED YAMS IN ORANGE SHELLS*
GREEN BEANS, SOUTHERN STYLE
BUTTER ROLLS*
JAPANESE FRUITCAKE*
PUMPKIN CHIFFON PIE*
FRESH-FRUIT BOWL
COFFEE

*Recipes given for starred dishes.

ANNA'S CHEESE BISCUITS

1 lb grated sharp Cheddar cheese
1 lb (4 sticks) butter or margarine, softened
1½ teaspoons paprika
¾ teaspoon ground red pepper
4 cups self-rising all-purpose flour
Pecan halves

1. Preheat oven to 325F. Grease two baking sheets. In large bowl of electric mixer, combine cheese, butter, paprika and red pepper. At medium speed, beat until smooth and fluffy.

2. At low speed, gradually add flour, beating just until combined. (If dough seems very soft, chill ½ hour, or until manageable.)

3. Turn out dough onto a lightly floured surface or pastry cloth. Roll dough to ¼-inch thickness. Cut dough with 1¼- or 1½-inch round biscuit cutter.

4. Place on prepared baking sheet, 1 inch apart. Press a pecan half in top of each biscuit.

5. Bake 10 to 12 minutes, or until firm when pressed gently with fingertips. *Makes about 10 dozen.*

Note: These biscuits freeze well—can be made ahead.

OYSTER PIE

36 saltines
36 oysters, drained
3 tablespoons butter or margarine
Pepper
2 cups milk

1. Break 12 crackers into fourths; layer in bottom of an 8¼-inch round glass baking dish.

2. Arrange half of the oysters on top. Dot with 1 tablespoon butter; sprinkle lightly with pepper.

3. Repeat layering with 12 more crackers (broken into fourths), remaining oysters, 1 tablespoon butter and a light sprinkling of pepper.

4. Arrange rest of crackers (broken into fourths) over oysters. Dot with remaining butter. Pour milk over all. Refrigerate one hour.

5. Preheat oven to 400F.

6. Bake 15 to 20 minutes, or until golden-brown but not dry. *Makes 6 to 8 servings.*

ANNA'S ROAST LOIN OF PORK
(pictured)

5-lb loin of pork (see Note)
Salt
Pepper
3 quarts boiling water
1 cup white vinegar
3 to 4 tablespoons currant jelly, melted, or apricot or guava jam
Brown Gravy, recipe follows
Watercress
Cranberries on a String, recipe follows

1. Wipe pork with damp paper towels. Sprinkle all over with ½ teaspoon salt and ⅛ teaspoon pepper.

2. Pour boiling water and vinegar into an oval Dutch oven (about 8-quart size). (Or use a heavy kettle, large enough for roast and liquid to almost cover, with a tight-fitting lid.) Place pork, fat side down, in liquid. Bring to boiling; reduce heat, and simmer, covered, very gently (liquid should barely bubble) 2 hours.

3. Preheat oven to 375F.

4. Remove pork to shallow baking pan; stand upright, resting on bones. Sprinkle surface with ½ teaspoon salt and ⅛ teaspoon pepper.

5. Bake 20 minutes, basting every 5 minutes with vinegar mixture. Brush surface with melted jelly. Bake 10 minutes longer, until shiny and glazed.

6. Meanwhile, make Brown Gravy.

7. Remove roast to heated platter. Garnish with watercress and Cranberries on a String. Serve with gravy. *Makes 6 to 8 servings.*

Note: Have butcher crack bones for easier carving.

BROWN GRAVY

2 tablespoons all-purpose flour
¼ cup (½ stick) butter or margarine, melted
1 can (10½ oz) condensed beef broth, undiluted

1. In medium saucepan, stir flour into hot butter until smooth. Cook, stirring, over low heat, to brown flour slightly. Remove from heat.

2. Gradually stir in broth. Bring to boiling, stirring; reduce heat; simmer 1 or 2 minutes, until slightly thickened. *Makes about 1½ cups.*

CRANBERRIES ON A STRING

Thread washed cranberries on a string, using a large darning needle and heavy-duty thread.

JELLIED CRANBERRY RELISH
(pictured)

4 cups (1 lb) fresh cranberries
1 cup sugar
1 env unflavored gelatine
½ cup apple juice
¼ cup finely chopped celery
¼ cup chopped pared apple
¼ cup chopped pecans or walnuts

1. Wash cranberries; drain and remove stems; chop coarsely. Add sugar; let cranberry mixture stand 15 minutes, stirring occasionally.

2. Sprinkle gelatine over apple juice in small saucepan, to soften for 5 minutes. Place over low heat, stirring until gelatine is dissolved.

3. Add gelatine mixture, celery, apple and nuts to cranberries; mix well. Turn into 3½-cup mold. Refrigerate until firm— 6 to 8 hours or overnight.

4. To unmold: Run a small spatula around edge of mold. Invert on a serving plate; place a hot, damp dishcloth on bottom of mold; shake to release. Repeat procedure, if necessary. *Makes 8 servings.*

SOUFFLEED YAMS IN ORANGE SHELLS
(pictured)

6 large yams or sweet potatoes (about 4 lb), or 1 can (40 oz) yams in syrup, drained
Boiling water
1 teaspoon salt
5 large navel oranges
¾ cup sugar
½ cup (1 stick) butter or margarine
1 tablespoon vanilla extract
½ cup raisins
Marshmallows (optional)

1. Wash yams. Place in large saucepan; cover with boiling water; add salt.

2. Bring to boiling; reduce heat, and simmer, covered, 35 to 40 minutes, or until tender.

3. Drain yams; let cool. Peel and slice. (If using canned yams, omit Steps 1 and 2.)

4. Cut oranges in half, and squeeze juice; save juice. Reserve shells for serving.

5. Preheat oven to 350F.

6. In large bowl, combine yams, sugar, butter and vanilla. Mash with potato masher, or beat with portable electric mixer, until smooth.

7. Add enough orange juice (about ½ cup) to make a light mixture (not runny); stir in raisins.

8. Mound high in reserved orange shells (¾ cup per serving). Swirl tops with fork. Place in baking pan.

9. Bake 30 minutes, or until hot. (If desired, place marshmallows on top, and place under broiler, 6 inches from heat, just until marshmallows are lightly browned.) *Makes 10 servings.*

BUTTER ROLLS
(pictured)

1 cup boiling water
½ cup shortening
¼ cup warm water (105 to 115F)
1 pkg active dry yeast
4½ cups sifted self-rising all-purpose flour
½ cup sugar
1 egg
6 tablespoons (¾ stick) butter or margarine, melted

1. In small bowl, pour boiling water over shortening; stir until shortening is melted; cool to lukewarm.

2. If possible, check temperature of warm water with thermometer. Sprinkle yeast over water in large bowl, stirring until dissolved.

3. Into large mixing bowl, sift together flour and sugar. Stir in cooled shortening, yeast and egg; beat vigorously with wooden spoon until well blended. Knead in bowl until dough is smooth.

4. Cover with towel; let rise in warm place (85F), free from drafts, until double in bulk—about 1 hour.

5. Punch down dough, and refrigerate several hours.

6. To shape: On sheet of waxed paper or very lightly floured pastry cloth, roll half the dough ¼ inch thick.

7. Cut with a 2-inch biscuit or cookie cutter. Dip in melted butter; fold over so that larger part overlaps. Repeat with remaining half of dough.

8. Place, 1 inch apart, on lightly greased cookie sheet. Cover with towel; let rise in warm place (85F), free from drafts, until double in bulk—1½ to 2 hours. Meanwhile, preheat oven to 400F.

9. Bake 15 to 20 minutes, until golden-brown. Serve hot. *Makes about 7 dozen.*

JAPANESE FRUITCAKE
(pictured)

Lemon-Coconut Filling, recipe follows

WHITE LAYER
4 egg whites (½ cup)
1½ cups sifted all-purpose flour
1½ teaspoons baking powder
1 cup sugar
½ cup (1 stick) butter or margarine, softened
1 teaspoon vanilla extract
½ cup milk

SPICE LAYER
1¼ cups sifted all-purpose flour
1¼ teaspoons baking powder
1 teaspoon ground cinnamon
1 teaspoon ground cloves
1 teaspoon ground nutmeg
½ cup citron, finely chopped
½ cup pecans, finely chopped
½ cup (1 stick) butter or margarine, softened
1 cup sugar
4 egg yolks
½ cup milk

Seven-Minute Icing, recipe follows
¾ cup freshly grated coconut or canned flaked coconut

1. Make Lemon-Coconut Filling; refrigerate several hours.

2. Meanwhile, make layers. For White Layer: In small bowl of electric mixer, let egg whites warm to room temperature—about 1 hour.

3. Preheat oven to 350F. Grease well bottoms and sides of two (9-by-1½-inch) round cake pans. Line bottoms with waxed paper. (Trace bottom of pans on paper, and cut two rounds.) Sift 1½ cups flour with 1½ teaspoons baking powder.

4. At high speed, beat whites until foamy. Gradually beat in ½ cup sugar, beating well after each addition. Beat until soft peaks form when beaters are slowly raised; set aside.

5. In large bowl of electric mixer (don't wash beaters), at high speed, cream ½ cup butter with ½ cup sugar and the vanilla until light and fluffy.

6. At low speed, beat in flour mixture (in fourths) alternately with ½ cup milk (in thirds), beginning and ending with flour mixture.

7. Using wire whisk or rubber spatula, gently fold egg whites into batter, using an under-and-over motion, just until combined.

8. Pour batter into one prepared pan; bake 30 to 35 minutes, or until surface springs back when gently pressed with fingertip.

9. Cool in pan 10 minutes. Remove; cool completely on wire rack.

10. Make Spice Layer: Preheat oven to 350F. Sift 1 cup flour with baking powder, cinnamon, cloves and nutmeg. Toss remaining flour with citron and pecans.

11. In large bowl of electric mixer, at medium speed, beat butter, sugar and egg yolks until smooth and fluffy—about 2 minutes.

12. At low speed, beat in flour mixture (in fourths) alternately with milk (in thirds), beginning and ending with flour mixture. Stir in citron-nut mixture; stir until well blended.

13. Pour batter into remaining prepared pan. Bake 30 to 35 minutes, or until surface springs back when gently pressed with fingertip.

14. Cool in pan 10 minutes. Remove; cool completely on wire rack.

15. Place Spice Layer, bottom side up, on cake plate. Spread with Lemon-Coconut Filling. Place White Layer, right side up, on first layer.

16. Make Seven-Minute Icing. To frost: With spatula, frost side first; use rest of icing on top, swirling decoratively. Sprinkle coconut on top. *Makes 12 to 14 servings.*

LEMON-COCONUT FILLING

2 tablespoons cornstarch
1 tablespoon all-purpose flour
½ cup sugar
⅔ cup water
1 egg yolk, slightly beaten
3 tablespoons lemon juice
1 teaspoon grated lemon peel
1 tablespoon butter
1 cup grated fresh coconut or canned flaked coconut

1. In small saucepan, combine cornstarch, flour and sugar, mixing well. Gradually add water, stirring until smooth.

2. Over medium heat, bring to boiling, stirring occasionally; boil 1 minute.

3. Remove from heat. Quickly stir some of hot mixture into egg yolk. Return to hot mixture; stir to blend.

4. Return to heat; Cook over low heat 5 minutes; stirring occasionally. Mixture will be stiff.

5. Remove from heat. Stir in lemon juice, lemon peel, butter and coconut.

6. Turn into a small bowl. Refrigerate, with waxed paper placed directly on surface of filling, until chilled and stiff—about 2 hours, or until ready to assemble cake.

continued on page 309

Winter Wonderland

Here is a fantasy bakeshop in the very best holiday tradition: Even the bricks, top left, are Lebkuchen. As in every good bakery, there's something for everyone. Cake lovers will be delighted with the fabulous selection: A rich, dark fruitcake, below the Lebkuchen; then clockwise from below the bakery sign, Austrian Butter Cake; cream-and-chocolate-covered Black Forest Cake; Linzer Torte; a sinfully delectable Chocolate Roll; and a splendid Hazelnut Torte, at center. For breakfast, there are three kinds of coffeecake—almond twist, right; streusel, lower center; and apricot, far left—all baked from the same coffeecake dough. Since it wouldn't be Christmas without cookies, our selection ranges from Gingerbread Boys and Girls to a treasure chest of Tyrolean Honey Cookies. And there's also a tray of other seasonal sweets: from bottom, buttery Spritz Wreaths, chocolate-frosted Toffee Bars, Chocolate-Dipped Rings, Hazelnut Balls, Viennese Cookies, Springerle dusted with sugar and Chocolate Pretzels. These scrumptious bakeshop recipes begin on page 294.

continued from page 292

1. *Lebkuchen Tiles.* 2. *Fruitcake.* 3. *Austrian Butter Cake.* 4. *Black Forest Cherry Cake.* 5. *Linzer Torte.* 6. *Chocolate Roll.* 7. *Hazelnut Torte.* 8. *Almond-Twist Coffeecake.* 9. *Streusel-Filled Coffeecake.* 10. *Apricot-Filled Coffeecake.* 11. *Gingerbread Boys and Girls.* 12. *Tyrolean Honey Cookies.* 13. *Spritz Wreaths.* 14. *Toffee Bars.* 15. *Chocolate-Dipped Rings.* 16. *Hazelnut Balls.* 17. *Viennese Cookies.* 18. *Springerle.* 19. *Chocolate Pretzels.*

LEBKUCHEN TILES

3 cups all-purpose flour
½ teaspoon baking soda
½ teaspoon salt
1 teaspoon ground cinnamon
½ teaspoon ground nutmeg
½ teaspoon ground ginger
½ teaspoon ground cloves
1 jar (8 oz) chopped candied orange peel
1 jar (8 oz) chopped candied lemon peel
½ cup ground unblanched almonds
2 tablespoons fresh lemon peel, grated
½ cup light molasses
1 cup light-brown sugar, firmly packed
2 whole eggs
Candied red cherries
Blanched almonds, halved
1 egg yolk, beaten with ½ teaspoon water
Decorating Icing, recipe page 298
Marzipan Hearts, recipe follows
1 egg white, lightly beaten

1. On sheet of waxed paper, sift flour with baking soda, salt and spices.

2. Toss candied peels with almonds and grated fresh lemon peel, to mix well.

3. In small saucepan, warm molasses; remove from heat.

4. In large bowl of electric mixer, at high speed, beat brown sugar and whole eggs until smooth and fluffy. Add molasses; beat well. Add 1 cup flour mixture; beat at low speed just until smooth.

4. In large bowl of electric mixer, at high speed, beat brown sugar and eggs until smooth and fluffy. Add molasses; beat well. Add 1 cup flour mixture; beat at low speed just until smooth.

5. Using a wooden spoon, stir in rest of flour mixture until well combined. Then stir in peel-and-nut mixture.

6. Refrigerate dough, covered, overnight.

7. Next day, preheat oven to 375F. Lightly grease several cookie sheets.

8. On lightly floured pastry cloth, roll out dough, one-half at a time, ¼ inch thick. (Refrigerate remaining half until ready to roll out.)

9. Using floured, sharp knife, cut out cookies, 3½ inches square. Place, 2 inches apart, on prepared cookie sheets. Decorate half of cookies with candied cherries and blanched almonds, as pictured. Brush surface of all cookies with beaten egg. Bake 10 to 12 minutes. Remove cookies to wire rack. Let cool completely.

10. Decorate candied-cherry cookies with a line of Decorating Icing, as pictured; decorate rest of cookies, as pictured, with Decorating Icing and Marzipan Hearts.

11. To store: Store in a glass jar or crock or cookie tin, tightly covered, in a cool, dry place for several weeks. Store cookies with a piece of apple, to make them more moist. *Makes about 2 dozen.*

Note: Lebkuchen tiles were designed by Albert W. Hadener, Elk Candy Co., New York City.

MARZIPAN HEARTS

Knead together 4 ounces almond paste and 1 drop red food color until smooth and pink. Roll out between two sheets of waxed paper to ⅛ inch. With 2-inch heart-shape cutter, cut out 12 hearts. Attach to cookies with beaten egg white.

BEST-OF-ALL FRUITCAKE

1 lb golden raisins
½ lb seedless raisins
¼ lb currants
½ cup dark rum or brandy
1 lb candied pineapple
½ lb candied red cherries
¼ lb candied citron
⅛ lb candied lemon peel
⅛ lb candied orange peel
2 cups all-purpose flour
½ teaspoon ground mace
½ teaspoon ground cinnamon
½ teaspoon baking soda
¼ lb almonds, shelled, blanched and coarsely chopped
¼ lb walnuts or pecans, shelled and coarsely chopped
½ cup (1 stick) butter or margarine, softened
1 cup granulated sugar
1 cup brown sugar, firmly packed
5 eggs, slightly beaten
1 tablespoon milk
1 teaspoon almond extract
Rum or brandy
1 can (8 oz) almond paste
Frosting Glaze, recipe follows

1. Day before: In large bowl, combine raisins and currants. Add ½ cup rum; toss to combine. Let stand, covered, overnight.

2. Next day, line a 10-inch tube pan: On heavy brown paper, draw an 18-inch circle and cut out. Set pan in center of circle; draw around base of pan and tube. With pencil lines outside, fold paper into eighths; snip off tip. Unfold circle; cut along folds to second circle. Grease well both the tube pan and unpenciled side of paper. Fit paper, greased side up, into pan.

3. Prepare fruits: With sharp knife, cut pineapple in thin wedges; cut cherries in half; cut citron and lemon and orange peels into very thin strips. Add to raisins and currants; mix well.

4. On sheet of waxed paper, sift 1½ cups flour with spices and baking soda. Preheat oven to 275F.

5. Combine remaining ½ cup flour with nuts and fruits; toss lightly.

6. In large bowl of electric mixer, at medium speed, beat butter until light. Gradually beat in granulated sugar, then brown sugar, beating until very light and fluffy.

7. Beat in eggs, milk and almond extract until thoroughly combined.

8. At low speed, beat in flour mixture, mixing just until combined. Turn batter into fruits and nuts. Mix well with hands.

9. Turn into prepared pan, pressing batter down in pan evenly all around.

10. Bake 3 hours and 15 minutes, or until a cake tester inserted near center comes out dry.

11. Let cake stand in pan on wire rack 30 minutes to cool slightly. Turn out of pan, and gently remove brown paper. Let fruitcake cool completely.

12. To store: Wrap cake in cheesecloth soaked in rum or brandy. Place in a cake tin with a tight-fitting cover. Add a few pieces of raw, unpeeled apple. (As cheesecloth dries out, resoak in rum or brandy.) Store in a cool place several weeks.

13. To decorate cake for serving: Roll almond paste between two sheets of waxed paper into an 8-inch circle. Remove top sheet of paper. Invert paste onto cake; remove paper. With sharp knife, trim edge of paste; then press paste to cake. Spread paste with Frosting Glaze, letting it run down side. *Makes a 5-pound fruitcake.*

FROSTING GLAZE

Combine 1½ cups confectioners' sugar, 2 tablespoons light cream or half-and-half and ¼ teaspoon almond extract; beat until smooth.

AUSTRIAN BUTTER CAKE

1 cup egg whites (8 eggs)
¼ cup packaged dry, unflavored bread crumbs
3 cups sifted all-purpose flour
1 teaspoon baking powder
Salt
2 cups granulated sugar
2 cups (4 sticks) butter or margarine, softened
2 tablespoons grated lemon peel
1 teaspoon vanilla extract
8 egg yolks
2 tablespoons lemon juice
1 tablespoon water
Confectioners' sugar

1. In large bowl of electric mixer, let egg whites warm to room temperature— about 1 hour.

2. Meanwhile, preheat oven to 350F. Grease well and sprinkle with bread crumbs a 10-inch tube pan or bundt pan.

3. Sift flour with baking powder and ½ teaspoon salt.

4. With electric mixer, at high speed, beat egg whites with ¼ teaspoon salt until foamy. Gradually beat in 1 cup granulated sugar, ¼ cup at a time, beating after each addition. Continue beating until soft peaks form when beaters are slowly raised. Gently transfer egg whites to medium bowl.

5. In same bowl of electric mixer, at high speed, beat butter, remaining granulated sugar, the lemon peel and vanilla until light and fluffy—about 5 minutes. Beat in egg yolks until light and fluffy. Add lemon juice and water; beat until smooth.

6. At low speed, beat in flour mixture, one-third at a time, just until smooth and well combined.

7. At low speed, gradually beat in egg whites just until blended, scraping side of bowl and guiding batter into beaters with rubber spatula.

8. Turn batter into prepared pan: bake 60 minutes, or until cake tester inserted in center comes out clean.

9. Cool in pan on wire rack 15 minutes. Remove from pan; cool thoroughly on wire rack.

10. Serve plain, or sprinkle with confectioners' sugar, as pictured. To serve, cut into thin slices. *Makes 12 to 16 servings.*

BLACK FOREST CHERRY CAKE

6 eggs, at room temperature
1 cup granulated sugar
1 teaspoon vanilla extract
½ cup sifted all-purpose flour
½ cup unsweetened cocoa
⅔ cup (1⅓ sticks) sweet butter or margarine, melted

SYRUP
⅓ cup granulated sugar
½ cup water
3 tablespoons kirsch or Cointreau

Glazed Cherries, recipe follows

FILLING
3 cups heavy cream
½ cup confectioners' sugar

1 (8 oz) milk-chocolate bar
Maraschino cherries with stems, well drained, or whole candied cherries

1. Preheat oven to 350F. Grease well and flour three (8-by-1½-inch) layer cake pans.

2. In large bowl of electric mixer, at high speed, beat eggs until light and fluffy. Beat in 1 cup granulated sugar gradually;

continue beating until very thick—about 10 minutes. Add vanilla.

3. Sift flour with cocoa. Then fold into egg mixture in fourths, using a wire whisk or rubber spatula. Also fold in butter, in fourths, just until combined. Turn into prepared pans. Bake 15 minutes, or until surface springs back when gently pressed with finger.

4. Let layers cool in pans on wire rack 5 minutes. Then loosen edges with metal spatula; turn out on wire rack to cool completely.

5. Meanwhile, make Syrup: In small saucepan, combine ⅓ cup granulated sugar with ½ cup water. Stir over medium heat, to dissolve sugar. Then bring to boiling; boil, uncovered, 5 minutes. Set aside to cool; add kirsch.

6. Also, make Glazed Cherries.

7. To assemble: Place layers on cookie sheets. Make several holes with toothpicks; spoon syrup over cake layers.

8. Make Filling: Beat cream with confectioners' sugar until stiff. Invert one cake layer on cake plate for bottom. Spread Glazed Cherries over bottom layer. Then spread with 1 cup whipped cream.

9. Place second layer on top; spread with 1 cup whipped cream. Place third layer on top. Spread top and side with remaining whipped cream, making 12 whipped-cream rosettes around top edge, as pictured. You may use a spoon or put some of whipped cream through a pastry tube with a number-5 tip. Refrigerate.

10. Make Chocolate Curls: Let chocolate bar soften slightly. Using vegetable parer, scrape across chocolate to make curls; refrigerate.

11. To serve: Place chocolate curls around side of cake, covering completely. Place cherry on each rosette. *Makes 12 servings.*

GLAZED CHERRIES

1 cup canned pitted Bing cherries, drained
2 tablespoons kirsch or Cointreau
1 tablespoon cornstarch
⅔ cup cherry juice

1. In small bowl, combine cherries and kirsch; let stand about 1 hour.

2. Meanwhile, in small saucepan, combine cornstarch and ⅓ cup cherry juice; stir to dissolve cornstarch. Stir in remaining juice.

3. Bring to boiling, stirring; reduce heat and simmer 5 minutes, or until thickened and translucent. Let cool completely.

4. Add cherries in kirsch to cooled cornstarch mixture; mix well. Use to fill Black Forest Cherry Cake.

continued on page 296

continued from page 295

LINZER TORTE

1½ cups sifted all-purpose flour
½ teaspoon ground cinnamon
Dash ground cloves
½ cup granulated sugar
1 cup ground unblanched almonds
2 hard-cooked egg yolks, sieved
2 teaspoons grated lemon peel
1 cup unsalted butter, softened
2 uncooked egg yolks
1½ cups raspberry jam
1 egg yolk, slightly beaten
1 tablespoon cream
Confectioners' sugar

1. Into large bowl of electric mixer, sift flour with cinnamon and cloves. Add granulated sugar, almonds, sieved yolks and lemon peel; mix well.

2. At medium speed, beat in butter and 2 egg yolks; beat until smooth. Form dough into ball; refrigerate several hours, or until it can be rolled out.

3. Lightly grease a 9-inch springform pan. Press about three-fourths of dough evenly on bottom and side of pan. Spread jam over bottom to make an even layer.

4. On a lightly floured surface or pastry cloth, with a stockinette-covered rolling pin, roll remaining dough to form a rectangle 9 by 6 inches.

5. Cut 6 strips, 1 inch wide and 9 inches long. Lay 3 strips across the pan, spacing evenly. Lay remaining 3 strips diagonally across first strips, spacing evenly to form diamonds.

6. With fingers, press edge of pastry all around to form a rim.

7. Combine beaten egg yolk with cream; mix with fork. Use to brush lightly over lattice and rim of torte. Refrigerate about 1 hour, or until ready to bake.

8. Preheat oven to 350F. Bake torte 45 to 50 minutes, or until lightly browned. Let cool slightly on wire rack. Then remove outer edge of pan. Let cool completely before serving. Sprinkle with confectioners' sugar. Set torte, still on bottom of pan, onto a serving plate. *Makes 8 servings.*

CHOCOLATE ROLL

6 egg whites
¾ cup granulated sugar
6 egg yolks
⅓ cup unsweetened cocoa
1½ teaspoons vanilla extract
Dash salt

Confectioners' sugar

FILLING

2 cups heavy cream, chilled
⅓ cup confectioners' sugar
1 teaspoon vanilla extract

1 bar (8 oz) milk chocolate

1. In large bowl of electric mixer, let egg whites warm to room temperature—1 hour. Grease bottom of a 15½-by-10½-by-1-inch jelly-roll pan; line with waxed paper; grease lightly.

2. Preheat oven to 375F.

3. At high speed, beat egg whites just until soft peaks form when beaters are slowly raised.

4. Add ¼ cup granulated sugar, 2 tablespoons at a time, beating until stiff peaks form when beaters are slowly raised. With same beaters, beat yolks at high speed, adding remaining ½ cup granulated sugar, 2 tablespoons at a time. Beat until mixture is very thick—about 4 minutes.

5. At low speed, beat in cocoa, 1½ teaspoons vanilla and the salt just until smooth. With wire whisk or rubber spatula, using an under-and-over motion, gently fold cocoa mixture into beaten egg whites just until blended.

6. Spread evenly in pan. Bake 15 minutes, or until surface springs back when gently pressed with fingertip. Sift confectioners' sugar in 15-by-10-inch rectangle onto a clean tea towel. Turn cake out on sugar; lift off pan; peel paper off cake.

7. Roll up, jelly-roll fashion, starting with short side, towel and all. Cool completely on rack, seam side down—at least ½ hour.

8. Meanwhile, make Filling: Combine heavy cream and ⅓ cup confectioners' sugar in medium bowl. Beat with electric mixer until thick; add vanilla; mix well. Refrigerate.

9. Unroll cake; spread with three-fourths of the filling, 1 inch from edge. Reroll. Place, seam side down, on serving plate. Spread remaining filling evenly over the top. Refrigerate for 1 hour before serving.

10. Make Chocolate Curls: Place chocolate bar, still wrapped, in a warm spot just until soft, not melting. With a vegetable peeler, pressing lightly, pare along bar in a long, thin stroke to form a curl. Make enough to cover top and sides of roll; refrigerate.

11. To serve: Arrange chocolate curls over entire roll, as pictured. Sprinkle lightly with confectioners' sugar. *Makes 8 to 10 servings.*

HAZELNUT TORTE

TORTE LAYERS

7 eggs
¾ teaspoon salt
1 cup granulated sugar
1 teaspoon vanilla extract
1¼ cups ground hazelnuts
1¼ cups ground pecans
¼ cup packaged dry bread crumbs
1 teaspoon baking powder

FILLING

1 cup heavy cream, chilled
½ cup confectioners' sugar
1 teaspoon vanilla extract

CHOCOLATE FROSTING

4 squares unsweetened chocolate
¼ cup (½ stick) butter or margarine
3 cups sifted confectioners' sugar
½ cup hot water
1 teaspoon vanilla extract

1 cup raspberry preserves
½ cup whole hazelnuts

COFFEE FROSTING

2 teaspoons instant coffee
2 tablespoons hot water
¼ cup (½ stick) butter or margarine, softened
1¾ cups sifted confectioners' sugar

1. Separate eggs, putting whites into large bowl of electric mixer, yolks in smaller one. Let whites warm to room temperature—about 1 hour.

2. Preheat oven to 375F. Line bottom of three (8-inch) round layer cake pans with circles of waxed paper.

3. With mixer at high speed, beat whites with ¼ teaspoon salt until soft peaks form when beaters are slowly raised. Gradually beat in ½ cup granulated sugar, 2 tablespoons at a time, beating until stiff peaks form.

4. With same beaters, beat yolks until thick and light. Gradually beat in rest of granulated sugar, beating until thick—3 minutes; beat in 1 teaspoon vanilla.

5. Combine ground nuts, crumbs, baking powder and ½ teaspoon salt; turn into yolk mixture; mix well. With an under-and-over motion, fold into the egg whites just to combine.

6. Pour into prepared pans, dividing evenly; smooth surfaces. Bake 25 minutes, or until surface springs back when gently pressed with fingertip. To cool, hang each pan upside down between two other pans—1 hour.

7. Make Filling: In medium bowl, combine cream, ½ cup confectioners' sugar and 1 teaspoon vanilla. Beat until stiff; refrigerate.

8. Make Chocolate Frosting: In top of double boiler, over hot water, melt chocolate and ¼ cup butter. Remove from water; add 3 cups confectioners' sugar, the hot water and vanilla; mix until smooth. Set

in larger bowl of ice cubes to chill. Stir until thickened.

9. Loosen sides of layers from pans with spatula. Turn out of pans; peel off paper. On plate, assemble layers, spreading bottom and middle layers first with half of raspberry preserves, then with half of filling. Add top layer.

10. Frost torte with Chocolate Frosting; refrigerate 1 hour.

11. Slice hazelnuts, reserving 6 whole ones for top. Make Coffee Frosting: In medium bowl, dissolve coffee in hot water. Add butter and confectioners' sugar; mix until smooth.

12. Place Coffee Frosting in pastry bag with number-4 star tip. Decorate as pictured, making ruching around bottom of cake and three even triangles on top, as pictured. Arrange sliced hazelnuts inside the three triangles. Place whole hazelnuts in center.

13. For easier cutting, refrigerate 2 hours before serving. *Makes 12 servings.*

ALMOND-TWIST COFFEECAKE

FILLING
¼ cup (½ stick) butter or margarine
1 cup blanched almonds, ground
7 zwieback, ground
¼ cup light-brown sugar, firmly packed
1 egg white, slightly beaten
½ teaspoon almond extract

TWIST
1 recipe Basic Coffeecake Dough, ready for
   shaping; recipe follows
2 tablespoons butter or margarine, melted
1 egg white
1 tablespoon water
¼ cup sliced blanched almonds

1. Make Filling: Melt ¼ cup butter in small skillet. Add ground almonds and zwieback; sauté until butter is absorbed and mixture is golden-brown (be careful not to scorch).

2. Turn into bowl. Add brown sugar, egg white and almond extract, mixing well.

3. Make Twist: Roll dough into a 20-by-12-inch rectangle. Brush with 1 tablespoon melted butter. Cut lengthwise into two strips.

4. Spread half of each strip crosswise with some of almond filling; fold over other half. (You now have two rectangles, each approximately 10 by 6 inches.)

5. Spread top of rectangles with more filling, reserving 3 tablespoons filling for later use. Press down lightly, so filling will adhere.

6. Starting with a corner, roll each rectangle diagonally toward opposite corner. Pat reserved filling evenly over surface of one roll. Place rolls parallel. Overlap at one end; pinch together. Twist rolls together, to form a rope.

7. Brush top with remaining melted butter. Place on greased cookie sheet. Cover with towel; let rise in warm place (85F), free from drafts, until double in bulk—about 1 hour.

8. Meanwhile, preheat oven to 350F. In small bowl, beat egg white with water. Use to brush surface. Sprinkle with sliced almonds.

9. Bake 35 minutes, or until golden-brown. Cool on wire rack. *Makes 1 twist.*

STREUSEL-FILLED COFFEECAKE

FILLING
4 teaspoons butter or margarine, softened
⅓ cup light-brown sugar, firmly packed
1 egg yolk
4 teaspoons milk
2 drops vanilla extract
½ teaspoon grated lemon peel
1 cup ground pecans

1 recipe Basic Coffeecake Dough, ready for
   shaping; recipe follows
2 tablespoons butter or margarine, melted

TOPPING
1 tablespoon granulated sugar
Dash ground cinnamon
2 tablespoons chopped pecans

Confectioners' sugar

1. Make Filling: In small bowl, with wooden spoon, mix 4 teaspoons butter, the brown sugar and egg yolk. Stir in milk, vanilla and lemon peel; blend in ground pecans.

2. Make loaf: Lightly grease a 9-by-5-by-3-inch loaf pan.

3. Roll dough into a 12-by-9-inch rectangle. Brush with 1 tablespoon melted butter. Spread with pecan filling.

4. Cut crosswise into 3 strips, 4 inches wide. Roll each, from long side.

5. Place rolls, seam side down, side by side in prepared loaf pan. Brush with remaining melted butter. Cover with towel; let rise in warm place (85F), free from drafts, until double in bulk—about 1 hour.

6. Meanwhile, preheat oven to 350F.

7. For Topping, sprinkle loaf with mixed granulated sugar and cinnamon. Cover the loaf with chopped pecans.

8. Bake loaf 35 minutes, or until it is golden-brown and sounds hollow when rapped with knuckle. Remove from pan at once; let cool slightly on wire rack. Then sprinkle with confectioners' sugar. Serve warm. *Makes 1 loaf.*

APRICOT-FILLED COFFEECAKE

FILLING
1 cup dried apricots, cut up
1 cup granulated sugar
1 cup water
¼ cup light-brown sugar, firmly packed
Dash ground cinnamon
Dash ground nutmeg

COFFEECAKE
1 recipe Basic Coffeecake Dough, ready for
   shaping; recipe follows
2 tablespoons butter or margarine, melted
½ cup chopped pecans

ICING
½ cup confectioners's sugar
2 teaspoons milk
⅛ teaspoon vanilla extract

1 tablespoon warm water
¼ cup pecan halves

1. Make Filling: Bring apricots, granulated sugar and water to boiling; then simmer, covered, until tender—10 minutes. Drain; reserve ½ cup liquid.

2. Press apricots and reserved liquid through sieve, or purée in electric blender. Add brown sugar, cinnamon and nutmeg; let cool completely.

3. Make Coffeecake: Butter an 8-inch springform pan.

4. Roll dough into a 28-by-8-inch strip. Brush with 1 tablespoon butter.

5. Reserve ⅓ cup apricot filling for later use, and spread remainder over entire surface of dough. Sprinkle with chopped pecans.

6. Roll dough from long side, forming a long rope; pinch edge of rope to seal well.

7. With sealed edge down, spiral the rope into springform pan, beginning in center of pan. Brush top with remaining butter. Cover with towel; let rise in warm place (85F), free from drafts, until double in bulk—1 hour.

8. Preheat oven to 350F.

9. Bake coffeecake 35 to 40 minutes, or until browned. Remove from pan at once; cool on wire rack.

10. Make Icing: Combine confectioners' sugar, milk and vanilla.

11. Blend reserved apricot filling with 1 tablespoon warm water. Spoon along spiral crease on coffeecake. Top with icing and pecans. *Makes 1 coffeecake.*

continued on page 298

continued from page 297

BASIC COFFEECAKE DOUGH

¼ cup milk
¼ cup sugar
½ teaspoon salt
¼ cup (½ stick) butter or margarine
¼ cup warm water (105 to 115F)
1 pkg active dry yeast
1 egg
2½ cups sifted all-purpose flour

1. In small saucepan, heat milk just until bubbles form around edge of pan; remove from heat. Add sugar, salt and butter, stirring until butter is melted. Let cool to lukewarm (a drop sprinkled on wrist will not feel warm).

2. If possible, check temperature of warm water with thermometer. Sprinkle yeast over water in large bowl, stirring until dissolved. Stir in lukewarm milk mixture.

3. Add egg and 1½ cups flour; beat with wooden spoon until smooth. Add rest of flour; beat until dough is smooth and leaves side of bowl.

4. Turn out dough onto lightly floured pastry cloth. Knead until dough is satiny and elastic and blisters appear on surface.

5. Place in lightly greased large bowl; turn to bring greased side up. Cover with towel; let rise in warm place (85F), free from drafts, until double in bulk—1 to 1½ hours.

6. Punch down dough with fist. Turn out onto lightly floured pastry cloth; knead 10 to 15 times.

7. Shape and fill, as directed for Almond-Twist Coffeecake, Apricot-Filled Coffeecake or Streusel-Filled Coffeecake (recipes above).

GINGERBREAD BOYS AND GIRLS

COOKIE DOUGH
4 cups sifted all-purpose flour
¾ teaspoon baking soda
½ teaspoon salt
1 teaspoon ground ginger
1 teaspoon ground nutmeg
1½ teaspoons ground cinnamon
½ teaspoon ground cloves
½ cup light-brown sugar, firmly packed
½ cup (1 stick) butter or margarine, softened
1 cup dark molasses

DECORATING ICING
⅓ cup egg whites (4 eggs)
3¾ to 4 cups sifted confectioners' sugar
Assorted gumdrops
Assorted food colors

1. Day before, make Cookie Dough: Sift flour with soda, salt and spices.

2. In large bowl, with portable electric mixer at medium speed, beat brown sugar, butter and molasses until well combined.

3. With wooden spoon, stir in flour mixture; then mix with hands until well combined. Form dough into a ball. Wrap in waxed paper or plastic wrap; refrigerate overnight.

4. Next day, preheat oven to 375F. Lightly grease cookie sheets.

5. Divide dough into four parts. Refrigerate until ready to roll out.

6. On lightly floured surface, roll out dough, one part at a time, ⅛ inch thick.

7. Using 5-inch gingerbread-man cutter, cut out 3 gingerbread figures from each part of dough. Use assorted small cutters to cut out rest of dough.

8. Place cookies, 1 inch apart, on prepared cookie sheets. Bake 6 to 8 minutes, or until lightly browned. Remove to wire rack; let cool.

9. Meanwhile, make Decorating Icing: In medium bowl, with portable electric mixer at medium speed, beat egg whites with 3¾ cups sugar, to make a smooth, stiff frosting. If frosting seems too thin, beat in a little more sugar. Cover with damp cloth.

10. To decorate cookies: Pipe frosting through number-4 small tip to make facial features. Spread aprons onto figures. Decorate with bits of gumdrops and frosting tinted green, yellow and pink. *Makes 1 dozen gingerbread boys and girls and 7 to 8 dozen smaller cookies.*

TYROLEAN HONEY COOKIES

¼ cup candied orange peel
¼ cup candied lemon peel
1½ cups whole unblanched almonds
¾ cup honey
1¼ cups granulated sugar
1 tablespoon grated fresh lemon peel
¼ cup lemon juice
1½ tablespoons kirsch or brandy
4 cups sifted all-purpose flour
Dash salt
1 teaspoon baking soda
1 teaspoon ground cinnamon
Dash ground cloves
Dash ground nutmeg
2 cups confectioners' sugar
3 tablespoons water
Decorating Icing (see Gingerbread Boys
    and Girls, recipe above)

1. Put candied orange and lemon peels and almonds through fine blade of food grinder. Or grind in blender or food processor until very fine.

2. In medium saucepan, bring honey and granulated sugar just to boiling, stirring (do not boil). Add fresh lemon peel and lemon juice. Set aside to cool—10 minutes. Then add ground candied peel and almonds and the kirsch.

3. Into a large bowl, sift flour with salt, baking soda, cinnamon, cloves and nutmeg. Make well in center of flour mixture; pour in fruit-and-honey mixture. Work together, with a kneading motion, until well combined. Dough will be quite stiff.

4. Preheat oven to 350F.

5. Divide dough into four parts. Refrigerate three parts until ready to use. Between two sheets of waxed paper, on slightly dampened surface, roll out one part to form a rectangle 6 by 8 inches, ¼ inch thick. Cut into squares or crescents or stars or hearts. Place, about 1 inch apart, on ungreased cookie sheets.

6. Bake about 10 minutes, or just until golden.

7. Repeat with rest of dough.

8. In small bowl, combine confectioners' sugar with water; stir to mix well. Brush over cookies while they are still warm. Make glaze thinner, if desired, by adding 1 or 2 more tablespoons water.

9. Store in a tightly covered jar or plastic container, in a cool, dry place, several weeks. To serve, decorate, as pictured, with Decorating Icing, tinted in pastel colors. *Makes about 5 dozen assorted cookies.*

SPRITZ WREATHS

2 cups sifted all-purpose flour
¼ teaspoon salt
¾ cup (1½ sticks) butter or margarine,
    softened
½ cup sugar
1 egg yolk
1 teaspoon vanilla extract, or ½ teaspoon
    almond extract
Cinnamon candies
Angelica

1. Refrigerate ungreased cookie sheets until ready to use.

2. Preheat oven to 375F. Sift flour with salt.

3. In large bowl, with electric mixer at medium speed, beat butter, sugar, egg yolk and vanilla until smooth and fluffy.

4. At low speed, beat in flour mixture until smooth and well combined. Fill cookie press with dough.

5. To make wreaths: Use the star disk. Force dough onto cold cookie sheet in a 15-inch strip; cut strip into three parts. Form each part into a circle. Decorate wreaths with cinnamon candies and bits of angelica.

6. Bake cookies 8 to 10 minutes, or until light golden. Remove to rack; cool. Store in airtight container. *Makes about 3 dozen.*

TOFFEE BARS

COOKIE CRUST
½ cup (1 stick) butter or margarine,
    softened
½ cup light-brown sugar, firmly packed
1 egg yolk
1 teaspoon vanilla extract
½ cup sifted all-purpose flour
½ cup raw quick-cooking oats (not instant)

TOPPING
3 squares semisweet chocolate
1 tablespoon butter or margarine

FROSTING
2 squares semisweet chocolate
2 tablespoons butter or margarine
1½ cups sifted confectioners' sugar
¼ cup hot water

1. Preheat oven to 375F. Lightly grease a 13-by-9-by-2-inch pan. Line bottom with foil.

2. Make Cookie Crust: In large bowl, with wooden spoon or portable electric mixer at medium speed, beat ½ cup butter, the brown sugar, egg yolk and vanilla until smooth.

3. Add flour and oats; stir until well combined.

4. Press mixture evenly in bottom of prepared pan.

5. Bake 15 minutes, or until golden. Cool slightly.

6. Meanwhile, make Topping: Melt 3 squares chocolate and 1 tablespoon butter over hot, not boiling, water.

7. Spread over warm cookie crust.

8. With sharp knife, cut into bars while still warm. Let cool completely in pan before removing.

9. Meanwhile, make Frosting: In top of double boiler, over hot water, melt chocolate and butter. Remove from water; stir in confectioners' sugar and hot water, mixing until smooth. Refrigerate, covered, about 10 minutes. Put frosting into pastry bag with number-27 tip. Decorate as pictured. *Makes 32.*

CHOCOLATE-DIPPED RINGS

Chocolate Pretzels dough, page 325
Chocolate Glaze, see Chocolate Pretzels,
    page 325
Multicolor nonpareils

Make dough for Chocolate Pretzels, as directed. Form dough into 6-inch rolls. Shape into rings on lightly floured pastry cloth. Bake as directed for Chocolate Pretzels. Make half of Chocolate Glaze. Dip warm cookies halfway into glaze, then into multicolor nonpareils. Let glaze set before storing rings in refrigerator. *Makes 4 dozen.*

HAZELNUT BALLS

1 cup sifted all-purpose flour
½ cup (1 stick) butter or margarine,
    softened
1 cup finely chopped hazelnuts or pecans
2 tablespoons granulated sugar
⅛ teaspoon salt
1 teaspoon vanilla extract
Confectioners' sugar

1. In large bowl, combine all ingredients except confectioners' sugar. With hands, mix until thoroughly blended. Refrigerate 30 minutes.

2. Meanwhile, preheat oven to 375F. Using hands, roll dough into balls 1¼ inches in diameter. Place, 1 inch apart, on ungreased cookie sheets.

3. Bake 15 to 20 minutes, or until cookies are set but not brown. Let stand 1 minute before removing from cookie sheets. Remove to wire rack; cool slightly.

4. Roll in confectioners' sugar while still warm; cool completely. Just before serving, reroll in sugar. *Makes about 20.*

continued on page 325

YOUR FAVORITE YULETIDE TREATS

From all over the country come the recipes pictured on these four pages: Sweet delights that have become traditions in many homes. Here, special breads, cakes and cookies. Below, Czechoslovakian Hoska, studded with raisins and almonds. Then, right: deep-fried Honey Bubbles dipped in syrup, Mama's extra-rich Fruitcake, Norwegian Sweet Bread and an Italian Nut Roll shaped like a cane.

More special recipes to share: Below, a sunny lemon mock-cheesecake and a plate of flaky Pizzelles (thin, sweet, wafflelike wafers). At right, a tumble of Anise Cookies: luscious Old-World favorites cut in festive shapes and dusted with sugar for a white Christmas. Recipes for these and other adaptations enjoyed from Connecticut to California begin on page 304.

continued from page 302

CHRISTMAS CAKE (HOSKA)
(Mrs. David Powell, Texas)
(pictured)

1 cup milk
1 pkg active dry yeast
¼ cup warm water (105 to 115F)
4 cups all-purpose flour
½ cup sugar
1 teaspoon salt
½ cup (1 stick) butter, at room temperature
1 egg, slightly beaten
1 tablespoon grated lemon rind
1 teaspoon vanilla extract
¼ cup blanched slivered almonds
½ cup seedless raisins
¼ cup chopped maraschino cherries (optional)

GLAZE
1 egg
1 tablespoon milk

1. In small saucepan, over medium heat, heat milk until small bubbles form around edge of pan. Remove from heat; let cool to lukewarm.

2. In a small bowl, sprinkle yeast over warm water to soften.

3. In a large bowl, combine flour, sugar and salt. With a pastry blender or two knives, cut in butter until mixture resembles coarse cornmeal.

4. Add slightly beaten egg to warm milk; stir in softened yeast, lemon rind and vanilla extract.

5. Add milk mixture to flour mixture. Beat with a wooden spoon until well combined. Turn out onto lightly floured surface; knead until smooth—about 5 minutes.

6. Place dough in a lightly greased bowl; turn to bring greased side up. Cover and let rise in a warm place (85F), free from drafts, until double in bulk—2 to 2½ hours.

7. Lightly grease a large baking sheet.

8. Turn risen dough out onto a lightly floured surface; knead in almonds, raisins and, if desired, well-drained maraschino cherries.

9. Divide dough into nine parts; roll each piece by hand into strips 16 to 17 inches long. (Length of loaf will depend on size of your baking sheet.) Make three layers of twists: the bottom one of four strands (twist two together and place side by side), the middle one of three strands (braid together) and the top layer of two strands (twist together). Transfer the bottom layer of twists to the greased baking sheet, placing on the diagonal if necessary to fit pan. Form the cake, stretching and shaping the layers so they sit firmly on top of each other. Pinch edges together.

10. Let cake rise again until double in bulk. Meanwhile, make Glaze: Beat 1 egg with the tablespoon of milk.

11. Preheat oven to 350F.

12. Brush loaf with glaze to cover top and layers of twists completely.

13. Bake 35 to 40 minutes, until golden-brown. Carefully lift loaf off baking pan and set on a wire rack to cool. *Makes 1 large braid.*

HONEY BUBBLES
(Mrs. Sally Fester, Maryland)
(pictured)

3 cups sifted all-purpose flour
1 tablespoon sugar
½ teaspoon salt
¼ cup (½ stick) butter or margarine, melted
4 eggs
Vegetable oil for deep frying

HONEY SYRUP
¾ cup honey
⅓ cup sugar
⅓ cup water
1 tablespoon lemon juice

Multicolored nonpareils (round shape)

1. Into a large bowl, sift flour, the tablespoon of sugar and salt.

2. Make a well in center of flour mixture; pour in melted butter and drop in the eggs. Stir with a fork to gradually combine flour with the butter and eggs.

3. When dough is stiff enough to handle, turn out onto a floured board; knead until smooth—five minutes. Wrap dough in plastic wrap or foil and refrigerate 1 hour.

4. Divide chilled dough into 10 pieces. Roll each piece into a rope 18 inches long. Cut each rope into 36 (½-inch) pieces.

5. In large heavy saucepan or deep fryer, slowly heat oil (3 inches deep) to 375F on deep-frying thermometer.

6. Drop in enough pieces of dough to cover surface of oil in one layer; stir to separate pieces if necessary. Cook until evenly golden-brown—2 to 5 minutes. Drain on paper towels. Continue cooking until all dough pieces have been fried.

7. Meanwhile make Honey Syrup: In a large saucepan, combine honey, sugar, water and lemon juice. Set over medium heat; bring to a boil, stirring constantly until sugar is dissolved. Continue cooking, uncovered, without stirring, for about 15 minutes until syrup is thick. Remove from heat.

8. Add fried bubbles to syrup; stir until syrup is absorbed and bubbles stick together.

9. Pile onto a serving plate (covered with a paper doily if desired) in a cone or ring shape. Sprinkle with nonpareils.

When syrup is hard and no longer sticky, cover Honey Bubbles loosely with waxed paper. *Makes 12 to 16 servings.*

MAMA'S FRUITCAKE
(Mrs. Louise C. Farrow, North Carolina)
(pictured)

2 containers (8-oz size) diced mixed candied fruit
2 containers (8-oz size) candied pineapple, chopped
1 jar (8 oz) candied red cherries, halved
1 jar (8 oz) candied green cherries, halved
1 box (15 oz) golden raisins
1 cup chopped pecans
1 cup chopped Brazil nuts or walnuts
1 pkg (14 oz) sliced almonds
2 cups sifted all-purpose flour
1½ teaspoons baking powder
1 teaspoon salt
½ cup (1 stick) butter
½ cup (1 stick) margarine
1 cup sugar
5 eggs
½ cup unsweetened pineapple juice
2 cups flaked coconut
1 teaspoon rum flavoring

1. Lightly oil a 10-inch tube pan. Line bottom and side with heavy brown paper; lightly oil paper.

2. In a very large bowl, combine the fruits and nuts; toss until well mixed. Sift ½ cup of the flour over them; toss to coat evenly. Set aside.

3. Sift together the remaining 1½ cups flour, baking powder and salt onto a sheet of waxed paper. Set aside.

4. Preheat oven to 275F.

5. In large bowl of electric mixer, at medium speed, cream butter and margarine. Gradually add sugar, beating until light and fluffy. Add eggs, one at a time, beating well after each addition.

6. With the mixer at low speed, alternately blend in flour mixture (in fourths) and pineapple juice (in thirds), beginning and ending with flour mixture.

7. Pour batter over fruits and nuts; add coconut and rum flavoring. Stir with a wooden spoon just until evenly blended.

8. Turn into prepared pan, packing lightly.

9. Bake, in center of oven, 2½ hours, or until a cake tester inserted near the center comes out clean.

10. Set cake pan on wire rack. Allow cake to cool completely. Remove from pan and peel off paper.

11. Store 2 to 3 weeks in an airtight container lined with waxed paper, to mellow. Put a wedge of fresh apple in the center of the cake to keep it moist; replace apple wedge weekly. *Makes about 5 pounds of cake.*

NORWEGIAN SWEET BREAD

(Mrs. D. Ewert, Wisconsin)
(pictured)

2 cups milk
1 cup granulated sugar
1 cup (2 sticks) butter or margarine
1 teaspoon salt
3 pkg active dry yeast
½ cup warm water
About 8 cups all-purpose flour
2 teaspoons cardamom or vanilla extract
½ cup (3-oz container) candied cherries, coarsely chopped
½ cup (3.5-oz container) candied pineapple, coarsely chopped
1½ cups golden raisins
3 eggs, beaten

ICING
1½ cups sifted confectioners' sugar
1½ tablespoons milk

1. In a 1-quart saucepan, over medium heat, heat milk until small bubbles form around edge of pan; remove from heat. Stir in granulated sugar, butter and salt. Let cool to lukewarm.

2. In large bowl of an electric mixer, sprinkle yeast over warm water; let stand to soften.

3. Add lukewarm milk mixture to yeast. Stir to blend. With mixer at medium speed, gradually add 3 cups of the flour. Continue beating until batter is smooth and well blended—about 5 minutes. Do not underbeat.

4. Cover bowl with a damp cloth; let dough rise in a warm place (85F), free from drafts, until double in bulk—about 1 hour.

5. Meanwhile, mix cardamon with ¼ cup of flour (to use vanilla, see Step 6). In a medium bowl, combine candied fruits and raisins. Sprinkle the flour mixture over them and toss to mix well; set aside.

6. Stir down dough; add beaten eggs (and vanilla, if using). With mixer at medium speed, gradually add four cups of the flour, enough so dough can be handled easily. You may have to beat in the last of the flour with a wooden spoon. (This will not take long if the first addition of flour—Step 3—was beaten adequately.)

7. Turn dough out onto a floured board and knead, using remaining flour as needed to make a smooth, soft, but not sticky, dough. Knead in floured fruits to distribute evenly.

8. Place dough in a large greased bowl; turn dough to bring greased side up. Cover and let rise again—about 1 hour.

9. Grease two 9-by-5-by-3-inch loaf pans.

10. Punch down dough and divide into two equal parts; place in loaf pans. Let rise again until double in bulk—about 45 minutes.

11. Preheat oven to 400F.

12. Bake loaves 10 minutes; reduce heat to 325F and bake 50 minutes longer, until nicely browned. (If bread is browning too quickly, lay a sheet of foil or rectangles of brown paper over tops of loaves.)

13. Turn baked loaves out of pans. Set on a wire rack to cool.

14. Meanwhile, make Icing: In a small bowl, combine confectioners' sugar and milk; mix well. With the tip of a spoon, drizzle icing over tops of loaves (see Note). *Makes 2 large loaves.*

Note: This bread has a very firm crust and a light, almost cakelike interior. If desired, you may wrap the loaves in foil overnight to soften crust. Omit icing or ice before serving.

TRADITIONAL ITALIAN NUT ROLL

(Rosalie Gaziano, West Virginia)
(pictured)

1 cup dry white wine
½ cup salad oil
¼ cup shortening
4 cups sifted all-purpose flour
3 eggs
2 tablespoons granulated sugar
1 tablespoon whiskey
1 box (15-oz size) and 1 box (7-oz size) golden raisins
5 cups (1¼ lb) chopped walnuts
Dash ground cinnamon
¼ cup light-brown sugar, firmly packed
1 jar (12 oz) honey
¼ cup honey for glazing

1. In a medium saucepan, over medium heat, bring the wine, salad oil and shortening to a boil; boil ½ minute; remove from heat and set aside to cool.

2. Measure sifted flour into a large bowl.

3. In a small bowl, with a portable electric mixer, beat eggs until light and frothy. Gradually add granulated sugar, beating until mixture is well combined.

4. Add egg mixture to cooled wine mixture. Pour over flour in the large bowl; mix well; beat until dough is smooth. (Dough will be soft.)

5. Divide dough into three balls. Leave them in bowl; cover and refrigerate.

6. Meanwhile, in a medium bowl, mix the whiskey, raisins, nuts, cinnamon, brown sugar and the jar of honey. Stir with a wooden spoon to combine evenly.

7. Preheat oven to 300F; lightly grease 1 or 2 baking sheets.

8. Remove one ball of dough from refrigerator. On a lightly floured pastry cloth, roll the dough into a rectangle 16 by 12 inches; it will be about ½ inch thick. Spread one-third of the raisin-nut mixture on dough. From the wide end, roll up rectangle tightly. Transfer to a prepared baking sheet; pinch ends of roll closed. Shape into a wreath or a candy cane.

9. Continue to fill, roll and shape remaining dough. Bake about 1½ hours, or until golden-brown, brushing frequently with honey for last 20 minutes of baking.

10. Carefully remove from baking sheets. Cool on wire racks. *Makes 3 wreaths or canes, 10 servings each.*

LEMON 'CHEESE' CAKE

(Mrs. Edna A. Peavy, Georgia)
(pictured)

3 cups sifted cake flour
1 tablespoon baking powder
6 egg whites, at room temperature
1 cup (2 sticks) butter
2 cups sugar
¾ cup milk

FILLING
½ cup (1 stick) butter or margarine
1 cup sugar
6 egg yolks, beaten
¾ cup fresh lemon juice
4 teaspoons grated lemon rind

Seven-Minute Frosting, recipe follows

1. Grease and flour three 9-inch round layer cake pans.

2. Sift measured flour and baking powder together onto a sheet of waxed paper.

3. In the large bowl of an electric mixer, at medium speed, beat egg whites until soft peaks form. With mixer at high speed, beat whites until stiff peaks form when beaters are slowly raised. Gently transfer beaten whites to another clean bowl. Set aside.

4. Preheat oven to 350F.

5. In same large mixer bowl (no need to wash bowl or beaters), at medium speed, cream butter; gradually add sugar, beating until mixture is light and fluffy.

6. With mixer at low speed, add flour mixture (in fourths) alternately with milk (in thirds), beginning and ending with flour mixture. Mix just until smooth; do not overbeat.

7. With wire whisk or rubber spatula, using an under-and-over motion, gently fold egg whites into batter.

8. Divide batter evenly into prepared pans. Bake 25 minutes, or until top springs back when gently pressed with fingertip.

continued on page 306

continued from page 305

9. Let layers cool in pans 10 minutes. Turn out on wire racks to cool completely.

10. Meanwhile, make Filling: Melt butter in the top of a double boiler over direct heat. Remove from heat and stir in sugar. Add beaten egg yolks, lemon juice and rind. Stir to mix well; set top over simmering water in bottom of double boiler (bottom of top pan should not touch water). Cook and stir filling mixture until thickened. Remove from heat; cool.

11. Make Seven-Minute Frosting.

12. Assemble the cake: Spread one-third of filling on a cake layer; top with second layer and spread with another third of filling. Add top layer and spread with remaining filling.

13. Frost side with Seven-Minute Frosting. *Makes 1 cake.*

SEVEN-MINUTE FROSTING

2 egg whites
1½ cups sugar
1 tablespoon light corn syrup or ¼
 teaspoon cream of tartar
⅓ cup water
1 teaspoon vanilla extract

1. In top of double boiler, combine egg whites, sugar, corn syrup and water.

2. With portable electric mixer or rotary beater, beat about 1 minute to combine ingredients.

3. Cook over rapidly boiling water (water in bottom should not touch top of double boiler), beating constantly, about 7 minutes, or until stiff peaks form when beaters are slowly raised.

4. Remove from boiling water. Add vanilla; continue beating until frosting is thick enough to spread—about 2 minutes.

5. Use to frost side of Lemon "Cheese" Cake.

PIZZELLE

(Rosalie Gaziano, West Virginia)
(pictured)

6 eggs
1¾ cups granulated sugar
1 cup salad oil
1 tablespoon lemon extract
1 tablespoon orange extract
½ teaspoon vanilla extract
⅛ teaspoon salt
3 cups all-purpose flour

Confectioners' sugar (optional)

1. In the large bowl of an electric mixer, at medium speed, beat eggs until

light and frothy; gradually add sugar, beating until smooth and creamy. Add oil; beat until well blended.

2. Stir in lemon, orange and vanilla extracts and salt.

3. With mixer at low speed, add the flour, a half cup at a time, mixing just until smooth.

4. Chill batter at least 2 hours to enrich flavor. (Batter may be stored, refrigerated, overnight or several days.)

5. When ready to bake, preheat a pizzelle iron. Pour a thin layer of batter on hot iron (for a 4-inch pizzelle use approximately 1 tablespoon of batter); bake 2 to 3 minutes, or until done.

6. If desired, sprinkle with a light dusting of confectioners' sugar while pizzelles are warm. *Makes 5 dozen.*

ANISE COOKIES

(Mrs. Jack Thompson, Pennsylvania)
(pictured)

4 cups sifted all-purpose flour
½ teaspoon salt
2 teaspoons baking powder
4 teaspoons anise seeds
4 eggs
2 cups granulated sugar

Confectioners' sugar (optional)

1. Day before: Sift measured flour, salt and baking powder onto a sheet of waxed paper. Sprinkle with anise seeds.

2. In the large bowl of an electric mixer at high speed, beat eggs and granulated sugar for 10 minutes.

3. With mixer at low speed, gradually beat in the flour mixture. It may be necessary to stir in the last of the flour with a wooden spoon.

4. On a lightly floured surface, roll out dough, a third at a time, to ½-inch thickness. Cut with star-, bell- or heart-shaped cookie cutters. Let cookies stand, uncovered, 12 hours or overnight. Cookies will develop a hard crust while standing.

5. Next day: Preheat oven to 350F. Lightly grease baking sheets.

6. With a spatula, transfer cookies onto prepared baking sheets. Bake 12 minutes.

7. Remove to wire racks. If desired, lightly dust warm cookies with confectioners' sugar. Let cookies cool completely before storing in an airtight container. *Makes 3 dozen (3-inch) cookies or 6 dozen (2-inch) cookies.*

SWEDISH CAKES

(Mrs. W. Peters, Wisconsin)

1 cup (2 sticks) butter or margarine, at
 room temperature
½ cup sugar
2 egg yolks, slightly beaten
2 cups sifted all-purpose flour
2 egg whites
1½ cups chopped walnuts
Red and green candied cherries, chopped

1. Preheat oven to 300F.

2. In a medium bowl, with wooden spoon or portable electric mixer, cream butter until soft and fluffy.

3. Beat in sugar until well combined. Add egg yolks and beat until light and fluffy.

4. Gradually stir in the flour, ½ cup at a time, until dough is soft and smooth.

5. With hands, roll dough, a tablespoon at a time, into balls. Roll each ball in unbeaten egg whites, then in chopped nuts.

6. Place balls about 2 inches apart on ungreased cookie sheets.

7. Before baking, flatten balls with the bottom of a glass; decorate centers with small pieces of red and green candied cherries.

8. Bake 15 minutes. Remove from pans to wire rack to cool. *Makes 2 dozen cakes.*

ITALIAN WINE CAKE

(LaVerne P. Morris, California)

2 cups cooked seedless raisins
4 cups sifted all-purpose flour
4 teaspoons unsweetened cocoa
4 teaspoons baking soda
2 teaspoons ground cinnamon
1 teaspoon ground allspice
1 teaspoon ground nutmeg
1 cup (2 sticks) butter or margarine, at
 room temperature
1 cup shortening
2 cups granulated sugar
3 eggs
2½ cups Burgundy
2 cups chopped nuts

1. Put 2 scant cups raisins into a medium saucepan; cover with cold water and bring to a boil. Remove from heat; drain well. Measure after draining. Set aside.

2. Preheat oven to 350F. Grease and flour 3 (9-by-5-by-3-inch) loaf pans (see Note).

3. Sift together flour, cocoa, soda and spices onto a sheet of waxed paper. Set aside.

4. In your largest mixing bowl, with a portable electric mixer or wooden spoon,

cream butter and shortening together; blend in sugar gradually, beating until mixture is light and fluffy. Add eggs, one at a time, beating well after each addition.

5. With the mixer at low speed, stir in flour mixture (in fourths) alternately with wine (in thirds), beginning and ending with flour, until mixture is smooth and well blended.

6. Stir in raisins and chopped nuts.

7. Divide batter into prepared pans. Bake 50 minutes or until surface springs back when gently pressed with fingertip. Do not overbake.

8. Cool in pans about 10 minutes. Turn out on wire racks to cool completely. *Makes 3 loaves.*

Note: This batter may also be baked in smaller loaves for gift-giving. Recipe makes 8 small (6-by-3¾-by-2-inch) loaves, plus 1 medium (8½-by-4½-by-2½-inch) loaf.

CHRISTMAS WHISKY CAKE
(Mrs. Marie Price, Tennessee)

1 lb candied red cherries, chopped
½ lb golden raisins
½ lb chopped dates
1 pint bourbon
5 cups sifted all-purpose flour
1 lb chopped pecans or walnuts
1 teaspoon ground nutmeg
1 teaspoon ground cinnamon
1 teaspoon baking powder
6 eggs, at room temperature
1½ cups (3 sticks) butter or margarine, at
    room temperature
2 cups granulated sugar
1 cup light-brown sugar, firmly packed

1. Day before: In a medium bowl, combine cherries, raisins, dates and bourbon. Cover and let soak overnight.

2. Next day: Grease a 10-inch tube pan and line bottom and side with brown paper. Grease paper lightly. Preheat oven to 275F.

3. Combine ½ cup of the flour with the chopped nuts; set aside. Sift together the remaining flour, nutmeg, cinnamon, and baking powder onto a sheet of waxed paper.

4. Separate the eggs, putting yolks in a small bowl and whites in the large bowl of an electric mixer.

5. With the mixer at medium speed, beat the egg whites until soft peaks form; with the mixer at high speed, continue to beat the whites until stiff peaks form when the beaters are slowly raised. Turn the beaten whites into another clean bowl.

6. In the large bowl of the mixer (no need to wash bowl or beaters), at high speed, cream the butter. Add sugars and beat until the mixture is light and fluffy.

7. With a rotary beater, beat the egg yolks until they are light and lemon colored.

8. Add beaten yolks to butter-sugar mixture; beat well to combine.

9. With a wooden spoon, stir in soaked fruit and bourbon. Add flour mixture, gradually, beating until batter is smooth and well blended.

10. With a wire whisk or rubber spatula, fold in egg whites using an under-and-over motion. Fold in floured nuts.

11. Pour batter into prepared pan. Bake 3 to 3½ hours, or until a cake tester inserted near center comes out clean.

12. Set cake on a wire rack; cool completely in pan. When cake is cool, remove from pan and gently peel off paper.

13. To store: Wrap cake in cheesecloth soaked in bourbon. Place in a cake tin with a tight-fitting cover. As cheesecloth dries out, resoak in bourbon. Store in a cool place several weeks. *Makes a 7½ pound cake.*

FILLED COOKIES
(Mrs. Barbara Hayes, Connecticut)

DOUGH
4 cups sifted all-purpose flour
2 tablespoons baking powder
5 eggs
⅔ cup salad oil
1 cup granulated sugar
½ teaspoon vanilla extract

FILLING
½ cup (1 stick) butter or margarine
2 cups chopped, pitted prunes
1 cup chopped walnuts
½ cup granulated sugar
1 cup seedless raisins
½ cup (2-oz jar) finely chopped orange peel

Confectioners' sugar (optional)

1. Make Dough: Sift flour and baking powder together onto a sheet of waxed paper.

2. In the large bowl of an electric mixer, at medium speed, beat eggs, oil, sugar and vanilla until light and creamy.

3. With mixer at low speed, gradually beat in flour mixture until dough is smooth.

4. Form dough into a ball and let stand, covered.

5. Make Filling: In a medium saucepan, melt butter over low heat; add remaining filling ingredients and cook, stirring, until filling is well blended. Remove from heat; let cool.

6. Preheat oven to 375F.

7. Divide dough into six equal pieces. Roll one piece into a rectangle about 12 inches long, 5 inches wide. Spread with ½ cup filling. Roll up from long side as for jelly roll. Repeat to make six rolls in all.

8. Place rolls, seam side down, on ungreased cookie sheets, about 2 inches apart.

9. Bake 15 minutes. Carefully remove rolls to wire racks to cool completely.

10. To serve: Cut each roll at an angle into 12 pieces. Sprinkle with confectioners' sugar if desired. *Makes 6 dozen cookies.*

FRESH-CRANBERRY-WHIPPED-CREAM PIE
(Hazel Gurney, Iowa)

1 navel orange
2 cups fresh cranberries
1¼ cups granulated sugar
1 env unflavored gelatine
¼ cup cold water
2 egg whites, at room temperature
¼ teaspoon salt
1 cup heavy cream
1 teaspoon vanilla extract
1 9-inch pie shell, baked and cooled
    (see Note)

1. Lightly grate the orange-colored rind from the orange onto a sheet of waxed paper; set aside.

2. With a small knife, remove and discard white membrane from orange. Cut orange into quarters.

3. Remove and discard stems from cranberries; wash berries and drain well.

4. Put cranberries and orange quarters through the medium blade of a food grinder. Add 1 cup sugar and the orange rind to the cranberry-orange mixture. Stir to blend well.

5. In a small bowl, sprinkle gelatine over cold water to soften. Place bowl in a shallow pan of hot water; stir gelatine until completely dissolved.

6. Add gelatine to cranberry mixture; stir to blend well. Set into refrigerator to chill until mixture begins to thicken.

7. In the small bowl of an electric mixer, at medium speed, beat egg whites with salt until soft peaks form. With mixer at high speed, gradually beat in ¼ cup sugar until stiff peaks form when beaters are slowly raised.

continued on page 308

continued from page 307

8. With a wire whisk or rubber spatula, fold egg whites into chilled cranberry mixture.

9. In same small bowl of mixer (no need to wash bowl or beaters), beat ½ cup of the heavy cream with vanilla until stiff. Fold whipped cream into cranberry mixture.

10. Turn cranberry mixture into baked pie shell; chill until firm.

11. Just before serving, whip remaining ½ cup of heavy cream. Use to garnish pie. *Makes 8 servings.*

Note: You may use ½ pkg (11 oz) piecrust mix, prepared and baked according to package directions, or a purchased frozen pie shell, baked as directed on package.

DATE ROLL
(Mrs. Wanda Kuhn, Washington)

3 cups granulated sugar
1 cup evaporated milk
3 tablespoons butter or margarine
3 tablespoons light corn syrup
1 cup chopped dates
1 teaspoon vanilla extract
1 cup chopped walnuts

1. In a medium saucepan, combine sugar, evaporated milk, butter and corn syrup. Cook over medium heat, stirring; bring to a boil.

2. Add dates; continue boiling, stirring often, to 238F on candy thermometer, or until a little of the syrup forms a soft ball when dropped into cold water. Remove from heat.

3. Cool slightly; add vanilla.

4. With a wooden spoon, beat candy until thick; stir in walnuts. Turn out on board.

5. Shape candy into two rolls, about 1¾ inches in diameter. Wrap tightly in waxed paper or plastic wrap. Place in refrigerator.

6. To serve, cut in slices, ⅓ inch thick. *Makes 2¼ pounds.*

EURIEKA'S SUGAR COOKIES
(Diane I. Fague, New York)

3 cups sifted all-purpose flour
1 teaspoon ground nutmeg
2 tablespoons sour cream
1 teaspoon baking soda
1 cup (2 sticks) butter or margarine, at room temperature
1½ cups granulated sugar
2 eggs
1 teaspoon vanilla extract

1. Sift measured flour with nutmeg onto a sheet of waxed paper. Set aside.

2. In a small bowl, combine sour cream and baking soda. Set aside.

3. In the large bowl of an electric mixer, at medium speed, cream butter; add sugar gradually, beating until mixture is light and fluffy. Add eggs and beat well.

4. With mixer at low speed, slowly add flour, a little at a time, alternating with the sour-cream mixture.

5. Add vanilla and mix well.

6. Wrap dough in waxed paper or plastic wrap; refrigerate 1 hour.

7. Preheat oven to 375F.

8. On lightly floured surface, roll dough, one-third at a time, to ⅓-inch thickness. Cut with 2-inch cookie cutters. Keep remaining dough refrigerated until ready to roll out. Reflour work surface as necessary.

9. Bake on ungreased cookie sheets, 6 to 8 minutes. Remove to wire racks to cool. *Makes about 6 dozen cookies.*

PEANUT-BUTTER FUDGE
(Rollie Wood, Virginia)

1 tablespoon plus 1 teaspoon butter
2 cups light-brown sugar, firmly packed
1 cup granulated sugar
1 cup light cream or evaporated milk, undiluted
1 teaspoon vanilla extract
2 to 3 tablespoons peanut butter
½ cup chopped pecans or walnuts

1. Using a small amount of the butter (a teaspoon or less), butter a 9-by-9-by-2-inch pan. Line pan with waxed paper; lightly butter paper.

2. In a heavy, 3-quart saucepan, over low heat, cook brown sugar, granulated sugar and cream, stirring constantly with a wooden spoon, until the sugar dissolves and the mixture comes to a boil.

3. Cook, stirring occasionally, until candy thermometer registers 234F, or until a little syrup dropped in cold water forms a soft ball.

4. Remove from heat and add remaining butter.

5. When butter is melted, add vanilla and peanut butter. With wooden spoon, beat until thick and creamy. Stir in nuts.

6. Quickly turn into prepared pan; cool completely; refrigerate.

7. Turn out of pan in one piece. Remove waxed paper. With sharp knife cut into squares. *Makes about 1½ pounds.*

ROPE COOKIES
(Mrs. Fred A. Ludwig, Texas)

3 cups all-purpose flour
1 teaspoon baking powder
1 cup (2 sticks) butter
1 cup sugar
2 eggs
Grated rind of 1 lemon

1. Sift 3 cups flour with baking powder onto a sheet of waxed paper. Set aside.

2. In the large bowl of an electric mixer, at high speed, cream butter and sugar until mixture is light and fluffy. Add eggs, beating well after each addition.

3. With mixer at medium speed, gradually beat in sifted flour mixture. Stir in lemon rind. (Dough will be soft.)

4. Refrigerate, covered, at least 2 hours or until you are ready to bake cookies.

5. Preheat oven to 350F.

6. With lightly floured hands, take about 2 teaspoons of dough and roll into a rope 5 inches long; rope will be a little thicker than a pencil.

7. On an ungreased cookie sheet, shape the rope into an "S." Repeat until all dough is used.

8. Bake about 10 minutes, or until edges are lightly browned; cookies will not be browned.

9. Let cool slightly before removing from pan. Cool completely on wire racks.

10. Store in an airtight metal tin; cookie flavor improves with age. *Makes 3½ dozen.*

CUBAITA (ITALIAN ALMOND BRITTLE)

(Rosalie Gaziano, West Virginia)

3½ cups shelled, unblanched almonds (2 lb unshelled)
Peel from 2 oranges
Peel from 1 tangerine
1½ teaspoons ground cinnamon
3½ cups (1¼ lb) sugar
1 jar (12 oz) honey (1 cup)

1. Preheat oven to 350F.
2. If necessary, shell almonds. Spread the nuts on a jelly-roll pan or cookie sheet. Bake 10 to 12 minutes, or until golden-brown. Chop almonds coarsely; put in a small bowl and set aside.
3. With a swivel-blade vegetable parer, remove the peels from the oranges and tangerine in long strips. Chop peels fine. (Wrap oranges and tangerine and refrigerate for another use.)
4. Add chopped peel and cinnamon to almonds; toss to mix well.
5. Set out a large board (22 by 16 inches) and moisten it with ice water.
6. In a heavy skillet, melt sugar just until golden. Remove from heat.
7. Quickly stir in honey. Add almond mixture; stir in.
8. Immediately pour candy onto chilled board; spread out mixture. Let it cool slightly; then, while it is still pliable, quickly cut into bite-size pieces.
9. Store in box or cookie tin lined with waxed paper. Place waxed paper between candy layers. *Makes 3 pounds.*

SWEDISH NUTS

(Mrs. Gail B. Rando, Massachusetts)

2 egg whites
1½ cups (½ lb) blanched almonds
Dash salt
1 cup sugar
½ cup (1 stick) butter or margarine

1. Preheat oven to 325F.
2. Put egg whites in large bowl of an electric mixer; let stand to come to room temperature—about 1 hour.
3. Spread almonds on a large baking sheet; toast in oven until lightly browned—about 25 minutes. Remove and let cool on pan.
4. With electric mixer at medium speed, beat egg whites and salt until soft peaks form. With mixer at high speed, gradually add sugar, a few tablespoons at a time, beating until stiff peaks form when beaters are slowly raised. (Meringue should be very stiff and shiny.)
5. With a rubber spatula, fold nuts into meringue, using an under-and-over motion.
6. Melt butter in a jelly-roll pan.
7. Spread meringue mixture evenly in pan.
8. Bake in slow oven (325F) for 30 to 40 minutes, stirring every 10 minutes to separate nuts. When done, all butter will have been absorbed and nuts will be coated with a browned sugar-coating.
9. Cool to serve. *Makes 1½ pounds.* ∎

CHRISTMAS DINNER WITH A SOUTHERN ACCENT

continued from page 291

SEVEN-MINUTE ICING

2 egg whites (¼ cup)
4 cups sifted confectioners' sugar
¼ teaspoon cream of tartar
1 tablespoon vanilla extract
⅓ cup water

1. In top of double boiler, combine egg whites, confectioners' sugar, cream of tartar, vanilla and water.
2. With portable electric mixer, beat about 1 minute, to combine ingredients.
3. Cook over rapidly boiling water (water in bottom should not touch top of double boiler), beating constantly, about 7 minutes, or until stiff peaks form when beaters are slowly raised.
4. Remove from boiling water. Continue beating until frosting is thick enough to spread—about 1 minute.

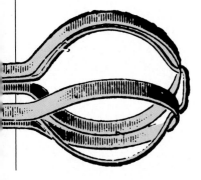

PUMPKIN CHIFFON PIE

(pictured)

GINGERSNAP CRUST
1¾ cups gingersnap crumbs (about 30)
½ cup (1 stick) butter or margarine, melted
¼ cup confectioners' sugar

PUMPKIN FILLING
1 env unflavored gelatine
¼ cup cold water
3 eggs
1½ cups canned pumpkin
1¼ cups granulated sugar
½ cup milk
½ teaspoon salt
½ teaspoon ground cinnamon
½ teaspoon ground ginger
½ teaspoon ground nutmeg

¾ cup heavy cream, whipped stiff
Candied red cherries
Ground nutmeg

1. Make Gingersnap Crust: In medium bowl, combine crumbs, butter and confectioners' sugar, stirring with fork to mix well.
2. With back of metal spoon, press crumb mixture on bottom and side (not on rim) of 9-inch pie plate. Refrigerate until ready to fill.
3. Make Pumpkin Filling: Sprinkle gelatine over cold water in measuring cup; set aside to soften.
4. Separate eggs, placing whites in large bowl of electric mixer, yolks in double-boiler top. Set whites aside to warm to room temperature.
5. Beat egg yolks slightly with wooden spoon. Stir in pumpkin, ¾ cup granulated sugar, the milk, salt, cinnamon, ginger and nutmeg.
6. Cook over boiling water (water should not touch bottom of double-boiler top), stirring frequently, until mixture becomes very thick—30 minutes.
7. Add gelatine, stirring until gelatine is dissolved. Remove pan from hot water. Turn into medium bowl; set in a larger bowl of ice cubes to chill, stirring occasionally, until mixture mounds when dropped from spoon—20 minutes.
8. Meanwhile, at high speed, beat whites until soft peaks form when beaters are slowly raised. Beat in remaining ½ cup granulated sugar, 2 tablespoons at a time, beating well after each addition. Continue beating until stiff peaks form when beaters are raised.
9. With rubber spatula or wire whisk, gently fold gelatine mixture into egg-white mixture just until combined.
10. Turn into pie shell, mounding in center. Refrigerate until firm—2 hours.
11. To serve: Decorate edge with whipped-cream ruching, put through pastry bag with number-5 rosette tip. Garnish with candied cherries and a sprinkling of nutmeg. *Makes 8 servings.*

Note: This pie is better if not held overnight before serving. ∎

These ten enchanting cookies—
shown amid their real, nonedible
counterparts—were inspired by
toys in a charming London antique shop.
Use them as stocking stuffers or decorations for your Christmas tree, table or
mantel…or just enjoy eating them!
They're all made from a basic cookie
dough in three varieties—sugar, spice
and chocolate—and cut from patterns
that you trace from our pages. For the
recipes and instructions,
please turn the page.

'TOYS'
WITH A TIMELESS FLAVOR

'TOYS' WITH A TIMELESS FLAVOR

continued from page 310

All patterns for tracing are found on pages 312, 313, 318 and 319.

ANTIQUE-TOY COOKIES
(pictured)

1 recipe Spice-Cookie Dough, recipe follows
1 recipe Chocolate-Cookie Dough, recipe follows
1 recipe Sugar-Cookie Dough, recipe follows
Tracing paper for patterns
Cardboard and confectioners' sugar, if desired (see Note)

1. Prepare cookie dough. Refrigerate.

2. Trace and cut out each pattern twice from outlines on pages 312, 313, 318 and 319. Trace inside lines on only one pattern of each set. Preheat oven to 350F.

3. *To make Engine:* With lightly floured rolling pin, on a greased cookie sheet, roll out some of Spice-Cookie Dough to a generous ⅛-inch thickness. Lay paper pattern for engine on dough; cut around it with a sharp knife. Lift off dough trimmings. Cut remaining pattern on interior lines; use to cut out individual pieces. On a lightly floured board, roll out some of Chocolate-Cookie Dough to ⅛-inch thickness. Cut out cab, wheels, cowcatcher and smokestack. Roll out some of Sugar-Cookie Dough. Cut out roof of cab and bottom of engine. Lightly brush cab, wheel and smokestack areas of spice-cookie cutout with water. Pat chocolate- and sugar-cookie pieces in place. Score front of engine, cowcatcher and top of smokestack, as pictured. Roll a little chocolate dough into a ball. Fasten on front of engine with a little water. Bake 10 to 12 minutes, or until edges are golden. Cool several minutes on cookie sheet. Remove to wire rack, and cool completely.

4. *To make Jack-in-the-Box Doll:* With lightly floured rolling pin, on a greased cookie sheet, roll out some of Sugar-Cookie Dough to a generous ⅛-inch thickness. Lay paper pattern for jack-in-the-box doll on dough; cut around pattern with a sharp knife. Cut remaining pattern on interior lines; use to cut out individual pieces. If possible, fit face pattern and side-box pattern on Sugar-Cookie Dough already rolled out. Cut around pattern; remove dough trimmings. On lightly floured board, roll out more Sugar-Cookie Dough. Cut out front of box and any of above pieces that did not fit. Roll out some Spice-Cookie Dough. Cut out spring and hat brim. Brush sugar-cookie cutout lightly with water. Place spring, front and

back of box, hat brim and face on sugar-cookie piece, using patterns to aid in placement. Break off little pieces of chocolate dough. Roll in balls, and place on front and sides of box. Press to flatten slightly. Make several thin rolls of chocolate dough. Place on top of face for "bangs." Make 2 large rolls. Place one on each side for hair. Flatten a little chocolate dough. Cut out ends of ribbon. Fasten in place with a little water. Make 2 rolls of chocolate dough 1¼ inches long. Form each into a circle, and set in place for top of bow. Make 2 small rolls of chocolate dough. Set in place for eyes. Make a small roll of spice dough, and set in place for mouth. Score nose, spring and hat brim. Bake and cool as in Step 3.

5. *To make China Doll:* With lightly floured rolling pin, on a greased cookie sheet, roll out some of Sugar-Cookie Dough to a generous ⅛-inch thickness. Lay paper pattern for china doll on dough; cut around it with a sharp knife. Cut remaining pattern on interior lines; use to cut out individual pieces. Place arm pattern beside doll on Sugar-Cookie Dough; cut out. Lift off dough trimmings. On a lightly floured board, roll out some Spice-Cookie Dough. Cut out hat brim, cape and a 4-by-1-inch rectangle. Cut rectangle into 8 half-inch pieces. Roll out some chocolate dough. Cut out hair, shoes, end of ribbon and a 3-by-¼-inch strip. Brush sugar-cookie cutout with a little water. Place hat brim, hair, arms, cape, shoes and ribbon ends on cookie. Make pleats at bottom of dress by overlapping spice-dough strips. Flatten at top, and fit chocolate strip in place. Make 3 small balls of chocolate dough. Press in place for buttons. Make two 1¼-inch rolls of chocolate dough. Form into rings for top of bow. Make 2 small chocolate rolls for eyes and one small spice roll for mouth; press in place. Score hat brim, nose, hands, shoes, cheeks. Bake and cool as in Step 3.

6. *To make Toy Drum:* With lightly floured rolling pin, on a greased cookie sheet, roll out some Sugar-Cookie Dough to a generous ⅛-inch thickness. Lay paper pattern for drum on dough; cut around it with a sharp knife. Lift off dough trimmings. Cut remaining pattern on interior lines; use to cut individual pieces. On a lightly floured board, roll out a little Spice-Cookie Dough. Cut out bands. Secure to sugar cookie with a little water. Make two 3½-inch rolls of spice dough for drumsticks; moisten bottoms, and arrange on drum as pictured. Roll out a little chocolate dough. Cut out seven ½-inch triangles. Press into place. Score sides of drum. Bake and cool as in Step 3.

7. *To make Noah's Ark:* With lightly floured rolling pin, on a greased cookie sheet, roll out some Spice-Cookie Dough to a generous ⅛-inch thickness. Lay paper pattern for ark on dough; cut around it with a sharp knife. Carefully lift off dough trimmings; set aside. Cut remaining pattern on interior lines; use to cut out individual pieces. On a lightly floured board, roll out some Sugar-Cookie Dough. Cut out pieces for front and side of cabin. Brush top of spice-dough ark lightly with water. Press front and side of cabin in place. With a 1¼-inch round cookie cutter, make 2 circles from Sugar-Cookie Dough trimmings and 2 circles from reserved spice-dough trimmings. Roll out a little chocolate dough, and cut 2 circles. Cut all circles into quarters. Arrange in pairs to fill opening at top of ark. Using a toothpick, mark eyes in each piece. Using cutout as a guide, score deck line on ark. Bake and cool as in Step 3.

8. *To make Ox Cart:* With lightly floured rolling pin, on a greased cookie sheet, roll out some Spice-Cookie Dough to a generous ⅛-inch thickness. Lay paper pattern for ox and cart on dough; cut around it with a sharp knife. Lift off dough trimmings. Cut remaining pattern on interior lines; use to cut individual pieces. On a lightly floured board, roll out some Sugar-Cookie Dough. Cut out wheel, yoke and horn. Make 3 rolls of chocolate dough ¼ inch thick. Flatten slightly; cut to 2-inch, 3-inch and 3½-inch lengths. Lightly moisten horn, yoke area and cart on spice-cookie cutout. Press horn and yoke in place. Put chocolate logs in place. Flatten slightly where wheel will go. Press wheel in place. With Chocolate-Cookie Dough, make a small ball for the eye and 2 larger balls for nose and hub of wheel. Press them in place. Score tail. Bake and cool as in Step 3.

9. *To make Tin Horn:* With lightly floured rolling pin, on a greased cookie sheet, roll out some Sugar-Cookie Dough to a generous ⅛-inch thickness. Place paper pattern for horn on dough; cut around it with a sharp knife. Lift off dough trimmings. Cut out bell opening of horn and holly-leaf pattern from remaining pattern. Roll out some spice dough on a lightly floured board. Cut out bell opening and 3 holly leaves. Lightly moisten areas on sugar cookie where cutouts will go. Press pieces in place. Make a thin roll of Sugar-Cookie Dough, 6 inches long. Fit around bell opening. Press into place, flattening slightly. Make a thick roll of Sugar-Cookie Dough, 6 inches long. Moisten handle; press roll into place, curling ends. Make a thin roll of spice dough 1¼ inches long. Press onto horn for branch design. Make 2 small rolls; press into place for leaves on branch. Make a thick ¾-inch-long roll of spice dough. Press into place for mouthpiece. Make small chocolate balls for holly berries. Bake and cool as in Step 3.

10. *To make Soldier:* With a lightly floured rolling pin, on a greased cookie sheet, roll out some Sugar-Cookie Dough to a generous ⅛-inch thickness. Place paper pattern for soldier on dough; cut around it with a sharp knife. Carefully lift off dough trimmings; set aside. Cut remaining pattern on interior lines; use to cut individual pieces. Cut out hat and epaulettes from reserved dough. Roll out some spice dough on a lightly floured board. Cut out jacket and feathers. Roll out a little chocolate dough. Cut out hat brim, collar, belt and shoes. Lightly moisten areas on cookie where cutouts will be placed. Press cutouts into place. Make 2 small thin rolls and 4 small balls of chocolate dough for eyes and buttons; press into place. Make one small thin roll of spice dough for mouth; press into place. Score arms, front of jacket, nose, pants and feathers. Make circular marks on hat with small round cookie cutter or cap of pen. Bake and cool as in Step 3.

11. *To make Toy Horse:* With lightly floured rolling pin, on a greased cookie sheet, roll out some Sugar-Cookie Dough to a generous ⅛-inch thickness. Place paper pattern for toy horse on dough; cut around it with a sharp knife. Lift off dough trimmings. Cut remaining pattern on in-terior lines; use to cut individual pieces. Roll out some Spice-Cookie Dough. Cut out tail, hooves, mane and saddle fringe. Roll out some chocolate dough. Cut out saddle and wheels. Moisten areas on sugar-cookie cutout where pieces will be placed. Press pieces into place. Make a 1¼-inch roll of spice dough; press into place for bridle. Make a 3-inch roll of spice dough for rein. Press into place. Make 3 small balls of Spice-Cookie Dough; press into place for eye and hubs of wheels. Make a small ball of chocolate dough. Place where bridle and rein meet. Score mouth, mane, tail and saddle fringe. Bake and cool as in Step 3.

12. *To make Top:* With lightly floured rolling pin, on a greased cookie sheet, roll out some Sugar-Cookie Dough to a generous ⅛-inch thickness. Place paper pattern for top on dough; cut around it with a sharp knife. Carefully lift off dough trimmings; set aside. Cut remaining pattern on interior lines; use to cut out individual pieces. Cut center of top from reserved Sugar-Cookie Dough. Roll out some spice dough on a lightly floured board. Cut out strips that fit on either side of center panel. Moisten center of cookie; press spice- and sugar-cookie panels in place. Press outer edges of spice panels down to meet sugar-cookie edges. Make a ball of spice dough, and place at top. Roll out some chocolate dough. Cut out tip; press in place. Make a 1¼-inch-long roll of chocolate dough. Fit below ball of spice dough, as pictured. Make a small ball of chocolate dough. Place at top. Bake and cool as in Step 3. *Makes 10 Antique-Toy Cookies.*

Note: If cookies are to be used for display, trace patterns onto cardboard and cut out. Stir 2 or 3 teaspoons water into 1 cup confectioners' sugar. Brush frosting onto cardboard. Press cookies onto cardboard. Set aside to dry.

SPICE-COOKIE DOUGH

½ cup (1 stick) butter or margarine, softened
⅔ cup dark-brown sugar, firmly packed
¼ teaspoon salt
1 egg
1 teaspoon vanilla extract
2 cups all-purpose flour
1 teaspoon ground cinnamon
½ teaspoon ground ginger
¼ teaspoon ground cloves

1. Measure butter, sugar and salt into bowl. With electric mixer at medium speed, beat until mixture is smooth.

2. Add egg and vanilla. Beat until fluffy—2 minutes.

3. Gradually add flour and spices, stirring until well combined and smooth.

4. With hands or spoon, shape dough into a ball. Place on waxed paper, plastic wrap or foil. Flatten dough, and wrap. Refrigerate 1 hour. Dough will be firm.

CHOCOLATE-COOKIE DOUGH

¼ cup (½ stick) butter or margarine, softened
⅓ cup sugar
⅛ teaspoon salt
1 egg yolk
1 teaspoon water
½ teaspoon vanilla extract
½ square (1-oz size) unsweetened chocolate, melted
1 cup all-purpose flour

1. Measure butter, sugar and salt into bowl. With electric mixer at medium speed, beat until mixture is smooth.

2. Add egg yolk, water, vanilla and chocolate. Beat until fluffy—2 minutes.

3. Gradually add flour, stirring until well combined and smooth.

4. With hands or spoon, shape dough into a ball. Place on waxed paper, plastic wrap or foil. Flatten dough and wrap. Refrigerate 1 hour. Dough will be firm.

SUGAR-COOKIE DOUGH

½ cup (1 stick) butter or margarine, softened
⅔ cup sugar
¼ teaspoon salt
1 egg
1 teaspoon vanilla extract
2 cups all-purpose flour

1. Measure butter, sugar and salt into bowl. With electric mixer at medium speed, beat until mixture is smooth.

2. Add egg and vanilla. Beat until fluffy—2 minutes.

3. Gradually add flour, stirring until well combined and smooth.

4. With hands or spoon, shape dough into a ball. Place on waxed paper, plastic wrap or foil. Flatten dough, and wrap. Refrigerate 1 hour. Dough will be firm. ∎

Forget about cookie cutters and complicated recipes. These simple, homespun, old-fashioned cookies are ideal for little helping hands: Just twist the dough into candy-cane shapes, roll it into wreaths and drop or spread into pans. Sugar sprinkles, licorice, candies and jams provide the colorful decorations. And those little hands won't need any help eating these wonderfully easy-to-make cookies.

Recipes begin on page 316.

SIMPLE MAKE-AND-BAKE COOKIES

continued from page 314

1. *Three-In-One Cookies (Trees, Bars, Stars).* 2. *Almond Macaroons.* 3. *Candy-Cane Cookies.* 4. *Pecan Diamonds.* 5. *Raisin Newton Bars.* 6. *Chewy Prune Bars.* 7. *Blondies.* 8. *Cranberry-Cereal Cookies.* 9. *Brown-Edge Wafers.* 10. *Jam Bites.* 11. *Walnut Wreaths.*

THREE-IN-ONE COOKIES
(Trees, Bars, Stars)

1 cup (2 sticks) butter or margarine, softened
1 cup granulated sugar
2 large eggs
2¼ cups all-purpose flour
1 teaspoon baking powder
Dash salt
1 tablespoon grated lemon peel
Red and green sugar crystals
Red licorice string
Small silver dragées
Multicolor nonpareils (long and round shapes)

ICING
1 cup confectioners' sugar
4 teaspoons water

1. In large bowl, with electric mixer at medium speed, beat butter and granulated sugar until light and fluffy. Add eggs, one at a time, beating well after each addition. At low speed, gradually beat in 1 cup flour, the baking powder and salt. With wooden spoon, stir in remaining flour and the lemon peel until smooth and well blended. Refrigerate dough, covered, several hours or overnight.

2. Divide dough into thirds. To make Trees: On waxed paper, form one-third dough into a cylinder 2½ inches in diam-

eter. Coat side of cylinder with red sugar crystals until dough is covered. Wrap cylinder in plastic wrap; chill until firm—about 1 hour.

3. With sharp, thin-bladed knife, slice cylinder into rounds ¼ inch thick. Place on ungreased cookie sheet, 1½ inches apart. Cut licorice into varying short lengths; arrange and press some on each cookie round to resemble a Chrismas tree. Sprinkle dragées over tree to resemble ornaments. At base of tree, sprinkle long nonpareils to resemble packages. Chill cookies on sheet while making bars. Preheat oven to 350F.

4. To make Bars: Using another third of dough, form into 1-inch balls. Cut balls in half; roll each piece into a 2½-inch rope. Place on another ungreased cookie sheet, 1½ inches apart. Bake trees and bars 10 to 12 minutes, or until edges start to brown. Remove to wire rack to cool.

5. To make Stars: Form remaining dough into 1-inch balls. With palms of hands, on lightly floured cloth or board, roll each to a 9-inch rope. Cut rope into thirds crosswise; place two pieces over the third in an X to form a star. Place on ungreased cookie sheet; sprinkle each star generously with green sugar crystals. Bake stars 10 to 12 minutes, or until edges start to brown. Remove to wire rack to cool.

6. Make Icing: In small bowl, combine confectioners' sugar and water until smooth. Spread ½ teaspoon icing on each bar cookie; sprinkle with round nonpareils; let dry. Store in airtight containers. *Makes 58 cookies (12 trees, 28 bars and 18 stars).*

ALMOND MACAROONS

1 can (8 oz) almond paste (about 1 cup)
2 large egg whites
½ cup sugar

1. Grease large cookie sheet. In large bowl, with wooden spoon, break almond paste into chunks. With electric mixer at low speed, beat in egg whites until mixture is smooth and well blended. Add sugar slowly, and continue beating until smooth.

2. Fill pastry bag, fitted with ¾- or ½-inch plain tip, with almond mixture. Holding pastry bag upright, close to cookie sheet, press mixture out in 1-inch mounds with peaks, about 1 inch apart. (Or, with spoon, drop mixture by teaspoonfuls.) Let stand, uncovered, at least 4 hours or overnight at room temperature, to dry.

3. Preheat oven to 300F. Bake 20 minutes, or until firm and golden-brown. Remove macaroons to wire racks to cool completely. Store in airtight container. *Makes about 4 dozen cookies.*

CANDY-CANE COOKIES

¾ cup (1½ sticks) butter or margarine,
  softened
1 cup confectioners' sugar
1 large egg
1 teaspoon vanilla extract
2¼ to 2½ cups all-purpose flour
2 tablespoons red cinnamon candies,
  chopped in blender
6 to 8 drops red food color
Red edible glitter or sugar crystals
  (optional)

1. In large bowl, with electric mixer at medium speed, beat butter and confectioners' sugar until light and fluffy. Beat in egg and vanilla until well blended. At low speed, gradually add 2 cups flour until mixture begins to form a dough. Stir or knead in enough remaining flour to make a smooth, not sticky, ball.

2. Cut ball in half; wrap and refrigerate one half. Knead or work cinnamon candies and food color into remaining half of dough. Mix until well blended; wrap and refrigerate at least 30 minutes.

3. Preheat oven to 350F. On lightly floured pastry cloth or board, with palms of hands, roll a rounded teaspoonful of the red dough into a 7-inch rope. Repeat with a rounded teaspoonful of the plain dough. Place the two ropes side by side; twist together; curve one end to form cane handle. Place on ungreased cookie sheet. Repeat with remaining dough. Sprinkle canes with red glitter.

4. Bake 12 to 15 minutes. Cool on wire rack. Store in airtight container. *Makes 2 dozen cookies.*

PECAN DIAMONDS
(Adapted from recipe of chef Dan Kucharski, Norwich Inn, Norwich, Connecticut)

CRUST
1⅓ cups (2⅔ sticks) unsalted butter or
  margarine, softened
⅔ cup granulated sugar
1 large egg
1 large egg yolk
1 teaspoon vanilla extract
3¾ cups all-purpose flour
2 teaspoons baking powder
Dash salt

FILLING
1⅓ cups (2⅔ sticks) unsalted butter or
  margarine
¾ cup honey
1⅓ cups lightly packed brown sugar
¼ cup granulated sugar
3 cups chopped pecans
¼ cup heavy cream

1. Preheat oven to 325F. Make Crust: In large bowl, with electric mixer at medium speed, beat 1⅓ cups butter and ⅔ cup granulated sugar until light and fluffy. Beat in egg, egg yolk and vanilla until well blended. At low speed, beat in flour, baking powder and salt until smooth.

2. On dampened surface, between two sheets of waxed paper, roll dough to 17-by-12-inch rectangle. Remove top sheet of paper; invert dough into 15½-by-10½-by-1-inch jelly-roll pan. Remove waxed paper; press dough onto bottom, ends and sides of pan. With fork, prick dough. Bake 20 minutes.

3. Meanwhile, make Filling: In 3-quart saucepan, melt butter; add honey and both sugars. Bring to boiling; boil 3 minutes. Remove from heat; stir in pecans and cream; mix well. Pour filling into partially baked crust; bake 40 minutes longer, or until top is bubbling and lightly browned. Cool in pan on wire rack.

4. To cut into diamonds: When cool, with sharp knife, cut into six lengthwise strips, about 1½ inches wide. From the cut line, 1½ inches from top lefthand corner, cut diagonally at a 45-degree angle to the right side of pan. Continue to cut diagonally across strips at 2-inch intervals above and below first diagonal cut until entire pan is cut into diamonds. (There will be 5 small triangular-shaped pieces at each end of pan.) *Makes 42 diamonds and 10 triangles.*

continued on page 318

continued from page 317

RAISIN NEWTON BARS

½ cup (1 stick) butter or margarine, softened
¼ cup lightly packed brown sugar
½ cup honey
1 large egg
2 cups whole-wheat flour
1 teaspoon baking powder
½ teaspoon baking soda
½ teaspoon salt
1 cup all-purpose flour

RAISIN FILLING
1 pkg (15 oz) dark seedless raisins
1¼ cups orange juice
1 teaspoon grated lemon or orange peel

1 large egg, beaten

1. In large bowl, with electric mixer at medium speed, beat butter and brown sugar until light and fluffy. Beat in honey and egg. At low speed, gradually add whole-wheat flour, baking powder, soda and salt; mix well. With wooden spoon, stir in all-purpose flour. Wrap dough in plastic wrap; refrigerate 1 to 2 hours.

2. Make Raisin Filling: In small saucepan, combine raisins, orange juice and peel; bring to boiling. Over medium heat, boil 10 minutes, stirring constantly the last 2 to 3 minutes, until all the juice has evaporated.

3. Pour mixture into food processor; process 30 to 60 seconds, or until finely chopped. Or place half the mixture in electric blender; blend 30 to 60 seconds; remove to bowl; repeat with remaining mixture. Refrigerate Raisin Filling until cold—about 30 minutes. Makes 1½ cups.

4. Lightly grease three small cookie sheets. Divide chilled dough in thirds; keep two-thirds refrigerated until ready to use. On dampened surface, between two sheets of waxed paper, roll one-third of dough to 14-by-6-inch rectangle. Remove top sheet of paper; spoon ½ cup filling lengthwise down center of dough to within ½ inch of ends.

5. Holding sides of waxed paper as a guide, fold long sides of dough over filling, overlapping slightly. Press to seal; seal ends well. With the waxed paper, lift cookie roll onto prepared cookie sheet. Cut away and discard waxed paper along one long side of cookie roll; holding other long side of waxed paper, lift and flip roll, seam side down, onto cookie sheet. Lift off paper.

6. Preheat oven to 400F. Roll out and fill another third of dough. Brush rolls with beaten egg. Bake 12 to 15 minutes, or until golden-brown. Meanwhile, roll and fill last third of dough; bake when first two are removed from oven.

7. Leave cookie rolls on cookie sheets 10 minutes after baking; slide onto large wire rack to cool completely. Cut each roll crosswise into eight bars. Store in airtight container. *Makes 2 dozen bars.*

CHEWY PRUNE BARS

CRUST
1¼ cups all-purpose flour
1 teaspoon granulated sugar
1 teaspoon baking powder
Dash salt
½ cup (1 stick) butter or margarine
1 large egg yolk
2 tablespoons cold coffee

1 pkg (12 oz) semisweet chocolate pieces

TOPPING
½ cup (1 stick) butter or margarine, softened
½ cup granulated sugar
2 large eggs
1 large egg white
1 tablespoon vanilla extract
1 cup chopped pitted prunes
1 cup finely chopped walnuts
Confectioners' sugar

1. Grease a 15½-by-10½-by-1-inch jelly-roll pan. Preheat oven to 350F.

2. Make Crust: In medium bowl, combine flour, 1 teaspoon granulated sugar, the baking powder and salt. With pastry blender or two knives, cut in ½ cup butter to resemble coarse cornmeal. With fork, stir in egg yolk and coffee just until mixture forms a dough.

3. Press dough evenly into bottom of prepared pan (crust will be thin). Bake 10 minutes. Remove pan from oven; sprinkle with chocolate pieces; bake 2 minutes longer. Remove pan from oven. With spatula, spread chocolate evenly over crust. Let crust cool on wire rack several minutes to set chocolate.

4. Make Topping: In medium bowl, with portable electric mixer, beat butter and granulated sugar until light and fluffy. Add eggs, egg white and vanilla; mix until well blended (mixture may look curdled). Stir in chopped prunes and walnuts. Spread mixture evenly over chocolate.

5. Bake 25 minutes longer, or until light golden. Cool completely in pan on wire rack. Cut into 32 bars; sprinkle confectioners' sugar over top. *Makes 32 bars.*

BLONDIES

¾ cup (1½ sticks) butter or margarine
1½ cups lightly packed light-brown sugar
2 large eggs
1 teaspoon vanilla extract
2 cups all-purpose flour
1 pkg (6 oz) semisweet chocolate pieces
1 cup chopped walnuts

1. Grease and flour 13-by-9-by-2-inch baking pan. Preheat oven to 350F.

2. In 3-quart saucepan, over medium heat, melt butter. With wooden spoon, stir in brown sugar until well blended; remove from heat. Let cool slightly, then stir in the eggs and vanilla until combined. Gradually stir in the flour until mixed. Stir in chocolate and walnuts. Pour into prepared pan.

3. Bake 20 to 25 minutes. Cool completely in pan on wire rack. Cut into 12 (3-inch) squares; cut each square diagonally in half. *Makes 2 dozen triangles.*

CRANBERRY-CEREAL COOKIES

1 cup (2 sticks) butter or margarine
½ cup granulated sugar
½ cup lightly packed dark-brown sugar
2 large eggs
1¼ teaspoons vanilla extract
2¼ cups all-purpose flour
1 teaspoon baking soda
¼ teaspoon salt
1 cup fresh or frozen cranberries
2¼ cups whole-wheat-and-bran cereal with fruit (any variety)
1 cup confectioners' sugar
2 to 3 teaspoons lemon juice

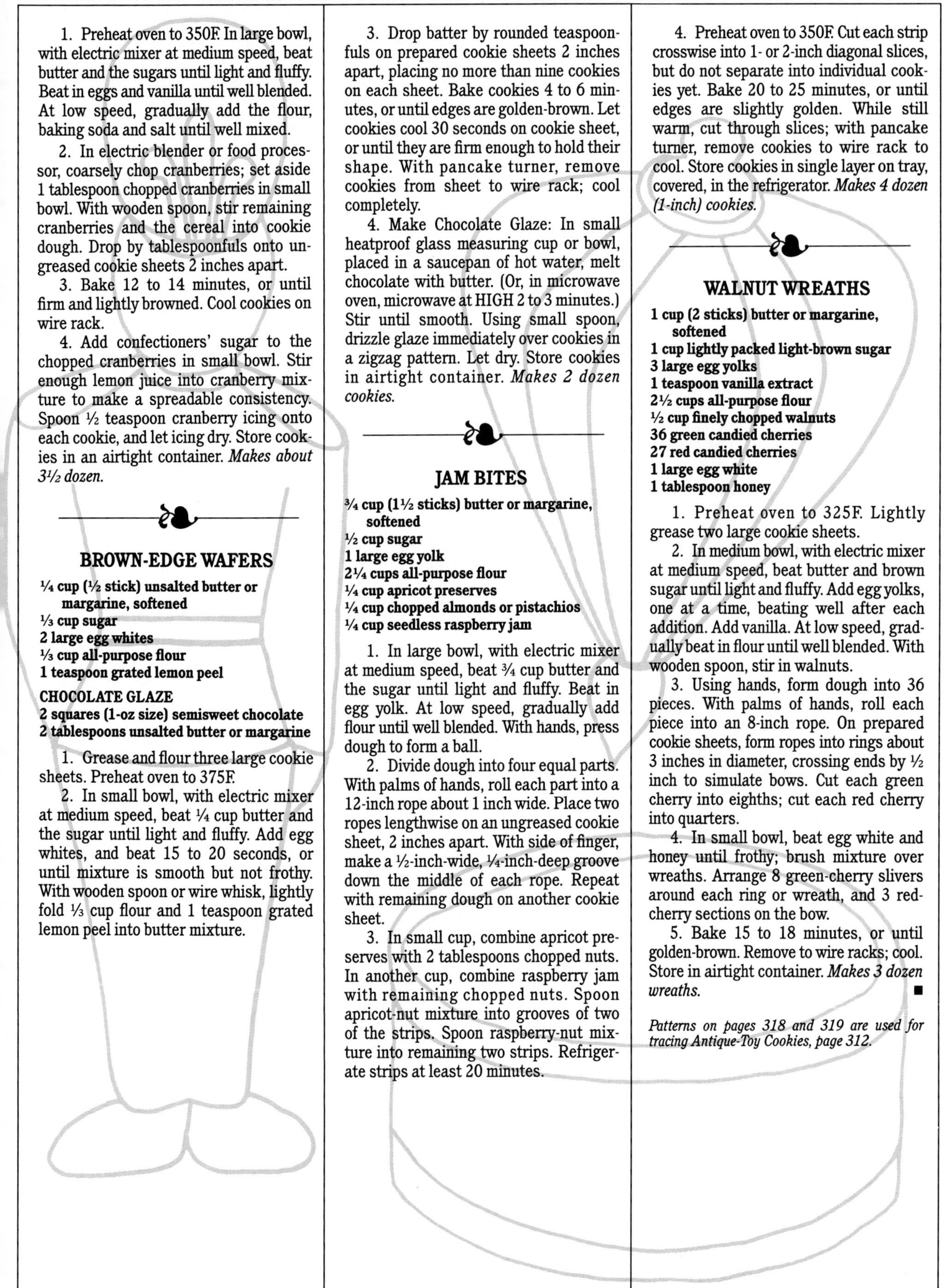

1. Preheat oven to 350F. In large bowl, with electric mixer at medium speed, beat butter and the sugars until light and fluffy. Beat in eggs and vanilla until well blended. At low speed, gradually add the flour, baking soda and salt until well mixed.

2. In electric blender or food processor, coarsely chop cranberries; set aside 1 tablespoon chopped cranberries in small bowl. With wooden spoon, stir remaining cranberries and the cereal into cookie dough. Drop by tablespoonfuls onto ungreased cookie sheets 2 inches apart.

3. Bake 12 to 14 minutes, or until firm and lightly browned. Cool cookies on wire rack.

4. Add confectioners' sugar to the chopped cranberries in small bowl. Stir enough lemon juice into cranberry mixture to make a spreadable consistency. Spoon ½ teaspoon cranberry icing onto each cookie, and let icing dry. Store cookies in an airtight container. *Makes about 3½ dozen.*

BROWN-EDGE WAFERS

¼ cup (½ stick) unsalted butter or
  margarine, softened
⅓ cup sugar
2 large egg whites
⅓ cup all-purpose flour
1 teaspoon grated lemon peel
CHOCOLATE GLAZE
2 squares (1-oz size) semisweet chocolate
2 tablespoons unsalted butter or margarine

1. Grease and flour three large cookie sheets. Preheat oven to 375F.

2. In small bowl, with electric mixer at medium speed, beat ¼ cup butter and the sugar until light and fluffy. Add egg whites, and beat 15 to 20 seconds, or until mixture is smooth but not frothy. With wooden spoon or wire whisk, lightly fold ⅓ cup flour and 1 teaspoon grated lemon peel into butter mixture.

3. Drop batter by rounded teaspoonfuls on prepared cookie sheets 2 inches apart, placing no more than nine cookies on each sheet. Bake cookies 4 to 6 minutes, or until edges are golden-brown. Let cookies cool 30 seconds on cookie sheet, or until they are firm enough to hold their shape. With pancake turner, remove cookies from sheet to wire rack; cool completely.

4. Make Chocolate Glaze: In small heatproof glass measuring cup or bowl, placed in a saucepan of hot water, melt chocolate with butter. (Or, in microwave oven, microwave at HIGH 2 to 3 minutes.) Stir until smooth. Using small spoon, drizzle glaze immediately over cookies in a zigzag pattern. Let dry. Store cookies in airtight container. *Makes 2 dozen cookies.*

JAM BITES

¾ cup (1½ sticks) butter or margarine,
  softened
½ cup sugar
1 large egg yolk
2¼ cups all-purpose flour
¼ cup apricot preserves
¼ cup chopped almonds or pistachios
¼ cup seedless raspberry jam

1. In large bowl, with electric mixer at medium speed, beat ¾ cup butter and the sugar until light and fluffy. Beat in egg yolk. At low speed, gradually add flour until well blended. With hands, press dough to form a ball.

2. Divide dough into four equal parts. With palms of hands, roll each part into a 12-inch rope about 1 inch wide. Place two ropes lengthwise on an ungreased cookie sheet, 2 inches apart. With side of finger, make a ½-inch-wide, ¼-inch-deep groove down the middle of each rope. Repeat with remaining dough on another cookie sheet.

3. In small cup, combine apricot preserves with 2 tablespoons chopped nuts. In another cup, combine raspberry jam with remaining chopped nuts. Spoon apricot-nut mixture into grooves of two of the strips. Spoon raspberry-nut mixture into remaining two strips. Refrigerate strips at least 20 minutes.

4. Preheat oven to 350F. Cut each strip crosswise into 1- or 2-inch diagonal slices, but do not separate into individual cookies yet. Bake 20 to 25 minutes, or until edges are slightly golden. While still warm, cut through slices; with pancake turner, remove cookies to wire rack to cool. Store cookies in single layer on tray, covered, in the refrigerator. *Makes 4 dozen (1-inch) cookies.*

WALNUT WREATHS

1 cup (2 sticks) butter or margarine,
  softened
1 cup lightly packed light-brown sugar
3 large egg yolks
1 teaspoon vanilla extract
2½ cups all-purpose flour
½ cup finely chopped walnuts
36 green candied cherries
27 red candied cherries
1 large egg white
1 tablespoon honey

1. Preheat oven to 325F. Lightly grease two large cookie sheets.

2. In medium bowl, with electric mixer at medium speed, beat butter and brown sugar until light and fluffy. Add egg yolks, one at a time, beating well after each addition. Add vanilla. At low speed, gradually beat in flour until well blended. With wooden spoon, stir in walnuts.

3. Using hands, form dough into 36 pieces. With palms of hands, roll each piece into an 8-inch rope. On prepared cookie sheets, form ropes into rings about 3 inches in diameter, crossing ends by ½ inch to simulate bows. Cut each green cherry into eighths; cut each red cherry into quarters.

4. In small bowl, beat egg white and honey until frothy; brush mixture over wreaths. Arrange 8 green-cherry slivers around each ring or wreath, and 3 red-cherry sections on the bow.

5. Bake 15 to 18 minutes, or until golden-brown. Remove to wire racks; cool. Store in airtight container. *Makes 3 dozen wreaths.* ∎

Patterns on pages 318 and 319 are used for tracing Antique-Toy Cookies, page 312.

A SWEET ENCHANTED FOREST

"I must be dreaming!" exclaims the little gnome in delight as he stumbles upon our mouth-watering array of confections nestled amid the greenery of this glade. All are molded and shaped to look like real denizens of the forest: marzipan-and-sliced-almond pinecones, caramel acorns (that squirrel can't wait to store these for the winter), a chocolate log, pecan-topped turtles, meringue mushrooms…and many more. To identify these delectable goodies and learn how to make them, turn the page.

FESTIVE FOODS 321

continued from page 321

1. *Chocolate Brazil Nuts.* 2. *Caramel Acorns; Burnt Almonds.* 3. *Chestnuts.* 4. *Marzipan Pinecones.* 5. *Marzipan Almonds.* 6. *Cocoa-Meringue Ladyfingers.* 7. *Turtles.* 8. *Chocolate-Dipped Peel.* 9. *Chocolate-Butterscotch Yule Log.* 10. *Penuche Walnuts.* 11. *Meringue Mushrooms.*

CHOCOLATE BRAZIL NUTS

¾ cup (1½ sticks) butter or margarine, softened
Sugar
½ teaspoon vanilla extract
2 squares unsweetened chocolate, melted
½ cup finely chopped walnuts or pecans
2 cups sifted all-purpose flour

1. In large bowl, with electric mixer at medium speed, or a wooden spoon, beat butter, ½ cup sugar and the vanilla until light and fluffy.
2. Beat in melted chocolate.
3. With spoon, stir in nuts. Add flour; mix until well blended. If dough is soft, refrigerate 1 hour, or until stiff enough to hold its shape.
4. Preheat oven to 350F. To shape: Use 1 level tablespoon dough for each. On ungreased cookie sheet, ½ inch apart, shape each into a crescent about 2½ inches long. With fingers, press along top edge to simulate shape of Brazil nut.
5. Bake 15 to 20 minutes, or just until set. Remove to racks; cool. *Makes 3 dozen.*

CARAMEL ACORNS

2¾ cups sifted all-purpose flour
½ teaspoon baking powder
1 cup (2 sticks) butter or margarine, softened
¾ cup light-brown sugar, firmly packed
3 egg yolks
1 teaspoon vanilla extract
½ cup finely chopped walnuts or pecans
½ lb vanilla caramels
¼ cup water
¾ cup finely chopped walnuts or pecans

1. Preheat oven to 350F. Sift together flour and baking powder.
2. In medium mixing bowl, combine butter, brown sugar and egg yolks. With electric mixer at medium speed, beat until smooth and fluffy.
3. Using wooden spoon, stir in vanilla, nuts and flour mixture. Mix well.
4. For each cookie, shape 1 slightly rounded teaspoon of dough into a ball. With fingers, pinch dough to a rounded point at one end to resemble an acorn.
5. Place 1 inch apart, on ungreased baking sheet, pointed side up. Bake 15 to 18 minutes, or until golden-brown. Remove from baking sheet to rack; cool completely.
6. In top of double boiler, combine caramels and water. Over hot water, stir until caramels are melted and mixture is smooth. Remove from heat.
7. Dip large end of cooled cookie into caramel, then into nuts. Store, covered, in refrigerator. *Makes 75.*

BURNT ALMONDS

1⅓ cups unblanched almonds
1 cup sugar
1 cup water

1. In heavy, medium-size skillet, combine almonds, sugar and water. Bring to boiling, stirring until sugar melts. Reduce heat; simmer until almonds make a popping sound—15 to 20 minutes.
2. Remove from heat. Stir until sugar crystallizes (mixture will become dry).
3. Return to heat; cook over low to medium heat until sugar starts to melt and clings to almonds, forming a glaze—15 minutes.
4. Turn out onto a greased cookie sheet. Separate almonds with fork. Cool completely. Store, in container with tight-fitting lid, in a cool, dry place. *Makes about 2 cups.*

CHESTNUTS

1 lb creamy peanut butter, at room temperature
1 cup (2 sticks) butter or margarine, softened
1½ lb (5½ cups) confectioners' sugar
1 pkg (12 oz) semisweet chocolate pieces

1. In large mixing bowl, combine peanut butter, butter and confectioners' sugar. Using wooden spoon, mix until smooth and well blended.
2. For large chestnuts: Shape 1 slightly rounded tablespoonful into a ball; flatten one side, to resemble a chestnut. Refrigerate several hours or overnight. *Makes about 40.*
3. For small chestnuts: Shape 1 slightly rounded teaspoonful into a ball. Refrigerate several hours or overnight. *Makes about 80.*
4. Next day: In top of double boiler, place chocolate pieces over hot, not boiling, water, stirring occasionally, until chocolate is melted. Remove from hot water.
5. Using a fork, dip cold "chestnuts" into chocolate just until two-thirds covered. Place on rack. When chocolate coating is firm, cover and refrigerate. If desired, freeze for later use.

MARZIPAN PINECONES

1 can (8 oz) almond paste
1⅔ cups confectioners' sugar
1 egg white
Blanched sliced almonds, toasted (see Note)
Water

1. In medium bowl, break the almond paste into smaller pieces. Knead to make it pliable.

2. Gradually knead sugar into almond paste, alternately with egg white, a little at a time.

3. To simulate a pinecone: With palms of hands, shape 1 scant tablespoon marzipan into a cone shape, about 1½ inches long (rounded at one end, pointed at the other end).

4. Starting at pointed end of cone shape, press almonds (pointed side in) into marzipan at slight angle and overlapping one another, in rows, to cover completely. (Before inserting into marzipan, dip tip of almond in water to hold in place better.) Refrigerate. *Makes 28.*

Note: To toast almonds: Place in a single layer in baking pan. Bake at 350F 10 to 12 minutes, or until golden.

MARZIPAN ALMONDS

Marzipan Pinecones, recipe above
⅓ cup semisweet chocolate pieces

1. Follow recipe for Marzipan Pinecones, above (Steps 1 and 2).

2. With fingers, shape 1 teaspoon dough to look like half an almond, 1¾ inches long, using a real almond in its shell as a model. With back of spoon, press a ridge around the edge.

3. Melt ⅓ cup semisweet chocolate pieces in top of double boiler over hot water.

4. Put two halves together with melted chocolate to form a whole almond. Make tiny indentations in "shell" with toothpick. Refrigerate. *Makes 28.*

COCOA-MERINGUE LADYFINGERS (LOGS)

½ cup egg whites
1¼ cups sifted confectioners' sugar
½ cup sifted unsweetened cocoa
1 cup granulated sugar
½ cup water
Dash salt
½ teaspoon vanilla extract

1. In small bowl of electric mixer, let egg whites warm to room temperature.

2. Preheat oven to 275F. Line two large baking sheets with brown paper.

3. On sheet of waxed paper, sift together confectioners' sugar and cocoa.

4. In small, heavy 1-quart saucepan, combine granulated sugar and water. Cook, stirring, over medium heat until sugar is dissolved and syrup is clear. Continue cooking over high heat, without stirring, to 240F on candy thermometer, or until a little spins a thin, 6-to-8-inch thread when dropped from tip of spoon.

5. Meanwhile, with mixer at high speed, beat egg whites and salt until stiff, moist peaks form when beaters are slowly raised.

6. With mixer at high speed, slowly pour hot syrup in a thin stream over egg whites, beating constantly. Add vanilla.

7. Turn meringue into large bowl of electric mixer; continue beating about 5 minutes, or until mixture is cool and stiff.

8. At low speed, gradually add cocoa-sugar mixture, guiding mixture into beaters with rubber spatula and beating just until smooth and well blended. Don't overbeat.

9. Using a rubber spatula, turn meringue into large pastry bag with number-5 plain tip (½-inch opening).

10. Pipe meringue in strips, 1 inch apart, to make ladyfingers 3 to 3½ inches long and about ¾ inch wide.

11. Bake both sheets at the same time 30 to 35 minutes.

12. Turn off oven. Let meringues stay in the oven until cool (open oven door slightly)—about 30 minutes.

13. With spatula, remove ladyfingers from paper. Store, covered, in a cool dry place. *Makes 30.*

TURTLES

For recipe, see page 177.

continued on page 324

continued from page 323

CHOCOLATE-DIPPED PEEL

1 large grapefruit
3 large navel oranges
Water
3 cups sugar
¼ cup light corn syrup
6 squares semisweet chocolate
2 tablespoons butter or margarine

1. Cut grapefruit and oranges in half lengthwise; squeeze out as much juice as possible. Refrigerate juice to use as desired.

2. In heavy, 3-quart saucepan, place peel and 2 quarts water; bring to boiling. Reduce heat, and simmer, covered, 30 to 40 minutes, or until peel is tender.

3. Drain; cool slightly. Carefully scrape excess pulp from peel.

4. In same saucepan, combine 1 cup water, 2 cups sugar and the corn syrup. Cook over medium heat, stirring constantly, until sugar is dissolved and syrup comes to boiling. Continue cooking, without stirring, to 235F on candy thermometer, or until a little in cold water forms a soft ball.

5. Add grapefruit and orange peel; simmer gently, stirring frequently, 30 to 40 minutes, or until peel becomes translucent. (To prevent scorching during cooking, lift peel off bottom of pan several times.)

6. Turn peel and syrup into bowl. Let stand in a cool, dry place, covered, overnight.

7. Next day, remove peel from syrup to wire rack, and let drain 3 hours. Then, with scissors, cut into ¼-inch-wide strips. Roll in remaining 1 cup sugar, coating well. Place on rack to partially dry—about 3 hours. Roll in sugar again.

8. In top of double boiler, over hot, not boiling, water, melt chocolate and butter. Holding with tongs or impaled on a toothpick, dip each strip in the chocolate to coat half the strip; drain off excess chocolate. Place on waxed paper on tray. Cool. Store in refrigerator. *Makes about 2 pounds.*

CHOCOLATE-BUTTERSCOTCH YULE LOG

1 lb pitted dates, coarsely chopped
1¼ cups walnuts
5 pieces candied ginger, finely chopped (about 3 tablespoons)
¼ cup confectioners' sugar
4 squares (1-oz size) semisweet chocolate
2 tablespoons butterscotch or peanut-butter pieces
Angelica (optional)
Candied cherries (optional)

1. Combine dates, nuts and ginger. Process in food processor, one-half at a time, to chop all finely. Turn out on breadboard sprinkled with confectioners' sugar. Knead with hands to blend thoroughly.

2. Form into a roll 1½ inches thick. Cut a 1½-inch piece from the end; roll and place on top of roll to form a branch stub. Wrap in waxed paper; refrigerate at least 1 hour before coating with chocolate.

3. In top of double boiler, melt chocolate over hot, not boiling, water. Spoon over date roll, spreading to coat evenly all over.

4. With fork, draw lines on log to simulate bark. Refrigerate until chocolate is hard.

5. In small skillet, over low heat, melt butterscotch pieces. With small spatula, spread on each end of the log, as well as on the branch stub. If desired, decorate with bits of angelica and candied cherries. Refrigerate at least 2 hours before serving.

6. To serve, cut into thin slices while still cold. *Makes 1 log, about 1½ pounds.*

PENUCHE WALNUTS

3 cups light-brown sugar, firmly packed
1 cup light cream or half-and-half
2 tablespoons butter or margarine
1½ teaspoons vanilla extract
⅔ cup chopped walnuts

1. Lightly butter a 9-by-5-by-2¾-inch loaf pan. Line with heavy-duty foil; lightly grease foil with butter or margarine.

2. In heavy, 3-quart saucepan, cook brown sugar and cream over low heat, stirring constantly with a wooden spoon, until sugar dissolves and mixture comes to boiling.

3. Cook, stirring occasionally, until candy thermometer registers 234F, or until a little in cold water forms a soft ball.

4. Remove from heat and add butter. Set aside, without stirring, to cool to lukewarm (110F).

5. Add vanilla. With wooden spoon, beat until thick and creamy. Stir in nuts.

6. Quickly turn into prepared loaf pan; cool completely; refrigerate.

7. To make walnuts: Turn penuche out of pan in one piece. Remove foil.

8. Take 1 well-rounded tablespoon of penuche. Using a real walnut as model, shape penuche with fingers into a walnut. Form an oval 1½ inches long and tapered at one end. Then, using a toothpick, make lines and indentations, as on the walnut.

9. Refrigerate each walnut after it is made. If penuche is too soft to handle, refrigerate 1 hour. *Makes 24.*

MERINGUE MUSHROOMS

2 egg whites (¼ cup), at room temperature for one hour
⅛ teaspoon cream of tartar
½ cup sugar
½ cup semisweet chocolate pieces
1 tablespoon unsweetened cocoa

1. Line a cookie sheet with brown paper.

2. Preheat oven to 200F.

3. In small bowl of electric mixer, combine egg whites with cream of tartar. At high speed, beat until foamy. Gradually add sugar, 2 tablespoons at a time, beating well after each addition.

4. Turn meringue into a large pastry bag with a large plain tip, ½ inch in diameter.

5. To make caps: On prepared baking sheet, press out mounds of meringue, 1¼ inches in diameter each, 2 inches apart. With spatula, smooth tops.

6. To make stems: Hold pastry tube upright; press out meringue 1¼ inches long, 2 inches apart.

7. Bake 2 hours, or until dry. Remove with spatula from paper to rack.

8. To assemble mushrooms: Turn cap upside down; with sharp knife, poke a small hole in center (the stem will later fit in this hole).

9. In small saucepan, over low heat, melt chocolate pieces.

10. Spread a thin layer of melted chocolate over bottom of cap. Immediately insert smaller end of mushroom stem into the hole.

11. Place on rack upside down; let stand until chocolate is firm—about 1 hour. Sift cocoa lightly over tops of mushrooms.

12. Cover with waxed paper; store at room temperature. *Makes 24.* ■

continued from page 299

VIENNESE COOKIES

COOKIE DOUGH
2 cups all-purpose flour
1 cup (2 sticks) butter or margarine, softened
1 cup ground walnuts or pecans
½ cup confectioners' sugar
⅛ teaspoon salt
1 teaspoon vanilla extract
¼ teaspoon almond extract

CHOCOLATE GLAZE
1 pkg (6 oz) semisweet chocolate pieces
2 tablespoons light corn syrup
2 tablespoons light cream or half-and-half

Sliced almonds
Chocolate shot
Multicolor nonpareils
Coconut

1. Make Cookie Dough: In large bowl, combine flour, butter, nuts, ½ cup sugar, the salt and extracts. With hands, mix until thoroughly blended; shape into a ball. Refrigerate, covered, 1 hour.
2. Preheat oven to 375F.
3. Shape cookies: Form dough into 1-inch balls. Then, with palms of hands, roll each ball into a 3-inch-long roll.
4. Place rolls, 2 inches apart, on ungreased cookie sheets; curve to make crescent shapes or ovals.
5. Bake 10 to 12 minutes, or until set but not brown.
6. Let stand 1 minute; remove to rack; cool completely.
7. Make Chocolate Glaze: In top of double boiler, combine chocolate pieces, corn syrup and cream. Cook over hot water, stirring until chocolate is melted and mixture is smooth. Remove from heat.
8. Dip ends of cookies in Chocolate Glaze; sprinkle with sliced almonds, chocolate shot, nonpareils or coconut. Let stand on wire rack until glaze is set. Refrigerate, covered. Or drizzle Chocolate Glaze over cookies, as pictured. *Makes about 3½ dozen.*

SPRINGERLE

4 cups sifted all-purpose flour
1 teaspoon baking powder
½ teaspoon salt
4 eggs
2 cups granulated sugar
2 teaspoons grated lemon peel
2 tablespoons anise seed
Confectioners' sugar

1. Two days before: Sift flour with baking powder and salt twice.
2. In large bowl of electric mixer at high speed, beat eggs until thick and lemon-colored—about 5 minutes.
3. At medium speed, gradually beat in granulated sugar, 2 tablespoons at a time, beating after each addition. Continue to beat until mixture is thick and smooth—about 10 minutes—occasionally cleaning side of bowl with rubber spatula.
4. Add flour mixture and lemon peel to egg mixture; with a wooden spoon, mix well until mixture is smooth.
5. Refrigerate dough, covered, overnight. Also refrigerate springerle rolling pin.
6. Lightly grease two large cookie sheets; sprinkle each with 1 tablespoon anise seed.
7. Divide dough into three parts. Refrigerate until ready to roll out.
8. Sprinkle pastry cloth or wooden board lightly with confectioners' sugar.
9. Roll one part of dough on pastry cloth, to coat with sugar; then roll out to an 8-by-5½-inch rectangle. Repeat with remaining dough.
10. Remove springerle pin from refrigerator. Coat surface lightly with confectioners' sugar. Starting from long side, slowly roll pin once, firmly and evenly, over dough, to make designs. (If dough sticks to springerle pin, peel off with a spatula.)
11. With floured sharp knife, carefully cut along straight lines in dough, to make individual cookies.
12. With wide spatula, transfer cookies to prepared cookie sheets, placing them ½ inch apart. Let stand, uncovered, at room temperature overnight.
13. Next day, preheat oven to 325F. Bake cookies 15 minutes, or just until light golden. Remove to wire rack; cool completely.
14. Store springerle in tightly covered container in a cool, dry place two to three weeks before serving. *Makes about 4½ dozen.*

CHOCOLATE PRETZELS

1 cup (2 sticks) butter or margarine, softened
1 cup sugar
1½ teaspoons grated lemon peel
3 egg yolks
1 cup ground unblanched almonds
¼ teaspoon almond extract
2¼ cups sifted all-purpose flour

CHOCOLATE GLAZE
2 pkg (6-oz size) semisweet chocolate pieces
¼ cup light corn syrup
½ cup light cream or half-and-half

1. In medium bowl, combine butter, sugar and lemon peel; using portable electric mixer, beat until smooth and fluffy.
2. Add egg yolks, one at a time, beating well after each addition.
3. Add almonds and almond extract; mix well.
4. Gradually add flour, mixing until the dough is smooth.
5. Refrigerate dough, covered, 1 hour.
6. Meanwhile, make Chocolate Glaze: In top of double boiler, combine chocolate pieces, corn syrup and cream. Cook over hot water, stirring, until chocolate is melted and mixture is smooth. Remove from heat.
7. Preheat oven to 350F. Grease baking sheet. Remove dough from refrigerator. Form dough into balls, using 1 tablespoon for each ball. Then, with palms of hands, on lightly floured pastry cloth, form each ball into a roll 8 inches long.
8. Shape into pretzels. Place on prepared cookie sheet, 2 inches apart.
9. Bake 10 to 12 minutes, or until lightly browned. Remove cookies to wire rack.
10. To glaze: Place sheet of waxed paper under rack of cookies. Brush glaze over warm cookies, covering completely. If glaze is too stiff to spread, reheat over hot water. Let glaze set before storing cookies in refrigerator. *Makes 4 dozen.* ∎

Heavenly Holiday Desserts

*C*hristmas is the time for spectacular desserts,
like this scroll-topped Baked Alaska of orange chiffon cake
adorned with vanilla and strawberry ice cream and served
with rich hot Chocolate Sauce.

*A*bove, the splendor of a Gâteau St.-Honoré:
tiny cream puffs encircling a rich cream filling, glazed with
caramelized sugar and crowned with strawberries.

*T*he Four Seasons Fancy Cake—a glorious mound
of pineapple Bavarian cream wrapped in sheets of chocolate
—is named for the New York restaurant that invented it.

*F*resh sliced oranges poached in sugar syrup make
this glazed cream-filled citrus tart positively celestial. For
this and other recipes, see page 330.

continued from page 329

BAKED ALASKA
(pictured)

1 quart vanilla ice cream
1 quart strawberry ice cream
Orange Chiffon Layer
    Cake, recipe follows
Chocolate Sauce, recipe follows

MERINGUE
8 egg whites (1¼ cups)
¼ teaspoon cream of tartar
¼ teaspoon salt
1 cup sugar
½ teaspoon vanilla extract

Confectioners' sugar

1. Day ahead: Let ice cream stand at room temperature 20 minutes, to soften. On sheet of foil on cookie sheet, draw an oval 10 inches long and 7 inches wide. With spatula, spread oval with vanilla ice cream, mounding in center; layer strawberry ice cream on top; freeze, covered, several hours or overnight.

2. Next day, make Orange Chiffon Cake Layer: Bake in an ungreased 9-by-9-by-2-inch square baking pan. Cool completely. Make Chocolate Sauce.

3. About two hours before serving, start assembling. Make Meringue: Let egg whites stand at room temperature 1 hour. In large bowl of electric mixer, at high speed, beat egg whites with cream of tartar and salt just until soft peaks form when beaters are slowly raised.

4. Gradually beat in sugar, 2 tablespoons at a time, beating well after each addition. Continue beating until egg whites are shiny and stiff peaks form when beaters are raised. Add vanilla.

5. With spatula, carefully loosen cake from pan; remove. Cut cake, on the diagonal, into an oval 10 inches long and 7 inches wide.

6. Preheat oven to 425F. Place cake in bottom of ovenproof oval baking dish (12½ inches by 8 inches). (We used an oval metal au gratin dish.) Working quickly, remove foil from bottom of ice cream; place on top of cake.

7. With spatula, spread entire cake and ice cream with meringue (about 1 inch thick), sealing completely.

8. Spoon the rest of the meringue into a pastry bag with number-6 star tip. Decorate the top and side with swirls (as pictured) or in any pattern desired. (Freeze if not baking at once.)

9. On lowest shelf of oven, bake Alaska 6 to 8 minutes, or until lightly browned. Meanwhile, reheat Chocolate Sauce in double boiler over hot water.

10. Sprinkle Alaska lightly with confectioners' sugar. Serve at once with Chocolate Sauce. *Makes 12 servings.*

ORANGE CHIFFON CAKE LAYER

½ cup egg whites (3 or 4)
1 cup plus 2 tablespoons sifted cake flour
¾ cup sugar
1½ teaspoons baking powder
½ teaspoon salt
¼ cup salad oil
2 egg yolks
¼ cup plus 2 tablespoons orange juice
1½ tablespoons grated orange peel
¼ teaspoon cream of tartar

1. In large bowl of electric mixer, let egg whites warm to room temperature—about 1 hour. Preheat oven to 350F.

2. Sift flour with sugar, baking powder and salt into another large bowl; make well in center. Add, in order, oil, egg yolks, orange juice and orange peel; beat with spoon until smooth.

3. With electric mixer at high speed, beat egg whites with cream of tartar until very stiff peaks form.

4. With wire whisk or rubber spatula, using under-and-over motion, gradually fold orange batter gently into egg whites just until blended. Do not stir.

5. Pour into ungreased 9-by-1½-inch round layer cake pan; bake 30 to 35 minutes, or until cake tester inserted in center comes out clean.

6. Invert cake by hanging pan between two other pans; let cool completely—about 1 hour.

7. With spatula, carefully loosen cake from pan; hit pan sharply on table; remove cake. Wrap loosely in foil, or store in cake box, until ready to assemble.

CHOCOLATE SAUCE

½ cup sugar
¼ cup unsweetened cocoa
½ cup light cream or half-and-half
⅓ cup light corn syrup
¼ cup (½ stick) butter or margarine
2 squares unsweetened chocolate
Dash salt
1½ teaspoons vanilla extract

1. In small saucepan, combine sugar and cocoa; mix well. Add cream, corn syrup, butter, chocolate and salt.

2. Cook over medium heat, stirring constantly, until sauce is smooth and comes to boiling. Remove from heat; stir in vanilla. *Makes 1½ cups.*

GATEAU ST.-HONORE
(pictured)

Pastry Cream, recipe follows

CREAM-PUFF DOUGH
1 cup water
¾ cup (1½ sticks) butter or margarine
¼ teaspoon salt
1½ cups all-purpose flour
6 large eggs

CARAMELIZED SUGAR
1¼ cups granulated sugar
¼ cup water

1 to 2 pints strawberries, washed and hulled
Confectioners' sugar

1. Make Pastry Cream, and refrigerate.

2. Make Cream-Puff Dough: Preheat oven to 400F. In medium saucepan, combine 1 cup water, the butter and salt. Bring to boiling over medium heat.

3. Remove from heat. Immediately, with wooden spoon, beat in all the flour.

4. Return to low heat, and continue beating until mixture forms a ball and leaves side of pan.

5. Remove from heat. Add eggs, one at a time, beating until dough is shiny and satiny—about 1 minute.

6. On large ungreased cookie sheet, spread one-third of the dough (about 1 cup) evenly in an 8-inch circle, ¼ inch thick. On the same cookie sheet, for 12 medium-size cream puffs, drop another third of dough by rounded tablespoonfuls, 2 inches apart. Bake 30 to 35 minutes, or until puffed and nicely browned. Remove to wire rack; let cool.

7. For 12 small puffs, drop rest of dough in level tablespoons, 2 inches apart, on ungreased cookie sheet. Bake 25 to 30 minutes, or until puffed and nicely browned. Remove to wire rack; let cool.

8. Caramelize sugar: In medium-size, heavy skillet, place granulated sugar and ¼ cup water; cook over medium heat until mixture forms a light-brown syrup—takes about 8 minutes. Then stir to blend. Remove from heat.

9. To assemble Gâteau: Dip bottoms of 12 largest puffs into caramel syrup; arrange closely around edge of cream-puff round to make a border (cream puffs should touch one another).

10. Continue building gâteau (like building a wall, to hold cream filling) with 12 smaller cream puffs. Spoon rest of caramel syrup over top of each puff.

11. Just before serving, turn Pastry Cream into center. Mound whole strawberries on top of cream; sprinkle with confectioners' sugar. *Serves 12 to 16.*

PASTRY CREAM FOR GATEAU ST. HONORE

Pastry Cream, page 331
¼ teaspoon almond extract
½ cup heavy cream, whipped

1. Make Pastry Cream. Add almond extract with vanilla. Omit Grand Marnier.

2. After chilling pastry cream, fold in whipped cream just before using.

FOUR SEASONS FANCY CAKE

(pictured)

Pineapple Bavarian Cream, recipe follows
CHOCOLATE COATING
2 pkg (6-oz size) semisweet chocolate
   pieces
¼ cup (½ stick) butter or margarine
¼ cup light corn syrup

Orange Chiffon Cake Layer, page 330
2 tablespoons dark rum

1. Day ahead, make Pineapple Bavarian Cream and Chocolate Coating.

2. To make Chocolate Coating: Cut five pieces of waxed paper 8 by 7 inches; then cut one sheet 17 by 5 inches.

3. In top of double boiler, combine chocolate with butter and corn syrup. Cook over hot water, covered and stirring occasionally, until melted and smooth. Remove from heat; keep top in place over hot water.

4. Spread ⅓ cup Chocolate Coating evenly on 17-by-5-inch waxed-paper sheet. On 8-by-7-inch sheets, spread remaining Chocolate Coating evenly. Refrigerate until firm—overnight or until ready to assemble cake.

5. Next day: Make Orange Chiffon Cake Layer. Cool completely. Sprinkle top with dark rum. Place cake layer on top of Bavarian cream. Invert on cake plate; remove bowl; peel off plastic wrap.

6. Remove the 8-by-7-inch chocolate-coated sheets from refrigerator; let stand at room temperature 3 minutes, or until chocolate peels easily from waxed paper.

7. Place chocolate side of one sheet, long side up and down, against side of Bavarian and cake; using a knife, loosen paper from chocolate at top, and peel off. Press chocolate against side, and quickly make a fold at top by sliding finger or handle of wooden spoon under chocolate and loosely pinching together to make fold. Repeat with remaining 4 sheets, overlapping them. Refrigerate.

8. To make ruching on top: Remove long chocolate strip from refrigerator; let stand 2 or 3 minutes. Cut in half, lengthwise, to make two (2½-inch-wide) strips; then peel off paper. With fingers, push in and pull out chocolate to make 4-inch ruffle on top of cake. Set each ruffle on top of cake, as pictured. Refrigerate.

9. To slice, let cake stand at room temperature about 20 minutes before serving. To serve, slice in wedges, without disturbing the topknot. *Serves 16.*

PINEAPPLE BAVARIAN CREAM

3 env unflavored gelatine
3¾ cups milk
6 eggs, separated
¼ teaspoon salt
1¼ cups sugar
¼ cup dark rum
1 can (8½ oz) crushed pineapple, drained
1 cup heavy cream, whipped
½ cup crushed almond macaroons or
   vanilla wafers
⅓ cup finely chopped walnuts or pecans

1. Sprinkle gelatine over 1 cup milk; let soften.

2. Heat remaining milk in top of double boiler, over direct heat, until tiny bubbles appear around edge.

3. In medium bowl, beat egg yolks with salt and ½ cup sugar just until well blended. Add softened gelatine. Gradually add hot milk, stirring rapidly.

4. Return mixture to top of double boiler; place over simmering water; cook, stirring, until mixture coats a metal spoon—about 15 minutes. Remove from heat; cool slightly. Add rum and pineapple.

5. Hasten chilling by placing pan over ice water; stir occasionally, until mixture is thicker than unbeaten egg white, or until it mounds slightly when lifted with a spoon—about 30 minutes.

6. Meanwhile, line a 2½-quart bowl with plastic wrap or foil; set aside.

7. In large bowl of electric mixer, beat egg whites until they form soft peaks when beaters are slowly raised. Gradually beat in remaining ¾ cup sugar; continue beating until stiff peaks form when beaters are slowly raised.

8. Add whipped cream and chilled gelatine mixture; beat at low speed just until combined—about 1 minute. Turn into prepared bowl.

9. In small bowl, combine macaroon crumbs and nuts; mix well. Sprinkle over mixture in bowl; press gently. Refrigerate until firm.

GLAZED ORANGE TARTE

(pictured)

2 cups sugar
¼ cup light corn syrup
2 cups water
4 medium navel oranges, unpeeled, sliced
   ¼ inch thick
2 tablespoons Grand Marnier
PASTRY
1½ cups sifted all-purpose flour
¼ cup sugar
¼ teaspoon salt
½ cup (1 stick) butter or margarine
1 egg, slightly beaten

Pastry Cream, recipe follows
Candied red cherries
½ cup apricot preserves

1. Day ahead, prepare oranges slices: In 4-quart Dutch oven, combine 2 cups sugar, corn syrup and water. Bring to boiling, stirring constantly, until sugar is dissolved. Boil, uncovered, 10 minutes.

2. Add orange slices; reduce heat; simmer slowly 1½ hours, or until slices are glazed and peel is tender. Remove from heat. Add Grand Marnier. Turn into a shallow dish to coat orange slices.

3. Cover; let stand at room temperature overnight.

4. Make Pastry: With fork, blend flour, sugar and salt in medium bowl.

5. With pastry blender, cut in butter until dough is in small particles. Stir in egg; blend well. Form into a ball; refrigerate overnight or until ready to roll out.

6. Make Pastry Cream.

7. Next day, make pastry shell: Roll pastry on lightly floured pastry cloth to form a 14-inch circle. Lift into a fluted 12-inch pan with removable bottom in place. Press evenly to bottom and side; pastry should come halfway up the side. Prick all over with fork. Refrigerate.

8. Preheat oven to 400F. Bake pastry shell 15 minutes. Cool on wire rack.

9. About 1½ hours before serving, gently remove outer rim of pan from pastry, keeping shell on bottom.

10. Drain orange slices; save syrup.

11. Fill pastry with Pastry Cream. Overlap orange slices around edge, then in center, as pictured. Garnish with cherries.

12. In small saucepan, bring to boiling 1 cup reserved syrup; boil, uncovered, to reduce it to ¼ cup. Add apricot preserves; stir over low heat until melted.

13. Use to brush over orange slices, coating completely. Refrigerate about 1 hour, to chill well. *Serves 10 to 12.*

PASTRY CREAM

⅔ cup sugar
¼ teaspoon salt
3 tablespoons cornstarch
3 cups milk
6 egg yolks, slightly beaten
1½ teaspoons vanilla extract
3 tablespoons Grand Marnier

1. In medium-size saucepan, mix sugar, salt, cornstarch. Stir in milk.

2. Cook, stirring constantly, over medium heat until mixture begins to boil; boil 1 minute. Remove from heat.

3. Add a little hot mixture to egg yolks, mixing well. Return to pan.

4. Cook, stirring constantly, until mixture is thick and bubbly.

5. Stir in vanilla. Let cool to room temperature—about 1 hour. Add Grand Marnier. Refrigerate, with waxed paper placed directly on surface, until well chilled. *Makes about 3⅓ cups.* ∎

SEVEN

WE WELCOME THE NEW YEAR

As the clock ticktocks away the last few hours and minutes of the year, we look toward a new year filled with hopes of better things to come. To help celebrate this special eve, as well as the day after, we've collected a smorgasbord of food and drink ideas that will let you usher in the New Year in spectacular style.

If the festivities involve hors d'oeuvres, you'll love our freeze-ahead and low-calorie nibbles. For help-yourself entertaining, our salmon dinner is sheer elegance; our curried chicken buffet, wonderfully bountiful. And one of our mouth-watering desserts will make a perfect finale to the feasting. Since New Year's is not celebrated with food alone, we've set you up with tips and exciting drinks — both spirited and nonalcoholic — in our "Party-Givers Guide to Beverages."

Finally, our recipe-of-the-month calendar offers marvelous dishes to help keep the special spirit of the holidays alive all through the new year.

What's the secret to enjoying your own New Year's celebration? Doing as much as possible ahead of time. To help, here's a lavish array of hot and cold hors d'oeuvres to prepare in advance, pop into the freezer, then simply heat or let thaw at party time. They include, at top left, a tempting platter of hot, flaky pastries with a variety of delicious fillings; clockwise, creamy quiche squares; a colorful tray of cold canapés; flavorful rumaki; and two Mexican treats: guacamole dip and spicy meatballs in chili sauce. Recipes begin on page 336.

GEORGE RATKAI

continued from page 334

All recipes are pictured on pages 334 and 335. See diagram below.

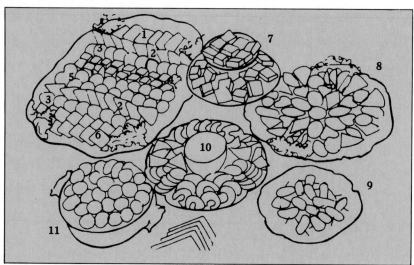

1. *Miniature Egg Rolls.* 2. *Triconas.* 3. *Hot Mushroom Canapés.* 4. *Cheddar-Cheese Puffs.* 5. *Golden Cheese Nuggets.* 6. *Shrimp Toast.* 7. *Quiche-Lorraine Squares.* 8. *Frozen Canapé Tray.* 9. *Rumaki.* 10. *Frozen Guacamole.* 11. *Mexican Meatballs With Chili Sauce.*

MINIATURE EGG ROLLS

BATTER
2½ cups water
2 cups all-purpose flour
1 egg
½ teaspoon salt

FILLING
¼ cup salad oil
½ cup finely chopped celery
¼ cup finely chopped scallion
1 clove garlic, pressed
¾ cup finely chopped cooked shrimp
¾ cup finely chopped cooked pork
¾ cup finely chopped water chestnuts
¾ cup bean sprouts
¼ cup soy sauce
½ teaspoon ground ginger
1 teaspoon sugar

Salad oil for deep-frying
Hot mustard (see Note)
Piquant Apricot Sauce, recipe follows

1. Make Batter: Gradually add 2½ cups water to flour in medium bowl, beating with portable electric mixer to make a smooth batter. Beat in egg and salt; beat until smooth, not frothy. Refrigerate until ready to use.

2. Make Filling: Heat 2 tablespoons oil in large heavy skillet; add celery, scallion and garlic. Cook, stirring, until tender—several minutes.

3. Add 2 tablespoons oil, the shrimp, pork, water chestnuts, bean sprouts, soy sauce, ginger and sugar; cook, stirring, 5 minutes. Set aside.

4. Lightly grease a 5-inch skillet (nonstick finish, if possible); heat slowly. Beat batter; pour 2 tablespoons batter into skillet, turning pan to spread batter all over. Cook several minutes; turn; cook on other side. Do not brown. Cool on wire rack; stack pancakes with squares of waxed paper between them. Continue making rest of pancakes. Lightly grease skillet in between.

5. Place 1 tablespoon filling in center of each pancake; fold four sides over filling.

6. Slowly heat oil (1 inch deep) in large skillet to 375F. Fry several egg rolls at a time just until crisp and golden-brown. Lift out with slotted spoon; drain on paper towels.

7. To freeze: Place egg rolls in single layer on tray; freeze until firm. Then freezer-wrap, label and store in freezer.

8. To serve: Preheat oven to 375F. Place as many frozen egg rolls as needed on cookie sheet. Bake 12 minutes, or until crisp and hot. Serve at once with hot mustard and Piquant Apricot Sauce. *Makes 26.*

Note: For hot mustard, use 2 tablespoons dry hot mustard mixed with ¼ cup water to form a smooth mixture.

PIQUANT APRICOT SAUCE

½ cup apricot jam, sieved
1½ tablespoons horseradish

In small bowl, combine jam and horseradish; blend well. Thin to desired consistency with 1 to 2 teaspoons water. *Makes ½ cup.*

TRICONAS
(Hot Cheese Pastries)

FILLING
2 pkg (8-oz size) cream cheese, softened
½ lb Greek cheese (feta), crumbled
1 egg
3 tablespoons butter or margarine, melted

1 pkg (1 lb) prepared phyllo-pastry or strudel-pastry leaves
1 cup (2 sticks) butter or margarine, melted

1. Make Filling: In small bowl of electric mixer, combine cream cheese, Greek cheese, egg and 3 tablespoons butter; beat at medium speed until well blended and smooth.

2. Preheat oven to 400F.

3. Place two leaves of phyllo pastry on board; brush with melted butter. Cut lengthwise into strips 2 inches wide.

4. Place 1 heaping teaspoon filling at end of a strip. Fold over one corner to opposite side, to make a triangle. Continue folding, keeping triangle shape, to other end of strip. Arrange on brown-paper-lined cookie sheets. Repeat with remaining strips.

5. Repeat with other pastry leaves.

6. Bake 20 minutes, or until golden-brown.

7. Cool on wire rack. Arrange in single layer on tray. Freeze. When frozen hard, remove from tray; freezer-wrap and label. Freeze until serving.

8. To serve: Preheat oven to 350F. Arrange frozen pastries on brown-paper-lined cookie sheets. Bake 10 minutes, or until heated through. Serve at once. *Makes about 7 dozen.*

HOT MUSHROOM CANAPES

1 lb mushrooms
¼ cup (½ stick) butter or margarine
1 cup finely chopped onion
⅓ cup all-purpose flour
⅓ cup milk
½ teaspoon salt
⅛ teaspoon pepper
1 loaf sliced white bread
Grated Parmesan cheese
Sliced stuffed olives

1. Wash mushrooms; dry on paper towels. Chop fine.

2. In some of hot butter in large skillet, sauté onion, stirring, until golden—about 5 minutes. Add rest of butter and the mushrooms; sauté, stirring, 5 minutes longer, or until tender and liquid has almost evaporated. Remove skillet from heat.

3. Add flour gradually, sprinkling over surface and stirring to mix well. Gradually stir in milk; add salt and pepper. Cook, stirring, until mixture is quite thick. Set aside to cool.

4. Using a 2-inch round cutter, cut bread into rounds. Spread with mushroom mixture, using about 1 tablespoon for each. Arrange in single layer on tray. Sprinkle with a little Parmesan cheese.

5. Freeze until firm. Remove to foil tray; freezer-wrap, label and seal. Store in freezer until serving.

6. To serve: Preheat broiler. Arrange frozen canapés on cookie sheets. Run under broiler 5 minutes, about 8 inches from heat, to brown top and heat through. Garnish each with olive slice. *Makes 30.*

CHEDDAR-CHEESE PUFFS

2 pkg (3-oz size) cream cheese
1 cup (2 sticks) butter or margarine
½ lb extra-sharp Cheddar cheese
1 teaspoon dry mustard
4 egg whites, beaten stiff
1 loaf (1 lb) unsliced white bread

1. In medium saucepan, over low heat, melt cream cheese, butter, Cheddar cheese and mustard. Remove from heat; let cool slightly; gently fold into stiffly beaten egg whites, to combine.

2. Trim crusts from bread; slice into 1-inch-thick slices; cut slices into 1-inch cubes.

3. Using fork, dip bread cubes into cheese mixture, coating evenly, but not on bottoms. Arrange on waxed-paper-lined tray. Place in freezer until frozen.

4. Remove to plastic bags; seal, label and store in freezer until ready to use.

5. To serve: Preheat oven to 400F. Place on lightly greased cookie sheet. Bake, frozen, 10 to 12 minutes, or until piping hot and golden-brown. Serve at once. *Makes 6 dozen.*

GOLDEN CHEESE NUGGETS

1 cup (¼ lb) grated sharp Cheddar cheese
¼ cup (½ stick) butter, softened
¼ teaspoon Worcestershire sauce
¾ cup sifted all-purpose flour
1 jar (6 oz) stuffed green olives

1. In small bowl, with fork, blend cheese, butter and Worcestershire; stir in flour to mix well. With hands, knead slightly to form a dough. Preheat oven to 400F.

2. Drain olives very well; dry on paper towels. Mold some dough around each olive, using about 1 teaspoon dough for each.

3. Arrange on cookie sheet. Bake 15 minutes, or until slightly golden. Cool on wire rack.

4. Place on tray; freeze 30 minutes, or until frozen. Remove to plastic bags; seal, label and store in freezer.

5. To serve: Preheat oven to 400F. Remove to cookie sheet. Bake, frozen, 15 to 18 minutes, or until heated through and crisp on the outside. Serve at once. *Makes 16.*

SHRIMP TOAST

12 slices white bread
1 lb deveined shelled shrimp
¼ cup finely chopped onion
1 tablespoon dry sherry
2 teaspoons salt
1 teaspoon sugar
Dash pepper
1 tablespoon cornstarch
1 egg, beaten
1 can (8 oz) water chestnuts, drained and finely chopped
Salad oil for frying
Chopped parsley

1. Trim crusts from bread; let slices dry out slightly.

2. Chop shrimp coarsely by hand; in medium bowl, toss with onion, sherry, salt, sugar, pepper and cornstarch; mix well. Stir in beaten egg and water chestnuts; mix well.

3. Spread mixture on bread; cut each slice into quarters (squares or triangles).

4. In a large heavy skillet or saucepan, heat oil (about 1 inch deep) to 350F on deep-frying thermometer.

5. Drop bread pieces, several at a time, shrimp side down, in hot oil. Fry until edges of bread begin to brown.

6. Drain well on paper towels. Cool. Arrange in single layer on foil tray. Freezer-wrap and label. Freeze until serving.

7. To serve: Preheat oven to 375F. Unwrap; reheat (still frozen) 10 minutes. Sprinkle with parsley. Serve at once. *Makes 48.*

QUICHE-LORRAINE SQUARES

1 pkg (11 oz) piecrust mix
1 egg white, slightly beaten
1 lb sliced bacon
3 cups (¾ lb) grated natural Swiss cheese
6 eggs
4 cups light cream or half-and-half
1½ teaspoons salt
¼ teaspoon ground nutmeg
¼ teaspoon white pepper
Dash ground red pepper

1. Prepare piecrust mix as package label directs.

2. On lightly floured surface, roll out pastry to an 18-by-15-inch rectangle. Use to line a 15½-by-10½-by-1-inch jelly-roll pan. Brush bottom and sides of pastry with egg white. Refrigerate.

3. Preheat oven to 375F.

4. Fry bacon until crisp. [...] per towels; crumble. Sprinkle [...] evenly over bottom of pie shell. Sprinkle cheese over bacon.

5. In large bowl, with wire whisk, beat eggs with cream, salt, nutmeg and peppers until well combined. Pour into prepared shell.

6. Bake 35 to 40 minutes, or until golden and center is firm when gently pressed with fingertip.

7. Let cool on wire rack 10 minutes. Cut quiche into squares—about 1½ inches. Cool completely. Remove from pan. Arrange on foil-lined cookie sheet. Freezer-wrap, seal and label. Freeze until ready to use.

8. To serve: Preheat oven to 400F. Unwrap; bake on cookie sheet, still frozen, until heated through—about 10 minutes. Serve at once. *Makes 54 squares.*

FROZEN CANAPE TRAY

Canapé Butters, recipes follow
Sliced white bread (use a firm type of bread)
Sliced rye bread (use a firm type of bread)
Thin-sliced ham, bologna, salami, olive loaf, turkey, Cheddar cheese, Swiss cheese
Sieved egg yolks
Red salmon caviar, drained
Chives
Canned pimiento, drained
Ripe olives
Stuffed green olives
Small gherkins
Cherry tomatoes, sliced
Cucumber slices

SALAMI-AND-CREAM-CHEESE CORNUCOPIAS
Cream cheese, softened

Lemon Glaze, recipe follows
Watercress sprigs

1. Make Canapé Butters.

2. Using pastry cutters, cut bread into various shapes (about 2-inch size): hearts, ovals, rounds, diamonds.

3. Spread with various canapé butters. (For example, Curry Butter for turkey, Mustard Butter for bologna, etc.)

4. Cut meats and cheese with fancy cutters to fit the bread bases. Arrange on matching bread bases. Cover half of some bread bases with egg yolk and red caviar at opposite ends. Garnish as shown, using cutouts of chives, pimiento, olives and small gherkins, leaving the tomato and cucumber garnish until serving time.

5. Make Salami-and-Cream-Cheese Cornucopias: Trim rind from large slice of salami. Spread with soft cream cheese. Roll up salami at one end, leaving other end open; fasten with toothpick. Freeze along with sandwiches.

continued on page 357

If one of your New Year's resolutions involves cutting down on calories, these light appetizers can get you and your willpower off to a great start. They all look spectacular, yet most have fewer than 20 calories each, and none has more than 75. Clockwise from top left: a platter of cucumber canapés with red caviar, tangy steak-tartare balls and cherry tomatoes stuffed with shrimp; a colorful bowl of seviche (strips of raw fish marinated in lime juice with onions, tomatoes and green peppers); shrimp and scallops in a lemon-tarragon dressing; vegetable-stuffed mushrooms; water chestnuts wrapped in slivers of steak teriyaki; and a glorious assortment of vegetables in a dill-scented marinade. Recipes and calorie counts begin on page 340.

Ring in the New Year...
The Low-Calorie Way

continued from page 338

CUCUMBER CANAPES
(pictured)

2 medium cucumbers
1 jar (4 oz) red caviar
Parsley sprigs

1. Pare cucumbers, leaving a small amount of green skin on. Slice crosswise into rounds ¼ inch thick, making about 50 rounds.

2. Arrange on tray; spoon ¼ teaspoon caviar in center of each round; top each with a parsley sprig. *Makes 50; 15 calories each.*

STEAK TARTARE
(pictured)

1 lb coarsely ground lean beef round or sirloin
½ cup finely chopped onion
½ clove garlic, crushed (optional)
1 teaspoon salt
1 teaspoon freshly ground black pepper
½ cup finely chopped parsley

1. In medium bowl, lightly toss beef with onion, garlic, salt and pepper just until combined.

2. Lightly form into 24 balls, 1 inch in diameter. Do not handle any more than necessary.

3. Roll each ball in parsley, covering completely. Refrigerate. *Makes 24; 71 calories each.*

SHRIMP-STUFFED TOMATOES
(pictured)

1 cup finely chopped, deveined, cooked shrimp
¼ cup finely chopped onion
½ teaspoon salt
¼ teaspoon pepper
2 tablespoons low-calorie mayonnaise
1 tablespoon lemon juice
1 box (1 lb) cherry tomatoes
Parsley sprigs

1. In small bowl, combine shrimp, onion, salt, pepper, mayonnaise and lemon juice; mix well. Refrigerate, covered, several hours to chill well.

2. Wash and dry tomatoes; refrigerate to chill well.

3. About 1 hour before serving, slice tomatoes across top to remove stem; scoop out some of seeds. Mound a little shrimp filling on top of each. Decorate each with parsley sprig. Arrange on tray. Refrigerate, covered, until serving time. *Makes 38; 17 calories each.*

SEVICHE
(pictured)

1 lb red snapper, halibut or sole (see Note), boned and skinned
2 medium onions, thinly sliced
½ lb cherry tomatoes, halved and seeded
½ green pepper, thinly sliced
1½ teaspoons salt
¼ teaspoon coarsely ground black pepper
½ cup lime juice

1. Cut fish fillets crosswise into ½-inch strips. Turn into a large bowl. Add onion, tomatoes, green pepper, salt and pepper; toss lightly to mix well.

2. Turn into a shallow baking dish. Sprinkle with lime juice. Refrigerate, tightly covered, overnight, tossing several times.

3. Drain; serve with wooden picks. *Makes 23 servings (2 pieces of fish); about 40 calories per serving.*

Note: Number of calories depends on fish; halibut is higher in calories than sole or snapper.

MARINATED SCALLOPS AND SHRIMP
(pictured)

1 lb sea scallops, halved
1 lb fresh shrimp (about 22), shelled and deveined
¼ cup finely chopped onion
1 bay leaf
1 teaspoon salt
¼ teaspoon white pepper
1 lb fresh mushrooms (about 80), thickly sliced right through stem

LEMON DRESSING
½ cup lemon juice
2 tablespoons olive or salad oil
2 teaspoons salt
½ teaspoon white pepper
½ to 1 teaspoon dried tarragon leaves
Chopped parsley

1. In medium saucepan, combine scallops, shrimp, onion, bay leaf, 1 teaspoon salt and ¼ teaspoon pepper. Add water to cover.

2. Bring to boiling; remove from heat; cover; let stand 5 minutes.

3. With slotted spoon, remove scallops, shrimp and onion to a shallow baking dish. Add sliced mushrooms; toss with shellfish mixture.

4. Make Lemon Dressing: Combine well all dressing ingredients except parsley. Pour over shellfish; toss to mix well. Refrigerate, covered, overnight.

5. Just before serving, toss well; turn into serving dish; sprinkle with parsley. Serve with picks. *Makes about 36 servings; 12 calories per shrimp, 15 calories per scallop half.*

STUFFED MUSHROOMS
(pictured)

16 small mushrooms (about ⅓ lb)
1 tablespoon butter or margarine
3 tablespoons finely chopped green pepper
3 tablespoons finely chopped onion
1 teaspoon salt
⅛ teaspoon pepper

1. Preheat oven to 350F.

2. Wipe mushrooms with damp cloth. Remove stems, and chop stems finely; set aside.

3. Heat butter in large skillet. Sauté mushroom caps, on bottom side only, 2 to 3 minutes; remove. Arrange, rounded side down, in shallow baking pan.

4. In same skillet, sauté chopped stems, green pepper and onion until tender—about 5 minutes.

5. Remove from heat. Stir in seasonings. Use to fill mushroom caps, mounding mixture high in center.

6. Bake 15 minutes. Serve warm from tray or chafing dish. *Makes 16 servings; about 2 calories each.*

TERIYAKI
(pictured)

2-lb flank steak (see Note)
½ cup chopped onion
2 cloves garlic, crushed
4 tablespoons soy sauce
2 tablespoons salad or peanut oil
2 tablespoons brown sugar
½ tablespoon crushed black pepper
2 tablespoons dry sherry
2 cans (8½-oz size) water chestnuts, drained
Scallion Flowers, recipe follows
Salt (optional)

1. Wipe steak with damp paper towels. Trim off any excess fat. Cut steak in half lengthwise. Slice across the grain in very thin slices, no more than ¼ inch thick.

2. In small bowl, mix well rest of ingredients, except water chestnuts and Scallion Flowers, for marinade.

3. Wrap each chestnut in a steak slice; fasten with wooden pick. Dip in marinade.

4. Arrange in shallow glass baking dish. Pour rest of marinade over steak-wrapped chestnuts, coating well. Let stand, covered, in refrigerator about 2 hours. Turn after 1 hour to marinate other side.

5. Place on ungreased rack in broiler pan. Broil four inches from heat, about 2 to 3 minutes on each side. Do not overcook. Arrange on warm platter; garnish with Scallion Flowers. Sprinkle with salt, if desired. *Makes 50; 43 calories each.*

Note: If you partially freeze flank steak, it will be easier to slice thinly.

SCALLION FLOWERS

Use the white part, 2 to 3 inches long, of 16 scallions. Make several crosscuts, about 1 inch deep, in one end. Cut lengths of green part of scallions the same way. Place scallion pieces in bowl of ice water; ends will open and curl. It will take about 1½ hours.

LOW-CALORIE ONION-SOUP DIP

1 cup (8 oz) plain yogurt
1 cup skim-milk cottage cheese
3 tablespoons dry onion-soup mix
¼ teaspoon chili powder
Chopped parsley

1. In medium bowl, combine yogurt and cottage cheese until well blended. Stir in soup mix and chili powder.

2. Refrigerate dip, covered, 3 hours, to chill well and to let flavor develop.

3. Arrange on tray with an assortment of crisp vegetables. Sprinkle dip with chopped parsley. *Makes 2 cups dip; 13 calories per tablespoon.*

YOGURT-DILL DIP

1 cup (8 oz) plain yogurt
½ cup low-calorie mayonnaise
2 tablespoons grated onion
2 tablespoons snipped fresh dill
¼ teaspoon salt

1. In small bowl, combine yogurt with rest of ingredients; mix well. Refrigerate, covered, several hours or overnight, or until thoroughly chilled.

2. Serve with an assortment of raw vegetables for dipping. *Makes 1½ cups dip; 11 calories per teaspoon.*

HERB-MARINATED VEGETABLES
(pictured)

Herb Marinade, recipe follows
Fresh green beans, ends trimmed
Green and red peppers, cut into strips ½ inch wide
Fresh cauliflower, separated into 1-inch flowerets
Fresh okra, ends trimmed
Eggplant, cut into 1-inch cubes, skin on
Fresh mushrooms, stems on, thickly sliced
Fresh broccoli, separated into 1-inch flowerets with stems
Frozen Brussels sprouts, thawed
Carrots, pared and cut into 5-inch sticks
Frozen artichoke hearts, thawed
Fresh zucchini, diagonally sliced ¼ inch thick
Radish roses, stems on
Fresh snow peas
Cherry tomatoes

1. Make Herb Marinade.

2. Wash and prepare an assortment of vegetables from the list above.

3. To blanch vegetables: Pour boiling water to cover green beans, red- and green-pepper strips and cauliflowerets; let stand 10 minutes; drain. Pour boiling water to cover okra; let stand 3 minutes; drain. Pour boiling water to cover eggplant; let stand 7 minutes; drain. The other vegetables need not be blanched.

4. Arrange vegetables in single layer in shallow baking dish or plastic container. Pour marinade over them, tossing gently to coat well. Refrigerate, covered, overnight, spooning marinade over vegetables four or five times.

5. To serve, drain vegetables; arrange on attractive platter.

About 3 calories each, according to vegetable, with marinade: green beans, 3 calories each; peppers, 2 calories; cauliflowerets, 3 calories; okra, 3 calories; eggplant, 2 calories; mushroom slices, 1 calorie or less; broccoli, 3 calories; carrots, 3 calories; artichoke hearts, 2 calories; zucchini, 2 calories; radishes, 2 calories; snow peas, 2 calories; cherry tomatoes, 2 calories.

HERB MARINADE

1 bottle (8 oz) low-calorie Italian-style or herb-and-garlic salad dressing
2 teaspoons snipped fresh dill
¼ cup lemon juice
½ teaspoon salt

Combine dressing, dill, lemon juice and salt; mix well. Refrigerate.

Makes 1 cup, enough to marinate 2 pounds assorted vegetables—about 16 calories per tablespoon of marinade. ■

AN ELEGANT NEW YEAR'S EVE

Show off your best on this special night and entertain your guests with this sumptuous buffet. The handsome whole salmon (you can also use striped bass) is poached in white wine, gloriously glazed and served with a creamy sauce verte. The sculpted tureen holds a fragrant, easy-to-make oyster stew afloat with, of course, crisp oyster crackers. Vegetables Parisienne, spirited fruits, assorted cheeses, fresh breads, holiday cookies and cake — plus champagne uncorked at midnight — complete this marvelous menu that salutes the New Year in style. For the recipes and menu, turn to page 372.

Celebrate New Year's — or any other winter's eve — with a hearty buffet for friends: steaming cups of spirited consommé; curried chicken breasts surrounded by fruit-and-chutney crêpes, all atop a bed of saffron rice; vinaigrette-dressed avocado salad; and a lush Grand Marnier soufflé. The complete menu and recipes begin on page 346.

A Bountiful Winter Buffet

continued from page 345

A HOLIDAY BUFFET

ROYAL CONSOMME MADRILENE*
BREAST-OF-CHICKEN CURRY
WITH SAFFRON RICE*
CREPES* WITH CHUTNEY-AND-
FRUIT FILLING*
TOSSED GREEN SALAD WITH
AVOCADO*
FRENCH BREAD
COLD GRAND MARNIER SOUFFLE*
CHILLED WHITE WINE   COFFEE
LIQUEURS

Recipes given for starred dishes.

ROYAL CONSOMME MADRILENE

ROYAL CUSTARD
2 eggs
⅔ cup light cream or half-and-half
¼ teaspoon salt
Dash white pepper

4 cans (13-oz size) consommé madrilène
1 cup dry sherry or Madeira
2 tablespoons lemon juice

1. Make Royal Custard: Preheat oven to 300F. In small bowl, with rotary beater, beat eggs, cream, salt and pepper until well blended but not foamy.

2. Strain into a buttered 8-inch pie plate. Set pie plate in shallow pan on oven rack. Pour hot water into pan to ½-inch level. Cover pie plate with piece of waxed paper.

3. Bake 40 to 45 minutes, or until knife inserted in center comes out clean. Remove pie plate from water. Cool; refrigerate until well chilled.

4. Just before serving: In medium saucepan, heat madrilène just to boiling.

5. Cut chilled custard into ⅓-inch cubes. Place cubes in eight consommé cups, dividing evenly.

6. Stir sherry and lemon juice into madrilène. Ladle over custard cubes. *Makes 8 servings.*

BREAST-OF-CHICKEN CURRY
(pictured)

4 whole boneless chicken breasts (3½ lb)
¼ cup (½ stick) butter or margarine
2 cans (10¾-oz size) condensed chicken
    broth, undiluted
Water

CURRY SAUCE
¼ cup (½ stick) butter or margarine
1 clove garlic, crushed
1 cup chopped onion
2 to 3 teaspoons curry powder
1 cup chopped, pared tart apple
¼ cup all-purpose flour
¼ teaspoon ground cardamom
1 teaspoon ground ginger
½ teaspoon salt
¼ teaspoon pepper
2 teaspoons grated lime peel
2 tablespoons lime juice
¼ cup chopped chutney

SAFFRON RICE
¼ teaspoon saffron, crumbled
Water
2 tablespoons olive or salad oil
2 tablespoons butter or margarine
1½ cups raw long-grain white rice
1½ teaspoons salt

Lime slices (optional)

1. Wash chicken; dry well on paper towels. Using a small sharp knife, carefully remove skin. Cut each breast in half, making eight pieces.

2. In ¼ cup hot butter in large skillet, over medium heat, brown chicken, a few pieces at a time, 5 minutes per side. Using tongs, remove chicken as it is browned. Then return all of chicken to skillet.

3. Add 1 can chicken broth; bring to boiling. Reduce heat; simmer, covered, 20 minutes, or just until chicken is tender. Remove chicken pieces; keep warm. Measure liquid in skillet; add remaining can of chicken broth and water to make 3 cups.

4. Make Curry Sauce: In ¼ cup hot butter in same skillet, sauté garlic, onion, curry powder and apple until onion is tender—about 5 minutes. Remove from heat.

5. Stir in flour, cardamom, ginger, ½ teaspoon salt and the pepper; mix well. Gradually stir in reserved liquid and lime peel and juice. Bring to boiling, stirring. Reduce heat; simmer, covered, 20 minutes, stirring occasionally.

6. Stir in chutney; add chicken. Cover and heat gently just to boiling, to reheat chicken—about 5 minutes.

7. Meanwhile, make Saffron Rice: Mix saffron with 1 tablespoon hot water; set aside. In hot oil and butter in medium saucepan, cook rice and salt, stirring occasionally, 5 minutes. Stir in the saffron mixture and 3 cups water; bring to boiling. Reduce heat; simmer, covered, 15 to 20 minutes, or until liquid is absorbed.

8. Turn rice into center of round platter. Arrange chicken breasts over rice, as pictured; spoon some of sauce over chicken. Pass rest of sauce. Garnish with slices of lime, if desired. *Makes 8 servings.*

CREPES
(pictured)

1 cup milk
¾ cup sifted all-purpose flour
¼ teaspoon salt
2 eggs
Salad oil

1. In medium bowl, with rotary beater, beat milk with flour and salt until smooth. Add eggs; beat until well combined.

2. Slowly heat a 5½-inch skillet until a little water sizzles when dropped on it. Brush pan lightly with salad oil. Pour about 1½ tablespoons batter into skillet, tilting pan so batter covers bottom completely.

3. Cook until nicely browned on underside. Loosen edge; turn; cook until browned on other side. Remove from pan. Lightly brush pan with oil before making each crêpe. Cool on wire rack; then stack with squares of waxed paper between crêpes. Repeat with rest of batter to make 14 to 16 crêpes.

CHUTNEY-AND-FRUIT FILLING
(pictured)

½ cup (1 stick) butter or margarine
½ cup light-brown sugar, firmly packed
2 teaspoons curry powder
1 cup chutney
1 cup green grapes, peeled and seeded
1 can (1 lb, 1 oz) apricot halves, drained
1 can (5¼ oz) pineapple chunks, drained
1 banana, sliced
1 tablespoon lemon juice

1. In medium saucepan, combine butter, brown sugar, curry powder and chutney.

2. Cook over medium heat, stirring, until sugar is dissolved and mixture starts to boil.

3. Add grapes, apricots and pineapple; cook over low heat just to heat.

4. Toss banana slices with lemon juice; add to mixture.

5. Use to fill crêpes. Fold crêpes in half, then in half again. Spoon about ⅓ cup fruit in each pocket. Keep warm.

TOSSED GREEN SALAD WITH AVOCADO

1 head Boston lettuce
1 small head romaine
2 Belgian endives
2 large ripe avocados (2 lb)

DRESSING
⅓ cup tarragon vinegar
⅔ cup salad or olive oil
2 teaspoons salt
½ teaspoon dry mustard
¼ teaspoon pepper
1 teaspoon sugar (optional)
1 clove garlic, split (optional)

Watercress sprigs

1. Wash greens thoroughly; separate into leaves, discarding discolored or bruised leaves. Drain well, shaking in salad basket or placing on paper towels to remove excess moisture.

2. Place cleaned greens in plastic bag or wrap in plastic wrap. Refrigerate until crisp and cold—several hours. Also, refrigerate avocados and bowl.

3. Make Dressing: Combine all ingredients in jar with tight-fitting lid; shake vigorously to blend.

4. Refrigerate, covered, at least 2 hours before using.

5. Remove garlic; shake just before using. Makes 1 cup.

6. To serve: Cut avocados in half lengthwise; discard peel and pits. Slice about ⅓ inch thick. Reserve 8 slices.

7. Tear greens and cut endive into bite-size pieces. Turn half into chilled salad bowl. Add half of the sliced avocado; then add remaining greens and endive. Add enough dressing to coat salad greens well; toss to combine.

8. Garnish with reserved avocado slices and watercress sprigs. Drizzle a little dressing over all. *Makes 8 to 10 servings.*

COLD GRAND MARNIER SOUFFLE
(pictured)

6 egg whites (¾ cup)
1 env unflavored gelatine
1¾ cups sugar
Dash salt
4 egg yolks
1½ cups orange juice
¼ cup grated orange peel
⅓ cup Grand Marnier
1 cup heavy cream
6 ladyfingers, split
Chocolate curls
½ cup chopped walnuts or pecans

1. Day before serving: Fold waxed paper, 28 inches long, in thirds, lengthwise. With string, tie collar around 1½-quart soufflé dish, to form rim 2 inches high. Let egg whites warm to room temperature—1 hour.

2. In double-boiler top, combine gelatine with ½ cup sugar and the salt.

3. In small bowl, with mixer at high speed, beat egg yolks until thick—3 minutes. Gradually beat in ½ cup sugar, 2 tablespoons at a time; beat until very thick. Slowly add orange juice; mix to combine.

4. Stir into gelatine mixture; mix well. Cook over boiling water (water in bottom should not touch top of double boiler), stirring constantly, until gelatine dissolves and mixture is thickened—15 to 20 minutes. Remove from hot water. Stir in orange peel and Grand Marnier.

5. Turn into bowl to cool slightly. Set bowl in a pan of ice cubes; stir mixture occasionally, 30 minutes. Then stir constantly until mixture thickens and mounds when dropped from a spoon.

6. In large bowl, at high speed, beat whites (clean beaters) until soft peaks form when beaters are slowly raised.

7. Beat in remaining ¾ cup sugar, 2 tablespoons at a time; beat well after each addition. Beat until stiff peaks form.

8. With wire whisk, using an under-and-over motion, gently fold gelatine mixture into egg whites just to combine.

9. Beat ½ cup cream until stiff. Gently fold into gelatine mixture. Turn one-fourth of mixture into soufflé dish. Top with a layer of split ladyfingers. Continue to layer soufflé and ladyfingers, ending with soufflé. Refrigerate overnight.

10. To serve: Remove collar. Whip remaining cream; put through pastry bag with number-6 tip to decorate soufflé. Garnish with chocolate curls. Press nuts gently around side. *Makes 8 servings.*

To make chocolate curls: Let a 1-ounce square of semisweet or unsweetened chocolate stand in paper wrapper in warm place about 15 minutes, just to soften slightly. For large curls, unwrap chocolate, and carefully draw vegetable parer across broad flat surface of square. ∎

PARTY-GIVERS GUIDE TO BEVERAGES

Holiday celebrations are synonymous with good food...and good drink. These next few pages contain beverage information and delightful recipes to help turn your New Year's Eve party—or any other special gathering—into a glowing success. Below are tips for planning and setting up a bar; opposite, a short course in serving champagne, along with three terrific punches. In keeping with the growing trend toward consuming less alcohol, we've gathered fabulous nonalcoholic drinks and punches that will dazzle—not dull—the senses. For coffee and tea lovers alike, there is information on proper brewing, the different varieties available, plus unique recipes to jazz up that plain cup. And, to warm your spirits, we have hot, spiced wine drinks. Cheers!

SETTING UP THE BAR

At pub or restaurant, you'd expect to find a fully stocked wet bar with tall, cushioned stools and mirrors on the wall. But very few of us have such an elaborate setup in our own homes, and it's not at all necessary for a successful party. Any rectangular table with an ample surface will make a good bar. Cover it with a plastic dropcloth for protection and then dress it up with a floor-length tablecloth so that you can store bottles underneath.

Place the table far enough away from the wall so that you (or your bartender) can stand comfortably behind it. If you want your guests to make their own drinks, try to arrange the bar so that several people can help themselves at one time.

If you are having more than 25 guests, it is a good idea to set up two bars to help alleviate congestion.

Count on having lots of coasters and twice as many glasses available as you have people (some guests are bound to set down a half-finished drink, abandon it and eventually get themselves another). At a sit-down dinner, don't forget additional wineglasses.

A variety of glasses is nice if you have them, but you can get by with just two sizes: 9- or 10-ounce wineglasses, which can also be used for highballs, and 7-ounce straight-sided old-fashioned glasses for drinks served on the rocks. (Paper and Styrofoam cups don't work well for alcohol; they can alter the taste.)

Traditionally, a bar is set up with ice bucket and glasses to the left, liquors and mixers to the right, garnishes in front of the bartender.

USEFUL EQUIPMENT FOR THE BAR:
Ice bucket with tongs
Bottle and can openers
Corkscrew
Water pitcher
Mixing pitcher
Long stirring spoon
Double-ended measure:
    jigger (1½ ounces) on one end;
    pony (1 ounce) on other end
Cocktail shaker
Measuring spoon
Napkins and several towels
Coasters
Paring knife and cutting board
Lemon and lime squeezer
Lemon stripper (optional)
Straws and toothpicks

HOW MUCH FOR HOW MANY?

How much liquor you'll need depends not only on the number of people you're expecting but also on the nature of the occasion. People will drink more at an informal social gathering than at a business get-together, and they will drink more at a cocktail party than at a sit-down dinner.

There's no rule that says you have to be able to concoct every exotic drink imaginable. It will be a lot easier to organize your bar—and stay within a budget —if you stick with the standards. (You might even want to offer just one special drink—a holiday libation such as eggnog or champagne punch.)

What does a well-stocked bar include? The following guidelines are for a cocktail party for 30 guests (multiply or divide the amounts as necessary):

LIQUORS
2 liters vodka
2 liters Scotch
½ liter dry vermouth
½ liter sweet vermouth
1 liter gin
1 liter blended whiskey or bourbon
WINES
4 liters white wine
2 liters red wine
BEER
1 to 2 cases beer
MIXERS
4 liters *each* club soda, tonic, ginger ale, cola (2 liters *each* diet mixers)
2 large cans juice (tomato, orange or grapefruit)
1 pitcher water
GARNISHES
Olives, cocktail onions, slices/wedges of lemon and lime, celery ribs (for Bloody Marys) and maraschino cherries (for Manhattans)

Some people may prefer a light aperitif before dinner, rather than hard liquor. While one bottle should be ample in a group of 30, you may want different kinds for variety.

If you are serving a sit-down dinner with wine, count on an additional half bottle of wine per person.

If you want to offer some after-dinner liqueurs or brandy, three bottles will be plenty; most people won't have more than two after-dinner drinks.

If you're serving champagne—for a special New Year's toast, for example— five or six bottles will be ample for 30 people; or, if you're on a tight budget, you can stretch a couple of bottles by serving a champagne punch. You might also want to look into less-expensive sparkling wines. ∎

A CHAMPAGNE TOAST TO THE NEW YEAR

Break out the "bubbly"…and enjoy it straight or in one of our taste-tickling punches. Whether it is a modest domestic champagne or a costly import, this wine's natural sparkle and distinctive flavor have made it everyone's choice for celebrating special occasions. But champagne is also a perfect dinner wine, since it can be served before, during and after the meal.

Whether your taste runs to sweet or dry, the bottle should be well chilled before it is opened—at least one hour in the refrigerator or 45 minutes in an ice bucket. Uncork it by holding a napkin around the neck (this prevents the heat of your hand from warming the wine) and pulling off the foil and wire muzzle. Tilt the bottle away from yourself and others and grasp the cork with one hand, while twisting the bottle (*not* the cork) with the other. The pressure in the bottle should force the cork out easily without causing any loss of wine. Contrary to popular belief, champagne corks should not pop out and careen across the room; not only does this cause spillage, but it also allows many of the bubbles to escape. The proper glass for champagne is not the open-bowl, saucer style formerly identified with champagne; instead, choose a tulip shape or flute champagne, which limits the wine's exposure to the air and thus allows it to keep its sparkle longer. Champagne should be stored in a cool place on its side to prevent the cork from drying out and crumbling.

AULD LANG SYNE PUNCH

2 bottles (25.6 fl-oz size) champagne
1 bottle (25.6 fl oz) sauterne
1 quart club soda
2 trays ice cubes
¼ cup brandy
¼ cup Cointreau
¼ cup light corn syrup
1 cup sliced hulled strawberries
Mint sprigs

1. Refrigerate champagne, sauterne and soda until well chilled.
2. Put ice cubes into large punch bowl.
3. Combine brandy, Cointreau and corn syrup, mixing well; pour over ice.
4. Add champagne, sauterne and soda; mix well. Garnish with strawberries and mint. *Makes about 4 quarts or 32 (4-oz) servings.*

FRUITED CHAMPAGNE PUNCH

1 large bunch seedless green grapes (about 1½ lb)
2 cups sauterne
1 cup cognac
2 tablespoons sugar
2 bottles (7-oz size) club soda, chilled
6 strawberries, hulls on, washed (optional)
1 bottle (25.6 fl oz) champagne, chilled

1. Day ahead: Wash grapes; place on small tray. Place in freezer.
2. Several hours before serving: In pitcher or bowl, combine sauterne, cognac and sugar; stir until sugar is dissolved. Refrigerate.
3. To serve: Pour sauterne mixture into punch bowl. Stir in soda. Add frozen grapes and the strawberries.
4. Pour champagne into punch just before serving. *Makes about 16 (4-oz) servings.*

PINK CHAMPAGNE PUNCH BOWL

STRAWBERRY ICE RING
2 quarts distilled or boiled water
1 dozen large strawberries, washed

8 bottles (25.6 fl-oz size) pink champagne, well chilled

1. Make Strawberry Ice Ring: Pour distilled water, to measure about 1 inch, into a 2-quart ring mold. Arrange unhulled berries in bottom. Freeze until firm. Gradually pour in distilled water to fill mold. Freeze until firm—several hours.
2. When ice ring is frozen, unmold: Place mold in warm water just until ice begins to loosen. Turn out ice ring onto waxed paper. Return to freezer at once, until ready to use.
3. At serving time, half fill punch bowl with champagne. Float ice ring in bowl. Add more champagne to fill bowl three-fourths full. Add more champagne as needed. *Makes about 50 (4-oz) servings.*

Note: If possible, refrigerate punch bowl or fill with ice water to chill. ∎

ILLUSTRATIONS BY DAVE JONES

NON-ALCOHOLIC BEVERAGES

Here are some beverages pretty enough for parties, special enough for a New Year's Eve celebration—and best of all, perfect for the whole family.

CRAN-APPLE PUNCH

(pictured)

This festive cranberry-apple punch boasts a fruit-studded floating ice bell to ring in the New Year.

3½ cups apple juice, chilled
2 cups cranberry juice, chilled
3½ cups ginger ale, chilled
Ice Bell, recipe follows, or 2 to 3 trays ice cubes

1. In large punch bowl, combine apple and cranberry juices.
2. Just before serving, add ginger ale and Ice Bell or ice cubes. *Makes 18 to 20 servings.*

ICE BELL

(pictured)

1 or 2 slices canned pineapple, drained
1 lime, thinly sliced, with skin on
About ¼ cup mandarin-orange sections, drained
Red and green maraschino cherries, drained (about 5)
Water

1. Use a 1½-quart decorative mold—a bell, Christmas tree or ring; choose one that will fit into your punch bowl. Place in freezer to chill well. Rinse inside of mold with cold water; return to freezer until thin coating of ice forms.

2. Covering bottom of mold as much as possible, arrange fruit in a decorative pattern.

3. Gently pour in enough water to just cover fruit. Freeze until firm.

4. Gently pour in more water to fill mold completely. Freeze until firm—overnight.

5. When ready to use, run cold water over mold to loosen; unmold; float on punch in bowl.

You may use any combination of colorful fruit in season, such as melon balls, preserved kumquats, strawberries, lemon and orange slices, etc.

FANCY CUBES

Fancy ice cubes give a lovely party touch, and they are very easy to make. Before freezing them, add a little green or red food color. Or add curls of lemon or orange peel; whole maraschino cherries with their stems; thin slices of orange, lemon or lime. It's best to use freshly boiled or distilled water if you want clear cubes.

FRUIT-PUNCH WARMER

4 cups apple cider
2 cups bottled cranberry juice
1 cup orange juice
1 can (12 oz) apricot nectar
1 lemon
36 whole cloves
10 sugar lumps (optional)
1 teaspoon ground cinnamon (optional)

1. In a large saucepan, combine cider, cranberry and orange juices and apricot nectar.

2. Wash lemon; cut thinly into 12 slices. Insert 3 cloves in each slice; add to fruit juices.

3. Over very low heat, bring just to simmer—15 to 20 minutes. Pour into prewarmed punch bowl.

4. In small bowl, toss sugar lumps with cinnamon. Drop a sugar lump into each punch cup. *Makes 10 (6-oz) servings.*

FRUITFUL PUNCH

2 cups orange juice
⅓ cup bottled lemon juice from concentrate
⅓ cup bottled lime juice from concentrate
½ cup honey
3 (3-inch-long) cinnamon sticks
2 whole cloves
1 bottle (1 quart) cranberry-juice cocktail, chilled
Ice cubes
1 bottle (1 quart) ginger ale, chilled

1. In large saucepan, combine orange juice, lemon juice, lime juice, honey and spices. Bring to boiling; simmer over low heat 15 minutes. Remove spices. Refrigerate until cold.

2. In large pitcher or small punch bowl, combine spiced mixture, cranberry-juice cocktail and ice cubes. Add ginger ale, and serve immediately. *Makes 12 (6-oz) servings or 16 (5-oz) servings.*

ORANGE SPRITZER

2 cans (6-oz size) frozen orange-juice concentrate
1 cup cold water
1 bottle (1 pt, 12 oz) club soda, chilled
3 tablespoons lemon juice
Ice cubes

1. In large pitcher, combine orange-juice concentrate and 1 cup cold water; stir until orange juice is thawed.

2. Add soda, lemon juice and 2 cups ice cubes. *Makes 8 (6-oz) servings.*

PINEAPPLE-ORANGE BLUSH

2½ cups orange juice
1 can (1 pt, 2 oz) pineapple juice
½ cup lemon juice
½ cup maraschino-cherry juice
1 bottle (12 oz) ginger ale, chilled
1 pkg (16 oz) frozen whole strawberries, thawed

1. In large punch bowl, combine orange, pineapple, lemon and cherry juices; mix well. Refrigerate several hours or overnight, or until well chilled.

2. To serve, add ginger ale and strawberries; mix well. Serve over ice, if desired. *Makes 8 (8-oz) servings.*

MOCK BLOODY MARYS

1 can (1 quart) tomato juice, well chilled
1 teaspoon Worcestershire sauce
2 tablespoons lemon juice

In large pitcher, combine all ingredients. Stir to mix well. *Makes 1 quart.*

TROPICAL CUP

3 tablespoons ginger ale
1 tablespoon lime juice
¼ cup pineapple juice, frozen or canned
1½ teaspoons maraschino-cherry juice
Cracked ice
Crushed ice
Pineapple chunk (optional)
Maraschino cherry (optional)

1. In a jar with a tight-fitting lid, combine ginger ale, lime, pineapple and maraschino-cherry juices. Add cracked ice and shake briskly.

2. Strain into a tall glass that is two-thirds full of crushed ice. If desired, garnish with a pineapple chunk and maraschino cherry. *Makes 1 serving.*

SPICY EGGNOG

½ cup sugar
Dash ground allspice
¼ teaspoon ground cinnamon
Ground nutmeg
3 eggs, separated
2 cups milk, chilled
1 cup light cream or half-and-half, chilled

1. Combine sugar, allspice, cinnamon and ⅛ teaspoon nutmeg.

2. In large bowl of electric mixer, at high speed, beat egg whites until soft peaks form.

3. Gradually beat in half of sugar mixture until stiff peaks form.

4. In small bowl, beat egg yolks until lemon-colored. Gradually beat in remaining sugar mixture until thick and smooth.

5. Thoroughly fold into whites. Stir in milk and cream; mix well.

6. Serve well chilled, each serving sprinkled with nutmeg. *Makes 12 servings.*

CORRIS' ORANGE EGGNOG

3 eggs
2 tablespoons sugar
⅛ teaspoon ground cinnamon
⅛ teaspoon ground ginger
⅛ teaspoon ground cloves
4 cups orange juice, chilled
¼ cup lemon juice
1 pint vanilla ice cream
2 cups ginger ale, chilled
Ground nutmeg

1. Beat eggs until lemon-colored. Stir in sugar, cinnamon, ginger, cloves, orange and lemon juices.

2. Cut ice cream in small cubes into punch bowl.

3. Pour in juice mixture and ginger ale. Sprinkle with nutmeg. *Makes 15 servings.* ∎

COFFEE

Whether it's black, mixed with sugar and cream or served as one of these favorite drinks, a cup of freshly brewed coffee is one of the world's greatest treats.

The Basic Brew

The secret is to start with fresh ground coffee (regular or decaffeinated), cold, clear water and clean coffee equipment. To keep your ground coffee fresh, store it in a tightly covered container in the refrigerator. When preparing coffee, run the water until it is very clear and cold. The time you save by using hot tap water isn't worth the loss of flavor.

For a percolator: Use 2 tablespoons of regular-grind coffee for every cup of water. Add another tablespoon of coffee for the pot.

For an automatic drip coffee-maker: Use 1 heaping scoop (the one provided with the set) of automatic-drip-grind coffee for every cup of water. Add an extra scoop for the pot.

For a nonautomatic drip coffee-maker: Use 2 tablespoons fine-ground coffee for every ¾ cup water. First bring the water to a roaring boil. Then add a few drops of cold water to it before pouring it into the filter. This method prevents the ground coffee from burning.

Never reuse the grounds. And, if possible, serve the milk or cream at room temperature so that the coffee will remain hot and steamy for as long as possible.

Fancy Beans

Beyond the regular selection in your supermarket there is a world of special coffee beans that awaits the curious coffee connoisseur. It doesn't cost much to be adventurous since you can usually purchase ground beans by the half- or quarter-pound. Be sure to tell the clerk what kind of pot you have (e.g., drip, percolator) so he or she will know how to grind the coffee. And if you really want to experiment, ask for suggestions on blending a few different kinds of beans together.

The major factor influencing the taste of coffee is how long it has been roasted. There are three main "roasts": The mildest is the American Roast (medium brown and somewhat darker than the typical canned coffees). The next strongest is the French, or Viennese, Roast (slightly darker and more tangy), which is recommended for demitasse or café au lait. The Italian Roast (definite bittersweet tang) is usually used for espresso. You'll find the widest selection of flavors among the American Roasts because the longer the beans are roasted, the less distinctive in flavor the different types of beans become.

Different kinds of coffee get their names from the degree to which the bean was roasted, the place where the bean was grown or the dealer's name for a special blend of beans. Blended coffees, like Mocha-Java, are a mixture of two or more straight coffees (beans from a single country, region or crop).

The strength of a cup of coffee refers to the proportion of coffee to water—not the flavor of the bean. The more coffee you use per cup, the stronger the brew.

Following are some flavors to try. As you read, remember that *acidity* refers to the slightly dry tang some coffees have (others may be almost sweet); *body* to the sense of richness and fullness (like a good aged Burgundy); *aroma* to the degree of fragrance.

AMERICAN ROAST

Santos Bourbon: Smooth-flavored Brazilian coffee with medium body and mild acidity.

Yemenite: Arabia is the home of those delicious Mocha coffees that have a rich, slightly chocolaty flavor but not overwhelming acidity. Real Mocha beans are very rare; most of the Mocha coffees you buy are high-quality beans that have been roasted with chocolate liqueur, cocoa beans or carob powder to produce a chocolaty flavor.

Indonesian: These are the famous Java coffees, which have a tart, pleasant flavor that lingers after the last sip.

Mocha-Java: A classic blend, usually made of one part Mocha and two parts Java; light and aromatic.

Colombian Medellin: This full, robust, world-renowned bean is grown on the slopes of the Andes and has a finely balanced acidity.

Colombian Supremo: Rich, extra-top quality grown at the tip of the Andes.

Ethiopian: This bean produces a beverage with a savory hint of wine. The most popular type is Harrar.

Hawaiian: Our native American bean is more commonly known as Kona coffee, and it is flavorful and light with a subtle, sweet, nutty flavor.

FRENCH ROAST

After roasting in oil, these shiny, dark brown beans are used to make strong coffee with a flavor that is richer, sharper, more robust, with a bittersweet tang.

New Orleans Blend: Dark-roasted coffee blended with up to 40 percent chicory, which gives it a bitter, almost peppery flavor—usually mixed with milk or cream.

ITALIAN ROAST

Even darker than the French Roast, this type of bean is the preferred blend for espresso. This darkest roast has a rich, bittersweet flavor and a full body.

IRISH COFFEE

Sugar
½ cup Irish whiskey
4 cups hot, strong black coffee
½ cup chilled whipped cream

1. Spoon 1½ teaspoons sugar into each of 4 (5-ounce) goblets.
2. Add 2 tablespoons whiskey to each. Fill with coffee to within ½ inch of rim.
3. Float a heaping tablespoonful of whipped cream on coffee in each goblet by sliding it off a spoon. Serve at once. *Makes 4 servings.*

CAFE BRULOT

2 (1½-inch) cinnamon sticks
2 whole cloves
¼ teaspoon ground nutmeg
¼ teaspoon whole allspice
Peel of 1 small orange, removed in a continuous spiral
1 lemon slice
12 sugar cubes
1 cup cognac
5 cups hot strong coffee (see Note)

1. In chafing dish, over direct heat, combine all ingredients except coffee. Heat until hot throughout—about 10 minutes.
2. In heated ladle, ignite a little of hot cognac mixture. Pour back into cognac in chafing dish to ignite.
3. While cognac is flaming, pour in hot coffee. Serve in brûlot or demitasse cups. *Makes 12 servings.*
Note: Coffee made from dark-roast Italian coffee, fine grind, in a special caffè espresso pot is preferred. Follow manufacturer's directions.

COFFEE CORDIAL

8 cups hot strong coffee
½ cup orange liqueur (or ½ to 1 cup Kahlúa)
Vanilla ice cream (optional)
Dried orange peel (optional)

1. Pour coffee and liqueur into pot.
2. Serve in heatproof glasses or mugs. Top with a small scoop of ice cream. Or serve without ice cream in demitasse cups with a twist of orange peel. *Makes about 8 servings in mugs; 16 in demitasse cups.*

CALIFORNIA COFFEE

8 oz brandy
1 pint chocolate ice cream
6 cups hot coffee

1. Into each of 8 large coffee cups or brandy snifters, pour 1 ounce brandy.
2. To each, add about ¼ cup ice cream and ¾ cup hot coffee. Serve at once. *Makes 8 servings.*

VIENNESE COFFEE

3 cinnamon sticks
8 cups strong hot coffee
Whipped cream
Ground cinnamon (optional)

1. Put cinnamon sticks in a serving pot and add the hot coffee. Let stand for about 5 minutes.
2. Pour coffee into mugs or cups and top with whipped cream. Add a sprinkle of ground cinnamon, if you wish. *Makes 8 servings.*

COFFEE NOG

4 cups milk
4 cups hot strong coffee
4 egg yolks
4 teaspoons sugar
Rum or brandy (optional)

1. Gently heat the milk and add it to the freshly brewed coffee.
2. In a medium-size bowl, beat egg yolks with sugar. Gradually add milk-and-coffee mixture, beating continuously with a fork or small whisk.
3. Pour into warmed mugs. For extra flavor, spike the drink with rum or brandy. *Makes about 8 servings.*

ICED COFFEE

½ cup instant coffee
¾ teaspoon ground cinnamon
⅛ teaspoon ground cloves
1 cup boiling water
3 cups cold water
2 trays ice cubes
6 twists lemon peel
Sugar (optional)
Cream (optional)

1. Combine coffee, cinnamon and cloves in a 1-quart measure. Add boiling water; stir until coffee mixture is dissolved.
2. Add 3 cups cold water; refrigerate the coffee, covered, until ready to serve.
3. To serve: Fill 6 tall glasses with ice cubes. Place a lemon twist in each; fill with chilled coffee. Serve with sugar and cream, if desired. *Makes 6 servings.*

SPICED ICED COFFEE

⅓ cup instant coffee
½ teaspoon ground cinnamon
⅛ teaspoon ground cloves
⅛ teaspoon ground allspice
1 cup boiling water
2 cups cold water
¼ teaspoon vanilla extract
Crushed ice or ice cubes
Sugar
Cream

1. In a 1-quart measure, combine coffee and spices; stir to mix well.
2. Pour in boiling water, stirring until coffee mixture is dissolved. Stir in 2 cups cold water and the vanilla.
3. Pour over ice in 4 tall glasses. Serve with sugar and cream. *Makes 4 servings.*

KAREN PRITZKER ∎

TEATIME

Once dumped overboard by our American Revolutionary forefathers, tea is enjoying a revolution of its own as more and more people are discovering the pleasures of this delicate brew.

The Proper Brew

To make a really good cup of tea:

1. Bring freshly drawn cold water to a full boil.

2. Use a teapot for brewing, even for one cup. Preheat the pot by filling it with very hot water and allowing it to stand for several minutes. Empty this when ready to brew tea.

3. Use one teaspoonful (in a tea ball or infuser) or 1 bag of tea for each cup of freshly boiling water.

4. Cover and let the tea brew 3 to 5 minutes. If you like weak tea, let the tea brew the full time and then add boiling water; don't cut the brewing time. Some teas brew light and some dark, so brew by time, not color.

5. Remove the infuser or bag. Stir tea before pouring it, to make the strength uniform.

6. Serve tea with sugar, lemon or milk, not cream.

A convenient way to make hot tea for a large crowd is to make a tea concentrate. To serve 25 people, bring 1 quart of fresh cold water to boiling. Pour it over ⅔ cup of loose tea or 30 tea bags. Cover, and let stand 5 minutes; then strain it into a 4- to 6-cup teapot and hold it at room temperature. (It is best made not more than four hours in advance.) To serve, pour 2 tablespoons of concentrate into a cup and fill the cup with boiling water.

Tea leaves will absorb up to seven times their weight in water, so give a gentle squeeze to the tea bag before removing to get every drop of delicious tea.

It's in the Leaves

The variety of teas available in this country has increased tremendously with the new interest in serving tea. Selecting a tea to serve can now be as exciting an experience as selecting a wine. Teas, like wines, often take their names from the areas in which they are grown—and there are more than 3,000 varieties grown around the world. All tea leaves come from the same plant: the *Camellia sinensis*. It is where they are grown, how they are processed and how they are blended that create a whole world of teas.

There are three general classifications of teas: black, green and brown, or oolong. The tea leaves can all come from the same bushes; it is the processing that makes them different. Black tea, the most popular in the United States, undergoes an oxidation process that turns the leaves black. It produces a rich, dark-looking tea. Green tea is not oxidized; it produces a mild tea that is very light green in color, even at full strength. Brown, or oolong, tea is in between. It is semiprocessed and produces a tea that is somewhere between black and green in flavor and light in color. In addition to processing, there are subtle differences in flavor produced by soil and climate in the area in which the tea plants are grown.

Following are some of the more popular teas to try and to enjoy.

- *Assam*—Most commonly brewed as an early-morning pick-me-up, this variety of black Indian tea has a rich, robust flavor.
- *Ceylon*—Ceylon teas are strongly flavored black teas. Those labeled "high grown" are the finest because they are cultivated above 4,000 feet, where tea grows best.
- *Darjeeling*—This fine Indian variety of black tea is consistently noted for its wonderful soothing flavor and exquisite bouquet.
- *Decaffeinated Tea*—Black tea undergoes an additional process that removes most of the caffeine from the leaves.
- *Earl Grey*—A highly aromatic blend of Chinese and Indian black teas distinctly scented with oil of bergamot, a citrus fruit.
- *English Breakfast*—This full-flavored blend is made of teas grown around the world. As its name suggests, it is most frequently served as a morning soother.
- *Flavored Teas*—There is a wide variety of flavored teas available. Generally, a base of black tea leaves is blended with natural spices and flavorings.
- *Herbal Teas*—Not technically true "tea," but a delicate blend of all-natural ingredients such as spices, herbs and fruit peels that is used to create herbal teas. Herbal teas are caffeine-free, since they do not contain tea leaves from the *Camellia sinensis* plant.
- *Jasmine*—Fresh jasmine blossoms are combined with a delicate blend of green and black Chinese teas to create this fragrant brew.
- *Keemun*—Chinese in origin, this highly distinguished black tea is normally not blended. It is superior in flavor and has an attractive deep amber color and has been termed by connoisseurs "the Burgundy of teas."
- *Lapsang Souchong*—Easily identifiable by its unique smoky flavor, this hearty black tea exhibits a pungent aroma and robust taste.

In the mood for something special? Try one of these tasty tricks in your next cup of hot tea:

- Add a slice of orange while brewing tea; then stir in a splash of Burgundy wine. Sweeten to taste.
- Stir a tablespoon of maple syrup into brewed tea; top with a scoop of vanilla ice cream.
- Add a slice of orange, lemon or grapefruit while brewing tea.
- Add 1 to 2 teaspoons Irish whiskey or your favorite fruit-flavored brandy or liqueur to brewed tea. Sweeten to taste.
- Stir 1 tablespoon strawberry, raspberry or your favorite flavor of preserves into brewed tea.
- Stir 1 tablespoon apricot preserves and 2 tablespoons apricot brandy into brewed tea; top with sweetened whipped cream and a dash of ground cinnamon.

FIRESIDE WARMER

1⅓ cups water
3 tea bags
1 cinnamon stick, broken
2 whole cloves
⅓ cup sugar
1⅓ cups cranberry-juice cocktail
1 cup Burgundy wine
Orange wedges (optional)

1. In medium saucepan, bring water to a boil.
2. Add tea bags and spices; cover and brew 5 minutes.
3. Remove tea bags. Stir in sugar, cranberry juice and wine; heat through.
4. Remove spices and serve, if desired, with orange wedges. *Makes about 6 servings.*

IRISH TEA

2 cups boiling water
4 tea bags
1 tablespoon sugar
2 to 4 tablespoons Irish whiskey
⅛ teaspoon angostura bitters (optional)
Sweetened whipped cream (optional)

1. In teapot, pour boiling water over tea bags; cover and brew 5 minutes.
2. Remove tea bags. Stir in sugar, whiskey and bitters.
3. Serve, if desired, with sweetened whipped cream. *Makes about 4 servings.*

MULLED-TEA PUNCH

4 cups boiling water
6 tea bags
1 quart cranberry-juice cocktail
1 cup brown sugar
6 whole cloves
6 whole allspice
1 cinnamon stick, broken
1 bottle (25.6 fl oz) Burgundy wine
Orange wedges studded with whole cloves (optional)

1. In large saucepan, bring water to a boil.
2. Add tea bags; cover and brew 5 minutes.
3. Remove tea bags. Stir in cranberry juice, brown sugar and spices.
4. Bring to a boil; then simmer, stirring occasionally, 5 minutes.
5. Remove spices; stir in wine and heat through.
6. Garnish, if desired, with clove-studded orange wedges. *Makes about 20 (5-oz) servings.*

SPICED APPLE TEA

1 can (46 oz) apple juice
1 tablespoon honey
10 whole cloves
1 cinnamon stick, broken
4 tea bags
Cinnamon sticks (optional)

1. In medium saucepan, bring juice, honey and spices to a boil.
2. Add tea bags; cover and brew 5 minutes.
3. Remove tea bags and spices.
4. Serve, if desired, with cinnamon sticks. *Makes about 8 servings.*

HOT SCOTCH RUMBA

1 quart water
5 tea bags
⅓ cup hard butterscotch candy
⅓ cup rum
Cinnamon sticks (optional)

1. In medium saucepan, bring water to a boil.
2. Add tea bags; cover and brew 5 minutes.
3. Remove tea bags. Add candy and cook over low heat, stirring frequently, until candy is melted.
4. Stir in rum. Garnish, if desired, with cinnamon sticks. *Makes about 6 servings.*

TEMPTING TEA-LIGHT

1½ cups boiling water
6 tea bags
¼ cup sugar
3 cups apple juice, chilled
2 cans (12-oz size) ginger ale, chilled
Vanilla ice cream

1. In teapot, pour boiling water over tea bags; cover and brew 5 minutes.
2. Remove tea bags; stir in sugar and set aside to cool.
3. In large pitcher, combine tea and juice.
4. Just before serving, add ginger ale and top with ice cream. *Makes about 8 servings.*

ICED TEA

8 to 10 tea bags, tags removed
1 quart cold water
Crushed ice or ice cubes
Sugar
Lemon

1. Combine tea bags and water in a glass pitcher; refrigerate, covered, at least 6 hours or overnight, no longer.
2. Remove tea bags, squeezing against side of container.
3. To serve, pour into ice-filled glasses. Add sugar and lemon to taste. *Makes 6 servings.*

SPICY ORANGE ICED TEA

6 whole cloves
8 whole allspice
½ cup sugar
1¼ cups water
1¼ cups orange juice, chilled
2 teaspoons lemon juice
1¾ cups tea, chilled
Ice cubes

1. In medium saucepan, combine spices and sugar with 1¼ cups water; bring to boiling. Reduce heat; simmer for 10 minutes.
2. Let cool; then strain.
3. Add the juices and tea. Serve over ice cubes in 4 tall glasses. *Makes 4 servings.* ■

Courtesy of Thomas J. Lipton, Inc.

HOT WINE DRINKS

For winter parties—or just to warm up after being out on a blustery day—few things taste as comforting, cheering and delicious as a hot wine drink.

Begin with table wine or fortified wine (sherry, port or Madeira). For tantalizing taste, add herbs and spices, honey or sugar, fruit, nuts, brandy or cider. Combine the ingredients, heat and pour into brandy snifters, wine glasses, mugs or punch cups. Here are some of our favorite recipes.

To start, here are some drink recipes that serve one.

VIN CHAUD

One of the simplest hot wine drinks is vin chaud, which means "hot wine" in French:

6 oz red wine (¾ cup)
¾ oz cognac (4 teaspoons)
Honey to taste
Slice of lemon
Light sprinkling of ground cinnamon

In a saucepan, combine all ingredients. Heat just to boiling, remove from heat and stir well.

HOT WINE LEMONADE

An easy-to-make delight:

1½ oz red wine
Juice of half a lemon (3 tablespoons, more if you like a tart flavor)
1½ teaspoons sugar
Boiling water
Twist of lemon peel

Combine wine, lemon juice and sugar in a warm mug. Add boiling water, and garnish with lemon peel.

MULLED WINE

Mull simply means to heat, sweeten and spice a drink — and wine works best for this purpose. Its fragrance alone will lift your spirits. A classic mulled wine:

4 oz (½ cup) red wine
7 oz (¾ cup plus 2 tablespoons) water
1 teaspoon sugar
Pinch ground allspice
Small piece of cinnamon stick, to taste
Twist of lemon peel
2 or 3 whole cloves
Dash of angostura bitters

In a saucepan, combine all ingredients. Stir and heat, but do not boil. Strain steaming mixture into a large, warm wineglass or mug.

BURGUNDY MINT

Here's a hot wine drink with added zest that serves two:

¾ cup red Burgundy
1 cup water
2 tablespoons sugar
1 teaspoon dried mint or six fresh mint leaves
2 twists lemon peel
2 cinnamon sticks
4 whole cloves

Combine all ingredients in a saucepan. Heat to steaming, and strain into mugs.

The following hot wine recipes are for larger gatherings and can be served in individual mugs or in a punch bowl.

WASSAILS In early England, a wassail was a toast offered to a person's good health, fortune or luck. "Waes haeil" was the shout in Old English. Over the centuries, the word evolved to mean big parties, and special drinks evolved, too. They were called, naturally enough, wassails. Here is our spicy recipe:

WASSAIL

1 gallon sherry
1 gallon cider or apple juice
1 cinnamon stick
Whole cloves to taste
3 baked apples

Combine the first four ingredients in a large saucepan; heat until mixture is steaming but not boiling. Place baked apples in a large, heatproof punch bowl, and strain the mixture from the saucepan into it. *Makes 64 punch-cup servings.*

GLOGG The Vikings were a hardy lot, and there are those who believe they were able to survive those long, bitter northern winters by glogg alone. Like wassail, glogg has a long history, and its recipe has taken many twists and turns through the centuries. Here are two versions of this Nordic warmer:

GLOGG I

1 orange, peeled and sectioned
1 bottle (25.6 fl oz) red wine
1 bottle (25.6 fl oz) ruby or tawny port
1 bottle (25.6 fl oz) aquavit
10 whole cloves
½ cup raisins
15 to 20 blanched almonds
2 cinnamon sticks
½ cup sugar
2 cups brandy (optional)

Combine all ingredients, except brandy, in a large saucepan; cover, and heat very slowly to steaming. Do not boil. Pour into a large, heatproof punch bowl. For a dramatic effect, float two cups of brandy on top, set aflame and serve. *Makes 20 to 24 punch-cup servings.*

GLOGG II

1 bottle (25.6 fl oz) red wine
1 bottle (25.6 fl oz) sherry
1 pint brandy
3 oz (6 tablespoons) angostura bitters
1½ cups sugar
Raisins
Blanched almonds

Combine the first five ingredients in a large saucepan. Heat, without boiling, until steaming. Pour into a heatproof punch bowl. Serve in punch cups, and add a few raisins and a blanched almond to each. *Makes 32 punch-cup servings.*

WINTER WINE PUNCH

Finally, this delicious concoction:

2 bottles (25.6 fl-oz size) red wine
¾ cup sugar
Peel from half a lemon
½ teaspoon ground cinnamon
6 whole cloves
10 thin slices of orange

Combine the first five ingredients in a large saucepan, and heat slowly. Simmer; do not boil. Pour hot mixture into warm mugs. Garnish each with an orange slice. *Makes 24 punch-cup servings.* ∎

EUNICE FRIED

continued from page 337

6. Arrange on cardboard trays. Cover with plastic wrap, then foil; seal with freezer tape and label. Freeze until ready to serve.

7. To serve: Remove sandwiches from freezer; let stand at room temperature, still wrapped, about ½ hour. While thawing, make Lemon Glaze.

8. Remove sandwiches to serving tray. Finish garnishing with cucumber rounds and cherry tomatoes. Brush sandwiches with Lemon Glaze. Garnish tray with watercress. Place a sprig of watercress in open ends of cornucopias.

CANAPE BUTTERS

CAPER BUTTER
⅓ cup (⅔ stick) butter or margarine, softened
1½ tablespoons finely chopped capers

In small bowl, combine butter and capers, mixing well. *Makes about ⅓ cup.*

CHIVE BUTTER
⅓ cup (⅔ stick) butter or margarine, softened
2 tablespoons finely chopped chives
1½ teaspoons lemon juice

In small bowl, combine butter, chives and lemon juice, mixing well. *Makes about ⅓ cup.*

CURRY BUTTER
⅓ cup (⅔ stick) butter or margarine, softened
½ teaspoon curry powder

In small bowl, combine butter and curry powder, mixing well. *Makes about ⅓ cup.*

MUSTARD BUTTER
⅓ cup (⅔ stick) butter or margarine, softened
½ teaspoon dry mustard

In small bowl, combine butter and mustard, mixing well. *Makes about ⅓ cup.*

LEMON GLAZE

1 env unflavored gelatine
1¼ cups water
¼ cup lemon juice

1. Sprinkle gelatine over water in saucepan; let stand 5 minutes to soften.

2. Over very low heat, melt gelatine; stir in lemon juice.

3. Pour into bowl; set in a larger bowl of ice cubes; stir until mixture begins to set slightly. Spoon a little over each canapé, just enough to moisten surface. *Makes about 1½ cups.*

RUMAKI

16 chicken livers
½ cup soy sauce
¼ cup cream sherry
16 slices bacon, halved crosswise

1. Wash chicken livers; dry well on paper towels.

2. Cut each liver in half, removing any stringy portion. Turn livers into a large bowl.

3. Combine soy sauce and sherry; mix well. Pour over chicken livers; toss lightly to mix well. Let marinate, refrigerated, 1 hour.

4. Wrap each halved chicken liver with half a bacon slice; secure with wooden pick. Arrange on broiler rack in broiler pan. Brush each side with soy mixture.

5. Broil, 3 inches from heat, 2 or 3 minutes on each side, turning once or twice, until bacon is crisp and livers are cooked through.

6. Drain on paper towels. Then arrange in single layer on foil tray. Freezer-wrap and label. Freeze until ready to serve.

7. To reheat: Preheat oven to 350F. Unwrap; bake (still frozen) on tray 10 minutes, or until heated through. Serve at once. *Makes 32.*

FROZEN GUACAMOLE

2 ripe avocados (about 1½ lb in all)
¼ cup finely chopped onion
1 tablespoon finely chopped canned chili pepper
1½ tablespoons white vinegar
1 teaspoon salt
1 ripe medium-size tomato, peeled

1. Halve avocados lengthwise; remove pits and peel. Mash avocado in bowl with potato masher. Add onion, chili pepper, vinegar and salt; mix well.

2. Place in plastic freezer-container; cover tightly, label and freeze.

3. To serve: Let thaw. Finely chop tomato; stir into avocado mixture. Serve with raw vegetables, cooked shrimp or tortilla chips. *Makes about 2 cups.*

Note: If using a processor, combine sliced onion and whole chili pepper; process to chop fine. Add avocado, vinegar and salt; process to blend. Freeze as directed above.

MEXICAN MEATBALLS WITH CHILI SAUCE

MEATBALLS
3 slices fresh white bread
¼ cup milk
1 lb ground chuck
1 lb ground pork
2 teaspoons salt
¼ teaspoon pepper
1 teaspoon chili powder
½ teaspoon dried oregano leaves
2 eggs, slightly beaten

CHILI SAUCE
2 tablespoons olive or salad oil
½ cup finely chopped onion
1 clove garlic, crushed
1½ tablespoons chili powder
1 teaspoon salt
¼ teaspoon dried oregano leaves
¼ teaspoon ground cumin
1 can (8 oz) tomato sauce
1¼ cups water

1. Make Meatballs: In medium bowl, soak bread in milk.

2. Mash bread with fork. Add remaining meatball ingredients; mix well with hands to combine.

3. With moistened hands, shape mixture into meatballs, 1¼ inches in diameter. Place meatballs in a 13-by-9-by-2-inch baking pan.

4. Make Chili Sauce: In hot oil in medium saucepan, sauté onion and garlic, stirring, until golden—about 5 minutes.

5. Add rest of sauce ingredients, except water; mix well. Bring mixture to boiling, stirring. Reduce heat; simmer, covered, 15 minutes, or until sauce has thickened. Preheat oven to 350F.

6. Add the water to sauce; return to boiling. Spoon sauce over meatballs in baking pan. Cover pan tightly with foil. Bake 30 minutes.

7. To freeze: Cool meatballs in sauce. Cover tightly with foil; seal, label and freeze until ready to use.

8. To serve: Place pan of frozen meatballs in 350F oven 30 minutes, or until heated through. Serve at once. *Makes 50 cocktail-size meatballs.* ∎

For a beautiful finale to your holiday table, here are six extravagant desserts made with the plentiful fruits and favorite flavorings of the season. At bottom left, a spicy pumpkin pie sweetened with maple syrup. Clockwise: royal meringue dessert — a cascading confection of fruits, nuts and fluffy meringues; a Nesselrode-flavored chocolate mousse; an ambrosia cake with orange filling and coconut frosting; a shimmering rosé-wine mold garnished with grapes; and, in the goblet, Danish fruit pudding made with frozen strawberries and raspberries. Recipes begin on page 360.

Sweet Endings For the New Year

continued from page 358

MAPLE PUMPKIN PIE
(pictured)

FILLING
3 eggs, slightly beaten
½ cup sugar
½ cup maple or maple-flavored syrup
½ teaspoon ground cinnamon
½ teaspoon ground ginger
½ teaspoon salt
1 can (1 lb, 13 oz) pumpkin
1 cup light cream or half-and-half

9-inch unbaked pie shell (with high fluted edge)
Whipped cream
Maple syrup

1. Preheat oven to 400F.
2. Make Filling: In large bowl, combine eggs, sugar, maple syrup, spices, salt, pumpkin and light cream. Beat with rotary beater until mixture is smooth.
3. Turn most of filling into unbaked pie shell. Place on lowest shelf of oven; pour in rest of filling. Bake 55 to 60 minutes, or until filling is set in center when pie is gently shaken.
4. Let cool on wire rack. Serve pie slightly warm or cold. Garnish with whipped-cream rosettes, drizzled with a little maple syrup. *Makes 8 servings.*

ROYAL MERINGUE DESSERT
(pictured)

6 large or 8 medium egg whites (1 cup)
½ teaspoon cream of tartar
½ teaspoon salt
1½ cups granulated sugar
¼ cup chopped pecans

Assorted fruits: 2 large navel oranges, sectioned; ¾ cup drained, canned pineapple chunks; ¾ cup seedless green grapes; 1 banana, sliced and dipped in orange juice
2 cups heavy cream
½ cup confectioners' sugar
Sweet cooking chocolate (optional)

1. In a large bowl, let the egg whites warm to room temperature—about 1 hour.
2. With electric mixer at high speed, beat egg whites with cream of tartar and salt until soft peaks form when beaters are slowly raised. Gradually beat in granulated sugar, 2 tablespoons at a time, until very stiff peaks form. Mixture should be moist and shiny.
3. Preheat oven to 275F. Lightly butter and flour two large cookie sheets. Drop meringue by tablespoonfuls, using rubber spatula to push meringue from spoon, to form mounds, 1 inch apart. There should be 40 to 50. Sprinkle each with a little of the chopped pecans. Bake about 1 hour, or until crisp and very light golden in color. Cool on wire rack.
4. Drain fruit; save juice for another use.
5. Beat cream with confectioners' sugar until stiff. Fold in three-fourths of drained fruit.
6. Arrange some of meringues on round serving platter to form a 9-inch round layer. Spoon some of whipped-cream mixture on center of meringues, mounding. Arrange more meringues around and on top of whipped-cream mixture.
7. Continue to make a pyramid with meringues and whipped-cream mixture (you will need about 40 meringues in all). Fill in spaces between meringues with more fruit. Decorate side with rest of fruit, as pictured.
8. Place one meringue on top. Sprinkle with chocolate curls or shaved chocolate.
9. Refrigerate to chill well—4 hours or overnight. *Makes 10 to 12 servings.*

Note: Meringues may be baked several days ahead, if desired, and stored in a cool, dry place until ready to assemble dessert.

CHOCOLATE-NESSELRODE MOUSSE
(pictured)

6 eggs
1½ pkg (6-oz size) semisweet chocolate pieces
½ cup (1 stick) unsalted butter
3 tablespoons cognac, brandy or rum
½ cup bottled Nesselrode sauce (see Note)
½ cup heavy cream, whipped

1. One or two days before serving: Separate eggs, turning whites into a medium bowl. Let whites warm to room temperature.
2. In top of double boiler, over hot, not boiling, water, melt chocolate and butter; stir to blend. Remove from hot water.
3. Using wooden spoon, beat egg yolks into chocolate mixture, one at a time, beating well after each addition. Set aside to cool. Stir in cognac. With rubber spatula, fold in ¼ cup Nesselrode just until combined.
4. When the chocolate mixture has cooled, beat egg whites with rotary beater just until stiff peaks form when beaters are slowly raised.
5. With rubber spatula or wire whisk, gently fold chocolate mixture into egg whites, using an under-and-over motion. Fold only enough to combine mixtures— there should be no white streaks.
6. Turn into an attractive 1-quart serving dish. Refrigerate mousse overnight.

7. To serve: Spread ¼ cup Nesselrode over top, leaving a 1-inch circle in center.

8. Put whipped cream through pastry bag with a number-6 decorating tip. Pipe cream in center and around edge. *Makes 12 servings.*

Note: If Nesselrode sauce is not available, use ½ cup finely chopped mixed candied fruits.

AMBROSIA CAKE
(pictured)

3 cups sifted cake flour
2½ teaspoons baking powder
½ teaspoon salt
1 cup (2 sticks) butter or margarine, softened
2 cups sugar
4 eggs
1 teaspoon vanilla extract
1 cup milk

ORANGE FILLING
1 cup sugar
3 tablespoons cornstarch
¼ teaspoon salt
¾ cup orange juice
¼ cup lemon juice
½ cup water
3 egg yolks
1 tablespoon grated orange peel

FROSTING
½ cup egg whites (4 eggs)
1½ cups sugar
½ teaspoon cream of tartar
½ cup water
½ teaspoon vanilla extract
½ cup shredded coconut

1. Preheat oven to 350F. Grease well and flour three 9-by-1½-inch round layer cake pans.

2. Sift flour with baking powder and ½ teaspoon salt. In large bowl of electric mixer, at high speed, beat butter and 2 cups sugar until light. Add 4 eggs, one at a time, beating well after each addition. Add 1 teaspoon vanilla. Continue beating, occasionally scraping side of bowl with rubber spatula, until mixture is light and fluffy—about 2 minutes.

3. At low speed, beat in flour mixture (in fourths) alternately with milk (in thirds), beginning and ending with flour mixture. Beat just until smooth—about 1 minute.

4. Pour batter into prepared pans; bake 20 to 25 minutes, or until surface springs back when gently pressed with fingertip. Cool in pans on wire racks 10 minutes. Remove from pans; cool thoroughly on wire racks.

5. Make Orange Filling: In small saucepan, combine sugar with the cornstarch and salt, mixing well. Gradually stir in orange and lemon juices and water.

Bring to boiling, over medium heat, stirring. Remove from heat. Cool slightly. Add egg yolks, one at a time, beating well after each addition. Bring to boiling, stirring; boil 1 minute. Remove from heat. Stir in orange peel. Cool completely before spreading between cake layers.

6. Make Frosting: In small bowl of electric mixer, let egg whites warm to room temperature. In medium saucepan, combine sugar and cream of tartar with water. Cook, stirring, over medium heat until sugar is dissolved and syrup is clear. Continue cooking over medium heat, without stirring, to 240F on candy thermometer, or until a little spins a thin thread 6 to 8 inches long when dropped from tip of spoon.

7. Meanwhile, with mixer at medium speed, beat egg whites until soft peaks form when beaters are slowly raised. With mixer at high speed, slowly pour hot syrup in a thin stream over egg whites, beating constantly. Add vanilla; continue beating until stiff peaks form when beaters are slowly raised and frosting is thick enough to spread. Spread frosting on top and side of cake. Sprinkle with coconut. *Makes 12 servings.*

ROSE-WINE MOLD WITH GREEN GRAPES
(pictured)

1 lb seedless green grapes
3 env unflavored gelatine
1 cup water
¾ cup sugar
1 bottle (25.6 fl oz) rosé wine

1. Wash grapes under cold water; drain well. Dry on paper towels. Remove stems from about 35 grapes. Reserve rest for garnish. Refrigerate a 6-cup decorative mold.

2. In small saucepan, sprinkle gelatine over 1 cup water to soften. Heat over low heat, stirring constantly, until gelatine is dissolved. Stir in sugar until dissolved.

3. In medium bowl, combine gelatine mixture and wine. Place bowl in larger bowl of ice and water. Chill, stirring occasionally, until mixture thickens and mounds slightly; takes about 20 minutes.

4. Spoon a layer of gelatine in bottom of mold; refrigerate to set—about 20 minutes.

5. Form seven grape clusters, using about five grapes for each one. Arrange on gelatine, spacing evenly, around bottom of mold.

6. Spoon remaining gelatine mixture into mold to fill. Refrigerate 3 hours or overnight, or until gelatine is firm enough to unmold.

7. To unmold: Run a small spatula around edge of mold. Invert over serving platter; place a hot, damp dishcloth over inverted mold and shake gently to release. Refrigerate if not serving at once. Garnish with small bunches of green grapes. *Makes 8 servings.*

DANISH FRUIT PUDDING
(pictured)

2 pkg (10-oz size) frozen sliced strawberries, thawed
2 pkg (10-oz size) frozen raspberries, thawed
Sugar
¼ cup cornstarch
½ cup cold water
Whipped cream or light cream or half-and-half

1. Drain berries; reserve juice (2 cups). Turn berries into six to eight dessert dishes or a medium serving bowl.

2. In large saucepan, combine 2 tablespoons sugar and the cornstarch; mix well. Stir in reserved fruit juice and cold water; mix well.

3. Cook over medium heat, stirring, until mixture is thickened and translucent (do not boil)—takes 10 minutes.

4. Pour over berries in individual dessert dishes or large serving bowl. Sprinkle surface of each lightly with sugar. Refrigerate several hours, or until well chilled.

5. To serve, decorate top of each with a mound of whipped cream, or serve with light cream. *Makes 6 to 8 servings.* ∎

A YEAR FULL OF SPECIAL DELIGHTS

For those of you who love to try new recipes but keep putting it off for "another day," here is a timely New Year's resolution: Beginning right now, surprise your family with at least one new dish each month. To help you keep your pledge, we present 12 tasty recipes — one for every month of the new year. This culinary calendar features fabulous main dishes and desserts made with seasonal meats, seafood, vegetables and fruits. To start, try this herbed and superb roast pork — a marvelous New Year's dinner. Other ideas-of-the-month follow; recipes begin on page 368.

Roast Loin of Pork —
bright and fragrant
in its blanket of
herbs and spices

JANUARY

WELCOME THE NEW YEAR   363

Creamy Apple Pie with a French accent
and a glaze of apricots over fresh apples

FEBRUARY

MARCH

Sirloin Dinner —
pot roast and vegetables
foil-wrapped and
roasted in a rich
red-wine sauce

First supper on the
terrace: Asparagus
Quiche with fresh
mushroom-and-
watercress salad

MAY

Rice Cream, with nuggets of
pineapple, topped with fresh
strawberries and slivered almonds

JUNE

Something new to spring: marvelously Mediterranean **Chicken Bouillabaisse** in white wine — perfect for dunking

APRIL

Something short, sweet and summery: **Peach Shortcake** with Melba Sauce

AUGUST

Bayou-style **Shrimp-And-Crab Soup,** highly flavored but low-caloried

JULY

SEPTEMBER

Chicken Basquaise with a garden harvest of onions, peppers, zucchini and tomatoes

OCTOBER

Scallops Provençal — *fresh-from-the-sea feast cooked in a matter of minutes with mushrooms, tomatoes and other tasty things*

NOVEMBER

For frosty November: **Gourmet Steak** *in a rich — and truly nourishing — wine-and-marrow sauce*

Scandinavian sensation: cider-basted **Swedish Glazed Ham** *served cold with festive rickracks of butter*

DECEMBER

continued from page 362
All recipes are pictured on pages 362 to 367.

ROAST PORK WITH HERBS

5-lb loin of pork
Salt
Dried rosemary leaves
Dried oregano leaves
Dried thyme leaves
Dried rubbed sage
Pepper
Ground nutmeg
1 cup thinly sliced onion
1 cup thinly sliced carrot
Sautéed Sweet Peppers, recipe follows

HERB GRAVY
¼ cup pan drippings
¼ cup all-purpose flour
Boiling water

1. Preheat oven to 325F. Wipe pork with damp paper towels.

2. In small bowl, combine 2 teaspoons each salt and rosemary; 1½ teaspoons each oregano, thyme and sage; and ¼ teaspoon each pepper and nutmeg. With paring knife, make ½-inch-deep slits on back of roast between ribs and on fat side of meat. Press half of herb mixture into slits; rub remaining herb mixture on surface of meat.

3. Insert meat thermometer in center of roast, away from bone. Place roast, fat side up, in shallow roasting pan without rack. (Roast will rest on bones.) Scatter onion and carrot around roast.

4. Roast about 3 hours, or until meat thermometer registers 170F.

5. Meanwhile, prepare Sautéed Sweet Peppers.

6. Remove roast to heated platter. Surround roast with peppers; keep warm in low oven.

7. Make Herb Gravy: Pour pan drippings with onion and carrot mixture through strainer. Reserve ¼ cup drippings; discard onion and carrot.

8. In 1-quart saucepan, combine reserved pan drippings and the flour; mix until smooth; set aside. Pour 2¾ cups boiling water into roasting pan. Return to boiling, loosening brown particles and brown drippings from pan. Continue boiling about 2 minutes.

9. Slowly pour boiling liquid into flour mixture, stirring briskly with wire whisk. Stir in ½ teaspoon salt, ¼ teaspoon rosemary, ⅛ teaspoon oregano, ⅛ teaspoon thyme, ⅛ teaspoon sage, ⅛ teaspoon pepper and dash nutmeg. Bring to boiling, stirring constantly.

10. Reduce heat, and simmer, covered, 5 minutes. Stir with wire whisk just before serving. (You should have about 2½ cups.) Serve with roast. *Makes 8 servings.*

SAUTEED SWEET PEPPERS

6 or 7 green and red peppers (2 lb)
½ cup salad oil
1 cup sliced onion
1 clove garlic, crushed
1 teaspoon salt
⅛ teaspoon pepper

1. Wash peppers. Slice into ¾-inch-wide strips, removing ribs and seeds.

2. In hot oil in large skillet, sauté onion and garlic, stirring occasionally, 5 minutes. Add peppers; sauté, stirring occasionally, 10 minutes. Sprinkle with salt and pepper.

FRENCH APPLE PIE

1 pkg (9½ to 11 oz) piecrust mix

FILLING
⅓ cup sugar
2 tablespoons all-purpose flour
1 cup milk
3 egg yolks
1 tablespoon butter or margarine
½ teaspoon vanilla extract

2 lb tart cooking apples
1 tablespoon lemon juice
2 tablespoons butter or margarine
2 tablespoons sugar
Dash ground nutmeg
¾ cup apricot preserves
1 egg yolk
1 tablespoon water

1. Prepare piecrust mix as package label directs. Form into a ball. On lightly floured pastry cloth, with a rolling pin covered with a stockinette, roll out two-thirds pastry to form a 12-inch circle. Use to line a 9-inch pie plate; refrigerate with rest of pastry.

2. Make Filling: In small saucepan, combine ⅓ cup sugar and the flour; mix well. Stir in milk. Bring to boiling, stirring; reduce heat; simmer, stirring, until slightly thickened—1 minute.

3. In small bowl, beat 3 egg yolks slightly. Beat in a little of hot milk mixture; pour back into saucepan, beating to mix well. Stir in 1 tablespoon butter and the vanilla. Turn into bowl to cool.

4. Pare, core and slice apples; sprinkle with lemon juice.

5. In medium skillet, heat butter with sugar and nutmeg. Add apple slices; sauté, stirring occasionally, until partially cooked—about 5 minutes. Remove from heat. Heat apricot preserves just until melted.

6. Preheat oven to 425F.

7. Turn filling into pie shell, spreading evenly. Arrange apple slices on top, mounding slightly in center. Spread with apricot preserves.

8. Roll out rest of pastry to form a 10-inch circle. With knife or pastry wheel, cut into 12 strips ½ inch wide.

9. Slightly moisten rim of pie shell with cold water. Arrange 6 strips across filling; press ends to rim of pie shell, trimming ends if necessary.

10. Arrange rest of strips at right angles to first strips, to form a lattice.

11. Bring overhang of pastry up over ends of strips; crimp edge.

12. Mix yolk with tablespoon water; use to brush lattice strips, not edge.

13. On lowest shelf of oven, bake 35 to 40 minutes, or until pastry is golden. Cool. Serve slightly warm. *Makes 8 servings.*

POT ROAST IN RED WINE

6-lb sirloin pot roast (silver tip)
½ teaspoon dried thyme leaves
¼ teaspoon pepper
1 bay leaf, crumbled
2 lb small new potatoes, scrubbed
1½ lb whole carrots (about 12), pared
½ cup dry red wine
1 env (1⅜ oz) dry onion-soup mix
Baked Stuffed Onions, recipe follows
2 pkg (9-oz size) frozen whole green beans
Dry red wine
2 tablespoons all-purpose flour
2 tablespoons water
Chopped parsley

1. Preheat oven to 350F.

2. Wipe roast with damp paper towels. Rub with thyme, pepper and bay leaf. Place 30-by-18-inch piece of heavy-duty foil in shallow, 15-by-10-inch roasting pan.

3. Center roast on foil. Arrange potatoes and carrots around roast. Pour ½ cup wine over roast. Sprinkle roast and vegetables with soup mix. Seal foil at top and sides.

4. Roast in oven 3 hours, or until fork-tender.

5. Meanwhile, prepare Baked Stuffed Onions.

6. About 30 minutes before serving, cook green beans according to package directions; drain; keep warm.

7. To serve: Remove roast from oven; fold back foil. Transfer roast to warm serving platter. Using slotted spoon, arrange vegetables around the roast, as pictured. Keep warm in oven.

8. Pour pan drippings into 2-cup measure; add wine to make 1¾ cups. Return to pan.

9. In small bowl, stir flour into 2 tablespoons water until smooth. Stir into pan juices; bring to boiling, stirring. Reduce heat; simmer 3 minutes. Strain, pressing any vegetable bits through sieve. Pass with meat. Just before serving, sprinkle vegetables with chopped parsley and spoon 1 tablespoon gravy over meat. *Makes 8 servings.*

BAKED STUFFED ONIONS WITH CHEESE

8 medium onions (2 lb), peeled
2 tablespoons butter or margarine
½ teaspoon salt
¼ teaspoon pepper
2 tablespoons grated Parmesan cheese
1 cup packaged croutons, crushed

1. With sharp knife, scoop out center of each onion, leaving a shell; chop center portions finely—should measure about 1 cup.

2. In hot butter, sauté chopped onion, stirring until golden—about 3 minutes. Remove from heat; add salt, pepper, cheese and croutons; mix well. Use to stuff center of each onion, mounding high.

3. Place onions in center of 24-by-18-inch piece of heavy-duty foil. Seal foil at top and sides. Place in 9-inch square baking pan. Bake 1½ hours, along with roast. *Makes 8 servings.*

CHICKEN BOUILLABAISSE

4 small white onions, peeled
4 whole cloves
1 can (10¾ oz) condensed chicken broth, undiluted
1 cup water
½ clove garlic, crushed
½ cup coarsely chopped celery
4 parsley sprigs
1 teaspoon dried thyme leaves
3-lb roasting chicken, cut in serving pieces
1 tablespoon olive or salad oil
2 shallots, chopped
5 tomatoes (2 lb), or 1 can (1 lb) whole tomatoes, undrained
½ teaspoon saffron threads
Pinch sugar
1⅓ cups dry white wine
6 slices French bread

1. Chop 3 onions; stud remaining onion with cloves.

2. In a 2-quart kettle, combine chicken broth, water, chopped onion, whole onion, garlic, celery, parsley and thyme. Bring to boiling; reduce heat, and simmer 30 minutes.

3. Meanwhile, wash chicken under cold running water; dry on paper towels. With sharp knife, carefully remove skin.

4. In hot oil in large skillet, brown shallot slightly. Arrange chicken in one layer in skillet; brown, turning once; then cook, uncovered, 10 minutes.

5. If using fresh tomatoes, place in boiling water a few minutes. Holding each tomato on a fork, peel with sharp knife. Remove and discard seeds; cut flesh into pieces, holding over bowl to catch juice.

Or break up canned tomatoes with a fork. Add juice and tomato pieces to chicken; cook 5 minutes.

6. Remove clove-studded onion and parsley sprigs from kettle; discard. Add chicken-tomato mixture to kettle, along with saffron, sugar and wine. Stir to combine well.

7. Over low heat, cook 30 minutes. Taste for seasoning; add salt if needed.

8. Toast bread lightly in broiler.

9. To serve, place a bread slice in each serving bowl; spoon some of chicken and soup over each one. *Makes 1½ quarts; 6 servings.*

ASPARAGUS QUICHE

1½ lb fresh asparagus, or 2 pkg (10-oz size) frozen asparagus spears
1 teaspoon salt
1 pkg (9½ oz) piecrust mix
8 slices bacon, quartered
½ lb natural Swiss cheese, grated
4 eggs
1½ cups light cream or half-and-half
⅛ teaspoon ground nutmeg
⅛ teaspoon salt
Dash pepper

1. Wash asparagus; break off and discard tough white portion. Scrape ends of asparagus with vegetable parer. Set aside 12 of the best spears for decoration— should be 5 inches long. Cut rest of asparagus into ½-inch pieces.

2. In large saucepan, bring 1 quart water to boiling; add salt and asparagus. Bring back to boiling; reduce heat; simmer, covered, 5 minutes. Drain; rinse asparagus under cold water.

3. Prepare piecrust as package label directs. On lightly floured pastry cloth, with a stockinette-covered rolling pin, roll pastry to form a 12-inch circle. Use to line an 11-inch pie plate. Flute edge. Refrigerate.

4. Preheat oven to 375F. Sauté bacon until crisp. Drain on paper towels.

5. Sprinkle bottom of pie shell with bacon, then cheese, then cut-up asparagus.

6. In medium bowl, with rotary beater, beat eggs with cream, nutmeg, salt and pepper just until combined.

7. Pour cream mixture into pie shell. Arrange reserved asparagus spears, spoke fashion, on pie, as pictured.

8. Bake 40 minutes, or just until puffy and golden. Serve warm. *Makes 12 servings.*

MOLDED RICE CREAM

⅓ cup raw regular or converted white rice
2¼ cups milk
¼ cup granulated sugar
½ teaspoon salt
1 env unflavored gelatine
1 can (8½ oz) crushed pineapple, undrained
½ teaspoon vanilla extract
Dash ground nutmeg
⅓ cup heavy cream, whipped

APRICOT SAUCE
1 cup apricot preserves
⅓ cup light-brown sugar, firmly packed
⅓ cup water
1 tablespoon lemon juice
¼ cup light or dark rum
½ teaspoon vanilla extract

2 tablespoons slivered almonds
1 pint fresh strawberries, washed, hulls on

1. Combine rice, 2 cups milk, the granulated sugar and salt in top of double boiler. Cook, covered and stirring occasionally, over boiling water until rice is tender—about 1 hour and 10 minutes. (Add more boiling water as needed to bottom of double boiler.)

2. Sprinkle gelatine over crushed pineapple in small bowl; let stand 5 minutes, to soften.

3. Turn into hot rice mixture, stirring until gelatine is dissolved. Add ½ teaspoon vanilla, the nutmeg and remaining ¼ cup of milk, stirring until well combined.

4. Turn into shallow baking dish; refrigerate until cool—1 hour.

5. With rubber spatula, gently fold whipped cream into rice. Turn into 1-quart mold or six (about ½-cup size) individual molds. Refrigerate until rice is firm— about 2 hours.

6. Make Apricot Sauce: In 1-quart saucepan, combine apricot preserves, brown sugar, water and the lemon juice. Bring to boiling; reduce heat; simmer 10 minutes.

7. Remove from heat; stir in rum and vanilla. Turn into small bowl; refrigerate, covered, until serving.

8. To unmold Rice Cream: Run a sharp knife around edge of mold; invert onto serving plate; shake mold to release. Spoon ½ cup sauce over large mold; about 1 tablespoon each over individual molds. Sprinkle top with slivered almonds; garnish with strawberries, as pictured. Pass rest of sauce. *Makes 6 servings.*

continued on page 370

continued from page 369

CREOLE SHRIMP-AND-CRAB SOUP

1 sweet red pepper
1 green pepper
2 carrots
5 medium tomatoes (2 lb), or 1 can (1 lb, 12 oz) whole tomatoes, undrained
1 white onion, peeled
4 whole cloves
2 shallots, peeled
5 cups water
2 cans (10¾-oz size) condensed chicken broth, undiluted
1½ cups chopped celery
½ teaspoon dried basil leaves
⅛ teaspoon dried thyme leaves
¼ teaspoon turmeric
1 bay leaf
¼ teaspoon crushed red pepper
1 teaspoon salt
1 lb unshelled fresh shrimp
1 can (7¾ oz) King-crab meat, drained and cartilage removed
¼ cup lemon juice
1 tablespoon chopped parsley

1. Wash peppers; remove ribs and seeds; cut into small pieces. Pare carrots; slice thinly crosswise—about 1 cup each of peppers and carrot.
2. If using fresh tomatoes, scald in boiling water; peel; remove and discard seeds; chop pulp coarsely. Break up canned tomatoes with fork.
3. Stud the onion with cloves. Slice shallots.
4. In large saucepan, bring 3 cups water and the chicken broth to boiling; add red and green pepper, carrot, tomato, onion with cloves, shallot, celery, basil, thyme, turmeric, bay leaf and crushed red pepper. Bring back to boiling; reduce heat, and simmer, uncovered, 30 minutes.
5. Meanwhile, cook shrimp: In small saucepan, bring 2 cups water with the salt to boiling. Add shrimp; cook over medium heat, uncovered, 3 to 5 minutes or just until tender. Drain, reserving 1 cup cooking liquid. Cool shrimp; remove shells, and devein.

6. Add shrimp, reserved cooking liquid, crabmeat and lemon juice to soup; cook gently, uncovered, 10 minutes. Add parsley at end of cooking time. Taste, and add salt, if desired. *Makes 2 quarts; 6 to 8 servings.*

PEACH-MELBA SHORTCAKE

MELBA SAUCE
1 pkg (10 oz) quick-thaw frozen raspberries
1 tablespoon cornstarch
2 tablespoons water
¼ cup currant jelly

2 lb ripe peaches; or 3 pkg (10-oz size) frozen sliced peaches, thawed; or 2 cans (1-lb, 14-oz size) sliced peaches, drained
¼ cup orange or lemon juice
Sugar
2 cups packaged buttermilk-biscuit mix
4 tablespoons (½ stick) butter or margarine, melted
¼ cup water
1 cup heavy cream, whipped, or soft vanilla ice cream

1. Make Melba Sauce: Thaw raspberries as package label directs. Drain, reserving juice.
2. In 1-quart saucepan, mix cornstarch with the 2 tablespoons water, stirring to mix well. Stir in raspberry juice.
3. Bring to boiling over medium heat, stirring; boil 3 minutes, or until mixture is slightly thickened and translucent. Stir in jelly.
4. Remove from heat; let cool slightly. Add drained raspberries; cool.
5. Peel and slice peaches into medium bowl; toss with orange juice and ¼ cup sugar.
6. Preheat oven to 450F. Lightly grease an 8-inch round layer cake pan.
7. In medium bowl, with fork, toss biscuit mix with 2 tablespoons sugar and 2 tablespoons butter until blended. Gradually add the ¼ cup water, tossing with fork, to form a soft dough. Gently pat dough into prepared pan, spreading evenly. Bake about 15 minutes, or until cake tester inserted in center comes out clean.
8. Let cool 5 minutes on wire rack; then remove from pan. Split while still warm, and spread cut sides with remaining butter.
9. Place bottom layer, cut side up, on serving dish; arrange about a third of peach slices on bottom layer; spoon on ½ cup Melba Sauce. Top with other layer, cut side down; arrange rest of peaches on top; pour on remaining Melba Sauce. Serve at once with whipped cream or ice cream. *Makes 8 servings.*

CHICKEN BASQUAISE

5-lb roasting chicken, with giblets
¼ cup (½ stick) butter or margarine, softened
2 teaspoons dried tarragon leaves
2 teaspoons dried oregano leaves
1 teaspoon salt
⅛ teaspoon pepper

2 cups water
1 teaspoon salt
½ teaspoon dried oregano leaves
½ teaspoon dried tarragon leaves
¼ teaspoon crushed dried hot red pepper
2 sprigs parsley
2 white onions, peeled
1 shallot, sliced
2 green or red peppers, sliced
2 lb zucchini, thickly sliced
2 tomatoes, quartered
¼ cup all-purpose flour
2 tablespoons butter or margarine

1. Preheat oven to 350F.
2. Wash chicken inside and out under cold running water; also wash chicken giblets. Dry on paper towels.
3. Combine ¼ cup softened butter with 2 teaspoons tarragon and 2 teaspoons oregano. Put half of butter mixture and the liver in cavity of chicken.
4. Rub outside of chicken with rest of butter mixture. Sprinkle with 1 teaspoon salt and the pepper.
5. Place chicken in shallow, 15-by-10-inch roasting pan without rack. Roast 2 hours, basting several times with pan drippings.
6. About 30 minutes before chicken is done, cook vegetables. In 11-inch skillet with tight-fitting cover, bring 2 cups water, 1 teaspoon salt, the oregano, tarragon, crushed pepper, giblets and parsley to boiling.
7. Add onions and shallot; cook, covered, over medium heat 15 minutes. Remove and discard giblets and parsley.
8. Layer peppers and zucchini over onions; cook, covered, 10 minutes. Add tomato; cook 5 minutes longer, or just until vegetables are tender. Drain, reserving liquid (about 2 cups).
9. In small saucepan, combine ¾ cup pan drippings with flour; mix well. Stir in reserved vegetable liquid. Bring to boiling, stirring. Serve as sauce.
10. Return vegetables to skillet, and continue cooking, uncovered, several minutes, to dry out vegetables. Toss with butter.
11. Serve chicken surrounded by vegetables. *Makes 6 servings.*

SCALLOPS PROVENCAL

1 lb bay or sea scallops
2 tablespoons lemon juice
½ lb fresh mushrooms
2 lb fresh tomatoes, or 1 can (1 lb) whole
    tomatoes, drained
5 tablespoons olive or salad oil
4 shallots, peeled and sliced
4 parsley sprigs, chopped
1 small clove garlic, crushed
½ teaspoon salt
Dash white pepper
½ teaspoon dried thyme leaves
½ teaspoon dried oregano leaves

1. In medium bowl, toss scallops with lemon juice.

2. Wipe mushrooms; slice lengthwise, right through stem, about ⅛ inch thick. Toss with scallops.

3. If using fresh tomatoes, scald in boiling water; peel; remove seeds; chop pulp coarsely. Break up canned tomatoes with a fork.

4. In 2 tablespoons hot oil in 8-inch skillet with tight-fitting cover, sauté half of shallot and parsley with the garlic just until golden. Add tomato, salt, pepper, thyme and oregano. Cook, covered, over low heat, 20 minutes, stirring occasionally to break up tomato. Uncover, and cook 5 more minutes.

5. In 3 tablespoons hot oil in large skillet, sauté remaining shallot and parsley, stirring, about 5 minutes. Add scallops and mushrooms; cook, uncovered, over high heat 10 minutes, shaking pan and stirring frequently.

6. Stir in tomato mixture; cook 2 minutes longer. Serve at once. *Makes 6 first-course servings. Or serves 4 with rice, as a main course.*

STEAK WITH MARROW SAUCE

2½ lb round steak, 1½ inches thick
    (see Note)
Freshly ground pepper

MARROW SAUCE
2 large marrowbones (about 1½ lb)
3 tablespoons butter or margarine
6 shallots, chopped
1½ tablespoons all-purpose flour
1½ cups red wine
1 tablespoon chopped parsley
½ teaspoon dried thyme leaves
½ teaspoon salt

2 tablespoons butter or margarine
1 shallot, chopped
1 teaspoon chopped parsley
½ teaspoon salt
Watercress

1. Wipe steak with damp paper towels. Sprinkle both sides with pepper, pressing in well. Let stand 30 minutes.

2. Make Marrow Sauce: In large saucepan, bring 1 quart water to boiling. Add marrowbones; bring back to boiling; reduce heat; simmer, uncovered, 10 minutes. Remove bones; cool. Scoop out marrow; chop finely.

3. In 3 tablespoons hot butter in small saucepan, sauté the 6 chopped shallots, stirring, until transparent—about 5 minutes. Remove from heat; stir in flour. Cook over low heat, stirring 1 minute. Slowly add wine, stirring constantly. Add 1 tablespoon parsley, the thyme and ½ teaspoon salt. Simmer gently 10 minutes. Stir in marrow. Keep warm over very low heat while cooking steak.

4. In 2 tablespoons hot butter in heavy skillet, sauté 1 shallot and the teaspoon of parsley about 1 minute. Add steak; cook over medium heat 10 minutes, turning once. Steak will be quite rare. Cook 5 minutes longer for medium rare. Place on hot serving platter; sprinkle with salt.

5. Pour about ¼ cup Marrow Sauce into skillet; bring to boiling, stirring to loosen brown particles. Add to rest of sauce. Spoon a little of hot Marrow Sauce over steak. Garnish platter with watercress. Pass rest of sauce. To serve, slice steak very thinly, on the diagonal. *Makes 8 servings.*

Note: Use prime or choice quality meat. If desired, you may use unseasoned meat tenderizer as package label directs.

SWEDISH GLAZED HAM

2 bay leaves, crushed
1½ teaspoons ground cloves
1 teaspoon ground ginger
10-to-12-lb fully cooked, bone-in whole
    ham
2 parsley sprigs
1 cup sliced onion
2 carrots, sliced
2 cups apple cider

MUSTARD GLAZE
1 egg
3 tablespoons spicy prepared mustard
3 tablespoons granulated sugar

¼ cup packaged unseasoned dry bread
    crumbs

BUTTER FROSTING
3 tablespoons butter or margarine
2 cups sifted confectioners' sugar
1 teaspoon vanilla extract

Whole cloves
Greens
Cranberries

1. Day before: Preheat oven to 325F. Combine bay leaves, ground cloves and ginger.

2. Carefully remove ham rind. Place ham, fat side up, in shallow, open roasting pan. Rub surface of ham with bay-leaf mixture. Insert meat thermometer in center of meat, away from bone.

3. Place parsley, onion and carrot around ham; pour cider into pan. Cover pan tightly with foil.

4. Bake, basting every 20 minutes with cider mixture in pan, until thermometer registers 130F, about 3 hours. Remove ham from oven; pour off liquid; discard vegetables. Increase oven temperature to 450F.

5. Make Mustard Glaze: In small bowl, beat together egg, mustard and granulated sugar.

6. Spread Mustard Glaze over ham. Sprinkle with bread crumbs. Bake, uncovered, 15 minutes, or until golden-brown. Remove from pan; cool completely. Refrigerate, covered, overnight.

7. Before serving, remove ham to serving platter. Make Butter Frosting: In small bowl, mix together butter, confectioners' sugar and vanilla until smooth.

8. Using pastry bag with small writing tip, ⅛ inch in diameter, filled with Butter Frosting, make zigzag lines on the diagonal, 1½ inches apart, to form diamond pattern. Insert a whole clove in the center of each diamond. Garnish with greens and cranberries as pictured.

9. To serve: Carve a few slices, and arrange around ham. Serve with additional mustard, if desired. *Makes 24 servings.* ■

continued from page 343

NEW YEAR'S EVE MENU

VIC'S OYSTER STEW*
COLD SALMON POACHED IN WHITE WINE*
SAUCE VERTE*
VEGETABLES PARISIENNE*
TRAY OF ASSORTED CHEESES AND BREADS
WINTER FRUIT BOWL WITH COINTREAU
CHRISTMAS COOKIES AND FRUITCAKE
COFFEE
CHILLED CHAMPAGNE OR WHITE WINE

Recipes given for starred dishes.

Mrs. Warren Vickery's
VIC'S OYSTER STEW
(pictured)

1 pint raw oysters with liquid
¼ cup (½ stick) butter
¾ teaspoon celery salt
¾ teaspoon salt
⅛ teaspoon white pepper
Paprika
1 quart light cream or half-and-half
Butter
Oyster crackers

1. Pick over oysters to remove any bits of shell.
2. In large skillet, heat ¼ cup butter; stir in celery salt, salt, pepper and ⅛ teaspoon paprika. Add oysters with liquid; heat just until edges of oysters curl slightly. Reduce heat to simmer.
3. Meanwhile, in top of double boiler, heat half-and-half. When hot, add oysters with seasoned liquid, and heat 15 minutes longer. Do not let stew come to a boil.
4. Serve in bowls or cups, each topped with a lump of butter and dash of paprika. Serve along with oyster crackers. *Makes 6 cups.*

COLD SALMON POACHED IN WHITE WINE
(pictured)

8-lb piece fresh salmon or striped bass, scaled, with tail left on

COURT BOUILLON
Water
3 cups chablis or dry white wine
1½ cups chopped celery
1 large onion, peeled and sliced
6 parsley sprigs
6 lemon slices
1 bay leaf
1 tablespoon salt

2 env unflavored gelatine
½ cup cold water
½ cup chablis or dry white wine
Large unpitted ripe olives
2 small unpeeled cucumbers, halved and thinly sliced
Watercress sprigs
Lemon wedges
Sauce Verte, recipe follows

1. Day before serving: Wipe salmon inside and out with damp paper towel. (If roasting pan is too small, cut off tail.) Wrap fish (with tail) in double thickness of cheesecloth, leaving 6 inches of cloth at each end; tie ends with string.
2. Prepare Court Bouillon: In large roasting pan, combine 2 quarts water with 3 cups chablis, the celery, onion, parsley, lemon slices, bay leaf and salt. Add salmon to pan; if not covered completely, add more water. Cover pan tightly, using foil if necessary.
3. Bring to boiling over medium heat (use two burners for more even cooking). Reduce heat, and simmer 30 to 35 minutes. Remove pan from heat.
4. Carefully remove 2 cups Court Bouillon from pan; strain through a triple thickness of cheesecloth. Refrigerate for later use.
5. Spoon Court Bouillon in pan over fish. Cover loosely with foil; let stand until completely cool. Then remove fish from liquid by grasping ends of cheesecloth. Discard cheesecloth and remaining Court Bouillon. Arrange fish with tail on large serving board or platter. Carefully remove skin, and scrape gray meat from the salmon to expose pink meat underneath. Do not remove skin from bottom. Refrigerate, covered with plastic wrap, overnight.
6. Next day: Sprinkle gelatine over ½ cup cold water; let soften.
7. In small saucepan, combine the reserved 2 cups Court Bouillon, ½ cup chablis and gelatine. Bring to boiling, stirring until gelatine is dissolved. Remove from heat. Set pan in ice cubes; stir gelatine mixture occasionally, until consistency of unbeaten egg white—10 minutes.
8. Carefully brush salmon and tail

with gelatine mixture, to make a thin glaze. Refrigerate 30 minutes. Place strips of waxed paper around salmon.
9. Reheat gelatine; chill. Cut olives into crescent shapes.
10. Decorate salmon with cucumber slices and olives, as pictured. Carefully spoon remaining thickened gelatine mixture over top and sides of salmon, to glaze evenly. Refrigerate until serving time. If any glaze is left, reheat, chill and spoon over fish.
11. Before serving, remove waxed paper. Garnish with watercress and lemon. Serve with Sauce Verte. *Makes 20 servings.*

SAUCE VERTE

2 cups mayonnaise
⅔ cup chopped parsley sprigs (no stems)
⅔ cup chopped watercress (no stems)
¼ cup capers, drained
¼ cup tarragon vinegar
2 tablespoons snipped chives

1. Combine all ingredients in medium bowl or blender container or food processor. At high speed, beat with electric beater or blend until smooth.
2. Turn into a serving bowl. Refrigerate, covered, at least 2 hours. *Makes about 2½ cups.*

VEGETABLES PARISIENNE

1 cup mayonnaise
¼ cup lemon juice
3 pkg (10-oz size) frozen petits pois
4 large stalks celery, cut on diagonal, ½ inch thick
1 lb small carrots, pared and cut in ½-inch rounds
Chopped parsley

1. Combine mayonnaise and lemon juice; mix well. Refrigerate, covered, to chill well—several hours.
2. Meanwhile, prepare vegetables: Cook peas as package label directs. Do not overcook. Drain; then plunge in ice water to cool rapidly. Drain well; pat dry on paper towels. Refrigerate.
3. In medium saucepan, bring ½ cup water to boiling; add celery. Simmer, covered, 5 minutes, or until just tender. Drain; chill in ice water and dry well, as in Step 2. Refrigerate.
4. Following directions for cooking celery, cook carrots about 8 minutes, or until just tender. Chill and drain well, as above. Refrigerate.
5. At serving time, combine vegetables in chilled bowl; toss with mayonnaise mixture. Sprinkle with parsley. *Makes about 16 servings.* ∎

RECIPE INDEX

A

adobe ranch (cookie house), 232
acorn squash:
  baked, 49
  with cranberries, steamed, 270
  slices, lemony, 55
almond(s):
  brittle (cubaita), Italian, 309
  burnt, 322
  macaroons, 316
  marzipan, 323
  -twist coffeecake, 297
ambrosia, 102
ambrosia cake, 361
anise cookies, 306
Anna's cheese biscuits, 290
Anna's roast loin of pork, 290
antipasto medley, 168
antique-toy cookies, 312
appetizers:
  Anna's cheese biscuits, 290
  Cheddar-cheese puffs, 337
  cherry-tomato hors d'oeuvres, 280
  chicken-tofu balls, 75
  Chinese egg rolls, 74
  chopped chicken livers, 259
  Christmas pâté, 281
  cocktail olives, 278
  cucumber canapés, 340
  dill-yogurt dip, 12
  fantasy bird holiday, 12
  frozen canapé tray, 337
  frozen guacamole, 357
  garlic-herb cheese, 169
  golden cheese nuggets, 337
  guacamole dip with crisp vegetables, 87
  herb-marinated vegetables, 341
  hot cheese balls, 75
  hot mushroom canapés, 336
  hot sardine and salmon crescents, 281
  liver pâté en gelée, 78
  low-calorie cheese spread, 169
  low-calorie onion-soup dip, 341
  marinated scallops and shrimp, 340
  Mexican meatballs with chili sauce, 357
  miniature egg rolls, 336
  oyster-filled artichokes, 89
  pâté en croûte, 75
  piquant apricot sauce, 336
  piquant cheese logs, 169
  puff-pastry olives, 74
  quiche Lorraine, our best, 75
  quiche-Lorraine squares, 337
  rumaki, 357
  seviche, 340
  shrimp-stuffed tomatoes, 340
  shrimp toast, 337

  steak tartare, 340
  stuffed mushrooms, 340
  teriyaki, 341
  three-cheese loaf, 74
  triconas, 336
  yogurt-dill dip (low-calorie), 341
apple(s):
  brown-sugar-glazed, 285
  candied sweet potatoes and, 36
  -cranberry cider, mulled, 97
  -cranberry-orange relish, 37
  -cranberry pie, 37
  -cranberry relish, 48
  -cranberry salad, 56
  -cranberry sauce, 261
  -cran punch, 350
  custard tarts, 101
  glazed, 49
  -mincemeat pie with flaming rum sauce, 38
  pie, French, 368
  pie, sour-cream, 106
  rings, sautéed, 35
  rosy cinnamon, 278
  tart, glazed, 93
  tart, Scotch, 107
  tea, spiced, 355
  wine-braised goose, 270
apricot:
  -filled coffeecake, 297
  glaze, 170
  -glazed noodle pudding, 259
  -pineapple-nut loaf, 170
  sauce, 369
    piquant, 336
artichokes, oyster-filled, 89
asparagus quiche, 369
aspic, breast of turkey in, 287
au gratin:
  creamed spinach and potatoes, 35
  parsnips, 36
auld lang syne punch, 349
Austrian butter cake, 295
avocado:
  -and-cauliflower salad, 113
  and orange salad, 117
  tossed green salad with, 347

B

bacon and scallops en brochette, 115
baked:
  acorn squash, 49
  Alaska, 330
  ham in crust with Cumberland sauce, 284
  stuffed onions, 35
    with cheese, 369
banana-pineapple cake, warm, 113
barbecued chicken with Mexican rice, 87
barbecue sauce, 87

barley-sugar twists, 175
bars:
  chewy prune, 318
  raisin newton, 318
  toffee, 299
basic coffeecake dough, 298
bean-sausage soup, hearty, 110
beef:
  Bourguignon, 78
  with cashews, oriental, 111
  empanadas, 88
  enchiladas, 88
  stroganoff, 79
  -and-Swiss-cheese rolls, corned-, 116
best-of-all fruitcake, 294
best quiche Lorraine, our, 75
beverages:
  auld lang syne punch, 349
  brandy-Alexander frappes, 39
  Burgundy mint, 356
  café brûlot, 353
  Cajun coffee, 91
  California coffee, 353
  coffee cordial, 353
  coffee nog, 353
  Corris' orange eggnog, 351
  cran-apple punch, 350
  field-mouse special, 287
  fireside warmer, 355
  frosted daiquiris, 287
  fruited champagne punch, 349
  fruitful punch, 351
  fruit-punch warmer, 351
  glogg I, 356
  glogg II, 356
  hot Scotch rumba, 355
  hot wine lemonade, 356
  iced coffee, 353
  iced tea, 355
  Irish coffee, 353
  Irish tea, 355
  mock bloody Marys, 351
  mulled ale, 287
  mulled cranberry-apple cider, 97
  mulled-tea punch, 355
  mulled wine, 356
  orange spritzer, 351
  pineapple-orange blush, 351
  pink champagne punch bowl, 349
  spiced apple tea, 355
  spiced iced coffee, 353
  spicy eggnog, 351
  spicy orange iced tea, 355
  syllabub, 285
  tempting tea-light, 355
  tropical cup, 351
  Viennese coffee, 353
  vin chaud, 356
  wassail, 356
  winter wine punch, 356

biscuits, Anna's cheese, 290
bisque:
    crabmeat, 78
    pumpkin, 270
    tomato, 109
Black Forest cherry cake, 295
blondies, 318
blueberry-and-peach shortcake, 115
Blum's coffee-toffee pie, 102
bouillabaisse, chicken, 369
bouillon, court, 372
braised:
    goose, apple wine-, 270
    turkey roll, 35
brandy-Alexander frappes, 39
brandy hard sauce, 271
bratwurst, 35
breadflats, crisp, 172
breads:
    challah (Sabbath twist), 259
    cranberry-nut, 171
    Danish kringles, 266
    date-nut, 171
    Fannie's mandel, 261
    Finnish Christmas dolls, 265
    herbed onion pita rounds, 110
    Italian panettone, 264
    kolach wreath, 264
    kugelhopf, 266
    lemon tea, 170
    Meg's Christmas braid, 278
    Norwegian Christmas, 265
    Norwegian sweet, 305
    pineapple-apricot-nut loaf, 170
    Portuguese, 92
    pumpkin loaves, 171
    Scandinavian Christmas, 266
    stollen, 267
breast-of-chicken curry, 346
breast of turkey in aspic, 287
brittle:
    California popcorn, 176
    cubaita, 309
broccoli:
    chicken and ham hollandaise, 109
    with lemon sauce, 36
brown-edge wafers, 319
brown gravy, 290
brown-sugar:
    -glazed apples, 285
    muffins, 278
Brussels sprouts, parsnips with, 55
Burgundy mint, 356
burnt almonds, 322

butter:
    cake, Austrian, 295
    caper, 357
    chive, 357
    curry, 357
    frosting, 371
    mustard, 357
    rolls, 291
buttered rice, 117
butternut-squash pie, 102
butterscotch:
    -chocolate Yule log, 324
    -pecan pie, 39
    sauce, hot, 97

C

cabbage, coleslaw-stuffed, 116
café brûlot, 353
Cajun coffee, 91
cakes:
    ambrosia, 361
    Austrian butter, 295
    baked Alaska, 330
    Black Forest cherry, 295
    chocolate-chestnut, 279
    chocolate-raspberry layer, 63
    chocolate roll, 296
    Christmas, (Hoska), 304
    Christmas whisky, 307
    clove, caramel frosting with, 37
    coconut-carrot, 271
    Four Seasons fancy, 331
    honey, 258
    Italian wine, 306
    kiwi-mandarin orange, 57
    lemon "cheese," 305
    lemon chiffon, 57
    low-calorie sponge-, 63
    pumpkin, 37
        spice, 56
    rolls, orange-, 57
    three-kings', 280
    warm banana-pineapple, 113
    warm plum kuchen, 116

California coffee, 353
California popcorn brittle, 176
canapé(s):
    butters for, 357
    cucumber, 340
    hot mushroom, 336
    tray, frozen, 337
candied:
    orange-ring chain, 16
    pineapple rings, 177
    sweet potatoes and apples, 36
candy. See confections
candy-cane cookies, 317
candyland house, 240
caper sauce, 286
capon:
    with herbs, roast, 61
    with pecan-herb stuffing, roast
        stuffed, 62
caramel(s):
    acorns, 322
    -custard mold, 89
    frosting, easy, 38
    hazelnut, 176
carrot(s):
    -coconut cake, 271
    maple-glazed, 91
casserole, roast stuffed pheasant and
    wild-rice, 48
cauliflower:
    -and-avocado salad, 113
    Polonaise, 51
    with shrimp sauce, 36
    soup, cream-of-, 114
challah (Sabbath twist), 259
Cheddar-cheese puffs, 337
Cheddar crackers, savory, 173
cheese:
    balls, hot, 75
    bell, jalapeño, 173
    biscuits, Anna's cheese, 290
    garlic-herb, 169
    loaf, three-, 74
    logs, piquant, 169
    marinated goat, 173
    nuggets, golden, 337
    pie, Greek, 280
    puffs, Cheddar-, 337
    rolls, corned-beef-and-Swiss-, 116
    spread, low-calorie, 169
    triconas, 336
cheesecakes:
    pumpkin, 17
    Ratner's famous marble, 259

cherry(ies):
  cake, Black Forest, 295
  glazed, 295
cherry-tomato hors d'oeuvres, 280
chestnut:
  -chocolate cake, 279
  -cranberry string, 60
  stuffing, 20
    -sausage, 60
chestnuts, 322
chewy prune bars, 318
chicken:
  barbecued, 87
  Basquaise, 370
  bouillabaisse, 369
  coq au vin with mushrooms, 79
  curry, breast-of-, 346
  egg-drop soup, 111
  fricassee, 261
  ham and broccoli hollandaise, 109
  livers, chopped, 259
  -tofu balls, 75
chili:
  for a crowd, 113
  sauce, 357
Chinese egg rolls, 74
chive butter, 357
chocolate:
  Brazil nuts, 322
  -butterscotch Yule log, 324
  -chestnut cake, 279
  clusters, holiday, 177
  coating, 331
  -cookie dough, 313
  crumb crust, 39
  -crunch squares, 175
  curls, 39
  -date Yule log, 178
  -dipped dried fruits, white- or dark-,
    169
  -dipped orange and grapefruit peel,
    176
  -dipped peel, 324
  -dipped rings, 299
  fudge, holiday, 176
  glaze, 319, 325, 325
  -Nesselrode mousse, 360
  pecan pie, 271
  pretzels, 325
  -raspberry layer cake, 63
  -raspberry torte, 100
  roll, 296
  sauce, 330
    dark, 39
    fudge, 107
    hot, 97
    quick, 97
  -sour-cream frosting, 100
  surprises, 176
chopped chicken livers, 259
chowder, New England clam, 91
Christmas cake (Hoska), 304

Christmas pâté, 281
Christmas pizza, 96
Christmas popcorn balls, 175
Christmas spiced oranges, 280
Christmas whisky cake, 307
chutney:
  cranberry, 168
  -and-fruit filling, 346
cider, mulled cranberry-apple, 97
cinnamon:
  apples, rosy, 278
  stars, 279
clam chowder, New England, 91
clove cake with caramel frosting, 37
cocktail olives, 278
cocoa:
  -meringue ladyfingers (logs), 323
  -shortbread dough, 237
coconut:
  bonbons, 177
  -carrot cake, 271
  -ice-cream mold, toasted-, 38
  -lemon filling, 291
coffee:
  café brûlot, 353
  Cajun, 91
  California, 353
  cordial, 353
  iced, 353
  Irish, 353
  nog, 353
  spiced iced, 353
  -toffee pie, Blum's, 102
  Viennese, 353
coffeecakes:
  almond-twist, 297
  apricot-filled, 297
  streusel-filled, 297
cold Grand Marnier soufflé, 347
cold salmon poached in white wine, 372
coleslaw-stuffed cabbage, 116
confectioners'-sugar icing, 265
confections:
  barley-sugar twists, 175
  burnt almonds, 322
  California popcorn brittle, 176
  candied pineapple rings, 177
  caramel acorns, 322
  chestnuts, 322
  chocolate Brazil nuts, 322
  chocolate-butterscotch Yule log, 324
  chocolate-crunch squares, 175
  chocolate-date Yule log, 178
  chocolate-dipped dried fruits, white- or
    dark-, 169

chocolate-dipped orange and
    grapefruit peel, 176
chocolate-dipped peel, 324
chocolate-dipped rings, 299
chocolate pretzels, 325
chocolate surprises, 176
Christmas popcorn balls, 175
cocoa-meringue ladyfingers (logs), 323
coconut bonbons, 177
crisp breadflats, 172
cubaita (Italian almond brittle), 309
date roll, 308
divinity fudge, 175
hazelnut caramels, 176
holiday chocolate clusters, 177
holiday chocolate fudge, 176
honey bubbles, 304
marzipan almonds, 323
marzipan pinecones, 323
meringue mushrooms, 324
old-fashioned hard candy, 176
peanut-butter fudge, 308
penuche walnuts, 324
pizzelle, 306
rocky roads, 175
seafoam, 178
speedy soft pretzels, 174
sugared nuts, 279
sugarplums, 177
Swedish nuts, 309
turtles, 177
consommé Madrilène, royal, 346
cookie houses:
  adobe ranch, 232
  candyland, 240
  log cabin, 237
  windmill, 235
cookies:
  almond macaroons, 316
  anise, 306
  antique-toy, 312
  blondies, 318
  brown-edge wafers, 319
  candy-cane, 317
  chewy prune bars, 318
  cinnamon stars, 279
  cranberry-cereal, 318
  Eurieka's sugar, 308
  filled, 307
  gingerbread boys and girls, 298
  hazelnut balls, 299
  jam bites, 319
  lebkuchen tiles, 294
  molasses cutout, 97
  pecan diamonds, 317
  raisin newton bars, 318
  rope, 308

springerle, 325
spritz wreaths, 299
Swedish cakes, 306
three-in-one, 316
toffee bars, 299
Tyrolean honey, 299
Viennese, 325
walnut wreaths, 319
coq au vin with mushrooms, 79
cornbreads: 90
  Indian, 48
  -oyster dressing, 32
  -sausage stuffing, 20
corned-beef-and-Swiss-cheese rolls, 116
Cornish hens with caper sauce, 61
cornmeal crust, 87
corn pudding, 92
Corris' orange eggnog, 351
court bouillon, 372
crab(meat):
  bisque, 78
  soup, Creole shrimp-and-, 370
crackers, savory Cheddar, 173
cranberry(ies):
  -apple cider, mulled, 97
  -apple pie, 37
  -apple punch, 350
  -apple relish, 48
  -apple salad, 56
  -apple sauce, 261
  Bavarian, frozen, 101
  -cereal cookies, 318
  -chestnut string, 60
  chutney, 168
  frosted, 101
  -nut bread, 171
  -orange-apple relish, 37
  -orange stuffing, 20
  -pear pie, deep-dish, 107
  -raisin relish, 60
  -raisin tart, 100
  relish, jellied, 290
  sauce, fresh-, 16
  sauce, molded, 36
  string, 33, 290
  -tangerine relish, 37
  whip with custard sauce, 92
  -whipped-cream pie, fresh-, 307

cream:
  -of-cauliflower soup, 114
  molded rice, 369
  pastry, 331
    for gâteau St.-Honoré, 330
  pineapple Bavarian, 331
  -puff dough, 330
  puffs, floating, 112
cream-cheese frosting, 37
creamed spinach and potatoes au gratin, 35
Creole shrimp-and-crab soup, 370
crêpes: 346
  curried-turkey, 41
crisp breadflats, 172
crusts:
  chocolate crumb, 39
  cornmeal, 87
  gingersnap, 309
  pizza, 96
cubaita (Italian almond brittle), 309
cucumber canapés, 340
Cumberland sauce, 284
curry(ied):
  breast-of-chicken, 346
  butter, 357
  sauce, 346
  -turkey crêpes, 41
custard:
  -caramel mold, 89
  filling, 100
  pie, old-fashioned pumpkin, 106
  royal, 346
  sauce, 92
  tarts, apple, 101

D

Danish fruit pudding, 361
Danish kringles, 266
Danish pastry wreaths, 172
dark chocolate sauce, 39
date:
  -nut bread, 171
  roll, 308
  Yule log, chocolate-, 178
Dearborn Inn fruitcake, 179
decorator frosting, 233
deep-dish cranberry-pear pie, 107
deep-dish picadillo pie, 87
deluxe turkey pie, 40
desserts:
  ambrosia, 102
  baked Alaska, 330
  caramel-custard mold, 89
  chocolate-Nesselrode mousse, 360
  chocolate-raspberry torte, 100
  Christmas spiced oranges, 280
  Danish fruit pudding, 361
  English trifle, 286
  floating cream puffs, 112
  frozen cranberry Bavarian, 101

fruit supreme with pink champagne, 103
gâteau St.-Honoré, 330
glazed apple tart, 93
grandpa's, 261
harvest fruit bowl, 39
hazelnut torte, 296
hot mincemeat pastries, 109
lemon sherbet with pineapple-mint sauce, 117
Linzer torte, 296
melon and grapes with lime sherbet, 111
miniature babas au rhum, 170
mint madeleines, 56
molded rice cream, 369
orange-cake rolls, 57
peach-and-blueberry shortcake, 115
peach-melba shortcake, 370
pig's-ear twists, 91
plum kuchen à la mode, warm, 116
plum pudding with brandy hard sauce, 271
praline parfaits, 114
pumpkin mousse, 50
rosé-wine mold with green grapes, 361
royal meringue, 360
dilled mustard sauce, 168
dill-yogurt dip, 12
dips:
  dill-yogurt, 12
  guacamole, 87
  low-calorie onion-soup, 341
  yogurt-dill (low-calorie), 341
divinity fudge, 175
doughs:
  basic coffeecake, 298
  chocolate-cookie, 313
  cocoa-shortbread, 237
  cookie (Viennese), 325
  cream-puff, 330
  gingerbread, 235
    cookie, 298
    -cottage, 239
    -village, 251
  peanut-butter-cookie, 233
  speculaas, 236
  spice-cookie, 313
  spiced cookie, 241
  sugar-cookie, 313
dressings. See stuffings
duck(ling):
  fricassee, 90
  with turnips, 62
Dundee cake, 161

E

easy caramel frosting, 38
egg:
   -drop soup, chicken, 111
   -nog, Corris' orange, 351
   -nog, spicy, 351
   rolls, Chinese, 74
   rolls, miniature, 336
eggplant Neapolitan, 112
English fruitcake, 179
English trifle, 286
Eurieka's sugar cookies, 308

F

fancy cubes, 351
Fannie's mandel bread, 261
fantasy bird holiday appetizer, 12
festive mushroom salad, 56
field-mouse special, 287
filled cookies, 307
fillings:
   chutney-and-fruit, 346
   custard, 100
   lemon, 63
     -coconut, 291
   orange, 57
   pastry cream, 331
     for gâteau St.-Honoré, 330
   pineapple Bavarian cream, 331
   pumpkin, 309
   raisin, 318
   turkey, 41
Finnish Christmas dolls, 265
fireside warmer, 355
fish, sweet-and-sour jellied, 260
flaming rum sauce, 38

floating cream puffs, 112
Four Seasons fancy cake, 331
frappes, brandy-Alexander, 39
French apple pie, 368
French-fried potatoes, 35
fresh-cranberry sauce in orange shells, 16
fresh-cranberry-whipped-cream pie, 307
fresh-mushroom stuffing, 20
fricassee:
   chicken, 261
   duck, 90
frosted cranberries, 101
frosted daiquiri pie, 103
frosted daiquiris, 287
frosted punch bowl, 287
frostings: 97
   butter, 371
   caramel, easy, 38
   chocolate, 296
     -sour-cream, 100
   coffee, 296
   cream-cheese, 37
   decorator, 233
   glaze, 160, 295
     Mrs. Halks', 160
   seven-minute, 306
   snow, 235, 251
   white fruitcake, 161
frozen canapé tray, 337
frozen cranberry Bavarian, 101
frozen guacamole, 357

fruit(s):
   bowl, harvest, 39
   filling, chutney-and-, 346
   garnish, glazed-, 34
   pickled dried, 168
   pudding, Danish, 361
   -punch warmer, 351
   supreme with pink champagne, 103
   white- or dark-chocolate-dipped dried, 169
fruitcakes:
   best-of-all, 294
   Dearborn Inn, 179
   Dundee, 161
   English, 179
   grandma's, 160
   Japanese, 291
   mama's, 304
   Mrs. Halks', 160
   small, 172
   sour-cream, 160
   white, 161
fruited champagne punch, 349
fruited pot roast, 258
fruitful punch, 351
fruit-punch warmer, 351
fudge:
   divinity, 175
   holiday chocolate, 176
   peanut-butter, 308
   sauce, 107
     hot, 97

G

garlic-herb cheese, 169
garnishes:
   chestnut-cranberry string, 60
   cranberry string, 33
   glazed-fruit, 34
   scallion flowers, 341
gâteau St.-Honoré, 330
giblet:
   gravy, 32
     goose, 60
   -orange sauce, 16
gingerbread:
   boys and girls, 298
   cookie dough, 298
   -cottage dough, 239
   dough, 235
   -village dough, 251
gingerbread houses:
   adobe ranch, 232
   candyland, 240
   chapel, 242
   cottage, 238
   log cabin, 237
   Swiss chalet, 239
   Victorian house, 233
   Victorian village, 246
   windmill, 235

gingersnap crust, 309
glacé, lemon zest, 92
glazed:
    apples, 49
        brown-sugar-, 285
    apple tart, 93
    carrots, maple-, 91
    cherries, 295
    -fruit garnish, 34
    ham steak with cornbread stuffing,
        114
    ham, Swedish, 371
    noodle pudding, apricot-, 259
    orange tarte, 331
    vegetables, 62
glazes:
    apricot, 170
    chocolate, 319, 325, 325
    frosting, 160, 295
        Mrs. Halks', 160
    lemon, 357
    mustard, 371
glogg I, 356
glogg II, 356
golden cheese nuggets, 337
golden potato pancakes, 258
golden roast turkey, 32
golden stuffed baked potatoes, 55
goose:
    apple wine-braised, 270
    giblet gravy, 60
    roast, 60, 285
        stuffed, 49
Grand Marnier soufflé, cold, 347
grandma's fruitcake, 160
grandpa's dessert, 261
gravies:
    brown, 290
    giblet, 32
        goose, 60
    herb, 368
Greek cheese pie, 280
green mayonnaise, 103
guacamole:
    dip with crisp vegetables, 87
    frozen, 357

H

ham:
    chicken and broccoli hollandaise, 109
    in crust with Cumberland sauce,
        baked, 284
    steak with cornbread stuffing, glazed,
        114
    Swedish glazed, 371

hard sauce: 17, 51, 172
    brandy, 271
harvest fruit bowl, 39
hazelnut:
    balls, 299
    caramels, 176
    torte, 296
hearty bean-sausage soup, 110
herb:
    -garlic cheese, 169
    gravy, 368
    marinade, 341
    -marinated vegetables, 341
    -pecan stuffing, 62
herbed onion pita rounds, 110
holiday chocolate clusters, 177
holiday chocolate fudge, 176
honey:
    bubbles, 304
    cake, 258
    cookies, Tyrolean, 299
    -walnut palmiers, 279
hors d'oeuvres. *See* appetizers
hot buttered rice, 111
hot butterscotch sauce, 97
hot cheese balls, 75
hot fudge sauce, 97
hot mincemeat pastries, 109
hot mincemeat pie, 17
hot mushroom canapés, 336
hot potato salad, 116
hot sardine and salmon crescents, 281
hot Scotch rumba, 355
hot wine lemonade, 356

I

ice:
    bell, 351
    cubes, fancy, 351
    ring, strawberry, 349
ice-cream desserts:
    brandy-Alexander frappes, 39
    mold, toasted-coconut-, 38
    -sundae pie, peppermint-, 107
iced coffee, 353
    spiced, 353
iced tea, 355
    spicy orange, 355
icings:
    confectioners'-sugar, 265
    decorating, 298
    Norwegian sweet bread, 305
    royal, 179
    seven-minute, 309
Indian cornbread, 48
Irish coffee, 353
Irish tea, 355
Italian panettone, 264
Italian wine cake, 306

J

jalapeño cheese bell, 173
jam bites, 319
Japanese fruitcake, 291
jellied:
    cranberry relish, 290
    fish, sweet-and-sour, 260
jelly, red-pepper, 168
Joanne's Maryland oyster stuffing, 20
julienne vegetables, 93

K

kapusta, 260
kasha varnishkes, 258
kiwi-mandarin orange cake, 57
kolach wreath, 264
kuchen, warm plum à la mode, 116
kugelhopf, 266
kumquats, preserved, 168

L

lamb, roast saddle of, 286
lebkuchen tiles, 294
lemon:
    "cheese" cake, 305
    chiffon cake, 57
    dressing, 340
    filling, 63
        coconut-, 291
    glaze, 357
    tea bread, 170
    zest glacé, 92
lemony acorn-squash slices, 55
Linzer torte, 296
liver(s):
    chopped chicken, 259
    Christmas pâté, 281
    pâté en croûte, 75
    pâté en gelée, 78
log cabin (cookie house), 237
lollipop syrup, 235
low-calorie cheese spread, 169
low-calorie onion-soup dip, 341
low-calorie spongecake, 63

M

macaroons, almond, 316
Madeira sauce, 286
make-ahead raisin stuffing, 21
mama's fruitcake, 304
maple:
 -glazed carrots, 91
 pumpkin pie, 360
-mandarin orange cake, kiwi, 57
marinade:
 duck fricassee, 90
 herb, 341
 lemon dressing, 340
 spiced sirloin, 286
 vegetable-salad platter, 103
marinated:
 goat cheese, 173
 -herb vegetables, 341
 scallops and shrimp, 340
marmalade, onion, 168
marrow sauce, 371
marzipan:
 almonds, 323
 hearts, 294
 pinecones, 323
 torte, 100
mashed-potato stuffing, 21
mayonnaise, green, 103
meatballs:
 Mexican, 357
 mole, 88
Meg's Christmas braid, 278
melba sauce, 370
melon and grapes with lime sherbet, 111
meringue:
 dessert, royal, 360
 ladyfingers (logs), cocoa-, 323
 mushrooms, 324
 pie, pumpkin, 38
 ring, 38
Mexican meatballs with chili sauce, 357
Mexican rice, 87
Mexican stuffed zucchini, 89
mile-high mincemeat glacé pie, 106
mincemeat:
 -apple pie with flaming rum sauce, 38
 glacé pie, mile-high, 106
 pastries, hot, 109
 pie, hot, 17
 Pontchartrain's, 51
miniature babas au rhum, 170
miniature egg rolls, 336
mint:
 Burgundy, 356
 madeleines, 56
 -pineapple sauce, 117
mock bloody Marys, 351
molasses cutout cookies, 97
molded cranberry sauce, 36
molded rice cream, 369

mousse:
 chocolate-Nesselrode, 360
 pumpkin, 50
Mrs. Halks' fruitcake, 160
Mrs. Halks' frosting glaze, 160
muffins, brown-sugar, 278
mulled:
 ale, 287
 cranberry-apple cider, 97
 -tea punch, 355
 wine, 356
mushroom(s):
 canapés, hot, 336
 coq au vin with, 79
 meringue, 324
 and noodles, 34
 salad, festive, 56
 stuffed, 340
 stuffing, fresh-, 20
mustard:
 butter, 357
 glaze, 371
 sauce, dilled, 168

N

nectarine tart, 110
Nesselrode:
 -chocolate mousse, 360
 pie, 106
New England clam chowder, 91
noodle(s):
 and mushrooms, 34
 pudding, 260
 apricot-glazed, 259
Norwegian Christmas bread, 265
Norwegian sweet bread, 305
nut(s):
 bread, cranberry-, 171
 bread, date-, 171
 loaf, pineapple-apricot-, 170
 roll, traditional Italian, 305
 rum pie, Trader Vic's, 101
 sugared, 279
 Swedish, 309

O

old-fashioned dressing, 32
old-fashioned hard candy, 176
old-fashioned pumpkin custard pie, 106
olives:
 cocktail, 278
 puff-pastry, 74
onion(s):
 baked stuffed, 35
 with cheese, 369
 marmalade, 168
 pita rounds, herbed, 110
 -soup dip, low-calorie, 341

orange(s):
 cake, kiwi-mandarin, 57
 -cake rolls, 57
 chiffon cake layer, 330
 Christmas spiced, 280
 -cranberry-apple relish, 37
 -cranberry stuffing, 20
 eggnog, Corris', 351
 filling, 57
 -giblet sauce, 16
 and grapefruit peel, chocolate-dipped, 176
 iced tea, spicy, 355
 -pineapple blush, 351
 -ring chain, candied, 16
 roast turkey à l', 16
 salad, avocado and, 117
 sauce, 33
 spritzer, 351
 tarte, glazed, 331
oriental beef with cashews, 111
oriental pecans, 169
oyster:
 -cornbread dressing, 32
 -filled artichokes, 89
 -and-pecan dressing, Pontchartrain's, 51
 pie, 290
 stew, Vic's, 372
 stuffing, Joanne's Maryland, 20

P

pancakes:
 potato, 261
 golden, 258
panettone, Italian, 264
parfaits, praline, 114
parsnips:
 with Brussels sprouts, 55
 au gratin, 36
partridge pie, 284
party popcorn mix, 174
pastry(ies):
 for baked ham, 284
 cream, 331
 for gâteau St.-Honoré, 330
 glazed orange tarte, 331
 honey-walnut palmiers, 279
 hot mincemeat, 109
 for partridge pie, 284
 pâté en croûte, 75
 pig's-ear twists, 91
 -puff olives, 74
 triconas, 336
 wreaths, Danish, 172
pâtés:
 Christmas, 281
 en croûte, 75
 en gelée, liver, 78
peach(es):
 -and-blueberry shortcake, 115
 -melba shortcake, 370
 spiced, 114

peanut-butter:
  -cookie dough, 233
  fudge, 308
peanuts, spiced sugar, 169
pear:
  pie, deep-dish cranberry-, 107
  pie with streusel topping, 102
peas and lettuce, 115
pecan(s):
  -butterscotch pie, 39
  diamonds, 317
  oriental, 169
  -and-oyster dressing, Pontchartrain's,
    51
  pie, chocolate, 271
  stuffing, 16
    -herb, 62
     sweet-potato-, 20
  -sweet-potato pie, 90
penuche walnuts, 324
peppermint-ice-cream-sundae pie, 107
peppers, sautéed sweet, 368
pheasant and wild-rice casserole, roast
  stuffed, 48
pickled dried fruit, 168
pies:
  Blum's coffee-toffee, 102
  butternut-squash, 102
  butterscotch-pecan, 39
  chocolate pecan, 271
  cranberry-apple, 37
  deep-dish cranberry-pear, 107
  deep-dish picadillo, 87
  deluxe turkey, 40
  French apple, 368
  fresh-cranberry-whipped-cream, 307
  frosted daiquiri, 103
  Greek cheese, 280
  maple pumpkin, 360
  mile-high mincemeat glacé, 106
  mincemeat-apple, 38
  mincemeat, hot, 17
    Pontchartrain's, 51
  Nesselrode, 106
  old-fashioned pumpkin custard, 106
  oyster, 290
  partridge, 284
  pear, 102
  peppermint-ice-cream-sundae, 107
  pineapple cloud, 39
  pumpkin chiffon, 309
  pumpkin meringue, 38
  rich squash, 40
  sour-cream apple, 106
  sweet-potato-pecan, 90
  Trader Vic's nut rum, 101
  turkey-and-vegetable, 40

pig's-ear twists, 91
pineapple:
  -apricot-nut loaf, 170
  Bavarian cream, 331
  cake, warm banana-, 113
  casserole, sweet-potato-and-, 36
  cloud pie, 39
  -mint sauce, 117
  -orange blush, 351
  rings, candied, 177
pink champagne punch bowl, 349
piquant apricot sauce, 336
piquant cheese logs, 169
pita rounds, herbed onion, 110
pizza, Christmas, 96
pizza-flavored popcorn, 169
pizza sauce, 96
pizzelle, 306
plum:
  kuchen à la mode, warm, 116
  pudding with brandy hard sauce, 271
  puddings, steamed, 171
  sauce, 285
Pontchartrain's hot mincemeat pie, 51
Pontchartrain's oyster-and-pecan
  dressing, 51
popcorn:
  balls, Christmas, 175
  brittle, California, 176
  mix, party, 174
  pizza-flavored, 169
pork:
  Anna's roast loin of, 290
  with herbs, roast, 368
Portuguese bread, 92
potato(es):
  French-fried, 35
  golden stuffed baked, 55
  au gratin, creamed spinach and, 35
  ovals, sautéed, 93
  pancakes, 261
    golden, 258
  pudding (kugel), 258
  salad, hot, 116
  stuffing, mashed-, 21

pot roast:
  fruited, 258
  in red wine, 368
  Yankee, 91
praline parfaits, 114
preserved kumquats, 168
preserves:
  antipasto medley, 168
  cranberry chutney, 168
  dilled mustard sauce, 168
  onion marmalade, 168
  pickled dried fruit, 168
  preserved kumquats, 168
  red-pepper jelly, 168
pretzels, speedy soft, 174
prune bars, chewy, 318
puddings:
  corn, 92
  Danish fruit, 361
  noodle, 260
    apricot-glazed, 259
  plum, 271
  potato (kugel), 258
  steamed plum, 171
puff-pastry olives, 74
pumpkin:
  bisque, 270
  cake, 37
  cheesecake, 17
  chiffon pie, 309
  custard pie, old-fashioned, 106
  loaves, 171
  meringue pie, 38
  mousse, 50
  pie, maple, 360
  soup, 48
  spice cake, 56
punches:
  auld lang syne, 349
  pink champagne, 349
  cran-apple, 350
  fruited champagne, 349
  fruitful, 351
  mulled-tea, 355
  warmer, fruit-, 351
  winter wine, 356

Q

quiche:
    asparagus, 369
    Lorraine, our best, 75
    -Lorraine squares, 337
quick brown sauce, 270
quick chocolate sauce, 97

R

raisin:
    -berry relish, 60
    -cranberry tart, 100
    filling, 318
    newton bars, 318
    stuffing, make-ahead, 21
raspberry:
    -chocolate layer cake, 63
    -chocolate torte, 100
    sauce, 97
Ratner's famous marble cheesecake, 259
red-pepper jelly, 168
relishes:
    apple-cranberry, 48
    cranberry-orange-apple, 37
    cranberry-tangerine, 37
    jellied cranberry, 290
    raisin-berry, 60
rice:
    buttered, 117
        hot, 111
    casserole, wild-, 48
    cream, molded, 369
    Mexican, 87
    ring, 90
    saffron, 346
rich squash pie, 40
roast capon with herbs, 61
roast goose, 60
    with sage stuffing and plum sauce, 285
roast loin of pork, Anna's, 290
roast pork with herbs, 368
roast saddle of lamb with caper sauce, 286
roast stuffed capon, 62
roast stuffed goose, 49
roast stuffed pheasant and wild-rice casserole, 48
roast turkey, Alsatian style, 34
roast turkey flambé, 50
roast turkey, golden, 32
roast turkey à l'orange, 16
roast turkey in white wine, 33
rocky roads, 175
roll(s):
    braised turkey, 35
    butter, 291
    Chinese egg, 74
    corned-beef-and-Swiss-cheese, 116
    date, 308
    miniature egg, 336
    orange-cake, 57
    traditional Italian nut, 305
rope cookies, 308
rosé-wine mold with green grapes, 361
rosy cinnamon apples, 278
royal consommé madrilène, 346
royal custard, 346
royal icing, 179
royal meringue dessert, 360
rum:
    pie, Trader Vic's nut, 101
    sauce, flaming, 38
rumaki, 357

S

saffron rice, 346
sage stuffing, 285
salad dressing: 347
    green mayonnaise, 103
    soy-vinaigrette, 56
salads:
    avocado and orange, 117
    cauliflower-and-avocado, 113
    cranberry-apple, 56
    festive mushroom, 56
    hot potato, 116
    tossed green, 93
        with avocado, 347
    -vegetable platter, 103
salmon:
    crescents, hot sardine and, 281
    with lemon butter, 93
    poached in white wine, cold, 372
salsa, 88
sardine and salmon crescents, hot, 281
sauces:
    apple-cranberry, 261
    apricot, 369
    barbecue, 87
    caper, 286
    chili, 357
    chocolate, 330
        dark, 39
        quick, 97
    Cumberland, 284
    curry, 346
    custard, 92
    dilled mustard, 168
    flaming rum, 38
    fresh-cranberry, 16
    fudge, 107
        hot, 97
    hard, 17, 51, 172
        brandy, 271
    hot butterscotch, 97
    Madeira, 286
    marrow, 371
    melba, 370
    molded cranberry, 36
    orange, 33
    orange-giblet, 16
    pineapple-mint, 117
    piquant apricot, 336
    pizza, 96
    plum, 285
    quick brown, 270
    raspberry, 97
    strawberry, 96
    verte, 372
    white-wine, 49
sauerkraut with sausage, 49
sausage(s):
    -bean soup, hearty, 110
    -chestnut stuffing, 60
    -cornbread stuffing, 20
    sauerkraut with, 49
    sautéed link, 33
    stuffing, 49
    sweet and hot, 96
sautéed:
    apple rings, 35
    link sausages, 33
    potato ovals, 93
    squash slices, 90
    sweet peppers, 368
savory Cheddar crackers, 173
scallion flowers, 341
scallops:
    and bacon en brochette, 115
    Provençal, 371
    and shrimp, marinated, 340
Scandinavian Christmas bread, 266
Scotch apple tart, 107
seafoam, 178
seven-minute frosting, 306
seven-minute icing, 309
seviche, 340

shortcakes:
  peach-and-blueberry, 115
  peach-melba, 370
shrimp:
  étouffée with rice, 89
  marinated scallops and, 340
  soufflés, 117
  soup, Creole crab-and-, 370
  -stuffed tomatoes, 340
  toast, 337
small fruitcakes, 172
snow frosting, 235, 251
soufflé(s):
  cold Grand Marnier, 347
  shrimp, 117
  yam, 51
souffléed yams in orange shells, 290
soups:
  chicken egg-drop, 111
  crabmeat bisque, 78
  cream-of-cauliflower, 114
  Creole shrimp-and-crab, 370
  hearty bean-sausage, 110
  kapusta (hot cabbage), 260
  New England clam chowder, 91
  pumpkin, 48
  pumpkin bisque, 270
  royal consommé madrilène, 346
  tomato bisque, 109
  winter-squash, 32
sour-cream:
  apple pie, 106
  frosting, chocolate-, 100
  fruitcake, 160
soy-vinaigrette dressing, 56
speculaas dough, 236
speedy soft pretzels, 174
spice-cookie dough, 313
spiced:
  apple tea, 355
  cookie dough, 241
  iced coffee, 353
  oranges, Christmas, 280
  peaches, 114
  sirloin steak with Madeira sauce, 286
  sugar peanuts, 169
spicy eggnog, 351
spicy orange iced tea, 355
spinach, potatoes au gratin and
  creamed, 35
springerle, 325
spritz wreaths, 299
squash:
  baked acorn, 49
  with cranberries, steamed acorn, 270
  Mexican stuffed zucchini, 89
  pie, butternut-, 102
  pie, rich, 40
  slices, lemony acorn-, 55
  slices, sautéed, 90

soup, winter-, 32
steak:
  glazed ham, 114
  with marrow sauce, 371
  spiced sirloin, 286
  tartare, 340
steamed acorn squash with cranberries,
  270
steamed plum puddings, 171
stew, Vic's oyster, 372
stollen, 267
strawberry:
  ice ring, 349
  sauce, 96
streusel-filled coffeecake, 297
streusel topping, 102
stuffed:
  baked potatoes, golden, 55
  cabbage, coleslaw-, 116
  mushrooms, 340
  onions, baked, 35
    with cheese, 369
  zucchini, Mexican, 89
stuffings:
  chestnut, 20
    -sausage, 60
  cornbread-oyster dressing, 32
  cranberry-orange, 20
  fresh-mushroom, 20
  Joanne's Maryland oyster, 20
  make-ahead raisin, 21
  mashed-potato, 21
  old-fashioned dressing, 32
  pecan, 16
    herb, 62
  Pontchartrain's oyster-and-pecan
    dressing, 51
  sage, 285
  sausage, 49
    -cornbread, 20
  sweet-potato-pecan, 20
  for turkey, vegetable, 56
sugar:
  cookies, Eurieka's, 308
  peanuts, spiced, 169
  twists, barley-, 175
  -cookie dough, 313
sugared nuts, 279
sugarplums, 177
Swedish cakes, 306
Swedish glazed ham, 371
Swedish nuts, 309
sweet and hot sausage in pita bread, 96

sweet potato(es):
  and apples, candied, 36
  -pecan pie, 90
  -pecan stuffing, 20
  -and-pineapple casserole, 36
sweet-and-pungent turkey, 41
sweet-and-sour jellied fish, 260
syllabub, 285
syrups:
  honey, 304
  lollipop, 235

T

tangerine-cranberry relish, 37
tart(s):
  apple custard, 101
  cranberry-raisin, 100
  glazed apple, 93
  glazed orange, 331
  nectarine, 110
  Scotch apple, 107
tea:
  fireside warmer, 355
  hot Scotch rumba, 355
  iced, 355
    spicy orange, 355
  Irish, 355
  -light, tempting, 355
  punch, mulled-, 355
  spiced apple, 355
tempting tea-light, 355
teriyaki, 341
three-cheese loaf, 74
three-kings' cake, 280
three-in-one cookies, 316
timetable for roasting (un)stuffed turkey,
  21
toasted-coconut-ice-cream mold, 38
toffee:
  bars, 299
  -coffee pie, Blum's, 102
tofu-chicken balls, 75
tomato(es):
  bisque, 109
  hors d'oeuvres, cherry-, 280
  shrimp-stuffed, 340
torte:
  chocolate-raspberry, 100
  hazelnut, 296
  Linzer, 296
  marzipan, 100
tossed green salad with:
  avocado, 347
  hazelnut dressing, 93
Trader Vic's nut rum pie, 101
traditional Italian nut roll, 305
triconas, 336
trifle, English, 286
tropical cup, 351

turkey:
Alsatian style, roast, 34
in aspic, breast of, 287
crêpes, curried-, 41
flambé with oyster-and-pecan
dressing, roast, 50
golden roast, 32
à l'orange, roast, 16
with orange sauce, 33
paprikash, 34
pie, deluxe, 40
roll, braised, 35
sweet-and-pungent, 41
terrine, 174
-and-vegetable pie, 40
in white wine, roast, 33
turkey tips, 17
turnips, duckling with, 62
turtles, 177
Tyrolean honey cookies, 299

V

veal, stuffed breast of, 260
vegetables:
asparagus quiche, 369
baked acorn squash, 49
baked stuffed onions, 35
with cheese, 369
broccoli with lemon sauce, 36
candied sweet potatoes and apples, 36
cauliflower-and-avocado salad, 113
cauliflower Polonaise, 51
cauliflower with shrimp sauce, 36
coleslaw-stuffed cabbage, 116
creamed spinach and potatoes au
gratin, 35
eggplant Neapolitan, 112
glazed, 62
guacamole dip with crisp, 87
herb-marinated, 341

julienne, 93
lemony acorn-squash slices, 55
maple-glazed carrots, 91
Mexican stuffed zucchini, 89
oyster-filled artichokes, 89
Parisienne, 372
parsnips with Brussels sprouts, 55
parsnips au gratin, 36
peas and lettuce, 115
pie, turkey-and-, 40
-salad platter, 103
sauerkraut with sausage, 49
sautéed squash slices, 90
sautéed sweet peppers, 368
souffléed yams in orange sauce, 290
stuffing for turkey, 56
sweet-potato-and-pineapple casserole,
36
yam soufflé, 51
Vic's oyster stew, 372
Victorian village (gingerbread houses),
246
Viennese coffee, 353
Viennese cookies, 325
-vinaigrette dressing, soy, 56
vin chaud, 356

W

walnut(s):
palmiers, honey-, 279
penuche, 324
wreaths, 319

warm banana-pineapple cake, 113
warm plum kuchen à la mode, 116
wassail, 356
white- or dark-chocolate-dipped dried
fruits, 169
white fruitcake, 161
frosting, 161
white-wine sauce, 49
windmill (cookie house), 235
wine:
-braised goose, apple, 270
cake, Italian, 306
cold salmon poached in white, 372
mold, rosé-, 361
pot roast in red, 368
roast turkey in white, 33
sauce, white-, 49
wine drinks:
Burgundy mint, 356
glogg I, 356
glogg II, 356
hot wine lemonade, 356
mulled, 356
vin chaud, 356
wassail, 356
winter wine punch, 356
winter-squash soup, 32
winter wine punch, 356

Y

yam(s):
in orange shells, souffléed, 290
soufflé, 51
Yankee pot roast with onions, 91
yogurt-dill dip, 341

Z

zucchini, Mexican stuffed, 89

CRAFT INDEX

*Page numbers in bold-face type following
main entries refer to pictures with no accompanying directions. These pictures are included to give you a variety of ideas for holiday decorating and to stimulate your
creativity.*

A-C

angels:
counted cross-stitch, "joy," **188**,
196-197
wall hanging, **189**, 194-195
animals: **130**, **133**
striped teddy bears (crocheted bears),
184-185, 186-187
felt (tree ornaments), **147**, 148-149
tiny toy wreath, **137**, 155

baskets: **122**, **123**, **133**
cinnamon-stick, **182**, 209
to make and take, bountiful (gift
ideas), 180-181
ornaments
berry-pine, **151**, 153
cinnamon-sticks, **151**, 152
golden-cones, **151**, 155
teddy bear, **151**, 152
white-rose, **151**, 153
peppermint-stick, **183**, 209
surprise package, **214**, 215
Thanksgiving flower, **64**, 65
bow, tie-your-own: **145**, 145
boxes, ribbon-decorated:
diagonal, **199**, 201
lattice, **198**, 201
mitered, **198**, 201

sewing, **199**, 201
candleholder, Della Robbia: **136**, 155
centerpieces. *See* table decorations
clay carolers: **126**, **127**
crèches: **127**, **131**
crochet:
scarf (for teddy bear), **184**, 187
stockings
cowboy boot, **202**, 204
high-button shoe, **203**, 207
hiking boot with knitted sock, **203**,
208
penny loafer with argyle sock, **202**,
206
slipper with knitted leg, **202**, 204
running shoe, **203**, 207
striped teddy bears, **184-185**, 186-
187

D-F

Della Robbia: **132**
    candleholder, **136**, 155
    wreath, **136**, 155
flowers (dried): **120, 121, 122, 123, 126, 128, 132, 135**
    basket, Thanksgiving, **64**, 65
    mantelpiece, silky poinsettia, **141**, 144
    ornaments
        cinnamon-sticks basket, **151**, 152
        golden-cones basket, **151**, 155
        teddy bear basket, **151**, 152
        white-rose basket, **151**, 153
    wreath
        grapevine, **137**, 138
        scented "Victorian," **188**, 193
        statice spice, **137**, 139
flowers (fresh):
    autumn glory arrangement, **68**, 69
    Christmas carnation centerpiece, **140**, 143
    pumpkin-in-bloom, **66**, 67
frames, ribbon-decorated:
    padded, **198**, 201
    shadow-box, **198**, 200

G-L

garlands: **125, 129, 132**
gift packaging:
    basket, **214**, 215
    big pencil, **217**, 221
    carry-out container, **214**, 215
    cube, **214**, 215
    double torpedo, **214**, 215
    house, **214**, 215
    shopping tote, **214**, 215

gift wrap (paper):
    border wraps, **218, 219**, 221
    buttons & bows, **211**, 213
    calendar, **218**, 220
    Christmas-card decal, **219**, 221
    crushed-foil package, **218**, 220
    cutout paper snowflake, **218**, 220
    cutout-trees overwrap, **218**, 220
    cutout-trees stencil, **218**, 220
    decorative doily, **210**, 212
    fit to be tied, **211**, 221
    fold-and-cut decorations, **218, 219**, 220

golden holly leaves, **210**, 212
horn of holly, **211**, 213
lacy & lovely, **210**, 212
photo hang tag, **218**, 220
read all over, **211**, 213
record wrap, **211**, 213
shooting stars, **210**, 213
silver sack, **210**, 212
strips and stripes, **211**, 221
trivet trim, **218**, 220
gingerbread houses: **126**. *See also*
    Recipe Index, gingerbread houses
lace:
    "hats," **150**, 155
    sachet hoops, **188**, 192

O-P

ornaments: **122, 123, 124, 126, 129, 130, 133**
    basket
        berry-pine, **151**, 153
        cinnamon-sticks, **151**, 152
        golden-cones, **151**, 155
        teddy bear, **151**, 152
        white-rose, **151**, 153
    fabric
        calico Christmas tree, **150**, 153
        holiday heart, **150**, 152
        ribbon-tail balloon, **150**, 153
        stocking for stuffing, **150**, 152
    felt animals, **147**, 148-149
    foil
        cookie-cutter, **190**, 191
        folk-art, **190**, 191
        pinwheel, **190**, 191
    lace "hats," **150**, 155
    ribbon, **146**, 154
    tiny toy, **137**, 155
paper. *See* gift wrap
pillow, ribbon cover: **199**, 209
potpourri: **124**
    clove-and-spice, 197
    lace sachet hoops, **188**, 192
    lavender-rose, 197
    scented "Victorian" wreath, **188**, 193

R-S

ribbon: **124, 125, 129**
    address book, **198**, 201
    blotter, **198**, 200
    breakfast tray, **199**, 209
    diagonal box, **199**, 201
    lattice box, **198**, 201
    mat, **198**, 200
    mirror, **199**, 209
    mitered box, **198**, 201
    ornaments, **146**, 154
    padded frame, **198**, 201
    paper-clip holder, **198**, 200
    pencil holder, **198**, 200
    pillow, **199**, 209
    planter, **199**, 201
    sewing box, **199**, 201
    shadow-box frame, **198**, 200
    wreath, **135**, 154
stockings
    crocheted, **202-203**, 204-208
    for stuffing (ornament), **150**, 152
straw: **123, 126, 133**

T-Z

table decorations: **121, 123, 129**
    autumn glory arrangement, **68**, 69
    Christmas candle wreath, **140**, 142
    Christmas carnation centerpiece, **140**, 143
    Della Robbia candleholder, **136**, 155
    pumpkin-in-bloom, **66**, 67
    silky poinsettia, **141**, 144
    Thanksgiving flower basket, **64**, 65
trees, Christmas: **121, 123, 124, 125, 126, 129**
wall hanging, angel: **189**, 194-195
wreaths: **120, 122, 123, 125, 126, 128, 130, 132, 133**
    bubble-gum, **135**, 154
    chili-pepper, **135**, 154
    Christmas candle, **140**, 142
    cork, **135**, 154
    Della Robbia, **136**, 155
    dried-herb, **135**, 154
    grapevine, **137**, 138
    ribbon, **135**, 154
    scented "Victorian," **188**, 193
    statice spice, **137**, 139
    tiny toy, **137**, 155
    Williamsburg, **134**, 154